T0336646

Information Communication Technology Law, Protection and Access Rights:
Global Approaches and Issues

Irene Maria Portela
Polytechnic Institute of Cávado and Ave, Portugal

Maria Manuela Cruz–Cunha
Polytechnic Institute of Cávado and Ave, Portugal

INFORMATION SCIENCE REFERENCE

Hershey · New York

Director of Editorial Content:	Kristin Klinger
Director of Book Publications:	Julia Mosemann
Acquisitions Editor:	Lindsay Johnston
Development Editor:	Julia Mosemann
Publishing Assistant:	Natalie Pronio
Typesetter:	Michael Brehm
Production Editor:	Jamie Snavely
Cover Design:	Lisa Tosheff
Printed at:	Yurchak Printing Inc.

Published in the United States of America by
Information Science Reference (an imprint of IGI Global)
701 E. Chocolate Avenue
Hershey PA 17033
Tel: 717-533-8845
Fax: 717-533-8661
E-mail: cust@igi-global.com
Web site: http://www.igi-global.com

Library of Congress Cataloging-in-Publication Data

Information communication technology law, protection, and access rights : global approaches and issues / Irene Maria Portela and Maria Manuela Cruz-Cunha, editors.   p. cm.
 Includes bibliographical references and index.
 Summary: "This book identifies key issues in the relationship between ICT and law, ethics, politics and social policy, drawing attention to diverse global approaches to the challenges posed by ICT to access rights"--Provided by publisher.
 ISBN 978-1-61520-975-0 (hardcover) -- ISBN 978-1-61520-976-7 (ebook) 1. Information superhighway--Law and legislation. 2. Information superhighway-- Moral and ethical aspects. 3. Information superhighway--Social aspects. 4. Information superhighway--Political aspects. 5. Internet--Law and legislation. 6. Electronic records--Access control. 7. Data protection--Law and legislation. 8. Privacy, Right of. 9. Intellectual property. I. Portela, Irene Maria, 1965- II. Cruz-Cunha, Maria Manuela, 1964-
 K564.C6I543 2010
 343.09'944--dc22
                              2010016304

British Cataloguing in Publication Data
A Cataloguing in Publication record for this book is available from the British Library.

List of Reviewers

Table of Contents

Section 1
ICT Law and Regulation

Irene Portela, Polytechnic Institute of Cávado and Ave, Portugal
Maria Manuela Cruz-Cunha, Polytechnic Institute of Cávado and Ave, Portugal & University
of Minho, Portugal

Áurea Anguera de Sojo, Escuela Universitaria de Informática, Spain
Francisco Serradilla, Escuela Universitaria de Informática, Spain

Francisco Andrade, University of Minho, Portugal
Paulo Novais, University of Minho, Portugal
Davide Carneiro, University of Minho, Portugal
José Neves, University of Minho, Portugal

Witold Abramowicz, Poznan University of Economics, Poland
Piotr Stolarski, Poznan University of Economics, Poland
Tadeusz Tomaszewski, Poznan University of Economics, Poland

Section 2
Policies, Models, Frameworks and Rules

Section 3
Protection of Privacy and Trust

Section 4
Access Rights

Section 5
ICT Ethics

Detailed Table of Contents

Section 1
ICT Law and Regulation

This section discusses implications, challenges, barriers and opportunities of the Information Society and ICT, namely the legal aspects in the field of intellectual property rights, conflict resolution in electronic commerce and electronic transactions, authentication of digital contents.

Chapter 1

        Irene Portela, Polytechnic Institute of Cávado and Ave, Portugal
        Maria Manuela Cruz-Cunha, Polytechnic Institute of Cávado and Ave, Portugal & University
            of Minho, Portugal

The Data Retention Directive (2006/24/EC) provides the obligation for providers of publicly available electronic communications services or of public communications networks to retain traffic and location data for six months up to two years for the purpose of the investigation, detection and prosecution of serious crime. In the regulatory framework imposed by this Directive, the Portuguese Law no. 32/2008, of 17 July, requires that providers of publicly available electronic communication services or of public communications networks retain specific communication data, so that such data can be accessed by competent authorities, exclusively for the purpose of investigation, detection and prosecution of serious crime. Retained (via digital storage) metadata of telecommunications acts change and transform into the content of something else: a surveillance program. The concept of a data space that provides movement within and between data described here illustrates the powers of data retention in an imaginable way. Considering potential uses and misuses of retained data such as traffic analysis, social network analysis and data mining, this chapter examines the degree of interference with the right to privacy posed by the data retention laws.

Áurea Anguera de Sojo, Escuela Universitaria de Informática, Spain
Francisco Serradilla, Escuela Universitaria de Informática, Spain

Due to the development of the information society, there has been a substantial change in regulating certain legal aspects in the field of intellectual property. Focusing on the Internet, there is the need to protect, on the one hand, user interests in use and private access to information in order to ensure security and protection of the data exchanged on the Web and, on the other hand, to ensure respect and protection of copyright of the work as well as the sui generis right of database makers. The picture is extremely complicated as interests and rights that may collide with each other must be combined. In the case of Internet access to different content that is offered on the Web, there is also another problem. In many cases we are not only faced with the problem of determining who owns the rights or who is the author, but a new way of creating content through collaboration or automated software agents is spreading that is radically different from the traditional model which makes it even more complicated to establish the intellectual property regime and the rights derived thereof, as we will understand in the second chapter.

Francisco Andrade, University of Minho, Portugal
Paulo Novais, University of Minho, Portugal
Davide Carneiro, University of Minho, Portugal
José Neves, University of Minho, Portugal

The growing use of telematic ways of communication and of the new developments of Artificial Intelligence, brought along new ways of doing business, now in an electronic format, and requiring a new legal approach. Thus, there is an obvious need for legal changes and adaptations, not only concerning a new approach of traditional legal institutes, but also concerning a need for new developments in procedural means. Transactions are now undertaken in fractions of seconds, through the telematic networks, requiring more efficient ways for solving conflicts; on the other hand, the fact that we must now consider commercial transactions totally undertaken within an electronic environment ("online transactions") leads to an obligation of rethinking the ways of solving disputes, that will inevitably arise from electronic commerce. Chapter 3 discusses a whole new evolution towards a growing use not only alternative dispute resolution, but also, towards the so-called on-line dispute resolution.

Witold Abramowicz, Poznan University of Economics, Poland
Piotr Stolarski, Poznan University of Economics, Poland
Tadeusz Tomaszewski, Poznan University of Economics, Poland

As discussed in the fouth chapter, re-usability is frequently declared as sine qua non feature of modern ontology engineering. Although thoroughly examined in general theory of knowledge management models the re-usability issue is still barely a declaration in the domain of legal ontologies. The similar situation also applies to statute-specific ontologies. Those knowledge modeling entities are well described especially as an opposition to the general application legal ontologies. Yet it is trivial to say that most of the developed legal ontologies so far are those generic ones. And this sole fact should not surprise as the very specialized knowledge models – usually harder to develop – are at the same time narrowed with their utility. Of course in terms of re-usability this simply means that this feature may be largely disabled in this kind of knowledge models. In this chapter the authors face both challenges, i.e. as an excuse for presentation of the most interesting in their opinion trends and works in the field the authors demonstrate the practical approach to modeling copyright law case by re-using statute-specific ontologies.

Chapter 5

Masakazu Ohasji, Chuo University, Japan
Mayumi Hori, Hakuoh University, Japan

In our modern clock-ruled culture, it is not too much to say that no society can exist unless based on "time". Computers, which are the key device of an information society, are equipped with high precision clocks to synchronize their entire circuit function. In an electronic environment or digital society built on computers, recordkeeping relates inevitably to the time that is ticked away by the clocks embedded in the computers. Time is thus the infrastructure of this information society. To save the situation, a notion of time for the digital society should be properly defined and popularized, specifying the way and conditions of using it safely. The scope of discussion here focuses on some specific industries and applications for time-stamping technologies. The study here presented in Chapter 5 will be further refined step by step as their validity is verified in actual use. Meanwhile, authors are planning to work on this study for standard time distribution, which is as important as time-stamp to time business.

Chapter 6

Fernando Díez Estella, Universidad Antonio de Nebrija, Spain

Chapter 6 analyses how Antitrust is applied to ICT, in order to grant access to so-called "essential facilities", promote consumers' welfare and enhance undertakings' R&D investments. Our contentions are underscored by the recent Microsoft ruling. First the authors summarize the basic principles underlying Article 82 EC Treaty, and the way in which European antitrust authorities are trying to "reshape" it in order to achieve a more economic understanding of abusive practices, specifically refusals to deal. The the authors focus on the protection of IPRs, essential to the pivotal role ICT plays in our modern and developed world, and –closely linked to it- the consequences of this landmark case in incentives for innovation and investment. In addition to these, there is the always-present concern for consumers' welfare, which of lately has become the cornerstone for antitrust decisions; which is also addressed here.

The novelty of "new realities", such Virtual Worlds, presents a challenge to the law. Many transactions are made every day on Virtual Worlds, but no taxation is applied to them. Chapter 7 argues, firstly, that the object of such transactions is subject to the right of property and secondly that the electronic currency used to buy such property is electronic money. For both conclusions, one important issue considered will be the legal strength of the EULA. The issues of property and electronic money form the basis of this approach to VW taxation. It is argued that virtual transactions should be taxed, and that is possible to create a legal solution that does not endanger the principal of taxing only profit, and does not tax mere entertainment. Tax law must be applied to these transactions. The author considers these two issues, which allow us to view VW as an electronic commerce marketplace.

Support for research and development in information technology is considered today as critical by most governments in the industrially advanced countries. Traditionally the way of stimulating research has been to ensure to the investor the appropriability of the returns generated. Such appropriability is typically implemented by means of the Intellectual Property Rigths. Nevertheless the protection of such rights is heterogeneous worldwide. Today two different legal systems for the protection of software coexist: the system of patents and the system of author's copyrights. Chapter 8 explains these two main systems of 'intellectual property' to provide legal protection to a software, including the licenses to transfer rights on software. The end of the chapter presents the most recent trends of the EU government to replace the current European software protection system, including a discussion onf the software patents and the legal initiatives on the subject. In addition, legal issues linked with new ways in software comercialization are presented.

The price of privacy intrusion and security breaches is often due to the ubiquitous connectivity of networks. National entities as well as other governing bodies have passed laws and regulations to assist individuals in their quest to protect their information as it is being transmitted as well as received over these networks. An international perspective of information privacy and security laws and regulations can provide an insightful view concerning how each country differs as well as the important drivers for these differences. Policy makers can learn from the comparisons made in relation to similarity and/or differences of privacy and security laws as well. In chapter 9, authors have selected different countries and regions around the world due to the growth of security and privacy threats that has grown over the past 10 years as well as their legislative practices.

Chapter 10
Intellectual Property Protection and Process Modeling in Small Knowledge Intensive
Riikka Kulmala, Turku University of Applied Sciences, Finland
Juha Kettunen, Turku University of Applied Sciences, Finland

As discussed in chapter 10, knowledge-based assets, intellectual property, and capital play a fundamental role in an enterprise's competitiveness, especially in small knowledge intensive enterprises. Small knowledge intensive enterprises need to create new ways of operating in order to manage the intellectual and knowledge-based assets in their organizations more efficiently. Organizational knowledge and intellectual property can be protected, either formally via IPR, or informally via efficient knowledge management. Successful IP protection requires systematic intellectual property and knowledge management. Intellectual property protection via efficient knowledge management affects the entire organization rather than being just a separate task. It needs to be embedded in organizational work routines, practices, and processes as an overall operational strategy. When embedded in organizational work processes, IP protection and knowledge management become a continuous part of work routines and tasks in the enterprise, not a separate action.

Chapter 11
Jeremy Pitt, Imperial College London, UK
Arvind Bhusate, Imperial College London, UK

Pervasive computing aims to saturate ambient environments with sensors and processors; affective computing aims to infer emotive and intentional states from physiological readings and physical actions. The convergence of pervasive and affective computing offers genuine promise for creating ambient environments which (re-)configure themselves according to user's emotive states. On the downside, there is a real risk of privacy invasion if emotions, behaviours, and even intentions are recorded and subject to the same content-access rules as telephone calls, IP logs, and so on. Based on an experiment to enhance Quality of Experience (QoE) in a visit to a public collection enhanced with pervasive and affective computing, chapter 11 discuss the subtle interactions and requirements of enhanced service provision vis-à-vis privacy rights. The outcome will contribute to the discussion on ensuring an effective relationship between technologists and application developers on the one hand, and those concerned with privacy rights, ethical computing and formulation of social policy on the other, to promote and protect the rights and interests of citizens.

   Paulo Novais, University of Minho, Portugal

   Francisco Andrade, University of Minho, Portugal

   José Machado, University of Minho, Portugal

   José Neves, University of Minho, Portugal

Inter-systemic contracting may be based upon autonomous intelligent behaviour. Autonomy is an important advantage of software agents. Yet, it brings along several issues concerning the legal consideration (e.g. legal personality/attribution) and the legal consequences of software agent's behaviour. The intervention of software agents in corporate bodies and the consideration of its roles must also be referred. All this intends interactions based on contracts and relations of trust, at an individual, at a community and at a systemic level. In this regard, it does make sense to speak of the relation between good faith and trust in inter-systemic contracting. And at the systemic level there is a need to focus on special protocols intended to enhance trust in electronic commerce. Chapter 12 proposes smart contracts as a way of enhancing trust and of achieving enforcement in electronic contracting.

   Pedro Pina, Consultant, Portugal

As a reaction to the challenges of digitization, recent developments of international copyright law are characterized not only by its strengthening and proliferation but also by the protection of technological protection measures against circumvention acts. Consequently, in the digital context, copyright is being deconstructed and converted into a mere access right to legally and technologically protected information. Considering that copyright must represent a compromise between holders and users interests, the desired balance has been lost to the disadvantage of the users, potentially harming fundamental and human rights such as freedom of expression and freedom of access to information. In chapter 13, the author describes the conflict between copyright and freedom of expression, how the classic compromise achieved by the conflict's internalization within copyright law and the provision of copyright exemptions may no longer exist and how the users tend to find legal protection externally, outside copyright law.

   Beatriz Sainz de Abajo, University of Valladolid, Spain

   Isabel de la Torre Díez, University of Valladolid, Spain

   Miguel López-Coronado, University of Valladolid, Spain

The objective of chapter 14 is the study of the art of e-commerce, analyzing the different existing commercial models in the market such as Business to Business (B2B), Business to Consumers (B2C), Business to Business to Consumers (B2B2C), Consumers to Business (C2B), Business to Employee (B2E), Administration to Business/Consumers/Administration (A2/B/C/A), Consumers to Consumers

(C2C), Peer to Peer (P2P), Mobile to Business (M2B) and Small Office Home Office (SOHO) amongst others, the level of implementation in the work place as well as the level of acceptation in society and the regulatory framework for the development of the activity. After this study, the central theme will be one of carrying out a study of the pros and cons that e-commerce brings to the client and to the company. Moreover, a study is carried out of the implementation of e-commerce in a Small and Medium Enterprise (SME), analyzing the technological possibilities and the market of the company which is the object of the study, as well as the associated barriers and risks.

Section 2
Policies, Models, Frameworks and Rules

The second section includes five chapters that introduce new practices, new models and new approaches to data security, to information and knowledge sharing and to collaborative processes.

Business intelligence is the most powerful part of enterprise information systems (ERP). It is shown that the absence of the counterpart of business intelligence in e-government called civic intelligence (CI) has important negative consequence that are probably more severe than the absence of business intelligence for enterprises. Missing CI threatens the prosperity of countries and nations as it has crucial negative effects on social processes like the quality of education, health-care research, and research and control of economic processes. Data security of CI is an issue. Current practices of data security are to a high degree equivalent to virtual massive data shredding. It is a big obstacle for the development of CI. An architecture of CI allowing satisfactory level of data security is proposed in chapter 15, together with organizational and legislative preconditions of CI, and the barriers of CI are analyzed.

Chapter 16 focuses on sharing information through global communication systems in the context of computer-aided academic research: more specifically, on cross-disciplinary research primarily involving collaborations between natural scientists and colleagues in computational science. The authors interest lies in the visualization and high performance computing (HPC) communities, branches of computational science providing enhanced ways of organising, analysing and presenting materials, models and results of research in other disciplines.

Chapter 17

Pawan Chhabra, Infosys, India
Chetan Jagatkishore Kothari, Infosys, India
Subhadip Sarkar, Infosys, India

In recent times, the focus of innovation is increasingly moving beyond the centralized R&D programs of large firms to more of a collaborative innovation. This is true even in the Information Communication Technology (ICT) industries. With this approach in mind, the technical strategy has to be laid down to design appropriate architectural models that act as key foundations of building large software systems without compromising on access rights, privacy, confidentiality, ethics, policies, IP, etc. A platform that can enable researchers to share their views, ideas, thoughts or products in seamless manner is the need of the hour. Chapter 17 examines the ways and means of creating a standard model which focuses on well proven software design practices to leverage full potential of open innovation platform; while focusing upon the evolution of IP trends and without compromising on access rights, privacy, confidentiality, ethics, policies, IP, etc.

Chapter 18

Sam De Silva, Taylor Walton LLP, UK

Developments in technology and the global nature of business means that personal information about individuals in the UK may often be processed overseas, frequently without the explicit knowledge or consent of those individuals. This raises issues such as the security of such data, who may have access to it and for what purposes and what rights the individual may have to object. The Data Protection Act 1998 provides a standard of protection for personal data, including in respect of personal data that is being transferred outside of the UK. Chapter 18 focus on how a UK data controller (the organisation that controls how and why personal data is processed and is therefore legally responsible for compliance) can fulfil its business and operational requirements in transferring personal data outside the EEA, whilst ensuring legal compliance.

Chapter 19

Murat Erdal, Istanbul University, Turkey
Gulşah Ekiz, Galatasaray University, Turkey
Selim Aksin, Turkey Telecommunication Council, Turkey
Necmi Murat Güngör, Turkey Telecommunication Council, Turkey

In Turkey, access blocking to websites by judicial orders has especially come into spotlight with the blocking of globally renowned websites such as www.youtube.com and www.wordpress.com. After the police operations in 2006 concentrating on internet child pornography, the need for legal provisions to regulate internet has started to be widely discussed and Law No. 5651 on the Regulation of Publications on the Internet and Suppression of Crimes Committed by means of Such Publications was enacted on 25 May, 2007. This law has generally defined the actors related to internet and has regulated the access blocking in the scheme of suppression of the crimes listed below. Telecommunications Communication Presidency is entitled to the enforcement of the law that has come into effect as of 23 October 2007. Chapter 19 aims to trace the short history of access blocking and try to assess the subject in the light of cases from the applications in Turkey.

Section 3
Protection of Privacy and Trust

The third section includes three chapters concerned with unauthorized accesses to sensible digital information, privacy rights and trust and presents tools and techniques to prevent or control these aspects.

Chapter 20

J. A. Álvarez Bermejo, Universidad de Almería, Spain
J. A. López Ramos, Universidad de Almería, Spain
F. Gálvez Sánchez, Universidad de Almería, Spain

In chapter 20 the authors propose a powerful yet inexpensive method for protecting and discriminating unauthorized accesses to sensible digital information (or even to the entire system) via common and conventional tools such as USB devices. The result of this work allows that the access to servers or the execution and access to specific data, take place only under a controlled and defined scenario.

Chapter 21

Louis B. Swartz, Robert Morris University, USA
Michele T. Cole, Robert Morris University, USA
David A. Lovejoy, Robert Morris University, USA

There is no clear right to privacy, confidence, and reputation in United States case law or in legislation for students in the online environment. While some privacy interests are protected under a variety of legal theories, none expressly applies to online education. The study presented in chapter 21 examines pertinent issues concerning the privacy rights of students while engaged in online learning. A survey of students using online tools in their courses demonstrated a widespread belief that their communications were private. A second survey of business law instructors using online tools revealed a lack of awareness of the potential for abuse by third parties able to access users' information. Survey results were inconclusive with regard to the existence of policies and procedures within the institutions with regard to protecting users' privacy rights in online instruction. Survey respondents made several recommendations for action to mediate the lack of existing protections for privacy in online learning.

Georgios V. Lioudakis, National Technical University of Athens, Greece
Francesca Gaudino, Baker & McKenzie, Italy
Elisa Boschi, Hitachi Europe, France
Giuseppe Bianchi, University of Rome Tor Vergata, Italy
Dimitra I. Kaklamani, National Technical University of Athens, Greece
Iakovos S. Venieris, National Technical University of Athens, Greece

Passive network monitoring is very useful for the operation, maintenance, control and protection of communication networks, while in certain cases it provides the authorities with the means for law enforcement. Nevertheless, the flip side of monitoring activities is that they are natively surrounded by serious privacy implications and, therefore, they are subject to data protection legislation. Chapter 22 investigates the challenges related to privacy protection in passive network monitoring, based on a joint technical and regulatory analysis of the associated issues. After introducing the issue and its special characteristics, the chapter provides background knowledge regarding the corresponding legal and regulatory framework, as well as some related work. It then delves into the description of the legal and regulatory requirements that govern network monitoring systems, before providing an overview of a reference monitoring system, which has been designed with these requirements in mind.

Section 4
Access Rights

The fourth section discusses both web accessibility legislation and standards, and legal aspects of access to digital contents and intellectual property rights.

P. Chías, University of Alcalá, Spain
T. Abad, University of Alcalá, Spain
E. Rivera, University of Alcalá, Spain

The Council of the European Union is developing some strategies about the European Digital Libraries considered as a common multilingual access point to Europe's digital cultural heritage. The project introduced in chapter 23, of a digital cartographic database accessed through GIS looks for the integration of digital technologies with the cartographic heritage providing new approaches to, and new audiences for the history of cartography. The online presence of this cartographic material will be a rich source of raw material to be re-used in different sectors and for different purposes and technological developments; but we must also afford some legal challenges because digitisation presupposes making a copy, which can be problematic in view of intellectual property rights (IPR). As the transparency and clarification of the copyright status of works is very relevant to us, those legal challenges and their solutions will be the main subjects of this chapter.

Nowadays, in contrast with centralized or hierarchical certification authorities and directory of names, other solutions are gaining momentum. Federation of already deployed security systems is considered the key to build global security infrastructures. In this field, trust management systems can play an important role, being based on a totally distributed architecture. The idea of distributed trust management can be confronted with the concept of trusted computing. Though having a confusingly similar denomination, the different interpretation of trust in these systems drives to divergent consequences with respect to system architectures and access policies, but also to law, ethics, politics. While trusted computing systems assure copyright holders and media producers that the hosting system will respect the access restrictions they defined, trust management systems, instead, allow users to grant trust to other users or software agents for accessing local resources, as discussed in chapter 24.

Web accessibility is a major question in present ICT legislation. An ageing population is a known phenomenon that makes older people become a specific interest group. In chapter 25 the authors present the evolution encountered in laws and standards due to specific concern about older people. This publication is related to the works of the W3C WAI-AGE group. The authors focus mainly in the adaptations encountered in W3C accessibility guidelines (WCAG) while considering the difficulties related to ageing. The chapter also proposes some practical recommendations for web designers that want to develop websites targeting seniors, and finally gives some perspectives about accessibility legislation and standards.

Section 5

ICT Ethics

The last section includes two chapters that discuss legal, privacy and security aspects related to ICT ethics in the information and knowledge society.

Chapter 26 describes the present situation of E-Health at home taking into account legal, privacy and security aspects. As a first step, some background and a general description of E-Health activities at home are presented. In order to have a general idea of the current status of this field, we analyze the general legal situation in terms of ICT for E-Health and several related issues on data mining privacy and information recovery aspects. The topics covered include the taxonomy for secondary uses of clinical data and a description of the role that controlled vocabularies play. Concerning the provision of E-Health at home, the chapter revises the current situation in the digital home evolution including topics on sensors and sanitary devices. Furthermore the challenge of digital identity at home and the differences between the domestic environment and the professional one are considered. Finally some ethical considerations under the "InfoEthics" concept and future lines of work are addressed.

"Informational Society" is unceasingly discussed by all societies' quadrants. Nevertheless, in spite of illustrating the most recent progress of western societies the complexity to characterize it is well-known. In such societal evolution the "leading role" goes to information, as a polymorphic phenomenon and a polysemantic concept. Given such claim and the need for a multidimensional approach, the overall amount of information available online has reached an unparalleled level, and consequently search engines become exceptionally important. Search engines main stream literature has been debating the following perspectives: technology, user level of expertise and confidence, organizational impact, and just recently power issues. However, the trade-off between informational fluxes versus control has been disregarded. Chapter 27 discusses such gap, and for that, the overall structure of the chapter is: information, search engines, control and its dimensions, and exploit Google as a case study.

Preface

ABOUT THE SUBJECT

In the digital age, ICT raise new concerns that are not accounted for within the existing data protection/privacy legal framework, so some action is therefore necessary to ensure individual rights. After providing an overview of ICT as a new development that creates opportunities and also risks, this book discusses the need to integrate, at a practical level, data protection and privacy from the very inception of new information and communication technologies.

Information and communication technologies (ICT) are enabling tremendous capabilities in virtually every aspect of our lives–how we work, play, socialize and educate. They are essential for today's information economy and for society in general. ICT have been compared to other important inventions of the past, such as electricity. While it may be too early to assess their real historical impact, the link between ICT and economic growth in developed countries is clear. ICT have created employment, economic benefits and contributed to overall welfare.

The impact of ICT goes beyond the purely economic, since it has played an important role in boosting innovation and creativity. But individuals should be able to rely on ICT's ability to keep their information secure and control its use, as well as be confident that their privacy and data protection rights will be honored in the digital space.

MISSION AND OBJECTIVES OF THIS BOOK

The mission of this book is to provide comprehensive coverage of the latest and most relevant knowledge, developments, solutions and practical approaches related to this topic that are able to transform society and the way we live from a technological, legal and ethical perspectives.

Some of the most significant objectives of this book include:

- to overcome the fragmentation of knowledge concerning the latest developments on the theme and document the most impact contributions, from legal and regulative developments to its concrete applications, from the discussion of frameworks, approaches and models, to its impact on society and organizations, from technology to people.
- to incentive and to support future trends for research and development
- to discuss advantages, opportunities, challenges, results and future trends
- to support for higher education courses.

The resulting publication is a valuable and multi-faceted resource that gives the reader good insight about where technological developments and legal aspects are taking us in this emerging and more and more relevant expanding domain.

ORGANIZATION OF THE BOOK

This book is a compilation of 27 contributions that discuss several dimensions: Information and Technology law and regulation, Knowledge and Information Society aspects related to protection and access rights both for individuals and digital contents, and accessibility issues related to ethics, regulation and standards.

These 27 chapters are written by 68 authors from academe, industry and professionals, related to the different dimensions of the book's theme: from law to ICT experts, including policy makers.

Information Communication Technology Law, Protection and Access Rights: Global Approaches and Issues is organized in five sections:

- **Section 1:** ICT Law and Regulation discusses implications, challenges, barriers and opportunities of the Information Society and ICT, namely the legal aspects in the field of intellectual property rights, conflict resolution in electronic commerce and electronic transactions, authentication of digital contents.
- **Section 2:** Policies, Models, Frameworks and Rules introduces new practices, new models and new approaches to data security, to information and knowledge sharing and to collaborative processes.
- **Section 3:** Protection of privacy and trust is concerned with unauthorized accesses to sensible digital information, privacy rights and trust and presents tools and techniques to prevent or control these aspects.
- **Section 4:** Access Rights discusses both web accessibility legislation and standards, and legal aspects of access to digital contents and intellectual property rights.
- **Section 5:** ICT Ethics discusses legal, privacy and security aspects related to ICT ethics in the information and knowledge society.

The first section, ICT Law and Regulation, discusses implications, challenges, barriers and opportunities of the Information Society and ICT, namely the legal aspects in the field of intellectual property rights, conflict resolution in electronic commerce and electronic transactions, authentication of digital contents. This section includes the 14 chapters summarized below.

The Data Retention Directive (2006/24/EC) provides the obligation for providers of publicly available electronic communications services or of public communications networks to retain traffic and location data for six months up to two years for the purpose of the investigation, detection and prosecution of serious crime. In the regulatory framework imposed by this Directive, the Portuguese Law no. 32/2008, of 17 July, requires that providers of publicly available electronic communication services or of public communications networks retain specific communication data, so that such data can be accessed by competent authorities, exclusively for the purpose of investigation, detection and prosecution of serious crime. Retained (via digital storage) metadata of telecommunications acts change and transform into the content of something else: a surveillance program. The concept of a data space that provides movement within and between data described here illustrates the powers of data retention in an imaginable way.

Considering potential uses and misuses of retained data such as traffic analysis, social network analysis and data mining, the first chapter of this book examines the degree of interference with the right to privacy posed by the data retention laws.

In the second chapter, *"Information Agents, Social Web and Intellectual Property,"* the authors argue that due to the development of the information society, there has been a substantial change in regulating certain legal aspects in the field of intellectual property. Focusing on the Internet, there is the need to protect, on the one hand, user interests in use and private access to information in order to ensure security and protection of the data exchanged on the Web and, on the other hand, to ensure respect and protection of copyright of the work as well as the sui generis right of database makers. The picture is extremely complicated as interests and rights that may collide with each other must be combined. In the case of Internet access to different content that is offered on the Web, there is also another problem. In many cases we are not only faced with the problem of determining who owns the rights or who is the author, but a new way of creating content through collaboration or automated software agents is spreading that is radically different from the traditional model which makes it even more complicated to establish the intellectual property regime and the rights derived thereof, as we will understand in the first chapter.

The growing use of telematic ways of communication and of the new developments of Artificial Intelligence brought along new ways of doing business, now in an electronic format, and requiring a new legal approach. Thus, there is an obvious need for legal changes and adaptations, not only concerning a new approach of traditional legal institutes, but also concerning a need for new developments in procedural means. Transactions are now undertaken in fractions of seconds, through the telematic networks, requiring more efficient ways for solving conflicts; on the other hand, the fact that we must now consider commercial transactions totally undertaken within an electronic environment ("online transactions") leads to an obligation of rethinking the ways of solving disputes that will inevitably arise from electronic commerce. Chapter 3, *"Conflict Resolution in Virtual Locations"* discusses a whole new evolution towards a growing use not only alternative dispute resolution, but also, towards the so-called on-line dispute resolution.

As discussed in the fourth chapter, *"Legal Ontologies in ICT and Law,"* re-usability is frequently declared as sine qua non feature of modern ontology engineering. Although thoroughly examined in general theory of knowledge management models the re-usability issue is still barely a declaration in the domain of legal ontologies. The similar situation also applies to statute-specific ontologies. Those knowledge modeling entities are well described especially as an opposition to the general application legal ontologies. Yet it is trivial to say that most of the developed legal ontologies so far are those generic ones. And this sole fact should not surprise as the very specialized knowledge models – usually harder to develop – are at the same time narrowed with their utility. Of course in terms of re-usability, this simply means that this feature may be largely disabled in this kind of knowledge models. In this chapter the authors face both challenges—by presenting the most interesting trends and works in the field, the authors demonstrate the practical approach to modeling copyright law case by re-using statute-specific ontologies.

According to the authors of chapter 5, *"Certified Originality of Digital Contents by the Time Authentication,"* in our modern clock-ruled culture, it is not too much to say that no society can exist unless based on "time." Computers, which are the key device of an information society, are equipped with high precision clocks to synchronize their entire circuit function. In an electronic environment or digital society built on computers, recordkeeping relates inevitably to the time that is ticked away by the clocks embedded in the computers. Time is thus the infrastructure of this information society. To save the situation, a notion of time for the digital society should be properly defined and popularized, specifying the way and conditions of using it safely. The scope of discussion here focuses on some specific industries and applications for time-stamping technologies. The study presented here will be further refined step by step as its validity is verified in actual use. Meanwhile, authors are planning to work on this study for standard time distribution, which is as important as time-stamp to time business.

Chapter 6, "*Antitrust Applied to ICT: Granting Access, Promoting Consumers' Welfare and Enhancing Undertakings' R&D Investments*" analyses how Antitrust is applied to ICT in order to grant access to so-called "essential facilities," promote consumers' welfare and enhance R&D investments. Our contentions are underscored by the recent Microsoft ruling. First, the authors summarize the basic principles underlying Article 82 EC Treaty, and the way in which European antitrust authorities are trying to "reshape" it in order to achieve a more economic understanding of abusive practices, specifically refusals to deal. The authors focus on the protection of IPRs, essential to the pivotal role ICT plays in our modern and developed world, and–closely linked to it–the consequences of this landmark case in incentives for innovation and investment. In addition to these, there is the always-present concern for consumers' welfare, which has become the cornerstone for antitrust decisions and is also addressed here.

The novelty of "new realities" such as Virtual Worlds presents a challenge to the law. Many transactions are made every day on Virtual Worlds, but no taxation is applied to them. Chapter 7, "*Taxation of Virtual Worlds: An Approach to Face Virtual Worlds as Electronic Commerce*" argues, firstly, that the object of such transactions is subject to the right of property and secondly, that the electronic currency used to buy such property is electronic money. For both conclusions, one important issue considered will be the legal strength of the EULA. The issues of property and electronic money form the basis of this approach to VW taxation. It is argued that virtual transactions should be taxed, and that is possible to create a legal solution that does not endanger the principal of taxing only profit, and does not tax mere entertainment. Tax law must be applied to these transactions. The author considers these two issues, which allow us to view VW as an electronic commerce marketplace.

Support for research and development in information technology is considered today as critical by most governments in industrially advanced countries. Traditionally, the way of stimulating research has been to ensure to the investor the appropriability of the returns generated. Such appropriability is typically implemented by means of Intellectual Property Rights. Nevertheless, the protection of such rights is heterogeneous worldwide. Today, two different legal systems for the protection of software coexist: the system of patents and the system of author's copyrights. In chapter 8, "*Intellectual Property Systems in Software,*" the authors explain these two main systems of intellectual property to provide legal protection for software, including the licenses to transfer rights on software. The end of the chapter presents the most recent trends of the EU to replace the current European software protection system, including a discussion on software patents and legal initiatives on the subject. In addition, legal issues linked with trends in software commercialization are presented.

The price of privacy intrusion and security breaches is often due to the ubiquitous connectivity of networks. National entities as well as other governing bodies have passed laws and regulations to assist individuals in their quest to protect their information as it is being transmitted and received over these networks. An international perspective of information privacy and security laws and regulations can provide an insightful view concerning how each country differs as well as the important drivers for these differences. Policy makers can learn from the comparisons made in relation to similarities and differences between privacy and security laws. In chapter 9, "*A Global Perspective of Laws and Regulations Dealing with Information Security and Privacy,*" the authors have selected different countries and regions around the world due to the growth of security and privacy threats over the past 10 years as well as their legislative practices.

As discussed in chapter 10, "*Intellectual Property Protection and Process Modeling in Small Knowledge Intensive Enterprises*," knowledge-based assets, intellectual property, and capital play a fundamental role in an enterprise's competitiveness, especially in small knowledge intensive enterprises. Small knowledge intensive enterprises need to create new ways of operating in order to manage the intellectual and knowledge-based assets in their organizations more efficiently. Organizational knowledge and intellectual property can be protected, either formally via IPR, or informally via efficient knowledge management. Successful IP protection requires systematic intellectual property and knowledge management. Intellectual property protection via efficient knowledge management affects the entire organization rather than being just a separate task. It needs to be embedded in organizational work routines, practices, and processes as an overall operational strategy. When embedded in organizational work processes, IP protection and knowledge management become a continuous part of work routines and tasks in the enterprise, not a separate action.

Pervasive computing aims to saturate ambient environments with sensors and processors; affective computing aims to infer emotive and intentional states from physiological readings and physical actions. The convergence of pervasive and affective computing offers genuine promise for creating ambient environments which (re-)configure themselves according to user's emotive states. On the down-side, there is a real risk of privacy invasion if emotions, behaviours, and even intentions are recorded and subject to the same content-access rules as telephone calls, IP logs, and so on. Based on an experiment to enhance Quality of Experience (QoE) in a visit to a public collection enhanced with pervasive and affective computing, chapter 11, "*Privacy in Pervasive and Affective Computing Environments*" discusses the subtle interactions and requirements of enhanced service provision vis-à-vis privacy rights. The outcome will contribute to the discussion on ensuring an effective relationship between technologists and application developers on the one hand, and those concerned with privacy rights, ethical computing and formulation of social policy on the other, to promote and protect the rights and interests of citizens.

Inter-systemic contracting may be based upon autonomous intelligent behaviour. Autonomy is an important advantage of software agents. Yet, it brings along several issues concerning the legal consideration (e.g. legal personality/attribution) and the legal consequences of software agent's behaviour. The intervention of software agents in corporate bodies and the consideration of its roles must also be referred. All this intends interactions based on contracts and relations of trust, at an individual, at a community and at a systemic level. In this regard, it does make sense to speak of the relation between good faith and trust in inter-systemic contracting. And at the systemic level there is a need to focus on special protocols intended to enhance trust in electronic commerce. Chapter 12, "*Agents, Trust and Contracts*," proposes smart contracts as a way of enhancing trust and of achieving enforcement in electronic contracting.

As a reaction to the challenges of digitization, recent developments in international copyright law are characterized not only by its strengthening and proliferation but also by the protection of technological protection measures against circumvention acts. Consequently, in the digital context, copyright is being deconstructed and converted into a mere access right to legally and technologically protected information. Considering that copyright must represent a compromise between holders' and users' interests, the desired balance has been lost to the disadvantage of the users, potentially harming fundamental and human rights such as freedom of expression and freedom of access to information. In chapter 13, "*Between Scylla and Charybdis: The Balance between Copyright, Digital Rights Management and Freedom of Expression*," the author describes the conflict between copyright and freedom of expression, how the classic compromise achieved by the conflict's internalization within copyright law and the provision of copyright exemptions may no longer exist and how the users tend to find legal protection externally, outside copyright law.

The objective of chapter 14, "*Analysis of Benefits and Risks of E-Commerce: Practical Study of Spanish SME*," is the study of the art of e-commerce, analyzing the different existing commercial models in the market such as Business to Business (B2B), Business to Consumers (B2C), Business to Business to Consumers (B2B2C), Consumers to Business (C2B), Business to Employee (B2E), Administration to Business/Consumers/Administration (A2/B/C/A), Consumers to Consumers (C2C), Peer to Peer (P2P), Mobile to Business (M2B) and Small Office Home Office (SOHO) amongst others, the level of implementation in the workplace as well as the level of acceptance in society and the regulatory framework for the development of the activity. After this study, the central theme will be one of carrying out a study of the pros and cons that e-commerce brings to the client and to the company. Moreover, a study on the implementation of e-commerce in a Small and Medium Enterprise (SME) is conducted, analyzing the technological possibilities and the market of the company which is the object of the study, as well as the associated barriers and risks.

The second section, "Policies, Models, Frameworks and Rules," includes five chapters that introduce new practices, new models and new approaches to data security, to information and knowledge sharing and to collaborative processes.

Business intelligence is the most powerful part of enterprise information systems (ERP). It is shown in chapter 15, "*Data Security Legislative as Data Shredding Mill*," that the absence of the counterpart of business intelligence in e-government called civic intelligence (CI) has important negative consequence that are probably more severe than the absence of business intelligence for enterprises. Missing CI threatens the prosperity of countries and nations as it has crucial negative effects on social processes like the quality of education, healthcare research, and research and control of economic processes. Data security of CI is an issue. Current practices of data security are to a high degree equivalent to virtual massive data shredding. It is a big obstacle for the development of CI. An architecture of CI allowing a satisfactory level of data security is proposed in chapter 14, together with organizational and legislative preconditions of CI, and an analysis of barriers to CI.

Chapter 16, "*Collaborative Practices in Computer-Aided Academic Research*," focuses on sharing information through global communication systems in the context of computer-aided academic research: more specifically, on cross-disciplinary research primarily involving collaborations between natural scientists and colleagues in computational science. The authors' interest lies in the visualization and high performance computing (HPC) communities, branches of computational science providing enhanced ways of organising, analysing and presenting materials, models and results of research in other disciplines.

In recent times, the focus of innovation is increasingly moving beyond the centralized R&D programs of large firms to more collaborative innovation. This is true even in the Information Communication Technology (ICT) industries. With this approach in mind, the technical strategy has to be laid down to design appropriate architectural models that act as key foundations of building large software systems without compromising access rights, privacy, confidentiality, ethics, policies, IP, etc. A platform that can enable researchers to share their views, ideas, thoughts or products in a seamless manner is needed. Chapter 17, "*Designing Appropriate Frameworks, Models, Strategies and Solutions*," examines the ways and means of creating a standard model which focuses on well proven software design practices to leverage the full potential of an open innovation platform while focusing upon the evolution of IP trends and without compromising on access rights, privacy, confidentiality, ethics, policies, IP, etc.

Developments in technology and the global nature of business means that personal information about individuals in the UK may often be processed overseas, frequently without the explicit knowledge or consent of those individuals. This raises issues such as the security of such data, who may have access to it and for what purposes and what rights the individual may have to object. The Data Protection Act 1998 provides a standard of protection for personal data, including in respect of personal data that is being transferred outside of the UK. Chapter 18, "*International Transfers of Personal Data: A UK Law Perspective,*" focuses on how a UK data controller (the organisation that controls how and why personal data is processed and is therefore legally responsible for compliance) can fulfill its business and operational requirements in transferring personal data outside the EEA, whilst ensuring legal compliance.

In Turkey, access blocking to websites by judicial orders has especially come into spotlight with the blocking of globally renowned websites such as www.youtube.com and www.wordpress.com. After police operations in 2006 that concentrated on Internet child pornography, the need for legal provisions to regulate the Internet has been widely discussed and Law No. 5651 on the Regulation of Publications on the Internet and Suppression of Crimes Committed by means of Such Publications was enacted on May 25, 2007. This law has generally defined the actors related to the Internet and has regulated access blocking in the scheme of suppression of crimes. Telecommunications Communication Presidency is entitled to the enforcement of the law that has come into effect as of October 23, 2007. Chapter 19, "*Restricted Access and Blocking Websites, Internet Regulations and Turkey Practices,*" aims to trace the short history of access blocking and try to assess the subject in the light of cases from the applications in Turkey.

The third section, "Protection of Privacy and Trust," includes three chapters concerned with unauthorized accesses to sensible digital information, privacy rights and trust, and presents tools and techniques to prevent or control these aspects.

In chapter 20, "*Hardware Secure Access to Servers and Applications,*" the authors propose a powerful yet inexpensive method for protecting and discriminating unauthorized accesses to sensible digital information (or even to the entire system) via common and conventional tools such as USB devices. The result of this work is that access to servers or the execution and access to specific data takes place only under a controlled and defined scenario.

According to chapter 21, "*Ensuring Users' Rights to Privacy, Confidence and Reputation in the Online Learning Environment: What Should Instructors Do to Protect Their Students' Privacy?*" there is no clear right to privacy, confidence, and reputation in United States case law or in legislation for students in the online environment. While some privacy interests are protected under a variety of legal theories, none expressly applies to online education. The study presented examines pertinent issues concerning the privacy rights of students while engaged in online learning. A survey of students using online tools in their courses demonstrated a widespread belief that their communications were private. A second survey of business law instructors using online tools revealed a lack of awareness of the potential for abuse by third parties able to access users' information. Survey results were inconclusive with regard to the existence of policies and procedures within the institutions with regard to protecting users' privacy rights in online instruction. Survey respondents made several recommendations for action to mediate the lack of existing protections for privacy in online learning.

Passive network monitoring is very useful for the operation, maintenance, control and protection of communication networks, while in certain cases it provides the authorities with the means for law enforcement. Nevertheless, the flip side of monitoring activities is that they are natively surrounded by serious privacy implications and, therefore, they are subject to data protection legislation. Chapter 22,

"*Legislation-Aware Privacy Protection in Passive Network Monitoring,*" investigates the challenges related to privacy protection in passive network monitoring based on a joint technical and regulatory analysis of the associated issues. After introducing the issue and its special characteristics, the chapter provides background knowledge regarding the corresponding legal and regulatory framework, as well as some related work. It then delves into the description of the legal and regulatory requirements that govern network monitoring systems, before providing an overview of a reference monitoring system, which has been designed with these requirements in mind.

The fourth section, "Access Rights," discusses both Web accessibility legislation and standards, and legal aspects of access to digital contents and intellectual property rights.

The Council of the European Union is developing some strategies about the European Digital Libraries considered as a common multilingual access point to Europe's digital cultural heritage. The project introduced in chapter 23, "*The Project of the Ancient Spanish Cartography E-Library: Main Targets and Legal Challenges,*" concerning a digital cartographic database accessed through GIS, looks for the integration of digital technologies with the cartographic heritage providing new approaches to and new audiences for the history of cartography. The online presence of this cartographic material will be a rich source of raw material to be reused in different sectors and for different purposes and technological developments; but we must also afford some legal challenges because digitisation presupposes making a copy, which can be problematic in view of intellectual property rights (IPR). As the transparency and clarification of the copyright status of works is very relevant to us, those legal challenges and their solutions will be the main subjects of this chapter.

In contrast with centralized or hierarchical certification authorities and directory of names, other solutions are now gaining momentum. Federation of already deployed security systems is considered the key to build global security infrastructures. In this field, trust management systems can play an important role, being based on a totally distributed architecture. The idea of distributed trust management can be confronted with the concept of trusted computing. Though having a confusingly similar denomination, the different interpretation of trust in these systems drives to divergent consequences with respect to system architectures and access policies, but also to law, ethics, and politics. While trusted computing systems assure copyright holders and media producers that the hosting system will respect the access restrictions they defined, trust management systems instead allow users to grant trust to other users or software agents for accessing local resources, as discussed in chapter 24, "*Trusted Computing or Distributed Trust Management?*"

Web accessibility is a major question in present ICT legislation. An aging population is a known phenomenon that makes older people become a specific interest group. In chapter 25, "*Senior Web Accessibility: Laws, Standards and Practices,*" the authors present the evolution encountered in laws and standards due to specific concern about older people. This publication is related to the works of the W3C WAI-AGE group. The authors focus mainly on the adaptations encountered in W3C accessibility guidelines (WCAG) while considering the difficulties related to aging. The chapter also proposes some practical recommendations for Web designers that want to develop websites targeting seniors, and finally gives some perspectives about accessibility legislation and standards.

The last section, "ICT Ethics," include two chapters that discuss legal, privacy and security aspects related to ICT ethics in the information and knowledge society.

Chapter 26, "*E-Health at Home: Legal, Privacy and Security Aspects,*" describes the present situation of e-health at home, taking into account legal, privacy and security aspects. As a first step, some background and a general description of e-health activities at home are presented. In order to have a general idea of the current status of this field, we analyze the general legal situation in terms of ICT for E-health and several related issues on data mining privacy and information recovery aspects. The topics covered include the taxonomy for secondary uses of clinical data and a description of the role that controlled vocabularies play. Concerning the provision of e-health at home, the chapter revises the current situation in the digital home evolution including topics on sensors and sanitary devices. Furthermore the challenge of digital identity at home and the differences between the domestic environment and the professional one are considered. Finally, some ethical considerations under the "InfoEthics" concept and future lines of work are addressed.

"Informational Society" is unceasingly discussed by all societies' quadrants. Nevertheless, in spite of illustrating the most recent progress of western societies the complexity to characterize it is well-known. In such societal evolution, the "leading role" goes to information as a polymorphic phenomenon and a polysemantic concept. Given such claims and the need for a multidimensional approach, the overall amount of information available online has reached an unparalleled level, and consequently search engines become exceptionally important. Mainstream search engine literature has been debating the following perspectives: technology, user level of expertise and confidence, organizational impact, and, just recently, power issues. However, the trade-off between informational fluxes versus control has been disregarded. Chapter 27, "*Controlling Informational Society: A Google Error Analysis!*" discuss such gaps, and the overall structure of the chapter is: information, search engines, control and its dimensions, and exploiting Google as a case study.

EXPECTATIONS

This book offers an exhaustive coverage on the theme, providing researchers, scholars, and professionals with some of the most advanced research discussions, developments and solutions on the domain of ICT law, protection and access rights in a very comprehensive way.

This book intends to support the academic audience (teachers, researchers and students, mainly of post-graduate studies), law, IT and ICT professionals and managers and policy makers of a broad range of sectors.

We sincerely expect that this work will stimulate further research and development on the theme by law and IT professionals and researchers, academics and doctoral students, policy makers and top managers.

The Editors,

Irene Maria Portela
Polytechnic Institute of Cávado and Ave, Portugal

Maria Manuela Cruz-Cunha
Polytechnic Institute of Cávado and Ave, Portugal

Acknowledgment

Editing a book is a quite hard but compensating and enriching task, as it involves an set of different activities like contacts with authors and reviewers, discussion and exchange of ideas and experiences, process management, organization and integration of contents, and many other, with the permanent objective of creating a book that meets the public expectations. And this task cannot be accomplished without a great help and support from many sources. As editor I would like to acknowledge the help, support and believe of all who made possible this creation.

First of all, the edition of this book would not have been possible without the ongoing professional support of the team of professionals of IGI Global. I am grateful to Dr. Mehdi Khosrow-Pour and to Ms. Jan Travers for the opportunity. A very very special mention of gratitude is due to Ms. Julia Mosemann for her professional support and friendly words of advisory, encouragement and prompt guidance.

Special thanks go also to all the staff at IGI Global, whose contributions throughout the process of production and making this book available all over the world was invaluable.

We are grateful to all the authors, for their insights and excellent contributions to this book. Also we are grateful to most of the authors who simultaneously served as referees for chapters written by other authors, for their insights, valuable contributions, prompt collaboration and constructive comments. Thank you all, authors and reviewers, you made this book! The communication and exchange of views within this truly global group of recognized individualities from the scientific domain and from industry was an enriching and exciting experience!

We are also grateful to all who accede to contribute to this book, some of them with high quality chapter proposals, but unfortunately, due to several constraints could not have seen their work published.

A special thanks to our institution, the Polytechnic Institute of Cávado and Ave, for providing the material resources and all the necessary logistics.

Thank you.

The Editors,

Irene Maria Portela
Maria Manuela Cruz-Cunha

Barcelos, November 2009

Section 1
ICT Law and Regulation

Chapter 1
What about the Balance between Law Enforcement and Data Protection?

Irene Portela
Polytechnic Institute of Cávado and Ave, Portugal

Maria Manuela Cruz-Cunha
Polytechnic Institute of Cávado and Ave, Portugal & University of Minho, Portugal

ABSTRACT

The Data Retention Directive (2006/24/EC) provides the obligation for providers of publicly available electronic communications services or of public communications networks to retain traffic and location data for six months up to two years for the purpose of the investigation, detection and prosecution of serious crime. In the regulatory framework imposed by this Directive, the Portuguese Law no. 32/2008, of 17 July, requires that providers of publicly available electronic communication services or of public communications networks retain specific communication data, so that such data can be accessed by competent authorities, exclusively for the purpose of investigation, detection and prosecution of serious crime. Retained (via digital storage) metadata of telecommunications acts change and transform into the content of something else: a surveillance program. The concept of a data space that provides movement within and between data described here illustrates the powers of data retention in an imaginable way. Considering potential uses and misuses of retained data such as traffic analysis, social network analysis and data mining, this chapter examines the degree of interference with the right to privacy posed by the data retention laws.

INTRODUCTION

The EU adopted the Data Retention Directive in March 2006. The purpose of the Directive is to achieve an EU-wide harmonisation of national requirements for the mandatory retention of communications data. Seen from a broader scope, data retention fits well into the post-9/11 war on terror measurements. The shift toward an omniscient surveillance-state has generally often been compared to scenarios familiar from the prophetic novel 1984 by George Orwell (1949).

DOI: 10.4018/978-1-61520-975-0.ch001

After the terrorist attacks in Europe in 2004 and 2005, the EU passed the Directive because of the legal and technical differences between national provisions for data retention[1]. The European Union Directive on data retention[2], though less than 10 pages long, is invested with considerable authority[3]. The Data Retention Directive requires EU governments to retain data for assistance in the investigation, detection and prosecution of serious crime3 and covers both telephones and the internet. It directs the member states to pass a law compelling each provider of telecommunications services to retain traffic and location data for at least the past six, and at most, the last 24 months.

Two key privacy protections were removed. The first of which said that data could only be held for the purposes of billing (ie: for the customer to check the details), usually only for a few weeks. The second allows member states to adopt national laws to require communications providers to retain data for a specified period so that law enforcement agencies can get access to it.

As stated in the first sentence of Article 1: This Directive aims to harmonise Member States' provisions concerning the obligations of the providers of publicly available electronic communications services or of public communications networks with respect to the retention of certain data which are generated or processed by them, in order to ensure that the data are available for the purpose of the investigation, detection, and prosecution of serious crime, as defined by each Member State in its national law (2006/24/EC: 56).

- And what are the data object of the EU Directive[4]?

The "Data" as is defined in this text is "data generated by or during an act of telecommunication with a mobile phone, a landline, or via the Internet", minus the content, means traffic data and location data.

These inquiries around data ask who, when, where, with whom, how long, and so forth — but do not ask about the nature of the communication. The data generated during unsuccessful acts of telecommunication is also similarly analysed. (Davies & Trigg, 2006).

This differentiation between data that contains the structural components of communication and data that relates to content is that traffic data consists only of the information needed to technically initiate, sustain, and terminate an act of communication.

However, as the Directive aims at "the investigation, detection, and prosecution of serious crime," the relevant data is divided into the following categories[5] as we can see at the article 5[6] of the 2006/24/EC:

1. data necessary to trace and identify the source of a communication. For example:
   - The telephone number and subscriber name and address (telecoms);
   - The user ID and name and address of the subscriber or registered user (Internet);
2. data necessary to identify the destination of a communication. For example
   - the number called, any number to which a call is rerouted, name and address of subscriber/user (telecoms); user ID or telephone number of the intended recipient(s) of an Internet telephony call, name and address of subscriber/user (Internet);
3. data necessary to identify the date, time, and duration of a communication;
4. data necessary to identify the type of communication: the telephone or Internet service used;
5. data necessary to identify users' communication equipment or what purports to be their equipment: the calling and called telephone numbers, identifiers of mobile telephone and SIM card; the date, time and place of initial activation of prepaid card;

6. data necessary to identify the location of mobile communication equipment: cell ID and geographic location of cell.

The Directive also requires the retention of data relating to unsuccessful call attempts where those data are generated or processed, and stored (e.g. telephony data) or logged (e.g. Internet data). This is not data that would normally be held, for example, by telecommunications companies for billing purposes[7].

Article 6, Sentence 2, of the Directive states: "No data revealing the content of the communication may be retained pursuant to this Directive." But the person calling the crisis line is not ordering pizza, or a cheeseburger with coke!. There are undeniably semantic elements in the mass of so-called traffic data. Data identifying the person calling the crisis line unavoidably reveals content (by virtue of the nature of the call.) This is one of the reasons why such data is protected under privacy legislation in the European Union.

As far as retention periods are concerned, the Directive states that Member States may set a retention period of not less than six months and not more than two years from the date of the communication. However, Member States can, if circumstances dictate, and for a limited period of time, extend the maximum period as long as they inform the other Member States and the Commission that they have done so, and their reason for doing so. The Commission will then check after 6 months to ensure that the extended retention period is not being used as a disguised trade restriction. It appears that where such an extension is approved by the Commission, it may be continued indefinitely. Previous experience, in arenas such as data privacy, suggests that the broad scope of the discretion over time periods may not bode well for uniformity of retention and the harmonisation process[8]. The Directive indicates that data retained must be kept subject to appropriate technical and organisational measures to ensure that they can be accessed by specially

authorised personnel only and, except for data that has been accessed and preserved (presumably for the purposes specified under the Directive), retained data must be destroyed at the end of the period of retention. With regard to the former point, it has been noted that given that data generated or processed by communications service providers in the process of supplying communications services is likely "to include items such as billing data, and that this might mean either designating billing clerks as specially authorised personnel, or requiring separate systems for business purpose data and data retained pursuant to the Directive". (Davies & Trigg, 2006).

A final area of interest lies with the use of the retained data. The Directive provides that data retained under the Directive is to only be provided to "the competent national authorities in specific cases and in accordance with national law." It does not specify any criteria for "competent authorities", which means that some Member States may choose to widen access beyond law enforcement agencies, nor does it provide guidance as to the reasons for which retained data may be accessed, again leaving this to the discretion of the Member States[9]. (Davies & Trigg, 2006; Kosta & Valcke, 2006)

THE PORTUGUESE DATA RETENTION LAW AS A SPECIAL CASE OF LEGALITY

Two years latter, by the Law nº 32/2008, of 17 July, Portugal transposes to the national legal order the Directive 2006/24/EC, of the European Parliament and the Council, of 15 March 2006, on the retention of data generated or processed in connection with the provision of publicly available electronic communications services or of public communications networks, and amending Directive 2002/58/EC of the European Parliament and of the Council of 12 July 2002 concerning the processing of personal data and the protection of privacy in the electronic communications sector.

In the regulatory framework imposed by this Directive, Law no. 32/2008, of 17 July, requires that providers of publicly available electronic communication services or of public communications networks retain specific communication data, so that such data can be accessed by competent authorities, exclusively for the purpose of investigation, detection and prosecution of serious crime.

Acknowledging that the values at stake and the retention of data are both sensitive subjects, Law no. 32/2008, of 17 July, adopted special restrictions, cautions and security measures as regards the access to and processing of data and the supervision and monitoring of compliance with the obligations provided for under the law, among which the following must be highlighted: inclusion of an exhaustive list of types of crimes that integrate the notion of "serious crime"; the strict prohibition to retain data revealing the content of communications; the provision that the access to data can only be requested by the Public Prosecution Office or by the competent criminal police authorities and is always dependant on a judicial decision; the establishment of a one-year-period as the time limit for data retention; the requirement that personnel responsible for carrying out the tasks associated to compliance with the obligations legally provided for, in the scope of providers of publicly available electronic communications services or of public communications networks, must be authorized by and registered at the "Comissão Nacional de Protecção de Dados" - CNPD (National Data Protection Commission).

So, first of all, by this Law, the Portuguese government stablish the legal framework to regulate the retention and transmission of traffic and location data on both natural persons and legal entities, and of the related data necessary to identify the subscriber or registered user, for the purpose of the investigation, detection and prosecution of serious crime by competent authorities.

The retention of data revealing the content of electronic communications is prohibited, without prejudice to provisions laid down in Law no. 41/2004 of 18 August[10] and in penal procedure law on recording and interception of communications.

The Law 32/2008 define several concepts at article 2. According to the law «data» means traffic data and location data and the related data necessary to identify the subscriber or user; «Telephone service» means any of the following services: "Call service, including voice, voicemail and conference and data calls, Supplementary services, including call forwarding and call transfer, Messaging and multi-media services, including short message services (SMS), enhanced media services (EMS) and multi-media services (MMS); «User ID» means a unique identifier allocated to persons when they subscribe to or register with an Internet access service or Internet communications service; «Cell ID» means the identity of the cell from which a mobile telephony call originated or in which it terminated; «Unsuccessful call attempt» means a communication where a telephone call has been successfully connected but not answered or there has been a network management intervention.

As we said ahead, the Directive does not specify any criteria for "competent authorities", but the portuguese law specifies this this concept at article 2, e). So, «Competent authorities» means judicial authorities and criminal police authorities of the following bodies:

1. Polícia Judiciária (Judicial Police);
2. Guarda Nacional Republicana (Republican National Guard);
3. Polícia de Segurança Pública (Public Security Police);
4. Polícia Judiciária Militar (Military Judicial Police);
5. Serviço de Estrangeiros e Fronteiras (Aliens and Borders Department);
6. Polícia Marítima (Maritime Police);

These Authorities shall retain data concerning categories provided for in article 4 in such a way that they can be provided without undue delay to the competent authorities, by reasoned Court order; Ensure that the retained data are of the same quality and subject to the same security and protection as those data on the network; Take all appropriate technical and organisational measures to protect the data provided for in article 4 against accidental or unlawful destruction, accidental loss or alteration, or unauthorised or unlawful storage, processing, access or disclosure; Take all appropriate technical and organisational measures to ensure that data provided for in article 4 are accessed by specially authorised personnel only; Destroy data at the end of the period of retention, except those that have been preserved by court order; Shall prepare records of data retrieved and provided to competent authorities and send them to CNPT on a quarterly basis. And they shall retain data provided for therein for a one-year-period from the date of the communication (article 6). But as it is written at article 3, nº 2, the transmission of data to competent authorities may only be ordered or authorized by reasoned Court order, pursuant to article 9.

Accordind to the Law 32/2008, the retention and transmission of data is exclusively intended for the investigation, detection and prosecution of serious crime by competent authorities. And «Serious crime» means "terrorist crime, violent crime, highly organised crime, illegal restraint, kidnapping and hostage-taking, cultural identity or personal integrity crimes, crimes against national security, counterfeiting currency or equivalent securities, and crimes covered by conventions on safety of air or sea navigation" (article 2, g). Files intended for data retention in the scope hereof must be stored separately from other files with different purposes.

The article 5 of the Directive 2006/24/EC determine what are the relevant data, and the Portuguese law, at article 4, specify all the six cathegories of data presented by the Directive, but the legislator make a distinction of criteria about the type of retention of data in order to foresee the kind of equipment used, such as, if it is a fixed network telephony or a mobile telephony, or if is concerning Internet access, Internet e-mail or/and Internet telephony.

So the Law 32/2008, at article 4, says that the providers of publicly available electronic communications services or of public communications networks shall retain the following categories of data:

- Data necessary to trace and identify the source of a communication; The data necessary to trace and identify the source of a communication are of two types:
  1. the ones concerning fixed network telephony and mobile telephony, as the the calling telephone number and the name and address of the subscriber or registered user;
  2. and the data concerning Internet access, Internet e-mail and Internet telephony, such as the user IDs allocated, the user ID and telephone number allocated to any communication entering the public telephone network and the name and address of the subscriber or registered user to whom an Internet Protocol (IP) address, user ID or telephone number was allocated at the time of the communication.
- Data necessary to trace and identify the destination of a communication are of two types:
  1. the data concerning fixed network telephony and mobile telephony, as the numbers dialled, and, in cases involving supplementary services such as call forwarding or call transfer, the number or numbers to which the call is routed; the name and address of the subscriber or registered user and

2. The data concerning Internet e-mail and Internet telephony, as the user ID or telephone number of the intended recipient of an Internet telephony call, the names and addresses of subscribers or registered users and user ID of the intended recipient of the communication;

• Data necessary to identify the date, time and duration of a communication are of two types:

1. Concerning fixed network telephony and mobile telephony, the date and time of the start and end of the communication;

2. Concerning Internet access, Internet e-mail and Internet telephony, as the date and time of the log-in and log-off of the Internet access service, based on a certain time zone, together with the IP address, whether dynamic or static, allocated by the Internet access service provider to a communication, and the user ID of the subscriber or registered user and the date and time of the log-in and log-off of the Internet e-mail service or Internet telephony service, based on a certain time zone;

• Data necessary to identify the type of communication are of two types:

a. The ones oncerning fixed network telephony and mobile telephony: the telephone service used;

b. The ones oncerning Internet e-mail and Internet telephony, the Internet service used.

• Data necessary to identify users' communication equipment or what purports to be their equipment are of three types:

a. the data concerning fixed network telephony, the calling and called telephone numbers;

b. the data concerning mobile telephony, as the calling and called telephone numbers, the International Mobile Subscriber Identity (IMSI) of the calling party, the International Mobile Equipment Identity (IMEI) of the calling party, the IMSI of the called party, the IMEI of the called party and in the case of pre-paid anonymous services, the date and time of the initial activation of the service and cell ID from which the service was activated;

c. Concerning Internet access, Internet e-mail and Internet telephony, as the calling telephone number for dial-up access and the digital subscriber line (DSL) or other end point of the originator of the communication;

• Data necessary to identify the location of mobile communication equipment are of two types:

a. the cell ID at the start of the communication;

b. The data identifying the geographic location of cells by reference to their cell ID during the period for which communications data are retained.

Telephony data and Internet data relating to unsuccessful call attempts must be retained where those data are generated or processed and stored by bodies referred to in paragraph 1 of article 4, in the context of provision of communication services. Data relating to unconnected calls shall not be retained (see article 5° of the Law 32/2008).

All these data, except for data on subscribers' names and addresses, shall be blocked as from the moment they are retained, and shall only be unblocked in order to be provided to competent authorities, pursuant to provisions hereof. And they shall be provided by means of an electronic communication, under technical and security conditions set out in a joint administrative rule of members of the government for internal administration, justice and communications, which must meet the highest possible degree of codification and protection, according to the state of the art at the moment of transmission, including codification or encryption methods, or other (article 7, nº 3)[11].

A year after, pursuant to paragraph 3 of article 7 of Law no. 32/2008, of 17 July, to paragraph 3 of article 94 of the Criminal Procedure Code, the portuguese Government has foreseen the Administrative Rule no. 469/2009 of 6 May. This Administrative Rule lays down the technical and security conditions under which electronic communications for the transmission of traffic and location data on natural persons and legal entities, as well as of related data necessary to identify the subscriber or registered user, must operate.

In implementing the Law 32/2008, of 17 July, the administrative rule nº 469/2009 of 6 May, introduces important measures, aiming to set out the technical and security conditions of the electronic communications of traffic and location data on natural persons and legal entities, as well as of the related data necessary to identify the subscriber or registered user. Consequently, it is hereby determined, in the first place, that the electronic communication must be processed on the basis of a specific software, through which the judge sends out the data request (see article 2)[12] and the providers of publicly available electronic communications services or of public communications networks notify the transmission of the file that corresponds to the search result (see article 3)[13].

In the second place, the placing of a digital signature, both in the reasoned Court order that orders or authorizes the transmission of data - the rule in paragraph 1 of article 17 of Administrative Rule no. 114/2008, of 6 February, being applied to this subject-matter - as well as in the reply file to the data request sent by providers, is made compulsory.

In the third place, it is established that all electronic communications under this Administrative Rule, as well as in the reply file to the data request sent by providers, must be encrypted, thereby providing to this matter the strongest possible guarantees[14].

In the fourth place, the electronic record of sent data requests is made mandatory, with the indication of who sent the request and the time and date when it was sent. The access to reply files is also subject to an electronic record, also with the indication of who requested the access and when.

Lastly, security audits to the software have been provided for, thereby expressly laying down herein a good practice being currently applied by computer systems of the judicial system.

This Administrative Rule enables also the judge to use the established technological platform to send data requests concerning crimes for which is not possible to order or authorize the transmission of data retained pursuant to Law no. 32/2008, of 17 July.

It is thus ensured that the judge is able to send data requests to providers under the same security conditions and always by electronic means, regardless of the type of crimes that the data concern.

The Comissão Nacional de Protecção de Dados - CNPD (National Data Protection Commission) shall be the public authority incumbent for the monitoring of provisions of security and protection of the colected data.

The CNPD shall maintain and permanently update an electronic record of personnel specially authorised to access data, and the providers of publicly available electronic communications services or of public communications networks shall submit exclusively by electronic means to CNPD the necessary elements to identify personnel specially authorised to access data.

The CNPD shall provide the Commission on a yearly basis with statistics on the retention of data generated or processed in connection with the provision of publicly available electronic communications services or a public communications network. For this purpose the criminal police authorities shall convey to the CNPD by 1 March every year, the information, concerning the preceding year about the cases in which information was provided to the competent authorities, the time elapsed between the date on which the data were retained and the date on which the competent authority requested the transmission of the data; and the cases where requests for data could not be met, but the information provided shall not contain personal data.

At the end of each period of two years, the CNPD, in collaboration with Instituto das Comunicações de Portugal - Autoridade Nacional de Comunicações (ICP-ANACOM), shall assess all procedures provided for herein and prepare a detailed report including recommendations, which shall be submitted to the Assembly of the Republic and to the Government.

The article 9 sets that the transmission of data shall only be authorized, by reasoned order of the investigating judge, where there is reason to believe that such a step is crucial to the truth-finding process, or that otherwise it would be impossible or very difficult to secure evidence in the scope of the investigation, detection, and prosecution of criminal offences. The authorization provided for the transmition may only be requested by the public prosecutor or by the competent criminal police authority. The authorization for data transmission shall only concern:

a. The suspect or defendant;
b. The person who acts as an intermediary, where there are clear grounds for believing that such person receives or transmits messages to or from the suspect or defendant;
c. The crime victim, through his/her actual or presumed consensus.

The judicial decision to provide data shall meet the requirements of adequacy, necessity and proportionality, namely as regards the definition of categories of data provided and competent authorities with access to data and the protection of professional secrecy, under the law, in accordance to pursuant to article 252-A of the Penal Procedure Code.

According to the Article 11, the judge shall determine, of his own motion or upon request by any interested party, the destruction of data held by competent authorities, as well as data preserved by the criminal police authorities, as soon as they are no longer required for their intended purpose.

The Law 32/2008 consider that the data are deemed to be no longer required for their intended purpose where one of the following circumstances occurs:

a. Definitive closure of criminal proceedings;
b. Final acquittal;
c. Final conviction;
d. Proceedings that becomes time-barred;
e. Amnesty.

There is breaches of the law, without prejudice to criminal liability, when there is a failure to retain categories of data provided for in article 4; Non-compliance with the period of retention provided for in article 6; Failure to provide data to competent authorities holding authorization under article 9; Failure to send data necessary to identify specially authorised personnel, pursuant to article 8. Breaches provided for in the preceding paragraph are punishable by penalties between (Euro) 1.500 and (Euro) 50.000 or between (Euro) 5.000 and (Euro) 10.000.000, according to whether a natural person or legal entity is concerned, and attempt and negligence are punishable.

Under the Article 13, the Law consider as "a crime", punished by imprisonment of up to two years or fine up to 240 days, the failure to comply with any of the provisions on data protection or security provided in article 7; the access to data by an unauthorised person under the article 8. Ant the penalties shall be doubled where the crime is committed through infringement of safety technical standards; Has made personal data available to the infringer or third parties; or Has provided the infringer or third parties with material benefits or advantages. Attempt and negligence are punishable. The CNPD is incumbent for examining the breach procedures and for the corresponding application of penalties concerning actions provided for, and the amounts of penalties imposed shall be distributed as follows: 60% to the State and 40% to the CNPD. The sanction regimes provided for in Law no. 67/98, of 26 October, and Law no. 41/2004, of 18 August is applicable without prejudice.

WHAT ABOUT THE RIGHT TO PRIVACY?

The European Court of Human Rights has interpreted Article 8's reference to respect for private life expansively. «Private life» does not consist only of an individual's innermost thoughts—those that he chooses not to share with the outside world... It extends to the right to establish and develop relationships with other human beings. Intrusions into an individual's personal or business affairs that interfere with this right therefore fall within the protection of Article 8.

Article 8[15] of the European Convention on Human Rights (ECHR) guarantees every individual the right to respect for his or her private life, subject only to narrow exceptions where government action is imperative. (Privacy International, 2003)[16].

An individual's use of communications services falls squarely within this zone of privacy. The telephone, the Internet and other communications services are quintessentially about bringing people together, in a personal or a business capacity. Government regulation that chills use of these services is accordingly an interference with the right to respect for private life protected by Article 8. Retention of data by the authorities is interference in private life, whether or not the State subsequently uses that data against the individual[17].

The retention of these data for law enforcement purposes, beyond what is necessary for communication purposes, without consent of the person concerned, is an exception to the strict rules on the deletion of such data that applied before and were intended to protect the privacy and confidentiality of communications.

Article 8 of the ECHR guarantees the individual's right to respect for his private and family life[18]. The Article specifies that public authorities may only interfere with this right in narrowly defined circumstances. In particular, any interference must be in accordance with law and necessary in a democratic society, in view of such public interests as national security and the prevention of crime.

It means that both the Directive itself and the national legislation implementing it should meet the conditions laid down in Article 8 for a lawful restriction of the right to respect for private life and correspondence: any such restriction should be "in accordance with the law" and "necessary in a democratic society'" for a legitimate purpose, such as for example the prevention or repression of crime[19]:

- The first condition – "in accordance with the law" - does not only require a formal legal basis, but one that meets certain quality criteria, such as clarity, precision, predictability and existence of adequate safeguards against possible abuse.
- The second condition – "necessary in a democratic society" - is perhaps even more relevant in this discussion. It means that a measure should not only be useful, but necessary and proportionate in a democratic society to satisfy a pressing social need[20].

This is why, more in general, it is crucial that the applicable national law ensures a fully adequate and effective data protection in the business reality of telecom and internet providers and in the way access for law enforcement is implemented and provided in practice.

If the risks of security breaches or irregular or unlawful conduct is underestimated, there can be little doubt that both breaches and irregular conduct will happen in practice and that this will certainly undermine the legitimacy and credibility of data retention, also where it would be fully justified[21].

CONCLUSION

The Portuguese Law is an example for the others national Laws in the UE. The Legislator had the notion that the law 32/2008 and the Administrative Rule 469/2009 are exceptionals acts. But we have not only good news!

The question becomes more sensitive when the Member States of the UE has to transmite or make available the personal data by the competent authority of another Member State, or may be transferred to third States or international bodies[22]. The transmition of personal data must be possible only when it is necessary for the prevention, investigation, detection or prosecution of criminal offences or the execution of criminal penalties, and when the receiving authority in the third State or receiving international body concerned ensures an adequate level of protection for the intended data processing. The question is that, no national data protection law may "restrict or prohibit" the exchange of personal data with agencies in other EU states, so "national security matters" (internal security agencies) is exempt from control. And there is no obligation to correct errors or mistakes in data passed to EU states or third countries.

There is an analogy between the historical concept of the panopticon (Bentham, 1785) and popularised by Foucault (1977), and the retention of these data for law enforcement purposes, beyond what is necessary for communication purposes, without consent of the person concerned. The panopticon draws its power from the fact that the surveilled never know if they are surveilled, and therefore internalise habits as if they were surveilled, the present situation, fostered by ongoing modalities such as data retention, should more accurately be referred to as panspectron (Sandra Braman, 2006)[23].

It is currently an open question as to whether a significant portion of European mobile phone users know about data retention at all or are sufficiently aware of its repercussions.

This is not only true of data retention, but also of most data collecting, processing, and mining practices. This significant lack of knowledge, understanding, and consciousness about new paradigms of technologically-enabled surveillance and related governmental practices and commercial business is comparable to a situation of betrayal: While the people communicating assume that their privacy is strongly protected, a permanent but virtual eavesdropping operation is in the making that might become all too real later[24].

The fact is that data retention of telecommunications data belongs to an assemblage of new emerging forms of control endemic to a networking society. Its power results from the wide acceptance and usage that electronic communications media have gained in the last years. Yet each link within this megaweave of omnipotent cyber-connectivity is a single, tenuous, finite, vulnerable strand: the voice of the person at the other end of the line. To take part in this connected world is coupled with a number of drastic consequences that have been described above. Calling someone produces data far beyond the call. And while the call might be forgotten to have taken place within a couple of days by the people who have spoken to one another, the technical infrastructure implemented for data retention ensures for up to 24 months that it has happened, regardless of whether or not any human being remembers the call.

The retention of numbers dialled, length of calls, the location of the transmission, as well as email and internet activity raises issues of privacy as it allows those with control over communications systems to build up a profile of the user and target them for commercial purposes, criminal investigation or other reasons.

Although records and logs are a natural by-product of advanced telecommunications systems – billing and systems maintenance are standard beneficiaries of this data retention – the information that is retained and its possible transfer to a third party requires regulation to ensure users privacy is protected.

The retention of traffic data by communications providers also greatly enhance the risk that personal information can be stolen and exploited by third parties. Stored traffic data present an attractive target for hackers, who can to access multiple personal details about individuals in one place. Moreover, because the information is stored, hackers are able to sort through stolen data at their leisure, rather than trying to intercept valuable personal details in real time. Thus, in the name of facilitating the investigation and prosecution of crimes, mandatory data retention laws are making the job of the cybercriminal considerably easier. The development of various databases by state and non-state actors could lead to a culture of "Dataveillance" i.e. surveillance through the use of databases. In this respect, it is essential that the data retained under provisions of the Law are used for those specified purposes only.

REFERENCES

2006/24/EC. (European Union Directive 2006/24/EC of March 2006 on the retention of data generated or processed in connection with the provision of publicly available electronic communications services or of public communication networks and amending Directive 2002/58/EC). *Official Journal of the European Union, L* 105, 56-63.

Administrative Rule no. 469/2009, of 6 of May-Administrative Rule no. 915/2009, August 18. Lays down the technical and security conditions under which electronic communications for the transmission of traffic and location data on natural persons and legal entities, as well as of related data necessary to identify the subscriber or registered user, must operate. Retrieved January 21, 2010 from http://www.anacom.pt/render.jsp?contentId=951486

Andrejevic, M. (2007). iSpy: Surveillance and Power in the Interactive Era. Kansas: University of Kansas Press.

Bentham, J. (1995). *The Panopticon Writings*. London: Verso.

Bignami, F. (2007). Protecting Privacy against the Police in the European Union: The Data Retention Directive. *Duke Law School Science, Technology and Innovation Research Paper Series,* Research Paper No. 13.

Braman, S. (2006). Tactical Memory: the Politics of Openness in the Construction of Memory. *First Monday, 11*(7). Retrieved from http://firstmonday.org/issues/issue11_7/braman/index.html.

Curry, M. R. (2004). The Profiler's Question and the Treacherous Traveler: Narratives of Belonging in Commercial Aviation. *Surveillance & Society, 1*(4), 475–499.

Davies, G., & Trigg, G. (2006). Being Data Retentive: A Knee Jerk Reaction. *Communications Law, 11*(1), 18–21.

Feiler, L. (2008). *The Data Retention Directive.* European and International Technology Law Seminar: Intellectual Property Rights, Information Technology Law, Biotechnology Law. Retrieved from www.rechtsprobleme.at/doks/feiler-DataRetentionDirective.pdf

Foucault, M. (1977). *Discipline and Punish: The Birth of the Prison.* New York: Vintage.

Haggerty, K., & Ericson, R. (2000). The surveillant assemblage. *The British Journal of Sociology, 51*(4), 605–622. doi:10.1080/00071310020015280

Jordan, J. M., III. (2006). *EU Personal Data Protection Laws Require Deleting Data When No Longer Needed.* Retrieved from www.cyberscrub.com/.../Legal_Requirements_to_Delete_EU_Personal_Data_Jim.pdf

Korff, D. (2008). The Standard Approach under Articles 8 – 11 ECHR and Article 2 ECHR at http://ec.europa.eu/justice_home/news/events/conference_dp_2009/presentations_speeches/KORFF_Douwe_a.pdf

Kosta, E., & Peggy Valcke, P. (2006). Retaining the Data Retention Directive. *Computer Law & Security Report, 22,* 370–380. doi:10.1016/j.clsr.2006.07.002

Law 32/2008, July 17. Transposes to the national legal order Directive 2006/24/EC of the European Parliament and of the Council of 15 March 2006, on the retention of data generated or processed in connection with the provision of publicly available electronic communications services or of public communications networks at. Retrieved January 21, 2010 from http://www.anacom.pt/render.jsp?contentId=951486

Law no. 41/2004, August 18. Legal provisions transposing to the national legal order Directive 2002/58/EC, of the European Parliament and of the Council, of 12 July, concerning the processing of personal data and the protection of privacy in the electronic communications sector. Retrieved January 21from http://www.anacom.pt/render.jsp?contentId=951486. View: 21.01.2010

Law no. 67/98, October 26. Transposing into the Portuguese legal system Directive 95/46/EC of the European Parliament and of the Council of 24 October 1995 on the protection of individuals with regard to the processing of personal data and on the free movement of such data. Retrieved January 21, 2010 from http://www.anacom.pt/render.jsp?contentId=951486

Orwell, G. (1949). *Nineteen Eighty-Four.* New York: Penguin.

Privacy International. (2003). *Data Retention violates human rights convention.* Retrieved from http://www.privacyinternational.org/article.shtml?cmd%5B347%5D=x-347-57875

ENDNOTES

[1] So the question has to be asked: does this mean that all telecommunications have not been under surveillance since 11 September? Of course they have, not by the law enforcement agencies but by the security and intelligence agencies. The National Security Agency (USA) and the Government Communications Headquarters (GCHQ, UK) have been surveilling global communications since 1947 (UKUSA agreement). During the Cold War this was for military and political purposes, later through the new Echelon system political and economic intelligence was targeted. Echelon, NSA and GCHQ were already moving to cover terrorism (and associated serious crime) before 11 September - after it became a new priority. But even then, for example, with the new, huge, NSA online storage system (Petraplex) designed to hold all the world's communications for 90 days, this is almost useless unless the agencies know (through gathering human intelligence on the ground, HUMINT) what to look for. (see: Answer to questionnaire on data retention, General Secretariat to Multidisciplinary Group on Organised Crime (MDG), doc on 14107/02, 20.11.02. at http://www.statewatch.org/news/2002/nov/euintercept-2002-11-20.htlm).

[2] European Union directive 2006/24/EC of March 2006 on the retention of data generated or processed in connection with the provision of publicly available electronic communications services or of public communication networks and amending directive 2002/58/EC.

[3] Directive has passed as a so-called First Pillar directive using the single market power of the European Union, and not as a Third Pillar directive pursuant to the Union's power fighting crimes. "Once the choice was made

to go ahead with the Directive as a First Pillar initiative, the Commission and the Council took the position that, legally speaking, the Directive could not regulate police access to communications data. Anything having to do with the police was strictly Third Pillar" (Bignami, 2007, p. 12). In 2005, the Commission adopted a proposal for a directive of the European Parliament and of the Council, based on art. 95 EC, on the retention of data processed in connection with the provision of public electronic communication services and amending Directive 2002/58. The Council opted for a directive on the legal basis of the EC Treaty, rather than for the adoption of a framework decision. After the European Parliament issued its opinion in accordance with the co-decision procedure under art. 251 EC, the Council adopted Directive 2006/24 by qualified majority.

4   Being aware of significance of personal data and the necessity to protect private life of every person, two directives were adopted in the European Union. *Directive 95/46/EC (on protection of individuals with regard to the processing of personal data and on the free movement of such data and Directive 2002/58/EC.* The further processing of these data without the consent of the identified person is allowed only in particular cases according to respective legislative acts. As the significance of traffic data increased, several countries (France, Sweden, Great Britain, Ireland) - reacting to the reduction of the safety- made an initiative for an EU Framework decision for the retention of traffic data. At the end of 2005, following extensive debates and changes of opinions, the draft Framework decision and directive were combined. The Directive 2006/24/EC adopted on 21 February 2006. See Directive 95/46/EC of the European Parliament and of the Council of 24 October 1995 on the protection of individuals with regard to the process-

ing of personal data and on the free movement of such data (OJ L 281, 23.11.1995, p. 31–50); See Directive 2002/58/EC of the European Parliament and of the Council of 12 July 2002 concerning the processing of personal data and the protection of privacy in the electronic communications sector (Directive on privacy and electronic communications, OJ L 201, 31.7.2002, p. 37–47). See Directive 2006/24/EC of the European Parliament and of the Council of 15 March 2006 on the retention of data generated or processed in connection with the provision of publicly available electronic communications services or of public communications networks and amending Directive 2002/58/EC, OJ L 105, 13.4.2006, p. 54–63).

5   Pursuant to the Data Retention Directive, the data to be retained can be divided into three main groups: 1) user identifying data; 2) traffic data; 3) location data.

6   In case of "Internet access" no data is to be retained "to identify the destination of a communication" (Art 5(1)(b)) or "to identify the type of communication" (Art 5(1)(c)). Internet communication therefore is only to be retained if it is Internet e-mail or Internet telephony, but the directive does not define either term. As e-mail is a technical term is should also be interpreted in accordance with the relevant technical standards. While RFC 2822 specifies the format of an e-mail the RFCs 2821, 1939 and 3501 specify the standard e-mail protocols SMTP, POP3 and IMAP respectively. The term Internet e-mail as used in the Directive has to be construed as data that conforms to RFC 2822 and is being transferred in accordance with RFC 2821, 1939 or 3501. Data transferred over the Internet that does not conform to the aforementioned RFCs is not an "Internet e-mail" and – unless it falls under "Internet telephony" – is not to be retained under Art 5. As the term "Internet telephony" is not

defined in the directive one might recourse to Art 2(2)(c) which defines the term "telephone service" as "calls [...], supplementary services [...], and messaging and multi-media services (including short message services, enhanced media services and multi-media services)". The term "telephone service" is only used in Art 5(1)(d)(1) to give meaning to the term "type of communication" with respect to fixed network and mobile telephony. The term "telephone service" therefore cannot be used to give meaning to "Internet telephony". If the definition of "telephone service" was applied to the Internet it would effectively cover all services offering audio-visual content. See ITU-T Recommendation H.323, Packet-based multimedia communications systems, http://www.itu.int/rec/T-REC-H.323/en. and *Schulzrinne/ Casner/Frederick/Jacobson*, RFC 3550, RTP: A Transport Protocol for Real-Time Applications (2003). To construe the terms "Internet e-mail" and "Internet telephony" using applicable technical standards is not only a matter of practicality and legal certainty. The whole purpose of the Directive is to obligate providers to retain certain traffic data. To fulfill this obligation providers cannot perform a case-by-case determination of every communication or even every data packet. They have to use automated means to read, analyze, filter and store network traffic data. The implementation of these automated means requires explicit rules as to what data has to be retained. If every provider is not to use his own interpretation of what constitutes "Internet e-mail" or "Internet telephony" they have to use common standards. The aim of the Directive is to harmonize Member States' provisions concerning the obligations of providers with respect to the retention of traffic and location data. As the Directive does not define any technical standards itself, the aim of

harmonization can only be fulfilled if already existing generally accepted standards are used. The purpose of the Directive therefore requires that technical terms left undefined in the Directive be construed using technical standards. As the following means of online communication are neither "Internet e-mail" nor "Internet telephony" they are not to be retained under Art 5: Blogs, message boards, videos on platforms like YouTube, communication via social networking platforms, instant messaging, IRC, Usenet, all HTTP traffic in general and peer-to-peer services. *Schulzrinne/Casner/Frederick/Jacobson*, RFC 3550, RTP: A Transport Protocol for Real-Time Applications (2003).

[7] Location data of mobile phones might be the most important trace for the profiler, as location becomes the lingua franca in the surveillance and profiling community (Curry, 2004). This data is of specific value and shows most precisely the difference between metadata and the actual data used in data retention: "... as long as the phone is turned on, it serves as a passport into a monitored electromagnetic enclosure" (Andrejevic, 2007, p. 100)

[8] "harmonise" means to implement technical standards of retention, and to do so for data access from anywhere in the EU. It was determinated to aid the prevention, investigation, detection and prosecution of criminal offences between the Member States. Member States must implement the provisions of the Directive concerning fixed network and mobile telecommunications in their national laws by 15 September 2007. (2006/24/EC: 56). Member States have been given the option to delay the application of the Directive to retention of communications data relating to Internet access, Internet telephony and Internet e-mail until 15 March 2009, and the UK has made a Declaration

9   to the Commission that it intends to utilise that option. (2006/24/EC: 56)

Germany has already indicated that access to traffic data will be permitted not just for the investigation of "substantial" offences, but also for the investigation of any offence committed using telecommunications networks - including the sharing of copyrighted content. (Davies & Trigg, 2006; Kosta & Valcke, 2006).

10   The Legal provision transposing to the national legal order Directive 2002/58/EC, of the European Parliament and of the Council, of 12 July, concerning the processing of personal data and the protection of privacy in the electronic communications sector is the Law n° 41/2004, of 18 of August.

11   The retention of data must be execute to compliance with principles or rules on quality and safeguard of confidentiality and security of data, provided for in Law n° 67/98 of 26 October, and Law n° 41/2004, of 18 August.

12   The "request for data" consists of the reasoned Court order that orders or authorizes the transmission of data, in portable document format (pdf) or in a text file, bearing a digital signature, pursuant to paragraph 1 of article 17 of Administrative Rule n° 114/2008, of 6 February; and the electronic form, filled in according to the Court order. The judge that ordered or authorized the transmission of data under article 9 of Law n° 32/2008, of 17 July, shall issue the corresponding request by means of software specifically made available for this purpose ("the software"). The request for data is carried out by filling in the electronic form available in the software, to which must be attached the reasoned Court order that orders or authorizes the transmission of data (article 2 of the Administrative Rule n° 469/2009 of 6 May).

13   Upon receipt of a request for data, the provider of publicly available electronic communications services or of public communications networks ("the provider") shall immediately carry out the respective search, according to the chronological order in which requests are received or to the degree of urgency determined in the reasoned Court order. As soon as the data search has been finalised, the provider shall transfer the file that corresponds to the search result, through a secure and encrypted connection, authenticated with a user name and password; and send the notification of the reply file transfer through the software, indicating the name of the transferred file. The reply files shall comply with the following technical requirements: (a) files must be produced in portable document format (pdf); (b) Files must bear a digital signature; (c) Files must be encrypted by means of asymmetric keys, made available through digital certificates. The provider shall request, through the software, the rectification or completion of the request for data where: The reasoned Court order and data filled in the electronic form do not match. (see article 3 of the Administrative Rule n° 469/2009 of 6 May). The software shall notify the provider that the reply file was successfully received and stored. Upon receipt of the notification referred in the preceding paragraph, the provider may remove from his system the copy of the file under consideration, without prejudice to the obligation to retain data pursuant to Law no. 32/2008, of 17 July (see article 4 of the Administrative Rule n° 469/2009 of 6 May). Note that, the Administrative Rule n° 469/2009 was amended by the Administrative Rule n° 915/2009, of 18 August. Administrative Rule no. 469/2009, of 6 May, laid down the technical and security conditions under which electronic communications for the transmission of traffic and location data on natural persons and legal entities, as well as related data necessary to

identify the subscriber or registered user, must operate, pursuant to Law no. 32/2008, of 17 July, so the Administrative Rule n° 915/2009, of 18 August, on its turn, aims to establish a trial period of about three months, in order to further address the functionality and usability of the software, as well as to enable a steady adjustment of professionals to the new working procedures, and added to Administrative Rule no. 469/2009, of 6 May the following Article 6-A: «The use of the software provided for in the preceding paragraphs is optional during the respective trial period, which runs up to 30 November 2009. In the course of the trial period, requests for data and replies from providers which were not submitted through the software, shall be performed in the traditional way, reply files, prepared pursuant to paragraph 3 a) and b) of article 3, being submitted in CD-ROM.»

14 The Article 5 of the Administrative Rule set down the security rules of the information, so it determines that " In the interests of security of data contained in the electronic communication referred to in article 1, the following measures must be adopted: (a) Encryption of all electronic communications performed pursuant to the present Administrative Rule; (b) Encryption of the reply file, pursuant to paragraph 4c) of article 3, thus assuring that the data on that file may only be viewed electronically through the software; (c) The reasoned Court order and the reply file of the provider must both bear a digital signature in order to guarantee the integrity of these files; (d) Electronic record of sent data requests, with the indication of who sent the request and the time and date when it was sent; (e) Electronic record of all accesses to reply files, with the indication of who requested the access and the respective time and date; (f) Storage of reply files in separated folders according to

each provider, which must be provided with security mechanisms to avoid the interconnection of data; (g) Security audits to the software; (h) Further measures provided for in Law no. 67/98, of 26 October, and Law no. 32/2008, of 17 July. Court judges shall access the software by introducing a user name and password.

15 The text of the Article 8 of the ECHR. Right to respect for private and family life. "(1) Everyone has the right to respect for his private and family life, his home and his correspondence. (2) There shall be no interference by a public authority with the exercise of this right except such as is in accordance with the law and is necessary in a democratic society in the interests of national security, public safety or the economic well-being of the country, for the prevention of disorder or crime, for the protection of health or morals, or for the protection of the rights and freedoms of others"

16 The indiscriminate collection of traffic data offends a core principle of the rule of law: that citizens should have notice of the circumstances in which the State may conduct surveillance, so that they can regulate their behavior to avoid unwanted intrusions. Moreover, the data retention requirement would be so extensive as to be out of all proportion to the law enforcement objectives served. Under the case law of the European Court of Human Rights, such a disproportionate interference in the private lives of individuals cannot be said to be necessary in a democratic society. These and related protections are clearly affirmed in such cases as Klass v. Germany, Amann v. Switzerland, Rotaru v. Romania, Malone v. United Kingdom, Kruslin v. France, Kopp v. Switzerland and Foxley v. United Kingdom. (Privacy International, 2003).

17 The indiscriminate collection of traffic data offends a core principle of the rule

of law: that citizens should have notice of the circumstances in which the State may conduct surveillance, so that they can regulate their behavior to avoid unwanted intrusions. Moreover, the data retention requirement would be so extensive as to be out of all proportion to the law enforcement objectives served. Under the case law of the European Court of Human Rights, such a disproportionate interference in the private lives of individuals cannot be said to be necessary in a democratic society. These and related protections are clearly affirmed in such cases as Klass v. Germany, Amann v. Switzerland, Rotaru v. Romania, Malone v. United Kingdom, Kruslin v. France, Kopp v. Switzerland and Foxley v. United Kingdom. (Privacy International, 2003).

[18] In complete text, ECHR Article 8 provides as follows: "(1) Everyone has the right to respect for his private and family life, his home and his correspondence." (2) There shall be no interference by a public authority with the exercise of this right except such as is in accordance with the law and is necessary in a democratic society in the interests of national security, public safety or the economic well-being of the country, for the prevention of disorder or crime, for the protection of health or morals, or for the protection of the rights and freedoms of others."

[19] For processing for the purposes of direct marketing, data subjects must be given an opportunity "to object, on request and free of charge," to such processing or (if they prefer) to ask to be "informed before personal data are disclosed for the first time to third parties or used on their behalf for the purposes of direct marketing, and to be expressly offered the right to object free of charge to such disclosures or uses." The data subject may opt-out of direct marketing without meeting any particular standard of scrutiny

for his objection. For processing for purposes other than direct marketing, the data subject must be extended the opportunity to object at any time, but the objection will only be considered "justified" if the data subject has "compelling legitimate grounds relating to his particular situation," in which case the controller must stop the data processing that is the subject of the justified objection. Since "processing" includes "storage," this may require "blocking" of access to the data or even "erasure" of the data (Jordan III, 2006)

[20] See the ecerpt from S. & Marper v. The United Kingdom (European Court of Human Rights Judgment [GC] of 4 December 2008, paras. 101-104) "(1). Principal facts: The applicants, S. and Michael Marper, are both British nationals, who were born in 1989 and 1963 respectively. They live in Sheffield, the United Kingdom. The case concerned the retention by the authorities of the applicants' fingerprints, cellular samples and DNA profiles after criminal proceedings against them were terminated by an acquittal and were

[21] Industry has already responded to these challenges with new products that ISPs can purchase to implement the Directive. See OSS News Reviews, EM and Intec and SenSage Technology to Identify Terrorist Activity in Call Detail Records, http://www. ossnewsreview.com/telecom-oss/emc-and-intec-and-sensage-technology-to-identify-terroritst-activity-in-call-detail-records/ (last visited Sept. 21, 2009).

[22] The United States (US) and the European Union (EU) have been, and in the future will continue to be, engaged in discussions on transatlantic exchanges of information, including personal information collected commercially but used for security purposes. There is widespread understanding of the US approach to privacy within the Federal government, including oversight of law en-

forcement, security, and intelligence agency use (collectively, security service use) of personal information, because of the accepted government practice of transparency within government. Far less is understood in the US about the EU approach to data protection and oversight within its security services. Pursuant to the Department of Homeland Security's 2007 agreement with the Council of the European Union regarding the transfer of Passenger Name Record (PNR) data to the Department of Homeland Security (DHS) by air carriers operating flights between the US and the EU, the DHS Privacy Office recently published a comprehensive report on PNR. Mindful of this responsibility in 2007, the DHS Privacy Office looked for an analogous situation in which commercial entities collected PII for security service use.

23   The term "panspectron", as introduced by Sandra Braman (2006), refers to a state of things where no surveillance subject is specifically invoked in order to trigger an information collection process. Rather, information is collected about everything and everyone *all the time*. An individual subject appears only when a particular question needs to be answered, triggering data mining for particular information within the mass already gathered, in order to precisely answer that question. And while populations remain generally aware of the unmoved and intimidating presence of the panopticon,

they tend to be unaware of the aggressive efficiency of specific modes of information collection. Data retention exactly fits into this conceptual frame, just as with Passenger Name Records and SWIFT financial data. These are sustained and augmented without any specified trigger, and therefore, potentially infinite.

24   The Directive's scope is limited in regional terms to the territory of the Member States. This means that providers in third countries have no obligation to retain any data under the Directive. If somebody was to use a dial-up Internet access provided by a third country provider and applies link level encryption then no traffic data could be retained. Another example would be somebody employing end-to-end encryption when communicating with his mail service provider located in a third country. The user's European Internet access provider would be unable to find out to whom e-mails are being sent or from whom they are being received. A much more drastic limitation of the Directive's scope results from the fact that the categories of data listed in Art 5 are only to be retained with respect to fixed network telephony, mobile telephony, Internet access, Internet e-mail and Internet telephony. These means of communication may be the most obvious but by far not the only ones. E-mail and Internet telephony (VoIP) are actually only a very small subset of the means of communication available on today's Internet. (Feiler, L. 2008)

Chapter 2
Information Agents, Social Web and Intellectual Property

Áurea Anguera de Sojo
Escuela Universitaria de Informática, Spain

Francisco Serradilla
Escuela Universitaria de Informática, Spain

ABSTRACT

In recent years, due to the development of the information society, there has been a substantial change in regulating certain legal aspects in the field of intellectual property. Focusing on the Internet, legally it is trying to protect, on the one hand, user interests in use and private access to information in order to ensure security and protection of the data exchanged on the Web and, on the other hand, to ensure respect and protection of copyright of the work as well as the sui generis right of database makers. The picture is extremely complicated as interests and rights that may collide with each other must be combined. In the case of Internet access to different content that is offered on the Web, there is also another problem. In many cases we are not only faced with the problem of determining who owns the rights or who is the author, but a new way of creating content through collaboration or automated software agents is spreading that is radically different from the traditional model which makes it even more complicated to establish the intellectual property regime and the rights derived thereof.

1. INTRODUCTION

In recent years we have witnessed a tremendous development of technologies that enable user groups to disseminate, share and reuse information on the Web. Moreover, we are also witnessing the increasingly significant expansion of automated techniques for capturing and reusing the information that is currently on the Web to develop new tasks for which the original information was probably not conceived.

An everyday example of these types of systems is search engines, currently led by the Google

DOI: 10.4018/978-1-61520-975-0.ch002

search engine, which captures information presently on the internet to carry out a "simple" task: making this information accessible to users. For this task, Google software downloads, stores and processes the contents of sites and shows part of this in the search results; it has even made this into a business through receiving large amounts of advertising revenue by showing information for which it does not own the intellectual property.

The development of the information society has also brought a substantial change in regulating certain legal aspects in the field of intellectual property and especially copyright and the *sui generis* right derived thereof. The European Union has been making a great effort since the '90s to try to harmonise Member State legislation relating to intellectual property and the information society in general. This has been done in such a way to ensure both the development and growth of the information society as well as the free movement of goods and services by respecting in all cases both the economic as well as personal rights that may arise in favour of the owners or authors of the data or information. Since the European Council summit in Corfu in June 1994, the need to harmonise the laws of different States in order to ensure free movement of goods and services has been stressed. This harmonisation should be based on establishing a general and flexible legal framework to encourage the development of the information society and in turn ensure the protection of rights of the authors and owners of the work and content. This is due to the fact that protecting these rights is considered to be the basis for stimulating development and marketing new products and services as well as creative activity. Within this effort being made in Europe to harmonise legislation, Directives 96/9/EC on the legal protection of databases and 2001/29/EC relating to harmonising certain aspects of copyright and related rights in the information society are worth noting, among others.

The European Commission has been tracking how the different E.U. Member States have been transposing the Directives into their legal systems as well as how these have been applied by the courts in the different States. (Report on the application of the Directive on the harmonisation of certain aspects of copyright and related rights in the information society [2001/29/EC]).

Focusing on the Internet, we can say that legally it is trying to protect, on the one hand, user interests in use and private access to information in order to ensure security and protection of the data exchanged on the Web and, on the other hand, to ensure respect and protection of copyright of the work as well as the *sui generis* right of database makers. The picture, as can be seen, is extremely complicated as interests and rights that may collide with each other must be combined and the regulation that exists in relation to these poses unclear boundaries which are often difficult to regulate.

In the case of Internet access to different content that is offered on the Web, there is also another problem. This is because in many cases we are not only faced with the problem of determining who owns the rights or who is the author, but a new way of creating content through collaboration is spreading that is radically different from the traditional model (the best known example is Wikipedia) which makes it even more complicated to establish the intellectual property regime and the rights derived thereof.

Taking these two fields into account (technology and legal), in this chapter we will analyse a number of actual cases in which the boundary is unclear, as well as the technical and strategic measures that are used to prevent agents accessing the information, in addition to the technical and strategic measures to access the information in spite of everything. This will be done from the perspective of applicable rules and interpretations that may shed some light on situations in which our laws are simply increasingly outdated.

2. BACKGROUND: INTELLECTUAL PROPERTY AS A BARRIER TO KNOWLEDGE USE

In recent years there has been a huge development in two fields: (a) the social web and (b) information agents.

The Social Web is made up of a combination of services and tools that allow people to interact and generate knowledge collectively, establishing user networks with common aims that share and disseminate information. In a very short period of time we have witnessed a Web transformation; from centralised services (portals) where content production is carried out traditionally, by professionals employed for that particular purpose, to distributed services that are generated by tens, hundreds or thousands of users.

One of these paradigmatic Social Web services is Wikipedia, that takes the idea to the extreme, making content creation a completely collaborative process. What we must ask ourselves is: Who owns a Wikipedia article? How can traditional legislation on Intellectual Property protect the inappropriate use of content created collaboratively? What rights do collaborators have over what they have contributed?

On the other hand, the information agents process, extract and reuse the knowledge on the website for their own purposes, which are ultimately the purposes of their users, and reorganise the information, making it accessible and making decisions using it. However, who owns the profits? Can the owner of the initial information legally claim rights over those profits? Should they share in the profits obtained from the use made out of it by the information agent? Is it legal to technically block access made by agents to the original information? No one in their right mind would try to stop a human being from reading a book, just because when making future decisions, this may conflict with the intellectual property of the author of the book, and yet, if the reader of the book is a machine, many would probably raise objections.

Nobody would claim against someone for rewriting an idea that was previously described using other words, but if it is a machine, it appears that the matter changes.

From the point of view of the creators, the legislation is also insufficient. What happens if the author of a book wants an individual, company or institution to commercialise their book without having to specifically ask for permission, or if a person who takes a photograph, wants anyone to be able to transform it, crop it, or process it to obtain a new image that perhaps improves on the original, also without having to specifically ask for permission? With the current legislation, this simply cannot be done. Intellectual Property is monolithic and not transferable, unless the author agrees. The author creates the piece and all rights are reserved. Perhaps some authors want it this way, but there are more and more creators that think otherwise, and that would like to reserve some rights, but not others. The socioeconomic context is inclined in this way, but the law, for the time being, does not provide for this possibility.

3. INTELLECTUAL PROPERTY AND COPYRIGHT IN DATABASES, SERVICES, AND AGENTS

3.1. Introduction

Generally speaking, intellectual property refers to the right over any creation of human intelligence, independent of the medium used to bring together said creation. As regards the type of creation, it may be literary, artistic, scientific, or industrial. In our legal system (Spain), the term is limited to the first three categories, and Industrial Property is treated independently, through patent legislation. The difference between the first three and the last is that in the first cases, pieces of work that are created to transmit ideas or feelings are protected, whereas industrial inventions are considered to improve on production processes and trade, and are fundamentally for protecting the creation's economic values from competitors, and therefore, in the case of Spain (as well as other countries), they are protected by a jurisdiction different to that of intellectual property.

Intellectual property is made up of personal and patrimonial rights, that gives the author full control and exclusive right to the use of the work created by him/her. Accordingly, we can deduce that copyright is made up of two types of authority: one is of a personal nature, and the other is patrimonial or economic.

3.2. Copyright

Referring to who the author of the piece of work is (understanding the term "piece of work" in its broadest sense), it is understood that the author is the natural person that creates a literary, artistic or scientific piece of work. As authorship is determined through an act of creation, this condition cannot correspond to a legal person nor to inanimate objects and the author is considered to be the person that appears on the piece, be it by name, signature or identification marks. When the piece is not signed, is disclosed anonymously, or under a pseudonym, the one to exercise the author's rights, is the person who makes it public, understanding that they have the author's consent, and only when the latter does not reveal his/her identity.

On occasions we encounter pieces created by several authors, for which the following basic cases should be distinguished:

a. **Collaborative work:** Several people participate in the creative activity to achieve a joint result. E.g.: a book divided into chapters. The rights over the work correspond to all of those who participate, being divided up in the manner in which they decide: they are all co-authors. Subject to the agreement reached between them, they may separately use their contributions, unless this causes damage to the common work.

b. **Collective work (Encyclopaedia, dictionary):** The authorship of a piece made up of contributions by several individuals, merged into one single autonomous creation is attributed to one sole individual. In cases like these, the contribution is normally made without contact with other participators. The is created due to the initiative and under the coordination of one person, who edits it and circulates it under their name (subordination), and the intellectual property rights belong to this person, unless agreed otherwise.

c. **Pieces created in the framework of a work relationship:** When an employed worker carries out a creative activity while exercising the duties to which they have been entrusted, or following orders from their employer, unless it has been agreed otherwise, the owner of the economic rights consequent to the use of the piece, will exclusively belong to the employer.

d. **Pieces carried out on commission:** The person who commissions the work acquires the property of the hardware in which it is contained, but this does not mean that they will acquire the copyright over the work. This occurs if it has been agreed in the contract. For example, in Spain, in a ruling on December 12th 1988, the Supreme Court determined that the copyright holder of a computer program created on request, will remain in the hands of the author, unless agreed otherwise. In the absence of agreements, there is no transfer of rights nor legal cession, contrary to what happens in the work relationship.

Applying this casuistry to collaborative content creation (such as Wikipedia), the author of each content will be the person who created it, even though, in order to use their own creation independently, no damage may be caused to the common work created in collaboration with the others. In other words, the personal content of the right belongs to the person who creates the content, independent of whether use of the economic rights or profits can be transferred to the person who disseminates or publishes it. Likewise, in the case of collaborative works, the different authors may freely agree on the rules for using the work.

As previously stated, the copyright has a personal content (or moral) and an economic one. The moral right means that the author has the following rights that are absolute: (1) To decide as to whether the piece is to be disseminated and in what way. (2) To decide if this dissemination should be done with his/her name, under a pseudonym or anonymously. (3) To demand to be acknowledged and respected as author of the piece. (4) To demand that the piece be respected in its entirety, and stop any modification or alteration being made to it, that may harm its rightful interests, or damage its reputation. (5) To modify the piece, respecting the rights acquired by third parties. (6) To withdraw the piece from stores due to a change in intellectual or moral convictions, upon providing compensation for damages caused to the holders of the user rights. (7) To access the only copy in the hands of someone else, in order to exercise dissemination rights or any others that correspond. The personal content (moral right) of copyright, as can be deduced from that stated above, refers to the acknowledgement of the creation of the piece by the person who holds the right, and is therefore a personal and non-transferable right, except in the case of the piece being disseminated or made public anonymously.

Returning to the case of the Social Web, as has already been pointed out, content creation is carried out collaboratively, with the copyright as it is defined today. Each one of the authors will have moral rights over the content created by him/her and will be considered as the author of this, except in the case of content published without the name of the author, in which case the person which makes the content in question public, has the user rights but not the moral rights. Therefore,

problems in the area of the Social Web referring to the contents of the moral rights of the author will be determined by the different opinions that the authors may have with respect to modifications or alterations of their works, or in the case of wishing to withdraw the piece from trade, due to a change in convictions. However, due to the nature of the Social Web itself and of the people that participate, it would be difficult for this type of problem to occur. Whatever the case may be, it would indeed be a good idea for the European Union to harmonise the different legislation to decide what should be the legal mechanism that defines the copyright of content created in this way, as it seems that the notion of working in collaboration does not include all of the nuances that currently exist in the Social Web.

As regards the other part of copyright, user rights, they also go exclusively to the author, and therefore, unless they have been yielded, they are acts that require authorisation from the author. (1) *reproduction rights:* reproduction is understood as being the transfer of the piece to a medium that allows for it to be communicated and for copies to be obtained. (2) *distribution rights:* the original or copies of the piece are made available to the public through sale, hire, loan, or by any other means. At community level, special importance is given to the principle of the exhaustion of intellectual property rights, meaning that if a copy of the piece is introduced into the market of any member state by the holder of the rights or an authorised third party, the previous distribution acts -excluding the hiring or lending- of this copy in community territory, remain outside the sphere of the holder's exclusive right to intellectual property. (3) *public communication rights:* any act that implies that a number of people may access the piece without prior distribution of copies. (4) *transformation rights:* all modifications to the piece which turn it into another. This includes translation and adaptation. The intellectual property rights over the work resulting from transformation fall on the person who performed it, without prejudice to the author's rights over the already existing work. (5) *participation right* in the resale price. (6) *remuneration right*, compensatory for the reproduction carried out exclusively for private use, which is usually reflected in a levy to those who manufacture mediums capable of storing the work and the apparatuses capable of reproducing or displaying it.

Conscious of the fact that extending the user rights in copyright may pose a problem for the development of the information society, as well as for the free circulation of goods and services, in the Directive 2001/29/EC of the European Parliament and Council, May 22nd 2001, dealing with the harmonisation of specific aspects of copyright and related rights in the information society, the European Union established exclusive reproduction, public communication and distribution rights, in favour of the copyright holders, whilst at the same time, establishing some exceptions and limitations to those rights. In article 5.1 of the abovementioned Directive, the European Union lays down an exception to the reproduction right that refers to provisional reproduction acts that are temporary or extra and form and integral and essential part of a technological process whose aim is to facilitate the transmission in a network between third parties using an intermediary or to facilitate the legal use of a piece or protected service and that do not themselves have an independent economic importance, which will be exempt from the reproduction rights. Therefore, this exception is applied in all States.

In addition to the above exception to reproduction rights, the Directive 2001/29/EC gives Member States the possibility of establishing either exceptions or limitations to the reproduction rights, to public communication, to public availability and distribution in particular cases, with each of them having the authority to include them into their legislation or not. Amongst the States' optional exceptions or limitations, some have been adopted by the majority of EU Member States. The following may be mentioned:

- Reproduction in any medium carried out by natural persons for private use and without directly or indirectly using it for commercial purposes, whenever the holders of the rights receive reasonable compensation.
- Reproduction acts carried out by libraries, teaching centres, or museums with public access, or by archives whose intention is not to obtain economic or commercial profit directly or indirectly.
- Exceptions or limitations to the reproduction and communication rights and making publicly available, referring to: use for educational or scientific research purposes, whenever the source and author's name is indicated (if possible); when it is used to benefit people with disabilities, being directly related to the disabled person and not being of a commercial nature; when the press reproduces or wishes to make publicly available articles published about current issues, or when the use of works or services is related to information on current events, in so far as it is justified as being for informative purposes and when the source and name of author (when possible) is indicated; when it is used for public safety or to guarantee the appropriate development of administrative, parliamentary or legal procedures; when it is used to communicate with specific members of the public or made available to them, for purposes of investigation or personal research, through terminals installed in education centres, libraries, etc. In any case, the member states will also be able to lay down exceptions or limitations on distribution rights whenever the purpose of the authorised reproduction act is justified.

With these exceptions and limitations (and some others that are not mentioned here), the Directive aims to establish a legal framework which, on the one hand guarantees the copyright content, but at the same time allows public access to different content, given that without these exceptions or limitations, we would find ourselves faced with a law that may be too extensive to be compatible with the information society.

The application of these exceptions should stop conflicts occurring, such as those demonstrated by Google News and certain newspapers: if information is public, and refers to the public and is made publicly available, being treated as a current issue and citing the source and the author, no protest can be made, nor should it be considered that a copyright violation has occurred. Once the author or authors have decided to make use of their exclusive right to communicate their work to the public, or to make their work publicly available, the exceptions and limitations analysed in the Directive come into play, as long as the limits are respected and the sources and author are cited.

Nevertheless, there is still another matter to be dealt with in this area, above all in order to leave room for new ways of creation and generation of content that have arisen in recent years and that, each day, have more of an influence over citizens. The exceptions and limitations should be re-evaluated in light of recent technological enhancements and the current legislation should be modified in this way, as otherwise, intellectual property will become a barrier to new forms of creation that we are currently experiencing.

3.3. Database and Sui Generis Rights

Within the protection of intellectual property, the Directive 96/9/EC of the European Parliament and Council, on March 11th regarding the legal protection of databases, extended the protection of database copyright, given that the legislation of the Member States in this area was very scattered, and gave different levels of coverage, thus negatively influencing the normal running of the internal market.

For the purposes of intellectual property, the Directive 96/9/EC establishes the database con-

cept, understanding "database" as compilations of works, of data, or of other independent elements systematically or methodically available, and individually accessible by electronic means, or in another way. Legal protection of databases is based on two rights: copyright and "sui generis" rights.

The subject of the copyright is the *author of the database,* with regard to the originality of the selection and the arrangement of the content. Databases are, after all, intellectual creations. However, the "sui generis" right protects the *manufacturer of the databases* against the appropriation of profits obtained from economic and work investments by those who searched and compiled the content. This protection is known as "sui generis" right, which is different to that of copyright.

The object which is protected under copyright is the database, as defined in Directive 96/9/EC. Ownership of the database does not necessarily imply ownership of the information stored in it or the programmes it uses, the right applies to the database itself independently of any copyrights which may apply to the content of the database. As such, the copyright for the database will not apply to:

- The information stored, it will only apply to the structure in terms of the expression of the selection or layout of the contents and other aspects.
- The programmes: Protection does not apply to the computer programmes used in the manufacture or operation of electronically-accessed databases.

The object of *"sui generis"* rights is to allow the manufacturer of the database to prohibit the extraction and/or re-use of all or of a substantial part of its content, evaluated quantitatively or qualitatively, when the verification or presentation of the content of the database implies a substantial investment. For the purposes of the Directive this will be understood as:

a.   "extraction" the permanent or temporary transfer of all or of a substantial part of the content of a database to another medium, whatever type of medium that may be and whatever way in which it is done;

b.   "re-use" any form of public disclosure of all or of a substantial part of the content of the database through the distribution of copies, leasing, online transmission or any other form. The first sale of a copy of a database in the Community by the owner of the rights, or with his consent, will nullify the rights of control for successive sales of that copy in the Community.

Whoever owns the copyright also owns the moral rights and user rights, unless these have been transferred. Among the user rights (transformation, communication, reproduction, distribution) the right of transformation is interesting as it includes the re-ordering of a database. This avoids the danger of the content of a database being copied and electronically re-ordered without the manufacturer's permission, in order to create a database with identical content but which does not infringe the copyright in respect of the ordering of the original database.

Public dissemination rights include access to the works included in the database in any form, even if the database is not protected by copyright.

As we have already mentioned, databases are protected by so-called sui generis rights. This is an exclusive economic right which protects the substantial investments made by the creators of a database. The goal is to protect the work of the database manufacturer given that, in principle, the whole database could be easily copied and used as a new one by changing the selected content, again protected by copyright. As a consequence of the recognition of sui generis rights, no indiscriminate or excessive use of a database is allowed which may prejudice the financial interests of its creator.

This protects the creator of the database given that he/she took the initiative and has assumed the risk for the investment made. These protective measures can be exercised in cases of:

•   User actions which exceed their legitimate rights and which therefore prejudice the investment made. These operations include the extraction and/or re-use of all or a substantial part of the content, evaluated qualitatively or quantitatively, when the acquisition, verification or presentation of said content represents a substantial investment from a qualitative or quantitative point of view. This right may be transferred, ceded or contractually licensed, but under no circumstances will repeated and systematic extraction or re-use of non-substantial parts of the database content which may unfairly prejudice the interests of the creator be allowed. What is meant by unfair prejudice will need to be interpreted in jurisprudence.

•   Actions by competitors. It may occur that a competing manufacturer commercialises a product which is a parasite of the original (Considering Article 42 of the European Directive on the legal protection of databases).

Sui generis rights have several exceptions, as do the user rights mentioned above, in that they allow a legitimate user of the database to extract and/or re-use a substantial part of the content in the following cases:

•   When data is extracted for private use from the content of a non-electronic database.

•   When data is extracted for illustrative purposes for teaching or for scientific research with no commercial gain and the source is cited.

•   For the purpose of ensuring public safety or for administrative or judicial purposes.

A substantial difference with the legal protection of databases is the fact that the time periods established have altered; copyright lasts for 70 years while the sui generis right lasts for a period of 15 years from the 1st of January of the year following the year during which the creation of the database was completed. This right can be extended if substantial new investment is undertaken. The directive establishes that the burden of proof, both for the time of completion of the database and proof of substantial modifications (implying a new database and therefore a new time period), falls on the manufacturer.

We can differentiate between two types of databases:

a. Online, in which the medium is the memory of a computer which users access remotely. A provision contract exists between the user and the distributor in that the distributor is obliged to offer to provide information in return for payment for a stipulated period of time, or at a price to be agreed; the user being obliged to pay a fee to be able to access the information for personal or professional use.

b. Stand-alone, where the information is contained on an independent medium and must be copied by each user to be able to be used on their own computers. A usage-rights contract would exist between the distributor and the user in that the user is empowered to perform any operation required for use, promising to pay a charge and to return the media and manuals as well as any recovery programs. In both these cases there is an obligation to provide technical support and to respect Intellectual Property rules which relate to copyright and sui generis rights. Free access is a growing trend in the online distribution of information. The owner of the database obtains profits by other mechanisms such as advertising or capturing users for other products or services offered by the same company.

One of the more serious questions arising at the moment, above all in terms of information agents with respect to copyright, is how to combine the use of these agents by users to obtain the information they want in accordance with their expectations and the copyright of the information and also for the manufacturers of the databases in which the information, or any part of it, is contained and which the user is searching for.

The trend in European legislation is to try to adapt to the new tools arising within the information society; but, as we have indicated, it is complicated to balance such diverse interests; on the one hand, those of the authors and manufacturers and, on the other hand, those of the users, including those of any intermediaries acting between them.

In the case of intelligent agents we need to consider two aspects; it is one thing to copy a database (extract all of the entries to create a duplicate copy of the content), but it is another thing to use it or to consult it to obtain information, conclusions or results. Such consultation is allowed when done by a user for non-commercial and private reasons, as we mentioned above; if a real person is able to use a database which has been shared on the Web for any purpose, it is also understood that an agent or robot may also enjoy this same right, even more so when we consider that its work implies satisfying a need of the person for which it is working.

In this context, the development of Web 2.0 has brought with it a new and extremely important concept: That of the "mashup" (Merrill, 2006; Rankin, 2007). A mashup or remix consists of combining two or more information sources in the provision of new services for users. Mashups take data from several providers and combine them to achieve some features lacking in the original services. The ability of building mashups is independent of the openness of the provider, although the provider could facilitate the task giving an API (Application Programming Interface) to the programmers. One example of a mashup is Panoramio (www. panoramio.com), this was developed at the end of 2005 and is a service that allows users to locate photographs geographically using the Google Maps service supplied by Google. This allowed them to provide a completely new service without having to deal with the problems associated with the creation, storage and management of the maps required for locating the photos. Two years later, at the end of 2007, Panoramio had around 5 million photos on its site. Panoramio was bought out by Google in July of 2007.

Despite the enormous potential of these initiatives and the drive for innovation they require, corporate positions surrounding the re-use of information are diverse and go from one extreme to the other, those which are most open include Google and 11870, while others are almost entirely closed, such as Tele 5, the Spanish television broadcaster (France Presse, 2008).

We think mashups will be in the near future one of the most important engines of knowledge society, because they increase the quality and possibilities of current services, and reuse information to build new level of capabilities on the Web. Therefore it's very important to develop laws that facilitate information reusability when the result is a new service or product, and so a social profit for the users. According with Lawrence Lessig (2004), the remix culture is a desirable ideal, and argues, among other things, that the health, progress, and wealth creation of a culture is fundamentally tied to this participatory remix process.

3.4. The Law and its Pitfalls: "Technical Limitations" on the Use of Information

Irrespective of whether the use of information by information agents is legitimate or whether it is legal to block their access to this information, suppliers have been using a series of mechanisms to try to (1) determine if the agent trying to access

the information is human or not and (2) to block non-human agents in order to prevent them accessing the information. These types of technological measures are covered under Directive 2001/29/EC which authorises their use for both copyright and sui generis rights for databases, however, legitimate users must always be provided with adequate provisions to be able to access the work or presentation. Although the owner of the database, according to this Directive, has the power to block access for non-human agents, we must ask ourselves if doing so does not prejudice the development of the information society by preventing the development of new products and services which add value by combining and re-creating information collected from various sources.

The following mechanisms are used by information providers:

- *Detection:* Detection uses a kind of reverse Turing Test to determine whether the person trying to access the information is human or not (Dowe and Hajek, 1997). We must remember that humans access Internet systems using a browser and that information agents "replace" browsers in ways that can be more or less complex, therefore the only clue we have as to the identity of the agent is its "behavioural pattern". More specifically, many suppliers can detect when a single IP address is using their services excessively, this will always be the case when a robot tries to download massive amounts of content, normally with the intention of replicating the service. From our point of view this replication is not reasonable because it does not add value to the information, it should therefore be covered by Directive 96/9/CE on databases.
- *Distribution:* However, when an agent is servicing a large number of clients, the use of the information service could trigger this type of blocking mechanism even when

the service is reasonably adding value to the original information. The tactic used by robots in this case is to go undetected by using cache mechanisms or, even better, by the use of agents which execute themselves in the machines of each user (client agents) and not centrally (server agents), meaning that the blocking mechanism will not notice a huge demand from a single IP address but rather a series of small downloads by the computers of each of the users. The disadvantages of the client agent include the fact that any modifications to it will require re-installation on all the user computers. Our group is working on an intermediate solution which we have called the Agent Resource Importation System (ARIS), this allows the agent to reside in the user's machine but also to execute instructions from a central server each time it runs (Figure 1). This makes it possible for each client to perform requests in such a way that the agent is not fixed but evolves over time depending on how it is configured by the server, it can even be personalized for each user or group of users.

- *Protocol:* Other simpler blocking mechanisms are based on specific HTTP protocol messages, which control transactions between the browser and the web servers; these include the name of the agent, the referrer and cookies. Providers can use these to block requests from simpler robots and agents which do not send the correct information or which do not comply with best practices in the development of software robots (Koster, 1993). These rules are only recommendations but, obviously, if they cause the provider to block it, the agent will be obliged to break these rules.

A more elaborated approximation to a machine intelligence test is what is called CAPTCHAs (Completely Automated Public Turing test to tell

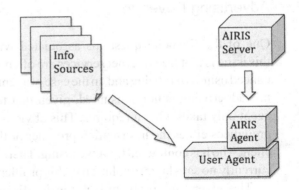

Figure 1. ARIS architecture

Computers and Humans Apart) (von Ahn et al 2002; von Ahn et al 2008). CAPTCHAs are any kind of simple question that can be easily answered by a human but not by current artificial intelligence technology. CAPTCHAs cannot be used for most of the tasks associated with an information agent because they require constant attention from the human user, probably causing him to leave the service. This technology can only be applied to occasional actions such as registration to a service for example, something which we can do with respect to our agent.

- *"Embedded" Information:* One way of preventing agents from capturing the information they need is to embed the information in non-textual files, this is similar to the concept used by CAPCHAS. As the information is not represented in the form of a text string but could be embedded in images, it is very difficult for an agent to extract it and re-use it. The two technologies which are most used for this are Flash and Adobe and, to a lesser extent, Java Applets. These make the information presented to the human appear as a "black box" to the agent.

The Background Problem: Advertising Revenue

One of the financial questions associated with this issue is that free Internet services are often financed using advertising and, in the case of agents, this advertising is not consumed, given that the agent only takes what it requires. This obviously prejudices either the information provider or the client who has contracted the advertising. There is currently no satisfactory solution to this problem.

The advertising problem is not insignificant; in the current climate traditional media outlets are fighting for survival in a clear context of decline and one of their options for survival revolves around the digital publication of free information financed by advertising. But, if this information can be captured and re-created by information agents, the advertising content is lost.

The Google News case is well-known and many information media outlets who wanted to be excluded from the news search engine or who asked for huge fees accused Google of infringing their copyright by including parts of their news content in search results. This demonstrates, among other things, a certain short-sightedness on the part of the media outlets as Google News is in fact a good revenue-earning opportunity when users follow the news link.

4. FUTURE TRENDS—NEW AND MORE FLEXIBLE IDEAS: CREATIVE COMMONS LICENSES

As an alternative, to the automatic "all rights reserved" copyright, David Berry and Giles Moss have credited Creative Commons with generating interest in the issue of intellectual property and contributing to the re-thinking of the role of the "commons" in the "information age". Beyond that Creative Commons has provided "institutional, practical and legal support for individuals and groups wishing to experiment and communicate with culture more freely" (Berry & Moss, 2005).

Creative Commons Licenses was developed by Creative Commons, a non-profit organization devoted to expanding the range of creative works available for others to build upon legally and to share. Founded in 2001 by Lawrence Lessig, Creative Commons' first project, in December 2002, was the release of a set of copyright licenses free for public use. Creative Commons Licenses allow certain rights to be reserved instead of all of them being reserved by default.

The rights established under Creative Commons licenses (Lessig, 2004) are the following:

- "Attribution" (by) requires users to attribute a work's original author. This is the only one that is obligatory.
- Authors can either not restrict modification, or use "Share-alike" (sa), which is a copyleft requirement that requires that any *derived works* be licensed under the same license, or "No derivatives" (nd), which requires that the work not be modified.
- "Non-commercial" (nc) requires that the work not be used for commercial purposes.

When an author publishes their piece of work, they decide which rights are reserved and which are granted by default. This does not mean that reserved rights cannot be granted at a later date by means of contractual agreements; these may include, for example, the commercial use of a work that was initially copyrighted. These licenses may be understood to be the *default* position as they are open to be modified by later agreements, as with traditional copyright this modifies the status if so authorized by the author.

For example, if we choose to use a by-nc license we will be permitting the work to be used for any purpose except commercial use. This means that the work may be included in any type of free product and may even be modified to produce a new work without the need for permission or consultation.

This new way of understanding copyright obviously has profound implications as it allows the re-use and modification of creative material which would otherwise not be used due to the need to contact the authors, even if they would be prepared to authorize the use of the material.

It might be that a photo is re-touched to be used as the logo for a programme, or an audio file might be used in a YouTube video which is broadcast by a television broadcaster. All of these are possible without the need to contact the author as long as the corresponding rights have been granted by default.

However, we need to be very careful when it comes to selecting the rights which are granted by default. The Seth Godin case is fairly well-known, he published an online book with a by type CC license, when he discovered that his book was being sold by a company on Amazon for 10$ he launched a litigation. During this public litigation (Godin, 2007) he stated that he was annoyed that the company had not asked for permission to publish the book. But this was inconsistent with the type of license he chose as he had granted this right by default. The author should actually have chosen a by-nc license, this would have meant that the company would have been obliged to ask his permission before putting the book on sale, the author could then have granted this right with no problems.

This issue is so important for the future use of information by software agents that in 2001 Tim Berners-Lee (Berners-Lee et al, 2001) proposed the construction of the Semantic Web, this would entail a new form of website design to make them easily understandable by programs, this would allow interaction and the recreation of the information included in them.

The Resource Description Framework (RDF) is a metadata W3C standard for describing information on the Web. The motivation behind the development of RDF was, to borrow the words Tim Berners-Lee used for the Semantic Web, "to have a common and minimal language to enable to map large quantities of existing data onto it so that the data can be analyzed in ways never dreamed of by its creators." (Gutierrez, 2008).

5. CONCLUSION

If we want to encourage serious development in the field of information agents and to create non-human assistants that improve the efficiency of our day-to-day work, it is essential that they have legal permission to access the same information under the same conditions as human users. Information providers should be obliged to guarantee the equal treatment of both humans and programs.

The mechanisms used by providers to obtain income from their services are another issue, this is fairly clear in the case of paid services but not so for services which are financed through advertising, as agents simply ignore it.

It is also important to be able to accurately differentiate an agent which is taking information for fair use and reprocessing, from one which is simply copying information in order to re-produce the service, in which case it would be in violation of the legislation included in Directive 96/9/EC on databases.

With the appropriate exceptions, we should not fall into the trap of defending obsolete business models and holding back the evolution of new types of services which, in the future, may become allies and empower information agents.

The truth is that, on a legislative level, the European Union is continuing with the job of harmonizing the legislation and issues concerning all parties involved; as we have already mentioned we believe that copyright protection is essential for the creation of intellectual property as it ensures that authors receive appropriate compensation for their work and that they have an incentive to carry on working. On the other hand we also need to promote the free circulation of knowledge and innovation as the "fifth freedom" of the single market.

6. REFERENCES

Berners-Lee, T., Hendler, J. & Lassila, O. (2001, May). The Semantic Web A new form of Web content that is meaningful to computers will unleash a revolution of new possibilities. *Scientific American*.

Berry, D., & Moss, G. (2005). *On the "Creative Commons": a critique of the commons without commonalty. Is the Creative Commons missing something?*Free Software Magazine.

Dowe, D. L., & Hajek, A. R. (1997). A computational extension to the Turing Test [Tech. Rep. #97/322]. Dept Computer Science, Monash University, Melbourne. France Presse. (2008, July). Spain's Telecinco wins lawsuit against YouTube. Inquirer.net. Godin, S. (2007). Please don't buy this book. Seth Godin Blog.

Gutierrez, C. (2008). Foundations of RDF Databases. *The Semantic Web: Research and Applications*. Koster, M. (1993). *Guidelines for Robot Writers*. Retrieved from http://www.robotstxt.org/guidelines.html

Legal Directives & European Commission papers COMMISSION STAFF WORKING: Paper on the review of the EC legal framework in the field of copyright and related rights. Directive 96/9/EC of the European Parliament and Council, on March 11th regarding the legal protection of databases. Directive 2001/29/EC of the European Parliament and Council, May 22nd 2001, dealing with the harmonisation of specific aspects of copyright and related rights in the information society.

Lessig, L. (2004). *Free culture: how big media uses technology and the law to lock down culture and control creativity*. Penguin Press. Retrieved from http://www.free-culture.cc/freecontent/

Merrill, D. (2006). Mashups: The new breed of Web app, an introduction to mashups. *The ultimate mashup - Web services and the semantic Web*. 2006. Retrieved from http://www.ibm.com/developerworks/xml/library/x-mashups.html

Rankin, B. (2007, November). What is a Mashup? *Ask Bob Rankin*. Retrieved from http://askbobrankin.com/what_is_a_mashup.html von Ahn, L., Blum, M. & Langford, J. (2002). Telling Humans and Computers Apart (Automatically) or How Lazy Cryptograhpers do AI. *Communications of the ACM*. von Ahn, L., Maurer, B., McMillen, C. & Blum, M. (2008, September 12). reCAPTCHA: Human-Based Character Recognition via Web Security Measures. *Science, 321*.

Report on the application of the Directive on the harmonisation of certain aspects of copyright and related rights in the information society [2001/29/EC].

Chapter 3
Conflict Resolution in Virtual Locations

Francisco Andrade
University of Minho, Portugal

Paulo Novais
University of Minho, Portugal

Davide Carneiro
University of Minho, Portugal

José Neves
University of Minho, Portugal

ABSTRACT

The growing use of telematic ways of communication and of the new developments of Artificial Intelligence, brought along new ways of doing business, now in an electronic format, and requiring a new legal approach. Thus, there is an obvious need for legal changes and adaptations, not only concerning a new approach of traditional legal institutes, but also concerning a need for new developments in procedural means. Transactions are now undertaken in fractions of seconds, through the telematic networks, requiring more efficient ways for solving conflicts; on the other hand, the fact that we must now consider commercial transactions totally undertaken within an electronic environment ("online transactions") leads to an obligation of rethinking the ways of solving disputes that will inevitably arise from electronic commerce. It is an important change already taking place, pointing out to various ways of alternative dispute resolution and, among all these ways, letting us already perceive different possibilities of using the new technologies in order to reach faster and more efficient ways (still also "fair") of solving commercial disputes. It is a whole new evolution towards a growing use not only alternative dispute resolution, but also towards the so-called on-line dispute resolution.

DOI: 10.4018/978-1-61520-975-0.ch003

INTRODUCTION

On-line activities, on-line contracting, will necessarily lead to on-line disputes, requiring new ways of solving conflicts. New ways of dispute resolution are thus appearing, so that the parties do not need neither to travel nor to meet in courtrooms or in front of arbitrators or mediators. Different forms or methods of alternative dispute resolution for electronic environments have been pointed out by legal doctrine. Thus being, we can now speak of Online Dispute Resolution (ODR) as any method of dispute resolution in which wholly or partially an open or closed network is used as a virtual location to solve a dispute (Katsh & Rifkin, 2001).

A relevant issue, in a first moment, will be to inquire in what way (and to what point) traditional mechanisms such as negotiation (Raifa, 2002), mediation (Brown & Marriott, 1999) or arbitration (Bennett, 2002) can be transplanted or adapted to the new telematic environments, taking advantage of all the resources made available by the newest information and communication technologies. But it will also be of the utmost importance to stretch our analysis to the point of foreseeing a real technologically advanced possibility, inquiring whether or not we can take advantage, for online dispute resolution, of the new developments in the area of Artificial Intelligence, facing this knowledge in two different perspectives: on one hand, as a tool of undeniable interest in order to help the parties and the decision makers to obtain the best possible results in solving commercial disputes, and on the other hand, considering a new way of autonomous dispute resolution through the use of autonomous and intelligent software, supported by a knowledge base and decision capabilities.

It must also be considered alternatives for dispute resolution arising from Artificial Intelligence models and techniques (e.g. Argumentation, Games Theory, Heuristics, Intelligent Agents, Group Decision Systems) (Peruginelli & Chiti, 2002; Lodder & Thiessen, 2003).

Among the possible methods for ODR, it must be referred the distinction between automated negotiation – specially the "blind bidding" procedure, by which both parties send confidential offers or proposals to the informatics system, being up to the system to detect and to declare whether or not the case gets settled – and assisted negotiation ("assisted" meaning here just providing communication facilities, trust marks, certification programs for the parties to use in their negotiation). A distinction must also be made between assisted negotiation and mediation, being the former based on technological tools, while the latter is based not only in technology (the parties and the mediator having access to different electronic communication tools, such as email, chat – with possibilities of private conversations - messenger, videoconferencing) but mainly on the intervention of a third neutral (mediator) intending to help parties to reach an agreement. If the third party appears to be a neutral party empowered to make a binding decision, through an enforceable award, as a form of privatised justice, then we must speak of arbitration (although, in theory, we might think of two possible different forms of arbitration, considering the possibilities of awarding a really binding and enforceable decision or just a contract like decision (binding only like a contract)).

In online dispute resolution it must be considered not just the parties themselves and eventual third parties (mediator, arbitrator) but of course there will be a significant focus on what Ethan Katsh and Janet Rifkin (2001) call "The fourth party", that is to say the technological elements involved. An important element of this "fourth party" will of course be the emergence of expert systems and intelligent software agents with capabilities for helping the parties and the mediator / arbitrator in reaching a fair solution. And as Arno Lodder (2006) already refers, it must be considered, as well, a "fifth party", that is to say the service providers, those who provide and deliver the technological elements. All this turning ODR in a quite new and somewhat complex (but eventually quite fast, cheap and advantageous) way of interaction and of solving conflicts.

Having in consideration all these experiences and the benefits of the technologies (but also its drawbacks), it must be analysed the main characteristics of the different ODR methods, the different types of communication used, the different types of interaction emerging from them, the advantages and disadvantages of the use of ODR. But it must also be foreseen the future trends for its development, the use of interactive, automated or intelligent technologies, the use of expert-systems, knowledge based systems and decision support systems, and the use of artificial intelligence, specially agents.

TECHNOLOGIES

Let us start by exposing some of the main technologies used in ODR. We will not be looking at any hardware in particular since all the hardware required is regular hardware that we use in our day-to-day: computers, networking hardware, telephones, webcams, among others. Although communication technologies are of main importance they will also not be mentioned here as they comprise technologies that are nowadays used and known by everyone: telephone, fax, video conference, E-mail, internet, forums, mailing lists, among others. We will instead pay special attention to three software technologies that have an important and promising role in ODR processes.

Multi-Agent Systems

Multi-agent Systems (MAS) emerged from the combination of Artificial Intelligence with distributed computational models, generating a new paradigm: distributed artificial intelligence (Wooldrige, 2002). There are several valid definitions for a multi-agent system so we will try to define a multi-agent system from the ODR point of view. A Multi-agent System is a group of entities (may be software or hardware) which will "feel" the circumstances they are in and make intelligent decisions in order to achieve some common goal (like proposing a solution for the parties in dispute) based on knowledge from every agent in the system. For an agent to be considered so, it must show some basic abilities: autonomy, reactivity, pro-activity and sociability which means agents must operate on their own, read their environment and react accordingly, they must show initiative and take their own actions and be able to relate to other agents in order to achieve their goals. Additionally, an agent may show characteristics such as mobility, learning, veracity, emotions, among others. In ODR characteristics like veracity are very important and the emotions-based agents are also being researched as one possible path for second generation ODR systems as the ability for understanding the feelings of the parties towards each topic of the dispute is essential.

In this paradigm, with simple agents or modules each one responsible for some part of the environment, the global objective is achieved through the cooperation of the agents (Olson et. al, 2001). They are able to make their simple individual decisions completely independently and we see the result of these decisions as a global intelligent behaviour. This paradigm rapidly started to play a major role in the design of any intelligent system. A lot of research has also been done in the field of argumentation with agent technologies (Rawhan et.al, 2004; Novais et. al, 2005). In argumentation, agents debate, defend their beliefs and try to convince the other agents into believing the same they do. In ODR this is especially useful as argumentation and debate may be important to parts in dispute resolution processes.

Agents may also implement negotiation techniques (Brito et. al, 2003). In MAS, negotiation refers to the modelling of Human negotiation techniques so they can be used for conflict resolution between agents. This type of agents is very used in auctions and eCommerce. In this specific case of dispute resolution, agents may represent the parties in a negotiated process and try themselves to negotiate and get to an outcome and suggest that outcome to the respective parties and this way trying to achieve a resolution for the dispute. MAS technology is suited for many different fields and specially suited for implementing distributed ODR systems mainly because agents may mimic social interactions between humans.

Decision Support Systems

With the constant growth of the information present in decision processes the need for tools that could provide support has also grown. Indeed, the new economy, along with increased competition in today's complex business environments, takes the companies to seek complementarities in order to increase their competitiveness and reduce risks (Bonczek et. al, 1981). In this scenario, planning takes a major role in a company life. However, effective planning depends on the generation and analysis of ideas (innovative or not) and, for this reason, the idea generation and management processes become a crucial tool in present days. The tools used may range from simple systems for compiling useful information from raw data to other more complexes that make suggestions on the best strategy to use or the fairest outcome.

Decision support systems may be used in virtually any knowledge based environment (Turban, 1993) and ODR is not an exception. More complex processes may involve much information that can become hard to deal with the parties and above all by the mediator. They can also be useful when the parties are not at ease with certain kind of information or there is too much information that can be summarized for a better understanding. Regardless their application area, these systems are known for improving the personal efficiency, fastening the problem resolution, increasing organizational control and facilitating interpersonal communication.

Expert Systems

Expert systems are software that try to replicate the skills of a human expert in a determinate field of expertise (Jackson, 1990). This is one of the fields of investigation of Artificial Intelligence. It is expected that an expert system is able to deal with information relating to the specific problem domain, analyze it and produce knowledge and then take actions and decisions based on that knowledge. It is also expected that these actions and decisions resemble the ones that the human would do.

Expert systems can be found in the fields of accounting, medicine, process control, financial service, production or human resources just to name a few. Examples of expert systems can be found in insurance companies which are replacing human experts by software ones. They are also commonly found in banks to decide whether a client asking for a loan should or should not receive it. In one hand companies started to replace human experts by software in order to save money but, in other hand, because it is nowadays impracticable to do this kind of decision based only on humans due to the current increase amount of cases to evaluate and the increasing amount information associated to each one.

Before these expert systems are ready to be used they must be trained (Hayes-Roth, 1983). This may be done using information from past cases and respective decisions provided by human experts. They can also learn while they are used in which case generally a human makes adjustments according to the input, expected output and actual output.

ADR

Abraham Lincoln once said "Discourage litigation, persuade your neighbour to compromise where you can. Point out to them how the nominal winner is often the loser... in expenses and waste of time". This is the sentence that probably better describes the need for an alternative to traditional courts and the appearing of ADR (Brown &Marriott, 1999). With its evolution, ADR has become very used and adopted by both the legal system and the parties involved as the first step for trying to solve a dispute. In some countries, parties are even encouraged or required to try some kind of mediation before advancing into a court.

There are three main types of ADR: negotiation, mediation and arbitration. The objective of each type is the same, although each one has its way of achieving it. They aim to put the parties into contact and get into a common agreement without having to recur to litigation thus saving money and time.

Negotiation

Negotiation is a collaborative and informal process by which the parties communicate and, without any external influence, try to achieve an outcome that can satisfy both. Negotiation is widely used in very different areas such as legal proceedings, personal situations like divorces or parental disputes or hostage situations just to name a few. Negotiation is however a non-binding process which means that the parties do not have to accept the outcome. There are many ways of organizing the several negotiation techniques. According to Walton & McKersie (1991), negotiation can be classified as distributive or integrative.

In distributive negotiation, one looks at the problem as something that can be divided and distributed by the parties in an attempt to maximize their satisfaction. In integrative negotiation, the problem is expected to have more solutions than the ones visible at first sight.

A good example of distributive negotiation can be a divorce process in which the parties sit down to divide the assets. There are a fixed number of items each one with a given value and they will be divided according to concepts like justice or equality. Another well known process of distributive negotiation is the one that goes on between Unions and the managers of companies. In this relation, there are a few scarce resources like wages, daily hours of work and other working conditions. In this process Unions defend the interests of the workers thus trying to maximize the income and working conditions. In the other hand, managers try to maximize the profit of the company. The common point is that the company needs the workers and the workers need the job so it is around that point that the negotiations will take its course. In this type of negotiation, what one part wins, the other looses, i.e., if the workers earn a higher wage, the company will lose that money thus decreasing the profit. In game theory, this situation is known as a zero-sum game. Two important concepts here are the ones of utility and resistance (Bellucci et al., 2004). Utility denotes the value that a given item being negotiated has to a party while resistance denotes the willingness of a party to change the utility of an item. A good negotiator usually tries to convince the other party that certain items do not have the value that they are given. The negotiator will succeed if the opponent has a low resistance in that item and if he does, it will be easier for the negotiator to win that item or he will at least have better conditions for the rest of the negotiation process (Jennings et al., 2001). Accordingly, utility functions can be formalized that help to understand how each party values the items being distributed and possible outcomes and evolution of the negotiation process (Zeleznikow & Bellucci, 2003).

In integrative negotiation, the parties try to bring to the table as much interests as possible so that there are more items and more valuable with which to negotiate. When the parties are increasing the value of what they put in the table, they take into account their interests which include the needs, fears, concerns, and desires. This type of negotiation is also known as interest-based as the parties try to combine their interests and find common points in which both interests are satisfied. By doing so, more satisfactory outcomes are achieved by both parties. This makes integrative negotiation processes more desirable than distributive ones.

A good example for illustrating this difference is the following one. Two old ladies have a dispute because of an orange. They both want the last orange that is in the fruiter. If they resolve the dispute using the distributive approach they will split the orange in two equal parts and each one will get half of what they wanted. If, in other hand, they use the integrative approach, each one will state what they want, listen to what the other part wants and try to reach a common point that would satisfy both. In this case, one of the ladies wanted to eat the orange while the other just wanted the peel for making a tea. By doing so, each one gets what they wanted and the outcome is optimum. An important concept in this field is the one of Pareto efficiency (Fudenberg & Tirole, 1983). In this case, the solution obtained with the integrative approach would have been a Pareto efficient solution as no better solution could have been made. This process eventually leads to what is known in game theory as a win-win game, i.e., all the parties are better at the end of the negotiation process than when it started.

Although these two approaches when analyzed this way may be understood as opposite, they may be used together as introduced by (Lax & Sebenius, 1986). In fact, even in an integrative approach the items have eventually to be split up. The joint use of these two approaches has however the advantage of creating a relationship of trust between the parts when they are expanding the values so that when they get to the phase of splitting the items, everyone knows the interests and fears of the others which makes it easier to divide in a fair way and reach a common agreement.

Mediation

Mediation refers to a form of alternative dispute resolution in which the parties in dispute are guided by a 3rd neutral and independent entity which tries to orient the process to an outcome that may satisfy both the parties. In this approach, like in negotiation, the parties decide about the outcome instead of it being imposed by another entity like in litigation, but with the assistance of the neutral part. This neutral part is chosen by both the parties and has no authority for deciding on the outcome of the dispute but only for guide and assist them throughout it. This should be done by maintaining the parties focused on the subject of the dispute and by facilitating all the interaction and communication between them. The mediators are hence very important as their skills and aptitudes may represent the success or failure of the dispute resolution process (Hammond, 2003).

A mediator must therefore be able to communicate and to be understood by both the parties, giving clear instructions to each one. He should provide strategic advices in the correct time with the objective of easing the process without forgetting to maintain its neutrality. For this purpose it is important that the mediator shows different perspectives, recognizes the expectations and frustrations of the parties and react to it, is able of calming down the parties when the discussion gets more exalted and at all time support and encourage them to reach a satisfactory outcome. For all this a mediator must have above all good communication skills so that ideas are correctly passed to the parties. A mediator should not be a cold outsider that simply examines facts and decides upon them since being able of reading the parties feelings about the subjects may be a very important skill for really understanding how important each subject is for the parties (Langer, 2005).

The mediation process, from the mediator perspective, generally has three phases and starts with the claimant presenting a claim to which the respondent answers. The first step for the mediator is to establish contact with both the parties and bring them into reality. In this phase, the mediator must introduce the parties if they do not know each other and expose how the process will take place. After this, the mediator must get to know the problem and understand it in the form of the objects in dispute, the claim and the expectations of each part. It is very important in this phase for the mediator to talk very closely with each part so that the characteristics of the problem and the disputants are correctly understood. In the last phase of the process the mediator must know the rules of the process and define a strategy for reaching the goal based on the observations done in the previous phase. If the mediator understood well the singularities of the problem and the disputants, the strategy should work otherwise, the mediator may adapt its strategy during the process if the goal is not being achieved (Hammond, 2003). It is therefore important that the mediator has the sensibility needed for perceiving how the process is being interpreted by each part in order to make adjustments to the strategy, if needed.

Mediation tools are often preferred by the clients for many reasons. One of the more important one has to do with the price and time consumed during a mediation process when compared with regular litigation processes. Although some mediators will demand a fee, the process will be certainly more money-saving than going into a court and it will also be faster, which translates into advantages for both the parties. The fact that the mediator can be chosen by the parties instead of being appointed also gives them some confidence on the entity chosen and may act as a first concordance point that may start to create a relationship of trust between the parties. Mediation may also offer more privacy than regular courts as it is a private process that involves only the two disputants and the mediator, leaving out elements like journalists, diminishing the exposure. This way, what happens during the case remains strictly confidential as the only ones that need two know are the three main elements. Furthermore, mediation often reaches better results for the disputants than the results obtained in litigations. This happens because in mediation the parties take an active role in the

definition of the outcome while in court a jury decides on the outcome which generally would not satisfy both or even any of the parties. Unlike negotiation, when two parties seek mediation as dispute resolution they are often more willing to achieve a solution. The simple fact of agreeing in a common mediator and giving him authority for conducting the process is a sign of good will and determination in achieving a solution for the common problem. Disputants in this situation usually are more willing to work together than against each other.

Hence, mediation is a tool often used in a variety of cases ranging from a mother trying to calm down two brothers that are fighting over a car to conflicts between countries (Zartman, 2007). One of the most recent and known examples is the one of U.S. mediating the Israeli-Palestinian conflict in the Middle East with the objective of achieving a long lasting cease fire (Feste, 1991). It is also important to say that mediation, as well as negotiation is a non-binding process, i.e., the parties do not have to legally accept the outcome.

Arbitration

In arbitration the two parties also use the help of a 3rd independent and neutral entity for solving a dispute but, contrary to mediation, this entity has no active role on helping the parties throughout the process. In this approach the neutral part, the arbitrator, simply hears the parts and, based on the facts presented, takes a decision without influencing the parts during their presentations. The outcome of the process in arbitration is also singular as it may be binding or non-binding (Kohler, 2003). If in a determinate case the outcome is non-binding, arbitration is similar to mediation except for the role of the 3rd party. However, if the decision of the arbitrator is binding, all the parties will have to accept it like they would if it was a court.

As the decision of the 3rd party may be definitive, its role is here even more important than in mediation. Its task can be compared to the tasks of a jury or a judge in a common litigation process in a court. Nevertheless, disputants find some advantages in using this approach. Like with other ADR tools, the costs and the time spent can be significantly smaller than in courts. One factor that definitively contributes to the smaller time spent has to do with the growing number of arbitration services providers. Confidentially may also be granted as these services providers are usually private. In a few words, arbitration may be a low cost trial.

However there are also disadvantages (Moses, 2008). One of the most known is that sometimes people, when buying an item or signing a job contract, do not know that the only way of solving an eventual dispute is through a binding arbitration process without the possibility to go into court, thus being a serious threat to the rights. Situations like these are mostly caused by people not reading the small prints in contracts and terms of agreement. This case is even worst when the persons have to pay for the arbitration service they are "forced" to use. Contrary to courts, the right to an attorney is not always granted so sometimes persons that cannot afford one end up without any legal representative. Another negative point is that there are not many ways for an appeal so that it may not be easy to overturn an erroneous decision, contrary to courts.

ODR

With the moving on to a global society based on computers, new needs appeared in the fields of alternative dispute resolution. This new reality raises some questions and certainly increases the possibilities for any of the parties involved in a dispute resolution process. Technologies can in one hand be used as a simple tool for ODR. In this approach, ODR is much like ADR except the parts are not in contact personally but instead through a mean of communication. We can think on each of the disputants in a different part of the globe, an

eventual 3rd one with mediator or arbitrator role in another location, all of them communicating via IM or video conference. Technologies here have no active role, they act only as a facilitator for the process.

In another approach, technologies can be used as a 4th participant that assists the 3rd part or even one of the parties (Rifkin, 2001; Sourdin, 2005). Although still not having here an active role, these tools can assist the parties in taking the right decisions or planning the right strategy. In this field the most important technology are the expert systems. They can provide the parties with knowledge about past cases and their outcomes, about the law or about other aspects. Technologies here can even consist of support decision systems that have the autonomy for guiding or even representing the parts throughout the process. These two types of ODR systems are called 1st and 2nd generation ODR systems, respectively.

Why ODR

ODR is a relatively new approach to dispute resolution since the technologies it builds in are also recent. It has however met a fast growth in its use due to its advantages (Schultz, 2001). ODR tools are generally easy to use. Most of the times, clients interact with intuitive interfaces that hide all the complexity of the laws and formalities behind these processes. This increases the willingness of the parties to solve their disputes online as they feel that it is a more transparent and controlled process. As these systems are available 24/24 the parties can submit documents and evidence and use the services at any time, from any place. By having the possibility to communicate synchronously and asynchronously, these tools can be used by parties to communicate even when the time zones are very different what certainly makes the whole process easier (Katsch & Rifkin, 2001). Evidently, these tools, by being available online, make it possible for the parties to communicate with each other and with the 3rd part from any part of the world. This reduces the costs with transportation and accommodation. Regarding costs, these tools are generally cheaper and faster than common litigation since they are based on cheap and available technologies and avoid all the costs associated to courts (Schultz, 2002).

Another important characteristic is that by being behind an interface instead of being in front of a judge, the environment is less intimidating (Schultz, 2001). In these conditions people tend to be less afraid of talking and being true. At the same time, because the parts are not in contact personally, they tend to be more focused on the subject that on the opponent, more focused on the facts than on the sorrows. There are some extreme cases in which the parts even refuse to sit together at the same table so this is the only possible way of trying to solve the dispute, avoiding any fight or violence. When persons are not in the presence of others that might have a suppressor or inhibitor effect (such as the relations in the cases of domestic violence) they also tend to speak more freely and without the fear of the consequences.

Using these tools the parties tend to reflect more and take wiser decisions than when the meetings are personal. This is due to the fact that the parties have more time to think about what they are going to do or say than if they were in the presence of the interlocutors. This is even truer when asynchronous communication mechanisms like forums or E-mail are being used. It is also easier for all the parties to manage and have access the information of the case since everything is available online all the time. The creation of formal documents is also easier since there may be digital assistants that help the parties through the process or that even create the documents automatically. All the communications are also stored so they can be later analyzed and can even act as evidence for later phases.

Summarizing, ODR tools can be a more accessible, fast, economic and transparent way of solving disputes. However, some points that are considered as advantages may also be disadvantages (Goodman, 2003). If in some cases moving from a paper based process to an online one brings it closer to people, in others that does not happen, namely to population slices that do not have access or that do not have the proper training for using the tools, leading to inequalities. Training can be provided in these cases but the time spent to do it could delay the cases. If it is true that in most of the developed countries technologies used by ODR are cheap and available, in developing countries that is not necessary true and might lead to higher costs than in developed countries. This may also be an inequality and make inhibit some parts to go on or even start the dispute resolution process. In some cases, storing the information online means that there is more security but sometimes it means the opposite. If one part has access to the login information of the other it becomes very easy to access and change confidential information of the other part, it gets even easier than entering into a court and trying to access the paperwork. This raises the problems of online identity: when we communicate with someone online, how can we be sure that it is really with that person that we are talking? How do we know that someone did not steal the login information and is now using it instead?

Another major disadvantage has to do with the online communications. If in one hand one does not feel as intimidated by not speaking in front of a jury or an opponent and may speak truer, it also becomes easier to lie online since there is not the intimidating presence of a judge or an entity with a higher authority. One maybe even more important issue is the one of the body language. Mehrabian (1980) states that most of the meaning that we derive from a face-to-face conversation comes from other aspects than the words spoken, namely the tone of voice, the loudness, the facial expressions and body gestures. Evidently that all this important information in a conversation is lost if technologies like IM, E-mail, forums or others similar are being used. The best approach to follow here would be to use more recent technologies like video conference or TelePresence that are the most similar to a face-to-face conversation. Important here is more how things are said instead of what is said.

Although these disadvantages, ODR has been growing in its users. It is not expected that any of the parties in a dispute resolution process is replaced by intelligent agents in a near future but these tools should be more and more used and its integration will eventually lead to that reality.

How ODR Works

An ODR process starts when one of the parties contacts an ODR provider with the intention of starting an online dispute resolution process (Lodder & Zeleznikow, 2005; Peruginelli & Chiti, 2002). This litigant must in this phase provide information about the other or other litigants. The system must therefore contact all the intervenient putting them into contact and determine if they are willing to participate on the dispute resolution process. If all the parties agree, the system moves into the next phase where it tries to gather as much information about the problem as possible.

In this phase, the parties are asked about all the details of the dispute, including eventual monetary values. It is very important in this phase that the system understands how each part feels about each subject and to understand what are the expectations of each one. This is probably the hardest phase for a totally autonomous ODR provider, i.e., without human intervention. This phase is easier and more efficiently conduced, at this moment, by a Human expert that can more easily understand the emotions of the persons towards each subject covered. The parties are also asked for documents that can act as evidence or facts to the case being solved.

Having done this the system may enter into the 3rd phase where the data collected in the previous phase is analyzed. This is the central phase of the ODR process since it determines the outcome based on previous known cases and their out-

comes. The presence of the Human is in this phase also important. However, there are already many implementations of Case-based reasoning models that look into a knowledge base of previous cases and autonomously decide the probable outcome of a case with given characteristics. However, as this is the most important and determinant phase of the process, there is a lot of reluctance in entrusting it to computer systems (Kolodner, 1993).

In the last phase the decision taken is presented to the parties. In this phase the effectiveness of the algorithms and strategies used is studied in terms of the success or failure of the ODR process. This information can later be used for improving the strategies and algorithms for future use. If the process succeeded to satisfy both parties, the case is closed and they should do what they agreed on. If the decision is binding, the parties should do the same even if they do not agree on the outcome. There may still be however the chance to an appeal and the resolution of the dispute in a normal court.

First Generation ODR

First generation ODR systems describe the systems that nowadays are more or less implemented. The main idea of first generation ODR systems is that the Human remains the central piece in the planning and decision making process (Peruginelli & Chiti, 2002). Because of that, human mediators are carefully chosen according to their skills, aptitudes and previous cases that they participated in since they will have a determinant role in the process. Electronic tools are evidently used but are seen as no more than tools, without any autonomy or major role. Their only purpose is to assist the parties and make the management of the information and the communications between them easier. In this first generation the main technologies used are instant messaging, forums, video and phone calls, video conference, mailing lists and more recently VideoPresence. Agent technologies and other autonomous systems may be used but have no active role and no autonomy. These systems are common nowadays and are usually supported by a web page. They represent a first necessary step before a more autonomous role of intelligent systems (Lodder & Zeleznikow, 2005).

The evolution towards second generation ODR systems has been slow because in one hand of the difficulty of implementing into software agents the complex cognitive processes that a Human mediator has and, in other hand, because of the reluctance we humans have against letting computer systems deciding our us. This might even be the main barrier to this evolution as one would be more prone to disagree with an unfavourable outcome if it was decided by a computer system instead of being decided by an expert Human. Due to this, the second generation of ODR systems seems yet a bit far to reach.

Second Generation ODR

The second generation of ODR systems is essentially defined by a more active role of technology (Peruginelli & Chiti, 2002; Lodder & Thiessen, 2003). It is not used for the mere role of putting the parties into contact and making access to information easier. It goes beyond that and is used for idea generation, planning, strategy definition and decision making processes. Humans have here a secondary role whether they are one of the parties in dispute or they are the neutral. They will be represented by intelligent agents that will have the legal authority and the autonomy for representing the wills and desires of the humans. These agents will try to behave and pursue the same objectives that the humans they represent would. The technologies used in this new generation of ODR systems will comprise not only the communication technologies used nowadays but also many of the AI subfields like neural networks, intelligent agents, case-based reasoning, logical deduction, methods for uncertain reasoning and learning methods.

Although the path to this second generation of ODR is traced and the technologies needed are already more or less known and explored, there is still a long way for reaching it, most likely because of our reluctance to be replaced by computer systems and the consequences of it. It is expected that ODR tools slowly move towards this new generation giving small but solid steps bringing it closer to reality.

Categories of ODR Systems

ODR systems can be categorized according to the way they assist the parts in a dispute resolution process (Thiessen & Zeleznikow, 2004):

- **Information systems:** These kinds of system simply provide information that can be used by the parties to solve the dispute. This information may comprise the laws of a given country towards the subject in dispute, information about all the parties, about the status of the process, among other.
- **Blind bidding:** The systems included in this category aim at the automation of simple purely monetary questions. This may include cases such as divorces without children, failed buy or sell operations, among others. The parties make bids without the knowledge of the other part and the system is responsible for deciding when a possible agreement point has been reached.
- **Document management:** These systems include facilitators working online or offline with parties, providing services for the creation and management of contracts and other structured documents. The clients of these systems tend to be entities with some difficulty in creating documents that need to meet a specific standard or structure.
- **Automated negotiation:** These systems rely on advanced optimization algorithms that try to find the optimum solution for

complex problems. These systems generally work by asking the user their preferences about the items in dispute, i.e., a quantification of how much they want each item. They can be used in a variety of different cases, ranging from divorces on which people need to agree on who gets what, to unions and managements trying to agree on wages and working conditions for the workers of a given company.

- **Customized systems:** These systems are custom systems built for specific purposes or requisites. Some processes have very particular characteristics that are not fit by any system so that specific systems have to be developed.
- **Virtual mediation rooms:** These systems are very similar to traditional mediation except that the meetings take place in virtual rooms using tools such as instant messaging or email. The mediator will try to work out a favourable outcome without meeting the parties, just by means of the communication technologies.
- **Arbitration systems:** These systems are equivalent to traditional arbitration services except for the fact that they are provided online. In this approach, human arbitrators work from any point of the world solving cases with the help of communication technologies like E-mail, telephone or instant messaging.

ODR PROJECTS/SITES

In this section we will look at a number of sites of ODR providers for consumers currently available and research projects that through small steps try to improve the current ODR systems, approaching them to what is expected of the second generation systems.

ODR Systems for Consumers

- **ADNDRC:** The Asian Domain Name Dispute Resolution Centre is a joint undertaking by the China International Economic and Trade Arbitration Commission (CIETAC), the Hong Kong International Arbitration Centre (HKIAC) and the Korean Internet Address Dispute Resolution Committee (KIDRC) that is credited by the ICANN as a dispute resolution provider. http://www.adndrc.org
- **Electronic Courthouse:** This is an American dispute resolution service provider created in 2000 which offers services of mediation, arbitration and evaluation of cases. Evaluation is used when the parties are not aware of the laws and are simply looking for some legal framework, being therefore a non-binding and merely informative process. Customers of this service include employees, unions, professional associations, individuals, sole proprietors, governments, public agencies, businesses and enterprises. http://www.electronic-courthouse.com
- **eucon:** Europäisches Institut für Conflict Management e.V., (European Institute for Conflict Management) headquartered in Munich is a non-profit organisation and was formed in October 2006. This company provides mediation services that may be used by customers such as institutions, professional organizations, law firms and corporate business. The eucon site also offers a comprehensive explanation about mediation and its advantages, including a film intended to provide a practical case study showing the advantages of mediation and illustrating how a case proceeds. http://www.eucon-institute.com
- **HKIAC:** Hong Kong International Arbitration Centre was established in 1985 to assist disputing parties to solve their

disputes. Besides arbitration, parties can chose alternative ways such as negotiation, conciliation, mediation and finally litigation. The company also has a free service for providing information about the alternative dispute resolution methods. The Centre maintains a growing information Services Centre of books and publications which are available for reference to interested members of the public. http://www.hkiac.org

- **ICC:** The International Chamber of Commerce is a global business organization whose activities cover a broad spectrum, ranging from arbitration and dispute resolution for open trade and the market economy system, business self-regulation, fighting corruption or combating commercial crime. The arbitration services provided are on increase use, having received cases at a rate of more than 500 a year since 1999. http://www.iccwbo.org

- **The Mediation Room:** This company provides a virtual mediation space for parties trying to solve their disputes. Users of TheMediationRoom.com software include The Ministry of Justice (UK), The National Institutes of Health (USA), The Law Council of Australia (Australia), The National Mediation Board (USA), The Commonwealth Telecommunications Organisation, The European Consumer Centres and eBay/PayPal (Europe and Australia). Each of these entities has very different disputes but the software, by being very dynamic, may be used by all of them. http://mediation.orcawebsites.com

- **ODRWorld:** The lemma of this company is that "justice is paramount and should be available to all". It therefore provides ODR services for solving any type of dispute, ranging from simple and trivial to higher value ones. Disputes can be solved online and offline through assisted negotia-

tion, mediation and arbitration. ODRWorld focuses on disputes that emerge from the global online activities and defends that these disputes should be solved online. The site includes tools such as a case message board and an online chat. http://www.odrworld.com

- **Smartsettle:** Smartsettle is an online negotiation system (eNegotiation) that can be described as a generic tool for decision-makers with conflicting objectives that wish to reach a formal agreement. This platform can be used to solve problems relating to family, insurance, real estate, labor-management, contract negotiations, among others. In the site it is possible to find a few simulations that explain and show how the platform works. The Smartsettle suit is organized into SmartsettleOne which deals with simple and single-issue disputes, and the SmartsettleInfinity which deals with complex and multivariate cases. http://www.smartsettle.com

ODR Research Projects

In this section we will be looking at a few research projects that are being developed at the moment. Most of the projects analyzed here are maintained by universities and other institutions and focus on particular questions and not on the whole of the problem since only this way can progresses be made.

- **Geneva Law School:** Geneva University has a Research Team on Online Dispute Resolution, Arbitration, and Information Technology. One of the projects developed in this group did research on the fields of Online Dispute Resolution on a first stage and on IT on a second phase. This project was financed by the Swiss National Science Foundation and ended in December 2005. This research group continues to do research on these topics mainly driven by the executive director Dr. Thomas Schultz who did his academic career in the fields of ODR. The results can be seen in many published articles and books such as (Schultz et. al 2001; Schultz, 2006). http://www.mids.ch/school/university.html

- **Lauterpacht Centre:** The Centre is part of the Faculty of Law in the University of Cambridge and one of the Faculty's specialist law centres. The Centre is the scholarly home of international law at Cambridge University. International law is a major aspect of the Law Faculty's teaching programme at undergraduate, LLM and research level. The Centre's objectives are to promote the development of international law through research and publication, to serve as a forum for the discussion of current events and issues in international law and to provide an intellectual home in Cambridge for scholars of international law from around the world to pursue their research in a stimulating and congenial atmosphere. http://www.lcil.cam.ac.uk

- **MeRC:** The mission of the McMaster eBusiness Research Centre is to provide leadership and infrastructure support for eBusiness research to academic and industry partners. To accomplish this, MeRC focuses on three main activities: Research, Education and Outreach. There is currently a large number of research projects being held at MeRC that cover a wide range of disciplines, among them are mobile commerce, identity theft, online trust or online negotiation (Hassanein, 2004; Sproule & Archer 2006; Wang et. al 2004). In these projects better and more secure ways of doing online transactions are investigated as well as the dispute resolution methods to apply when these fail. This research project is based in Ontario, Canada at MacMaster University. http://www.merc-mcmaster.ca

- **Victoria University:** The Victoria University's Faculty of Law develops research in the areas of business and law with special focus on ODR procedures, namely in the work of Prof. John Zeleznikow who is responsible for the Family_Winner project (Zeleznikow & Bellucci, 2003). Some key areas of research include developing software tools to support negotiated decision making, building ethical standards into corporate governance, assessing the economic impacts of climate change, studying the impact of WorkChoices legislation on Victorian workers or analysing the social impact of tourism. http://www.businessandlaw.vu.edu.au/index.asp

- **National Center for Technology and Dispute Resolution:** This center is located at the University of Massachusetts at Amherst and provides an interdisciplinary approach to the study of law and society. Research efforts of faculty have included the impact of new information technologies on law, alternative dispute resolution, law and multinational corporations, law and popular culture, law and education, law and indigenous peoples, the legal profession, and law and education (Katsh, 1995, 1999). The Department organizes a clinical project in conjunction with the Massachusetts Fair Housing Center (MFHC) and it also sponsors the National Center for Technology and Dispute Resolution. One of the main figures behind ODR investigation in this university is professor Ethan Katsh who besides being professor of legal studies in this university is also Director of the National Center for Technology and Dispute Resolution. http://www.odr.info

- **Minho University:** The CCTC (Computer Science and Technology Center) research centre develops research in the areas of Computer Science and the Law with special focus on ODR procedures, namely in with TIARAC (Telematics and Artificial Intelligence in Alternative Conflict Resolution) research project. The key areas of research include the consideration of possibilities for solving disputes through telematics, having in consideration both Portuguese and European legal frameworks and also considering alternatives for dispute resolution arising from Artificial Intelligence models and techniques, applied to civil and labour Law. http://cctc.di.uminho.pt/

FUTURE OF ODR

The future of ODR is somehow uncertain. The path to follow is clear and the desirable behaviour of future ODR systems is already defined: second generation ODR (Peruginelli & Chiti, 2002). The question however is more if we really want that this generation to become a reality. This is the same to say: do we want that software agents play a major role, deciding on our lives and on the outcome of our disputes? Should they be granted a more important role than mere electronic tools that make our life easier? Should they be given authority similar to the one of a judge in a court?

All these questions are evidently very problematic and controversy. One of the main questions is about how much can we trust on the decisions of automated software agents. Evidently, one can state that the degree of confidence that one may have on software agents is proportional to the confidence of the developer that wrote those agents. That may be truth until a certain point. But, when we are talking about intelligent agents that may develop its own behaviours, its own will, how can we control them? How can we be sure that they do not develop unwanted behaviours? Human mediators may also develop unwanted behaviours but, although this may sound strange, it is more acceptable for us if a human takes a

wrong or unfair decision than if it is a computer doing so. In the case that a computer shows this behaviour, the damaged parts would without any doubt appeal with more conviction than if it happened with a human mediator. This happens because we respect more the human than the computer, which is natural, but may be a barrier for the acceptation of these systems.

It is indeed a very big step to give an agent autonomy and legal representation powers so that it may replace us in disputes. Agents will have autonomy for deciding about the best strategies to use, will be able of changing strategies by analyzing previous cases, will consult expert systems in order to collect knowledge and will take their own decisions (Jennings et.al., 2001). As problematic as representing us is an agent acting as the 3rd part since in some cases, it may decide on the outcome of the parties which gives him the major role on the process.

The case that won't be so problematic is on autonomous agents with mediator roles. The mediator does not have a preponderant role on the process, it acts merely as an intermediary and facilitator, therefore having no power on the decision of the outcome. Agents may make its way into ODR processes by automating mediation. The first tasks may be to arrange dates for conversations and to ask for documents and managing, moving then to higher level tasks like mediating conversations and generating ideas and strategies for solving the disputes. Having succeeded here, agents may start to have more and more important roles being even trusted to arbitrate cases.

CONCLUSION

The use of telematics in electronic commerce will inevitably lead to conflicts arising in virtual locations and new tools for dispute resolution will be required. The use of such tools will certainly have parties being faced with new challenges, some clear advantages but also some disadvantages.

The ways of solving disputes online will necessarily become different from what happens in traditional dispute resolution. Even the so-called power imbalances may become very different "from what they would be if the parties were interacting offline" (Rifkin, 2001).

Some clear advantages and disadvantages may easily be pointed out: cost savings and convenience, on one side, but also impersonality and potential inaccessibility on the other (Goodman, 2003). Face to face contact, the spoken words, voice tone and body language will tend to be replaced by written words and computer screen dimensions. Speed and ease of communication may be a clear advantage, although online messages can also become easily ambiguous or misinterpreted. Of course, time and money can be a relevant factor in the moment of choosing ODR specially in order to solve disputes between parties geographically located very far away from each other. But difficulties related to accessing technologies or even software disparities must be considered.

An interesting advantage, especially in online mediation, is the possibility of private meetings and caucusing, at the same time with both parties. Interestingly, parties will tend to feel calmer, more confident, less intimidated in online dispute resolution (Hammond, 2003). The use not only of synchronous but also asynchronous communication will offer parties alternatives leading to a reduction of impulsive replies, although paradoxically it may also be stated the appearance of an electronic distance on the parties. And all the parties involved in online dispute will have to be confronted with the need to interact with a very special and different kind of partner: the technological elements will always have to be considered (Katsch & Rifkin, 2001).

ACKNOWLEDGMENT

The work described in this paper is included in TIARAC - Telematics and Artificial Intelligence in Alternative Conflict Resolution Project (PTDC/JUR/71354/2006), which is a research project supported by FCT (Science & Technology Foundation), Portugal.

REFERENCES

Bellucci, E., Zeleznikow, J., & Lodder, A. R. (2004). Integrating artificial intelligence, argumentation and game theory to develop an Online Dispute Resolution Environment. In *Proceedings of the 16th IEEE International Conference*.

Bennett, S. C. (2002). *Arbitration: Essential concepts*. ALM Publishing.

Bonczek, R. H., Holsapple, C. W., & Whinston, A. B. (1981). *Foundations of decision support systems*. Academic Press.

Brito, L., Novais, P., & Neves, J. (2003). The logic behind negotiation: from pre-argument reasoning to argument-based negotiation. In *Intelligent agent software engineering* (pp. 137–159). Hershey, PA: Idea Group Publishing.

Brown, H., & Marriott, A. (1999). *ADR Principles and Practice*. Sweet and Maxwell.

Feste, K. A. (1991). *Plans for peace*. Greenwood Publishing Group.

Fudenberg, D. A., & Tirole, J. (1983). Game Theory (Chapter 1, Section 2.4). MIT Press.

Goodman, J. W. (2003). *The pros and cons of online dispute resolution: an assessment of cyber-mediation websites*. Duke Law and Technology Review.

Hammond, A. M. (2003). How do you write "yes"? A study on the effectiveness of online dispute resolution. *Conflict Resolution Quarterly, 20*(3). doi:10.1002/crq.25

Hassanein, K., Head, M., & Centre, M. E. R. (2004). *Manipulating social presence through the Web interface and its impact on consumer attitude towards online shopping*. McMaster eBusiness Research Centre.

Hayes-Roth, F., Waterman, D. A., & Lenat, D. B. (1983). *Building expert systems*. Boston, MA: Addison-Wesley Longman Publishing Co., Inc.

Jackson, P. (1990). *Introduction to expert systems*. Boston, MA: Addison-Wesley Longman Publishing Co., Inc.

Jennings, N., Faratin, P., Lomuscio, A., Parsons, S., Wooldridge, M., & Sierra, C. (2001). Automated Negotiation: Prospects, Methods and Challenges. *Group Decision and Negotiation, 10*(2), 199–215. doi:10.1023/A:1008746126376

Katsch, E., & Rifkin, J. (2001). *Online dispute resolution – resolving conflicts in cyberspace*. San Francisco, CA: Jossey-Bass Wiley Company.

Katsh, E., Rifkin, J., & Gaitenby, A. (1999). E-Commerce, E-Disputes, and E-Dispute Resolution: In the Shadow of eBay Law. *Ohio State Journal on Dispute Resolution, 15*, 705.

Katsh, M. E. (1995). *Law in a digital world*. Oxford University Press.

Kohler, G. K. (2003). La resolución de los litigios en línea – perspectivas y retos del contencioso internacional contemporáneo. Revista Latino-Americana de Mediación y Arbitraje, vol. III – Número 4

Kolodner, J. L. (1993). *Case-based Reasoning*. Morgan Kaufmann Publishers.

Langer, A. (2005). *The Importance of Mediators, Bridge Builders, Wall Vaulters and*. Frontier. Una Città.

Lax, D., & Sebenius, J. (1986). *The Manager as Negotiator: Bargaining for Cooperation and Competitive Gain*. Free Press.

Lodder, A. R. (2006). The Third Party and Beyond. An Analysis of the Different Parties, in particular The Fifth, Involved in Online Dispute Resolution. *Information & Communications Technology Law, 15*(2), 143–155. doi:10.1080/13600830600676438

Lodder, A. R., & Thiessen, E. M. (2003). The role of Artificial Intelligence in Online Dispute Resolution. In D. Choi & E. Katsh (Eds.), *Proceedings UN forum on ODR*.

Lodder, A. R., & Zeleznikow, J. (2005). Developing an Online Dispute Resolution Environment: Dialogue Tools and Negotiation Systems in a Three Step Model. *The Harvard Negotiation Law Review, 10*, 287–338.

Mehrabian, A. (1980). *Silent Messages: Implicit Communication of Emotions and Attitudes*. Wadsworth Pub Co.

Moses, M. L. (2008). *The principles and practice of international commercial arbitration*. Cambridge University Press.

Novais, P., Brito, L., & Neves, J. (2005). Pre-Argumentative Reasoning. *The Knowledge-Based Systems Journal, 18*(2-3), 79–88. doi:10.1016/j.knosys.2004.07.007

Olson, G. M., Malone, T. W., & Smith, J. B. (Eds.). (2001). *Coordination Theory and Collaboration Technology*. Mahwah, NJ: Erlbaum.

Peruginelli, G., & Chiti, G. (2002). Artificial intelligence in alternative dispute resolution. In *Proceedings of LEA 2002. Workshop on the Law of Electronic Agents* (pp. 97–104). CIRSFID, Bologna.

Rahwan, I., Ramchurn, S., Jennings, N., McBurney, P., Parsons, S., & Sonenberg, L. (2004). *Argumentation-based negotiation*. The Knowledge Engineering Review.

Raiffa, H. (2002). *The Art and Science of Negotiation*. Harvard University Press.

Rifkin, J. (2001). Online dispute resolution: theory and practice of the fourth party. *Conflict Resolution Quarterly*, *19*(1).

Schultz, T. (2002). *Online Dispute Resolution: An Overview and Selected Issues*. Economic Commission for Europe. Retrieved from http://ssrn.com/abstract=898821

Schultz, T. (2006). *Information Technology and Arbitration: A Practitioner's Guide*. The Hague: Kluwer Law International.

Schultz, T., Kaufmann-Kohler, G., Langer, D., & Bonnet, V. (2001). *Online Dispute Resolution: The State of the Art and the Issues*. Geneva: Report of the E-Com / E-Law Research Project of the University of Geneva.

Sourdin, T. (2005). *Alternative Dispute Resolution* (2nd ed.). Lawbook Co.

Sproule, S., & Archer, N. (2006). Defining Identity Theft–A Discussion Paper. *McMaster eBusiness Research Centre (MeRC), McMaster University*.

Thiessen, E., & Zeleznikow, J. (2004). Technical aspects of online dispute resolution challenges and opportunities. In M. Conley Tyler, E. Katsh, & D. Choi (Eds.), *Proceedings of the Third Annual Forum on Online Dispute Resolution*.

Turban, E. (1993). *Decision support and expert systems: management support systems*. Upper Saddle River, NJ: Prentice Hall PTR.

Walker, D. (1980). *Oxford Companion to Law* (p. 301). Oxford University Press.

Walton, P. R. E., & McKersie, R. B. (1991). *A behavioral theory of labor negotiations*. Cornell University Press.

Wang, W. J., Yuan, Y., Archer, N. P., & Centre, M. E. R. (2004). *A Theoretical Framework for Combating Identity Theft. McMaster eBusiness Research Centre (MeRC)*. DeGroote School of Business.

Wooldrige, M. (2002). *An Introduction to Multiagent Systems*. John Wiley & Sons.

Zartman, I. W. (2007). *Peacemaking in international conflict*. US Institute of Peace Press.

Zeleznikow, J., & Bellucci, E. (2003). Family_Winner: integrating game theory and heuristics to provide negotiation support. In *Proceedings of Sixteenth International Conference on Legal Knowledge Based System* (pp. 21-30).

Chapter 4
Legal Ontologies in ICT and Law

Witold Abramowicz
Poznan University of Economics, Poland

Piotr Stolarski
Poznan University of Economics, Poland

Tadeusz Tomaszewski
Poznan University of Economics, Poland

ABSTRACT

Re-usability is frequently declared as sine qua non feature of modern ontology engineering. Although thoroughly examined in general theory of knowledge management models the re-usability issue is still barely a declaration in the domain of legal ontologies. The similar situation also applies to statute-specific ontologies. Those knowledge modeling entities are well described especially as an opposition to the general application legal ontologies. Yet it is trivial to say that most of the developed legal ontologies so far are those generic ones. And this sole fact should not surprise as the very specialized knowledge models – usually harder to develop – are at the same time narrowed with their utility. Of course in terms of re-usability this simply means that this feature may be largely disabled in this kind of knowledge models. In this chapter we face both challenges, i.e. as an excuse for presentation of the most interesting in our opinion trends and works in the field we will demonstrate the practical approach to modeling copyright law case by re-using statute-specific ontologies.

INTRODUCTION

The legal information and knowledge computer representation is still an open issue. In this chapter we decided to introduce a global view on problems and challenges which have been solved so far contrasting them to those which in our opinion are still awaiting some constructive approaches.

DOI: 10.4018/978-1-61520-975-0.ch004

Moreover it is our intention to present matter within the scope of the topic together with the important background information incorporated as well, ergo in the context of legal ontologies we felt obliged to present also selected facts and materials which concerns less specific (broader) range – the ontologies – as necessary[1].

This chapter shows the background works of modern legal ontologies state of art. We thoroughly discuss legal ontology knowledge engineering methods. We demonstrate how ontologies are useful for modeling the legal knowledge and normative aspects of reality described in various types of documents. We discuss logical formalisms that can be used mutually as a part of ontologies or together with them in order to provide environments for legal reasoning. Finally we are analyzing some real legal logic-based problems and give examples of solutions on the basis of our own research and lessons learned from those experiments. Unlike the other works on this topic we selected a specific strategy of approaching to the presented above issues, taking into account an aspect which is very often declared by the authors of knowledge models but at the same time does not obtain the expected attention. By the aspect we mean the re-usability feature of ontologies. Therefore we examine what is the potential of existing ontologies – both our own and those of external authors – in modeling legal knowledge straight ahead without the very costly burden of new legal ontologies creation.

BACKGROUND

Ontologies are "an explicit specification of a conceptualization" as states one of the most commonly known definition by Gruber (Gruber, 1993). Being based on the OWA assumption the ontological formalisms are well fitted to meet some of the challenges of legal knowledge representation. What is more – the wide spread of web standards introduced into development of ontology life-cycle guarantees that the fulfillment of the vision of automated sharing of knowledge and the reuse of that knowledge between software components and human agents is not far from realization. In terms of legal domain the vision of accessing pieces of codified knowledge from different sources in a standardized manner can be tempting esp. on account of possibilities of making automated inference on a larger scale.

In the field of legal knowledge management and representation the problem of representing legal knowledge in the form of variety of knowledge bases or ontologies has been vastly recognized (Despres, 2004). As a consequence a number of generally elaborated methods of ontology engineering have been tested to produce legal ontologies. Some of those methods were also used to create specific solutions for legal domain embedded tasks of building semantic knowledge repositories.

Legal ontologies have been formed to fulfill numerous aims (Gangemi, 2007) and to provide support for various functions. Those functions coupled with the aims delimit the outline and structure of the ontology. Those mentioned properties define content and expressivity in addition. Thus, methods used to construct the knowledge models are to reflect the needs and intentions of constructors.

The already developed methods of creating ontologies in the legal domain that reflects a specific highly expertise knowledge models form small domains connected to single statutes or other legal documents. In the context of works of (Guarino, 1998) our ontologies should be considered as a mixture of domain and application specific ones. The aim of research is to look closer to the problems of not only creating a common semantic platform as a set of symbols and concepts but to be able to built logical theories around it. The creation of legal ontologies (or rights and norms representing knowledge models) overcomes a number of obstacles. Thus, although the efforts of creation of legal ontologies are intensified for the last decade and there exists a rather large resource of those, containing and dealing with a general legal vocabulary (Breuker et al., 2006) we perceive a lack of oriented models describing more precisely matters of a concrete branch of law, a statute or even only some specific regulations. It is certain that with new opportunities of use arising and with demand from the software systems for facilities enabling easy to re-use dedicated expert knowledge which additionally will be change-proof such ontologies will be of great value.

The models incorporating legal knowledge ought to be viewed as exceptional. The challenges that stand before the knowledge engineers make them especially particular even in the world of semantic knowledge modeling. The main cause of this fact is that legal ontologies must properly reflect the exact meaning of legal terms. And those latter on the other hand are extraordinarily vulnerable to even subtle changes in the way they are defined or used in contexts. This means that slight nuances and divergences have to be taken care of in the process of ontology engineering as their expression has major influence on usefulness of the produced models.

The early attempts of automating the legal reasoning are under way for more than decade (Zeleznikow, 1996) yet as the task in any more general approach is very extensive and it is mainly based on the gathered legal knowledge models. For a longer period of time the possibilities of making such reasoning was largely limited due to wide-ranging resources of knowledge from different domains needed to make any sophisticated inference.

The initial interesting resume of works in the field of legal knowledge description with the use of ontologies is contained in the paper of Visser and Bench-Capon (1999). This paper summarized the results of works done by – among others - Valente (1995), McCarty (1989), Visser (1995), Kralingen (1995, Visser, Kralingen, et al. 1997). The mentioned work dated 1999 apart from introducing the results of the ten-years period of extensive researches went further by formulating numerous remarks and truthful guidelines addressing the challenges of proper legal knowledge models constructing. For instance Visser and Bench-Capon present the list of minimal – in their opinion - features of an adequate legal ontology which should be: epistemologically adequate (understood as epistemological clarity, intuitive-

ness, relevance, completeness and discriminative power); operational (encoding bias, coherence, computationability); and reusable (by task-and-method and domain) – the vital keyword from the point of view of our later deliberations.

Those given criteria are in fact reflections of earlier deliberations done by Gruber (Gruber, 1995). The authors of the cited work (Visser and Bench-Capon) also elaborate on different types of legal ontologies referencing them to general views on types in ontology engineering in general.

Another relevant text - is the one written by Boer (2003). Though the paper is less focused on knowledge models construction methods it is by contrast mainly on the idea of employment legal ontologies in order to build frameworks on their basis. The result frameworks are then better adjusted to the tasks of making comparisons and harmonization of legislation. The text also raises the problem of differences between legal systems and diversified ways of expressing norms and regulations. In the cited work the reader should turn the attention to a number of interesting factors – like namely - the enlistment of frames of regulations comparison and harmonization. The authors give a formal introduction to representing systems of norms through ontologies.

Moreover, they pay attention to the problem of legal concepts similarity as well which is an important one on the account of the earlier mentioned nuances in possible legal interpretations and argumentations. The similarity of ontological elements is widely explored in the works connected to the field of ontology[2]. Yet, this issue is much more complex to cope with within the legal applications than in other fields and domains as the similarity measures in this case ought to take into consideration the system of norms as a whole rather than fragmentary one which the elements are connected with.

Bourcier et al. in the article of (2005) cast light on specific techniques and methods of building legal ontologies. The authors commence with the statement, that the design of this type of ontologies raises problems of both knowledge management but also jurisprudence. After this opening remark they start to show the effects of work of two groups of 25 researchers in total which aim was to produce two types of legal ontologies. The group used and shared different resources in the course of the engineering. The conclusion of the analysis of the researchers' ontologies was the need of stressing the fact of taking into account the points of view on law. Those points of view may be differentiated, which is essential when doing the conceptual work. As a result a 3-dimensional space is considered for situating this kind of modeling problem. The dimensions should reflect three types of modeling perspectives:

- Legal perspective,
- Action perspective,
- Logical perspective.

The authors of this text suggest also bearing in mind another 3-dimensional space when building legal ontologies. In the other case the axes are connected with the ontology goals perspective. This means that knowledge experts should take into account the factors of:

- Lexicographic opposed to computational modeling,
- Detail biasing by presenting upper-level concepts against descriptive ontology,
- More versus less decision-making approach.

Finally, there is also another one vital distinguishing in the cited paper of Bourcier. It is the differentiation between two types of legal knowledge engineering:

- Operational and,
- Cognitive.

The most common ontology typologies are usually combining different dimensions that might characterize any ontology. The most fundamental from the point of view of the world of discourse's generality (and robustness) is the distinction between top-level, domain and applicational. On the other hand sophistication of the modeling techniques allows ranging ontologies from lightweight (Corcho et al., 2003) or simple taxonomies through typical tree-structured - terminological ontologies to the latter expanded with additional logical rules or constraints. In terms of legal ontologies we may indicate large lexicons corresponding to top-level ones and smaller specialized domain specific with specialized legal vocabulary.

There are a number of positive cases where the ontologies proved to be a useful tool in the modeling of knowledge in the legal domain. Yet most of the cases are connected to the very general tasks and thus the employed ontologies are also top-level ones rather than specialized models. Also a thorough reference of works related to legal ontologies may be found in (Despres, 2004).

Surden (2007), together with his co-authors claims that certain norms coming from given legal systems or branches of regulation tends to be more challenging to represent and apply in computable contexts than others (Kowalski, 1985). They suggest that is possible to identify discrete legal rules which are likely to be, from a legal theoretical standpoint, amenable to simpler computational representation. The text is also important on account of introducing the idea of representational complexity – a measure offering information on the degree to which legal theoretical issues are likely to complicate the task of computationally modeling a given legal rule. They also extend this idea be presenting the factors that influence this measure by applying framework which reflects the stages of rule life-cycle model.

Above all, the work deals with the issue of accurate representation of provisions in the perspective of sophistication and complexity of legal regulations. The authors turn the attention to two excluding options of modeling legal knowledge:

- By creating sophisticated models which are capable of representing rules of arbitrary legal complexity,
- By focusing on a subset of individual legal rules which are more amenable to simplified computational representation from a legal theoretical perspective.

The work on Commercial Companies Code Ontology (Abramowicz et al., 2007) was dedicated to make an OWL DL based inference over the knowledge description of main parts of Polish Commercial Companies Code – the main statute of the commercial law branch. By Using the environment combined of OWL DL editor (Protege) and the Racer Pro reasoning system as the inference engine we have successfully built a statute-specific legal ontology in the domain of commercial law and secondly, we depicted how some basic real-life problems may be solved on the top of it.

Another paper dated the same year (Warnier, 2007) aims to merge three fields, suggesting to use artificial intelligence technologies to provide further support for verification of consistency and completeness within processes in the legal domain. This means the document flow within prosecution and court institutions. The authors propose to build and employ a legal ontology which would describe the type of information and knowledge in the documents and then are stored in the meta-data of those documents. The next phase then will use fuzzy-matching techniques in order to enforce internal consistency.

In the Tax Legal Ontology (Tomaszewski et al., 2008) experiment we further studied the possibilities of manual creation of ontologies from legal sources with the assumption that the resulting knowledge model is focused on resolving given legal problems situations. The presented Tax Legal Ontology was also built with the use of OWL DL but during the work we recognized the promising effects of using the OWL full formalism. Unfortunately the capabilities of the latter

flavor of the language are mostly still beyond use when employing reasoning engines.

The Insurance Case Ontology proposed in (Stolarski et al., 2008) was an experiment to show that ontology mapping formalisms can be used to denote the many interpretations of a given legal concept; secondly, we provide a short case, justifying the potential need of using such formalisms in modern legal knowledge models. This approach may be especially useful for coding knowledge about specific legal cases.

Modeling Legal Cases by Ontologies Re-Using

The ontologies have a number of typically enlisted features. The re-usability is one of them. It is especially important (Cantador, 2007; Doran, 2006). Most of the methods of building ontologies take into account that the resulting product – an ontological schema – might be in the future reused for some other purposes. The rationale for such approach is obvious as the resources, which have to be devoted to the development of even a medium-sized ontology, are not to be passed over (Bontas, 2005).

Of course the very idea of reusing the existing constructs is extremely attractive[3] although in practice it yields a lot of problems in general[4]. The legal domain in this respect overlaps some additional challenges as both the knowledge to be modeled as well as knowledge models itself are to high extent specific.

Regardless of the actors performing the task of ontology reusing[5] there is a number of views on how the reusing processes should be executed and handled. In (Doran, 2006) it is called for two major ways of ontology reusing. These are: with the use of ontology editors which allow the reuse of another ontology by inclusion into another model; by the specific virtues of ontology languages which can offer the possibility to import desired ontology[6].In (Bontas, 2005) you can find that the content of the knowledge sources as well as their domain overlapping are decisive factors in choosing between ontology merging and integration. While the integration should be considered a similar process to importing – esp. in the light of the full reading of Doran's work[7] – the merging is often seen as a more comprehensive approach (de Brujin, 2003).

Ontologies are typically constructed with the use of methods which are based on gathering and analysis of knowledge sources. The knowledge sources are often taking form of domain texts. In the legal domain the source texts are mainly dominated by those written in a very specific form of natural language – the language of law. This type of language is widely characterized and adds its traits to national[8] languages[9]. This is even more interesting as reusable ontological components are commonly deemed to be another kind of knowledge sources; which in case of constructing legal knowledge models imply that other legal ontologies will take part in ontology engineering cycle. That is why, legal knowledge should be considered as a domain requiring high expertise – the knowledge sources, i.e. texts – constitute highly-specialized corpuses which constitute an obstacle in ease of processing and as a result make the ontology engineering process costly.

The Copyright Case

A very interesting inspiration comes from the idea and need of studying the possibilities of using legal ontologies in the domain of copyrights and electronic access rights. This need is inevitable in order to be able to construct components and frameworks that on the one hand ultimately enable search engines to robust retrieve resources (documents, software, information) on the basis of access rights and content use criteria[10]. On the other hand intellectual protection rights (IPR) ontologies are heavily wanted to fuel the digital rights management (DRM) systems.

In this subsection we endeavor to make the sum up of the theoretical speculations in the form of an

example and experiment at the same time. We are going to model a case from the copyright domain by using the earlier created ontologies – both ours and publicly available created by other authors. The experiment and its results are intriguing because of at least three facts: firstly, as stated in (Ding, 2007) few studies on practically reusing ontologies have been conducted and reported[11] and the one of few research that has implicitly addressed the domain-specific ontology reuse problem is the mentioned earlier work by Bontas and colleagues (Bontas, 2005). While there are some statements (Visser, 1996) that esp. in the legal appliances the statute-specific ontologies[12] cannot be a subject for reuse for other domains, and should always be created for each legal sub-domain under consideration (though it should support various tasks in that sub-domain). Secondly, one should be aware that the particularity of legal ontologies covers not only the engineering of connected processes but also the whole maintenance as well as the reusability issues. We have written earlier why ontology creation is more complicated and crucial because of the unique features of material the process is based on. But there is more to it, as not only the legal language has its differences in usage. The law is a system – highly organized and diversified (Huxley-Binns, 2008).

Apart from the two major possibilities of how the system is arranged[13] there is no doubt that each legal system is different moving from one jurisdiction to another. Every state has in the long history formed its particular procedures, institutions, precedents. Much of them are similar in general yet – the legal knowledge is not about generality. Fortunately, the copyright law domain in this context is in the privileged position as it is highly regulated on the beyond-national basis (Paris, 2008; EU, 2004; Berne 1886).

The description of the story standing behind the case is as follow[14]:

A student being at the end of her study at an Art School named Eva is asking for the legal advi-

sory. The authorities of the School requested her to repeat the last year classes as a penalty for breaching the copyrights during the works on her diploma. Eva herself gives an account of the situation as following: at the time when she was preparing the diploma work to defend it in the Department of Graphics, she accidentally has found abandoned, already used copper engraving plates. The plates had been used previously probably by other students for the purposes of their work. However the plates – as worn out and not needed any more – have been moved to the garbage of the University and left alone. But Eva during inspection came to the idea that she might use them for the purposes of her diploma work. Just then she had already a number of works that she could present to defend the academic title, yet she wanted to use the found plates to produce a new work. The concept of Eva was that she would use the plates with the pickled pictures as a kind of background beneath which she wanted to create an original work of her own. In result each instance of the work will be produced in two stages – the found plate and another plate of Eva. After few experiments Eva obtained the expected result – the old plate was hardly visible. The presentation at the Department went very well and Eva was granted the highest note.

After then the selected works have been showed publicly – meaning everyone was invited to come and see the performance of University's students. Eva's composition was exhibited as well. The one person among visitors was Adam. During the observation of the works he discovered in the one of them a familiar motif. After closer scrutinize he had no doubt – his work has been copied within the work of Eva. After paying special attention to the works of Eva he came to the conclusion that there exists another work that might have something in common with his diploma work. He was extremely irritated as he obtained the information that the Eva's diploma was highly scored while Adam himself got the lowest passing grade.

After that he decided to inform the Department's authorities of the whole situation and within the letter he requested explanation together with the punishment for the "plagiarist". The authorities without a further delay decided the punishment as stated at the beginning of the case description[15].

Before we try to model the case we should note a number of facts and suppositions. Firstly, the case is embedded in and based on Polish law. While Polish copyright law incorporates international treaties and thus implements the minimal regulations, it still – as other national level regulations - has its own particularities. Secondly, before the case modeling we need to consider which norms have been violated and what are the consequences. This is vital as obtaining this knowledge enable us to turn attention in the direction of significant elements of the case while omitting the irrelevant ones. The key statements about the copyright law and its connections to the case matter are:

- The copyright law is connected to this bundle of rights that are immanently associated with intangible goods. Therefore it protects works in the form of intangible, abstract entities rather than pieces or instances[16] of such. As a result being entitled to posses or use of a given piece of work is not in any case related to the rights of any kind to the work itself. In other words – being the owner of a tangible good is not equivalent to being the possessor of the copyrights to the conceptual work[17] expressed in the property[18].
- A grant of permission by the copyrights owner is necessary in order to be lawfully permitted to use the work (or any of its instances) for the purposes other than personal.
- Making any alteration or changes to the piece of work by the person who is not an author or has no legitimation in the form of adequate permission for such use is

Figure 1. Adam's work initial legal situation

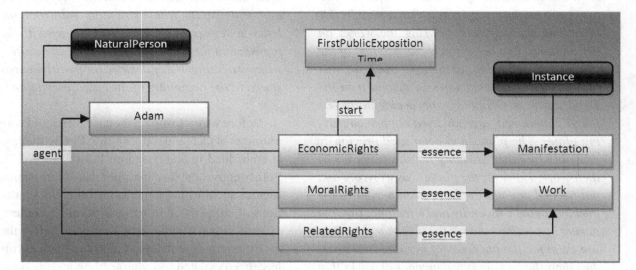

breaching of rights of the author towards the work.

- There are some forms of work that legitimize co-authoring[19]. These are: derived work – if the work is created subsequently, which means that the work of one author is reused by another creator; mutual work – if the final work is formed by more than one author.

Having the above in mind we may sketch the model for the description of this particular set of circumstances. For this purpose we need ontologies for the reuse[20] and have chosen the below enlisted for this purpose.

- Copyright Ontology[21] – is according to its author a contribution towards the realization of the vision of copyright-aware Digital Rights Management (DRM) systems. The model is well developed since four years and – what is even more important in the context of reuse – it is abundantly documented as it is major part of the García's PhD contribution (García, 2007).

- Civil Law Ontology[22] – is the extension built for the purpose of modeling parts of Commercial Law that describe language necessary for expressing some primitive aspects of legal relationships within civilistic scope.

- LKIF-Core[23] – the core ontology for the LKIF language[24].

Let us start with the original work of Adam. The domain of this creation is depicted on the Figure 1[25].

Most of the jurisdictions recognize three types of rights connected to the sphere of copyrights. These are economic, moral and related rights. The copyrights ontology makes no difference here thus we are able to include the instances of those rights into the model. All the rights associated to a given work are erected with the moment of first publication of the work. This very moment is vital and can be modeled as an instance describing a point in time or as a raw coordinate[26]. As there exists a number of models of passing from an abstract idea into work's instances, the completeness of those models with all the possible stages depends on the medium and type of art[27]. The visual arts however

Figure 2. Adam's ownership model

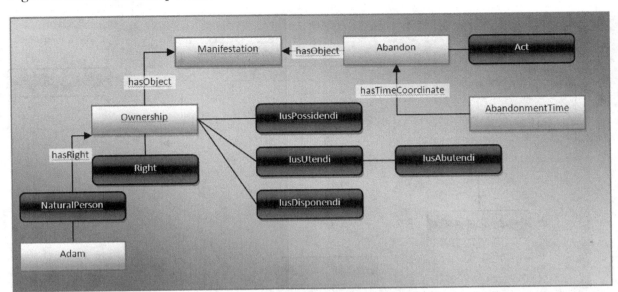

are rather mean taking into account the entities that can be recognized within creation chain. As a result we may equate the Manifestation of the work with its sole Instance.

As presented on the Figure 2, form the ownership model's perspective – Adam is a NaturalPerson and as such may have a bunch of rights. The Ownership is one of them. Each right to own a property is according to some Roman tradition a number of specific rights for the title, which are right to possess, right to utilize and right to dispose. The particular form of IusUtendi is the right to destroy a given thing (IusAbutendi). The act of abandonment of the property (Work) at the AbandomentTime time was legitimized from the point of view of the model and Polish law[28].

On the Figure 3 the situation after taking possession by Eva is given. The Possession concept[29] is an Action when considering it as the space-time event while it can also be interpreted as a State but not the Right. Nevertheless under some strict circumstances the state of possession may by legible coined into Ownership as indicated earlier[30]. This is reflected on the same figure thanks to the use of createsRight property. With the use of an

SWRL axiom[31] the knowledge about the state of possession is induced into knowledge about property rights.

On the other hand, after taking the possession of the Manifestation of Adam's abandoned Work, Eva creates a derived Work' with its Manifestation'. This is because of her Derive Action done on the original Work as a theme. The observer should note that on the Figure nothing has been said about the CopyRights (EconomicRights, MoralRights, RelatedRights). This is because the state of Eva's Possession has nothing in common with the passing or making changes in the state of those rights.

As a result even though – as said in (García, 2007) – that the *"resulting derivations are themselves works protected by copyright (...) derive is thus also a rights generation action"* which is also true within Polish realm of jurisdiction, Eva has no legitimating for taking use of the copyrights to the final creation. This can be better understood once taking into account the Derive-Rule of Copyrights Ontology (Table 1).

This rule encodes the knowledge on how copyrights may be derived from the authors of

Figure 3. Eva's acting

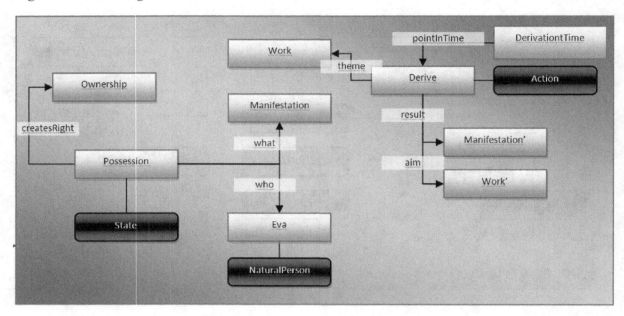

Table 1. Derive-Rule - assign author rights (García, 2007)

(∀v:Derive)
((∃mr:MoralRights)(∃er:EconomicRights)
((∀p:Person)(∀w:Work)(∀w':Work)(∀m:Manifestation)(∀t:Time)
(w≠w') ∧ agent(v,p) ∧ theme(v,w) ∧ result(v,m) ∧ aim(v,w') ∧ pointInTime(v,t) ∧ location(v,l)
→
agent(mr,p) ∧ agent(er,p) ∧ essence(mr,w') ∧ essence(er,m) ∧ start(mr,t) ∧ start(er,t) ∧ location(mr,l) ∧ location(er,l) ∧
isManifestationOf(m,w') ∧ isDerivationOf(w',w)))

base works for derived ones creating a chain of derived rights. As the author of the rule points it out: *"from the legal point of view it is required, prior to any derivation, that the author of the derivation follows this chain in order to get the authorizations from the owner of the copyright of the original work".*

The tables: Table 2 and Table 3 sums up the concepts and relations that have been reused for modeling the case. As it appears from the analysis of the two tables two more Concepts and one relations have had to be added in order to describe the whole case – these are namely: Possession and IusAbutendi concepts together with the createsRight realtion.

Further conclusions that can be drawn from this case include the two below. Firstly, when analyzing the reuse process some measures may be used to assess the efficiency of the process. This can be applied to measure the quality of statute-specific ontologies.

Secondly, it is very favorably if the documentation of ontology subject to reuse purposes have some examples of use cases or modeled typical scenarios. This is especially vital as the legal domain often operates on such level of abstraction that reading of documentation with concepts and relations described only may be insufficient or at least contribute to much greater effort needed in order to employ the targeted ontological components for own purposes. This is true even for

Table 2. List of concepts reused in the copyright case

Ontology Used	Reused Concepts
Copyright Ontology	Instance, Manifestation, Work, EconomicRights, MoralRights, RelatedRights, Derive, Action
Civil Law Ontology	NaturalPerson, Ownership, IusPossidendi, IusUtendi, IusDisponendi
LKIF	Right, Act, State

Table 3. List of relations or attributes reused in the copyright case

Ontology Used	Reused Relations / Attributes
Copyright Ontology	agent, start, essence, theme, result, aim, pointInTime
Civil Law Ontology	hasObject, hasRight, hasTimeCoordinate
LKIF	what, who

experienced knowledge engineers who have dealt earlier with the legal domain models particularity and law as general branch of knowledge[32].

FUTURE TRENDS

One of the employments of the modern designed legal ontologies is being the abstract models enabling the legal documents representation. As the legal documents we mean the acts establishing the law. Among major practical actions and research initiatives aiming at making the comprehensive approach to the issue presented we should include such programs and approaches as: Akoma Ntoso[33], LKIF, MetaLex, xmlLegalEditor as well as MetaVex.

LKIF (The Legal Knowledge Interchange Format) is a framework devoted to representation of legal knowledge sensu largo, which means that the elements of the LKIF are independent of application and does not focus on any particular aim like content representation. The developed formalisms are designed to work in the Semantic Web environments. The framework itself is made up of a number of levels (terminology, rules and norms), among which the central one is the core ontology LKIF-Core. The LKIF-Core ontology

is a binding building block which defines all the most fundamental concepts and unites the other elements of the LKIF thus the ontology is the center of LKIF language. While the core is formalized with the use of OWL language another layer – the rules layer is introduced with the employment of SWRL[34] formalism. Although much more expressive the SWRL language does not exhaust the needs for norms description in law. Therefore the next layer - norm level – is enriched with the developed, partly novel rule formalism, called LKIF-rules. LKIF-rules supports among others rules with exceptions, assumptions, and exclusionary conditions, and enables meta-level information about rules to be represented. The framework is developed within the ESTRELLA project[35].

Akoma Ntoso (Architecture for Knowledge-Oriented Management of African Normative Texts using Open Standards and Ontologies) is an overall framework for the representation of different types of legal documents, including: parliamentary, legislative and individual cases manuscripts. The standards are being prepared under auspice of most of African continent countries that are at the same time the initiators of the project aiming at technological support for the administrations and governments of those countries. The mains goals of the initiative are to define the date schemas, meta data as well as common formats and models for accessing the legal documents with the legal acts foremost. As a consequence of the employment and widespread replication, the new levels of interoperability should be reached together with the positive impact on openness through the propagation of common mechanisms of co-reference to the diversified types of resources connected to legislation processes and initiatives.

Another direction of applications – although related to the above mentioned – is the Bungani 2.0 initiative. Bungeni is the legislative and parliamentary information system platform. It is a twin development with Akoma Ntoso which means that similarly to the latter it is open source. Bungeni is a set of solutions aiming to systematic support of authoring, amendments and dissemination of legislative "products". The system is intended to cover the whole life-cycle of legal documents with the parallel support of tools for citizens that will allow them to give feedback about the product's quality and changes postulates.

MetaLex is a generic scope, extensible and open format for serialization of legal documents and legal acts. The format allows containing some meat information and the description of the structure of documents. The main idea lying behind this development is that the format is to be jurisdiction- and document language-independent.

The last two described Project: MetaVex and xmlLegalEditor are the representers of the recently growing on popularity solutions commonly addressed to as legal editors. The author of the article devoted to the description of the developed MetaVex environment (Hoekstra, 2008) notice at the beginning that the legislation bodies nowadays is forced to using the popular office software for text processing for the purpose of legislation process. He points out also a number of drawbacks resulting from such a state of things. No top of those negative consequences a theory for aim-targeted information processing is introduced and then comes the description of software that impale-

ments partially the developed ideas. The resulted environment is projected in order to facilitate and improve processes within the regulating bodies. There are a number of functionalities described that should be delivered by the final product of such type. The editor itself uses the MetaLex as a document representation layer and has been tested within the finished SEAL project.

On the other hand the xmlLegalEditor is a part of a new EU initiative – project DALOS. From the functional point of view it conveys similar functions and possibilities as the mentioned MetaVex. The general aim of the whole project is to provide the regulators and law creators with the sufficient linguistic and knowledge-management tools in order to employ them in the legislative chain (especially in its initial stages – the law drafting). In the consequence it is expected that the rule makers will be given a better control over the legal language on the national and international levels. The legal editor with ontological support places itself perfectly within the initiative's goals.

There is a certain reason why we enlisted those projects in the "future trends" section. All of them have at least two common features. The first one is that they are very practically oriented on the usage of theoretical achievements of last years in the field of legal knowledge modeling and legal ontologies. Though still prototypical solutions the projects are aiming at incorporation of ontologies into larger frameworks. Thus, making the legal knowledge models the important if not central part of the systems. Secondly, those projects eventually push the more-than-ten-year's efforts from computer science laboratories into real applications, where often the legal ontological components are the heart of the whole systems or frameworks.

CONCLUSION

In our view the matters that were raised in this chapter are crucial for the future development of legal knowledge modeling methods as well as overall use of such knowledge in a number of applications.

In our judgment, after the more than decade of efforts it is now time to push the ontology engineering technologies in the legal domain form laboratories to real test-beds in practical applications. This is already being done – slowly but inevitably. This of course will generate a lot of new challenges and practical problems. While generic legal ontologies are very fine in testing and research environments. The real-life solutions will need knowledge encoding on much higher level of details. This will be a major step forward but it will be occupied with the toil of encoding the knowledge. This "inflation shock" may result in the need of revising some of today's approaches and attitudes towards legal knowledge engineering methods. In exchange for the effort a lot of promises of Semantic Web and semantic technology vision may soon come true to the satisfaction of legal applications users.

REFERENCES

Abramowicz, W., Stolarski, P., & Tomaszewski, T. (2007). Reasoning Using Polish Commercial Companies Code Ontology. In Lodder, A. R., & Mommers, L. (Eds.), *Legal Knowledge and Information Systems, JURIX 2007* (pp. 163–164). Amsterdam: IOS Press.

Berne (1886). Berne Convention for the Protection of Literary and Artistic Works.

Boer, A., Engers, T. v., & Winkels, R. (2003). *Using ontologies for comparing and harmonizing legislation* (pp. 60–69). ACM.

Bontas, E. P., Mochol, M., & Tolksdorf, R. (2005). *Case Studies on Ontology Reuse.*

Bourcier, D. & de, M. D., Legrand, J. (2005). *Methodological perspectives for legal ontologies building: an interdisciplinary experience.* (pp. 240-241). ACM.

Breuker, J., & Boer, A. Hoekstra R & van den Breg K. (2006). Developing content for LKIF: Ontologies and frameworks for legal reasoning. In T.M. van Engers (Ed.), Legal Knowledge and Information Systems. Jurix 2006. IOS Press.

Breuker, J., & Winkels, R. (2004). *Use and reuse of legal ontologies in knowledge engineering and information management.*

Cantador, I., Fernández, M., & Castells, P. (2007). Improving Ontology Recommendation and Reuse in WebCORE by Collaborative Assessments. In *Proceedings of the 1st International Workshop on Social and Collaborative Construction of Structured Knowledge (CKC 2007), at the 16th International World Wide Web Conference (WWW 2007).* Banff, Canada, May 2007. CEUR Workshop Proceedings, vol. 273.

Corcho, O., Fernández-López, M., & Gómez-Pérez, A. (2003). Methodologies, tools and languages for building ontologies. Where is their meeting point? *Data & Knowledge Engineering, 46*(1), 41–64. doi:10.1016/S0169-023X(02)00195-7

de Bruijn, J., Martın-Recuerda, F., Manov, D. & Ehrig, M. (2003). *D4.2.1 State-of-the-art survey on Ontology Merging and Aligning.*

de Hoekstra, S., Winkels, R., Maat, R., & Kollar, E. (2008). MetaVex: Regulation Drafting meets the Semantic Web. In *Computable Models of the Law. Languages, Dialogues, Games, Ontologies* (LNCS 4884). Fitterer, R., Greiner, U. & Stroh, F. (2008). Towards Facilitated Reuse of Ontology Results from European Research Projects – a Case Study. In *Proceedings of the 16th European Conference on Information Systems (ECIS).*

Despres, S., & Szulman, S. (2004). Construction of a Legal Ontology from a European Community Legislative Text. In *Legal Knowledge and Information Systems. Jurix 2004: The Seventeenth Annual Conference* (pp. 79-88).

Ding, Y., Lonsdale, D., Embley, D. W., & Xu, L. (2007). *Generating ontologies via language components and ontology reuse.*

Doran, P. (2006). *Ontology reuse via ontology modularisation.*

EU(2004). Directive 2004/48/EC of the European Parliament and of the Council of 29 April 2004 on the enforcement of intellectual property rights.

Gangemi, A. (2007). Design patterns for legal ontology construction. In *Proceedings of LOAIT '07 II Workshop on Legal Ontologies and Artificial Intelligence Techniques.* Retrieved from http://ftp.informatik.rwth-aachen.de/Publications/CEUR-WS/Vol-321/paper4.pdf.

García, R. (2007). *A Semantic Web Approach to Digital Rights Management.* PhD Thesis. Retrieved from http://rhizomik.net/~roberto/thesis

Gruber, T. R. (1993). A Translation Approach to Portable Ontology Specifications. *Knowledge Acquisition, 5*(2), 199–220. doi:10.1006/knac.1993.1008

Guarino, N. (1998). Formal Ontology and Information Systems. In N. Guarino (Ed.), *Formal Ontology in Information Systems. Proceedings of FOIS'98* (pp. 3-15). Trento, Italy, 6-8 June 1998. Amsterdam: IOS Press.

Huxley-Binns, R., & Martin, J. (2008). Unlocking the English Legal System (2nd ed.).

Karpowicz A. (2001). *Podręcznik Prawa Autorskiego dla Studentów Uczelni Artystycznych.* RTW 2001.

Kowalski, R., & Sergot, M. (1985). Computer Representation of the Law. In. *Proceedings, IJCAI-85,* 1269–1270.

Nagy, M., Vargas-Vera, M., Stolarski, P., & Motta, E. (2008). DSSim results for OAEI 2008. In *Proceedings of the 3rd International Workshop on Ontology Matching (OM-2008), Karlsruhe, Germany, October 26, 2008, CEUR WS vol. 431.*

Paris (2008). *Paris Convention for the Protection of Industrial Property.*

Stolarski, P., Tomaszewski, T., Zeleznikow, J., & Abramowicz, W. (2008). *A Description of Legal Interpretations in Risk Management with the Use of Ontology Alignment Formalisms. ODR Workshop 2008 (Vol. 430).* CEUR-WS.

Surden, H., Genesereth, M., & Logu, B. (2007). *Research abstracts 2: Representational complexity in law* (pp. 193–194). ACM.

Tomaszewski, T. (1998). *Wyszukiwanie Informacji Prawnej w Systemach Hipertekstu.* PhD Thesis. Poznan University of Economics.

Tomaszewski, T., & Stolarski, P. (2008). Legal Framework for eCommerce Tax Analysis. In L. M. Camarinha-Matos & W. Picard (Eds.), *Pervasive Collaborative Networks, IFIP TC 5 WG 5.5 Ninth Working Conference on Virtual Enterprises, Poznan, Poland.* Springer.

Visser, R. S. P., & Bench-Capon, J. M. J. (1999). *Ontologies in the Design of Legal Knowledge Systems.* Retrieved from https://eprints.kfupm.edu.sa/55792/1/55792.pdf

Visser, R.S.P., & Bench-capon, T. (1996). *On the Reusability of Ontologies in Knowledge-System Design.*

Warnier, M., Brazier, F., Apistola, M., & Oskamp, A. (2007). *Towards automatic identification of completeness and consistency in digital dossiers* (pp. 177–181). ACM.

Zeleznikow, J., & Stranieri, A. (1996). Automating legal reasoning in discretionary domains. In Legal Knowledge Based Systems JURIX'96 Foundations of legal knowledge systems (pp. 101-110).

ENDNOTES

[1] We support our views by use of works on ontologies in other domains or of general use

as long as there lacks the relevant research reported strictly on legal ontologies or the authors lack the information about the findings in this specific field of research.

2   See for instance (Nagy, 2008).

3   (Ding, 2007) enumerates some of potential gains of knowledge models reuse, including such advantages as: reduction of human labor involved in formalizing ontologies out of nothing; an improvement in quality of new ontologies on the account that the used components have already been tested; enabling wide-range knowledge updates by updating commonly reused components simultaneously within multiple ontologies; simplification of mapping between product ontologies as they share components through ontology reuse.

4   We will point some of them later.

5   This can be a human being doing the incorporation of earlier found relevant ontologies manually or at the other end – a fully automated process with the continuum of tasks between those two extreme situations referred to as semi-automated.

6   For instance, OWL offers the possibility to import by means of the <owl:imports> statement.

7   The work is on method of automatic ontology partitioning into ontology modules contain some selected aspects of knowledge for the purpose of importing them as reusable components.

8   or ethnic

9   For instance in Polish the legal texts have been characterized as less verbose with having up to 100-300% of words in an average phrase. Additionally, the mean length of sentences in legal texts are 100% greater than comparing to typical day-to-day written text language and a typical legal text have up to 75% less usage of infrequent exploited vocabulary (Tomaszewski, 1998). There are also other particularities of knowledge

sources to be used for ontology engineering in the context of legal domain comparing to any other one – like legal definitions, interpretational modes, attention to precision and so forth … On the other hand most of the legal texts have additional more or less strict document structure as well as graphical layout which both convey some additional information and thus can be used for special purposes.

10   Note that such features of retrieval engines are already in use, though the results are, so far, much below expectations, mainly because of much unsophisticated capabilities and methods employed. See the "usage rights" search facility description of Google - http://www.google.com/support/websearch/ bin/answer.py?answer=29508. Especially indicative is the information at the end of explanation of the capability: "The Usage Rights feature identifies websites whose owners have indicated that they carry a Creative Commons license. By returning these search results, Google isn't making any representation that the linked content is actually or lawfully offered under a Creative Commons license (…)".

11   The authors represent probably the same line of thought by differentiating the intention of ontology engineer to create a new ontology not necessarily with the additional help of other ontologies and re-using in its strict sense.

12   Defined by the authors as „the ontology providing the vocabulary for describing the knowledge of the (legal) sub-domain".

13   Two main ways reflects the distinction between continental and common system of law.

14   The case is a real case based on the description given In (Karpowicz, 2001).

15   In fact the case description ends up reporting that after the lawyer's intervention the punishment has been widely reduced. The

University' authorities acknowledge that they are co-responsible for the occurrence as there were absolutely no copyright matters discussed at any time with the students during the course of study.

16   Later on we will be using the terms „piece of work" and "instance of work" as synonyms.

17   Plans, design, ideas, etc.

18   This is usually obvious in the case of such replicable wares as DVD movies, music CDs or copies of computer software. Yet it may be less intuitive when it comes to pieces of art as many works of art may have in fact only one instance.

19   At the same time they however convey some restrictions in the individual use of copyrights by the authors separately and some additional obligations. Like in the case of Eva – if she wanted to reuse the work of Adam she needed to have his permission on that in order to author the derived work.

20   For techniques and resources possible to be employed for the task of looking for the relevant reusable ontology components, see for instance (Fitterer, 2008).

21   http://rhizomik.net/ontologies/2008/05/copyrightonto.owl

22   http://www.semiramida.info/ontologies/law/polish/civil.owl

23   http://www.estrellaproject.org/lkif-core/lkif-core.owl

24   More thoroughly described later on.

25   On the pictures the arrows represent an explicitly named relations; a line stands for "is a" relation; the black boxes are concepts; while the silver one are instances.

26   As is done in the examples from (García, 2007).

27   For instance, within literature there are some by-products like manuscripts.

28   Polish Civil Code of 23 April 1964 (Dz.U.64.16.93) says in **Article** 180 An owner may renounce the ownership of a movable thing by abandoning the thing with that intent. **Article** 181 The ownership of an ownerless movable shall be acquired by anyone by taking independent possession of it.

29   On the Picture only its instance is shown.

30   see note 24.

31   Not given here. Using the DL inference is too weak in this case.

32   We expect that an inexperienced individual building the model cases for its own purposes has little chances of success with today's techniques and available ontologies with regard to their usually poor documentation.

33   www.akomntoso.org

34   Semantic Web Rule Language (SWRL) is a combination of the OWL DL and OWL Lite sublanguages of the OWL Web Ontology Language with the Unary/Binary Datalog RuleML sublanguages of the Rule Markup Language. SWRL includes a high-level abstract syntax for Horn-like rules and thus it extends the limited possibilities of OWL models for defining rules / norms. More on SWRL here: http://www.daml.org/2003/11/swrl/

35   http://www.estrellaproject.org/

Chapter 5
Certified Originality of Digital Contents by the Time Authentication

Masakazu Ohashi
Chuo University, Japan

Mayumi Hori
Hakuoh University, Japan

ABSTRACT

In our modern clock-ruled culture, it is not too much to say that no society can exist unless based on "time." Computers, which are the key device of an information society, are equipped with high precision clocks to synchronize their entire circuit function. In an electronic environment or digital society built on computers, recordkeeping relates inevitably to the time that is ticked away by the clocks embedded in the computers. Time is thus the infrastructure of this information society. To save the situation, a notion of time for the digital society should be properly defined and popularized, specifying the way and conditions of using it safely. The scope of discussion here focuses on some specific industries and applications for time-stamping technologies. We focused mainly on time-authentication (time-stamp). This study will be further refined step by step as their validity is verified in actual use. Meanwhile, we are planning to work on this study for standard time distribution, which is as important as time-stamp to time business.

1. INTRODUCTION

The future direction, and agendas for e-Local Governments are to re-build the deteriorated fiscal structure in public administration with innovative management minds, and to promote administrative autonomy by decentralizing the society, while many Local governments suffer from their depreciated financial situation. Under

these situations, IT systems should be mutually worked between central and local government. It avoids overlapping investments of the ICT utilization and development by determining the development methods. In this paper, we discuss the potentialities of standardization for promoting the certification of digital contents and originality.in order to swiftly and appropriately satisfy a central and local organizations, further development and utilization of IT and its infrastructure in the local municipalities

DOI: 10.4018/978-1-61520-975-0.ch005

In our modern clock-ruled culture, it is not too much to say that no society can exist unless based on "time". Computers, which are the key device of an information society, are equipped with high precision clocks to synchronize their entire circuit function. In an electronic environment or digital society built on computers, recordkeeping relates inevitably to the time that is ticked away by the clocks embedded in the computers. Time is thus the infrastructure of this information society. However, the importance of securing evidential authority of electronically determined time, and synchronizing clocks of multiple computers working in cooperation are not recognized enough.

To save the situation, a notion of time for the digital society should be properly defined and popularized, specifying the way and conditions of using it safely. Time Business Forum was established to diffuse the time notion for the digital society. We focused mainly on time-stamp use by national and local governments to produce a general study for both users and providers.

2. BACKGROUND: IMPORTANCE OF DIGITAL TRACE OF TIME

In transactions, applications, personal promises or whatever we experience daily, notion of time is of the essence, whether or not we are aware of it. And physicochemically or socially obtained trace of time is recorded on paper. In other words, we are recording analog trace of time in terms of media, methods and forms.

Recent progress of information technology has rapidly promoted document digitization. Unfortunately, digital data or documents, unlike paper documents, are essentially impossible to distinguish a copy from the original. This raises problems such as securing originality and preventing alteration of information. Securing authenticity of trace of time is also one of the biggest problems. To activities in the society, completing digital data in an electronic environment means that digital

trace of time independent of any medium must be realized. This means that trace of time must be a piece of digital data that is digitally documented. Technical methods for this have been proposed and applied to practical tools, with some of them introduced into actual operation. However, the electronic trace of time has not yet obtained a high standing as the traditional one, which is supported by the time-honored custom and rules rooted deeply and widely in the society.

3. DIGITAL INFORMATION PROBLEMS

Importance of digital information in the advanced network society is steadily growing. Information network infrastructure that guarantees security of transaction is vital to the growing opportunity of e-commerce. Secrecy of channel, authentication of document correspondent, and authenticity of exchanged documents are indispensable to security of transaction. Especially, securing digital documents' authenticity is a serious agenda, as they are distributed easily and rapidly, and copied without difficulty.

3.1 Possible Threats

The following threats are possible in digital information distribution:

1. **Spoofing:** This means an act done by some ill-intentioned person in the disguise of the right person. On e-commerce network, one may incur damage from some unknown transaction unless personal identification is strictly conducted. This can be avoided by digital signature that secures personal authenticity.

2. **Alteration:** Some ill-intentioned person may alter important information in a digital document. If the alteration is easy to make but hard to detect, one may incur damage

from false information in, for instance, an electronic application form. Alteration can be detected through securing document authenticity with digital signature.

3. **Repudiation:** This means that someone denies or contradicts the fact of having done something. This can be a denial of the fact of having received or submitted an electronic application form, or a contradiction of the fact of having signed a contract. It is likely that these will happen frequently in network activities unless evidence of certain facts is recorded. Repudiation can be avoided by digital signature that secures personal authenticity.

3.2 Digital Signature Technology

(1) Authenticity of Digital Document

In traditional paper society, a document is regarded to be "an authentically produced document" or "an authentic document" when it has been produced truly by the one presenting him/herself as the author. In addition, a document with the professed author's seal allows a presumption of the contents' authenticity. Enforced in 2001, the Digital Signature Law (the Law concerning Digital Signature and Certification Services) gave digital documents (electromagnetic records) the effect of presumptive authenticity of private documents, which is provided in 228-4 of the Civil Proceedings Act. Since then, digital document authenticity can be legally recognized if signed with a key secured under a Public Key Certificate, which is issued from a well-trusted Certification Authority based on the Public Key technology (or PKI: Public Key Infrastructure). The Digital Signature Law also defines the service requirements for trusted Certification Authorities.

(2) Digital Signature Technology

Digital signature is a technology to secure authenticity of digital document author and contents.

PKI enables identification of a digital document's signer, producer, and risk of having been altered, by using Public Key Certificate information issued by a trusted Certification Authority.

In traditional paper society, authenticity of a sealed document is verified by identifying the imprint of a registered seal, which can be generated only by its genuine owner. An interested party in a transaction examines the identity of the other's seal imprint on the document with that on a registered seal certificate issued from a municipal office. In PKI-based digital signature system, in contrast, a trusted Certification Authority issues a public key certificate to the key pair (public key and private key) after implementing a strict personal verification of its owner. An interested party in a transaction uses the private key of its exclusive possession when generating its digital signature, and can view digital document contents only by using the public key that matches the private key.

In the digital signature system to secure digital document authenticity, a digital document producer degenerates the document to a message digest by hash function, and encodes it with the private key unique to him/her. The recipient of a digitally signed document acquires both the document producer's public key certificate and Certification Authority's public key certificate in order to verify that the certificate has been validly issued by a trusted CA. Then, using the producer's public key, the recipient verifies authenticity of the received electrically signed document. Damage from transmission to or alteration of the one-directional message digest can be detected during the digital signature verification.

(3) Limitations of Digital Signature

Digital signature has been adopted by national and local e-government infrastructure as a technology to verify authenticity of documents, which is essential for Internet uses such as electronic application. However, documents with digital signature based on PKI have the following limitations.

- With an absence of time-related information in itself, digital signature does not provide evidence that a document existed at the time when it is supposed to have. (Accuracy of the time axis of Figure 2-2 cannot be verified.)
- A PKI-based CA's guarantee for a digitally signed document does not last beyond the public key certificate's period of validity, which represents the period that the relevant private key is valid. In the case that the certificate's validity is lost before the period is over, the guarantee expires when the revocation notice has been accepted and settled by the CA. (Figure 1)
- PKI-based digital signature system to secure document authenticity can eliminate alteration by third parties, but it cannot prevent mala fide alteration by the document producer in person.

To solve these problems, existence of a digital document at a specific point of time must be proved by time-stamp. This is the time-stamping technology, which realizes existential evidence of digital information.

3.3 Time-Stamp

As already mentioned, digital signature is a means to enable personal verification and content authenticity of digital documents, which are involved in transactions and procedures to be secured. For security of transactions and procedures taking place on the digital network, evidence of the existence of relevant facts and proof of document delivery are also necessary. Therefore, along with digital signature, time-stamp is essential to authenticate (guarantee) that a digital document existed at a certain time(Ohashi,M.,2003a).

It is expected that time-stamp will be effective in the following functions and services:

- Evidence of the existence: To guarantee that a digital document existed at a certain point of time.
- Proof of delivery: To prove that a transmitted document has reached the recipient, as well as that the recipient have received the document. Also known as "delivery evidence" which is equivalent to delivery certificate used in existing postal service. This contributes to avoiding repudiation threat.
- Long storage of electrically signed documents: To secure authenticity of a digital document over time by providing existential evidence. The proper time of document verification information is authenticated in order to cope with digital documents exceeding the PKC validity period or key algorithm compromised.

4. ROLE OF TIME-STAMP

While contributing to securing digital document authenticity, digital signature technology has the following problems as mentioned in Chapter 3. To solve these problems, there needs to be a service to prove existence of digital information at a certain point of time.

Time of Digital Signature Generation is Left Unproved

Digital signature verifies the person who produced a document and that the contents are just as they were at the time the document was signed. However, it does not verify when the document was produced.

Authenticity of a digitally signed document is not secured after expiration or revocation of PKC.

To secure authenticity of a digitally signed document after validity period or revocation of PKC, the following are necessary: proof that PKC,

Figure 1. Period that Authenticity of Document is Guaranteed (Time Business Forum (Ed.)2003)

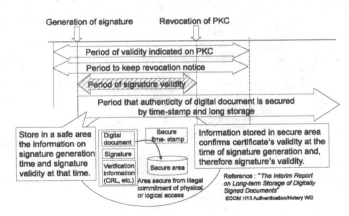

revocation information, etc. did exist at a certain point of time; and evidence that the digitally signed document really exists.

The person who digitally signed a digital document can alter it by him/herself.

If there is a third party who guarantees that a digitally signed document existed at a certain point of time, an attempt of alteration made later by the document author him/herself will never succeed.

In addition, time-stamp is indispensable for establishing evidence of the existence of digital facts, proof of digital document delivery, etc. This chapter will discuss models, technological trends, standardization and structure of time-stamping service.

4.1 Time-Stamping Service Model

(1) Functions Required of Time-Stamping Service

Time-stamping service provides a proof that a certain piece of digital information existed at a specific point of time. The service must satisfy the following two essential requirements(Ohashi,M. (Ed.)2004).

- Existential evidence of a certain piece of digital information at a specific point of time must be supported by a technically traceable connection between time information and digital information.
- The service will have no concern with digital information contents.

The first requirement includes the use of cryptographic technology, which essentially needs security management requirements.

(2) Time-Stamping Service Component

A Time-stamp Authority (TSA) provides the service as in the model case that Figure 2 illustrates.

- **NTA:** National Time Authority to generate, maintain and distribute national standard time. It distributes national standard time to TA or TSA. Some NTAs periodically audit the time managed at TAs.
- **TA:** Time Authority to distribute standard time to TSA. TAs periodically audit the time managed at TSAs. TA is a trusted third party.
- **TSA:** Time-Stamping Authority to produce and issue time-stamp token (TST) for digital data submitted from users. A TSA

Figure 2. Time-stamping Service Model [13]

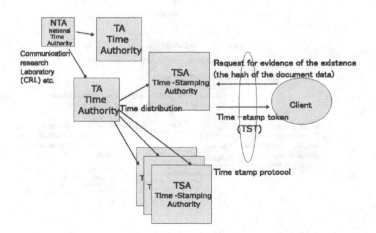

may also act as a TST verification player, which will be described later, depending on time-stamping system adopted. TSA is a trusted third party.

4.2 Technological Trends

Time-stamping technology is controlled by the following standards:

1. International Standards: ISO/IEC 18014-1 Information technology – Security techniques – Time-stamping services
    ○ **Part 1:** Framework: Provides frameworks for requirements, scope, and components/functions of time-stamping services. It also outlines Independent Token and Linked Token, the two different token systems to support authenticity of time-stamp.
    ○ **Part 2:** Mechanisms producing independent tokens: Defines three different mechanisms of independent token system: digital signature-based token (RFC3161 compatible), Message Authentication Code (MAC) -based token, and archive-based token.

    ○ **Part 3:** Mechanisms producing linked tokens: Defines two mechanisms of linked token system: digital signature-based token and digital signature-free token.
2. Internet Standards (IETF: Internet Engineering Task Force)
    ○ RFC3161 Internet X.509 Public Key Infrastructure Time-Stamp Protocol (TSP): One of the standards groups for PKI use on the Internet, defining protocols and time-stamp tokens which represent procedures and formats of time-stamping models.
    ○ IETF Policy Requirements for Time-Stamping Authorities (draft – ietf – pkix – pr – tsa-00.txt) (2002-03): Provides requirements on TSA operational policies.
3. European Standards
    ○ ETSI TS 101 861v1.2.2 Time-stamping Profile: Specifications based on RFC3161. Defines requirements that time-stamp clients and servers should fulfill.

Figure 3. Time-stamp by Independent Token System (digital signature-based) (Time Business Forum (Ed.) 2003)

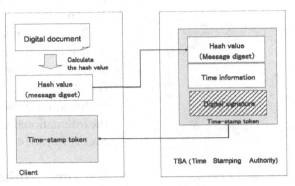

4.3 Time-Stamping Systems

ISO18014 defines two time-stamping systems with different time-stamp token types, which are called independent token and linked token. Typical examples of the two systems are as follows.

(1) Independent Token System

Independent token system (a.k.a. Simple Protocol) is represented by PKI-based time-stamp, which provides clients with a third-party guaranty by giving TSA's digital signature to the time information. A client sends TSA a time-stamp request in a prescribed format along with a hash value (a message digest) of the document to be time-stamped. TSA produces a time-stamp token (TST) with the received message digest, a digital certificate of the time of acceptance and TSA's digital signature included in a prescribed format (TST type), and sends it back to the client. The client receives and stores the TST, so that the original document's existence at the time of the TST issuance can be verified by using TSA's public key certificate (PKC), when necessary in the future.

This system is characterized by simplicity of TST validation, which requires only the PKC for the public key cryptography used to produce TST and its certificate. For effective performance of the system, the TSA here needs to be a Trusted Third Party (TTP) (Ohashi,M.2003b).

Independent token system also includes MAC-based time-stamp and archive-based time-stamp.

(2) Linked Token System

Linking Protocol is a system depending on security of hashing algorithm. Having received a digital document's hash value from a client, TSA sends back a linked token to use as evidence. Also, it periodically reports in the papers a total of hash values to provide a chronological linkage of the tokens.

Figure 4 shows a system, where TSA issues a client with a time certificate in linkage with the message digest and hash function of another time-stamp request, which has been accepted just or shortly before. In this system, a newly issued time-stamp token is consequently linked to all those issued in the past. Therefore, no forgery of time-stamp token is possible unless coordinated with all the previous ones. In addition, with periodical publication of the linking information in papers, forgery becomes even more difficult while the linkage has to be verified only during the regular publication period. This system always needs TSA for verification of a time-stamp token.

Figure 4. Linked token system (Time Business Forum (Ed.) 2003)

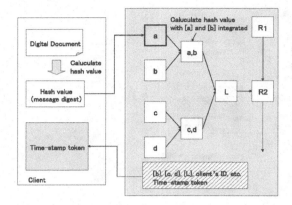

4.4 Non-Repudiation System

Time-stamp, which provides evidence of the existence of digital documents, is effective in preventing repudiations. ISO/IEC 10181-4 and 13888 standardize the framework and technology of non-repudiation services. Figure5 shows a typical non-repudiation service, illustrating the players and systems concerned to data transmission, non-repudiation service provided, and the technologies used in the service provision. The facts of the data submission, receipt and transfer are stored respectively in the form of token. Time-stamping and digital signature technologies applied to verify that the data have been properly received.

5. MECHANISM OF TIME AUTHENTICATION INFRASTRUCTURE

Time authentication infrastructure can be technically defined as a system infrastructure for providing standard time distribution, time-stamping, and other related services. The standard time distribution service is conducted by Time Authorities (TAs) in place of National Time Authority (NTA), while the time-stamping service provides evidence

that a data item existed before a certain point in time, based on the time source distributed from NTA or TAs.

This chapter describes the mechanism of time authentication infrastructure, which supports time-stamping services. Time-stamping service systems (i.e. time-stamp token issuance and validation systems) described here are based primarily on the international standards such as RFC 3161 and ISO/IEC 18014.

5.1 Time Authentication Service Model

The following paragraphs outline a time authentication service model applied to e-application system of a local e-government. Players in this model are defined as follows, except for NTA, TA and TSA, which have been already defined in 3.1 (2).

- **CA:** Certification Authority, which issues NTA, TA and TSA with appropriate certificates or PKCs for digital signatures. Some time-stamping systems do not involve this player.
- **TST verification player:** Verifies the validity of time-stamp tokens. The entity of this role can be different depending on time-stamping system. TSTs based on simple protocol system can be verified on PKI by clients themselves. In the case of the TSTs based on linking protocol system, TSA, who issues the tokens, or some other third party becomes the player.
- **Applicant (resident):** Local residents making applications or the residents' software and tools. They follow application formalities in communication with the application acceptance system of the local government. They can make a request to TSA for time-stamps to prove their applications' existence. In the case of some trouble, they verify the validity of TSTs is-

Figure 5. Non-repudiation services model (Time Business Forum (Ed.) 2003)

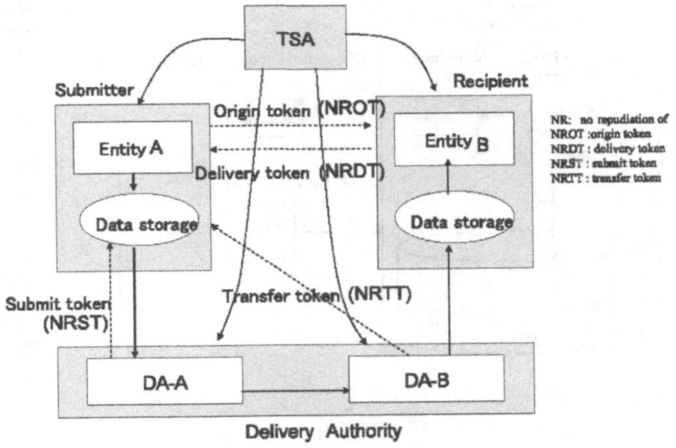

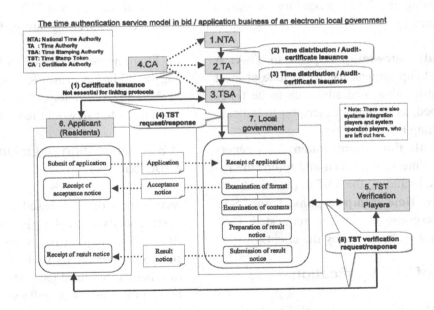

Figure 6. Time authentication service model for e-application transaction (Time Business Forum (Ed.) 2003)

sued from the local government, by using the TST verification player.

- **Local government:** Local government providing application services for residents, or the application system itself. Based on time-stamping services provided by TSA, the local government gives time-stamps to application forms from applicants, acceptance notice, result notice and other documents produced during the application transaction. In the case of trouble, it verifies the validity of TSTs it has issued, by using the TST verification player.

Figure 7. Flow of Time-Stamp Token Issuance (Time Business Forum (Ed.) 2003)

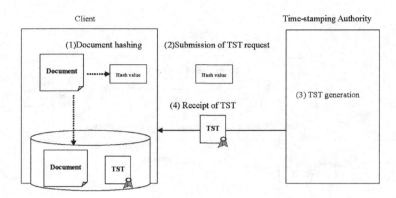

5.2 Flow of Time-Stamp Token Issuance

A client acquires time-stamps for their digital data, following the basic procedure as shown below (Figure 7).

- **Submit time-stamp request to TSA:** A time-stamp request has to include at least the hash value of digital data to be time-stamped, as well as a descriptor to indicate a hashing algorithm.
- **Generate time-stamp token:** TSA generates a time-stamp token and return the response including the TST to the client.
- **Receive time-stamp response from TSA:** The response carries the requested TST, which shall be stored by the client.

4.3 Flow of TST Verification

Procedure of verification of the validity of a time-stamp token differs by time-stamping system.

4.3.1 Verification of Simple Protocol TST

TSTs based on simple protocol system can be verified on PKI by clients themselves. The basic procedure is as follows (See (1) in Figure 8).

- Examine if the TST is syntactically well-formed.
- Examine if the hash value of digital data to be verified is identical to the equivalent hash value in the TST.
- Verify TSA's signatures found in the TST.

Examine the validity of TSA's PKC. Then, using the public key in the PKC, verify the signatures in the TST. Alternately, clients may ask a trusted third party to carry out the verification for them.

5.3.2 Verification of Linking Protocol TST

Verification of TST based on linking protocol system needs to involve players who possess the linking information necessary for the verification. Specifically, TSA who has issued the TST or other trusted third party should take part. The basic procedure is as follows (See (1), (2) and (3) in Figure 8).

- Examine if the TST is syntactically well-formed.
- Examine if the hash value of digital data to be verified is identical to the equivalent hash value in the TST.
- Submit the request for verification of the TST' validity to TSA who has issued the

Figure 8. Flow of TST verification (Time Business Forum (Ed.) 2003)

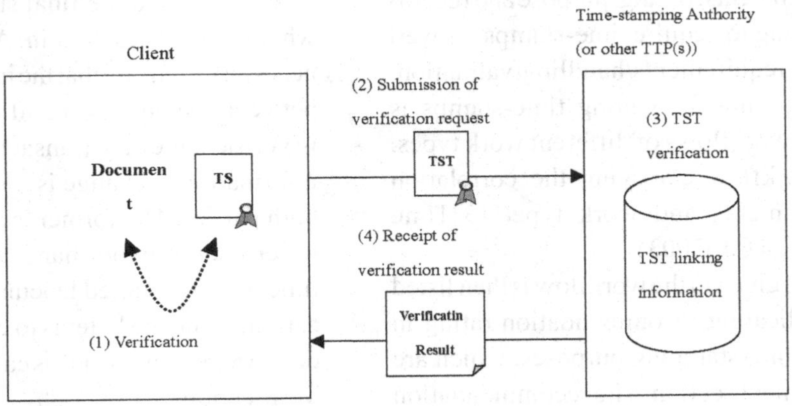

TST or other trusted third party that has access to the issuing TSA's linking information (i.e. TSA's summary links).

- Receive the validation result from the TST or other entrusted third party.

5.4 Traceability of Time Authentication

Traceability of time authentication means the traceability of time information included in time-stamp tokens. The followings are the requirements for the traceability of time:

- It is provable that the time source of time-stamp token issued by a TSA has a logical connection with that of a TA or, if possible, NTA.

- It is provable that the difference between the time used by a TSA for time-stamp token issuance and the national standard time is within a prescribed permissible range.

Traceability of time authentication can be realized by the following methods:

- Include traceability information within time-stamp tokens.

TSAs produce evidence of undergoing periodical time audit by a TA or NTA.

6. BUSINESS MODEL OF TIME-STAMP

6.1 Framework

We will introduce time-stamp user Business Model for e-bidding, which is one of the primary targets of the e-Japan Project efforts being made by local governments. The guideline will specify the cases where time-stamps should be used within business applications, as well as the proper way to use them. To begin with, time-stamp information common to different work types is provided in this section (Ohashi,M.2004).

(1) Structure of the E-Bidding

Occasions demanding time-stamps and action taken on such occasions are almost the same in any work type, even if the causes and processes differ. Although detailed elements of time-stamps and time-stamping are specific to each work type, they can be integrated into a common concept of framework. Based on the common framework described below, we define the elements for each work type: documents, timing, purpose and recommendation rating to acquire time-stamps, as well as time-stamp requirements/handling/validation.

First, the timing for getting time-stamps is pointed out in workflows of different work types, with each workflow clarifying the correlation between documents and work type([13]Time Business Forum(Ed.)2003)

Documents given in the workflow is then listed with signs indicating recommendation rating in relation with time-stamping purposes, which are detailed in the next section. The recommendation rating is on three levels: "strongly recommended", "recommended" and "preferable" Requirements for time-stamps are numerically specified about performance and validity period according to purpose. A time-stamp will not work effectively by merely acquiring it. It must be properly verified in relation with the lifecycle of a document it has been given to. In this guideline, verification necessary for the time of acquiring a time-stamp on a document, receiving the time-stamped document, storing the time-stamped document is detailed.

For the purpose of document delivery/receipt certification, delivery and receipt shall be time-stamped on every individual act, partly overlapping with system logging, or a log file of such acts shall be time-stamped for non-alteration and non-repudiation, while improving the log file clock accuracy over the standard.

(2) Purpose of Time-Stamp in E-Bidding

To e-bidding explained here, time-stamps are important not only to verify the past status of a certain piece of information, but also to certify its existence in order to avoid the risk of alteration, spoofing or repudiation potential in the course of transaction. To avoid troubles from the above-mentioned risk, status of information must be confirmed at each transaction step after its submission to the local government, specifically: (1) what it was like initially, (2) how it changed

in the course of transaction, (3) what it was like when it reached the final step of transaction, (4) what notice it resulted in. At the same time, it is necessary to ensure that the information exchanged between the applicant and the local government is verified at every transaction step, and that the information exchange is mutually recognized by both parties. The former is a time-stamp purpose to verify information handled at different points of time, which is called Document Existence Verification, while the latter is to confirm the document delivery/receipt, which is called Delivery/Receipt Verification.

Separate from the above, by giving time-stamp to digitally signed documents, the limited validity period of PKI-based digital signature is extended, securing document validity for a longer period of time. This is another time-stamp purpose called Long-term Storage Verification, which enables long retroactive verification that the document has been non-altered, and that digital signature and digital certificate were valid at the time of issuance.

7. CONCLUSION

To become widely approved in society, the time notion for an electronic environment needs to win public awareness, trust and daily opportunity as well as technical support. Given that the modern world is based on "time", an electronic/digital world can be based on an integral structure that authorizes "digital trace of time". We call the whole such structure as "time authentication infrastructure", establishment of which is the objective of this chapter. Through describing the feature, importance and effects of time-stamp as a trace of time given to digital documents/data stored for future use. Consequently, time-stamp users will know business application standards for appropriate time, documents/data, trace of time and certified originality of digital contents, while providers will be suggested service quality standards such as type and reliability of time-stamp they offer.

REFERENCES

Hori, M., & Ohashi, M. (2005). Adaptive Collaborative Work and XML Web Services. In Guah, M. W., & Currie, W. L. (Eds.), *Internet Strategy: The Road to Web Services* (pp. 86–100). Hershey, PA: IRM Press.

Hori, M., & Ohashi, M. (2007). Knowledge Creation and Adaptive Collaboration Based on XML Web Services. In Putnik, G. D., & Cunha, M. M. (Eds.), *Knowledge and Technology Management Virtual Organizations: Issues, Trends, Opportunities, and Solutions* (pp. 292–305). Hershey, PA: IDEA Group Publishing.

Ohashi, M. (2003a). *Time Business*. Tokyo, Japan: NTT Publication.

Ohashi, M. (Ed.). (2003a). *Knowledge-Based Collaborative Work*. The Report of Supplementary Budget Project of the Ministry of Post and Telecommunications.

Ohashi, M. (2003b). *Public iDC and c-Society*. Tokyo, Japan: Kogaku Tosho.

Ohashi, M. (Ed.). (2003b). *The Report of Society for the Advance Study on e-Society*. The Society of the Basis for e-Community.

Ohashi, M. (2004). The Time Authentication of Digital Contents. *Journal of Policy and Culture*, *11*, 69–85.

Ohashi, M. (Ed.). (2004). The Report of the Advanced Studies for the Social Capital of e-Society. The Society of theBasis for the e-Community, Japan.

Ohashi, M. (Ed.). (2005). *XML Web Services for Next Generation & A view of Citizen Centric*. Japan: Kinokuniya Co.Ltd.

Ohashi, M., & Hori, M. (2005). The Theory of Economics for Network Society (pp. 2-5; 106-118). Japan: Kinokuniya Co., Ltd.

Ohashi, M., & Nagai, M. (2001). *Internet Data Center Revolution*. Tokyo, Japan: Impress.

Ohashi, M., Sasaki, K., & Hori, M. (2004). On the Study of Knowledge Structualization and Adaptive process Based on Project Based Learning. *Journal of Policy Studies*, *11*, 55–78.

Time Business Forum (Ed.). (2003). *Time Ausentication Infrastructure Guidelines*. Japan: Time Business Forum.

KEY TERM AND DEFINITIONS

Time Authentication: Time Authentication is a technology, services and business model of time-stamp.

Time-Stamp: Time-stamp is the effective technology in the following functions and services:

Evidence of the existence: To guarantee that a digital document existed at a certain point of time.

Proof of delivery: To prove that a transmitted document has reached the recipient, as well as that the recipient have received the document. Also known as "delivery evidence" which is equivalent to delivery certificate used in existing postal service. This contributes to avoiding repudiation threat.

Long storage of electrically signed documents: To secure authenticity of a digital document over time by providing existential evidence. The proper time of document verification information is authenticated in order to cope with digital documents exceeding the PKC validity period or key algorithm compromised.

Certified Originality: Digital data or documents, unlike paper documents, are essentially impossible to distinguish a copy from the original. This raises problems such as securing originality and preventing alteration of information. Timestamp is certified originality of the content.

E-Government: E-Government (electronic government) is the use of ICT(information communication technology) to provide and improve government services, transactions and interactions with citizens, businesses, and other arms of government.

Digital Signature: Digital signature is a technology to secure authenticity of digital document author and contents. PKI enables identification of a digital document's signer, producer, and risk of having been altered, by using Public Key Certificate information issued by a trusted Certification Authority.

Chapter 6
Antitrust Applied to ICT:
Granting Access, Promoting Consumers' Welfare and Enhancing Undertakings' R&D Investments

Fernando Díez Estella
Universidad Antonio de Nebrija, Spain

ABSTRACT

This chapter analyses how Antitrust is applied to ICT, in order to grant access to so-called "essential facilities," promote consumers' welfare and enhance undertakings' R&D investments. Our contentions are underscored by the recent Microsoft ruling. First, we summarize the basic principles underlying Article 82 EC Treaty, and the way in which European antitrust authorities are trying to "reshape" it in order to achieve a more economic understanding of abusive practices, specifically refusals to deal. We then focus on the protection of IPRs, essential to the pivotal role ICT plays in our modern and developed world, and –closely linked to it- the consequences of this landmark case in incentives for innovation and investment. In addition to these, there is the always-present concern for consumers' welfare, which of lately has become the cornerstone for antitrust decisions; which is also addressed here.

INTRODUCTION

Article 82 of the EC Treaty prohibits any abuse of a dominant position in the Common Market, and is frequently compared with the declaration in Section 2 of the American Sherman Act, that it is unlawful "to monopolize" (15 U.S.C. § 2). Both provisions deal with the behavior of single firms. "Monopoly" seems comparable to "domi-

nant position". Both the wording and the goals of these provisions seem quite close.

However, the differences arise sooner than expected. The well known examples listed of "abuse" (to which we will refer in detail in a following section) reflect a variety of public policies that have led European antitrust authorities in several directions simultaneously, while it seems that in the United States efficiency is the only power driving enforcement of "monopolization" cases. Also, the ways in which both antitrust agencies as courts apply this provision suggest a higher

DOI: 10.4018/978-1-61520-975-0.ch006

regulatory policy of control of the adverse effects of market power in the EU than in the US. Finally, a more formalistic approach is perceived in the European enforcement, and the way both the Commission and the Courts have interpreted the different provisions of Article 82 than the typical effects-based approach that characterizes American view of Section 2.

It is not the aim of this chapter to do a lengthy and full comparison between the two systems, but the reference to the other side of the Atlantic will be underpinning our study of Article 82 EC Treaty, concerning the so-called "duty-to-deal" as regards disclosure of essential specification for certain protocols that Windows workgroup servers use, since it provides a quite adequate analytical framework.

The lack of guidance in this field both for undertakings and enforcers led the European Commission to issue in 2005 the well known *Discussion Paper* on exclusionary abuses; although also announced, a further notice on the so-called exploitative abuses is still waited. We are, therefore, in a critical juncture in the reform of EU policy on abuse of dominance; against this backdrop, the recent *Microsoft* landmark ruling may –or may not- shed some light and clarify both the law and the policy to a great extent.

A fact which speaks for itself as to what extent we lack that clarity, is the recent issuing by the Commission of a second document, the *Guidance on the Commission's Enforcement Priorities in Applying Article 82 EC Treaty to Abusive Exclusionary Conduct by Dominant Undertakings* (Brussels, 3 December, COM 2008). Its precise scope and weight is yet to be seen.

The proposed "change" in the understanding competition policy regarding Article 82 can be summarized in the shift from a form-based approach to an effects-based approach. Such an approach would focus on the presence of anti-competitive effects that harm consumers, rather than searching for behaviors that are listed in a certain category of prohibited conducts. It is based

on an examination of each specific case (based on sound economics and grounded on facts) and, consequently, advocates for a *rule of reason* enforcement rather than establishing a series of *per se* prohibitions. Finally, it avoids Type I and II errors (as long as it ensures that anti-competitive behaviour does not outwit legal provisions, as well as guarantees that the statutory provisions do not unduly thwart pro-competitive strategies).

In addition to it –and this is an issue we want to underscore here, since it's going to be one of the main topics dealt with in this chapter- this new economic approach should led competition authorities to avoid the "regulatory temptation", and therefore refrain from intervening against monopolistic pricing in itself (absent demonstrable adverse welfare effects). Only when the dominant firm is owner of assets considered indispensable for other competitors to operate business –such as the so-called *essential facilities*, whenever properly identified as such- antitrust intervention may be required. However, the ongoing supervision –when behavioral remedies are imposed- is a task for which regulatory agencies are better equipped.

The Court of First Instance's ruling in the *Microsoft* saga represents on of the latest "big" Article 82 cases decided by European antitrust authorities; it involves one of the most controversial anticompetitive practices in the abusive catalogue, refusal to deal; it has happened to occur in one of the paradigmatically characterized markets of "our time" (in terms of network effects, involvement of Intellectual Property Rights, high sector-specific regulation, etc.): software industry. This is why we will deal with this case specifically to illustrate the contentions we present in this chapter.

The general organization of this chapter goes as follows. After this introduction, the next section summarizes the basic principles underlying Article 82 EC Treaty, and the way in which European antitrust authorities are trying to "reshape" it in order to achieve a more economic understanding of abusive practices. We'll focus –in the next section-on the one that is going to be later underscored by the *Microsoft* case: refusals to deal. Next section addresses the issues of the *Microsoft* case worth considering for our purpose: the protection of IPRs, essential to the pivotal role ICT plays in our modern and developed world, and –closely linked to it- the consequences of this landmark ruling in incentives for innovation and investment. Of course, in order to offer some guidance to those who are not familiar with the main features of the *Microsoft* ruling, an overview is presented at the beginning of this section. Some lessons which can be drawn from this landmark ruling are also offered. In addition to these, there is the always-present concern for consumers' welfare, which of lately has become the cornerstone for antitrust decisions; which is also addressed here. The next section suggests some future trends for the protection of IPRs and the status of R&D's incentives after the doctrine settled in the *Microsoft* case. The final section offers some concluding remarks.

BACKGROUND: ARTICLE 82 AND ABUSIVE PRACTICES UNDER EC LAW

A) General Framework of the Provision

We've noted earlier the similarities between European and American regulation of abusive practices. Major differences between Article 82 and Section 2 are also apparent from their language alone. Article 82 contains no provision comparable to the attempt language in Section 2, and thus one may think that the European provision appear to be less far-reaching. Accordingly, under Article 82 a firm must be dominant in order to be declared it has incurred in some sort of liability. Under Section 2, it is enough in some cases that a firm is trying to be dominant. To some, under the attempt provision a firm may be held in violation of the Sherman Act even when its effort has failed.

But surely what is more unique about Article 82 is its recitation of four specific examples of "abuse", examples which –as we've thoroughly studied somewhere else (DÍEZ, 2003) - reflect a variety of goals and public policies and have led the European Commission and the Court of Justice in several directions simultaneously. Section 2, however, reflects an almost single-minded focus on price and output effects.

Following that "list", it is commonplace today to place abusive conduct into one of two categories: *exploitative abuses* –expressed mainly by the prohibition in paragraph 82 (a) - and *exclusionary abuses* –expressed mainly by the prohibition in paragraph 82 (b)-. The second group of abuses have, as their anticompetitive outcome, harm inflicted upon competitors, especially market foreclosure. The first group is about anticompetitive effects upon consumers, especially in the form of higher prices.

That is how the *DG Competition discussion paper on the application of Article 82 of the Treaty to exclusionary abuses* (hereinafter, *Discussion paper*) classifies the examples of abusive practices, dealing only with the second group, and within it only with the most common ones (n. 52): predatory pricing, single branding and rebates, tying and bundling, and refusal to supply. It is also a more "economic" than "formal-legalistic" classification, and as such is celebrated by the economists (GUAL et. al., 2005) who have assessed the Commission in the preparatory works for issuing the Discussion paper.

Virtually, all the proposed classifications follow this pattern (GYSELEN, 1990). Much of what the Commission and the Court of Justice have done does fit one or both of these categories. It should be also said that, as some commentators have pointed out (TEMPLE LANG, 2005), while the first category seems easy and clear in its formulation and application, the second one, the exclusionary abuses, present more difficulties when distinguishing a legitimate –albeit, aggressive- unilateral conduct from an anticompetitive one.

Paragraph (d) of Article 82, the final example in the abusive practices catalogue is closer to those familiar about the provision in Section 2. Its primary focus is on tying arrangements, which are seldom attacked under Section 2 but are an example of a broader leverage principle which has long been a part of established Section 2 doctrine. Interestingly, the other big "part" of the Microsoft ruling deals precisely with tie-ins, since it has been accused –and condemned- of illegally bundling its multimedia player (the *Windows Media Player*) with the ubiquitous *Windows* Operating System. According to both the Commission and the Court, this sort of tying arrangement would "leverage" Microsoft's dominance in one market (operating systems) to the adjacent one (media players).

One may conclude that the examples of abuses under Article 82 virtually assure that its interpretation must vary from that of Section 2. The Commission and Court have been required to accommodate the policies they reflect within a broader concept of abuse that lacks the single-minded focus on conduct directed toward competitors –to which we have referred earlier- which has characterized the enforcement of Section 2. Indeed, the Court of Justice has struggled to distinguish legitimate competitive conduct from "abuse" just as American courts have sought to identify conduct which is "predatory" or "exclusionary". But Article 82 reaches well beyond predation and the bounds of Section 2.

This is hardly coincidence. As pointed out by the most authorized doctrine (FOX, 1986), article 82 was not born of the same tradition as Section 2. Within the European Community, and in the very earliest stages of the "building" of the Common Market, competition policy was seen as one of several instruments aimed at achieving the full integration of the Member States' economies. As a result, heavy emphasis has been placed on firm conduct which seemed to reestablish national or regional boundary lines. National economies were relatively small and barriers between them relatively high. Firms were thought to be suboptimal in scale. Greater size was thought desirable. Market power was inevitable, particularly since significant national protections remain. The solution, consistent with a long regulatory tradition, was to deal directly only with the abuse of that power.

This solution, which is embodied in the first two examples of abuses in Article 82, also reflects both a great confidence in the correctness of government intervention in markets and a strong belief that monopoly once created will endure. This, if ever can be said about the European Union, cannot be said in the United States. American antitrust is hostile to judicial evaluation of the reasonableness of prices. Also, and thanks surely to the influence of the Chicago School, they have generally assumed that normal market forces will cause the erosion of monopoly power except in cases where such power is the result of greater efficiency (which the law ought not condemn), government protection, or predatory conduct (As stated by the Supreme Court in *Standard Oil Co. v. United States*, 221 U.S. 1, [1911]). In recent years, the law of monopolization under the Sherman Act has been directed almost exclusively at conduct targeted at competitors, conduct which might be viewed as predatory.

Although today the reach of Article 82 is significantly broader than that of Section 2, it has often been described as the more tolerant provision, dealing only with abuses by dominant firms whose dominance must be accepted, in contrast to the emphasis on market structure under Section 2. In addition, with its emphasis on conduct targeted at rivals, Section 2 is significantly less restrictive in conduct terms than Article 82. Both provisions may be viewed as imposing a special set of duties on dominant firms (in the competition law jargon, this is called the "especial responsibility") duties not shared by non-dominant undertakings, firms operating in more competitive markets.

B) The Control of Pricing Schemes Under Article 82

A dominant firm which charges an excessive price, or a below-cost price, or a discriminatory price, is guilty of an abuse under Article 82. The way antitrust authorities deal with these prohibitions shows much of how they understand competition principles, and as such how the Microsoft case has been handled. Take, for example, the ban against excessive pricing.

While most of the cases in which price has been directly at issue have involved dominant positions protected to some degree by government action –cases where monopoly is likely to persist- nothing in Article 82 confines the principle of abuse through excessive pricing to such cases. The principle is always stated in terms applicable to any firm holding a dominant position, however derived or maintained. A price is excessive when it bears "no reasonable relation to the economic value of the product supplied" (*United Brands v. Commission*, 1978 E.C.R. 207). The assessment of this relationship has been based on a variety of comparisons, such as between the dominant firm's costs and its competitors' prices, or prices in another geographic market.

We have examined the issue of excessive prices elsewhere (DÍEZ, 2006) and will not repeat the analysis here, but it is interesting at least to make some remarks about this category of abuse because we can trace here the remote origin of something essential to the *Discussion Paper*, the "as efficient" clause. Accordingly, "*the principles for assessing alleged price based exclusionary conduct are based on the premise that in general only conduct which would exclude a hypothetical "as efficient" competitor is abusive*" (n. 63).

In its decision, in *SACEM II* (Cases 395/87 et. al.) the Court of Justice built into the standard of abuse a direct evaluation of the dominant firm's efficiency. Beginning with the commonly-held view that one of the costs of monopoly is inefficiency (as stated, half a century ago, in *United States*

v. Aluminium Co. of America, 148 F.2d 416, 2d Cir., 1945) the Court was led almost inevitably to conclude that an excessive price may be justified in terms of costs only if those costs themselves are not inflated by inefficiencies. Thus direct proof that a firm is acting efficiently (or at least as efficiently as comparable firms) may be required.

The Court's logic is compelling, given its assumption that monopolists tend to have higher costs than other firms. But the *SACEM II* standard at least magnifies the practical difficulties of dealing with excessive pricing under Article 82, and opens the door for the difficult –if possible?- task of comparing efficiency between undertakings. This analytical framework also underscores the contrast between Article 82 of EC Treaty and Section 2 of Sherman Act. A monopolist does not violate Section 2 by restricting output and increasing price. A firm acquiring monopoly power through greater efficiency or other lawful means is free to set prices at monopoly levels. It is assumed that it will do so, and that such prices serve the beneficial purpose of inducing entry.

For these and a variety of other often repeated reasons, American courts have been unwilling to undertake the tasks of determining whether prices are reasonable, and of the continuous supervision of a monopolist's pricing (*United States v. Trenton Potteries Co.*, 273 U.S. 392 [1927]). Article 82 requires just such determinations, and one of the critics that the recent CFI's ruling in the Microsoft case is precisely stating the "fair and reasonable" prices at which the firm has to share the interoperability information with its competitors.

SACEM II, of course, went even further, suggesting that courts are capable of evaluating and measuring efficiency. As some commentators have pointed out, "this, too, would be anathema to American courts, which have generally succeeded in avoiding such issues" (KAUPER, 1990).

It is also noteworthy that American courts have always sought to distinguish between monopolies based on source of their power. The central element in the distinction is basically the presence of the exclusionary conduct we are dealing with. Economic theory shows that the monopoly which is not insulated from normal market forces through the use of such conduct will likely disappear over time. If it does not, it is likely that its power rests on greater efficiency. To condemn monopoly based on efficiency creates disincentives to innovation and efficiency gains by firms already dominant as well as those which might become so.

Again, many think this is exactly what has happened in the *Microsoft* case. Although there is room for some misinterpretation in her statement, some said the first words said by the Competition Commissioner after knowing the outcome of the CFI were "now we can expect a significant drop in Microsoft's market share". Again, does EC competition law penalize *bigness*? Is business success something that, in itself, raises antitrust concerns?

Finally, the conclusion we can draw from this considerations is, essentially, the same as obtained in a previous section of this chapter: when greater integration of the Common Market is achieved, efficiency concerns will need to be directly addressed. Firms which have been protected by national boundaries will need to achieve grater efficiency to survive. Consequently, fewer firms may be subject to Article 82, as markets grow larger. But a greater concern with efficiency than the Court of Justice has so far shown will be necessary to keep the treatment of excessive pricing and other similar pricing policies as an abuse from deterring efforts to enhance the competitiveness of firms.

THE CONTROVERSIAL ARTICLE 82 AND REFUSALS TO DEAL

Until recently, the treatment of refusals to deal by dominant firms as abuses under Article 82 has had little to do with economic efficiency in the price-output, consumer welfare sense. The Commission and Court of Justice cases concluding that refusals to deal were abusive have been mainly based on concerns over fairness or, in some cases, the threatened exclusion of direct rivals. In sum, these cases reflect the mix of concerns to we have already referred to, the ones that gave Article 82, because it is multi-valued and simultaneously oriented at several directions, a highly regulatory quality.

The effects of a refusal to deal vary, depending in large part on whether the target of the refusal is a potential o or actual competitor. Virtually all of the early decisions finding refusals to deal abuses did not involve direct competitors, but were vertical in nature. The target of the refusal was a distributor or other middleman who did not compete in the dominant firm's market. In such cases adverse welfare effects could only occur if the terminated party had a very large share of its market, was also a significant outlet for the seller's competitors, and therefore would not be able to remain in the market without access to the dominant firm's product. Refusals to deal with distributors might also involve vertical integration by the seller, with the harms and benefits identified with vertical integration. It seems clear that, absent one of these circumstances, a vertical refusal to deal like the ones we've described is likely to harm no one but the terminated enterprise.

In a series of vertical refusal to deal cases -*Commercial Solvents* (1974 E.C.R. 223, *United Brands,* (1978 E.C.R. 207), and *Hugin-Liptons* (1979 E.C.R. 1869)- in which the seller terminated a long-standing relationship, the Court paid scant attention to harm the refusal to supply distributors might have on the seller's own competitors –in the Robinson Patman Act terminology, *primary line injure-*, basically, we want to imagine, because such harm was hard to imagine. The emphasis in these cases was on hardship suffered by the buyer and on need to preserve the "independence of small and medium-sized firms" as an end value in itself. Undoubtedly the refusals were thought unfair because of the frustration of future expectations born out of the continuated commercial relationship. We need to bear this in mind in order to understand CFI's attitude towards *Microsoft*.

As the latest –and, to our opinion, more comprehensive and complete- doctrine has put it (PADILLA and DONOGHUE, 2006), basic notions of 'fairness' and the idea that large, well-resourced firms should not unduly hamper the activities of small and medium-sized undertakings feature more prominently under Article 82 EC than the equivalent provision in Section 2 of the Sherman Act.

If we conclude that the explanation for these decisions must rest on considerations of fairness, preservation of small business firms, and similar concerns, Article 82 comes then close to a per se condemnation of vertical refusals to deal by dominant firms, at least in cases where the parties have had a long-standing relationship and have previously dealt regularly over a substantial period of time.

Although there are decisions al the other side of the Atlantic reaching more or less similar outcomes under Section 2, particularly where a monopoly seller is vertically integrated (such as the 1927 Supreme Court decision in *Eastman Kodak* (273 U.S. 359, 1927), and the "leverage into a second market" principle of *United States v. Griffith* (334 U.S. 100, 1948) it seems clear that today American courts would not decide *Commercial Solvents, United Brands*, and *Hugin-Liptons* as they were decided by the Court of Justice.

Lately, the Commission has turned its attention to refusals to deal of a different sort. In a series of decisions dealing with the refusal by dominant firms to deal with direct competitors (*Magill, Oscar Bronner* and *IMS Health*), it has evoked themes which seem to track elements of *Aspen Ski* (472 U.S. 585, 1985) and the rejuvenated "essential facility" doctrine of American antitrust law. Generally, even a monopolist has no duty to deal with a competitor. See *Official Airline Guides v. FTC* (450 U.S. 917 [1981]). The Supreme Court has further recognized that a monopolist has "no general duty to engage in a joint marketing program

with a competitor", in *Aspen Skiing Co. v. Aspen Highlands Skiing Corp.*, 472 U.S. 585 (1985). As we have noted in previous works (DÍEZ, 2003), the relation between the so called "abuse in neighboring markets" and the monopoly leveraging (both present in the *Microsoft* ruling) goes through the "essential facilities" doctrine (see also, in this regard, DOHERTY, 2001; LANG, 1995).

While these decisions still seem to embody some of the multidimensional and nonefficiency concerns of the Court's previous rulings, they much more clearly involve concerns over accretions to market power through horizontal effects. These decisions are therefore closer to current American developments, and they're at the head of the way that leads to *Microsoft*.

The Decision in *ITP, BBC, and RTE* (O.J. L 78/43 [1989], hereinafter *Magill*) is considered, with all justice, the test under EC law for a refusal to deal. The fact that the asset to which access was required was not a physical one –say, an industrial plant- but an "intangible" one, information protected by intellectual property rights, only makes it even more suitable as the precedential to the *Microsoft* case.

In this leading case each of the defendants is a television broadcasting company, or subsidiary of such companies. They control the six major television channels available to viewers in Ireland and Northern Ireland. As part of their programming, the broadcasting companies also produce information about the scheduling of programs on the channels they control. Each defendant supplies scheduling information to daily newspapers well in advance of the date on which programs are to appear, and licenses the newspapers to publish such information under its copyright, which extends to these program listings, in *daily* comprehensive television guides that list the programs on all networks for that date. The defendants each also publish and sell *weekly* guides listing only their own programs. They refused to license their copyrights to firms desiring to publish *weekly* comprehensive guides (guides showing programs on all channels). When

Magill, a publisher, marketed such a guide in Ireland, defendants obtained preliminary injunctions barring its publication. Television program listings have been held entitled to copyright protection under British copyright law.

The Commission concluded that the refusal to license by each of the defendants was an abuse. The Commission found a strong potential demand for comprehensive weekly guides. The defendants' actions clearly prevented the marketing of such a product, since third parties' only means of access to such listings was through the defendants who generated the information as a byproduct of their programming. Through their refusals, the defendants each protected their individual weekly guides, with which no one else competed, frustrating the desires of consumers for a single weekly comprehensive guide. The refusals were found to be outside the scope of the copyright. While none of the defendants offered a comprehensive weekly guide, and thus might have difficulty competing with such a guide, the Commission apparently believed that they could provide such a guide through cross-licensing.

Diverging from previous rulings, we must not that *Magill* does not rest on a disruption of expectations based on an established pattern of dealing. The defendants had never supplied the firms which it now refused to license. Therefore, no element of unfairness was suggested. The effect was felt by potential competitors, a horizontal effect to be sure, but in circumstances in which the dominant firms were required to assist the development of a new product which they themselves did not offer, could not offer without the assistance of their own competitors, and that was likely superior in terms of consumer acceptance than the product they offered themselves.

Also importantly, the Commission treated scheduling information as though it were a kind of essential facility, access to which was necessary to "generate" a product that the Commission concluded consumers would want. The generation of information was not the result of the defendants'

dominant position; such information would be generated by any broadcaster, whether dominant or not. It is al least dubious, therefore, to see how the refusal to license had anything to do with market dominance. Moreover, the Commission's cryptic statement that "defendants' conduct was outside the scope of copyright protection" seemed at the moment both inconsistent with the fundamental concept of copyright protection and with prior Court decisions concerning the rights of copyright holders. As an example of these issues, see *CICRA v. Renault* or *AB Volvo v. Erik Veng*. As we'll show in the next section, it has lead to a sort of intrusion of antitrust law in the sphere of Intellectual Property Rights (IPRs) whose ultimate consequences nobody can foretell.

The ECJ's ruling *Oscar Bronner* (Case C-7/97, E.C.R. I-7791 [1999]) is, in turn, the standard setting decision for the European "essential facilities" doctrine and one of the closest ground in which the Microsoft ruling is founded.

The conflict rose when Mediaprint, an undertaking owner of a daily press home delivery distribution system –created and developed by it- refused to grant access to the newspaper owned by Mr. Oscar Bronner. He deemed this behaviour as abusive under Article 82 EC Treaty, and demanded Mediaprint to the Austrian *Kartellgericht*, invoking –inter alia- the "essential facilities" doctrine. The suit followed its due course, and it ended under the ECJ who assumed the task of deciding whether or not the defendant's behaviour constituted an anticompetitive refusal to deal.

Although embodied in its landmark ruling, no explicit mention is said about the essential facilities doctrine. The ECJ concluded (paragraph n. 47) that, in order to be held as abusive, such a refusal to deal should meet the following conditions:

a. It has to eliminate all the effective competition in the downstream market (the one in which operates the undertaking who request access or supply);

b. It has to involve some sort of economic resources deemed indispensable (essential) for profitably operate in the downstream market.

c. It lacks objective justification.

The ECJ considered these conditions were not met in the case at stake, since the newspapers can be easily distributed in other ways different from the home delivery, and therefore claiming that establishing an alternative distribution method was not profitable –or, by the same reasoning, economically feasible- was an unjustified aspiration.

Finally, the ECJ's *IMS Health* judgment (Case T-181/01, [2005]), confirms all the previous pronouncements, and firmly establishes the doctrine and the standard when analysing refusals to deal under EC Law, specifically if IPR of any sort are involved. The conflict here rose when IMS, an undertaking leader in the German market of pharmaceutical regional sales statistical surveys, refused access (by a negative to grant a licence) to one of its competitors to the so-called "1860 brick structure", namely, a data base that under German Law is protected by Copyright.

Relying on the *Magill* doctrine, the ECJ affirmed that, in order for such –that is, engaged in by a dominant company, being its dominance precisely derived from rightly holding an IPR over the asset to which access is requested- a refusal to deal to be abusive, the asset at stake must be indispensable for the business of the firm who asks the licence, and three conditions –again- must be cumulatively met:

a. the undertaking who is requesting the licence has the intention to offer a new product or service in the marketplace, which is not currently offered by the holder of the IPR, existing a potential or actual demand for such a product;

b. the refusal to deal has the consequence of eliminating all the competition in an adjacent market;

c. it lacks of objective justification.

As some commentators (FINE, 2002) have pointed out, this is a logical corollary of the principles established previously in Oscar Bronner and Magill, and others that are also relevant, but will not be examined here. In any case, as we have already said, they lead the way to *Microsoft*. We turn to it in the following section.

As a conclusion to this section, we can say that, taken together, these recent Commission decisions and Courts rulings do suggest a shift of emphasis from a vague and generic concern over fairness and an outright suspicion of refusals to deal to a more direct focus on the exclusion of the dominant firm's own rivals. This is consistent with the similar emphasis in Commission and Court decisions concerning predatory pricing, fidelity rebates, and exclusive dealing, and clearly shows a certain degree of alignment with the emphasis placed under Section 2 on conduct with horizontal effects. But it would be premature to suggest that Article 82 is no longer concerned with fairness.

In any event, the willingness of the Commission and Court to mandate continued dealing, displacing private decision-making, and taking on the obligation to supervise the terms of dealing, which is inherent in requiring firms to deal, far exceeds the willingness of American courts to do the same. In this sense, the "refusal to deal" cases are of a piece with the excessive pricing decision. Although we'll come back to this issue –it's one of the main contentions of this work- let's say, for the moment, that they both manifest a directly regulatory approach to antitrust.

THE MICROSOFT CASE: GOOD NEWS FOR ICT UNDER ANTITRUST LAW?

A) Overview of the Case

As we have noted previously, the Court of First Instance's ruling in the *Microsoft* saga represents on of the more important Article 82 cases decided by European antitrust authorities. We may add now that it involves one of the most controversial anticompetitive practices in the abusive catalogue, refusal to deal. Finally –and this suits perfectly with this Chapter's aim- it has happened to occur in one of the paradigmatically characterized markets of "our time" (in terms of network effects, involvement of Intellectual Property Rights, high sector-specific regulation, etc.): software industry.

The case originated with a December 1998 complaint from Sun Microsystems alleging that Microsoft was refusing to supply it with interoperability information necessary to interoperate with Microsoft's dominant PC operating system. In February 2000, following information obtained from the market, the Commission broadened the scope of its investigation to examine Microsoft's conduct with regard to its Windows Media Player product.

On 1 August 2000, on the basis of an initial investigation, the Commission sent Microsoft a Statement of Objections alleging that Microsoft was denying disclosing interface information which rival work group server operating system vendors needed to interoperate with Microsoft's dominant Windows PC operating system.

On 30 August 2001, the Commission sent Microsoft a second Statement of Objections. This document (mandatory in all EC Antitrust proceedings):

1. confirmed and expanded the interoperability objections of the first Statement of Objections, in particular by taking into account Microsoft's recently released Windows 2000 generation of PC and server operating systems; and
2. alleged that Microsoft had engaged in anticompetitive tying of its Windows Media Player product with its Windows PC operating system.

On 6 August 2003, on the basis of additional evidence that the Commission had gathered, a third Statement of Objections confirming both the interoperability and tying objections of the second Statement of Objections was sent to Microsoft.

Following an extensive analysis of the evidence on the file, the Commission concluded its investigation on 24 March 2004 by way of the Decision we have been referring to in this chapter, which found that Microsoft had abused its dominant position in the PC operating system market by:

- refusing to supply competitors in the work group server operating system market interface information necessary for their products to interoperate with Windows, and hence to compete viably in the market. The Decision ordered Microsoft to disclose, within 120 days, complete and accurate interface information which would allow rival vendors to interoperate with Windows, and to make that information available on reasonable terms;
- harming competition through the tying of its separate Windows Media Player product with its Windows PC operating system. The Decision ordered Microsoft to provide, within 90 days, a version of Windows which did not include Windows Media Player.

Intellectual property rights are at the heart of the ruling on Microsoft regarding software interoperability. According to the Commission, Microsoft had abusively refused to supply Sun Microsystems and other rivals with the specification for certain protocols that Windows workgroup servers use. According to Microsoft, the information required by Sun Microsystems is protected by several patents and involves many trade secrets. Such a protection justifies its refusal to disclose. In this chapter we therefore aim at discussing the intersection between intellectual property law and competition policy in the European Union as highlighted by the Microsoft case.

In appeal, the Court of First Instance confirmed (Case T-201/04, *Microsoft v. Commission*, [2007]

5 C.M.L.R. 846) in all its terms the Commission's Decision. More specifically, the peculiar configuration of the "duty-to-deal" resulting from the CFI's ruling in the landmark *Microsoft* case may be a milestone in the history of antitrust law applied to ICT. As we suggest in the title of this chapter, the aim of such a duty is to grant access to competitors to an asset considered essential. However, other equally important goals should not be overlooked, such as promoting consumer's welfare and enhancing undertakings budgets in R&D. Regarding these issues, the recent U.S. Supreme Court's judgment in *Trinko* is widely seen as significantly narrowing the scope of the duty to deal under U.S. antitrust law.

Going back to Europe, the Commission's decision and the CFI's ruling are going to be assessed from an economic perspective, analyzing the application of the "essential facilities" doctrine to the case. Accordingly, we will also discuss whether Microsoft has leveraged its dominance in the market of operating systems for desktop computers into the market of operating system for workgroup server. Finally, we will also focus our analysis on compulsory licensing as a remedy.

Supposedly, both EU and U.S. antitrust laws and enforcement are fairly closely aligned on both the underlying principles and the notion that enforcement is merited in only exceptional cases. However, regarding this "exceptional cases", the CFI ruling appears to have followed the long-standing criteria in this regard under EU law. The current test consists in four requisites to be met, to which we have devoted our attention in a preceding section.

B) The "Duty-to-Deal" Under *Trinko* and the New *Microsoft* Doctrine

As we have already noted, intellectual property rights are at the heart of the recent CFI ruling regarding software interoperability. It confirms, virtually in all its terms, the previous Commission's Decision in 2004. According to it, Microsoft had abusively refused to supply Sun Microsystems and other rivals with the specification for certain protocols that Windows workgroup servers use. By contrast, according to Microsoft, the information required by Sun Microsystems is protected by several patents and involves many trade secrets. Such a protection justifies its refusal to disclose. Intellectual property is at stake in the decision in two ways: in the first place, as concerning the remedies imposed –we've already referred to the importance of this issue in antitrust enforcement-, the European Commission asked for a compulsory licensing, and now the CFI has endorsed such decision.

Secondly, in order to prove liability, the Commission investigated whether exceptional circumstances were present to force Microsoft to license. It firmly concluded –using much of the language and ideas comprised in the decisions we've been looking at earlier, such as *Oscar Bronner*, *IMS*, and more specifically, *Magill*- that those circumstances were present. Now, the CFI has also endorsed this course of analysis. As we shall see now, although the outcome may be correct, the opportunity to clarify this crucial point in the "duty-to-deal" configuration has been unfortunately missed.

We've already discussed the intersection between intellectual property law and competition policy in the European Union as highlighted by the Microsoft case in other work (DÍEZ and BACHES, 2006). What we'll focus on now is, in the context of the interaction between regulation and antitrust to which we've referred in previous sections, the peculiar configuration of the "duty-to-deal" resulting from the CFI's ruling in the landmark *Microsoft* case.

We have already pointed out the main facts in this case, so there's no need to repeat them here. Basically, the points which we consider worth discussing in this Chapter are the following:

1. Under the *Microsoft* recently established doctrine, up to what extent there's a sort of

"duty-to-deal" under EC Law? Moreover, how closely is aligned with US antitrust law and principles?

2. After the somehow confusing line of decisions in this area, it is not reckless saying that EU case law is unclear whether intellectual property rights require a different or a similar antitrust treatment vis-à-vis Article 82 infringement when compared to other forms of property. Following the test set in *Magill* (as expressed in previous sections in this Chapter), it is unclear whether the offering of a "new product" by a competitor as a condition to force refusal to supply is specific to cases involving IPRs (patents or copyrights) or if it applies whatever the forms of property the bottleneck is featured with.

3. What about Microsoft's incentives to innovate? What reading can dynamic and innovative enterprises are going to do of this ruling, in terms of their comprised budget for R+D programmes?

Concerning the first of the lessons we can draw from the *Microsoft* ruling, the duty to deal, and following our earlier discussion in this paper comparing the provisions –and the way they're understood and applied by both agencies and courts- contained in Article 82 of the EC Treaty and Section 2 of the Sherman Act, some have already suggested –not without some doses of irony- that "the EU record in respect of refusals to deal is really no worse than U.S. enforcement history" (O'DONOGHUE, 2007).

The recent U.S. Supreme Court judgment in *Trinko* (540 U.S. 398 [2004]), is widely seen as significantly narrowing the scope of the duty to deal under U.S. antitrust law. But it leaves many questions unanswered and the precise scope of the duty to deal under US antitrust law remains a major issue in the on-going review of Section 2 of the Sherman Act by the U.S. enforcement agencies. It seems unlikely that, even in the US, anybody

could claim that there can never be a duty to deal in the case of a single firm. Consequently, EU and U.S. antitrust laws and enforcement are fairly closely aligned on both the underlying principles and the notion that enforcement is merited in only exceptional cases.

Regarding this "exceptional cases", the CFI ruling appears to have followed the long-standing criteria in this regard under EU law. The test is whether:

1. Access to the input in question is "essential";
2. The refusal to deal risks the "elimination of competition";
3. The refusal to deal would prevent the emergence of a "new product";
4. There is "objective justification" for the refusal.

On each of these points, the CFI assessed a huge amount of evidence, from both sides, before concluding that the conditions were satisfied. In conclusion, it has properly been said (O'DONOGHUE, 2007) that the CFI ruling does not really change the existing EU law on refusal to deal in any material respect and, in assessing the application of the existing legal rules, appears to have undertaken a level of factual review that was very detailed and reasonably balanced.

In addition to it, if the "essential facilities" doctrine is to be applied here, as some have suggested (STOTHERS, 2001) and is envisaged in *Aspen Skiing* and "monopoly leveraging" is considered an abusive practice in itself, Microsoft's leveraging strategy should be well-documented and corroborated with a convincing economic mechanism of foreclosure. Not having access to the complete file is difficult to say so. At least the CFI thinks that the Commission did a good work on this issue.

Thus, to answer the first of the questions we've raised, it should be said that the CFI does not emphasize enough that the conditions for a duty to deal will only ever be met in the very rarest

–or exceptional- circumstances. True, the ruling makes extensive reference to the unique position of Microsoft, and its persistent near-monopoly position held in PC operating system software. But, is this ruling *lex Microsoft*? To what extent serves as precedential guidance for other dominant–albeit, non "super dominant"- undertakings?

What the US Supreme Court did in *Trinko* was precisely expressing in very clear terms how the duty to deal is configured under American antitrust law. By not establishing precise and clearer guidance in the configuration of the "duty to deal" under EC law (in the same way as the doctrine was set up in the first place in *Oscar Bronner*, and later confirmed by *Magill* and *IMS*) risks "normalizing" it, and that's surely wholly inappropriate as a matter of general policy.

As has been suggested (GERADING, 2004), and in the same way it was said about the "essential facilities" doctrine some decades ago, the need for "limiting principles" regarding the application of the abuse of dominant position ban in European law is imperative. As we are trying to show here, enforcement of such a provision regarding practices such as excessive prices (*margin squeeze*) and refusals to deal still remains uncompleted and largely vague in its boundaries and scope.

C) Final Assessment

In its 2004 decision, the Commission established that Microsoft's refusal to supply information on interoperability was abusive. It followed two lines of arguments. Firstly, although it has not explicitly applied the *Magill* test, it has referred to the specific circumstances under which a refusal to supply may infringe article 82 EC Treaty. It has also claimed that Microsoft's disruption in disclosing information to rivals reflects a leveraging strategy, by which it expands its actual market power –close to a de facto monopoly- in PC's Operating Systems to the related market of Work-Group Server's operating systems.

Instead of applying the "new product" test, as established in *Magill*, discussing openly whether Microsoft's non-disclosure of information impedes to put on the market services or products for which there is an actual or potential demand, the Commission introduced an assessment on incentives to innovate. The Commission also shifted the burden of proof. Defendants, not competition authorities, would have the difficult task to demonstrate that their refuse to supply does not reduce incentives to innovate in the industry.

It remains to be seen up to what extent that shifts is appropriate, since, as some commentators have suggested (LÉVÊQUE, 2004) "it too largely opens the gate to apply the essential facility doctrine, especially when intellectual property rights are at stake in. The granting of high value patents protecting blockbuster innovations are featured with an absence of actual and potential substitutes and a high risk to eliminate competitors. The allocating of the 'easy' criteria to demonstrate to competition authorities –whereas the difficult one is under the burden of the innovative firm- will result in a misbalance".

When this "essential facilities" doctrine experienced an unsustainable rise in American antitrust jurisprudence, many claimed for the necessity of limiting principles (AREEDA, 1990); precisely now, in the *Microsoft* decision, to limit the extension of the essential facility doctrine, the required test consists in following the set of conditions as established in prior decisions. It was therefore the task of the European Commission to prove: (1) that the input is indispensable; (2) that the refusal to supply eliminates competition; (3) that there is no objective justification not to supply. In addition to these, one new feature is added to the test: (4) that the refusal to supply reduces incentives to innovate in the industry. If any, possibly only the finding of the objective justification must remain the burden of defendants.

It is a long-standing discussion whether intellectual property law stifles innovation; it seems that modern microeconomics theory proves so, in some circumstances. As the test goes, issued by the Commission and now endorsed by the CFI in its *Microsoft* ruling, the antitrust authorities are now empowered to *ex post* intervene in reassessing the granting of intellectual property rights by patent offices if right-holders refuse to license. It seems clear that this issue remains open for debate.

Among the "particular circumstances" of the case, the Commission stated that this case differed in some issues from previous cases, as long as Microsoft was "superdominant", the suit involved not only a question of access to an IPR but also a question of "interoperability", Microsoft's IPRs were "tenuous". However, in its ruling the CFI indicates that it does not matter whether Microsoft argues on the protection granted by IPRs, or if the allegedly protected technology is really innovative. According to the CFI, the key for assessing the abusive practice –the refusal to deal- is merely if this negative to license makes it more difficult for competitors to innovate.

As some commentators put it (WAELBROECK, 2008), in view of this extremely wide test, the Court logically finds that this is the case, and due to the IPRs owned by Microsoft its competitors are at a competitive disadvantage; however, this will always be the case whenever any dominant company refuses to license any IPR, unless such IPR is entirely useless.

Finally, according to the Commission –in a line of reasoning fully confirmed by the CFI- Microsoft leveraging intention and doing was well-documented by facts, especially regarding Microsoft's intent, the dependence of developers and users vis-à-vis network effects and compatibility, and the evolution of market shares in the market of operating systems for Work-Group servers. All these facts taken together supposedly corroborate a dynamic economic mechanism of foreclosure which is, as we've explained earlier in this paper, the greatest foe of antitrust authorities when faced to exclusionary abuses. If all this is true –and it seems so- it renders useless, or to put

it more gently, unnecessary, the always-troubling application of the essential facilities doctrine.

FUTURE TRENDS FOR THE PROTECTION OF IPRs AND INCENTIVES FOR R&D

It seems clear that one of the more –if not the most- far reaching issues at stake in the post-Microsoft's case world is the role IPRs are going to play under antitrust law.

In Microsoft's appeal it is persistent the allegation of IPRs concerning the information it is obliged to disclose by the Commission's decision, specifically as regards certain communication protocols. To this aim, the American company invokes a number of patents obtained both in Europe and the United States, as well as others still pending (paragraph 270). In the proceedings also the consideration of trade secrets is asserted (paragraph 285), demanding the same sort of legal protection against the compulsory disclosure –to which we have referred before, as a new way of expressing the traditional "duty-to-deal" obligation.

The Commission's counter-argument is that Microsoft has not sufficiently argued that the alleged innovations contained in its protocols are subject to the protection granted by a patent. However, the Commission does not object to the fact that the communications specifications and features dealt with in its decision may be subject to some kind of patent or copyright. Yet, this would not mean that the use of such protocols constitutes and infringement of IPRs (paragraphs 278 and 279).

It's interesting to point out that the Free Software Foundation Europe (FSFE), in its allegations –aligned with the plaintiff- states that Microsoft's invocated technology is neither new nor innovative. The FSFE goes on saying (paragraph 282) that Microsoft's usual policy is just adopting existing and current standards and protocols, and then introducing minor –and useless- modifications in order to impede interoperability.

As we have already said, unfortunately the CFI does not consider this question worth discussing (paragraph 283); it just admits the possibility of existence of IPRs over Microsoft's protocols, but states that the only relevant issue is whether the abovementioned requisites for a "duty-to-deal" obligation are met in this present case (paragraph 290).

As regards the protection of IPRs, and consequently the need to protect Microsoft's incentives to innovate, maybe the CFI's Sentence is not as sound as one expected. The argument of "objective justification" in this pretty singular refusal to deal case is not thoroughly addressed. The CFI simply notes that the mere fact that a duty to deal involves intellectual property rights is not a defense (paragraphs 690-691) and that Microsoft's arguments about the impact on innovation incentives were "*general, vague, and theoretical*" (paragraph 698). Accordingly, the above mentioned need to protect Microsoft's incentives to innovate cannot constitute an objective justification that would offset the exceptional circumstances identified (paragraph 707).

The Commission addressed this issue in the already cited *Discussion Paper* of 2005 on exclusionary abuses, when it stated (n. 235) that: "*The risks facing the parties and the sunk investment that must be committed may thus mean that an dominant firm should be allowed to exclude others for a certain period of time in order to ensure an adequate return on such investment, even when this entails eliminating effective competition during this period*", a statement which is –to our understanding, surely limited and definitely lacking of first-hand evidentiary support- simply at odds with the scarce treatment of this issue in the CFI's ruling in the *Microsoft* case.

Finally, regarding the "long-term" reading and consequences of the *Microsoft* ruling, there is probably no reliable way, in practice, that an antitrust authority or court can balance *ex post* the benefits of a duty to deal against its adverse effects on *ex ante* incentives for innovation and investment. We have already transcribed the somehow "harsh" words of the CFI, stating that arguments of this kind will by nature always be "general, vague, and theoretical." However, given the key role in our modern world of innovation, even more importantly if it can be said so in this software industry, it can be seriously questioned whether a general duty to share essential IPRs –even when the refusal to deal may cause some impediment to the development of new kinds of products- is appropriate as a matter of public policy. As some commentators have laconically said, "some basic recognition by the CFI of this fundamental point was essential" (O'DONOGHUE, 2007).

We have also mentioned before the existence, under EC Competition Law, of the so-called objective justification defence, which would have –ultimately- exonerated Microsoft from the allegedly anticompetitive conduct. In this regard, the undertaking first claimed that such justification lied precisely in the existence of IPRs on the protocols at stake, and since the developing of such technology required a lot of investment in R&D budgets, it was legitimated to refuse granting access to them. Secondly, also accused the European Commission of lacking a competitive trade-off, since it had only considered the short-term benefits derived from the public knowledge of Microsoft's interoperability codes, but had neglected the long-term disincentives that such a compulsory disclosure would mean in innovation expenditures (see paragraphs 666 et. seq.).

Again, the CFI does not accept this line of reasoning, stating that while the Commission should assert the existence of the abusive conduct, the proof of the existence of objective justification relies on the defendant (paragraph 668). In this regard, the mere invocation of existing IPRs does not amount to an objective justification as established by the *IMS* and *Magill* doctrine (paragraph 690).

To some commentators, this is some sort of a "one-two punch to incentives to innovate" (SPULBER, 2007). First, by penalizing Microsoft for bundling its Media Player with Windows –we are not dealing with this issue in this Chapter-, the court will make companies reluctant to add innovative features to their products. Second, as previously explained, by sanctioning Microsoft for not disclosing fundamental innovations to its server software to its rivals, it seems that the court will make companies think twice before investing in costly research and development.

CONCLUSION

One of the proposed areas to be covered by this book is precisely the boundaries and overlaps between economic ICT and competition law (and policy). In this Chapter, at the light of recent –and, by all standards, landmark decisions- events in the antitrust arena, such as the Commission's decision and the CFI's ruling in the *Microsoft* case, we've tried to show an example of that overlap.

In a highly sophisticated market, such as the software industry, where innovation plays a key role in economic growth, and the leading undertakings are those who expend greater sums in research and development, stating precisely up to what extent one should share its assets –even when they're protected by IPRs- is imperative, in order to clarify economic incentives. Given there's a "duty to deal" under EC law, and therefore a "refusal to deal" is –under certain circumstances- deemed an abusive practice, those circumstances should be expressed in very clear terms. Thus, it is at least dubious up to what extent the *Microsoft* ruling represents a step forward.

The reasons of these failures in the interaction between ICT and competition in the *Microsoft* case, with both the Commission and the CFI role of market regulators, telling the undertakings with whom and in which terms should deal, are, in our opinion, three-fold.

First, there's the problem of the not-so-easily-achieved market integration. As the Common Market comes closer to reality, the assumptions underlying its competition policy will come to be questioned. Once fuller integration has been achieved, the need to utilize competition policy as a means to accomplish such integration will be reduced. If remaining barriers created by Member States fall, locally dominant firms whose position is dependent less on efficiency than local protection will find their position eroding. The belief that dominance will persist, and that direct regulation is necessary to control conduct which is brought about by such dominance, may well give way to a greater faith in the ability of competitive forces to eliminate monopoly power in the absence of such protection.

Second, there's the problem of our multisecular-tradition of a form-based approach to abuse of dominant position. A more economic approach to Article 82 is needed, to focus on improved consumer welfare. In so doing, it avoids the long-standing confusion between the protection of competition versus the protection of competitors. Ultimately, it stresses that the ultimate yardstick of competition policy is in the satisfaction of consumer needs. Thus considered and implemented, competition would be a key element in the promotion of a faster growing, consumer-oriented and more competitive European economy, in the same way antitrust has been the driving force of American economic development.

The greater emphasis in Commission decisions on conduct which harms rivals is some indication that a shift toward a consumer welfare standard is beginning. The economics-based approach to the application of article 82 that we're advocating implies that the assessment of each specific case will not be undertaken on the basis of the form that a particular business practice takes but rather will be based on the assessment of the anti-competitive effects generated by business behaviour.

The ability of firms within the Common Market to ward off the intrusions of firms outside the

Common Market, and to become more effective competitors in other markets, will also turn on enhanced efficiency. Competition policy within the Common Market thus will confront the same efficiency concerns which helped redirect American antitrust policy away from concerns over fairness and protection of small and medium-sized firms and in the direction of the consumer welfare standard now applied by American courts. Fairness as a value in itself may become a luxury competition policy can no longer afford, a value trumped by the need to satisfy demands for efficiency.

Regarding the specific IPR-related issue, it seems clear that the obligation for a dominant undertaking to disclosure information and hence provide its IPRs to competitors whenever they constitute an advantage may encourage free-riding on technology-leading firms. Instead of investing huge amounts of money and efforts in R&D, it's easier to request for it, and threaten to complain to the antitrust authorities if you don't get full compliance. This scheme does not seem the best scenario for providing incentives to innovation.

In the third place, and finally, there's the antitrust authorities' "regulatory" bias in itself. Steps in the right direction have been taken, but they may, of course, go no further. As we have seen, the Commission and Court cannot be expected to abandon their control of excessive pricing by dominant firms. The wording itself of Article 82 expressly declares such conduct as an abuse. There are, in this sense, a lot of decisions and ruling –some of them have been cited in this work- paradigmatically representative of this trend, alien to American antitrust, with its scrutiny of the appropriateness of the dominant firm's costs, and its efficiency, and the "fair" price level, which seems to manifest an even more encompassing regulatory posture than the regulatory agencies themselves.

Because the regulatory tradition is well entrenched in the EU, we should not fall into the trap of active intervention and fine-tuning; whenever possible, competition is to be preferred to detailed regulation as the best mechanism to avoid inefficiencies and foster productivity and growth; as some commentators have put it, this calls for a "non-dirigiste" approach to competition policy that focuses in most cases on entry barriers; in the context of Article 82, it is then natural to focus on competitive harm that arises from exclusionary strategies. The possible exceptions allowed concern some natural monopoly industries which may require ongoing supervision of access prices and conditions by regulatory agencies, better-equipped for this task than the antitrust authorities. And regulatory solutions may be viewed as inferior to those imposed by the market itself.

Whether the pressures for greater efficiency, the shift to focus on consumer welfare, a rule of reason approach, and the abandoning of regulatory intentions will overcome this tradition, and refocus competition policy at least on issues not resolved by the text of Article 82, only time will tell.

REFERENCES

Areeda, P. (1990). Essential facilities: an epithet in need of limiting principles", *58 Antitrust L. J. 841.*

Díez Estella, F. (2003, Mar-Apr). Los objetivos del Derecho antitrust. *Gaceta Jurídica de la Unión Europea y de la Competencia, 224.*

Díez Estella, F. (2003, Apr-Jun). La doctrina del abuso en los mercados conexos: del "monopoly leveraging" a las "essential facilities." *Revista de Derecho Mercantil, 248.*

Díez Estella, F. (2006). Abusos mediante precios: los precios excesivos. In Pons, M. (Ed.), *El abuso de posición de dominio.* Fundación Rafael del Pino.

Díez Estella, F., & Baches, S. (2006, Apr-Jun). La aplicación del derecho "antitrust" al ejercicio unilateral de los derechos de propiedad intelectual e industrial: el estado de la cuestión en la Unión Europea y en los EE.UU. *Revista de Derecho Mercantil, 260.*

Doherty, B. (2001). Just What are Essential Facilities? *CMLR, 38*.

Fine, F. (2002). NDC / IMS: A Logical Application of Essential Facilities Doctrine. *European Competition Law Review, 23*(9).

Fox, E. M. (1986). *Monopolization and Dominance in the United States and the European Community: Efficiency, Opportunity and Fairness,* 61 NOTRE DAME L. REV. 981.

Geradin, D. (2004). Limiting the Scope of Article 82 EC: What Can The EU Learn From the US Supreme Court's Judgment in *Trinko*, in the Wake of Microsoft, IMS, and Deutsche Telekom? *Common Market Law Review, 41*(6), 1519–1533.

Gual, J., Hellwig, M., Perrot, A., Polo, M., Rey, P., Schmidt, K. & Stenbacka, R. (2005, July). *An Economic Approach to Article 82*. Report by the EAGCP.

Gyselen (1990). Abuse of Monopoly Power within the Meaning of Article 86 of the EEC Treaty -- Recent Developments. In B. Hawk (Ed.), 1990 *Fordham Corporate Law Institute* (pp. 598-599).

Kauper, T. (1990). EC Competition law - the road to 1992: article 86, excessive prices, and refusals to deal. *59 Antitrust L.J., 441*.

Lévêque, F. (2004, September). The Application of Essential Facility and Leveraging Doctrines to Intellectual Property in the EU: The Microsoft's Refusal to License on Interoperability. *CERNA Working Paper*. Retrieved from http://www.cerna.ensmp.fr

O'Donoghue, R. (2007, September). *Microsoft v. EU Commission*: Sounds Good In Theory But...." *eCCP Publication*. Retrieved from http://www.globalcompetitionpolicy.com/index.php

Padilla, J., & O'Donoghue, R. (2006). *The Law and Economics of Article 82 EC*. Oxford: Hart Publishing.

Spulber, D. (2007, September). Competition Policy in Europe: Harming Incentives to Innovate. *eCCP Case Note*. Retrieved from http://www.globalcompetitionpolicy.com/index.php

Stothers, C. (2001). Refusal to Supply as Abuse of a Dominant Position: Essential Facilities in the European Union. *European Competition Law Review, 22*(7).

Temple Lang, J. (1995). Defining Legitimate Competition: Companies' Duties to Supply Competitors, and Access to Essential Facilities. In B. Hawk (Ed.), 1994 Fordham Corporate Law Institute, 245.

Temple Lang, J., & O'Donoghue, R. (2005, June 10). The Concept of an Exclusionary Abuse under Article 82. *Research Paper on the Modernisation of Article 82 EC*. Colegio de Europa (Brujas).

Waelbroeck, D. (2008, January). The *Microsoft* Judgment: Article 82 Revisited? *GCP Online Magazine*. Retrieved from http://globalcompetitionpolicy.org

Chapter 7
Taxation of Virtual Worlds:
An Approach to Face Virtual Worlds as Electronic Commerce

Daniel Torres Gonçalves
Consultant, Portugal

ABSTRACT

The novelty of "new realities" such Virtual Worlds presents a challenge to the law. Many transactions are made every day on Virtual Worlds, but no taxation is applied to them. This chapter argues, firstly, that the object of such transactions is subject to the right of property and secondly that the electronic currency used to buy such property is electronic money. For both conclusions, one important issue considered will be the legal strength of the EULA. The issues of property and electronic money form the basis of this approach to VW taxation. It is argued that virtual transactions should be taxed, and that is possible to create a legal solution that does not endanger the principal of taxing only profit, and does not tax mere entertainment. Tax law must be applied to these transactions. I consider these two issues, which allow us to view VW as an electronic commerce marketplace.

INTRODUCTION

Virtual Worlds (VW) are still a stranger to the law. In several different fields, VW present challenges to lawyers, as there is not currently a straightforward application of the existing law.

Concurrently, VW bring new risks to society, copyright, identity theft and money laundry, for example. This chapter proposes a solution to one of those problems, that of taxation.

Inside VW, it is common to trade virtual goods in exchange for virtual currency, or other virtual goods. However, behind such 'virtuality' of goods and currency stands *real money*. Considerable amounts of money are currently exchanged in virtual environments. Even so, there are no regulations being applied to those transactions. However, new situations arise, giving VW a higher profile. Indeed, exchanging virtual currency for material (i.e. real) goods is not science fiction, as accepting virtual payments as an alternative to credit cards or PayPal is easy to envisage. These issues show the

DOI: 10.4018/978-1-61520-975-0.ch007

inability of current solutions to deal with taxation of VW. Thus, the present thesis establishes a new approach to tax virtual transactions.

When tax systems intend to tax trade, they pursue any kind trade, it does not matter if the trade is "in person" or "by phone". This fact drove tax systems to be able to cope with electronic commerce. Having this in mind, one should not be tempted to exclude, the possibility of virtual worlds being subject to tax.

"Western" tax systems intend to tax a person each time they undertake some kind of trade, and this may happen in a virtual world context also, as Nuttall (2007) states: "If someone reproduces, through their combined efforts in the real world and in-world what would clearly be a trading activity in the real world, it seems likely that this would be accepted as a trading activity".

In fact, in an "in-world environment", residents have the chance to add value to what they own. They may build some kind of object and sell it, or just be wise in the exchange of virtual things and earn in-world money with it. One may consider this just as e-commerce but placed in a different place; or one may think this has nothing to do with commerce because it is *monopoly money* and not *real things* in the equation.

Still, it seems commonly accepted that "player activity in virtual worlds undoubtedly produces measurable economic value to the player" (Camp, 2007, p.2). The real question is if such economic value should be taxed or not.

After introducing Virtual Worlds, two main issues will be presented. In the first place, it is argued that virtual property is actual property, and so property rights exist in virtual goods.

Secondly, it is argued that virtual currency used in VW is electronic money and not any 'unit of play'.

These two arguments are supported by considering the legal strength of the End-Use License Agreement (EULA). I propose that they (EULAs) can be considered contracts of adhesion and any unfair terms therein should not be enforced.

Property and electronic money are the starting point for consideration of taxation. These two issues will mould the approach to the principals applied of taxation as applied to VW. Thus, current legislative and theoretical solutions will be addressed.

This approach shows that to deal with the taxation of VW one should rely on the general rules of electronic commerce. Thus, it is understood that VW is an environment which can and should be taxed, then the question must be: how?

"Code" plays an important role, as it can be used as a way of enforcing tax rules in the environment of VW.

Any legal approach to VW faces a major difficulty. The ubiquity of the Internet, and thus of VW, makes it available to almost anyone in the world with a network connection and therefore jurisdictional problems arise. It is never simple to find the applicable law, and even more problematic is that the same reality may be viewed differently in different countries. There is never a perfect approach to this problem. In the current chapter the approach will be made mainly from a European Union perspective, noting certain US and UK-specific points where relevant.

I. Virtual Worlds

1. Definition of Virtual World

When considering taxation of transactions occurring inside Virtual Worlds (VW), one must first try to understand Virtual Worlds.

According to Lastowka and Hunter (in press), VW are places where "millions of people with Internet connections are currently living large portions of their lives, forming friendship with others, building and acquiring virtual property, and forming social organizations" (p.3).

A possible definition of Virtual World is:

"Virtual worlds are online digital environments in which large numbers of users, represented by

their 'avatars', socialise, participate in events and activities and, most interestingly from a legal perspective, create and trade virtual property and services" (Naylor & Jaworski, 2007, p.262).

Several elements can be discerned from both definitions:

- *online* means that not only the world is virtual but also it can only be accessed connecting to a network;
- *digital environments* – all the context is digital, including the traded property and services;
- *large numbers of users participate in events and activities* – VW are place of socialization and interaction, thus with no users or no relations between them, there is no VW;
- *avatars* – each user is digitally represented by a character;
- *create and trade* – users are not passive, they play an active role in the content and life inside the VW.

VWs should not be confused with mere games. VWs exist, change and evolve even when a given user is not "in-world": VW are *persistent* and *dynamic,* as "even when you are not [there] (...) the environment continues to exist and changes over time" (Lastowka & Hunter, in press, p.7)

The base unit for living in-world is the avatar. It is designed to fit the main purpose of VW, i.e. socialising.

VWs known today are packed with high-quality graphics and many potential actions available to the avatar. It was not always like that: VW are not a new concept. Their origins lay in the old Multi-User Dungeons (MUD) (Birch, 2005), which are almost as old as the Internet.[1] At that time, the action happened in a text-based environment in which a player could type their own actions into the VW. It was basically a role-playing game but also provided chat rooms. Thus, from the beginning, most of the characteristics of modern VWs were present in the MUDs, namely social interaction components.

Two Kinds of Virtual World

Today, VW can be divided in two types. "Scripted worlds" are VW which are structured and more closely resemble a game. The player must complete tasks, or quests, usually in cooperation with others to achieve certain objectives. These VWs are, "games complete with objectives and storylines fit for the setting (...) journey typically entails participating in quests and raids, confronting enemies, and gaining experience and accomplishment in the game" (Lederman, 2007, p.1626).

The second type of VW is the "unscripted world". In this category, there is neither storyline nor objective. VW are a place of socialization in which each resident opts for his "kind of life". Usually there is more room for residents to be creative than in scripted worlds, namely to produce virtual objects and trade them; these objects will keep the user "attached" to that particular world. In this case, "A world's creator can simply provide a virtual environment and basic avatars along with tools to create items, allowing participants to undertake virtual activities such as attending a concert, shopping, building a house, or making and selling items useful in the world" (Lederman, 2007, p.1626).

I will focus on unscripted worlds. Applying the findings of this chapter to scripted worlds can take place, if adjustments are kept in mind. Though, such analysis is not in the scope of this chapter.

Second Life (SL) will be used as an example. It is one of the most representative VW of its kind.

However, the findings of this paper shall not be limited to this example. Conclusions about taxation may be extended to several other VW and even new online realities that might arise where transactions between users exist.

2. THE STATE OF THE ART

In 2007, the major Virtual Worlds were worth more than US$2 billion (Naylor & Jaworski). Scholars became aware of the risks that might arise from VW, namely tax evasion (Lederman, 2007) and money laundry (Birch, 2007c).

The large number of users and companies that have participated in VW, and are engaging in commerce and making profit made the present author realise that is important to determine how law can cope with "in-world reality". The consequences are truly material – it is possible to make a living from virtual world businesses (Birch, 2007b), and crime may also therefore be a reality.

Exchanges that take place in VW are unregulated – there is no taxation being applied to them. However, in the U.S. the 2008 Annual Report to the Congress by the National Taxpayer Advocate, considers the issue in a section "The IRS Should Proactively Address Emerging Issues Such as Those Arising from 'Virtual Worlds'" (Vol. I, pp.213-226). In addition, in the European Union, VAT is being charged on some Second Life transactions, but not to transactions made between residents. Thus, the bulk of transactions are not included.

Although this is a very relevant matter, there are not plenty of solutions. One possible solution is the "betting theory" (Nuttall, 2007). Another one, more elaborated and more substantial, is the cash-out rule (Camp, 2007; Lederman, 2007). This theory embodies an out-world taxation system, where VW transactions should be taxed but such taxation occurs when virtual currency is cashed out as a real world currency.

Difficulties faced by the cash-out rule relate to the fusion between virtual and real life. The cited National Taxpayer Advocate Annual Report states that "businesses now accept virtual dollars in exchange for real property or services".

Consequently, in-world taxation should be evaluated and considered. It is also important to measure the burden that such a policy intervention would bring to residents of VW.

Considering in-world taxation, several questions should be addressed. Most importantly, virtual property and electronic money need to be considered. If one is before actual property and money then it will be possible to get profit inside the VW, and taxation should happen there. On the other hand, if one is dealing with property and money, the only difference to the real world is the utilised medium.

This paper will address those two issues in presenting an alternative approach to taxation. First, it will be shown that virtual property is actual property. Thus, in VW there is exchange of property, to which monetary value is linked. Then, it will be proved that virtual currency is electronic money. This means that the trade of property will occur in exchange for real money. This is critical to the taxation considerations that will follow.

II. The Starting Point: Property and Money

In their works, neither Camp (2007) nor Lederman (2007) address directly the question of taxation mainly for two reasons.

In the first place, Virtual Property can be seen as actual property or as something else. While Camp skips to answer the question, Lederman remits it to the interpretation of the EULA.

Secondly, currency of VW is usually considered as a mere *unit of play* or even *play money*, in the words of Camp (2007). The fact that such currency can be "real money" changes, necessarily, the approach of taxation to these transactions and will be considered later.

1. Property

The first issue to be addressed must be the analysis of virtual goods as subject to a property regime, what is relevant for taxation – Lederman (2007) states that if "Second Life residents actually have ownership rights in copies of Second Life items, these trades (...) will be taxable". Following these considerations, reflection will be given to the contractual regulation that property is subject to.

One of the most obvious characteristics of *virtual goods* is their intangibility. Indeed, a virtual object does not have any physical existence, at least in the 'real world'.

This fact could tempt us to argue that virtual goods do not constitute real property. However, this should not be an issue, as our system is capable of dealing with the intangibility of property. Thus, "the objections to virtual property sounding in tangibility or in time are descriptively implausible. Our property system cheerfully accommodates these characteristics, in one form or another, in various types of property interests" (Lastowka & Hunter, in press).

Intangibility should present no problem, note for example the recognition of intellectual property rights, such as copyright, trademarks and patent rights.

There is proximity between intellectual property and virtual property. This can make it more difficult to regulate the latter (Dougherty & Lastowka, 2007), because it is tempting to regulate virtual property based on the principles of intellectual property. This is pointed to by Fairfield (2005), who explains that "virtual property is governed under a regime where initial rights are allocated to intellectual property holders, and subsequent rights are governed by license agreements" (p.1050).

Virtual property is a concept broader than "property inside virtual worlds", and can exist outside the Internet. Focusing on the Internet, one can find several types of property – from internet domain names to email addresses, from an avatar in a virtual world to the pair of shoes she wears. Aware of this, Hunt (2007) proposes to divide virtual property in two categories: -open environment; -and, closed environment.

Closed environment virtual property is the one present in the virtual worlds. In this case, property exists only in the context of a determined world, which for access one needs to connect with a certain supplier through a website or software provided for that purpose.

In contrast, a domain name and an email address, examples of open environment property, are independent of such conditions for there is no great limitation on the way of accessing it.

I believe this distinction is most significant. A closed environment sets a more controlled background, where it is easier to define the rules that apply to property. For example, "Code", in the definition of Lessig (2006), might be used in a way of enforcing rules about property and taxation. VW shall be considered a closed environment for purposes of virtual property.[2]

Taxation principals, it is argued, should be applied not only to virtual worlds presently known but to all realities that come within the closed environment category. Limiting the rules to closed environments is due to not being possible, or desirable, to find rules that suit also to open environment property.

Virtual Property as Other Property

To consider virtual property as regular property, one needs to find if the first resembles the second. In fact, some fundamental properties of the second are found in the first one. Fairfield (2005) believes that "Virtual property shares three legally relevant characteristics with real world property: rivalrousness, persistence, and interconnectivity".

VW property can present each of these properties. Through code such characteristics can be achieved easily. The relevance of this is understandable:

Rivalrousness gives me the ability to invest in my property without fear that other people may take what I have built. Persistence protects my investment by ensuring that it lasts. Interconnectivity increases the value of the property due to network effects. (Fairfield, 2005)

Finally, it is substantial to point the reasons why one should protect virtual property as any other property.

Some virtual worlds, such as SL, have no goals, i.e. there is no game purpose when playing it. The purpose is social and commercial. The protection of virtual property would benefit users, and probably stimulate transactions and confidence on them.

Residents of virtual worlds expect to have possession of their virtual goods. Seeing themselves as the avatar, they rely on the premise that they have power over virtual property in the same way they have power over their physical objects. To quote Hunt (2007), "the average player instinctively thinks about virtual property as if it were like any other property".

Professor Fairfield (2005) understands that the base unit for virtual property is in the code itself – "the appropriate package of property rights also appears at the level of code. That is the right that matters. That is the right that is saleable" (p.1077). Thus, the property rights should be recognised at the level of code. Note however, that the considerations made by Fairfield are for virtual property in general.

It is imperative to import Fairfield theory to the context of Virtual Worlds, and apply it specifically.

Code, in this context, means the material stored in some server. This material, in computer language, is the palpable counterpart of the virtual object. It is stored somewhere in a computer owned by the developer of the VW. Such material can be divided in two types. Firstly, there is the software created by the VW developers. Secondly, there is the data created by third parties, namely residents of VW. It is about the latter that problems arise. Residents should have access to the code of their property and oppose the access by others, should be able to delete it and oppose to the deletion of it, etc.

The property of the user is divided in two moments. The first one is when he can access his virtual objects in the VW environment. Secondly, those objects are materialised in a computer owned by the VW developer. Thus, the property of code must be brought into compliance with the right of possessing the code by the owner of the VW, as that code will be kept in the VW server. However, the user must keep a range of rights concerning his property.

So, to achieve a proper property right, the proprietor should hold a strong power. This means that he shall keep more than the mere intellectual property rights on the virtual items. He must hold actual property rights on the code that correspond to his virtual objects.

Thus, property of virtual objects shall give the owner several rights, namely (Hunt, 2007, pp.162-164):

- *Right to Exclude* – which can be achieved through Code itself;
- *Right to Transfer* – residents could sell or offer the property, including through means different than the VW (for instance: auction sites)
- *Right to Own and Possess* – inside the VW and in the real world. In the real world it should mean to own the Code, however possessing it in cooperation with the developer.

This section has attempted to demonstrate that virtual property is indeed actual property: "these types of objects are indistinguishable from other legally recognized property interests" (Lastowka & Hunter, in press, p.13). Each object placed in a virtual world is an object subject to the right of property. To whom belongs such property? "Regardless of how the property is conceptualized and what theory it best fits under, most, if not all, commentators agree the law ought to recognize virtual property as property and vest someone with those rights" (Vacca, 2008, p.3). Developers of virtual worlds try to settle this with the EULA, which I now turn to consider.

EULA

Having concluded that property rights exist in the context of virtual worlds, it is time to question where such rights lay. This question does not have a straightforward answer, mainly because VW is a closed environment. To go in-world a user must *log in* to a service provided by the developer, in the case of SL, that occurs through a piece of software. This is a feature of closed environment property.

The use of this Service is always regulated by terms presented by the developer to the user, who must agree to it, in order to have access to the world in the first place. Such terms are usually called End User License Agreement (EULA) or, simply, Terms of Use (ToS).

Users will be in different countries and so in different jurisdictions. The first problem faced to enforce the EULA is its interpretation. Depending on the jurisdiction, provisions of the EULA will, probably, be interpreted differently.

Among other things, the EULA manages the allocation of the property rights. As the EULA is written by the service provider it is expectable that it is more favourable to this party. Indeed, the paradigm is users not keeping any property rights.

This is justified by not considering virtual property to be actual property, or simply for unspecified and possibly spurious "security" reasons.

Fears of Developers

Usually proprietors of virtual worlds do not concede any rights to users because they fear three things (Vacca, 2008, pp.19-20).

First, proprietors fear the liability of possible losses of property of residents or players. Loss of virtual property might have their origin in software problems, viruses or some incompatibility. If this property belongs to the VW proprietor, there

should be no problem of liability; however if it belongs to the user, he could sue the VW owner.

However, I would add that if the property right is on the developers' sphere they might be subject to other types of liability. For example, because of copyright infringement of objects made by residents.[3] If they hand out such property, there would be no room for law suits.

Secondly, the developers might fear the loss of control of the Virtual World. This means that: "their need to develop and expand the virtual environment necessitates locking out private property interests" (Fairfield, 2005, p.1097). This could be easily solved with a well-elaborated EULA which could specify "limitations on users' virtual property exist or the scope of the licenses the users must grant to developers" (Vacca, 2008, p.20).

Finally, it is pointed that granting property rights to residents could drive the developers to have to "innovate at a faster pace to keep their users' interests" (Vacca, 2008, p.21). This will not necessarily happen – if tools to generate content are in reach of users, they will innovate the world by themselves. Users will create new things, not demanding anything from the VW developers and that will "feed" other users thirst for content.

I believe that only the fear of liability is a meaningful worry. But, even for this, solutions can be found. One example is that presented by Vacca (2008) who proposes the creation of a safe harbour for VW developers.

Second Life innovated, perhaps because they understood this problem. Linden Lab decided to grant some rights to residents of Second Life. Indeed, as there is no defined storyline, there is no fear of loss of control or of need of innovation. In fact, something like "an estimated 99% of SL content is user-generated" (Camp, 2007, p.7).

Innovation of Second Life

The innovation brought by SL was granting to users certain intellectual property rights. However, is not clear exactly which rights residents keep;

the Terms of Service are not a great help in this matter (Sutin, 2007).

SL develops by the content generated by users. The service provides tools that allow users to produce objects within the virtual worlds. The difference in this virtual world is that users keep the intellectual property rights on what they produce.[4] SL Terms of Service (ToS) state:

3.2 You retain copyright and other intellectual property rights with respect to Content you create in Second Life, to the extent that you have such rights under applicable law. (...) you will retain any and all applicable copyright and other intellectual property rights with respect to any Content you create using the Service.

Several rights and licenses are also granted in favour of Linden Lab and the other users of SL. Term 3.2. grants the "perpetual and irrevocable right to delete any or all of your Content from Linden Lab's servers and from the Service, whether intentionally or unintentionally, and for any reason or no reason, without any liability of any kind to you or any other party".

Even if those dispositions impose some limitations, they do not collide totally with the property rights. Thus, from the referred dispositions, even being minded that they limit user rights, one should infer that the user detains property rights on the virtual objects created by him.

However, such a conclusion is contested by a later ToS term – 3.3:

[Y]ou do not own the account you use to access the Service, nor do you own any data Linden Lab stores on Linden Lab servers (including without limitation any data representing or embodying any or all of your Content). Your intellectual property rights do not confer any rights of access to the Service or any rights to data stored by or on behalf of Linden Lab.

This term intends users not to *own any data embodying his own content*. So, even if the user has the intellectual property rights of the object, the ToS establishes that she does not own it. This happens because the object is materialised in the code, placed on Linden Lab computers; and, as pointed above, code is the base of virtual property rights.

For the purposes of taxation, is not enough to focus on the goods made by the user. What matters is profit, therefore all property is important – including goods owned by the user but produced by someone else.

Related to the objects created by other users, term 3.2 of the ToS states:

[S]ubmitting your Content to any area of the Service, you automatically grant (or you warrant that the owner of such Content has expressly granted) to Linden Lab and to all other users of the Service a non-exclusive, worldwide, fully paid-up, transferable, irrevocable, royalty-free and perpetual License, under any and all patent rights you may have or obtain with respect to your Content, to use your Content for all purposes within the Service. (emphasis added)

This means that the ToS, "grants residents a mere license to use copies of others' creations" (Lederman, 2007, p.1656). This implies that no property rights shall be held relating to objects made by others, even detaining its possession (or a copy of it).

Analysing the treatment given to either self-made and other user's objects, one concludes that "Second Life ToS implicitly attempts to create different types of property, expressly recognizing **substantial rights only in residents' own creations**" (Lederman, 2007, p.1641) (emphasis added).

Thus, the user will have access to the object only by a license of use. When a user sells a virtual item it is giving the other user a license to use a copy of the item (or the item itself). This has impact for taxation purposes, as owning a license is not having the right of property.

Nevertheless the SL ToS, or indeed any EULA, is not free standing law. Firstly, the SL ToS may be considered unconscionable. It is important to determine if the ToS is an adhesion contract, what can drive some of its terms to be unlawful. Finally, one has to bear in mind that the concept of property takes precedence over the ToS. These three issues are considered below.

Putting the EULA in its Place

Looking at the terms of SL EULA it is arguable that they are inconsiderate towards virtual property in three different aspects: (1) *ownership*; (2) *rights of transfer and deletion*; (3) *value* (Hunt, 2007, pp.150-152).

Is this acceptable in the context of a contract? This is of major importance to taxation purposes. Lederman (2007) accepts that this point has impact as "the [U.S.] federal income tax questions turn partly on whether participants are transacting in property" (p.1641).

One argument supporting the validity of the ToS might be that, despite the apparent harshness of the terms, residents freely accepted them.

However, this is not clear. If terms are too restrictive they might be unlawful, and consequently rejected by courts, namely if they are "overly restrictive upon economic interests of participants within the world" (Lastowka & Hunter, in press, p.68).

Simply put, EULA terms will be valid until it is considered to be a contract of adhesion. In fact, there are some who consider that the SL ToS is in fact a contract of adhesion (Fairfield, 2005). In Bragg v Linden[5] a court of Pennsylvania found the arbitration clause unconscionable because the ToS were a contract of adhesion.

Besides unconscionability, one can find two other important contractual issues with the EULA: *misrepresentation* and *estoppel* (Hunt, 2007, pp.153-155).

Contracts of Adhesion

The EULA sets one-sided rules for the use of VW, but is this unfair?

A user must agree with the EULA in the form of a click-wrap contract. This contract is pre-written and there is no chance of the user negotiating individual clauses. The contract is the same for every user, and all must agree with it – it is a 'standard form contract'. Thus, in this case, users see their power of bargaining limited to effectively nothing.

Of course, in the market usually consumers don't have much choice to argue about the content of a contract – for the TV service, train ticket, etc. This is no different; although usually they can select from several providers. This fact makes the protection of the consumer all the more crucial.

The user pays a service and makes a contract with a provider, so the user is a consumer. In the European Union, this matter is regulated by the Unfair Contract Terms Directive.[6] The Directive, in its preamble, approaches consumer protection in the sense that "acquirers of goods and services should be protected against the abuse of power by the seller or supplier, in particular against one-sided standard contracts and the unfair exclusion of essential rights in contracts".

In its article 3(1), the Directive states:

A contractual term which has not been individually negotiated shall be regarded as unfair if, contrary to the requirement of good faith, it causes a significant imbalance in the parties' rights and obligations arising under the contract, to the detriment of the consumer.

None of the EULA terms were negotiated with the user; so, there was no 'individual negotiation'. Furthermore, the situation in question can be subsumed to the first part of the article 3(2) of the Directive.[7]

More than that, to be seen as unfair, terms must be contrary to the good faith and causing a significant imbalance.

To assess the good faith, the preamble of the Directive provides further guidance. It is not in the scope of this chapter to analyse the concept of good faith in the context of the Directive. However, I find it arguable to consider that the content of some EULA terms violate that concept. Namely, the terms in the SL ToS concerning property and Linden Dollars – for instance, terms 3.2. and 3.3.

There is the issue of significant imbalance in favour of the provider, as proved above: indeed, SL ToS reserve too many rights to Linden Lab in prejudice of the residents.

The fact that some individual terms may be unfair is not fatal to the contract as a whole. The terms not considered unfair should remain untouched, enforceable, as defined by the article 6(1) of the Directive.

Yet, enforcement measures should be stressed to prevent further use of unfair terms. This means that Linden Lab should be obliged, by the Directive, to remove abusive terms from the ToS presented to European users. See article 7(1) of the same Directive.

Most EULA terms appear to impose limitations to the right of property, as seen. Property law rules exist to avoid undesirable external effects to the right of property[8], especially by contract. Therefore, if property rights exist, it was not expected to see it conveyed to the developer, owner of the VW, merely due to a EULA.

This section has argued that the SL ToS, and possibly other EULAs, are contracts of adhesion. When found that terms are unfair, for the sake of consumer protection, they should be removed. Thus, the EULA does not override property law; what means that it cannot take the property from the resident and give it to the developer. As such, virtual property rights exist and belong to the user. Whilst here, the SL ToS was analysed, the findings of this section can easily be applied to other VW EULAs.

2. Electronic Money

The second key issue to analyse is the possibility that virtual currency is electronic money, which is a question with a growing debate. "[S]pecial circumstances might mean that new forms of money might arise to meet the needs of a new economy" (Birch, 2007a). As a "new form of money", law considers electronic money as *real money* – namely to what concerns to taxation.

Electronic money is a new way of looking at money. One can argue that more than being a *replacement* it is an alternative to "physical cash in the shape of coins and banknotes with an electronic equivalent" (Guadamuz & Usher, 2005, p.174), set by evolution of new technologies.

In the European Union, the framework for electronic money is the Electronic Money Directive[9] (EMD). It defines electronic money in article 1.3(b), setting four elements:

- monetary value;
- stored on an electronic device;
- issued on receipt of funds of an amount not less in value than the monetary value issued;
- accepted as means of payment by undertakings other than the issuer.

Analysis of each of these elements is necessary to determine if virtual currency is e-money, as defined by the directive, using the example of SL.

Monetary Value

Monetary value is commonly accepted as the property of having material worth. Doubts might arise when approaching that concept of material worth in an environment like SL.

Linden Dollars are used to buy virtual objects in SL. If your avatar owns currency he can go to *virtual stores* (that can be owned by other avatar, or by actual brands: -such as Reuters, Bershka among others) and buy something like *clothes*, *shoes*, *cars*, but also *hair* or *skin*. Here is the point of intangibility again, as referred above.

Secondly, one should not forget the SL market place, called LindeX, where one can exchange *real Dollars* for *Linden Dollars*, and vice-versa. This will be dealt below.

Therefore, if L$ have material worth, they also have monetary value.

Stored on an Electronic Sevice

There are many ways to store e-money *on an electronic device* (Guadamuz & Usher, 2005); however, I will look only at those relevant in the context of SL.

Each resident of Second Life has their own account, where information about several issues is stored– like the avatar, Linden Dollar and land owned. So, it's easy to fit this situation into the *Account-based* technology of storing electronic money that is characteristic for, "consumers having access to an account by means of user authentication" (Guadamuz & Usher, 2005, p. 177).

Recital 5 of the EMD states that the Directive is "technology-neutral" considering the "wider context of the rapidly evolving electronic commerce". This must mean that the Directive intends to be applicable to the broadest scope of technologies possible. Thus, it would be wrong to argue that a virtual world account is different from the concept of an *electronic storage device*.

Amount no Less in Value than the Monetary Value Issued

In contrast to the two first criteria, the remaining elements are more debatable.

The wording of art.1/3(b) ii) of the Directive, "issued on a receipt of funds of an amount not less in value than the monetary value issued", must mean that e-money issued can't be more valuable than the amount of money paid for it. One can infer that the objective is to "deter issuers from creating artificial value by giving out more e-money

than customers pay for" (Kohlbach, 2004). The concern here is to avoid the issuer of e-money becoming a credit institution, what would throw it to an "entirely different regulatory system" (Guadamuz & Usher, 2005, p.175).

Further, "no less in value" means that it can be higher in value. In another words, one might pay more to the issuer than the monetary value of e-money issued. So, this means that there is a chance of the issuer gaining some profit, as defended by Kohlbach (2004)[10], though opposed by Guadamuz and Usher (2005)[11].

Now, one should understand how to acquire Linden Dollar currency; how the virtual currency is issued, to find if the requirement is respected. Thus, two different issues should be considered – the membership and the exchange system of the currency.

Membership

To become a *full citizen* of the Second Life community, one must acquire 'Premium Membership'. This plan is based on a monthly payment (although one can pay by semester or by year). This scheme attributes among other things, some Linden Dollars to the avatar (to one's account).

Here, one is paying to have an *unlimited* access to the virtual world, and with that comes an extra – some L$; one is not paying *Dollars* to get *Linden Dollars*: here the requirement does not have to be fulfilled.

It is still important to analyse the situation. Membership[12] costs approximately $10/month (L$ 2600). The avatar will earn: -$3,85 (L$1000) one time; -and, $1,16 (L$300) per week. The amount paid is certainly not lower than the amount issued, so here the problem doesn't arise.

However, in the "First Basic" membership, the resident does not pay anything (it is the membership anyone gets when opening an account in SL) and still receives, once, L$250. This is the equivalent to $0,96, so it is next to worthless. But, once again, I believe in this situation the requirement (of the Directive) does not apply.

Exchange System

SL provides a service, LindeX, to exchange *real money* for L$.

The value of L$ is not always the same. It is defined by the market place (LindeX), where, as in any *real* market place, the *price of money* can go up as well as down. When one wants to buy L$, fees apply. In the end, one will get less L$ than what he has paid for.

This is a way of 'Linden Lab' making some profit, respecting, as seen above, the third requirement about electronic money.

Is important to notice that today LindeX is not the only place to trade L$. Other market places can be found on the Internet.[13]

Accepted as Means of Payment by Undertakings Other Than the Issuer

One should question whether L$ are only accepted by the issuer ('Linden Lab'). The key point here is the fact that the use of L$ is limited to SL environment.

Nevertheless, when one purchases something inside the virtual world he is dealing with someone, another resident, that's on the *other side of the line*. Those people and companies accept L$... Is that enough to fulfil this requirement?

Every move in the *world* of SL is made under the auspices of SL itself, or if you prefer of 'Linden Lab'. This is the starting point.

A sale of a *virtual object* is made, let's say, between two avatars. There will be a direct exchange of L$ from one avatar to another. 'Linden Lab' won't even notice that exchange. In fact most products and services available to purchase in SL are not provided by 'Linden Lab', whom only offers the "Service". In a nutshell, when a virtual object is made available in SL for purchase by an avatar, the "Service" of Second Life will offer a product that, in fact, is provided by a third party (another avatar or company).

The Analogy

The position of SL being a medium where a third party product is made available to the user may be considered analogue to what happens with Mobile Network Operators (MNO). In this case, mobile phone users buy products such as ringtones, music files and images through the MNO. Although users make the purchase via the MNO service, those products are provided by a third party.

In fact, the way Casanova (2006) describes MNO reality – "mobile network operators (MNOs) who offer products and services on mobile phones provided by third parties" can be extended to SL.

While today there is no real debate or regulation about the application of the EMD to virtual worlds, that is not the case with MNO. "[T]here is an ongoing debate over whether the provisions of the E-Money Directive apply to certain 'hybrid issuers', who offer electronic payment services to compliment their core business, such as with MNOs" (Casanova, 2006). One should determine if VW can also be a *hybrid issuer*.

The application of the EMD to MNO is still uncertain. For example, a report concerning the review of the EMD[14] refers to art.1/3(b)iii of the Directive that, "The definition will need to be clarified in this respect to ensure that the same services carrying the same systemic and consumer risks are subject to the same rules...".

The strongest argument in favour of the non-application of the EMD to the MNO to relates to the fact that the payment is made directly to it and not to the actual *seller*. "MNOs argue that the E-Money Directive does not apply where the payment is made direct by a customer to the MNO" (Casanova, 2006). Nevertheless this problem is not important to our analysis – in SL the payment is made directly to the *seller*.

But even if it was relevant, MNO argument is debatable, since there are those who argue that "the 'transfer' of e-money is also fulfilled for the purposes of the Directive if the transfer is done indirectly (through the MNO)" (Mansour, 2007).

I consider that electronic money applies to the MNOs. Furthermore, the most relevant position is that presented by the DG Internal Market in the report "Application of the E-money Directive to mobile operators" of 2004: "the e-value stored on mobile phone pre-paid cards that is used to pay third party products and services is indeed likely to be e-money".

The DG Internal Market report states that "products and services are supplied by an undefined number of merchants, which are not necessarily controlled or linked to the mobile operator". One can easily fit, "not necessarily controlled or linked to", to the developer of VW.

The analysis of this fourth criterion is not straightforward since it "has proved the most problematic in practice" (Casanova, 2006), and it "is arguably the [criterion] most open to interpretation", in the words of the Commission Staff Working Document. But, summarising, I believe that using mobile phone credit to purchase third part goods fulfils the criteria of being accepted by someone other than the issuer. Simultaneously, MNO and SL realities are alike. Thus, I must conclude that Linden Dollars fulfil the criterion now analysed.

I have undertaken an objective analysis of the issues surrounding L$, and concluded that this is *real* electronic money. Addressing each requirement the EMD sets for electronic money, I found it easily L$ meets each requirement.

Conclusions made about L$ are extendable to other VW currencies. The four elements will be found, in general, in an unscripted world currency, making it electronic money. In the case of scripted worlds, like World of Warcraft, a deeper analysis should be undertaken, particularly in the case of the fourth criterion.

EMI Requirements and Redeemability

The EMD requirements for 'Electronic Money Institution' and Redeemability will not be analysed in depth here.

The EMD, (see particularly article 4), sets a number of requirements for the issuer of e-money, with the goal of protecting consumers by ensuring the *financial integrity* of the issuer of the Electronic Money Institutions (EMI). "[T]he main aim of the E-Money Directive was to introduce the necessary regime to ensure the financial integrity of non-bank issuers of electronic money without stifling developments, and at the same time protecting consumers" (Casanova, 2006). If VW developers, such as Linden Lab, issue virtual currency, that is e-money; then, at a first glance, there are two possibilities: developers should become EMIs; -or, they should stop issuing L$.

However, some of EMI requirements are very strict. This approach results in stifling development. For instance, it is not understandable that EMI requirements apply to MNO – "the application of the Directive to MNOs would be disproportionate to the risks and would fail to recognise that third party payments only account for a very small percentage of pre-paid funds for MNOs" (Casanova, 2006). The same reasoning should be used when addressing VW and specifically the issue of Linden Lab becoming an EMI.

Secondly, art.3 of the EMD addresses redeemability as a characteristic of electronic money. Electronic money should be exchangeable for "coins and bank notes or by a transfer to an account" (emphasis added). For most SL players this is what occurs in the virtual world, in LindeX. However, in article 1.4 of the ToS, Linden Lab, not innocently, state that L$ are not "redeemable for any sum of money or monetary value from Linden Lab at any time".

The legal redeemability requirement is acceptable, but should not be understood to be very strictly. It ends addressing to the issue of barter transactions, dealt below. Thus, redeemability should be held in a lower extent. There should not be a requirement that electronic money be convertible at any and all times.

The Terms of Service relating to Electronic Money leads us to a discussion concerning the EULA, as it would be unconscionable to allow Linden Lab to regulate all aspects of users' e-money (See article 5.3 of ToS).

Being L$ electronic money, and belonging to the users of SL, Linden Lab must abstain from exercising such power. This causes uncertainty to the holders of this "value". The same applies to the regulation of LindeX; article 1.5 of ToS allows Linden Lab to do anything at its *sole discretion*. However, such a terms should be considered unfair, thus unenforceable. Considerations made about the EULA in a previous section fit here.

III. Taxation

1. Taxation Issues

A simplistic consideration of tax law might cause one to think that those rules have no application to VW, for two main reasons. Firstly, there are no objects (or property) in a material way. Furthermore, frequently trade in VW will relate to an exchange of virtual objects and will not involve currency and, even where it does, some argue that such virtual currency is not real money.

There is no validity to such arguments. Firstly, there is no need of tangibility in trade for taxation purposes. Indeed, above I devoted a section to prove that property rights can subsist in virtual property.

Secondly, the exchange of objects forms a barter exchange, which is taxable:

You do not have to receive currency in order to generate a profit from a sale. If you are paid 'in-kind', you may still have been paid from a tax point of view. You could be taxed on the 'fair value' of what you receive even though it is not immediately convertible into money. (Nuttall, 2007)

VW are much more than a social environment. Freedom given to residents in unscripted worlds is a key determinant that allows them to produce, sell and buy objects. This offers a whole 'game reality' which can be accessed with money, in-world. This means that in-world commerce plays a vital role too:

Current estimates suggest that the economies of the world's major online multi-user environments could have been worth more than US$2 billion in 2006. In July 2007, there were over 12.5 million transactions in Second Life alone, all of which had real money value. And, at the same time as some people are making money in-world, others may be losing it; in August 2007, Ginko Financial, a virtual bank, collapsed with approximately US$740,000 in liabilities. (Naylor & Jaworski, 2007, p.1)

The amount of money exchanged in-world makes one wonder if it should be considered solely a 'game' or entertainment place, for even millionaires have been made there.[15]

The expectation of growth and possible establishment of businesses inside VW should make us realise that such an environment cannot remain untouched by law.

One should bear in mind several problems might arise in the unregulated environment of VW. Tax evasion may especially be a problem: "If sales of virtual items for Lindens were untaxed, the enforcement difficulties would also give rise to opportunities for intentional tax evasion" (Lederman, 2007, p.1668).

Despite this, law should not be used to try and regulate all matters.

What should this mean when considering tax law? If one finds a large number of transactions and profit-making in VW, tax should be considered. However, it cannot be the intention of the law to regulate every individual trade. The critical point here is that entertainment should not be taxed, but profit should generally be taxed.

Today, businesses based online face different regulation from conventional offline business. It might be a mistake to try to regulate VW strictly by these general rules, as the realities now appear so different.

In fact, Virtual Worlds are a unique form, for which there is no specific legislation to deal with, but neither should there be. Before devising a *'Virtual Worlds law'* one should try to determine the similarities and differences between VW and other realities, already regulated by law.

The argument presented here is that VW are analogous to e-commerce – these regulations shall be considered here.

E-Commerce Regulations

VAT

From an EU perspective, one should consider EU Council Directive 2006/112/EC of 28 November 2006 on the common system of value added tax (VAT Directive), as amended by Directive 2006/138/CE.

VAT is a consumption tax on the supply of goods and services. VAT is "designed, as a single consumption tax for the whole of the European Union, to be effective across, borders between businesses, and ultimately consumers" (Craig, 2001, para.3.3).

VAT treatment will vary with the categorisation of the transaction object in 'goods' or 'services'. This presents a challenge to the approach to virtual property, and will be considered below. Presently, it is important to notice that "under presently agreed international rules for e-commerce, products in digitised format (...) are bizarrely categorised as services..." (Craig, 2001, para.3.5).

The VAT taxation will vary, also, depending on the form of supply (for business [B2B] or for consumer [B2C]) and the place of supply (Eden, 2005).

Income Tax

The electronic environment does not generate so many difficulties with respect to Income tax as it does in the case of VAT. Here the tax falls upon the profit; if a person has made a profit they will be taxed regardless of the way of obtaining it (online or offline).

Cyberspace brings an issue about income tax that is not different in virtual worlds and in electronic commerce. It is the point of the *tax nexus* between the profits and a State. "E-commerce presents problems for this methodology because in electronic trading it is questionable to what extent an electronic presence can be said to constitute a tax nexus" (Craig, 2001, para.3.13). This is no different to what happens in a VW environment, and will be considered within the solution presented.

In spite of this possible regulatory approach to VW, some other solutions are possible. In the next section I will point to those potential solutions, and explain why they are not preferred.. Following this, I will consider if transactions in VW can be considered within the definition of ordinary electronic commerce and the relevant rules can be applied.

Cash-Out Rule

Despite the scarcity of scholarly work in the area, some helpful concepts have emerged.

One example is the 'betting theory', by which the income earned in VW is due to a prize or betting system. Thus, taxing income from a VW would be the same as taxing income from a bet or prize. However, this option is not suitable for unscripted worlds like SL, "unless you can show, say, significant instability in the Second Life environment" (Nuttall, 2007), what is not the case.

The most important theory is the cash-out rule (Camp, 2007; Lederman, 2007). As the name indicates, this theory looks at the moment of exchanging virtual currency into actual currency as the moment to apply the taxation.

"When the play ceases, taxation begins" (Camp, 2007, p.2). This means that transactions which take place inside the world should not be taxed.

Camp (2007) argues that the cash-out rule, or *Taxing Real Money Trades (RMT)*, is the best option both for scripted and unscripted worlds. He analysis the three limits on the legal concept of income (in the US context), where he comes to the conclusion that most of the in-world transactions are imputed income, and as such they should not be taxed.

For his theory, the author builds a 'magical circle', a 'fourth wall' that represents the boundaries of the virtual world. If there is respect for such boundaries, the taxation should not be an issue. So, Camp (2007) states that "There is time enough to tax Leeroy and Zelda when they cash out, when the magic circle is broken, the fourth wall breached" (p.63). He understands that *usable profit* will exist only when there is cash-out.

Problems

There are several problems with this approach – the most important concerns the limitations of the fourth wall.

Trading L$ for real-life objects is not a hypothesis, it is a reality. And this reality jeopardises the cash-out rule, as the author himself suggested. For example, in a Portuguese university the issue of payments made in-world for real world sweaters arose.[16] In a previous section, it was pointed that, in the U.S., the National Taxpayer Advocate Annual Report refers that "businesses now accept virtual dollars in exchange for real property or services".

Camp (2007) accepts that the trade of L$ for real-life objects would bring the fourth wall down, and so in-world transactions should be taxed – "The most likely evidence of that shift will be when account owners gain the ability to trade Linden Dollars for goods and services that are useful outside of Second Life, beyond the fourth wall" (p.69).

Moreover, it is not difficult to imagine a future where L$, or other virtual currency are a legitimate payment option among others, like PayPal. For example, eBay could allow its users to meet in-world and change L$ for a product, such as a CD, DVD or book.

Another problem with the cash-out rule is the risks of allowing a tax-free environment online. This easily can lead to cases of fraud, tax evasion, or money laundering (Birch, 2007c).

Advantages

Nevertheless the cash-out rule has a number of advantages.

Taxation should be devised in a way to tax profit but not entertainment, i.e. fun or joy *per se*. By taxing RMT there is no risk of taxing someone who is in-world just for fun and will not be making any profit on that activity. When the resident is 'cashing-out' he is looking to extract value and bring it into the real world, so he is more than merely entertaining himself.

That goal, of taxing only profit, is achieved by another feature of this rule: it avoids taxation of exchanges that do not involve any money. Accordingly, even if residents have the right of property on virtual objects, they will not be taxed on the mere exchange of such objects.

In contrast, applying in-world taxation, even if the goal is to tax only money-transactions, the exchange of objects will also be taxed, as barter exchanges are also taxable. This makes it difficult to separate transactions that happen purely for fun from those where the user intends to make profit.

Looking for an alternative taxation option I will regard such issues, to make sure that the proposed solution is as useful in these matters as the cash-out rule.

2. The Solution

The previous section questioned the usefulness of the cash-out rule. Indeed, I conclude that it is not an adequate solution, and I support an in-world taxation mechanism.

One is dealing with a virtual environment. Nevertheless, I concluded that *actual property* exists and such property is traded with *actual money*. Thus, the only issue that is different from trading in a VW as compared to trading in real world is the medium i.e. the context where trade happens.

Trade happening in a different form from in-person is not new, starting with the long-distance sales, by post or phone, ending in electronic commerce. Trading in VW is very close to trading in conventional electronic commerce.

The best aspect of this analogy with traditional electronic commerce is that tax law already can cope with it. So, it is time to determine if these taxation rules can apply to VW trades.

Knowing that most of in-world transactions are made by avatars that are owned by individuals that are not merchants, one can conclude that in-world trading is mainly C2C commerce. In this sense, VW are very similar to C2C commerce sites such as eBay. eBay is already regulated for tax purposes, so one should find if such regulations are capable of dealing with VW.

Note that in VW there will be also some B2C commerce, as is the case with eBay.

HMRC (2007) issued guidance on the taxation of online sales in the UK, such as eBay. This can be used as the starting point for the taxation in the case of VW. Note that in the following discussion, legislation considered will be, mainly drawn from the EU.

Income Tax

The first point to consider is the act of trading. One will be trading, according to the HMRC (2007), if she:

- sells goods you have bought for resale
- makes items yourself and sell them, intending to make a profit

Applying this to the VW environment is quite straightforward. A resident who buys a virtual object with the purpose of selling it again is trading. The same applies to someone that creates virtual objects with the intention to gain profit.

However, the guide states, one is not trading when selling "occasional, unwanted personal items through Internet auctions or classified advertisements" and, I would add, VW.

In the UK, if a person is trading, she will be considered self-employed and will be taxed according to the Income Tax (Trading and Other Income) Act 2005.

If one considers a company, then it will be charged taxes under the Income and Corporation Taxes Act 1988 on profits "arising or accruing from any trade whether carried on in the UK or elsewhere" (Nuttall, 2007), including I would argue, VW.

Whilst it is difficult to connect profit made in a VW to a state, this is really no different to concerning profits made in a website such as eBay.

However, in the case of VW there is an issue that might help defining such a *tax nexus*. The server that a resident must log into to access the VW might be a useful means of tracking the *tax nexus*.

This might be a good example of the role of code as part of the enforcement of taxation rules in VW. Above I referred that Code, as conceptualised by Lessig (2006), might be a good way of enforcing regulation of VW. Keeping a record of the server where the user logs on might be an important way of finding the *tax nexus*.

VAT

When considering VAT, one must determine, are virtual items services or goods? (Craig, 2001, para.3.5.).

The answer to that question will determine which tax rules apply.

Accepting that right of property on virtual property exists, virtual items can be seen as goods, and indeed they are referred to as 'virtual goods'.

Furthermore, this categorisation is the best option: "There would be no need for uneasy re-categorisations, merely to treat the supply of a software package online the same way as the supply of the same package in a computer store: as supply of goods" (Craig, 2001, para.3.7.).

Even so, to make sure that the specific nature of taxation of non-corporeal goods do not escape VAT "cross border supply of goods from out with the EU would require to be re-written" (Craig, 2001, para.3.7.).

Therefore, the supply of virtual goods should be taxed in the same extent as material goods.

Thus, considering virtual property as goods, consumers will be taxed the VAT of the country of the supplier, in an in-EU transaction. If the consumer is from outside the EU the supply is zero-rated. Finally, if an EU consumer buys from outside the EU, the costumer should account for VAT on import.

Note that if a resident is trading he should keep records of his transactions and will have to register for VAT and pay it, if in a 12 month period the supplies exceed the annual VAT registration threshold.

This paper does not address enforcement issues. However, it should be acknowledge that the developers of the VW can create a system for users to keep records of transactions for purposes of helping authorities to enforce the law.

Once again, Code could be used to create a record of user transactions for purposes of taxation. Security of data and privacy must be a high priority, therefore, access to the record should be permitted only if there was some proof of undeclared transactions by the user.

3. ADVANTAGES OF THE SOLUTION

Extending the legal solution of taxing electronic commerce to the VW environment is desirable for several reasons.

Firstly, it easily allows VW to move fully within the scope of the law. Large amounts of money currently move through VWs and this is likely to continue rise in the immediate future.

Secondly, this is a mechanism for regulating VWs without creating significantly more regulations and laws, as I am simply expanding the scope of the eBay analogy.

This is not a very invasive approach; it is of the most importance that the law does not try to specifically deal with every particular issue. Further, I stress that profit should be taxed, but not mere leisure.

Considering income tax, if a person is trading, the income earned online will be considered for tax purposes. It must be stressed that, in general, the amount generated in the activity in a VW is quite small.

About VAT, most of the times, it will not even be taxed. This happens because VAT will only be charged if transactions are above a certain limit. This amount will not be normally achieved by someone selling virtual goods just for fun, and on an occasional basis.

A person trading objects in eBay just for fun shall not be in the range of the threshold, and will not pay any tax. Virtual items are, generally cheap and indeed much cheaper than material property. Thus, even a user making exchanges in a regular basis in a VW will not break through the tax thresholds. Only when those exchanges stop being incidental could be taxes applied.

This proposed solution creates few additional burdens for the average VW user. Most users probably will feel no impact whatsoever. In addition, for VW infrastructure, this solution does not bring any special additional liability. The developers could create an automated system to track the amount of transactions made, but the VW would not have to be changed in any way.

The solution defines an in-world taxation system. It copes with all concerns stressed by the defenders of the cash-out rule. It does not put VW user under an undue regulatory burden, they just have to keep record of transactions (what can be undertaken automatically by the Service) and only in limited circumstances will be subject to pay taxes. A user that uses a VW just for fun, trading every once in a while does not even have to worry about paying taxes, exactly in the same as people trading occasionally in eBay.

CONCLUSION

The issue of VW taxation has attracted many fans of the cash-out rule. However, I believe this option has two problems: it does not look at VW as a possibly evolving area nor as a reality which is fused with the 'real world'. These two problems were considered.

It is expectable that VW will evolve in different ways, Today, one sees closed VWs, and regard them as something similar to a game. The concept of VW should become more ubiquitous in the world of internet, namely with the opening of social networks.[17] The features of VW, as a social and trading place, with a virtual presence of users and virtual currency, shall spread beyond the terms of a mere game.

VWs growingly fusion with the real world has made the application of real world law to these VWs uncertain and opaque.

The existence of "new issues" generated by VW might tempt us to create specific 'VW law'. However, first, all remaining options should be weighted. This thesis shows that VW are close to other realities. Indeed, VWs are strongly fusing with other online places and with 'real world' – one important example pointed to in this chapter is the Mobile Network Operators.

This paper argued that there is right of property in virtual goods. And, in spite of developers trying to keep such property to themselves by means of the EULA, such a right truly belongs to the user. I have found EULAs to contain unenforceable terms as they are unfair. It was further argued that virtual money is electronic money, based, among other arguments, on the analogy created between VW and MNO.

These features demonstrate the fusion between VW and reality, and thus one doesn't need additional, specific laws for VW. Existing legal principles and laws are able to cope with the idea of VW taxation.

Defenders of the cash-out rule present several arguments in support of out-world taxation, namely the need to tax only profit made. Such features are present, also, in the solution proposed in this paper.

My proposed taxation system is applicable not only to Second Life, but to VWs in general, but mainly unscripted VWs. Application of the system to scripted worlds, like World of Warcraft, must be subject to further analysis and was not within the scope of the present chapter.

The conclusions made above might be extended to other realities beyond VW. Such realities may include Social Networks, such as MySpace and Facebook, which may become trading places where users exchange property using social network currency.[18]

New realities should not be underestimated by legal scholars. Something that could resemble a mere game might indeed bring new risks to society. Law must cope with these new situations. Even so, new realities shall not be considered a non-understandable matter or necessarily requiring whole new paradigms.. Analogy brings apparently dissimilar realities together, and avoids the various dangers of over-regulation, such as stifling of development and innovation.

I have no doubt that in the future, there will be further apparent challenges to the established law from new realities and online technologies more generally. However, I have faith in the strength of the existing principles of law and of the regulation of electronic commerce; I am confident that these principles can easily be extended to the taxation of new realities.

REFERENCES

Birch, D. (2005, June). *Opening a Branch in Narnia – You have no idea what is going on the virtual world*. Prepared for the 10th Annual Workshop on Economic Heterogeneous Interacting Agents at the Centre for Computational Finance and Economic Agents (CCFEA) and the University of Essex. Retrieved March 1, 2009, from http://digitaldebateblogs.typepad.com/digital_money/Birch_WEHIA.pdf

Birch, D. (2007a). A new dawn for digital money. *E-finance & payments. Law & Policy, 1*(5).

Birch, D. (2007b). Regulating virtual worlds: current and future issues. *E-Commerce. Law & Policy, 9*(1), 12–13.

Birch, D. (2007c). Virtual Money: Money laundering in virtual worlds: risks and reality. *E-finance & payments. Law & Policy, 1*(7).

Bragg v Linden Research, Inc., 487 F. Supp. 2D 593 (E.D. Pa. 2007).

Camp, B. T. (2007). The Play's the Thing: A Theory of Taxing Virtual Worlds. *The Hastings Law Journal, 59*(1).

Casanova, J. M. (2006). E-Money: EU reform of the E-Money Directive: the current state. *E-finance & payments. Law & Policy, 1*(1).

Commission of the European Communities. (2006). Commission Staff Working Document on the Review of the E-Money Directive (2000/46/EC). *SEC(2006) 1049*. Retrieved April 2, 2009, from http://ec.europa.eu/internal_market/bank/docs/e-money/working-document_en.pdf

Council Directive 2006/112/EC of 28 November 2006 on the common system of value added tax.

Council Directive 2006/138/EC of 19 December 2006 amending Directive 2006/112/EC on the common system of value added tax as regards the period of application of the value added tax arrangements applicable to radio and television broadcasting services and certain electronically supplied services.

Council Directive 93/13/EEC of 5 April 1993 on unfair terms in consumer contracts.

Craig, W. J. (2001). *Taxation of E-Commerce – Fiscal regulation of the Internet*. Tolley LexisNexis.

DG Internal Market. (2004). Application of the E-money Directive to mobile operators. Retrieved April 2, 2009, from http://ec.europa.eu/internal_market/bank/docs/e-money/2004-05-consultation_en.pdf

(2002, October). Directive 2000/46/EC of the European Parliament and of the Council of 18 September 2000 on the taking up, pursuit of and prudential supervision of the business of electronic money institutions. *OJEC, L275*(39), 27.

Dougherty, C., Lastowka, G. (2007). Copyright: Copyright issues in virtual economies. *E-Commerce Law & Policy, 9*(5).

Eden, S. (2005). VAT on Electronic Services Directive 2002/38/EC – Amending VAT Law for Electronic Transactions: A Simple Choice for a Simple Tax? In Edwards, L. (Ed.), *The New Legal Framework for E-Commerce in Europe* (pp. 203–238). Oxford: Hart Publishing.

Fairfield, J. (2005). Virtual Property. *Boston University Law Review 85*, 1047; Indiana Legal Studies Research Paper Number 35. Retrieved March 1, 2009, from http://ssrn.com/abstract=807966

Guadamuz, A., & Usher, J. (2005). Electronic Money: the European regulatory approach. In Edwards, L. (Ed.), *The New Legal Framework for E-Commerce in Europe* (pp. 173–201). Oxford: Hart Publishing.

HM Revenues & Customs. (2007). A guide for people who sell items online, through classified advertisements and at car boot sales. Retrieved April 2, 2009, from http://www.hmrc.gov.uk/guidance/selling/index.htm

Hunt, K. (2007). This Land Is Not Your Land: Second Life, CopyBot, and the Looming Question of Virtual Property Rights. *Texas Review of Entertainment and Sports Law, 9*, 141–173.

Income and Corporation Taxes Act 1988.

Kohlbach, M. (2004). Making Sense of Electronic Money. *The Journal of Information, Law and Technology, 1*.

Lastowka, F. G., & Hunter, H. (in press). The Laws of the Virtual Worlds. *California Law Review*. Retrieved March 1, 2009, from http://papers.ssrn.com/sol3/papers.cfm?abstract_id=402860

Lederman, L. (2007). 'Stanger than fiction': Taxing Virtual Worlds. *New York University Law Review, 82*, 1620–1672.

Lessig, L. (2006). *Code version 2.0*. New York: Basic Books.

Mansour, Y. (2007, April). *The E-Money Directive and MNOs: Why it All Went Wrong*. Prepared for the Bileta 2007 Annual Conference. Retrieved March 1, 2009, from http://www.bileta.ac.uk/Document%20Library/1/The%20E-Money%20Directive%20and%20MNOs%20-%20Why%20it%20All%20Went%20Wrong.pdf

Naylor, D., & Jaworski, A. (2007). Virtual worlds, real challenges. *Entertainment Law Review, 18*(8), 262–264.

Nuttall, G. (2007). Income earned in virtual worlds: taxation issues. *E-Commerce Law & Policy, 9*(5).

Sutin, A. N. (2007). Virtual Worlds: Issues and challenges presented by virtual worlds. *E-Commerce Law & Policy, 9*(3).

Income Tax (Trading and Other Income) Act 2005.

Vacca, R. (2008). Viewing Virtual Property Ownership through the Lens of Innovation. *Tennessee Law Review, 76*.

ENDNOTES

[1] The first MUD is dated from 1978 and still can be played online in www.british-legends.com/

[2] This does not jeopardise the possible future of standardise virtual worlds and the so-called passporting – *check* Kane, S. F. (2007). Virtual Worlds: 'Passporting' of avatars and property between virtual worlds. *E-Commerce Law & Policy, 9*(12).

[3] An example is the "Sex Gen Bed". *Check* Second Life gets its first copyright law suit *OUTLAW,* 17 July 2007. Note that Second Life argued that its users retain intellectual property rights over objects they produce.

[4] Usually users do not retain any intellectual property rights based on the argument that "If a user merely combines a limited number of developer-created objects, the result may be largely dictated by the options provided by the developer rather than by the user's creativity". In some cases however this shouldn't be the case, as "virtual world participants using complex software tools may become authors under copyright law - just as users of Microsoft Word are considered authors." (Dougherty & Lastowka, 2007)

[5] Bragg v Linden Research, Inc., 487 F. Supp. 2D 593 (E.D. Pa. 2007)

[6] Council Directive 93/13/EEC of 5 April 1993 on unfair terms in consumer contracts

[7] "A term shall always be regarded as not individually negotiated where it has been drafted in advance and the consumer has therefore not been able to influence the substance of

the term, particularly in the context of a pre-formulated standard contract."

[8] "The function of property law is in large part to resist contractual limitations on property use" (Fairfield, 2005, p.1084); *Check* Merrill, T. H., & Smith, H. E. (2000). Optimal Standardization in the Law of Property: The Numerus Clausus Principle. *The Yale Law Journal 110*(1)

[9] Directive 2000/46/EC of the European Parliament and of the Council of 18 September 2000 on the taking up, pursuit of and prudential supervision of the business of electronic money institutions. OJEC L275/39, 27 October 2002

[10] "The formulation (...) allows issuers to give out less e-money than customers pay for however. This was identified (...) as one of the ways for an issuer to make a profit" (p. 4).

[11] "The practical effect of this requirement is that it reduces the possibilities of the card issuer to profit from cards from the consumer." (p. 175).

[12] All data from www.secondlife.com, last access on the 31st March 2009. L$ conversion rate used is the one on that day, approximately L$260 for $1.

[13] For instance: www.dreamland.anshechung.com/; www.xstreetsl.com/; www.xchang-e4sl.com (all last access on the 31st March 2009).

[14] Commission Staff Working Document on the Review of the E-Money Directive (2000/46/EC) 19.07.2006 SEC(2006) 1049

[15] "Ailin Graef publicly claimed to have become Second Life's first US dollar millionaire in November 2006, through her in-world operations as property developer 'Anshe Chung', Graef's in-world avatar." (Naylor & Jaworski, 2007, p.1)

[16] In UTAD, "Universidade de Trás-os-Montes e Alto Douro", prof. Leonel Morgado, lecturer of Informatics, intends to set a UTAD store in SL, as a location for Computer Science students to try out pieces of management information systems; having faced the problem of taxation presented me such issues. The objective is to apply the solution proposed in the current chapter to the Portuguese reality in the given case, what is not in the scope of this chapter.

[17] *See* Break down these walls. (2008, March 22). *The Economist, 386*, 18.

[18] Hi5 (www.hi5.com), an U.S.-based social network, already launched a social network currency, even though it is not available for transactions between users.

Chapter 8
Intellectual Property Systems in Software

Ricardo Rejas-Muslera
University of Alcalá, Spain

Elena Davara
Davara & Davara Law, Spain

Alain Abran
University du Quebec, Canada

Luigi Buglione
University du Quebec, Canada

ABSTRACT

Support for research and development in information technology is considered today as critical by most governments in the industrially advanced countries. Traditionally the way of stimulating research has been to ensure to the investor the appropriability of the returns generated. Such appropriability is typically implemented by means of the Intellectual Property Rights. Nevertheless the protection of such rights is heterogeneous worldwide. Today two different legal systems for the protection of software coexist: the system of patents and the system of author's copyrights. This chapter explains these two main systems of 'intellectual property' to provide legal protection to software, including the licenses to transfer rights on software. The end of the chapter presents the most recent trends of the EU government to replace the current European software protection system, including a discussion onf the software patents and the legal initiatives on the subject. In addition, legal issues linked with new ways in software comercialization are presented.

I. INTRODUCTION

Originally, hardware and its corresponding software constituted an indivisible package and the use of early computers was limited to people with solid knowledge in computation, generally scientists or engineers. It was then quite typical for developers to share, interchange and improve software programmes freely: therefore, at that time, software was freely available and shared, not like a commercial transaction but as a personal favour.

DOI: 10.4018/978-1-61520-975-0.ch008

By the end of the 1970s, however, companies began viewing software as an independent product, and they commercialized it independently of the hardware by means of licenses agreements. This strategic move had its origin in IBM's decision of separating the production from software and hardware as a consequence of the pressures exercised by the USA anti-trust authorities (Mowery & Rosenberg, 1998).

Consequently, a new product of a nature entirely different from the hardware appeared: while hardware is a physical or tangible asset, the software presents a logical nature, and therefore it became necessary to look for a new system of legal protection. Initially in order to protect such products, companies decided to block access to the source code They also decided to shield their projects in confidentiality terms to avoid the flight of industrial trade secrets. This new working environment gradually limited the cooperation between programmers and created specific niches according to the necessities of the market.

Nowadays, governments of developed countries consider as extremely important for research and innovation in information technologies to position it as the masterpiece of the industrial economic and social development (Kalakota & Robinson, 2000). Information systems and specifically software are, nowadays, omnipresent in all the human activity's spheres, contributing in the surging, consolidation and future projection of the *Knowledge Era or Third Wave* (Toffler, 1980). The information is, from this perspective, the main asset for the development of the developed economies, and the software the instrument per excellence to treat the information (Faramarz, 2001).

Traditionally, the way of stimulating research and innovation, in any industrial or economic field, is to allow an investor to be involved in the appropriability of the benefits generated by the investment. The appropriability of products and benefits generated by an investment is materialized by the concession of property rights to the investor.

These property rights are appropriate not only to protect the material or tangible assets, but also to intangible or immaterial assets, specifically intellectual assets. Among these intellectual creations, new technologies, and specifically software, occupy a significant role because of their incidence on the development and well-being of modern society. In addition, software has an economic meaning in the sense of production means and as a product. The software industry is related to the codification of knowledge and information, its inputs and outputs being virtually immaterial. The outputs can be products or services, depending on the form in which they are provided. As an intellectual product, the way chosen to protect software was the Intellectual Property Rights. The majority of software was already intellectual property by the '80s.

Even though the intellectual property rights being the elected way, the software legal protection is not homogenous worldwide. At the moment, two normative frameworks or legal systems co-exist to control and protect the development and distribution of software:

1. patent systems in countries such as the USA or Japan, and
2. copyrights in the European Union (EU) and South American countries.

Within this environment, the discussion on the allocation of rights on software has going on within the information systems industry practically since its birth. However, in the 80's the debate intensified about creating appropriate normative frameworks to protect software by means of patents or copyrights.

The main objective of this chapter is to analyze the fundamental characteristics of both legal frameworks for software and, from such analysis, to explore the initiatives to patent software in Europe. More specifically, the second section discusses patents, copyrights and software licenses. The section II begins with an economic analysis of the software-like products and services: this is fundamental to understand its legal regulation. Once the software's legal framework is understood, the third section identifies the legal initiatives to patent software in Europe, examining the possible consequences in terms of market, specially to the free and open source software sector. Finally the *Future Trends* section presents the legal issues linked with new ways in software commercialization.

II. BACKGROUND: COPYRIGHTS AND PATENTS, TWO DIFFERENT SYSTEMS TO PROTECT SOFTWARE

As mentioned in the Introduction, two types of legal systems are currently in force to protect software: patents and copyrights. These two systems show important differences in key aspects such as the protection terms and depth of the recognized rights. But the way of transferring rights in both systems is similar: a specific kind of contracts named software licenses. However prior to discussing the specific of each legal system and corresponding software licenses, an economic understanding of the software industry is necessary: such an analysis enables to understand the legal framework of justification and consequences.

An economic analysis of the cost structures of the software industry allows to understand the fundamentals, the behavior and corresponding deficiencies of the current legal frameworks (patents and copyrights). Moreover, an economic analysis of the market structure of software products and services allows to understand how the legal differences between patents and copyrights move transversally to the markets, configuring very differently the mercantile structures.

1. Economic Issues

The software industry is heading towards the commercialization of knowledge as a raw material for the creation of inventions and new products and services. Even though the actual outputs of the software industry is essentially immaterial, such outputs will take the form of products or services to reach the market (Torrisi, 1998).

In software production the bulk of the costs required for its development are fixed costs and are associated to the R&D required to generate the precise knowledge necessary to come out with an innovative product on the market; with software the marginal costs of production (reproduction of software units) are comparatively negligible (Romer, 1993). This contrasts with what happens in more traditional industries.

In addition, in the software industry the innovative processes have often an accumulative character: i.e. the knowledge generated in the development of a product often serves as a basis for later developments in a cycle of incremental inventions (Hall, 2002). This cost structure generates lack of appropriability, in this context the incentives to invest in research are uncertain, but also providing certain beneficial effects.

On the one hand, two effects might be considered positive across-the-board:

1. The positive effects for the society appear under the form of externalities of knowledge *or spillovers*. In this way the knowledge spreads out in a rapid and easy transition from the innovators to the rest of the society. A significant case of such externalities of knowledge playing a highly beneficial role is the one belonging to the entrepreneurial clusters, considered like one of the most important and efficient business organization's form in the creation of wealth; this is essentially why clusters are entrepreneurial conglomerates which growth and competitiveness is based on the generation and transmission of externalities of knowledge; in turn, they attract other companies and qualified staff generating *spin's* off; it

generates knowledge in a virtuous circle of growth, competitiveness and efficiency.

2. *Increasing returns of scale*: once the product is developed, and once the maximum effort in terms of costs is expanded, the insignificance of the reproduction costs implies sales return practically net.

On the other hand, there is essentially the vulnerability of the rights that protect the knowledge generated; such a flaw configures an economic scenario impacted by appropriability's defects: insignificant reproduction costs imply that the copy of software is very inexpensive and make tremendously easy the systematic follow-up of market strategies. For this reason piracy (i.e. illegal copy of software) is advantageous because only needs insignificant investments in infrastructures in order to replicate the product. Similarly, the lack of appropriability in R&D has a major impact on the software's industry. This situation has been aggravated in recent times by the utilization of Internet as a distribution channel, internet being currently considered as a giant copying machine (Shapiro, 1999).

In addition, the legal system elected to protect software conditions the software market structure.

- Generally, if the elected system is copyrighted, the market tends to be formed by half of small size companies, which live together with large size companies. The protection offered by copyrights is less deep than patents: it is an eminently defensive system.

- In contrast, the patents system can be used as an offensive weapon to raise entry barriers to new competitors.

Such two circumstances favor the emergence of competitive markets. If the elected system is patents-based, the mercantile structure generally gets polarized, favoring the emergence of large size companies and making it difficult for new bidders to enter the market. This trend is clear when comparing the software market structure in Europe (copyrights system) and United States (patent system). This is well illustrated in a report on software patentability in Europe (Tang et al., 2001), as summarized next:

a. Small and medium-sized enterprises prefer to protect their programs by means of copyrights, because they consider the system of patents complex and expensive;

b. For their own innovative processes, small and medium-sized enterprises do not use extensively the information contained in someone else's patents;

c. Such companies consider time-to-market a strategic aspect; from this perspective, the patents is an inefficient system in stimulating innovative activities.

2. Legal Framework in Software Protection

This section presents an analysis of the differences between both legal systems by focusing on the following topics: (1) protected concepts, (2) terms of the rights, (3) obligation of exploitation (4) judicial process. To put such topics in context, a brief historical perspective is provided. At the end of this section the licenses are discussed as the main legal way to transfer software.

The Intellectual Property concept (that is: granting property rights on knowledge assets of intangible character) is not a modern creation of the knowledge society. Such an idea comes from an ancient concern that goes back a lot of centuries to preserve the creations from the intellect. This already existed in the year 25 b.c.: Marco Vitruvio in *De Architectura* (Vitrubio, 25 b.c.) requested protection and punishment against the theft of papers or other writers' thoughts misappropriating his authorship.

Recognition and consequently protection of Intellectual Property link up to the scientific, technological and social progress. However, the advent of the printing press and the possibility to make multiple copies of a work, led definitively to the protection of knowledge. The first legal system of intellectual property protection occured in England in the year 1710 when the English parliament conceded the first formal protection to intervening author's right: The Statute of Anne or Copyright Act of 1709 (the full title was *An Act for the Encouragement of Learning, by vesting the Copies of Printed Books in the Authors or purchasers of such Copies, during the Times therein mentioned*) (Wikisource, n.d). This law vested authors rather than printers with the monopoly on the reproduction of their works. It created a 21 year term for all works already in print at the time of its enactment and a fourteen year term for all works published subsequently; this law bestows upon the creators of a work the exclusive right to print it. The juridical protection of Intellectual property legal protection rapidly spread out over all of Europe.

The author rights on knowledge assets had in its origins a material and territorial character: to refer to literary works the idiom determined the geographic space of distribution. However, the universality of the literary works – i.e. the fact that they transcend the physical frontiers - encouraged the protection of copyrights in acquiring a double content: moral rights and economic rights. That led in 1886 to the *Berne Convention For The Protection Of Literary And Artistic Works* (WIPO, n.d.), also known as the Act of Paris (hereunder Berne Convention), being the international source for the legal protection of the intellectual property rights.

In short, Intellectual Property has been the legal tool to give an incentive to the authors in knowledge assets. However, an important technological change opened an intense debate that has lingered on to our days: the emergence of informational technologies and especially the appearing of software-like independent assets caused the need to look for the legal framework suitable for such new assets.

Since the 1960's when IBM decided to invoice software and hardware separately, there have been multiple attempts of figure out the suitable model for software legal protection. Software as an immaterial good presents a number of important peculiarities: peculiar structure of costs, strategic element for the economic and social development, high intellectual value, etc. Such circumstances have originated several positionings about how to protect sofware (Davara, 2008).

Finally, the mechanism elected to protect software was the granting to the authors of intellectual property rights, assimilating software to artistic scientific or literary works, due to his high intellectual value. According to the *Agreement on Trade-Related Aspects of Intellectual Property Rights* (WTO, n.d.) (hereunder referred as TRIPS), article 10 paragraph 1), a computer program is a type of work which is eligible for protection under the copyright law: "*Computer programs, whether in source or object code, shall be protected as literary works under the Berne Convention*. But article 27 paragraph 1 of TRIPS states that: "*...patents shall be available for any inventions, whether products or processes, in all fields of technology, provided that they are new, involve an inventive step and are capable of industrial application. (...) patents shall be available and patent rights enjoyable without discrimination as to the place of invention, the field of technology and whether products are imported or locally produced*". This article is seen like an open door to patent on software, fundamentally considering that software and computer-implemented inventions can be considered a *field of technology*. From this debate software legal protections have followed through two different ways: copyrights author's and patents.

The divergence in the EU's and the US's conventions for addressing ownership of software code can affect a variety of business-related activities between these entities. It can also affect the practices multinational corporations can safely and legitimately perform in different regions. For these reasons, an increased amount of attention has been paid to the divergences in these approaches.

Copyrights

Copyrights are in force in geographic areas, such as the European Union (EU) and in many South American countries. In order to analyze the content of copyrights systems, the EU legal framework is taken into consideration. The EU relies on the *Council Directive 91/250/EEC of 14 May 1991 on the legal protection of computer programs* (EurLex n.d.) (hereunder CD 91/250) as the basis for the regulation on software protection. The content of this Directive can be summarized in six points:

1. **Protected concepts:** The Directive compares software to literary work in accordance with the Berne Convention; software is therefore considered as an original creation because it is an intellectual creation of its author, and ownership/copyrights are held by the creator of the software.
2. **Contents of the copyrights:** The copyrights content is integrated by two types of rights:
   a. Patrimonial or economic exploitation rights, which represent the author's right to benefit economically from the created software.
   b. Morals rights, which are non-economic rights of personal character.
3. **Terms of the rights:** The copyright last for a term of the author's/creator's life plus seventy years after author's death, and once this time is up, the software will pass into the public domain where others can freely reproduce, distribute, or modify it.
4. **Obligation of exploitation:** Owners of copyrights do not need to exploit software for economic gain; rather, they can decide whether to commercialize the software they own and how to do so.
5. **Legal process to obtain copyrights:** Software copyrights are obtained automati-

cally, just by creating them, and the main reason for registering an item for copyrights with the government is to defend against prospective disputes over rightful ownership.
6. **The right to prepare derivative works:** CD 91/250 establishes the right to develop legally derivative works (i.e., items based on the work of others) so long as the creation of such derivative works is a function of the software being used (e.g., using the Microsoft Word program to write a story).

Patents

Patents permit the protection of ideas and algorithms as opposed to copyrights, which protect the implementation of such ideas and algorithms. Patents are a monopolistic concession on an invention and they last for a limited period of time in a particular geographic area. Once that time limit expires, the idea or the invention becomes freely available to the general public. In essence, the monopoly created by a patent covers the manufacture, distribution, commercialization and use of the process or product that has been patented, and for the duration of the patent.

During the past two decades, patents have been granted to protect a great diversity of software, from compilers to applications (Cohen, J. & lemley, M. 2001), as in Atari Games Corp. v. Nintendo Inc. America. Patents also permit the protection of both software processes (what functions a software performs) and methods for how individuals may legitimately implement software use. Focusing the analysis on the USA, as a pioneer country in this matter, four different stages can be identified in terms of software patentability (Tysver, 2008):

1. First stage: 1960s to 70s - Patents denied if invention used a calculation made by a computer;
2. Second stage: 1980s - The Supreme Court admitted patents on some computerized inventions;

3. Third stage: 1990s - The Federal Circuit recognized that almost all software is patentable;

4. Fourth stage: 2000s - Courts start pulling back.

The established legal doctrine on software patents involves four central concepts:

1. **Protected concepts:** The 1981 Diamond versus Diehr case delineated the basic requirement of patentability of a software product: a software process that includes a mathematical formula is patentable if such formula solely represents a step more in that process, but a mathematical formula itself is not patentable. For instance, the Supreme Court resolved the case Gottschalk versus Benson, denying software patentability on the basis that ideas and intellectual abstract concepts are not patentable. In the Freeman, Walter and Abele cases, a test for determining software patentability was established, focusing on two questions:

   a. Is the patent related to a mathematical algorithm in itself or is it an inherent or implicit invention element?

   b. Is the patent request for just the mathematical algorithm, which is not patentable, or is the algorithm part of a process or machine, which would be patentable?

2. **Contents of the rights:** A patent is a set of rights a government guarantees to the inventor of a new product (material or immaterial) that could be industrially profitable. Modern patent protections provide patent holders with the right to exclude third-parties from creating, using, selling, or dealing with a patented product.

3. **Terms of the rights:** In the US, patents are granted for 20 years (significantly shorter than copyrights terms) as patents have a higher level of legal protection that includes algorithms or processes that sustain software.

After this term, patented software passes into the public domain.

4. **Legal process to obtain patents:** Unlike the copyrights that are granted automatically, patents must be registered with a government patent office to have legal viability. Such patents registration process, moreover, tends to be more expensive than registering an item for copyrights.

Finally it is necessary to introduce a double nuance into what has been said previously: although the law in force in EU excludes software patentability, the European Patent Office (EPO) is granting patents on "computer-implemented inventions". Indeed, in the software domain, more than 30.000 patents have already been granting, but the problem with these patents is that their enforcement in the courts of EU members' states is extremely unlikely. On the other hand, the USA is a signatory member of the Agreement of Berne and therefore the copyrights system is also in force in USA.

3. Transferring Intellectual Property Rights: Licenses on Software

These intellectual property rights, both copyrights and patents, can be commercialized by their owner or transferred to third-parties. The conditions under which rights are transferred are specified in contracts or licenses. Software licenses offer very varied and heterogeneous contents, depending on the business model elected by the developer (Rejas & Cuadrado 2007). Software licenses can be classified into two major groups: Proprietary licenses and Free/Open Source Software Licenses.

Proprietary Licenses

The business model based on proprietary software has its origin in the '70s with IBM's decision of consolidating software as commercial products. Proprietary software licenses are mainly assignment of uses: the developer or author, in this way, ascribes the use of the product without transmitting the property in exchange for the payment of license fees. Such licenses are, generally, a contract of adhesion between the software developer/author and the end user; end user rights and obligations - generally restrictions, are fixed.

The end user's essential right is the right of use, without access to the software absolute property. Among the obligations/restrictions the following ones are often specified: prohibition of transmission, cession or lease to third parties, prohibition of the copy or reproduction, installation limited to one or two processors simultaneously or prohibition/restriction of reverse engineering. In addition, they often include releases from responsibility for damages derived in the installation and use, and guarantee exclusions or limitations.

Free/ Open Source Software (FOSS) Licenses

Free and open source software licenses present a system very different from the proprietary software licenses: it assigns certain rights to the end user related to the availability of the source code and the possibility of developing derivative software. Such rights are not present in the proprietary software licenses. The content of these licenses is very heterogeneous but they can be classified into three three main types of models:

(i) Permissive Licenses
This type of licenses allows users to use the software in any way they need without having to provide the new products as an open source product. It is permissible to copy, modify and distribute source code while only imposing a few minimum conditions such as copyrights information about the initial developers and collaborators, prohibition of using the names of the initial developers to endorse or promote the software and the inclusion of a clause to exempt previous developers of any responsibility. These

conditions do not prevent the final developers to assume responsibilities or extend guarantees about the final product; however, such modifications do not affect the original product.

The BSD (Berkeley Software Distribution) and MIT (Massachusetts Institute of Technology) licenses are two paradigmatic examples of permissive licenses. The BSD licence it is the most permissive authorising to use the software for any purpose; it also allows software modifications and its later distribution either as free software or as proprietary software, as long as the units include a determined type of license, in addition to a warning on the copyrights, a guarantee release and a limitation of responsibilities. They really allow the possibility of creating proprietary software based on open source software. The operating system UNIX is an example of software distributed using the BSD license, and the Sun Microsystems Solaris operating system is proprietary software derived from BSD UNIX.

(ii) Persistent Licences
The main characteristic of this type of licenses is that they cannot be modified in derived products, i.e., any software with a persistent license that is modified will automatically generate a license with the same conditions. This is known as the *viral effect* also known as *copyleft*.

The most extended persistent licenses are GNU General Public License (GNU GPL or just GPL) or its derived Lesser GPL (LGPL). The GPL has been defined by the Free Software Foundation. This model is more restrictive than the previous one, because it limits the right to copy, distribute and modify programs; it demands that any modified version inherits the same type of obligations and rights than the original software, i.e. it does not permit the development of proprietary software from open source. These licenses are denominated 'viral licenses' as they infect derived works. The objective is to guarantee that any derived software continue to grant to users the open source principles of the original software. The operating system

Linux is an example of open source code derived from UNIX under this license: it guarantees that any company or user that makes modifications and distributes them is forced to publish the source code. In addition many development tools of software known as GNU Compiler collection also are distributed using GPL. A variant of this model is the Lesser GPL license.

Both GPL and LGPL require to state the subsequent modifications introduced in the original software as well as its author(s). Also, these licenses include a clause to exonerate any responsibility which can be modified but will only affect the final developer or distributor. Both licenses do not permit to reconcile incompatibles legal resolutions or dispositions with the terms of the license. In those cases, developers need to stop further development of the affected software. However, there are some exceptions agreed by the FSF as long as the basic principles of open source are maintained. Most GNU software uses LPG. There are, however, some exceptions to certain libraries so proprietary software can link them. These exceptions are allowed if the combination complies with the GLP criteria. The LGPL is more flexible in these situations.

(iii) "Dual Licensing" Model

The software contains two different licenses according to the type of use. It is the most flexible model, because it permits, for example, to offer an open source software version and another version adapted to the customer needs, which version generally contains more restrictions. One of the pioneering companies using a "dual license" was Sleepycat Software: their product Berkeley BD is available under a free license which guarantees the access to the source code, with the condition of that the user publishes the source code of the applications that is developed using this product. On the other hand, if the objective is to use Berkeley DB to develop proprietary software, it is better to acquire a traditional license.

Intermediate licenses include the Mozilla Public License (MPL), Sun Public License (SPL) and the Artistic License. Open Source Software licenses allow users to copy, use, modify and distribute software. They must include information related to the copyrights, names of initial developers including information about the lack of support and guarantees from the initial developers to posterior modifications.

The Artistic License forces developers to make available any modification if the software is distributed. In the case of internal use, an agreement with the copyrights holder is required and the distribution is not needed. For SPL and MPL licenses, modifications in the code can be opened or not, but in any case, it is required to state its ownership. If the code is distributed, the source code must be made available. They also include some legal clauses for jurisdictional extensions, legal submissions, or notification of copyrights violation. They allow final developers or distributors to include clauses about guarantes, support and responsibilities.

The form of the license contract acceptance is common for all the licenses and is conditioned by certain particularities derived from their form of presentation. Generally licenses come together with the packaged product and are protected by plastic material: the rupture of the wrapping implies expresses acceptance of the contract, i.e the *shrink wrap licenses*. Another very common form is a text displayed during the installation process: in this case, the express acceptance is through selecting the option *I agree* by means of a mouse click; such licenses are named *click wrap licenses*.

III. TOWARD AN EUROPEAN PATENT-BASED SYSTEM?

The analysis in this section is mainly focused on the EU proposal for a directive on the patentability of computer programs: more specifically, this section discusses the benefits and potential side effects or contradictions that might take place in relation to the particular property.

Based on the opinions of the detractors of how the copyright protected works such as creating computer programs, and ensuring that it would be more desirable and necessary that they be protected by patents, we will study the regulatory oversight conducted in the EU. To this end, we begin by referring to the European Patent Convention.

On October 5 1973 an agreement was signed by several countries: the Convention on the Grant of European Patents, commonly known as the 'European Patent Convention or Munich Convention'(EPO, n.d.). Currently 35 states have signed it, including all EU Member States. As set forth in this Convention, any signatory country may apply for a patent to be valid in the other signatory countries designated. The result of this agreement led to the European Patent Office.

It is through this Convention that for the first time in Europe, the patenting of computer programs was not allowed. One of the most important article of the Convention is Article 52, which in its second paragraph which includes a list of items that may not be the subject of patents, including computer programs as listed in bullet c) - see Table 1.

That is, the Munich Convention does not accept the patentability of software, since it clearly states that programs for computers are not considered inventions for patentability basic premise. For such reason we cannot interpret this article as a closed list, but rather in a flexible manner, having to go to the European Patent Office to determine whether they are inventions: for example, the specifications and materials used.

It is well established that there is a number of exceptions to patentability: this leads once again to the old debate between the need or potential patentability of software, with advocates and detractors. To tackle this problem and to develop the necessary legislation and regulatory action in order to clarify the issue at the European level, the

Table 1. Article 52. Inventions patentable

1. European patents shall be granted for any inventions, in all fields of technology, provided that they are new, involve an inventive step and are susceptible of industrial application.

2. The following in particular shall not be regarded as inventions within the meaning of paragraph 1, including:
   a) discoveries, scientific theories and mathematical methods;
   b) aesthetic creations;
   c) schemes, rules and methods for performing mental acts, playing games or doing business, and programs for computers;
   d) presentations of information.

3. Paragraph 2 shall exclude the patentability of the subject-matter or activities referred to therein only to the extent to which a European patent application or European patent relates to such subject-matter or activities as such.

signatories of the Convention met in 1999 in Paris to try to regulate this issue in Europe, or at least for the signatory countries. The main objective of this meeting was to resolve any dilemma, issue or ambiguity arising from the application and granting of patents in a computer program. Although many countries were in favor of eliminating this Article 52 of the Convention of the software as an exception, it was announced the following year in 2000 that it was not going to proceed to amend this article to remove the software from it: as a consequence, it still appeared as an exception. This is the reason why the legislation of the signatory States follow the same guidelines and legal protection of software is carried out through the so-called intellectual property copyrights (and not through patents).

It is worth mentioning that the so-called free software (that must not to be confused with the other meanings of *free*), is the software that anyone can modify, distribute or use, either in its original version, as in the successive versions of the program developed by individual users: its creator so willed and made it available to the public with such characteristics. That is, 'free software' is a software that allows users to use and modify it to suit their needs, and to have the source code. Software freedom is therefore: free to use, at no charge. The fact that software is free and available to users of the source does not mean it is not protected by copyrights, as with proprietary software. This is where several experts believe that if the software could be patented, it would lose its status as free, since the existence of a patent on the computer program could limit the freedom to modify it: that freedom is implicit in the concept. In this respect, several experts are arguing that computer programs are already adequately protected by intellectual property rights.

Proposal for a Directive on the Patentability of Software

Aiming at a new or additional legal regulation of the software in the European Union in order to harmonize the various regulations of the Member States, the European Parliament and Council issued a draft directive in 2002 on the patentability of computer implemented inventions: this directive proposal is known as the *software patent directive*.

This proposal known as the Green Paper of 24 July 1997 on the Community patent and the patent system in Europe, aims at promoting innovation through patents. The Green Paper aim is threefold: to assess whether it meets the needs of users, to consider the need for further actions, and finally to explore the form and content that could take such further action.

In the same vein, the Commission in 1999 began to consider the need for a Proposal for a directive aimed at harmonizing the various laws of the Member States concerning the legal protection of software and especially considering the inclusion of computer-implemented inventions under the patent system.

Continuing in the same desire of harmonization of patentability, the Proposal directive on software patents, defines, in Article 2, the computer-implemented invention as "*any invention the performance of which involves the use of a computer, computer network or other programmable apparatus and having one or more prima facie novel features which are realised wholly or partly by means of a computer program or computer programs*".

This definition does not indicate to eliminate or amend Article 52 of the Convention under review, since the exemption was scheduled for the computer program, not the inventions herein.

This Proposal has undergone several amendments. It is noteworthy to highlight their most relevant aspects, that is, apart from including in its Article 2, indicated the need to make a technical contribution to occur implemented invention as defined in article 2, inventive that it actually had a new contribution to the state of the art in a certain field of technology, provided it was not evident to a skilled in the art, not just as the potential patentability of software in itself, while discussing the much-worn topic of computer-implemented inventions.

Finally, this proposal for a directive on software patents in the year 2002 contained 19 recitals and eleven articles. On September 2003, the first reading of the proposal in Parliament introduced many relevant amendments and led to 64 amendments, as a result of the analysis made by the House and by the Committees of Culture, Industry and Legal Affairs.

On May 2004 a new text was submitted to the Council, including the amendments above referred to; some of them were accepted directly, others with a change in wording, others were identified as negotiable, and some amendments were rejected. Again changes were made to this new text, highlighting the inability to patent a computer program as such. A qualified majority voted in favor of the text presented and amended, while Spain remained at odds, being the only country voting against it, which is not justified adequately reflect certain amendments proposed by the European Parliament on the scope of what we understand by patents or how to make a technical contribution the invention implemented in the computer. Also to be noted that Belgium, Italy and Austria abstained in the vote.

Despite reaching this agreement, several state members urged the Parliament to go through a second reading, expressing concerns about the text, particularly on the limits of patentability or the guarantee of interoperability, as well as about the potential impact that this agreement could have in small and medium enterprises.

So in February 2005, following a request by Parliament to restart the reading of the draft Directive, it was decided to reject it because it is considered that it did not guarantee the legal certainty necessary for new inventors or for those who are already owners of patents. The results of the voting were 648 votes in favor, 14 against and 18 abstentions. The European Commission has announced that it will not come back with a new initiative to establish common standards in granting patents for computer implemented inventions.

In summary, after several years of discussions on the issue, with different interests and positions, no solution entirely satisfied all parties. Therefore we must look to the Patent Convention and to see in which context to frame the patentability of software; Article 52 exclude such possibility as a clear exception in its second paragraph.

IV FUTURE TRENDS

Currently the legal protection systems on software (i.e. patents and copyrights) start from a traditional software view: software is an intellectual property asset – i.e. an intangible asset in business transactions as a product. From this perspective the legal way to protect software is to assimilate it with others intellectual assets such as scientific creations or industrial inventions. However, the software market, in present days, is experiencing a number of variations in the way this asset is commercialized and distributed: more and more the software is reaching the market as services - not as a product.

For instance, SaaS (Software as a Service) (O´Reilly, 2004) is an emerging business model based on the concept that the IT regular customer system is hosted in the developers' systems whereas, by means of a services contract, it supports the IT software requirements. According to (Gartner, 2007) SaaS represented in 2005 approximately five percent of business software revenues and it is forecasted that by 2011 up to twenty five percent of new business software could be delivered as SaaS. This trend in the software industry will affect its legal protection: for SaaS, the current legal schemes are not valid for they are designed for a product, not for a service.

Furthermore, cloud computing, as the entity integrated by the SaaS operations, needs a proper and comprehensive legal protection system, based in two relevant aspects:

1. **Services distribution channel:** In SaaS the IT systems and data are hosted in alien systems - possibly out of the customer country. Such circumstance generates several legal implications, both in substantive and procedural laws:

   a. **Substantive laws:** Cloud computing in general, and SaaS in particular, are new economic phenomena without a proper substantive regulation. Cloud computing and SaaS imply data transfers from the customer to the service provider who hosts such data. This data dynamic is relevant in legal terms. Data transfer and hosting are key concepts in personal data protection laws; for example international data transfer, in EU law, requires the fulfillment of restrictive conditions and establishes heavy penalties for infringement.

   b. **Procedural Laws:** In the SaaS business model, physical proximity between customer and service provider is not a relevant aspect. That way it is possible that customer and provider are not in the same country, nor even on the same continent. Such circumstance presents problems in terms of procedural law, especially in applicable law, in fields such as advertising, general hiring conditions, competition regulations or customer rights. In the same way, and in case of disagreements between customer and provider, court of competent jurisdiction would be a doubtful point.

2. **Legal act:** SaaS is a typical instance of a services contract, with relevant differences within sale contracts for software products or software licenses. Such contracts need, first, to fix in a clear way the ownership of the assets (i.e. software and hardware) which are used to render the hired service. Aspects such us the service level, maintenance conditions or responsibility in loss of data, demand a legal global framework, beyond patents and copyrights, that provide juridical certainty to this increasingly important sector of the software industry.

In an economy getting more and more globalized, the national laws are inadequate to regulate international phenomena such as SaaS. The old procedural rules from the international law are too complex; in addition the legal obsolescence rate is substantial, dragged along by their own rapid technological obsolescence rate. Besides, the law system in the EU is based on a prolific legislation of many social phenomena, with very detailed laws that become obsolete or inadequate when the realities they regulate change, more so when technology is involved. This converges to a panorama of juridical insecurity in which companies are threatened by important technology-related legal risks.

With software as a product as well as a service, the software legal protection system requires a major overhaul:

*   **for software as a product:** the patents negative effects have to be mitigated, in-

cluding for motivating R&D in knowledge assets and guaranteeing the economic rights to the developers;
*   **for software as a service:** the design of a proper and global regulation, both in substantive and in procedural laws.

V CONCLUSION

The investment in knowledge or immaterial assets related to software products needs to be protected using intellectual properties rights. It is essential to guarantee the benefits and products generated by an investment in knowledge as a way to stimulate the technological growth in a economic context characterized for lack of appropriability linked with a peculiar cost structure. Protection systems are applied to the software industry, which is at the moment one of the main sources generating innovation and knowledge.

Generally, intellectual property rights are shaped by means of the licensing agreements that regulate the commercial transactions in this economic sector, fixing rights and obligations of the contracting parties. Although the content of the proprietary software licenses is very different from the content of the open source software licenses, the legal framework is the same.

Currently, there are two legal frameworks to protect and control the software development and distribution: the copyright system, which is applied in the EU, and the patents system, which is applied in the USA. Patents and copyrights are two very different systems, both in terms of contents and protection depth. These differences in protection systems lead to differences in software markets in terms of competitiveness.

Nevertheless, in Europe there is a trend towards a patent system, led by the European Patent Office. Consequently, the European Council has deployed in the last years an intensive legislative and controversial activity with the objective to harmonize to European legislation and to introduce the software patentability like an added instrument for its protection. This initiative was rejected by the European Parliament in July of 2005, but it is foreseeable that European institutions will incorporate the possibility of patenting software at some point in time in the future. Software patentability will probably create a less competitive market dominated by large organizations because of the large budgets needed – i.e. patents are not affordable to small organizations and individual developers. In addition, new forms of software commercialization as a service announce future changes in software legal protection.

To design a worldwide standardized legal protection system and to organize a new legal framework to regulate the new ways of commercializing software, there remains a number of challenges and opportunities for the future of this industry.

REFERENCES

Cohen, J., & Lemley, M. (2001). Patent Scope and Innovation in the software industry. [from http://www.law.georgetown.edu/Faculty/jec/softwarepatentscope.pdf]. *California Law Review, 89*(1), 1–57. Retrieved on June 10, 2009. doi:10.2307/3481172

Davara, M. A. (2008). *Manual de Derecho Informático*. Spain: Thomson-Aranzandi.

EurLex. (n.d.). *Council Directive 91/250/EEC of 14May1991on the legal protection of computer programs*. Retrieved on June 10, 2009, from http://eur-lex.europa.eu/smartapi/cgi/sga_doc?smartap i!celexapi!prod!CELEXnumdoc&numdoc=3199 1L0250&model=guichett&lg=en

European Patent Office. (n.d.) Convention on the Grant Of European Patents (European Patent Convention). Retrieved on June 12, 2009, from http://www.epo.org/patents/law/legal-texts/html/epc/1973/e/ma1.html

Faramarz, D. (2001). E-businesse-commerce evolution: Perspective and strategy. *Managerial Finance, 27*(7), 16–18. doi:10.1108/03074350110767268

Gartner Inc. (2007). *Dataquest Insight: SaaS Demand Set to Outpace Enterprise Application Software Market Growth*. New York: Gartner.

Hall, B. H. (2002). On Copyright and Patent Protection for Software and Databases: A Tale of Two Worlds. In O. Granstrand (ed.), *Economics, Law, and Intellectual Property*. Kluwer. Retrieved on June 8, 2009, from http://www.iiasa.ac.at/docs/HOTP/Dec99/bhhiiasa4.pdf

Kalakota, R., & Robinson, M. (2000). *E-Business 2.0, roadmap to success*. Boston, MA: Addison-Wesley.

Mowery, D., & Rosenberg, N. (1998). *Paths of Innovation: Technological Change in 20th-Century America*. Cambridge, UK: Cambridge University Press.

O'Reilly, T. (2004). *Open Source Paradigm Shift*. Retrieved on June 8, 2009, from http://tim.oreilly.com/articles/paradigmshift_0504.html

Rejas, R., & Cuadrado, J. (2007). Licencias Software. *Otrosí. Ilustre Colegio de Abogados de Madrid., 84*, 60–70.

Romer, P. (1993). Two Strategies for Economic Development: Using Ideas and Producing Ideas. In *Proceedings of the World Bank Annual Conference on Development Economics*. Vitrubio, M. (25, b.c.). *De Architectura*. Retrieved on June 26, 2009, from http://www.latin.it/autore/vitruvio/de_architectura

Shapiro, A. (1999). *The Control Revolution*. New York: PublicAffairs.

Tang, P., Adams, J., & Paré, D. (2001). *Patent protection of computer programmes*. Final Report, ECSC-EC-EAEC. Brussels, Luxembourg: OMPI-CEPAL. Retrieved on June 26, 2009, from http://eupat.ffii.org/papers/tangadpa00/tangadpa00.pdf

Toffler, A. (1980). *The Third Wave*. Bantam Books.

Torrisi, S. (1998). *Industrial Organization and Innovation. An International Study of the Software Industry*. Cheltenham: Edward Elgar.

Tysver, D. (2008). The History of Software Patents: From Benson and Diehr to State Street and Bilski. *BitLaw Legal Resource*. Retrieved on May 2, 2009 from http://www.bitlaw.com/software-patent/history.html.

Wikisource (n.d.). *Statute of Anne*. Retrieved on June 16, 2009, from http://en.wikisource.org/wiki/Statute_of_Anne

World Intellectual Property Organization. (n.d.). *Berne Convention for the Protection of Literary and Artistic Works*. Retrieved on June 10, 2009, from http://www.wipo.int/treaties/en/ip/berne/trtdocs_wo001.html

World Trade Organization. (n.d.). *Trade-Related Aspects of Intellectual Property Rights*. Retrieved on June 10, 2009, from http://www.wto.org/english/docs_e/legal_e/27-trips_01_e.htm

Chapter 9
A Global Perspective of Laws and Regulations Dealing with Information Security and Privacy

B. Dawn Medlin
Appalachian State University, USA

Charlie C. Chen
Appalachian State University, USA

ABSTRACT

The price of privacy intrusion and security breaches is often due to the ubiquitous connectivity of networks. National entities as well as other governing bodies have passed laws and regulations to assist individuals in their quest to protect their information as it is being transmitted as well as received over these networks. An international perspective of information privacy and security laws and regulations can provide an insightful view concerning how each country differs as well as the important drivers for these differences. Policy makers can learn from the comparisons made in relation to similarity and/or differences of privacy and security laws as well. In this paper, we have selected different countries and regions around the world due to the growth of security and privacy threats that has grown over the past 10 years as well as their legislative practices.

INTRODUCTION

Managers and administrators responsible for securing data and applications on servers, desktops, and laptops have two broad strategic goals. The first goal is to prevent unauthorized access to information technology (IT) resources such as a consumer's or patient's information, and the second goal is to maintain IT services so that they are kept up-to-date.

DOI: 10.4018/978-1-61520-975-0.ch009

To address the first goal, access controls are an obvious tool for preventing unauthorized access; but less obvious practices, such as auditing for unauthorized hardware, are also important. As an example, consider an unauthorized wireless access point in an office transmitting confidential consumer or patient information over an unencrypted Wi-Fi network. Anyone with a wireless network card could intercept the traffic. This highlights the fact that all the effort that went into defining, implementing, and managing access control policies could easily be circumvented.

As previously mentioned, the second goal of the network administrator is the maintenance of IT services. This generally requires a multifaceted approach that includes firewalls and intrusion detection systems, as well as antivirus services, scanning for vulnerabilities, and system configurations for controlling system security. Another important measure is to ensure that operating systems are appropriately patched. Both of these goals are important in order to protect information and for the network to function effectively. If guidelines, policies, and management recommendations are not followed, systems are vulnerable to security breaches that can range from simple nuisances, such as the implanting of spyware that slows the performance of desktops, to the crippling of networks through a distributed DoS attack that can effectively disable network services.

Because we are a society governed by laws, in their striving to reach these aforementioned goals and repair breaches, managers and systems administrators must be aware of and address current laws, directives and regulations dealing with privacy and security issues. Certainly, the growth of the Internet as a file storage and transfer medium has forced society to reexamine the notions surrounding privacy and security.

We will discuss current laws and regulations applied to the general public in relation to the topics of security and privacy of personal information. This discussion includes areas such as health care, financial services and marketing that demonstrate the complexity of these questions and the ongoing search for answers. Understanding the progression of information security and privacy may allow for those individuals involved within the system to have a better idea of how to protect and secure information. If we can learn from history, we may be less likely to repeat the same mistakes.

We also recognize that not all countries are created equal with respect to their information privacy and security laws. The Internet is a global phenomenon and essentially affects almost every country in the world. A selection of countries and regions was made after researchers looked at an exhaustive list of security threats around the world. From this information as well as a comparison to prior lists developed by professional organizations that had already created listings of generally ten countries with the most threats, we offer a shorter list, but an informative one. Information privacy and security laws can offer an opportunity to explore how other international perspectives are applied to the issue of how to protect information privacy and security. Policy makers may also learn from one another through this comparison and together better secure the information privacy and security of information for all of the citizens of the world.

CONCEPTUAL FORMATION

Different countries have adopted disparate approaches in their approach to the implementation of information privacy laws and regulations. The U.S. delegated states to enact their own information privacy rules while the European Union attempted to enforce a common standard to regulate privacy across member countries. Australia adopted the third perspective of legalizing privacy laws and regulations at the Commonwealth and industry levels. Industry-specific privacy regulations supersede the jurisdiction of the Commonwealth's when coming to industrial relations. Unlike these three continents, Asia has largely ignored the importance of personal privacy, but has emphasized group interests over individual interests.

Because of the uncoordinated manner of regulating privacy practices around the world, many business issues such as transnational data transfer, search engine optimization, and censorship have dramatically affected the growth of international business. An international perspective of information privacy laws and regulations can offer an integrative view of these privacy laws their respectively related problems. Policy makers of different countries can learn from one another and propose effective solutions to address the existing as well as evolving privacy and security problems.

Information privacy laws generally include: (1) restriction of public access to another person's private information, (2) protection of an individual's personal identity, and (3) preservation of private communications. However, the execution of privacy law varies greatly with countries. For instance, it is illegal for checkout clerks to ask shoppers for their phone number in Europe; whereas the practice is common in the U.S.

European companies must register their data processing activities with their government, whereas it is not necessary for American companies to do so. Long-term visitors in major European countries (France and Germany) must register his or her address with the local police office, whereas the requirement is not necessary in the U.S. In general, Europeans distrust corporations in the protection of personal privacy and Americans generally distrust their government (Sullivan, 2006).

The fundamental difference in the attitude toward privacy laws has often resulted in dissimilar information in relation to privacy practices. As our society becomes more globally connected, citizens of the world need to understand the essence of information privacy rights and security that exist in different parts of the world.

United States

A chronological view of the evolution of information security and privacy laws can provide a rich observation and possible reason for the creation of each law or regulation. It is important to judge the rights of individual citizens and their right to privacy based on its sophistication without taking into consideration their historical and cultural backgrounds. The chronological approach can also provide insight as to how these laws have evolved over time as the United States society has evolved in its use of the Internet and other technologies.

Health Insurance Portability and Accountability Act of 1996

Every health care agency in the United States that handles protected patient health information is required to comply with the Health Insurance Portability and Accountability Act of 1996 (HIPAA). HIPAA security standards require health care agencies to adopt policies and procedures that will show how security methods will be implemented that in a way that is "reasonable and appropriate".

HIPAA consists of three sets of standards which include: (1) transactions and codes, (2) privacy, and (3) security. The objectives of these standards are to simplify the management and administration of health insurance claims, to lower costs, and to give patients more control and access to their medical information while protecting their information from real or potential threats of disclosure or loss. HIPAA also requires that healthcare organizations take reasonable and appropriate steps to limit the disclosure of an individual's personal health information, including training employees to follow privacy procedures, designating an individual to oversee the organization's privacy initiatives, and securing access to electronic patient records. The privacy deadline for HIPAA was April 2003; the security deadline was April 2005.

There are distinct differences between privacy standards and security standards. First of all, privacy is the patient's control over the use and disclosure of his or her own personal health information (PHI), whereas security is defined as the "policies, practices, and technology that must be in place for an organization to transact business electronically via networks with a reasonable assurance of safety" (Volonino & Robinson, 2004).

Personal health information or PHI is the HIPAA term for health information in any form (i.e., paper, electronic or verbal) which personally identifies a patient. This also includes individually identifiable health information in paper records that have never been electronically transmitted (http://www.medstarsystems.com/hipaa). Privacy may also include the right to determine when, how, and to what degree PHI is shared with others. The HIPAA privacy rules grant new rights to patients to gain access to and control the use and disclosure of their personal health information.

As required by HIPAA, security and privacy administrators, as well as management, must enhance the security of their networks by setting strong password policies and procedures. Password requirements such as length and strength should be built into every health care agency's security policies. Network administrators are required to regularly change or update employee passwords. Employees should also be frequently reminded about how easy it is for hackers to get passwords through social engineering techniques. New employees should also be taught good password practices. Providing intranet resources related to network security and password security may also be helpful. Finally, the organization's password policy should be integrated into the overall security policy, and all employees should be required to read and sign the policy as a part of their employment record.

Systems administrators should implement safeguards to ensure that people on their systems are using adequately strong passwords. This would require such actions as the setting of password expiration dates on all programs, keeping a password history to prevent reuse, and the lock out of accounts after 3 to 5 password attempts. Additionally, the organization should keep the number of people in the organization who have access to these passwords at a minimum. Finally, when installing new systems, they should ensure that default passwords are changed immediately.

On February 13th, 2009, The House of Representatives and Senate passed the American Recovery and Reinvestment Act to include new provisions to HIPAA. Inside the new provisions are regulations that address the protection of a patient's privacy. Listed below are these provisions (American Medical Association, 2009):

- Federal privacy/security laws (HIPAA) are expanded to protect patient health information.
- HIPAA privacy and security laws would apply directly to business associates of covered entities.
- Defines actions that constitute a breach of patient health information (including inadvertent disclosures) and requires notification to patients if their health information is breached.
- Allows patients to pay out of pocket for a health care item or service in full and to request that the claim not be submitted to the health plan.
- Requires physicians to provide patients, upon request, an accounting of disclosures of health information made through the use of an EHR.
- Prohibits the sale of a patient's health information without the patient's written authorization, except in limited circumstances involving research or public health activities.
- Prohibits covered entities from being paid to use patients' health information for marketing purposes without patient authorization, except limited communication to a patient about a drug or biologic that the patient is currently being prescribed.
- Requires personal health record (PHR) vendors to notify individuals of a breach of patient health information.
- Non-covered HIPAA entities such as Health Information Exchanges, Regional Health Information Organizations, e-Prescribing Gateways, and PHR vendors are required to have business associate agreements with covered entities for the electronic exchange of patient health information.
- Authorizes increased civil monetary penalties for HIPAA violations.
- Grants enforcement authority to state attorneys general to enforce HIPAA.

It is clear that information privacy and security issues continue to draw attention from the healthcare industry, the public, and the Obama administration. It is expected that as more and more patients records are being sent electronically and are being converted to digital formats that more laws will be enacted.

The Gramm-Leach Bliley Act 1999

As the Internet matures, more and more data is constantly being uploaded to it. Thus, it should not be surprising that every type of data from personal information to financial figures is located on computers that are linked globally via the Internet. Such information linking has a dramatic affect on Internet security. During the late 1990s, a citizen named Joe Barton began a movement that demanded better security allocated to financial data held by companies, particularly those located on the Internet. When, unknown to him, Barton's financial information was sold by his credit union to the Victoria's Secret intimate apparel merchandiser, Barton knew that legal action was necessary. Not only was Barton receiving catalogs from Victoria's Secret in the mail, but his wife and family began wondering if he had a secret partner to whom he was supplying lingerie. Tired of being harassed due to his personal information being sold, Barton took action (Hoofnagle, 2005). During Barton's legal battle, Representative Ed Markey of Massachusetts introduced an amendment that would add privacy restrictions to and protection of financial information. More specifically, the Markey Amendment was directed at the protection of people just like Joe Barton, citizens who had found that their financial data had been sold or traded to retail companies over the Internet. When Barton testified in court about his Victoria's Secret fiasco, the Markey Amendment was passed and later renamed as the Gramm-Leach Bliley Act (GLBA).

There are three subsets defined within the scope of the GLBA: the Financial Privacy Rule, the Safeguards Rule, and a provision against pretexting, defined by the FTC as the act of obtaining financial data under false pretenses (FTC, 2005). The Financial Privacy Rule limits what financial institutions and companies who obtain financial data can do with an individual's information. Financial data can no longer be sold or traded to other companies over the Internet. Not only can the aforementioned financial information not be sold, but it cannot even be displayed to the public or to any other entity on or off the Internet (FTC, 2005). Account numbers cannot be shared with affiliated companies unless so stated in a signed waiver under the Financial Privacy Rule. Within the stated waiver, an opt-out policy must be included allowing consumers to manually remove their name from any type of third party communication. Once manually removed from the list, the consumer will have his or her financial data secured in only one firm, i.e. the initial financial agency (FTC, 2005).

The Safeguards Rule pertains to the protection of customer financial information. Securing customer data is essential to the operations of a financial firm in today's world due to the overwhelming number of Internet abusers attempting to retrieve financial data. Companies that do not directly obtain financial data (such as credit agencies) are still liable under the Safeguards Rule to protect customer financial data at all costs (FTC, 2005). Physical data, such as paperwork contained in file cabinets, are a part of the Safeguards Rule as much as are electronic data (such as databases full of customer information). The confidentiality, integrity, and overall security of financial data are covered within the Safeguards rule (FTC, 2005).

The final provision against pretexting under the GLBA prohibits the act of falsely impersonating a customer to obtain financial data. Under no circumstances can a citizen, company, or entity use deceptive means to obtain data that could compromise sensitive information (FTC, 2005).

In Joe Barton's case, the Financial Privacy Rule was broken in numerous ways. Not only did

Barton's credit union sell his financial information to a credit agency using the Internet, but the credit agency in return sold his information to Victoria's Secret (Hoofnagle 2005). With such events occurring to everyday citizens, it is not unreasonable to conclude that most direct mail advertising is the result of a de facto breach in the Financial Privacy Rule of the GLBA. With financial data security covered, an in-depth look into another highly detailed Internet-related law is in order.

United States Patriot Act 2001

In September 2001, 45 days after the attack on the World Trade Center in New York City, President George Bush signed into public law the Uniting and Strengthening America by Providing Appropriate Tools Required to Intercept and Obstruct Terrorism Act of 2001, more commonly known as the Patriot Act (http://www.security-port.com/patriot-act.htm). Among the provisions of the Act that have specific relations with information security and privacy are the following sections (Martins, 2005).

- **Section 204:** allows stored voice mail communications to be obtained by a search warrant rather than by having to meet the more stringent wiretap requirements. However, messages on an answering machine tape are not accessible through this provision.
- **Section 210:** expands the type of information that an electronic communications provider must disclose. This could include records of session times and duration, temporarily assigned network addresses, and means of payment, and it is not limited to investigations of suspected terrorist activity.
- **Section 211:** makes cable companies that provide telephone or Internet services subject to existing laws that cover telecommunications providers and Internet service providers (ISPs).
- **Section 215:** allows the government to seek a court order to obtain personal records such as library, financial, phone, travel, and medical records. This is done by amending the Foreign Intelligence Surveillance Act and is based on a much lower probable-cause standard than that for a regular warrant.
- **Section 216:** applies telephone monitoring laws to Internet traffic, including e-mail, Web page, and Internet protocol addresses.
- **Section 314:** provides for information sharing among financial institutions and between the government and financial institutions.
- **Section 319(b):** amends Section 5318 of Title 31 of the U.S. Code to include a "120-hour rule." This provision requires that a financial institution must produce records relating to "any account opened, maintained, administered, or managed in the United States" upon request from an appropriate federal banking agency. This section also provides instruction on maintaining foreign bank records.
- **Section 326:** requires that financial institutions verify a person's identity when that person seeks to open an account and to maintain records of the information used in such identification, amending Section 5318 of Title 31, U.S. Code.
- **Section 505:** allows the government to seek personal records with no judicial approval through the use of an administrative subpoena. This provision does not expire at the end of 2005 and has been used many times since 2001. It was, however, struck down as unconstitutional by a New York Federal District Court in September 2004. The case is currently awaiting appeal.

Many of the act's provisions were set to sunset on December 31, 2005, and in July 2005, the U.S. Senate passed a reauthorization bill (S.1389) with substantial changes to several sections of the act, while the House reauthorization bill (H.R. 3199) kept most of the act's original language (http://www.cnn.com/2005/POLITICS/12/21/patriot.act/index.html) The two bills were then reconciled and a "compromise bill," was created which removed most of the changes from the Senate version. The new bill was passed in March 2006 and was signed into law by President Bush that same month.

Sarbanes-Oxley Act 2002

In the early 1990s regulatory examinations were primarily focused on IT issues and the core applications (e.g. deposits, loans, general ledger, etc.) as they related to in-house computer systems. After the preparation and completion of the century date change, more attention was directed towards risk management in the regulatory approach to IT examinations, especially risk management regarding the defining of responsibility for in-house core processing as opposed to activities outsourced to a third party vendor.

Certainly, outsourcing of any type works to overcome organizational obstacles to make operations more efficient. The opportunity to outsource can also provide banks with the opportunity to transfer execution of risk to their third-party service providers. However, on February 29, 2000, the Board of Governors of the Federal Reserve System issued the Supervision and Regulation Letter SR 00-04 that provided regulatory guidance related to the issue of the outsourcing of information and transaction processing activities to either third-party providers or affiliated institutions. The Federal Reserve stated that it expected institutions to ensure that controls over outsourced information would be handled the same as if the activity were handled in-house.

The Sarbanes-Oxley Act (SOX), which became law in July 2002, charged that publicly held companies must have strict corporate governance procedures that include financial disclosure, auditing and accounting. More specifically, Section 404 of SOX mandates that management assess the effectiveness of internal controls over financial reporting (http://www.sarbanes-oxley.com). Information technology plays a critical role in the financial reporting arena in most companies today and is often outsourced by community banks. Financial business processes that have been outsourced are of concern with respect to SOX requirements. When a financial process is transferred to another entity, corporate management assumes the responsibility for the accuracy of such processes and for the compliance of all parties under Section 404. This requires banks to assess whether a service provider is part of the company's internal control of financial reporting. Corporate management may not be aware that this would include any sub-contractors used by the service provider employed by the bank.

The Controlling the Assault of Non-Solicited Pornography and Marketing Act of 2003

The Controlling the Assault of Non-Solicited Pornography and Marketing Act of 2003 (or CAN-SPAM) was enacted in late 2003 due to the rampant growth of Internet e-mail spamming. Spamming is the sending out of massive waves of advertising e-mails in hopes of "hooking" a certain amount of sales with each wave. These e-mails, or spam, typically contain messages that may easily fool the average user and infect computers with malicious applications. The most recent wave of e-mail spam contains pornography and other adult content that should not be accessible to younger users.

In a staunch defense of consumer rights, the Federal Trade Commission (FTC) passed the

CAN-SPAM Act of 2003 to combat spamming and protect individuals from its effect. Within the CAN-SPAM Act of 2003, various issues ranging from misleading e-mails to sender identification are now legally binding on the e-mail creator. The header of every e-mail sent must now contain legitimate "To and From" information including the originating domain name (FTC, 2004). Further promoting the new legitimacy rules of the CAN-SPAM Act, e-mail subject lines can no longer be deceptive or misleading about the contents of the e-mail. In line with the Gramm-Leach Bliley Act, the CAN-SPAM Act now requires advertising or promotion e-mails to offer an opt-out choice allowing each recipient to remove his or her e-mail address from the e-mail list (FTC, 2004). Arguably the most demanding aspect of the CAN-SPAM Act relates to a physical address requirement. Not only do e-mails containing advertising have to be labeled as an official advertisement, but each e-mail sent out (every piece of spam) must contain the physical address of the spam sender (FTC, 2004).

As of January 1st, 2004, the CAN-SPAM Act of 2003 now imposes an eleven thousand dollar fine per instance for confirmed violations. In conjunction with the Gramm-Leach Bliley Act and the Digital Millennium Copyright Act of 1998, the Controlling the Assault of Non-Solicited Pornography and Marketing Act of 2003 is in place to clean up our digital frontier littered with false advertising and malicious electronic messages.

The Personal Data Privacy and Security Act of 2005

The United States Senate introduced the Personal Data Privacy and Security Act of 2005 which attempted to define security breaches and the handling of sensitive information as did HR 4127. However, the Senate bill included additional amendments. First, an individual who knowingly hides a security breach causing damage to one or more persons can be fined and/or imprisoned for up to five years. Second, those individuals who steal and use consumer information in a fraudulent manner can have up to two years tacked onto their mandatory prison sentence that is already in effect. Third, the bill would allocate $25 million annually nationwide for enforcement. This allocation of funds, in conjunction with other nuances of the law makes for a solid first try at requiring accountability from companies.

This bill is also significant in that it addresses the question of Government databases that are handled by private contractors. Requirements include an evaluation of potential contractors involved in handling personal data; an audit of commercial data brokers hired for projects involving personal data; and a privacy impact assessment on the use of commercial databases by federal departments.

The Financial Data Protection Act of 2005

Several members of the U.S. Congress introduced legislation in 2005 that would specifically address brokers of personally identifiable financial data. Essentially, H.R. 3997 is designed to stop data breaches by mandating a national standard for the protection of sensitive information concerning consumers (Moye, 2005). In order to accomplish this objective the Act requires institutions to notify consumers if data security breaches involving their information might be used to commit financial fraud and in addition requires institutions to provide consumers with a free six-month nationwide credit monitoring service upon notification of a breach (http://www.gao.gov/new.items/d06674.pdf).

It is apparent that the United States Congress, the Federal Trade Commission as well as other government agencies are making an earnest attempt to address the issues of privacy and security concerning personally identifiable information. Without the introduction and eventual adoption of laws and regulations such as the Gramm-Leach Bliley Act which has reinforced the foundation of security concerning financial data and protected individual consumers from having their information shared over the Internet and the CAN/SPAM Act which is currently slowing down the spread of spam e-mail, the issues of privacy and security would certainly be even more of a preoccupation to consumers and regulators alike. Over time it will be seen whether laws, federal and state, can effectively protect and secure information while allowing the Internet to continue to fulfill its potential as a legitimate information sharing medium.

European Union

The European Union (EU) centralizes the process of regulating information privacy. The 95/46/EC Directive is the general provision to regulate the personal data protection in EU. According to this Directive, all member states or countries within EU are obligated to share data with each other in order to protect the fundamental rights and freedoms of nature persons. This Directive stipulated two objectives as follows:

In accordance with this Directive, Member States shall protect the fundamental rights and freedoms of natural persons and in particular their right to privacy with respect to the processing of personal data.

Member States shall neither restrict nor prohibit the free flow of personal data between Member States for reasons connected with the protection afforded under paragraph 1(http://www.cdt.org/privacy/eudirective/EU_Directive_.html).

The EU Data Directive mandated that telecommunication firms and Internet service providers retain traffic data on users for at least two years. However, this privacy law is not applicable to content providers or search engines. Google has retained consumer data in order to improve search engine effectiveness. Because of the duality of compliance with information privacy laws, Google received many complaints about information privacy intrusion. According to the Privacy International, a London-based advocacy group, Google had the lowest privacy protection rating among all major Internet sites operating in United Kingdom (Swartz, 2007). The stringent data retention policy in EU has forced companies such as Google, Microsoft and Yahoo in shortening data retention period in order to address European regulators' concerns (Palmer, 2008).

The application of the European Union Data Directive which was developed before Internet commercialization, raised many transnational privacy issues related to the meaning of borders, territorial sovereignty and political space (Kobrin, 2002). Because of increasing number of disputes on personal privacy intrusion in cyberspace, the Working Party 29, the EU advisory body on data protection issues, clarified the general EU Data Protection Directive (95/46/EC) in 2008 as follows (Eecke and Truyens, 2008):

1. 95/46/EC applies not only to search engines established in the EU, but also to foreign search engines outside the EU;
2. 95/46/EC applies to activities of processing personal data (e.g. selling targeted advertising to EU residents) by an online company with a permanent establishment; and
3. 95/46/EC applies to companies making use of equipment located within the EU (e.g. instructing EU residents to store a cookie on their PCs).

In order to effectively crack down cybercrimes, the Council of Europe signed a transnational treaty with Canada, Japan, South Africa and the U.S. in order to regulate security threats, such as network attacks, digital copyrights, child pornography, computer-related fraud and viruses (Wall, 2002). This treaty allows participating countries to share information (e.g. email logs and hard drive contents) with each other about the suspect hackers. Governments also need to join hands to arrest and extradite hackers. This has strong implications of information privacy and security in the new economy.

The EU has continued its unified efforts to standardize the information privacy and security regulations on emerging technologies. The European Commission required that all companies that adopted RFID or Internet-enabled chips assess their potential privacy-related risks and use logos to indicate the presence of the adopted technology (Mason, 2009).

In addition, the aforementioned Directive also establishes the system opt-in. Article 13 affirms that only the use of systems of automatic call without human intervention, fax or electronic mail is authorized with the previous consent. This article has unified the market of the Union adopting, of obligatory form, the necessity to obtain consent independently of the communications.

The EU is further deploying RFID applications to protect personal information privacy and security via the ICAO-compliant electronic passport or electronic national identity (ID) card. Residents in eight EU countries, including Austria, Belgium, Estonia, Finland, Italy, the Netherlands, Spain and Sweden are currently using electronic ID cards in daily life (Naumann and Hogben, 2008). Other countries, including Germany, France and the UK, are also embracing this technology with new technical specifications. These new initiatives further substantiate EU's centralized approach to manage and legalize information privacy and security issues.

Asian Countries

Asia is the continent having the largest number of Internet users in the world. Internet World Stats (2009) estimated that about 3.7 billion Asians used the Internet in the year 2008, accounting for more than 40% of Internet users of the world. An examination of information privacy and security laws enacted in Asian countries can provide a general idea about their movement of privacy in Asia.

China's Constitution Law protects citizen's inherent dignity from damages and protects freedom and security of communication of us-ers. This fundamental law laid the foundation for today's personal privacy in China. The Civil Law General Principles is the law specifically detailing regulations regarding protection of privacy based on investigation, secrecy and public hearings. The Amendments to the Criminal Law (VII) expanded the scope of personal privacy by including the sales of personal information as criminal charges. This law mandated that People's Court put any accusations into a civil judicatory trial if any party makes a claim for infringement of privacy by others that cause psychological or reputation damage. This law provided a basis for a monetary compensation for the infringement of personal privacy. However, the decision on the extent of damages is up to the discretionary and subjective judgment in the courthouse. Privacy infringement without being able to make a case of causing psychological or reputation damage does not make the claimant liable for compensation. Therefore, the scope of privacy protection requires further clarification since what constitutes privacy infringement and/or compensation has no clear explanation.

In 2007, the First Intermediate People's Court of Beijing accepted an indictment against Microsoft Corporation and Microsoft (China) Co. Ltd., from a Peking University student for infringement of his personal information and privacy via the "WGA Notification" program (Zhang, 2007). Microsoft Co. Ltd. apparently had used the program to verify the legitimacy of his Windows XP system as they automatically provided users with software updates. Yet, the plaintiff was concerned that Microsoft also obtained his personal information during the verification process. The plaintiff asked for three actions from Microsoft: (1) delete all personal information of the plaintiff that resided in Microsoft's information systems, (2) make a public apology in a national newspaper, and (3) compensate him with 1,350 yuan (US$88.28) for psychological losses.

China is notorious for its high piracy rate according to the Fifth Annual BSA and IDC Global

Software Piracy Study (2008). The study reported China having an 82% piracy rate. In October 2008, China's desktop background would turn to black if user's installed operating system failed the online test of the Windows Genuine Advantage software. This new measure to combat the pirated software has created controversies among users regarding privacy infringement (Ye, 2008).

Individual privacy in Asia has a negative connotation because of its collectivism culture and the influence of Confucianism and Buddhism. Individual privacy involves shames, disrespect, losing face, shameful secret, and hidden, bad things (Ess, 2006). An individual should learn how to become Musi or "no-self" in order to fulfill the collective privacy of the family, group, company or the society. This connotation is a sharp contrast to the prevalent notion of privacy in the West that privacy is autonomous. Personal privacy in China is evolving as the country is increasingly becoming more open to the global community.

The "no-self" connotation of privacy has exerted influence on the practices of information privacy protection in Asia. Most Chinese websites do not post privacy policies or statements. Although a few websites have chosen to do so, the execution of the policy usually does not concur with the generally accepted principle of information practices (Kong, 2007).

China's first information privacy regulation was passed in the year 2003. One of Beijing's four districts, Xuanwu, was the first city to enact freedom of information rules that require any unclassified information disclosed to the public within 15 days (The Economist, 2003).

The Regulations of the People's Republic of China on Open Government Information (OGI Regulations) published on April 24, 2007 and effective one year later on May 1, 2008, mark a turning point away from the deeply ingrained culture of government secrecy toward making Chinese government operations and information more transparent (http://www.chinadaily.com.cn/china/2007-04/24/content_858745.htm) While

these Regulations, promulgated by China's executive body the State Council, do not have quite the status of a law promulgated by the National People's Congress, they nonetheless provide the legal basis for China's first nationwide government information disclosure system. Moreover, under China's unitary legal system, the OGI Regulations will apply not only to central government agencies but also extend the disclosure obligation downward through the Chinese government hierarchy to the provinces, counties and townships, the lowest level of government in China.

A mixture of economic and political motives has driven the authoritarian Chinese Communist Party leadership toward greater transparency. China's international and bilateral commitments require greater transparency and provide an external impetus toward greater openness. However, the main motivations underlying the OGI Regulations are largely domestic: broader sharing of government information in the service of economic development, improving people's lives, enhancing trust between the public and the government, curbing government corruption and promoting better governance at all levels of government.

Actions by the Chinese government still continue to ban Internet sites or other actions that do not agree with the government as seen by the banning of the YouTube service because of its anti-government content. Tudou.com, a leading video-sharing site in China, proactively restricts content that can potentially agitate government officials (Vascellaro and Fowler, 2009). Internet censorship standards vary with countries. China centrally manages website content by employing tens of thousands of people and having international companies cooperate with each other in order to implement a system of political censorship (Litvinsky, 2009). International companies participating in the Internet censorship include Yahoo!, Microsoft, Googel and Cisco. Failure to comply with the mandate of the Chinese government could subject these companies to criminal charges.

Australia

The Privacy Act 1988 was the first privacy law to address public's concerns with the use of personal information by Commonwealth agencies. This law became a general principal from which industry sector-specific information privacy laws were enacted. More specifically, they were enacted to regulate ways in which private industries collect, use, and disclose personal information. Legislators at different levels of the Australian government have passed privacy laws for different industries. Because of the dual system, a myriad of privacy-related laws emerged to cope with the general needs of the State-based agencies and the local needs of industries. Under the same principal of The Privacy Act 1988, individual states and territories of Australia as well as local governmental agencies localize the ways of how each deal with personal information. It therefore became a common practice to see the overlapping areas of information privacy between state and local laws. The multi-tier complexity of information privacy laws has resulted in a time-consuming review process for the Australian Law Reform Commission (ALRC) to enact any privacy laws in Australia.

Industry-specific privacy regulations often supersede general application of privacy protection for the public in Australia. The Howard Liberal-National Coalition Government enacted the Privacy Amendment for the private industry sectors in the year 2000. Section 7B (3) of the Act ruled that industrial relations laws are a better legislation than general one at addressing employee records protection (Pyman, O'Rourke and Teicher, 2008). This act resulted in the revoking of employee records from privacy protection. Many companies abused the predominance of industry-specific privacy regulations to their corporate benefits. Telstra (restrictive clauses) collected personal information of its employees on race, sexual preferences, and religious and political beliefs (Kerbaj, 2005). Mishandling of personal information by industry and professional sectors were widespread in Australia (Primedia, 2006). The number of employee complaints about unnecessary, unlawful or unfair collection of personal information had tripled from 2001-2003 (Office of the Privacy Commissioner, 2005).

The Australian Law Reform Commission (ALRC) continued the principles-based approach to regulate the information privacy practices at the state level, but adopted a "details-based" approach to regulate the same practices at the local-level. ALRC's recommendations made on August 11, 2008 are clear evidence to support the existence of the dual system. Within this recommendations are the three tiers of information privacy laws applicable to different geographical areas (Figure 1). The updated Privacy Act's Unified Privacy Principles (UPPs) serves as the foundation for privacy laws enacted in state and local levels. UPPs have general applications to privacy laws. Contingent upon UPPs, states enacted various laws to regulate the use of personal information for different industries, including healthcare, research and financial sectors.

Legal regulation of privacy in Australia is multi-faced, contradictory, and inconsistent among Commonwealth, states and industry sectors. A poorly orchestrated effort at these three levels has resulted in many unresolved privacy issues (e.g. drug testing, email monitoring in the workplace).

Australia has long centralized the development of privacy laws and regulations to fit the practical needs of different industries. The Commonwealth has dictated the legalization process in Australia. Although the U.S. has enacted industry-specific regulations on privacy protection, the approach adopted is opposite to that of Australia. The consumer pressure dictated the legalization process instead. EU and Asia are more interested in enacting comprehensive regulations to meet the unified needs of the public and industry.

The major differences between these two continents are that EU is taking proactive top-down approach and Asia is taking reactive bottom-up

Figure 1. Three-tiered approach of information privacy regulations

Figure 2. International perspective of information privacy laws and regulations

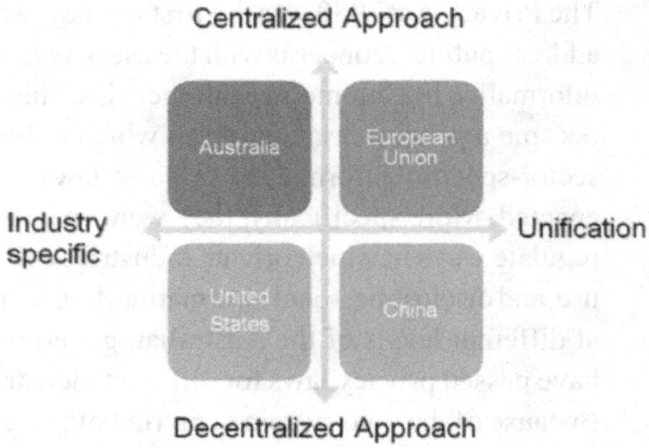

approach. Since the concept of privacy is largely ignored in Asia, using laws and regulations to govern the privacy protection practices is often absent. Unless privacy issues surfaced in the public, Asian governments often choose to ignore their existence.

IMPLICATIONS AND CONCLUSION

Attitude toward privacy ranges from "privacy fundamentalists" of the European Union to the "privacy ignorance" of Asia, Africa and the Middle East, with "privacy pragmatists" of Australia and the U.S. as seen as "in between" (Sheng, Nah and Siau, 2008). The cultural differences have exerted significant influence on each country's privacy laws and regulations. The abovementioned leads us to develop a theoretical framework to classify international privacy laws and regulations into four categories by two dimensions: centralized versus decentralized approach, and unification versus industry-specific development (Figure 2).

International governmental organizations have played an active role in privacy policy formation. Several countries have adopted or amended data protection legislation with an eye to entering the European Union or the European information technology market. The EU's adequacy requirement has played an important role in the development of international standards. In addition, international bodies such as APEC have also had significant impact on the development of data protection regimes, as is the case with recent proposed amendments to Australia's privacy legislation. International initiatives to combat spam, such as the StopSpam Alliance, have resulted in several new national anti-spam laws.

Many countries, especially in Asia, have developed or are currently developing laws in an effort to promote electronic commerce. These countries recognize that consumers are uneasy with the increased availability of their personal data, particularly with new means of identification and forms of transactions. These countries recognize consumers are uneasy with their personal information being sent worldwide. Privacy laws are being introduced as part of a package of laws intended to facilitate electronic commerce by setting up uniform rules.

To ensure laws are consistent with Pan-European laws. Most countries in Central and Eastern Europe are adopting new laws based on the Council of Europe Convention No. 108 and the EU Data Protection Directive. Many of these countries hope to join the European Union in the near future. Countries in other regions are adopting new laws or updating older laws to ensure that trade will not be affected by the requirements of the European Union Directive.

It is expected that if there is consistency in laws in relation to privacy and security issues that individuals information will be globally respected and protected. As the use of the Internet grows as well as cross-country e-commerce the importance of the issue of privacy and security laws will continue to grow.

REFERENCES

American Medical Association. (2009). American Recovery And Reinvestment Act of 2009 (ARRA) [Electronic Version]. Retrieved March 5, 2009 from http://www.ama-assn.org/ama/pub/legislation-advocacy/current-topics-advocacy/hr1-stimulus-summary.shtml.

Directive 95/46/EC of the European Parliament and of the Council of 24 October 1995 on the protection of individuals with regard to the processing of personal data and on the free movement of such data. Retrieved on April 9, 2009 from http://www.cdt.org/privacy/eudirective/EU_Directive_.html.

Eecke, P. V., & Truyens, M. (2008). Recent Events in EU Internet Law. *Journal of Internet Law*, *11*(12), 32–34.

Ess, C. (2006). Ethical pluralism and global information ethics. *Ethics and Information Technology*, *8*(4), 215–226. doi:10.1007/s10676-006-9113-3

Federal Trade Commission Protecting America's Consumers. (2004). Retrieved on March 22, 2007 from http://www.theiia.org/chapters/index.cfm/view.resources/cid/90.

Federal Trade Commission Protecting America's Consumers. (2005). Retrieved on March 22, 2007 from http://www.ftc.gov/privacy/privacyinitiatives/promises.htm

Fifth Annual BSA and IDC Global Software Piracy Study. (2008). Crime Statistics: Software piracy rate (most recent) by country. Retrieved from http://www.nationmaster.com/graph/cri_sof_pir_rat-crime-software-piracy-rate

Hoofnagle, C. J. (2005). *Privacy Self Regulation: A Decade of Disappointment*. Retrieved on March 13, 2007 from http://www.epic.org/reports/decadedisappoint.html.

http://www.medstarsystems.com/hipaa (n.d.). Retrieved on February 16, 2007.

http://www.security-port.com/patriot-act.htm (n.d.). Retrieved on February 15, 2007.

Internet World Stats. (2008, December 31). *Internet World Statistics: World Internet Users and Population Statistics*. Retrieved March 25, 2009, from http://www.internetworldstats.com/stats.htm

Kerbaj, R. (2005). *Telstra's secret dossiers on staff*. The Australian.

Kobrin, S. J. (2002, November). *The Trans-Atlantic Data Privacy Dispute, Territorial Jurisdiction and Global Governance*. Retrieved April 9, 2009 from http://ssrn.com/abstract=349561

Kong, L. (2007). Online Privacy in China: A Survey on Information Practices of Chinese Websites. *Chinese Journal of International Law*, *6*(1), 157–183. doi:10.1093/chinesejil/jml061

Litvinsky, M. (2009). *Internet boom in China has given citizens new avenues for self-expression*. NoticiasFinancieras.

Martins, C. S., & Martins, S. J. (2005). The Impact of the USA PATRIOT Act on Records Management. *Information Management Journal*, *39*(3), 52–58.

Mason, D. (2009). Chips Raise Privacy Concerns. *Ward's Auto World*, *45*(3), 15.

Moye, S. (2006). Congress Assesses Data Security Proposals. *Information Management Journal, 40*(1), 20-23.

Naumann, I., & Hogben, G. (2008). Privacy features of European eID card specifications. *Network Security*, (8): 9–13. doi:10.1016/S1353-4858(08)70097-7

New rules issued to require government transparency. (2007, April 24). Retrieved on March 18, 2009 from http://www.chinadaily.com.cn/china/2007-04/24/content_858745.htm.

Office of the Privacy Commissioner. (2005). *2004-05 Annual Report of the Office of the Privacy Commissioner*.

Palmer, M. (2008). EU targets online privacy fears. *Financial Times (North American Edition)*, 20.

Politics: Senate Gives Patriot Act Six More Months. (2005). Retrieved on March 13, 2007 from http://www.cnn.com/2005/POLITICS/12/21/patriot.act/index.html.

Primedia. (2006). Media Announcement: Privacy Commissioner publishes case notes 5-9 for 2006. *Primedia Email list*.

Pyman, A., O'Rourke, A., & Teicher, J. (2008). Information Privacy and Employee Records in Australia: Which Way Forward? *Australian Bulletin of Labour, 34*(1), 28–46.

Sarbanes-Oxley Financial and Accounting Disclosure Information. (2007). Retrieved on March 13, 2007 from http://www.sarbanes-oxley.com/

Sheng, H., Nah, F. F., & Siau, K. (2008). An Experimental Study on Ubiquitous commerce Adoption: Impact of Personalization and Privacy Concerns. *Journal of the Association for Information Systems, 9*(6), 344–376.

Sullivan, B. (2006). *'La difference' is stark in EU, U.S. privacy laws*. MSNBC.

Swartz, N. (2007, Sep/Oct). Google Reduces Data Retention Period. *Information Management Journal, 41*(5), 22.

The Economist. (2003). Asia: The right to know; China. *The Economist, 369*, 72.

United States Government Accountability Office. *Personal Information*. (2006). Retrieved on March 25, 2007 from http://www.gao.gov/new.items/d06674.pdf.

Vascellaro, J. E., & Fowler, G. A. (2009). China Blocks Local Access To YouTube, Once Again. *Wall Street Journal. (Eastern edition)* B1.

Volonino, L., & Robinson, S. R. (2004). *Principles and Practice of Information Security: Protecting Computers from Hackers and Lawyers*. Upper Saddle River, NJ: Pearson Prentice Hall.

Wall, B. (2002). An imperfect cybercrime treaty. *CIO, 15*(9), 102.

Ye, J. (2008). Going Dark: China's Computer Screens. Retrieved March 25, 2009, from http://blogs.wsj.com/chinajournal/2008/10/21/going-dark-chinas-computer-screens/

Zhang, M. (2007). University Student Sues Microsoft for Invasion of Privacy. *CHINA.ORG.CN*.

Chapter 10
Intellectual Property Protection and Process Modeling in Small Knowledge Intensive Enterprises

Riikka Kulmala
Turku University of Applied Sciences, Finland

Juha Kettunen
Turku University of Applied Sciences, Finland

ABSTRACT

Knowledge-based assets, intellectual property, and capital play a fundamental role in an enterprise's competitiveness, especially in small knowledge intensive enterprises. Small knowledge intensive enterprises need to create new ways of operating in order to manage the intellectual and knowledge-based assets in their organizations more efficiently. Organizational knowledge and intellectual property can be protected, either formally via IPR, or informally via efficient knowledge management. Successful IP protection requires systematic intellectual property and knowledge management. Intellectual property protection via efficient knowledge management affects the entire organization rather than being just a separate task. It needs to be embedded in organizational work routines, practices, and processes as an overall operational strategy. When embedded in organizational work processes, IP protection and knowledge management become a continuous part of work routines and tasks in the enterprise, not a separate action.

INTRODUCTION

Technological know-how alone is not enough to ensure success in competitive, rapid growth markets. Companies have to find other approaches to improve their performance and position in the markets and to remain competitive. Knowledge-based assets, intellectual property, and capital

play a fundamental role in an enterprise's competitiveness, especially in knowledge intensive enterprises. In the 1990s enterprise managers began to notice the importance of these assets. Knowledge-based assets are intangible and are often present only in employees' heads. This fact has led to two concerns: First, the risk of losing that key organizational knowledge (e.g., through employee mobility) and secondly, the need to develop that knowledge (Coleman & Fishlock,

DOI: 10.4018/978-1-61520-975-0.ch010

1999; Kalpic & Bernus, 2006; Randeree, 2006). The attention focused on this subject has created the need to manage organizational knowledge more efficiently and hence, to create new ways of operating in order to manage an organization's intellectual and knowledge-based assets. Small enterprises have certain advantages over larger corporate entities: they are able to respond quickly to changing market demand, they are organizationally flexible, and they often have efficient internal communications (Cordes et al., 1999; Mogee, 2003). As a result, small enterprises can more easily incorporate new working practices and processes into their operations.

The aim of this article is to examine the ways in which knowledge and *intellectual capital* is managed in small knowledge intensive enterprises and to discuss the factors that influence a small enterprise's propensity to adopt processes and practices[1] to secure their intellectual property and knowledge. Furthermore, the focus of this article is to make recommendations as to why and how small enterprises can secure their intellectual property and knowledge. The study emphasises knowledge protection and the development of knowledge management systems and processes that support knowledge sharing and creation, innovativeness, and knowledge protection. The analysis will focus on intra-organizational activity. In order to understand the phenomenon as a dynamic, tactical, and operational process; the phenomenon is investigated from two perspectives: Intellectual capital management and knowledge management (Wiig, 1997).

The article starts with a short introduction on the theoretical background of intellectual capital management and knowledge management; focusing on intellectual asset management strategy, intellectual property protection, knowledge creation, and transfer strategy. The main definitions and concepts are presented in this section. The first section also includes a brief description of the study sample and the methods used in the data collection and analysis. The second section dis-

cusses the methods, practices, and processes used by small enterprise managers in order to protect their embodied knowledge. Also, the value of these mechanisms in the process of intellectual property protection will be evaluated. Factors that might have an influence on an enterprise's propensity to manage and protect their knowledge will be discussed. The section will end with a discussion of the different knowledge categories; in addition to examining the knowledge process cycle and its relation to intellectual property protection. The final section of the article summarizes the results of the study.

BACKGROUND

The importance of capturing and managing intellectual capital (intangible assets) has been acknowledged in several research studies (e.g., Coleman & Fishlock 1999; Kitching & Blackburn 1998; Miles et al. 1999). However, the protection of knowledge has attracted very little attention among information systems and management researchers. The focus of the existing studies has been mainly on knowledge creation, knowledge acquisition, and knowledge sharing (Bloodgood & Salisbury, 2001; Liebeskind, 1996; Randeree, 2006). Small business and innovation researchers have investigated knowledge and intellectual property protection in small- and medium-sized enterprises (SMEs); focusing mainly on legal forms of intellectual property protection (IPRs) such as patents, trademarks, and copyrights. A central finding in previous research studies was the importance of the skills embodied in human capital: skills that cannot be protected through traditional, formal intellectual property protection (protection granted by national Intellectual Property Rights – IPRs). This intellectual capital is often only in employees' heads and it is not externalized or formalized in any particular way. Since the mobility of qualified employees is rather high, the need to capture and protect embodied knowledge is important. A strong dependence on employees is perceived as a problem, especially in small enterprises which have not developed an overlap in knowledge base. (Kuusisto, Kulmala, Päällysaho, 2005.) According to Teece (2000), the central role of knowledge management is to develop, capitalize on, and take advantage of intellectual capital – of which knowledge and intellectual property are the most important. Organizations are increasingly competing on the basis of their knowledge. Knowledge is a key asset for the knowledge intensive enterprise. Technology and new products can be copied and replicated fairly quickly, but knowledge has to be created by an individual. Consequently, knowledge is more difficult to replicate than technology and products, or even processes (Bender & Fish, 2000; Davenport & Prusak 1998).

The discussion on the subject of knowledge management is still quite unorganized (Lämsä, 2008) and there is still a lack of well-defined concepts. As this article focuses on the management of knowledge and intellectual property; knowledge, intellectual capital, and intellectual property are the key concepts. Table 1 presents the conceptual definitions of the study.

A great deal of organizational knowledge is embedded in practice (Lämsä, 2008). The value and importance of knowledge has been investigated in the strategic management field; for example, from a resource-based view (RBV). According to the resource-based approach, easily tradable knowledge is not as valuable to a company as a source of competitive advantage as knowledge that can be secured and not readily accessed by the markets (Kalpic & Bernus, 2006). As knowledge is a key asset for the knowledge intensive firm[2], enterprises have adopted various ways to protect that knowledge. Intellectual property is broader in scope and comprises a wider range of intangible assets than knowledge; in addition to being fundamental for knowledge intensive enterprises. In specific, intellectual property (IP) comprises the knowledge, skills, and other intangible assets

which a business can convert into usable resources to generate a competitive advantage (Teece, 2000). IP can be embodied or embedded in individuals, organizational products, systems, routines and practices, and processes or services.

Because intellectual property can take diverse forms, small enterprises adopt both formal and informal ways to protect it (Kitching, J. & Blackburn, R. 1998). By protecting intellectual property (including knowledge) either formally via IPRs and contracts, or informally via efficient knowledge management, enterprises can attempt to protect various tangible and intangible assets. Even though intellectual property itself is intangible, the object of protection can be either tangible (e.g., a product or machine) or intangible such as a service, a system, or knowledge (Kuusisto, Kulmala & Päällysaho 2005).

Ways to Protect Knowledge and Intellectual Property

The intellectual property right (IPR) system offers a way to protect intellectual property from misuse; whether in the form of theft, imitation, or modification. In other words, intellectual property rights allow people to own their intangible creativity and innovation in the same way that they can own their physical property. Intellectual property rights (IPRs) consist of two categories: industrial property and copyrights. Industrial property includes inventions (patents), trademarks, industrial designs, and geographic indications of source. Copyrights include literary and artistic works and architectural designs. As a result, IPRs are mainly based on *patents* (and *utility models)* for technical inventions, *trademarks* for brand identity, *design rights* for product appearance, and *copyrights* for artistic works. Besides, IPRs can be extended to include trade secrets, plant varieties, geographical indications, and performers' rights (World Intellectual Property Organization, Wipo). Contracts and contractual agreements are treated in this study as formal protection methods. They

Table 1. Definitions of key concepts of the study

Concept	
Knowledge	Knowledge originates in the head of an individual. Knowledge can be related to skills, know-how, processes, practises, products, customers and culture. Person is not always aware of the knowledge she/he posses or/and can't externalize (explain) it. This is noteworthy to consider when an enterprise is aiming to transfer/share/capture the knowledge that is embodied in employees. (Bender & Fish 2000; Choo,1996; Kalpic & Bernus, 2006.)
Knowledge management	Contains a range of practises that organisations use to identify, provide, share, store, create and transfer, and enable adoption and exploitation of knowledge (Choo, 1996). To be efficient, this process requires externalization of knowledge (converting tacit knowledge into explicit form).
Explicit knowledge	That part of knowledge that is externalised and formal and is easy to transmit between individuals and groups Through externalisation process tacit knowledge is converted into explicit form. (Nonaka & Takeuchi, 1995.)
Tacit knowledge	Part of knowledge that is personal and contextual. Contains technical and cognitive dimensions (Smith, 2001). Part of the tacit knowledge can be converted into explicit form.
Individual knowledge	Type of knowledge that is bound on an individual and owned by an individual.
Collective knowledge	Knowledge that exists rather between the members of an organization than in the members of an organization. Collectice knowledge is owned by an organization. (Lamm, 2000; Parsons, 2008.)
Components of knowledge	
Embodied knowledge	Knowledge and skills that are embodied in individuals (Blackler et al. 1998). Embodied knowledge is derived from an employee's experiences and the action-based processes of the organization (Tacit-individual.) (Lamm 2000; Parsons 2008).
Embedded knowledge	Collective form of tacit knowledge that is embedded in organisational working practises, routines and shared norms. This part of knowledge is relation-specific, contextual and dispersed (Lamm, 2000). Embedded knowledge is held within the knowledge management systems and documented processes of the organization (Parsons, 2008). Madhavan and Grover (1996) define embedded knowledge as a "potential knowledge resulting from the combination of the individual team members' stores of tacit knowledge" (Tacit-collective).
Encoded knowledge	Knowledge that is explicit and formalised and shown as a form of signs and symbols (books, manuals, databases). According to Parsons' (2008) typology, encoded knowledge is that part of embedded knowledge that is accessible for those who are familiar with the codification strategy of knowledge. (Explicit-collective.)
Embrained knowledge	Formal, abstract and theoretical knowledge of the individuals. Embrained knowledge is dependent on the skills of how individuals can conceptualize and articulate their knowledge. (Explicit-individual.) (Lamm, 2000.)
Encultured knowledge	The part of knowledge that is shared in an organization throughout organizations' social structure. (Parsons, 2008.) This part of knowledge is tacit on its nature and highly contextual (Tacit-collective).
Intellectual property (IP)	IP comprises the knowledge, skills and other intangible assets which business can convert into usable resources to generate a competitive advantage (Teece, 2000). IP can be embedded in individuals, organisational products, systems, routines or services. Whether this asset is service, system or know-how, it is owned, produced and protected (formally or informally) by the company or/and in the company.
Intellectual property protection (formal)	Formal IP protection methods *include legal forms of protection* and it consists of intellectual property rights (IPRs) and contracts. IPRs are assets that are protected by legal mechanism (Andersen, B. & Striukova, L. 2001; world Intellectual property Organization, WIPO). In other words, they provide protection that is granted by (traditional) national Intellectual Property Rights legislation. They can be protected, exploited, modified and transferred through contracts.
Intellectual property protection (informal)	Methods of knowledge management that do not entail legal rights.

are similar to IPRs in the sense that they *do entail legal rights*. However, while IPRs are targeted to protect products of the intellect, contracts are used to formalize and legalise the relationships between the enterprise and its employees or clients. In addition, the type of intellectual outputs that

IPRs protect is strictly defined, while a contract can be written to cover almost anything (Wipo).

In addition to formal IP protection, intellectual property can also be protected through informal protection methods *that do not directly entail an attempt to create legal rights* (Kitching, J. & Blackburn, R. 1998). As noted earlier, informal IP protection methods are extremely heterogeneous. They may take as their focus, for example, technical characteristics of products or relationships that are internal or external to the enterprise (Kitching, J. & Blackburn, R. 1998). As Blackburn (1999) concluded in his study of intellectual property and small and medium sized enterprises (SMEs), there are a substantial range of informal strategies available to, and used by owner-managers in their management of intellectual property. The principal informal methods of protecting IP and maintaining confidentiality are through working with customers, suppliers, and employees who can be trusted (Blackburn, R. 1998). Miles (2003) perceived that in IP protection informal methods are central for knowledge intensive business services KIBS. Professionalisation[3], employment relations, and relations with other organisations were the most common methods used. Miles, Andersen, Boden, and Howell (1999) mentioned six informal methods in their study that can be used by an enterprise to protect the key knowledge they have: Agreements with partners, suppliers and users; working with trusted partners; internal working practices; lead-time advantage; embodying knowledge in products; and membership in professional associations.

As the literature demonstrates, it has been noted in several research studies that informal methods of IP protection play a critical role for many small enterprises; particularly in certain business sectors. However, there exists a lack of research concerning informal intellectual property protection. This article examines how knowledge intensive small enterprises protect and manage their intellectual property via efficient knowledge management and intellectual property protection. The enterprises that were examined in this particular study represent small knowledge intensive enterprises from three industry sectors: Mechanical engineering, software, and knowledge intensive business services (KIBS). These enterprises were owner-managed and independent; and were located in the capitals of London, UK and Helsinki, Finland. Altogether 57 owner-managers were interviewed for the study. To obtain information rich data a snowball sampling technique was used. To avoid variation in responses and to facilitate the comparability of the information, the chosen design for interviews was a semi-structured open-ended format. The methodology chosen was a qualitative approach and the research design of the study incorporates a theory building focus.

MAIN FOCUS OF THE ARTICLE: INTELLECTUAL PROPERTY PROTECTION PRACTICES AND PROCESSES, AND THEIR RELATION TO THE KNOWLEDGE MANAGEMENT FRAMEWORK

The research results offer a good overview of the intellectual property (IP) protection practices and processes, formal and informal, adopted by small enterprises. Enterprises adopted various practices and processes to protect their IP. The rationale for the different practices and processes related to IP protection varied remarkably, and the practices often had a multi-dimensional function. While for one company the rationale for the adopted practice was to protect IP via efficient knowledge management; for another company it was just a way to support business operations and IP protection was of minor importance. Therefore, the motives behind the use of certain practices varied remarkably between business sectors and even between enterprises.

Intellectual Property Protection Practices and Processes Adopted by Small Enterprises

A heavy dependence on employees was perceived as a problem across the board. Since the mobility of qualified employees is rather high, the need to capture and protect embodied IP was seen as important. Enterprise managers in both countries had adopted various methods to protect and capture embodied IP and to decrease employee dependence.

Contrary to the common belief that small enterprises do not formally protect their IP and apply patents due to a lack of knowledge and time (Kitching & Blackburn, 1999), many of the interviewed managers were well aware of the different types of IP protection practices. They were even able to comprehensively evaluate[4] their rationale for IP protection and for other business operations. Even the managers (especially in the software industry) whose enterprise did not have patentable technology, were familiar with the patent system. However, the research sample does not allow for the generalization of the research results in a statistical manner and sample firms were selected with strict criteria to ensure the richness of the data. However, there were differences between the business sectors in the level of awareness of formal protection methods. Knowledge intensive business service (KIBS) managers who relied mainly on informal practices in IP protection were not very familiar with patents because they did not have patentable technology. Over half of the sample firms which had patentable technology used patent protection and had valid patents. However, patenting was mainly seen as a defensive method against other patents. In other words, the companies were patenting to make sure that the company itself was not infringing on other enterprises' patents. In addition to the case of possible patent infringement or when a company needed already patented technology, proprietary patents would have improved the enterprise's negotiating position and also made cross licensing possible. In addition, the other motive behind patenting was the objective of an enterprise to secure financing from venture capital markets. Venture capitalists often demand that the enterprise they are investing in has patented technology. The entrepreneurs felt that patents were not giving sufficient protection to their inventions, and in small enterprises the rationale for IP protection was seen as limited. Many of the business managers saw patenting as a threat because, when applying for a patent, they were forced to reveal their invention. In addition, they considered patenting to be unnecessary in cases where their products/processes included complex solutions. They felt that complexity, combined with a quick innovation cycle, secrecy, and efficient knowledge sharing; offered them a far better level of protection than patents. Contracts were widely used in all sample enterprises. The majority of Finnish, and one third of UK enterprises, used only simple employment contracts and collaboration agreements whose purpose was not to protect IP but rather to establish the working routines. Consequently, both employee and collaborator contracts were signed 'automatically'. The most used contracts, which aimed to protect intellectual property, were non-disclosure agreements, non-competition clauses[5,] agreements about IPRs, and agreements which prohibited reverse engineering and product-modifying.

Informal IP protection practices in small enterprises can be characterized as having a broad variety. These practices are very heterogeneous in nature and, as already mentioned, they may have multi-dimensional functions. The primary aim of informal practices in the context of human resources was to capture or share the information and knowledge throughout the organization and, at the same time, decrease dependence on employees. Informal practices that aimed to protect an enterprise's products, services, and systems in many cases focused on technical characteristics. In order to identify the protection methods used, the respondents were asked *which intellectual prop-*

Table 2. Protection practices adopted by small enterprises according to business sector

Protection practice/ Business sector	Formal	Informal
Mechanical engineering	Patents Contracts	Secrecy Technical protection Lead-time Documentation
Software	Patents Contracts	Technical protection Efficient knowledge and information sharing via databases and teamwork
KIBS	Copyrights Contracts	Confidentiality Client relationship management Task rotation

erty protection methods their enterprise is making use of and whether they are able to describe other possible methods for protecting IP than formal ones. Respondents were also asked to evaluate *how important role informal protection practices are in their enterprise's IP protection.* There was lot of variation between the responses. Some business managers employed informal IP methods systematically and these protection practices were built into the enterprise's IP strategy, including working routines and processes. As a result, they were using informal protection consciously and with consideration. In addition, they were able to evaluate the strengths and weaknesses in both formal and informal methods, and were able to employ both protection practices efficiently. However, some managers were not familiar with informal protection methods and, even while they were employing them, they were not able to 'identify' them. After a lengthy discussion it was revealed that many managers, who had initially responded that they were not protecting their IP at all because they were not able to utilize patent protection, actually employed several different forms of internally built practices. These practices aimed to protect IP by, for example, decreasing employee dependence. Many of the managers, especially in the UK, had a narrow definition of IP protection as being purely patent protection. Consequently, if they were not able or did not want to use patents, they considered that they

were not protecting their IP at all. That is why a qualitative research design was the only suitable method to approach this research problem. In-depth interviews allowed respondents to speak freely and describe in their own words which IP protection problems their company had faced and how they had addressed those problems. However, the important role of informal IP protection was recognized by the majority of respondents. Table 2 summarizes and defines the main practices, formal and informal, used by the sample firms.

According to the interview findings, confidential information, or key-knowledge, can simply be kept secret; either inside the enterprise (e.g. from particular employees) and/or from external collaborators such as competitors and clients. Most respondents expressed that they carefully evaluate which information they are giving out and, in many companies, secrecy played an important role in the firm's IP protection strategy. In the sample enterprises, a major element of this strategy involved preventing employee access, either virtually or physically, to certain defined pieces of information. According to the interview findings, the strict application of secrecy inside a company may result in limiting motivation and innovation because of insufficient knowledge sharing (Kulmala & Kettunen, 2007). In addition, failure to share knowledge makes small enterprises more vulnerable to a sudden loss of IP, for example through a key employee leaving. Nevertheless, this strategy was widely used within the service enterprises (excluding software enterprises that were included in the KIBS sector) metal enterprises, and electronics enterprises; especially in the UK. However, business managers from different business sectors approached the issue in different ways. While mechanical engineering managers were the most vigilant about keeping information secret from outsiders, software managers had the most negative attitude towards secrecy. In fact, many software managers felt that an open and co-operative approach, both internally and externally, was the most productive and beneficial way to do business. An open attitude allowed information and knowledge diffusion between the parties, and was therefore seen as supporting innovation within the company[6]. By a formation of contracts between the firm and its employees and collaborators, the firm can, by judicial means, prevent the transfer of confidential information. For example, many of the sample enterprises insisted that personnel and external collaborators sign a non-disclosure (NDA) or confidentiality agreement.

By seeking to create a short innovation cycle, enterprises can achieve 'lead time' advantages over competitors. By moving quickly and by bringing new products to market swiftly, the enterprise can reduce the risk of copying and imitation. A short innovation cycle played a significant role in the sample enterprises' business strategies, especially in rapid growth businesses such as software and mobile technology. In addition, a quick innovation cycle protected an enterprise's IP by reducing the risk of copying, and it was also seen as a considerable competitive advantage. Small enterprises are able to be more flexible and responsive than large enterprises. [7]

The business managers who were interviewed had adopted various ways to use technical protection to prevent the illegal use or copying of software codes or data. Copying software products is commonplace and the legal protection in relation to software is rather weak. This was why the software managers took copying seriously.

Since software is incorporated into many physical products, technical protection also played an important role in the mechanical engineering sector. The most commonly used methods for software protection were encryption[8] and obfuscation,[9] using specified keys called 'dongles' that have to be available for the program to run, and adding 'fake codes' in software.

Most managers preferred to use protection methods which were aimed to prevent unauthorized use and duplication of their software, or at least to make it difficult and time-consuming. Software products were also sold as a 'black box'. This means that the company sells the product without releasing the software code along with it.

Enterprises can protect their products by building in specialist know-how, which means that the products are so complex that they are very difficult and time-consuming to reverse engineer and copy. Complex product design, together with a quick innovation cycle, was seen as a very powerful protection strategy. Because of this, complexity may be linked to the niche market sector. When an enterprise's product is hard to reverse engineer and copy, and when the enterprise is operating in a niche market sector; it is more beneficial for competitors to buy a product from the enterprise, rather than copy it and develop their own product.

Embodied knowledge is formalized by embedding documentation into work processes. By using documentation, enterprises seek to transfer embodied tacit knowledge into an explicit form. Explicit knowledge is retained in written documents, tapes, and databases. These common methods used by enterprises to store explicit knowledge were seen as critical for an enterprise's operations and strategy. Documentation had two dimensions: First, it contributed to the efficiency and effectiveness of the organization by knowledge codification and knowledge sharing. When intellectual property is in the form of codified knowledge, it is fairly easy to replicate and distribute throughout the organization and hence, it is easy to restore. Secondly, by using documentation an enterprise can reduce the risk of losing IP through a key employee leaving[10]. The knowledge capture process should be as unobtrusive as possible, and also be easy and quick to administer. If possible, the documentation should be done at the time the experience happens. Efficient documentation can only be sustained if it is systematically incorporated into the work process. The big challenge for managers was how to identify and locate tacit knowledge and transfer it to explicit form. British metals and electronics companies had most formal documentation methodologies integrated into their processes and work practices. For example, in three UK metals and electronics companies documentation was made compulsory in the employment contract. As a result, employees had to produce formal written reports for their employer on a weekly or monthly basis. The documents were saved and secured both inside and outside the company. The reason for this was that the company needed a historical record of how things were done. In addition, documentation worked as 'an idea bank'; even assisting in the patenting process. Formally updated and signed documents worked as physical proof about inventions and, more importantly, they recorded the time when an invention or an innovation was created. This was viewed as being important in the case of possible patent infringement or dispute. The role of documentation in internal IP protection was central among metals and electronics companies: Documentation was formally organized and it was part of the working processes.

In order to diminish employee-dependence, a few service enterprises were rotating tasks between their employees and had established deputies for their key employees. Although only a few companies were using task rotation, it was seen as problematic in small enterprises which had not developed an overlap in knowledge structure. In small enterprises employees are often specialists in their own narrow field. However, some service managers were rotating tasks in order to diminish employee-dependence and to prevent both clients and the enterprise from becoming too committed to one or two key employees.

Business managers perceived that working with trusted partners and employees protected IP more efficiently than formalizing the relationship through collaboration agreements. They put a great deal of effort into developing high-trust relationships with collaborators, employees, suppliers, and customers. While confidential relationships were seen to protect IP, managers perceived that they also supported innovative and fruitful cooperation by allowing a certain degree of open discussion and information transfer between the parties. Also, efficient client relationship management was seen to be important; especially in the service sector. Service innovations are often born out of the client-supplier relationship,[11] and consequently both the client and the supplier share a lot of confidential information. In addition, innovations are often intangible, thus the ideas are easy to transfer to other enterprises once they are created. Client mobility can cause knowledge leaks to other enterprises. As a result, pragmatic client relationship management and client 'commitment' was seen as very important. The commitment of personnel is viewed as being especially important in businesses where the culture does not support formality and where the mobility of labor is high. For example, in the service sector, especially in marketing and advertising agencies, the role of contracts was seen as being mostly irrelevant, and infringements against the contracts were common. In these types of business the importance of positive methods of protection and different forms of incentives, are even more crucial than in other business sectors. It seems that, for these companies, the success of personnel management is critical for success. Consequently, these enterprises made a real effort to protect IP by retaining key members of staff.

Efficient knowledge sharing and transfer was seen as one way to support innovativeness, and also to protect IP. The sample enterprises promoted information and knowledge sharing, mainly through regular meetings and by setting up informal 'discussions'. The aim of efficient knowledge sharing, besides promoting efficiency, was to prevent the development of exclusive pools of knowledge in the enterprise.

Level of Tangibility and Internalization Related to IP Protection Activity

Enterprises that were included in this research study not only differ from business sector to business sector, but they vary inside their sectors as well. In order to find reasons to explain the behavior of the enterprises and their actions from the point of view of IP protection and knowledge management, the sample enterprises were analyzed carefully one by one. The research sample is large enough to provide some insight into the reasons that determine *'why enterprises operate the way they do'*. In order to find reasons that explain the behavior of the enterprises, the interviews were once again carefully read through. Enterprise specific factors which might have an influence on an enterprise's IP protection and knowledge management behavior were underlined. As a result, the following factors were identified for further analysis:

- **Business sector**. Is the business sector mature or immature? Are there standards for IP protection?
- **Age of the enterprise.** Does the age of an enterprise have an influence on IP protection activity in an enterprise?
- **Level of networking.** Does the enterprise co-operate mainly with its clients or does it also co-operate with other enterprises; for example, with universities? Is the nature of the co-operation horizontal, vertical, or both?
- **Competition.** Does the enterprise face competition? Is the enterprise operating in niche or mass markets?

- **International operations.** Does the enterprise operate in international markets or is it operating mainly in national or local markets?
- **R&D.** Does an enterprise engage in internal research and development work?
- **Manager.** How does the manager's education, experience, and competence influence IP protection in the enterprise? What kind of understanding does the manager have of IP protection? Does the manager consider IP protection important and if so, why?

To make sense of the massive amount of data, each interview was organized in table form by focusing on the issues presented above. On the basis of the organized data, a simple causal network was formed from each interview in order to understand the relationships between important variables. It must be pointed out that the relationships here are deterministic rather than being solely correlational. However, a simple causal network provides a visual rendering of the important variables in the study and of the relationships between them (Miles, B. & Hubermann, M.A.1984). This approach assisted in generating more qualitative insights into the reasons why some of the enterprises are behaving the way they are and, more importantly, why some outwardly similar enterprises are behaving differently.

Based on the analysis, it seems that, in mature business sectors where there is a tradition of protecting IP, the IP protection seems to be fairly well organized[12]. It also appears that, in business sectors like metals and electronics, where enterprises are active in patenting, enterprises are 'forced' to patent in order to avoid infringements. Also, it seems that those enterprises (in the mature business sector) that are using patents are active in protecting them in other IP areas as well. In comparison to the metals and electronics sectors, the software sector is fairly immature: standards for IP protection are still evolving, and general practices for IP protection have not yet been formed. Also, entrepreneurs have often a negative attitude towards IP protection in general. Even if entrepreneurs have a sufficient understanding of IP protection and the protection methods available, they are not necessarily utilizing them. In addition, if a software enterprise is using patent protection it is not necessarily using other IP protection methods in order to *protect IP*. Often, for this type of enterprise, patent protection was a 'separate' or 'disconnected' issue, and done purely for external reasons. However, the software sector is a rapid growth sector and new innovations go out of date quickly. Therefore, there is not the same pressing need for systematic IP protection as with business sectors where the lifecycle of innovations and the R&D cycles are longer. Efficient internal communications, the ability to respond quickly to market demands, and organizational flexibility are crucial; especially for enterprises in rapid growth business sectors. It is likely that these are the reasons why software managers often see IP protection as a negative, irrelevant issue; and are not willing to integrate IP protection practices and processes into their enterprise's daily routines. In regards to product protection they prefer to rely on technical methods, rather than patenting, which is seen to be a time-consuming process.

Based on these analyses, three different kinds of groups were identified. The groups are differentiated from each other on the grounds of the following interconnected issues: Level of internationalization, level of tangibility of final products, and nature of business sector.

Group 1 consists mainly of service enterprises (14) that were operating mostly in local or national markets. The majority of the managers in this group had little understanding of IP protection. Most of the managers, especially in the KIBS sector, perceived IP protection as important; although they have not developed a protection strategy for the company. Many of the managers had also problems in describing different protection methods. In general, the understanding of IP

protection was typically low amongst managers in this group. However, there were a few exceptions. One software and one metals and electronics manager had a good understanding of IP protection, but they did not consider it to be important. They had made a conscious decision not to protect their IP. Both enterprises were operating nationally and venture capital was not involved in the enterprise.

KIBS managers in this group evaluated IP protection as being important, but they perceived that there were not sufficient protection methods available. Enterprises did not use external assistance with IP issues. Contracts with personnel were simple and often out of date. NDAs and non-competition clauses were signed at the request of the clients', if at all. Typically, in the enterprises in the group there was not a tradition of IP protection. The common belief amongst KIBS managers was that they were not able to protect their IP because of the intangible nature of their intellectual property. Many of the managers had faced problems in IP protection when working with personnel and with the clients of the enterprise. Even so, the enterprises had not organized their operations in a way that they would have been able to diminish the employee dependence that was perceived as a big problem. IP protection in these enterprises was reactive or passive in nature. Enterprises in group 1 were relying on policies aimed at retaining key employees in the enterprise's customer relationship management, in addition to confidentiality. Although these enterprises did not have an IP protection strategy, protection was organized occasionally on an ad hoc basis, if at all. This indicates that many companies in the service sector recognize the importance of IP protection, but have not spent much time in thinking how to implement it.

Metals and electronics companies that were included in this group were operating either nationally or through an export agency. Three of the firms were subcontractors and they conducted their own research and development (R&D) work on a small scale. These enterprises only had a few main clients. One enterprise was a family business with three employees (all family members) and the business was built around one innovation that was created by the manager. That innovation was patented. The fifth enterprise was also operating nationally and it had only six employees. The manager of the fifth enterprise had a good understanding of IP protection, but he did not consider it important because the enterprise was small and it did not have any international operations. This enterprise was also operating in a niche market sector and was not facing competition in national markets.

Group 2 consisted of fourteen software and five metals and electronics enterprises. Typically the managers in this group were technologically oriented. Most of the managers had a good understanding of IP protection and they regarded preventing copying and imitation as being important. These enterprises had an explicit IP strategy, but they focused on the technological protection of a product or process. The majority of the managers in this group were opposed to patents. In regards to IP protection the managers in this group relied mainly on technical protection and lead time. They were not willing to integrate formalities into their enterprise's daily operations. These managers believed in open relations, confidentiality, and the exchange of knowledge. In the rapid growth software sector they did not see any reason for protection. They wanted to develop techniques and technology, and move the whole business sector forward. However, ten software enterprises in this group had patented technology, but the patenting was done for external reasons: because of the investors and to avoid infringements. The majority of the managers believed that patents are useless because they regarded them as being time-consuming and expensive. The enterprises in this group were relatively active in networking: they had joint research and development projects with other similar enterprises. The nature of this co-operation was mainly horizontal. Even though the relationships between collaborative parties were not usually formally governed, these enterprises had not experienced problems in these relationships. Taken together, it seems that the enterprises in this group managed sufficiently well without systematic IP protection.

Group 3 consisted of ten metals and electronics enterprises, four KIBS enterprises, and one software enterprise. Three of the KIBS were technology based content producers and one was a marketing and advertising agency.

Each enterprise had an explicit IP strategy which was integrated into the enterprise's work processes; and their employees were informed about these processes systematically. In addition, each enterprise used external professional help with IP issues. The managers had a comprehensive understanding of both formal and informal IP protection, and they were able to identify the strengths and weaknesses of different protection methods. They were able to use combinations of protection methods in different settings. Managers took employee mobility as a fact of business life, and precautions were taken to minimize employee dependence. The majority of the enterprises were operating internationally. Two KIBS were operating only in national markets, but they had a big international company as their client. The KIBS managers in this group were exceptional in the following ways: They had a comprehensive understanding of IP protection, and the managers had worked before in big international enterprises in a managerial position. One of the managers had a degree in law.

Figure 1 illustrates how the tangibility of intellectual property, the level of internationalization, and IP protection activity are interconnected.

Figure 1. Interconnection of tangibility of intellectual property, level of internationalization and IP protection activity

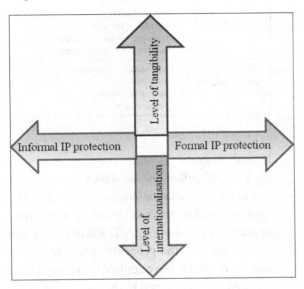

FUTURE TRENDS: WAYS TO PROTECT INTELLECTUAL PROPERTY AND THEIR RELATIONSHIP TO THE KNOWLEDGE MANAGEMENT FRAMEWORK

Informal IP protection is closely linked to knowledge management practices and is applicable to the knowledge management (KM) framework represented by Nonaka and Takeuchi (1995) (Kettunen & Kulmala, 2007). Knowledge processes and categories, including the relationship of core knowledge processes to knowledge categories, are defined in a knowledge process model. The main knowledge processes are internalization, externalization, combination, and socialization. In their study Holsapple and Joshi (2004) present four major categories of knowledge manipulation activities. The aim of these knowledge manipulation activities is to promote the development and use of knowledge resources (KR) in a way that produces value for an organization. How well an organization can utilize the knowledge

resource depends on the quality and availability of knowledge resources (Holsapple & Joshi, 2004). Knowledge can be classified into two main categories: tacit and explicit (see Table 1). The embodied§, encultured, and embedded components of knowledge are tacit in nature. Embedded and encultured knowledge is collective, which means that they exist between the members of an organization. This type of knowledge is organizational knowledge and, thus, owned by the organization. Collective knowledge is stored in organizational rules, routines, and processes. This knowledge is distributed and shared among the members of the organization (Lamm, 2000). The embodied component of tacit knowledge is individual. Individual knowledge resides in the heads of individuals and, thus, is owned by the individuals. Parts of this individual knowledge can be transferred to organizational (collective) knowledge through, for example, discussions, pair work, and task rotation. Individual knowledge moves with the employees. The tranferability of individual knowledge depends on the amount of 'embrained' knowledge that an individual possesses; and on the person's ability to conceptualize the knowledge that he/she possesses (Lamm, 2000). Encoded and embrained components of knowledge are explicit on their nature. Whereas the encoded knowledge that comprises written rules, documents etc. is collective, the embrained component of knowledge is individual. How well an organization can transform individual tacit knowledge depends on the amount of embrained knowledge in the organization and on the organization's ability to create mechanisms and processes to support knowledge transfer, sharing, and storing.

Tacit and explicit types of knowledge are complementary; explicit knowledge does not appear spontaneously, but it needs to be derived from tacit knowledge (Choo, 1996.). One of the main objectives of knowledge management is to explicate tacit knowledge (knowledge that is meaningful to an enterprise or an organization) in a way that it can be efficiently and meaningfully shared, internalized, and used by an enterprise; in order to create and generate new knowledge. The better the enterprise can transform tacit knowledge in an externalized form, the better that knowledge can be internalized and used. Table 3 presents how, according to the research results of this study, tacit knowledge can be transferred into explicit form or, how an enterprise can share, and thus utilize, the type of tacit knowledge that can't be formalized in formal processes or documents.

Tacit knowledge that can be formalized (the person is aware of that knowledge (Kalpic & Bernus, 2006)) can be transferred through documentation, process modeling, formal discussions (e.g. meetings), and by embedding knowledge in products; for example, via formal IP protection methods or technical protection in products. The explicit knowledge that is derived from tacit knowledge can be stored in databases and can be easily shared among the members of the enterprise. Tacit knowledge that cannot be formalized, can be shared via face-to-face contact and by creating organizational working routines. By creating working routines that promote knowledge transfer and sharing (e.g., task rotation or team work), an enterprise can create expectations for sharing knowledge. According to Smith (2001) employees are likely to share only explicit knowledge, unless management clearly state their expectations regarding the sharing of tacit knowledge. Also, by creating an open and friendly organizational culture and "high-trust-relations" among employees, an enterprise can support the sharing and transfer of tacit knowledge (Smith, 2001).

CONCLUSION

Knowledge-based assets play a fundamental role in the competitiveness of small knowledge intensive enterprises. To remain competitive and successful, small business managers are forced to find new approaches to maintain and develop their key organizational knowledge and intel-

Table 3. Formalisability of tacit knowledge

Tacit (formalisable)	Formal discussions e.g. meetings Process modeling Documentation Embedding knowledge in products (patenting, technical protection over products, copyrights, contracts,)
Tacit (not formalisable)	Task rotation "learning by doing" Team work Informal discussions Confidentiality

lectual property.

This article has discussed the practices and processes that small knowledge intensive enterprises have adopted in order to protect their intellectual property and knowledge. The aim of this article was to identify the processes and practices that small enterprises have applied to protect their IP in different situations and in the context of different types of knowledge. The goal was also to provide an understanding of why and how organizational IP and knowledge can be protected. The article has developed a better understanding of the practices and processes that can be used in intellectual property protection and knowledge management; and identified the strengths, weaknesses, and possibilities to improve existing practices. This article has also provided new information on the dynamics that characterize the different ways to protect IP and manage knowledge.

The characteristics of intellectual property and its value for small knowledge intensive enterprises emphasize the significance of retaining employee embodied knowledge and expertise in the organization. Successful IP protection requires systematic intellectual property and knowledge management. Intellectual property protection via efficient knowledge management is a operational process rather than a separate task. It needs to be embedded in organizational work routines, practices, and processes as part of an overall operational strategy. When embedded in organizational work processes, IP protection and knowledge management are a continuous part of work routines and tasks in the enterprise; not a separate action. Embedding IP protection and knowledge management in organizational work processes is not only important for knowledge and IP protection; but it also supports the transformation of tacit knowledge into explicit form, and hence, facilitates knowledge sharing, creation, and innovation in the enterprise (see also Kalpic & Bernus, 2006, s. 6). It seems that the most powerful IPprotection systems have a multi-dimensional function: These practices and processes protect employee embodied IP, which is a key-asset of most small knowledge intensive enterprises, and encourage knowledge acquisition and sharing.

REFERENCES

Andersen, B., & Striukova, L. (2001). *Where Value Resides: Classifying Measuring Intellectual Capital and Intangible Assets*. Birkbeck, University of London.

Autio, E., Sapienza, H. J., & Almeida, J. G. (2000). Effects of age at entry, knowledge intensity, and imitability on international growth. *Academy of Management Journal, 43*(5), 909–924. doi:10.2307/1556419

Bender, S., & Fish, A. (2000). The transfer of knowledge and the retention of expertise: the continuing need to global assignments. *Journal of Knowledge Management, 4*(2), 125–137. doi:10.1108/13673270010372251

Blackburn, R. A. (1998). *Intellectual Property and the Small and Medium Enterprise*. London: Kingston University.

Blacker, F., Crumb, N., & Macdonald, S. (1998). Knowledge, organizations and competition. In Krogh, G., Roos, J., & Kleine, D. (Eds.), *Knowing in Firms: Understanding, managing, and measuring knowledge* (pp. 67–86). London: SAGE Publications Inc.

Bloodgood, J. M., & Salisbury, W. D. (2001). Understanding the influence of organizational change strategies on information technology and knowledge management strategies. *Decision Support Systems, 31*(1), 55–69. doi:10.1016/S0167-9236(00)00119-6

Bontis, N. (2002). *World Congress on Intellectual Capital Readings*. Boston: Elsevier Butterworth Heinemann KMCI Press.

Choo, C. W. (1996). The Knowing Organization: How organizations use information to construct meaning, create knowledge and make decisions. *International Journal of Information Management, 16*(5), 329–340. doi:10.1016/0268-4012(96)00020-5

Coleman, R., & Fishlock, D. (1999). Conclusions and Proposals for Action Arising from the Intellectual Property Research Programme. The Department of Trade and Industry and the Intellectual Property Institute. London: Economics & Social Research Council (ESRC).

Cowan, R. & Harison, E. (2001). Intellectual property rights in a knowledge-based economy. *MERIT-Infonomics research Memorandum series*, 2001-027.

Davenport, T. H., & Prusak, L. (1998). *Working knowledge: How organizations manage what they know*. Boston: Harvard Business School Press.

Holsapple, C. W., & Joshi, K. D. (2004). A formal knowledge management ontology: Conduct, activities, resources, and influences. *Journal of the American Society for Information Science and Technology, 55*(7), 593–612. doi:10.1002/asi.20007

Kalpic, B., & Bernus, P. (2006). Business Process Modelling Through the Knowledge Management Perspective. *Journal of Knowledge Management, 10*(3), 40–56. doi:10.1108/13673270610670849

Kettunen, J., & Kulmala, R. (2007). Intellectual Property Protection in Software Business. In Pagani, M. (Ed.), *Encyclopedia of Multimedia Technology and Networking*. Hershey, PA: IGI Global.

Kitching, J., & Blackburn, R. (1998). Intellectual property management in the small and medium enterprise (SME). *Journal of Small Business and Enterprise Development*, 5(4), 327–335. doi:10.1108/EUM0000000006797

Kuusisto, J., Kulmala, R., & Päällysaho, S. (2006). Intellectual property protection and management in SMEs. In Pesonen, P. (Ed.), *Uutta tietoa ja osaamista innovaatiopolitiikan käyttöön. ProACT-tutkimusohjelma 2001-2005. Teknologiaohjelma-raportti 5/2006.*

Lämsä, T. (2008). *Knowledge creation and organizational learning communities of practice: An empirical analysis of a healthcare organization*. Faculty of Economics and Business Administration, Department of Management and Entrepreneurship, University of Oulu.

Liebeskind, J. P. (1996). Knowledge, strategy, and the theory of the firm. *Strategic Management Journal*, 17, 93–107.

Madhavan, & Grover, R. (1996). From embedded knowledge to embodied knowledge: New products development as knowledge management. *ISBM report*, 3.

Miles, I. (1998). *The management of intellectual property in Knowledge Intensive Business Service Firms. Final report to ESRC*. UK: University of Manchester.

Miles, I. (2003) *Knowledge Intensive Services' Suppliers and Clients*. Ministry of Trade and Industry, Finland.

Miles, I., Andersen, B., Boden, M., & Howells, J. (1999). Service production and intellectual property, *International Journal of services Technology and Management*, 1(1), 37-57.

Miles, M., & Huberman, M. (1984). Fit, Failure and the Hall of Fame. *California Management Review*, 26(3).

Mogee, M. E. (2003). *Foreign patenting behaviour of small and large firms: An update*. Restron, Virginia: SBA.

Nonaka, I., & Takeuchi, H. (1995). *The knowledge creating company: How Japanese Companies Create the Dynamics of Innovation*. Oxford: Oxford University Press.

Parsons, T. W. (2008). *Enhancing pharmaceutical innovation through the use of Knowledge Management*. Ph. D. Thesis, Loughborough University.

Randeree, E. (2006). Knowledge management: securing the future. *Journal of Knowledge Management*, 10(4), 145–156. doi:10.1108/13673270610679435

Smith, E. (2001). The role of tacit and explicit knowledge in the workplace. *Journal of Knowledge Management*, 5(4), 311–321. doi:10.1108/13673270110411733

Starbuck, W. H. (1992). Learning by knowledge intensive firms. *Journal of Management Studies*, 29(6), 713–740. doi:10.1111/j.1467-6486.1992.tb00686.x

Stewart, T. A. (1999). *Intellectual Capital: The New Wealth of Organizations*. New York: Doubleday.

Stewart, T. A. (2001). *The Wealth of Knowledge. Intellectual Capital and the Twenty-First Century Organization*. New York: Doubleday.

Swart, J., & Kinney, N. (2003). Knowledge Intensive Firms: the influent of the client on HR system. University of Bath. *Human Resource Management Journal*, *13*(3), 37–55. doi:10.1111/j.1748-8583.2003.tb00097.x

Teece, D. J. (2000). *Managing Intellectual Capital: Organizational, Strategic, and Policy Dimensions*. Oxford: Oxford University Press.

Teece, D. J. (2002). Knowledge and Competencies as Strategic asset. In Holsapple, C. W. (Ed.), *Handbook of Knowledge Management* (*Vol. 1*, pp. 129–152). Berlin: Springer-Verlag.

Wiig, K. M. (1997). Integrating Intellectual Capital and Knowledge Management. *Long Range Planning*, *30*, 399–406. doi:10.1016/S0024-6301(97)90256-9

Word Intellectual Property Organization (WIPO). (n.d.). Retrieved from http://www.wipo.org

Zack, M. H. (1999). *Knowledge and Strategy*. Boston, MA: Butterworth-Heinemann.

ENDNOTES

1 Practise is rather informal learning while process is strictly defined repeatable activity that can be measured.

2 Starbuck (1992) and Swart & Kinney (2003) defines knowledge intensive firm (KIFs) as a firm that place most importance on human capital as opposed to physical or financial capital These firms gain their competitive advantage by converting the skills and knowledge of their people into intellectual capital such as software solutions, business advise, patents etc. Thus their main input is knowledge and expertise. Autio, Sapienza and Almeida (2000) follow this definition by defining knowledge intensity of a firm as "the extent to which a firm depends on the knowledge inherent in its activities and outputs as a source of competitive advantage" (p913).

3 Professionalisation takes various forms; in general it means that firm or institution establish professional qualifications and accreditation systems to ensure that only certain people that meets the standards are able to get the certain information/ log in to service.

4 Many of the managers included in their evaluation for example following matters: Level of protection that certain protection practice offers, resources used (in the matter of time and money) to get protection, and distinct protection or level of protection that protection practise offers over enterprise's IP.

5 A non-competition clause is an agreement for which an employee promises not to start a competing business or work for a competitor for a given period of time after departing from his or her employer. At the most basic level, non-competition clauses are drafted in order to prevent a covenantee from competing with a covenantor following termination of a contract (usually an employment contract, although they are also widely used in the merger or acquisition of a business).

6 See also Miles et al. (1999).

7 See also Cowan, R. & Harison, E. (2001) and Miles, I. (2003).

8 An encryption means converting data from an understandable form to a non-understandable one in such a way that it can be converted back with no loss of information.

9 An obfuscation means converting a program into an equivalent one that is more difficult to reverse engineer.

10 See also Zack, 1999.

11 See also Miles, 2003.

12 Comparison is made between the business sectors that are included into this research.

Chapter 11
Privacy in Pervasive and Affective Computing Environments

Jeremy Pitt
Imperial College London, UK

Arvind Bhusate
Imperial College London, UK

ABSTRACT

Pervasive computing aims to saturate ambient environments with sensors and processors; affective computing aims to infer emotive and intentional states from physiological readings and physical actions. The convergence of pervasive and affective computing offers genuine promise for creating ambient environments which (re-)configure themselves according to user's emotive states. On the down-side, there is a real risk of privacy invasion if emotions, behaviours, and even intentions are recorded and subject to the same content-access rules as telephone calls, IP logs, and so on. Based on an experiment to enhance Quality of Experience (QoE) in a visit to a public collection enhanced with pervasive and affective computing, we discuss the subtle interactions and requirements of enhanced service provision vis-à-vis privacy rights. The outcome will contribute to the discussion on ensuring an effective relationship between technologists and application developers on the one hand, and those concerned with privacy rights, ethical computing and formulation of social policy on the other, to promote and protect the rights and interests of citizens.

1 INTRODUCTION

Miniaturisation and Moore's Law have combined to make a reality of ubiquitous or pervasive computing (ambient environments and artefacts saturated with sensors and processors); while advances in intelligent software (machine learning,

DOI: 10.4018/978-1-61520-975-0.ch011

autonomic systems, etc.) make adaptation of those pervasive computing environments correspondingly possible. This opens up a wide range of interesting and beneficial applications in health, commerce and entertainment; it also opens up the possibility of every behaviour and preference, and even emotions and intentions, being sensed and recorded digitally. This also raises the possibility that this data is then used in a way that is less desirable: for surveillance, invasions of privacy, reduction or removal of rights, unwanted advertising – even unexpected uses caused by inadvertent loss of the data.

Let us then assume a ubiquitous/pervasive computing infrastructure that provides location-based applications and delivers context-aware services to nomadic users. Clearly, there is added-value in both applications and services to those users if they can be customised and/or personalised to each user. Such customisation can be achieved by transmitting immediate personal information to the infrastructure, adding expressed preferences stored in a user profile, and delivering services according to user-defined policies. It is evident that users are willing to trade personal information in return for value-added services. Increasingly, though, as the sensor technology improves, physiological signals, from galvanic skin response to brain activity (via electroencephalograms) will be a type of personal information traded in return for such services, using the ideas of affective computing.

The premise of affective computing is that interaction — by desktop or ubiquitously — can be improved by sensing and responding to the user's emotive and intentional state (with respect to completion of, or engagement with, a task). If we seek to integrate ubiquitous computing with affective computing, an essential component of 'immediate personal information' to be transmitted is the physiological signals which can be processed (including fusion with sensed behaviour data) to infer a user's emotive and intentional state. This can be used as an input parameter to delivering the customised service. There are, however, well-documented security risks associated with revealing such personal information, and so, we have exacerbated the security risk, although now it is a matter primarily of privacy.

The transmission of affective data (physiological signals) is unlike, for example, the transmission of personal data like credit card information, or context data like location and device parameters.

We want to protect this information from eavesdroppers who would misuse it, and 'trust' the intended recipient of the signal not to misuse it. In any case, the interception of raw sensor data is less likely to be of any use unless one has that user's 'personal key' to interpret the data in order to make a sufficiently reliable estimate of a user's emotive state. This is not to say that eavesdropping on a personal transmission is a potential invasion of privacy, and steps should be considered to avoid this if necessary. However, the situation faced is distinctly more subtle and more serious than this, since the most likely exploiter might not necessarily be an eavesdropper on the channel, but is rather the intended recipient anyway.

Therefore it is too simplistic to respond that user-relevant contextual information should simply be transmitted over secure communication channels to assure user trust: no amount of security on the channel is going to protect the transmitter of information if the recipient intends to act in bad faith (e.g. a corporation intent on creating customer lock-in) or may be under pressure from an external authority to reveal data (e.g. ISPs in the UK required by law to reveal IP logs). Therefore, transmitting raw sensor data over encrypted channels is not the solution to assuring user trust and confidence in the system.

Instead, we have to assure the user that their privacy will be respected, and that the recipient of the sensor data, the computation of the emotive state, and the delivery of the service will all be within mutually agreed constraints. These constraints define how to achieve, on a per user basis, an optimal trade-off between the protection of privacy and the delivery of personalised services. However, there is also a subtle interaction between the principles of privacy and its interpretation and codification in computer law (Reidenberg, 2000), digital right managements (DRM) with respect to user-generated content, i.e., the affective data (Regner et al, forthcoming), and commercial law, involving the exchange of 'goods' (i.e., the same affective data) in return for personalised services.

This chapter addresses this issue by a in-depth investigation of the issue of privacy in pervasive and affective computing environments which entail revealing personal information (in particular, affective data) in return for personalised services. We present a system description (Section 2), set in the context of a visit to a public collection, in which data and behaviour are used to enhance Quality of Experience (QoE), and consider how affective data can also be gathered and used to enhance QoE. We will then show, through a number of scenarios elaborating on this system, that securing the channel is neither a necessary nor sufficient condition for safeguarding privacy, and by extension, establishing user trust and confidence in the service providers (Section 3). We will recommend instead an approach based on a combination of a user-centric privacy model, design contractualism and trust models integrated (Section 4).

The chapter contributes to the book by drawing attention to subtle issues of privacy rights as they pertain to pervasive and affective computing environments. The recommendations and conclusions (Section 5) contribute to the ongoing discussion on ensuring an effective relationship between technologists and application developers on the one hand, and those concerned with privacy rights, digital rights, ethical computing and formulation of social policy on the other, to promote and protect the rights and interests of citizens.

2 QUALITY OF EXPERIENCE IN A PUBLIC COLLECTION

Public collections (museums, galleries, etc.) everywhere are under increasing pressure to maintain visitor numbers, given the alternative presentation on websites, the alternative attractions of TV, cinema, etc., and the sense of expectation that stems from both alternatives. The requirement then is to enhance the Quality of Experience (Alben, 1996; Forlizzi and Battarbee, 2004; Beauregard et al, 2007) in a visit to (say) a museum (Hall and Bannon, 2005; Bhusate et al, 2006). One way of achieving this is to saturate (pervade) the museum environment, including the exhibits, with sensors; to define policies which allow both visitor and museum to personalise and customise their interactions with the exhibits; and then to use 'intelligent' decision making with respect to behaviour, emotive state, other sensed data and the expressed policies.

In this section, we describe a system architecture (from distributed system and physical standpoints) to achieve this, before going on to describe the automated system for 'intelligent' provision of services and content. We present first the distributed system architecture, called the APL platform, and then the specific physical instance built on this platform, called the iCars Exhibition.

2.1 System Architecture

This section presents the overall system architecture, called the APL platform (Section 2.1.1). It is generic in design, but is targeted at a specific exhibition, namely the iCars Exhibition (Section 2.1.2). For more details of both, see Bhusate and Pitt (2009).

2.1.1 APL Platform: Distributed System View

The APL Platform's purpose is two-fold. Firstly, it provides a means to deliver an experience and capture the reaction to this experience, and secondly it supports evaluation of the visitor's experience by collecting and storing user interaction data, which can later be retrieved and processed (e.g. in conjunction with other user feedback acquisition mechanisms, such as interviews and questionnaires, to determine enhancements to QoE).

Therefore, at a high level of functional abstraction, the APL Platform provides a user with a variety of personalised services and interaction mechanisms in a ubiquitous computing environment; and it provides the administrator a means to monitor and evaluate a user's experience in an unobtrusive manner.

The APL Platform itself is (logically) made up of software components and hardware components, which can include exhibit extensions (interactive exhibits), identification devices, video cameras and other interaction devices.

The APL Platform software consists of two parts: the server-side component, the APL System Server (APLSS) and the client-side components, the APL System Clients (APLSC).

The APL System Server (APLSS) allows for user registration, user log-in/log-out, and user/system policy creation and update using a built in policy configuration toolkit, as follows:

- Registration creates a user account on the APL Platform. This account initially stores a newly created policy and subsequently holds session interaction data and video data files. In addition, their personal details are also stored in a Registered Users Database.
- Log-in associates an IDDevice to a visitor and broadcasts their policy over the Bluetooth Communication Link to all available exhibits allowing them to start exploring the museum exhibits. Log out simply disassociates a visitor from the IDDevice and makes the IDDevice available to another visitor.
- The Policy Configuration Toolkit allows for the creation/modification of visitor/system (exhibit) policies catering for the personalisation and added-value of the service received by the visitor. The system also manages and monitors exhibits (APLSC instances) and their policies.

Each APL System Client (APLSC) provides the personalised services and content using its decision-maker in conjunction with fuzzy inference systems plus defined policies (see the next section). The APL System Client communicates with the APL System Server and the Exhibit Extension (if any) using Bluetooth.

An APL System Client (APLSC) instance is able to detect the presence of users that are registered and logged in via their IDDevice. It creates a session for this detected user and then captures the user's interactions through a variety of sensors and cameras. The APLSC also provides information content about the exhibit via its associated display (e.g. multimedia content using a display screen). Interaction data is collected and stored in the user's session file: after the user leaves the exhibit, the session file is sent to the APL System Server Software.

The automation and control of these capture and presentation processes is carried out using an intelligent decision-maker, which uses both the user and exhibit policies. The APLSC retrieves and loads user policies from the APLSS to be used when the corresponding user is detected. It then makes decisions about what content to serve and when, based upon the user's actions, overall inferred behaviour, and the user/exhibit policies.

The APL platform is generic and requires the designer to instantiate the APL platform for a specific planned exhibition. The hardware components therefore depend on the specific nature of the exhibits. In our test case, these are the exhibits that make up the iCars Exhibition.

2.1.2 The iCars Exhibition

The iCars Exhibition comprises a server and four constituent exhibits: three cars, one non-interactive, one partially interactive, and one fully-interactive; and an interactive quiz exhibit.

The physical architecture of the iCars Exhibition, i.e. in terms of machines, display, exhibits, controllers, etc, for the iCars Exhibition, is illustrated in Figure 1. There are four constituent exhibits, History, Security, Environment and Quiz. With four exhibits, there is one machine for each, each running a separate instance of the APL System Client. Each has its own local policies

Figure 1. iCars Exhibition: Physical standpoint

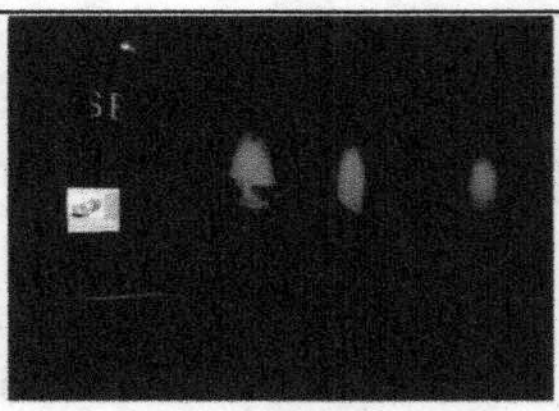

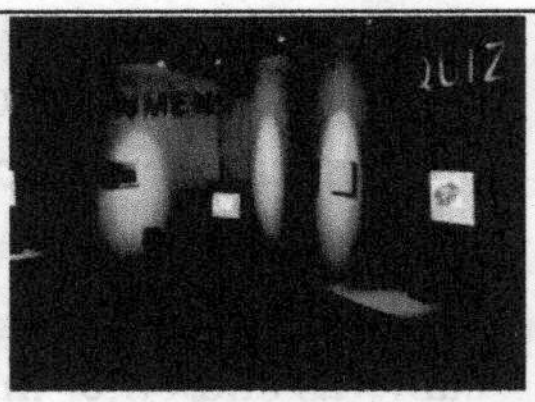

Non-interactive	Partially interactive	*Exhibit Extension* Fully interactive	*Exhibit Extension* Fully interactive

and content database, display screen to present information about the exhibit which it is associated with in the form of text, images, videos and CG models, depending upon the type of exhibit, video camera embedded unobtrusively in the display screen, which captures the user's focus and attention (its operation is automated and is triggered by the users presence).

For Exhibits 3 and 4, which are interactive, there is an Exhibit Extension which includes all the sensors and hardware required to implement an interactive exhibit.

The test for improved QoE through pervasive computing and intelligent service provision was through the sequence of more and more interactive cars. In the first exhibit (History), the car was kept in a traditional glass case. In the second exhibit (Safety), the car could be manipulated but had no effect. The third exhibit (Environment), the car was embedded with sensors: touch sensors, micro-switches, a compass, a 3-axis accelerometer, and a Bluetooth connection. Manipulating the exhibit changed the presentation of a computer-generated (CG) image (replicating the model car) on the exhibit's display (see Figure 2). The content of the

presentation was fully dependent on 'intelligent' decision support, as described in the next section.

2.2 Decision Support

We aim to enhance QoE through some 'intelligence' in the fully interactive exhibits. This is derived from fusing the behaviour and affective state of visitors, as derived from sensors, with other numerical data, using a fuzzy inference system (FIS). The output of the FIS, in conjunction with user policies, is interpreted by the Decision Maker, and used for example to change the view on the associated display. In the rest of this section, we review the three main components of the decision support system that make up this use case: the APL policies, the fuzzy inference system, and the decision maker.

2.2.1 APL Policies

An APL Policy can be written for several actors of the APL Platform. A policy encapsulates setup information for each entity. It also indentifies and define the responsibilities in terms of obligations

Figure 2. The iCars Exhibition Fully Interactive Exhibit

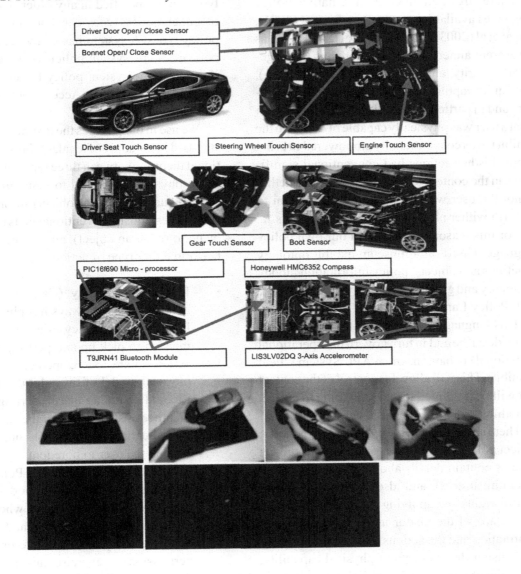

and sanctions for the system components; and actions in terms of physical capability, institutional power and permissions for the subjects (users). In particular:

- a policy represents the museum server in terms of its setup and main responsibilities, e.g. delivering system and subject policies as and when requested, keeping track of users movements etc.;

- a policy represents the exhibit in terms of how it must be set up, its responsibilities which importantly govern what reactions to carry out on certain actions from the user;

- a policy represents the user in terms of the actions they can/cannot perform whilst browsing or exploring an exhibit. A user can only have one policy file associated to them.

There are a number of alternative policy languages available (e.g. Damianou et al (2001), Kagal et al (2003), and Ushok et al (2004)), but as these were aimed at different domains (management, security, and web services, respectively), none quite captured this full range of representation, and in particular did not distinguish between what a user was physically capable of doing (to the exhibit), was conventionally empowered to bring about (his/her actions had conventional significance in the context of the museum), and whether or not the user was permitted, by the system to perform wither physical or conventional acts.

For this reason, we designed our own policy language, based on a museum/exhibit ontology of actions and objects, policy information model, dictionary and grammar, collectively defining the APL Policy Language.

This language is used to write APL Policies, which describe and in turn govern the operational (functional) behaviour of an APL System Client (Exhibit). This will allow for control of the content that will be presented to a user, helping to protect the exhibit from any potential harm etc.

There are essentially two types of APL policies: subject policies and system policies. The subject policies contain details about the users (visitors or administrators), and also define their access control rights for applying actions on exhibits. The details of the visitor include their personal information and the actions they are permitted to apply using the concepts of physical capability, institutional powers and permissions to exercise the former two. The system policies contain details about the various system components, and defines the systems control for automation of tasks such as delivery of content, denial of service, warning or aiding between system-user and system-system type interactions. The system uses obligations and sanction policies to control the delivery of content to the user, the general running of the system and finally what sanctions to apply when the user breaks a policy. The elements of either policy type can be specified in any order. The elements of either policy types can contain many other policy types. A system has many default system policies. Some system policies can be overruled if stated in the system policy by an administrator policy for example. Access control is a good example of this.

We use in our policies the distinction, which is standard in the study of legal, social and organizational theories, between three types of 'can'. This is the physical capability to manipulate objects (e.g. manually rotating an object), the institutional power to establish conventional facts (e.g. a command to rotate an object), and the permission to perform either type of action:

- Physical Capability (Can_1) Policy. We assume the user always has physical capability. However, they might not have permission to pick up and perform a physical action (rotate, touch, open/close etc) on the physical model of the exhibit – if they do, it could sound an alarm alerting a nearby member of staff to attend the scene. Or the virtual exhibit could simply not respond – leading the user to boredom.

- Institutional Power (Can_2) Policy. Power to request to rotate the CG model of the car (create a conventional fact), whether these requests are acknowledged and served by the system depends on if the user has the permission to exercise this power, if so the model will move appropriately. If this power is not granted the requests can't be made, however will be logged as part of the data collection. The CG model will be frozen.

- Permission (Can_3) Policy. The Museum gives the user permission to exercise his/her physical capability and institutional power on the physical exhibit in order to control the virtual exhibit i.e. open/close, rotate, touch and shake.

Permission can apply to both the physical capability and the institutional power. You can have permission to make a request, and you can have permission to pick up an object, or not, in both cases. The difference is, we can intercept in the system itself, the institutional power and permission, and grant/withdraw these accordingly. If the user has permission to make a request, a rotate request for example, the request that is made will be honoured and the relevant information will be provided (rotation of the CG model will occur, textual information will be displayed, video will start etc. at appropriate positions (zones) the model is rotated into). If the user does not have the permission to be able to perform 'Can_2', the request will not be honoured and the CG model will appear frozen.

We can *not* affect the physical capability of the users (short of "getting medieval" on transgressors); we can however monitor and control the permission to physically interact with exhibits, but can only do anything about it if we alert a Docent (i.e. back in the "real world", outside the system itself).

We will grant institutional power to specific users one at a time, so their movements do actually count as requests to the controller to perform actions of the appropriate type. This will also guide the user through the experience that was intended (so as for the user to systematically learn and query the exhibit) rather than just letting the user randomly explore it.

2.2.2 Fuzzy Inference System(s)

Fuzzy Logic, as developed by Takagi and Sugeno (1985) is a formalism which facilitates reasoning about imprecise facts, uncertainties, and value judgments. Fuzzy Logic is the basis of fuzzy inference systems, although there are different types of fuzzy systems as there are various different ways in which outputs can be determined.

In general, to build a fuzzy inference system (FIS), an engineer might start with a set of application- dependent fuzzy rules as specified by a domain expert. Fuzzy rules are expressed in the form "if … then …" that convert inputs to outputs, where both inputs and outputs are members of fuzzy sets (a fuzzy set is a set in which objects are members to some degree).

Given a set of such rules, it may be that a particular range of inputs fire (activate) any given subset of those rules. The rules which are fired then contribute proportionally to the fuzzy output: this is calculated by applying the implication method of fuzzy logic to the activated rules and aggregating all the results. The process of defuzzification converts the aggregated output into a 'crisp' value (the usual method is a centroid calculation, i.e. finding the centre of an area under a curve).

Several FISs are used to provide the user with a service (present information to the user), help and finally protect the exhibit if negative intentions are sensed by inferring a visitor's usage type and behaviour. The FIS is used to determine if: the user needs help, is mistreating the exhibit, or should be granted permission to be able to apply more advanced actions. If the user is determined to be mistreating the exhibit or not adhering to boundaries specified by instructions or warnings etc, the FIS will sanction the user. The severity levels of the sanctions are in the following order (1 being lowest level of severity):

1. Warning of removal of permission
2. Removal of permission
3. Warning of removal of power
4. Removal of power

For example, a user has the physical power to touch the steering wheel, they have the institutional power to touch the steering wheel and request information about it. However, they do not have the permission to touch the steering wheel when a door is not open. In this case the user will just be helped with a message such as: "this is not allowed, please open a door first". If this was the users first minor offence and is not doing any harm, then the FIS doesn't log this as a problem. If the user does this again, the FIS will see this as a warning should be provided as still no harm is done. But if the user decides to do this again the FIS will apply a heavier sanction and remove the permission of being able to perform Touch actions at all.

2.2.3 The Decision Maker (DM)

The DM uses several APL policies and FISs to make decisions about how the system (exhibit) should be controlled to cater for the user in the best possible way as to keep the users QoE high and to keep the systems (exhibits) safe from misuse. The FISs include 'checks' for the actions touch, shake, rotate, and open/close (door and bonnet). The decision maker gets raw data from a variety of sensors such as user presence, compass, accelerometer, touch, open/ close sensor readings from the exhibit extension, time etc. to infer or process data to infer meaningful behaviour or intentions, which can then be used to make decisions.

The combination of FISs work together to infer behaviours, such as if the user is 'normal' or whether they are potentially 'dangerous' and misusing the exhibit. This inferred behaviour may actually not mirror the reality, i.e. this misuse may not be intentional and therefore the system should not penalize the user on just some of the interactions and therefore must not appear to be a rigid system. The FISs use multiple rules to work out from many actions if the user is in need of help or should be heavily sanctioned for dangerous/ mischievous behaviour. Therefore the feedback/ response from the system varies from help and mild warnings, to strict warnings and even sanctions (denial of further interactions and/or even complete removal from using the exhibit). The administrator is able to intervene at anytime with the decisions of the system if something is clearly going wrong.

2.2.4 Affective Sensors

At this time, there are no affective sensors built into the iCars Exhibition or attached to visitors. Visitors are identified only by association with the IDDevice, and it is only their behaviour that is inferred and recorded.

However, it is not technically difficult to extend the range of sensors to include the following sorts of sensor which are commonly used in Affective Computing, e.g.:

- *AffectiveRings and AffectiveMouse (Mamdani et al, 2008):* sensors which are either permanently connected (the rings) or when used interact via devices (the mouse), which can be used to measure galvanic skin response, from which an estimate of affective state can be inferred (Goulev et al, 2004);
- *Tri-axial accelerometer (Trivino and van der Heide, 2008):* a sensor which can be attached to the body or clothing, and used to measure human activity.

Indeed there are a number of possible routes of using pattern recognition for inferring emotional and intentional states, including voice analysis, blood pressure and heartbeat, facial muscles, hand gestures and other physical actions, eye tracking, brain scans, and so on.

It is then no more technically difficult to integrate readings from such sensors into the FIS, the policies, and the Decision Maker. Then we have a system that can measure behaviours and record personal details (including profile information, preferences, and so on), and can even be used to infer emotions and intentions. Benignly, we can do much to improve Quality of Experience with this information, for example if personalising and customising the experience as described above. However, the development also raises privacy concerns, and these are the subject of the next two sections.

3 PRIVACY CONCERNS

The system presented above offers significant personal and community benefits in terms of enhancing quality of experience. However, the experience may be diminished if there is cost associated, that cost being manifest by an invasion of privacy through unintended use of personal information through inadvertent disclosure (cf. Lederer et al (2003)). In this section we look at how this might happen, and discuss the implications. We begin by presenting a series of interaction scenarios with these systems, and consider whether, or to what extent, an invasion of privacy has occurred.

3.1 Scenarios

Scenario 1. A visitor steps up to an information kiosk to access information about some of the special exhibitions on display at the museum. The mouse she uses is an affective mouse. She does not know that it is measuring her galvanic skin response. An eye-tracking camera detects where her attention is focussed. As she browses, the system notices that her focus is drawn to, and her emotive state changed by, an advertisement pushed on the screen. The system alerts the company of her interest. Two days later, she receives an unsolicited mailshot and an email, advertising the product.

Scenario 2. A user is exploring an interactive exhibit X, spends some time manipulating it and shows a positive affective response. Her affective reaction to exhibit X has been measured to be E, and has been stored in the museum's registered users database. She leaves the exhibit and approaches an interactive map of the museum. The IDDevice is used to recognise her. Based on the recordings of many visitors' affective responses, content-based data-mining system, the display proactively recommends: "people who felt like E about X, also felt E about exhibit Y". She browses

these recommendations, selects one, and is shown a map of how to navigate to the exhibition room.

Scenario 3. A schoolgirl explores the museum. At one exhibit in which she is particularly interested, there are a number of schoolboys already there, monopolising the exhibit extension and mucking about. There are several other schoolgirls present, they too are suffering in silence. Then the exhibit invokes clauses its security policy designed to protect the museum assets, and withdraws manipulation permissions and freezes, and so the boys leave. The system's user presence sensor recognise that these visitors have left, and that the only people left are the girls. The schoolgirl approaches the exhibit, and after detecting her with the IDDevice and consulting her behavioural record carried in her visitor profile, the system automatically restores the permissions. It also senses her dissatisfaction, as well as that of the other girls.

Scenario 4. A teacher takes a school class on a group visit to the gym. She wears a heart-rate monitor given to tour leaders by the museum. During the showround, due to the stress, the sensor notes an irregular heartbeat. The platform instructs the (electronic) agent of the teacher's doctor, and also the agent of her Health Insurance Company.

Scenario 5. A visitor walks into an exhibition space. She walks up to an information kiosk, puts on a set of AffectiveRings, and starts to browse the exhibits. Based on interest, the system automatically shows options that the visitor seems to prefer. When she has finished her visit, she goes browsing in the museum shop. The salesman approaches her and starts directing her to products related to exhibits in which the system registered she had an interest.

Scenario 6. A visitor borrows an electronic guide to provide personal information about exhibits. Suppose she is feeling E, where E is negatively pre-disposed. As she explores the museum, the system infers E from sensor data, and in-between exhibit commentaries plays personalised music intended to stimulate a feeling F, where F is a positive pre-disposition (essentially towards the museum).

3.2 Discussion

An informal, subjective assessment of Scenario 1 suggests that an invasion of privacy has occurred. There are a number of motivating factors: the fact that the user (the data subject) is not informed or aware that data is being captured or that she is being observed, and is not informed of what would be done with the data. Furthermore, there is a 'join' of information: the sensor data is being linked with location data and used to access personal information to send the unsolicited advertisements. In other words, the company has used affective information without the user's knowledge or consent to derive something of benefit to the company, not the user. In the UK, this might also contravene certain principles of the Data Protection Act [http://www.opsi.gov.uk/ACTS/acts1998/19980029.htm].

Scenario 2, on the other hand, appears structurally similar but the subjective consensus is that an invasion of privacy has not occurred. The visitor has an established beneficial relationship with the museum, the affective information is being willingly volunteered, and explanations can be offered as to why specific recommendations were being made. Information is stored *for* the visitor, not *about* the visitor, and this is a particularly important element of customer relationship management that can be leveraged by public collection to establish long-term trust and loyalty and repeated visits (Newell, 2000; Witkowski et al, 2001).

Scenarios 1 and 2 are also similar to an incident in the development Apple's iTunes. In one upgrade, Apple introduced — without notification — what was called the *ministore*. The idea was that every time the user listened to music, the details of the song were sent *without the user's knowledge or consent* to a central server, listening habits were then correlated against others, and this pattern was used to make personalised recommendations

through the ministore, users' reactions were primarily affront at the perceived intrusion, rather than gratitude for the potentially customised service. When it was claimed that this mechanism was supposed to mirror the recommendations system supported by Amazon, clear differences were identified, in particular that purchase on Amazon was a 'public' activity, whereas listening to music was 'private'. In addition, the clandestine nature of the installation and data transmission was especially objectionable: users considered this to be no better than spyware, or even worse, given the backdrop of the legal battle being waged over digital music. It might be considered a surprise that a company such as Apple should have made such a profound misjudgement over the way the 'service' was introduced and not anticipated the adverse reaction it would generate. This shows how fragile trusting relationships can be in practice.

Scenario 3 is not considered to be an invasion of privacy: indeed this is an ideal example of personalised service provision which integrates ubiquitous and affective computing in public spaces for groups. The most serious problem here is the correct identification of the source of dissatisfaction: the system might mistakenly associate it with the presentation and not the prior behaviour of the schoolboys. Scenario 4 is, on the other hand considered to be an invasion of privacy. Not, however, in alerting the doctor, but in alerting the Insurance Company. There are several reasons offered for this, for example it is considered that the GP (General Practitioner) has the user's best interests in mind, whereas the insurance company has a profit motive. However, most importantly, the GP (in the UK) has taken the *Hippocratic Oath*, of which one primary principle is the preservation of patient confidentiality.

In Scenario 5, we see both sides of the data collection coin. In the interaction with the kiosk, the subjective judgement is that appears to be no privacy invasion; in the interaction with the salesperson, the subjective judgement suggests there is. The distinction depends on the visitor's perspective: in the first case, the personal information is being used to tailor the 'sales care' in her favour; in the second case, the same (type of) information is being used against her. But there is a question over whether the salesperson is acting lawfully, as the visitor voluntarily put on the rings; or is this a case of 'caveat emptor'?

Scenario 6 is extremely ambiguous. It is one thing for a user to express a preference for feeling a certain emotion: it underlines radio station preferences, it is the basis of selection for a film to see at the cinema (hence 'scary' movie, 'feel-good' movie, etc.), and so on. There are already investigations into how to augment and enhance audio-visual search with emotions, and for music to affect mood in a workplace environment. However, the capacity for music to manipulate emotions is well-known, hence the 'Muzak' churned out in hotel lifts, supermarkets, etc., the music played in fast-food restaurants to 'encourage' customers to eat quickly, and so on. Therefore, one must be very cautious of emotion detection schemes which promise benefits to the user, but which are, or can be, subverted for other purposes (by analogy, some companies introduced appraisement schemes ostensibly to support personal career development; these schemes fell into disrepute when it was found that unscrupulous managers were setting workers unrealistic goals and then using the 'appraisement' as a justification for dismissal).

3.3 Summary

There are three important observations to make following this analysis of the scenarios.

The first observation is that securing the channel is not in and of itself enough to engender user trust. Therefore using https, for example, as the protocol on the communications channel is not, in this case, going to make much difference to the user's perception of trust, or assessment of the trustworthiness of the system, and their interactions with it.

There are four reasons for this. The first two reasons are simply practical. Firstly, given the number of sensors and the high data-rate of transmission, the sheer volume of sensor data makes it impractical to treat it all as sensitive information. Secondly, users are, in some circumstances, comfortable with revealing some information which makes them personally identifiable, and this applies in everyday interactions without computers, as well those that do (e.g. see Adams and Sasse (2001) for revealing personal information in multimedia communications).

The third reason is that as users become familiar with affective sensors and devices, they will recognize that transmitting raw sensor data is qualitatively different from other forms of personal information. For example, the AffectiveWare platform needs to be calibrated to a particular user in order for the fuzzy analysis of physiological signals to infer reliable estimates of user mood or emotive state, in the same way that speech recognition software works best when it is trained for each individual user. Therefore a phone call using VoIP could be recorded and speech processing software used to analyse the signal, but the accuracy of an untrained model will be much less than the trained model. The same applies with affective signals: some general inference could be made, but the estimate is likely to be much less accurate without the trained fuzzy analyser. Thus an eavesdropper could intercept some types of personal information, e.g. credit card details, and use it directly, but intercepting sensor data does not provide any information unless the personal 'key' is available to unlock it.

The fourth reason is that the Data Collector (to use the term of the UK Data Protection Act to designate any organization which collects, stores and uses personal data) must be responsible for the proper treatment of this data. This means, at the very least, complying with the eight principles of the UK Data Protection Act for example. However, there is a commercial imperative for doing so as well. If a company does collect affective data, then it is essential to keep/use it for the benefit of user, not for the benefit of Collector. There might be a temptation to try to create some form of customer lock-in based on years of personal data collected, based on a misguided notion that the Collector 'owns' this information. Similarly, the superficial attractions of so-called 'loyalty' schemes offering exiguous reward in return for information that has no intrinsic value on its own (but in the context of a vast customer base, is extremely valuable, e.g. for data mining) should be resisted. As the iTunes experience demonstrates, the rewards, in terms of best practice in online Customer Relationship Management, significantly outweigh other perceived benefits (Newell, 2000).

The second observation, which follows from the last of these reasons, is that it is not possible to build a system that is resistant to manipulation, malevolent deception, or wilful exploitation, if the Data Collector is determined to act in bad faith. Again, just as simply using a secure protocol is neither necessary, and certainly not a sufficient condition to indicate trustworthiness to a user, that same protocol alone is not going to ensure that a Data Collector complies with the provisions of the Data Protection Act. Therefore we need to appeal to other signs and signals. However, one of the scenarios does suggest a solution: just as the Hippocratic Oath is a statement binding a doctor to maintaining patient confidentiality, we need a similar mechanism for any system collecting and recording affective information.

The third observation is concerned with user empowerment. Arguably, the user 'owns' how she feels, irrespective of who supplies the equipment and software that process the signals to make an inference about that emotive state. The user is then trading those signals for personalised services. Therefore, from one perspective, there is a commercial relationship being entered into between the user and the service provider. Furthermore, the nature of the data being provided by the user is uniquely valuable: businesses go to some length (e.g. focus groups, questionnaires, surveys, etc.)

to get this information, and in many business sectors there is a distinct lack of empirical data about actual consumer trends and opinions. This is a substantial risk: for example the retail market in the UK has experienced substantial disruption in the clothing and food sectors due to an increased awareness of sustainable manufacturing and organic farming. Thus physiological data is potentially beneficial at an individual level, i.e. being able to personalise services, but also at a collective level, e.g. to understand and predict directions in which consumer trends are heading.

This suggests that in the domain of affective computing, a new business model is required. In this model, users should be aware of the value of what is essentially *their* data and should be empowered to exploit this value both at an individual and a social level.

In conclusion, we require the following:

- Mechanisms for communicating trust and reputation between communicating electronic components;
- Mechanisms for communicating trust and reputation between the people and/or organizations on whose behalf these components are operating; and
- A user-centric information model to inform systems development incorporating both types of mechanism.

In the next section, we review a number of basic building blocks which can be leveraged to provide a solution to supporting user-centric privacy and user empowerment in mixed affective/ubiquitous computing environments.

4 PRIVACY AND TRUST

Jiang and Landay (2002), for example, introduce information spaces to control both context flow and visibility. Information spaces are owned by both users and user agents. The latter protect the former by monitoring access to the information spaces and tagging the flow of data and metadata. However, as they pertinently note, the problem is that all software components that process the data must be trustworthy, and this is precisely the problem that motivates our analysis of privacy in this context.

4.1 Privacy Model

Much research and, indeed, legislation on privacy has focused on policies and mechanisms based on a presumption of *personal information*, i.e. data that can be used to identify an individual. However, from the summary at the end of the last section, it is clear that such a data-centric approach cannot function well in the domain of ubiquitous/affective computing delivering personalised services.

Instead, what is required is a user-centric approach as defined by Adams and Sasse (1999ab, 2001). Their Privacy Model emphasises three major privacy factors, namely the information sensitivity, receiver and usage, that interact modulo user and context to form the user's overall impression of privacy. In more detail, these factors are:

Information Sensitivity: defines the user's perception of the data transmitted and its interpretation as information by the information receiver. Contrary to legalistic definitions resulting in binary classifications (private/public), Adams and Sasse (op cit) show that users employ a flexible scale of what is personal/non-personal and are willing, in specific situations, to engage in trade-offs, making some privacy risks acceptable in return for received added-value benefits;

Information Receiver: defines the user's perception of the person or organization that receive, stores and/or manipulates their data. There are a number of factors that will influence this perception and the range of acceptable trade-offs user will make, but trust, reputation and recommendation are among the most important;

Information Usage: defines the user's perception of how their data is being used, both in the present and at some future date. Particular anxieties then rest on whether sensor data is being used for awareness or surveillance. If, for example, 20% (say) of the students are bored in a lecture, then it is one thing for the lecturer to know (present usage for awareness); it is another thing for a student's funding authority to know that that particular student has been bored in (say) 20% of her lectures (future usage for surveillance).

In ubiquitous computing, the term 'user' refers both to the person transmitting personal information and receiving personalised services. However, it is as a transmitter of information that an individual takes a privacy risk, but as a receiver or information that an individual receives a communication benefit. Therefore, in the context of a mixed affective/ubiquitous computing environment, the Adams and Sasse model emphasises the need to consider a user as someone who is transmitting data about themselves, and, with the trend towards entertainment-oriented rather than task-oriented systems, developers need to understand that a user not be actively engaged in a task, with the system, or even aware of data being transmitted. Furthermore, the user then has to be situated in a context where both social, organizational and cultural factors must be considered.

4.2 Design Contractualism

Adams and Sasse were primarily concerned with multimedia communications, and in that context they suggest it is then important for the user to receive some feedback and control over what is being transmitted. Reynolds and Picard (2004), on the other hand, concur with Adams and Sasse in various aspects of the privacy concerns of affective computing: in particular the designer's requirements to identify which emotions will be detected, who can access the results, and what use is made of them (corresponding to elements of information sensitivity, receiver and usage identified above).

However, Reynolds and Picard take the position that, unlike in multimedia communications, sensing affect is ultimately a designer's decision, and although those decisions should be guided by and framed within the given privacy model, it is not appropriate to give the user feedback and control. Instead, they propose to ground those decisions on mutual agreement. The form of this agreement is a contract.

Contractualism is the term used to describe philosophical theory that grounds morality, duty, or justice on a contract, often referred to as a 'social contract' (Rawles, 1971). Reynolds and Picard extend this notion to *Design Contractualism*, whereby a designer makes a number of moral or ethical judgements and encodes them, more or less explicitly, in the system or technology. The more explicit the contract, the easier it is for the user to make an assessment of the designer's intentions and ethical decisions. There are already a number of examples of (implicit and explicit) design contractualism in software systems engineering:

- *copyleft*: copyleft [http://www.gnu.org/copyleft/] is a licensing agreement which leverages copyright law by making it impossible for anyone to access software distributed with a copyleft licence from distributing software derived from the the the original except under the same or equivalent terms of the original licence;

- *ACM code of conduct*: the ACM (Association for Computing Machinery) code of conduct [http://www.acm.org/constitution/code.html] binds members to consider their work with respect to a number of guidelines and professional duties. This is often supplemented by other imperatives, e.g. the ACM Statement on E-voting, which recommends that electronic voting systems ACM developed by members should be resistant to manipulation (so undermining the democratic nature of public elections);

- *TRUSTe*: TRUSTe [www.truste.org] is an independent, non-profit organization which aims to facilitate trust based on privacy of personal information on the internet. For example, the organization certifies and monitors web sites privacy policies and practices; certification results in the award of a seal indicating that the awarded company complies with TRUSTe's privacy principles and will comply with their arbitration (dispute resolution) procedures. An informed user can interpret the seal in the same way as s/he would any other trademark (and use it to inform a trust decision);

- *agents*: a number of proposals have been developed in the domain of software agents, from the three laws of softbotics (Weld and Etzioni, 1994) to govern behaviour of mobile agents to the 'rule of law' being observed in norm-governed agent societies (Pitt, 2005);

- *shareware*: software distributed under a shareware licence can, in principle, be downloaded, installed, and trialled free of charge. If the user decides to retain the program or upgrade to a fully-functional version, then a fee is supposed to be paid. Shareware is an interesting case because the terms of the licence actually puts the ethical decision (pay or not) onto the user, not the designer.

Against this background, when designing interaction or service delivery in a ubiquitous computing environment using affective sensors, a designer will need to make a number of decisions with respect to privacy, according to his perception of the user's perception of information sensitivity, receiver and usage; and his perception of her willingness to make privacy trade-offs in return for received benefits. These decisions need to be coded in a contract, and in the case of privacy, we suggest the terms and conditions should be explicit. Whether the user 'signs up' to the terms and condition will depend on how well the designers perceptions match the user's expectations. As a mechanism for fostering this match, formal models of trust are required.

4.3 Trust

We have seen that there is a *prima facie* requirement for privacy in mixed ubiquitous/affective computing environments. We have described a privacy information model whose basic tenets can be encoded in a design contract to assure that user that the server behaviour was/is/will be compliant to that contract. (Indeed, the contract can be used to ensure that the server behaviour was/is/will be compliant to that contract; but this is a separate issue.) However, even with this assurance, the user is left with a decision: s/he needs to evaluate the contract and decide whether it is worth the risk of revealing personal information in return for an added-value service. This is a trust decision, and one way to resolve it is to use formal models of trust. However, trust has many facets, of which we analyse two here: the first aspect is trust for authentication and dependability; the second aspect is trust for reputation and reliability.

4.3.1 Authentication and Dependability

We have seen that to offer (transmit) personal, affective data in return for personalised services in mixed ubiquitous/affective computing environments involves a trade-off: surrendering personal information in return for added-value services, at the risk of an invasion of privacy. This requires *both* sides of the transaction to make a number of assessments:

- What is the 'real' identity of X? Is X who she claims to be?
- How dependable is X? Will X do "what it says on the tin"?

As Jonczy and Haenni (2005) point out, although both issues are a question of trust, the first is a matter of authentication, whereas the second is a matter of reliability. To address this issue, they propose to use what they call *credential networks*, as a way of managing issues of authenticity and reliability in decentralised open systems (i.e. systems with no centralised authority, and opaque, heterogeneous components).

In the Jonczy and Haenni framework, a *credential* is a statement which can fall into one of two classes: authenticity or trust. Each statement can carry one of three signs, positive, negative or mixed. A credential is then a 5-tuple consisting of a class, a sign, a weight, the issuer, and the mark (who it is the issuer is making a statement about, referred to as the recipient by Jonczy and Haenni). A credential network is then a 4-tuple consisting of the owner of the network, a set of users (network nodes, including the owner), a set of authenticity statements, and a set of trust-statements. Using the mathematical framework of probabilistic argumentation, the credential network can then be used, with respect to a particular user (*X* say), to make a quantitative judgement of both the authenticity of *X* and the trustworthiness (dependability) of *X*.

4.3.2 Reliability and Recommendation

A credential network, based on a system of ethical contracts implemented through credential statements, could be used to make judgements on the identity of a service provider and the likelihood and/or quality of provision. Thus credentials inform the decision to trust. However, the credential network is an 'expensive' computation, and there is another aspect of trust (reliability trust) is that trust is used as a 'short cut' to save the expensive computation. In this case, the decision to trust *first* takes the form of "do I trust?" which can implemented as a database look-up, before it takes the form "can I trust?" and implemented by a probabilistic reasoning algorithm.

The trust and reputation framework of Neville and Pitt (2003, 2004) works in this way: bilateral commercial relationships between unacquainted autonomous agents start with an economic assessment of risk exposure based on conventional signals (markers such as trademarks, guild membership) and third-party statements (i.e. credentials), which over time are outweighed by personal experiences. This is what we refer to as 'reliability' trust. Another issue is then how these reliability trust judgements are passed on as third-party statements — i.e. the recommendations that others use to make their "do I trust" judgements — which actually requires a finer-grained analysis than offered by credential networks.

Such a finer-grained analysis can be leveraged from attempts to create user-centric functionality for Digital Rights Management (DRM) systems operating in peer-to-peer networks. In such systems, the media player autonomously subscribes to nearby peers in order to receive recommendations from that peer and selected recommendations from third parties. This allows the original peer to discover content and to rank that content based on the opinions of nearby peers. As the original peer forms more opinions, software in the media player compares its user's tastes with those of their peers and then reorganises its connections and subscriptions based on the similarity of users' opinions. When passing on third party recommendations the client considers the source and its degree of shared preference, if it is not sufficient or the third party recommendation disagrees with their users' opinions then the recommendation is not propagated. The emergent collaborative filtering effect provides users with tailored content recommendations. In the privacy case, the 'content' can actually be an opinion on the extent to which a service provider is believed to respect the terms and conditions of the ethical contract, and on this basis a user can decide whether or not to reveal affective data.

Interestingly, the digital rights management in pervasive and affective computing is inverted compared to conventional DRM. In both cases the requirement is the protection of content. However, in conventional DRM, concerned with multimedia, the requirement is to protect content created by 'the few' for 'the masses'. In pervasive and affective computing we need to protect content — affective data — which is created *by* the masses for their own individual purposes. However, DRM solutions based on peer-to-peer trust frameworks can be used to ensure that, in this situation, the rights of the individuals are being respected. This assurance is likely to promote user confidence in the trust-worthiness of the system.

5 SUMMARY AND CONCLUSION

The dilemma of privacy protection versus personalised service delivery in pervasive and affective computing environments is going to be an increasingly important trade-off as such systems become more prevalent and the information exchanged increasingly valuable. The system that we have described indicates that the technology is feasible, and that the scenarios considered are likely to be realised.

However, these scenarios reveal that there is a subtle interaction between the principles of privacy, and the principles of digital rights management (as they apply to user-generated content), and the laws of commerce as applied to a market-based transaction, if that content is exchanged for added value services.

The point is this: the collection, storage and processing of affective data should be subject to a core set of fair information practices, as applied to digital information; for example that data is collected fairly, lawfully and knowingly; that it is used only for the purposes specified during collection; that it is subject to disposal after its purpose is served, etc. (these are established in OECD guidelines concerning the protection of privacy). This data is, arguably, user-generated content, just like any other uploaded audio or video, and so entitled to the same level of protection (and not the immediate property and copyright of whoever owns the web service to which it was uploaded). This protection can be encapsulated in DRM (digital rights management) systems for such user-generated content.

However, there is a question of what happens to these digital rights (and the inherent privacy rights), if the data is *traded* or *exchanged* for personalised services. If that is the case, then the rights are presumably traded with the data. Therefore, the idea that services are exchanged for data should be resisted, and personal data used to customise or enhance the delivery of personalised services should be treated as a 'personal belonging' whose ownership is retained after the service has been delivered.

In conclusion, the recommendations of this investigation can be summarised as follows:

- Securing a communications channel is neither necessary nor sufficient condition for assuring user trust or, by extension, privacy;
- Users are willing to reveal personal information in return for added-value personalised services, if they retain ownership of the personal information; moreover they want to make their own judgements on when to so and will make their own assessments on whether an invasion of privacy has occurred;
- We require a user-centric privacy model and suitable balance between user's feedback and control vs. the designer's decisions; that balance has to achieved and maintained through mutual agreement and implemented through customisable policies;
- We therefore need a code of conduct for designers and developers (i.e. a kind of

Hippocratic Oath for pervasive/affective computing environments) as a basis for design contractualism;
- The contract needs to be supported by automated trust mechanisms for authentication, reputation, repudiation, dependability and reliability.

In particular, a global solution is required, if, for example, affective data gathered on a school trip to a foreign country is to be subject to same set of privacy and data protection laws as in the home state (cf. Reidenberg, 2000).

REFERENCES

Adams, A., & Sasse, A. (1999a). Privacy issues in ubiquitous multimedia environments: Wake sleeping dogs, or let them lie? In *Proceedings of INTERACT'99*, Edinburgh (pp. 214-221).

Adams, A., & Sasse, A. (1999b). Taming the wolf in sheep's clothing: privacy in multimedia communications. In *Proceedings of ACM Multimedia'99*, Orlando (pp. 101-107).

Adams, A., & Sasse, A. (2001). Privacy in multimedia communications: Protecting users, not just data. In Blandford, A., & Vanderdonkt, J. (Eds.), *People and Computers XV - Interaction without frontiers. Joint Proceedings of HCI2001* (pp. 49–64).

Alben, L. (1996). Quality of experience: defining the criteria for effective interaction design. *Interactions (New York, N.Y.)*, *3*, 11–15. doi:10.1145/235008.235010

Beauregard, R., Younkin, A., Corriveau, P., Doherty, R., & Salskov, E. (2007). *Assessing the quality of user experience*. Intel Technology Journal.

Bhusate, A., Kamara, L., & Pitt, J. (2006). Enhancing the quality of experience in cultural heritage settings. Proc. 1st European Workshop Intelligent Technologies for Cultural Heritage Exploitation. *17th European Conf. on Artificial Intelligence* (pp. 1-13).

Bhusate, A., & Pitt, J. (2009). Pervasive Adaptation for Enhancing Quality of Experience. In *Proceedings 2nd PerAda Workshop on Pervasive Adaptation at the AISB Conventions*, Edinburgh. Retrieved from http://www.aisb.org.uk/convention/aisb09/Proceedings/PERADA/FILES/PittJ.pdf

Damianou, N., Dulay, N., Lupu, E. & Sloman, M. (2001). The Ponder policy specification language. *POLICY01*, 18-38.

Forlizzi, J., & Battarbee, K. (2004). Understanding experience in interactive systems. In *DIS '04: Proceedings of the 5th conference on Designing Interactive Systems* (pp. 261-268). ACM.

Goulev, P., Stead, L., Mamdani, A., & Evans, C. (2004). Computer Aided Emotional Fashion. *Computers & Graphics*, *28*(5), 657–666. doi:10.1016/j.cag.2004.06.005

Hall, T., & Bannon, L. (2005). Designing ubiquitous computing to enhance children's interaction in museums. In *Proceedings of the 2005 conference on Interaction design and children* (pp. 62-69). ACM.

Jiang, X., & Landay, J. (2002). Modeling Privacy Control in Context-aware Systems Using Decentralized Information Spaces. *IEEE Pervasive Computing / IEEE Computer Society [and] IEEE Communications Society*, *1*(3), 59–63. doi:10.1109/MPRV.2002.1037723

Jonczy, J., & Haenni, R. (2005). Credential Networks: a General Model for Distributed Trust and Authenticity Management. In *Proceedings Third Annual Conference on Privacy, Security and Trust*.

Kagal, L., Finin, T., & Joshi, A. (2003). A policy language for pervasive systems. *Fourth IEEE Int. Workshop on Policies for Distributed Systems and Networks*.

Lederer, S., Beckman, C., Dey, A., & Mankoff, J. (2003). *Managing personal information disclosure in ubiquitous computing environments* (Tech Rep IRB-TR-03-015). Intel Research, Berkeley.

Mamdani, A., Pitt, J., Vasalou, A., & Bhusate, A. (2008). Emotional Computing and the Open Agent Society. In L. Magdalena, M. Ojeda-Aciego, & J.-L. Verdegay (Eds.), *Proceedings of IPMU'08* (pp. 1575-1582). Torremolinos (Malaga), June 22–27, 2008.

Neville, B., & Pitt, J. (2003). A computational framework for social agents in agent mediated E- commerce. In A. Omicini, P. Petta & J. Pitt (Eds.), Engineering Societies in the Agents World: 4th International Workshop, ESAW 2003 (LNAI 3071, pp. 376-391). Springer Verlag.

Neville, B., & Pitt, J. (2004). A simulation study of social agents in agent mediated e- commerce. In *Proceedings AAMAS Workshop on Deception, Fraud and Trust in Agent Societies* (pp. 83-91). New York.

Newell, F. (2000). *Loyalty.com: Customer Relationship Management in the New Era of Internet Marketing*. McGraw-Hill.

Pitt, J. (2005). The open agent society as a platform for the user-friendly information society. *AI & Society*, *19*(2), 123–158. doi:10.1007/s00146-004-0306-1

Rawls, J. (1971). *A Theory of Justice*. The Belknap Press of Harvard University Press.

Regner, T., Barria, J., Pitt, J., & Neville, B. (forthcoming). An Artist Life-Cycle Model for Digital Media Content: Strategies for the Light Web and the Dark Web. *Electronic Commerce Research and Applications*.

Reidenberg, J. (2000). Resolving Conflicting International Data Privacy Rules in Cyberspace. *Stanford Law Review, 52,* 1315–1376. doi:10.2307/1229516

Reynolds, C., & Picard, R. (2004). Affective Sensors, Privacy, and Ethical Contracts. *Conference on Human Factors in Computing Systems* (CHI 2004), Vienna, Austria.

Trivino, G., & van der Heide, A. (2008). Linguistic summarization of the human activity using skin conductivity and accelerometers. In L. Magdalena, M. Ojeda-Aciego, & J.-L. Verdegay (Eds.), *Proceedings of IPMU'08* (pp. 1583-1589).

Uszok, A., Bradshaw, J., Johnson, M., Jeffers, R., Tate, A., Dalton, J., & Aitken, A. (2004). Kaos policy management for semantic web services. *IEEE Intelligent Systems, 19,* 32–41. doi:10.1109/MIS.2004.31

Weld, D., & Etzioni, O. (1994). The first law of softbotics. In *Proc. 12th Nat. Conf. on A.I.*

Witkowski, M., Pitt, J., Fehin, P., & Arafa, Y. (2001). Indicators to the Effects of Agent Technology on Consumer Loyalty. In Stanford-Smith, B., & Chiozza, E. (Eds.), *E-Work and E-Commerce: Novel Solutions and Practices for a Global Networked Economy* (pp. 1165–1171). IOS Press.

Chapter 12
Agents, Trust and Contracts

Paulo Novais
University of Minho, Portugal

Francisco Andrade
University of Minho, Portugal

José Machado
University of Minho, Portugal

José Neves
University of Minho, Portugal

ABSTRACT

Inter-systemic contracting may be based upon autonomous intelligent behaviour. Autonomy is an important advantage of software agents. Yet, it brings along several issues concerning the legal consideration (e.g. legal personality/attribution) and the legal consequences of software agent's behaviour. The intervention of software agents in corporate bodies and the consideration of its roles must also be referred. All this intends interactions based on contracts and relations of trust, at an individual, at a community and at a systemic level. In this regard, it does make sense to speak of the relation between good faith and trust in inter-systemic contracting. And at the systemic level there is a need to focus on special protocols intended to enhance trust in electronic commerce. Smart contracts may be considered in this respect as a way of enhancing trust and of achieving enforcement in electronic contracting.

INTRODUCTION

Inter-systemic contracting can be distinguished from other means of contracting by the degree of human involvement in the process of contract construction. In every conventional means of contracting, through conventional letters, fax, telex (and even in not so conventional ones, as electronic mail), the human intervention always appears at the beginning of any deal. However, in inter-systemic contractual relations the whole process of communication and contracting is "between applications" or "between agents" without any human intervention.

The party's computational systems are not only interconnected but are also able to relate among themselves without human intervention. The human beings limit their involvement to organize the computational systems in terms of their neces-

DOI: 10.4018/978-1-61520-975-0.ch012

sities of communication and action. Henceforth, the machines will act on their own, concluding contracts on behalf of the parties involved, either in terms of "automatic inter-systemic electronic contracting", which is classical case of contracting through EDI-Electronic Data Interchange, and "intelligent inter-systemic electronic contracting", where one has soft bots capable of acting, learning, modifying instructions and taking decisions Allen & Widisson, 1996).

Software agents are computational entities with a rich knowledge component, having sophisticated properties such as planning ability, reactivity, learning capabilities, cooperation, communication and the possibility of argumentation (Jennings & Wooldridge, 1996; Wooldridge, 2002). It is also possible to build logical and computational models having in consideration The Law norms (i.e., legislation, doctrine and jurisprudence). Agent societies may mirror a great variety of human societies, such as commercial societies with emphasis to behavioural patterns, or even more complex ones, with pre-defined roles of engagement, obligations, contractual and specific communication rules. An agent must be able to manage its knowledge, beliefs, desires, intentions, goals and values.

Software agents may be functioned as tools controlled by humans or faced as subjects of electronic commerce, they may be seen as legal objects or as legal subjects (Andrade et.al., 2007). Yet, in any case, it is important to legally consider their own and autonomous will. Thus, within the last years the vision of autonomous software agents conducting inter-systemic electronic contracts on behalf of their principals in the Internet has gained wide popularity and scientists have published a wide number of papers with possible application scenarios (Guttman et.al., 1998). However, when thinking about these scenarios one needs to keep in mind, that the Internet (as an extension of the real-word) and all its users are affected by

real-world regulations. Consequently, SAs that act on behalf of their human owners are subject to real-world regulations as well (Boella et.al, 2008). Neglecting the question of how legal acts by SAs should be interpreted, nevertheless the problem arises that SAs as actors in the Internet need to understand the legal context in which they are acting. Hence when performing legal acts for their principals, SAs need to understand the corresponding human regulations (Dignun, 2001) in order to be able to assess when and under which circumstances a regulation is violated and when not and what punishment might follow. One possible relevant issue is the mere consideration of rules and sanctions, specially when considering the communication platforms and the relations between SAs and platforms. But another important issue, especially when considering the will of the SA in legal relations, has to do with the consideration of legal rules and the possibility that SAs actually know them and adopt certain standards of behavior according to the legal rules. But is it reasonable to expect that SAs behave in accordance with legal rules? (Brazier et.al, 2002)

The fact is that we have to consider software agents operating without the direct intervention of human beings. And this brings us to another important issue that has to be considered: the one of good faith and trust. Autonomous agents may act with good faith or bad faith, may comply or not with certain standards of behaviour. In this sense it is important to understand if software agents comply with social or legal norms. Upon the activities and behaviour of software agents engaging in business, it will be built a certain "image" of the agent and trust will be a mandatory requirement for commercial dealings. Trust may be considered both at the individual and at the system level. And it may become quite interesting to consider the issue of smart contracts as a way of enhancing trust and of achieving enforcement in electronic contracting.

LEGAL PERSONALITY

We must, first of all, undertake an analysis of the meaning of "legal personality" and of the conditions under which law attributes it. In legal theory "personality" is not a "physical" or "natural" concept (Andrade, 1974), it is rather the capability of being a subject of rights and obligations, the capability of being a centre of production of legal effects. So our fist question must be: are intelligent agents capable of being personified? It is known that social roles evolve along with societies, and in the 21st century there must be a newer analysis of the social roles and needs played by different actors. So, it must be researched which actors have intervention in nowadays societies. And it seems obvious that intelligent agents are the newest actors in the global society of the 21st century, with a potential capability of intervention in the commercial and legal arena, and even of producing legal effects.

The issue of social roles looks determinant for the attribution of legal personality, maybe even more determinant than intelligence or self-consciousness. Human beings will (may) play – regardless of the ability to think and learn of each person – a social role. Legal persons, although instrumental to man interests, also play social roles. Intelligent software agents may as well, in a near future, engage on a relevant social role and take active part in many activities reserved, until now, to humans. It must be questioned which actors intervene in nowadays human societies. Indeed, it seems obvious that intelligent agents are the newest actors in the global society of the 21st century, with an impending capability of intervention in the commercial and legal arenas, and even in producing legal effects.

It is important to remember here the distinction between legal subjects and legal objects. As Wettig and Zehendner (2003) put it, "Legal subjects, usually humans, can be holder of rights and obligations. For legal objects (e.g. things, intellectual property rights) this is not possible. These can

only be object of legal owner rights". The issue is whether or not software agents may be seen as mere objects, or if they should be considered as real "subjects". According to their characteristics, they look much like real "subjects".

But can software agents be recognized as legal persons? Many difficulties would certainly arise if we intended that purpose. But the most crucial issue will always be the one related to liability for acts practiced by software agents (Wettig & Zehendner, 2003), since these are logical entities (whether or not physical entities) capable of multiple and autonomous intervention in the legal arena, whose personification under the law might be seen as a technical way of responding to a social need – the need for more efficient and reliable ways of undertaking actions that the man alone cannot perform or cannot complete in a sufficiently and economically not long time.

Civil Law Authors usually make reference to another way of conferring personality. C. Gonçalves (1929) considers legal persons (human or corporate) as "Technical Reality": Law considering "man as person, may as well attribute the same quality to other entities. Under such a point of view, it is correct Jehring's thought that personification is a technical instrument designed, not only to a unitarian regulation of man's multiple relations, but also to giving a stable basis to tasks of common interest". Nowadays, C. Fernandes also refers "the existence of technical means allowing to forming and manifesting a collective will in a legally relevant way" (Fernandes, 1996). And through this, this Author characterizes (collective) personality as a "technical instrument at the service of Law, through which it is achieved, in a practical and prompt way", a way of dealing with certain human interests, by attributing them to an autonomous and different being. Legal persons are thus a considered a reality, not at all a fiction, "a reality of the legal world", corresponding to a social need, to a social interest worth of being dealt with by law. And although legal personality may indeed be viewed as a legal creation, it is a useful creation and it may be attributed "to other beings worth of legal protection". Applying those arguments to intelligent software agents we could argue that those are physical and logical entities capable of multiple and autonomous intervention in the legal world, whose personification under the law might be foreseen as a technical way of responding to a social need – the need for more efficient and reliable ways of undertaking actions that man alone cannot perform or cannot perform in a sufficiently and economically short delay of time. From a man's point of view and man's interest must still be foreseen as the main point as far as legal personality is concerned, intelligent software agents may be viewed as useful creations well worth of some kind of legal protection.

We have to face the difficulties of legal doctrine speaking of "personal or patrimonial element" (Andrade, 1974). Does it exist in software agents? Of course a precision should be introduced about this element. Human persons have a personal element, composed of body and mind, capable of acting and reasoning. Intelligent software agents have a physical element composed of both a physical (hardware) structure and logical (software) structure, also capable of acting and reasoning. Corporate bodies don't have a personal element. They do not possess neither physical characteristics nor a will independent of its members or associates. They can not reason or act by themselves. They must be represented. But, in certain cases, they may be personified through the only existence of a patrimonial capability.

Another requirement that has been pointed out is the "teleological element", related to the finality presiding to the action of the "person". This finality must obey to certain requirements. It must be determined (Andrade, 1974), it must be legal or licit, it must be possible, it must be enduring, and the agents should exist with the possibility of being accessed over a more or less longer period of time. It is not at all impossible to foresee the attributing to a software agent of a finality that might correspond to such a "teleological element".

Still another pointed out requirement – as far as substratum is concerned – relates to the "intentional element", or the "intention of constituting a new legal being", a new and autonomous legal being that might become a new subject of legal relations.

The attribution of legal personality to intelligent software agents would have at least two clear advantages: First, by the recognition of an autonomous consent – which is not a fiction at all — it would solve the question of consent and of the validity of declarations and contracts enacted or concluded by electronic agents without affecting too much the legal theories about consent and declaration, contractual freedom, and conclusion of contracts (Felliu, 2003). Secondly, and also quite important, it would "reassure the owners-users of agents", because, by considering the eventual "agents" liability, it could at least limit their own (human) responsibility for the "agents" behaviour (Sartor, 2002). This solution might look rather convenient in all aspects. But, nevertheless, its adoption will not be without difficulties. One of the difficulties relates to the identification of the agents? We would need technical answers to some questions. What constitutes the agent? The hardware? The software? Both? And "what if the hardware and software are dispersed over several sites and maintained by different individuals?" (Allen & Widdison, 1996). Besides that, agents may have the capability of dividing themselves "into the modules they include" or multiplying themselves "into undistinguished copies" (Sartor, 2002). And if we consider mobile agents then we could speak of "ubiquitous agents" that can multiply themselves into undistinguished copies in order to distribute tasks among each other and to coordinate their own activities. That would inevitably put a tremendous problem relating to the domicile of the electronic agent. In order to be a legal person, the agent must have a residence or domicile. But mobile agents "do not have an established physical location" (Sartor, 2002).

Another relevant question concerning the legal personhood of electronic agents is that of its "patrimonial duties". In order to exist, a legal person must have, or at least be capable of having a patrimony. But does it make any sense to attribute a patrimony to an electronic device? Can we imagine a situation of these electronic devices having "patrimonial rights and also be subject to liability for negligent acts or omissions, just as natural persons would" (Weitzenboeck, 2001)? Is it possible for us to state that an electronic device acted in good faith, in bad faith, with "knowledge or ignorance of certain circumstances" (Miglio et.al, 2003) ? And how can electronic agents be sued in Court?

Of course these difficulties are possible to overcome. But laws would have to be prepared and approved accordingly. A non natural legal person surely must be object of a constitution / declaration act and eventually of registration. Through that registration procedure it could be attributed a physical location to the agent, and also the creators / owners of the device should be legally compelled to make a banking deposit, functioning as sort of an agents patrimony, "a capital or a certain amount of assets" (Lerouge, 2003) of the new legal person, in order to ensure that it could fulfil its financial obligations and liabilities. As Giovanni Sartor (2002) refers "this fund would represent a warranty for the counterparties, who would need to know its amount before finalizing a contract with the agent". A minimum amount of "capital" should be established, similarly to what happens to commercial corporations. Besides that, maybe the law should establish also a compulsory Insurance regime for Intelligent Agent's activities. And of course, the electronic agent should be attributed a way of being represented in case of legal actions in Court or legal executive procedures (Andrade et.al., 2007).

SUGGESTED SCENARIOS

All this could be very interesting when applied to electronic agents, having in mind the referred possibility of electronic agents cooperating among themselves or even multiplying or copying themselves in order to distributing or allocating tasks. But this scenario also presents a great deal of difficulties, considering that this might precisely constitute one of the bigger difficulties in the identification of electronic agents and thus in their eventual personification. Anyway, if the agents could be considered as legal persons, it seems obvious that they would be empowered to look for the cooperation required for the fulfillment of its designed goals and finalities. But that would require legal personality for electronic agents. And, although it might look really exciting, the truth is that we are not yet there. For the moment it is possible neither to consider the "electronic agents" as legal persons, nor to consider any sort of "agency paradigm" in relation to electronic agents. And yet, they exist and become more and more available for autonomous work in the electronic trading. Should we accept the fiction of considering them as mere tools the humans are using, even knowing humans may not be able to control them? Or is there another solution? For the moment, and considering that European jurisdictions have not yet decided what regime to adopt concerning electronic agents, I would mention like to appoint the optimistic suggestion of Giovanni Sartor (2002):

"An easier and less risky way for the agent to make contracts... and to limit the liability of the user (at least, to some extent) is available. This consists in creating companies for on-line trading, which would use agents in doing their business. Such agents would act in the name of a company, their will would count as the will of the company, their legally relevant location would be

the company's domicile, and creditors could sue the company for obligations contracted by those agents. The counterparties of an agent could then be warranted by the capital of the company and by the legal remedies available towards defaulting commercial companies".

But under this point of view, software agents are still seen as mere objects, belonging to corporate bodies instead of natural persons. In this view, the software agent is seen as a mere object the corporate body uses. And the consent given by the software agent (a consent that no one will be able to anticipate or control) will be the consent of the corporate body. In this sense, the will of the corporate body will still be formed by the will of its (human) members? Or will it be just the totally aleatory will determined by the action of a software program?

Of course further possibilities may be exploited. For instance, to foresee a new legal approach of the contract itself, considering not the agreement of wills but the result of the acts of machines or devices predisposed by human or corporate bodies. Or even to consider informatics systems as instruments capable of creating new forms of life, maybe new germs of legal personhood, even a sort of limited personhood, as it happens with some legal "realities" not personified but, for instance, capable of some kind of "process legitimacy" to be in Court, to demand and to be sued, such as it happens with branches, agencies or other commercial establishments or even condominium.

It is obvious that the existing legal norms are not fit for such an endeavouring challenge as the appearance of intelligent electronic agents in electronic relations. The debate about Intelligent Inter-systemic contracting is still beginning. New developments are arising in the field of Artificial Intelligence such as the "embodying" of electronic "conversational agents" (Ball & Breese, 2000). Virtual persons will get more and more sophisticated, but also more identifiable. An ultimate choice must be made between the fiction of

considering agents acts as deriving from human's will and the endeavour of finding new ways of considering the electronic devices own will and responsibility. And maybe in the virtual world – as it happened in the real world about corporate bodies – fictions will definitely be replaced by a more realistic approach of considering the challenging technical possibilities of software agents as new entities definitely requiring a particular legal approach in order to enhance the use of electronic commerce in a global world.

Another interesting possibility is pointed out by Allen and Widdison (1996), making a parallel once again with corporate bodies and speaking of the existence of a hybrid social person, "consisting of a computer and natural person operating in tandem. This "partnership" could exhibit behaviour which is not entirely attributable to either constituent, and yet is the product of their joint efforts. Here we might see something similar to the original idea of the collective of individuals as a single entity possessing social personality (and ultimately legal personality), but the collective would consist of a computer and a natural person".

This suggestion of considering the possibility of a hybrid person, a sort of natural persons and computers (actually software agents), capable of acting a will resulting from the joint efforts of men and software, points out to a new personality composed of man and machine, resulting in an interaction between natural biological (human) intelligence and artificial intelligence, forming thus a different kind of entity with a own will, different from merely human will.

There are interesting views on the constitution of collective entities, integrated not only by humans, but also by corporations and (why not?) by intelligent software, all this upon the idea that a corporate body never acts directly; it just acts upon the acting of the agents holding a role in its structure. And if human element plays a role in the corporate body, there is apparently no reason why software agents shouldn't also play an important role in a corporation. The question here is to know whether or not we may have not only the above referred hybrid society (constituted by human and by software) but also corporations constituted only by software agents. (Or, in the hypothesis of Sartor (2002), corporations constituted for the use of software agents). These are different possibilities that must be foreseen.

The truth is that is must be understood that corporate persons are non natural legal persons (and it is quite accurate that common law doctrine distinguishes natural persons and legal persons or corporations), but also that corporate persons are in fact organizations which may be viewed as "a set of interacting agents (human agents or not)" (Pacheco & Carmo, 2003). It may be assumed (at least the possibility of) that not only natural "persons can act for an organization; there is no reason why software agents ....cannot play some roles". Of course, the participation of software agents under current law is not yet possible, because software agents are not legal persons. On the other hand, participation of software agents in corporations would require not only the attribution of a "patrimony" to the agent, but also the rethinking of the rules of functioning and liabilities of the hybrid corporate person. Probably, a new type of corporation should have to be considered.

CONTRACTS AND TRUST

Software agent's intervention in electronic commerce intends interactions based on contracts and relations of trust (Teubner, 2001). But agents operate without the direct intervention of human beings and "have some degree of control over their actions and inner states" (Weitzenboeck, 2001). Indeed, it can be can assumed that agents behave upon mental states, that is to say their behaviour is a product of reasoning processes over incomplete or unknown information. In this sense, agents do make options and their behaviour can not be fully predicted.

Thus being, considering open distributed systems and autonomous agents that "act and interact in flexible ways in order to achieve their design objectives in uncertain and dynamic environments", is it possible to trust agents in electronic relations? Trust is mainly a belief in the honesty or reliability of someone ("a belief an agent has that the other party will do what it says it will…given an opportunity to defect to get higher payoffs"). It is clearly a requisite of the utmost importance to consider when deciding on "how, when and who to interact with" because it cannot be assumed in advance whether or not agents will behave according to rules of honesty and correctness. This issue leads us to consider the possibility of agents acting with good or bad faith. But also it forces us to view that ways of ensuring a high degree of reliability of electronic relations participants are required, namely the "need for protocols that ensure that the actors will find no better option than telling the truth and interacting honestly with each other". But trust can be perceived in different ways, from an individual perspective ("an agent has some beliefs about the honesty or reciprocities nature of its interaction partners"), or from a social or systemic perspective ("the actors in the system are forced to be trustworthy by the rules of encounter (i.e. protocols and mechanisms that regulate the system") (Figure 1 – adapted from (Ramchurn et.al., 2004).

At the individual level, trust arises from learning (agents do learn from experience), from reputation (a view "derived from an aggregation of members of the community about one of them") or from socio-cognitive models (mainly the belief that someone is competent or willing to do something).

At the community level, trust arises from ensuring that agents will act upon consideration of legal issues, rules and norms, that is to say that agent would abide upon a legal normativity (Brazier et.al, 2002).

At the system level, trust can be ensured by constraints imposed by the system, either by using

Figure 1. The different levels of trust

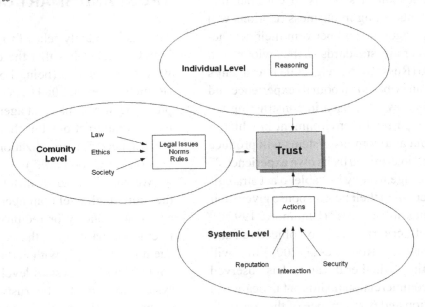

protocols that prevent agents from lying or colluding, or by making the system itself spreading agent's reputation as being truthful or liar, or even by using a system "proof" or "guarantee" of reliability "through the references of a trusted third party".

All these will be important elements to consider within open systems where agents with quite different characteristics may "enter the system and interact with one another", offering different services with different levels of efficiency.

In this regards, it will be of utmost relevance to consider a need, at the community level, of analysing the relation between good faith and trust in agent's behaviour. The same goes for the systemic level, with the possibility of using mechanisms to enhance trust (Smart Contracts (Andrade et.al, 2008)).

GOOD FAITH AND TRUST

Good faith is related to the ideas of fidelity, loyalty, honesty and trust in business (Lima & Varela, 1987). Good faith may be understood both in a psychological subjective sense and in an ethical objective sense (Lima & Varela, 1987). In the objective sense it consists "in considering correct behaviour and not actor's mental attitudes" (Rotolo et.al, 2005). It refers to both social norms and legal rules" (Rotolo et.al, 2005).

In the subjective sense it has to do with knowledge and belief. "It regards the actor's sincere belief that she/he is not violating other people's rights" (Rotolo et.al, 2005)

Good faith arises from general objective criteria related to loyalty and cooperation between parties. Good faith is an archetype of social behaviour; loyalty in social relations, honest acting (Barfield, 2005), fidelity, reliability, faithfulness and fair dealing "and it comprises the protection of reasonable reliance" (Teubner, 2001).

Acting in bad faith in business may either "lead to the invalidation of some of the contract clauses or of the whole contract" (Rotolo et.al, 2005) or even originate liabilities (Antunes, 1973).

The issue is not to wonder whether or not software agents may act in good faith or in bad faith; the question at stake is to consider that software agents acting in business relations will presumably negotiate and perform their acts according to certain standards of behaviour. Yet, according to (Russel & Norvig, 2003) "an agent's behaviour can be based on both its experience and the built-in-knowledge used in constructing the agent for the particular environment in which it operates", but autonomous systems will produce a behaviour "determined by its own experiences". Furthermore, agents may be "able to act strategically by calculating their best response given their opponents possible moves" (Binnmore, 1992).

Good faith criteria relate to "objective standards of conduct" (Rotolo et.al, 2005) that will help determine "whether the agent has observed reasonable commercial standards of fair dealing in the negotiation and performance of the contract" (Weitzenboeck, 2001).

"The form given to the correctness rules allows to impose both positive and negative requirements to be fulfilled" (Rotolo et.al, 2005).

Important issue is the one related to the attribution of the acts: should the acts of the electronic agent be attributed to the user who activated it, considering the electronic agent just as an instrument or tool at the disposal (and control??) of the user? Or should the volition of the agent be autonomously considered, since the user may not have been directly involved or consulted and may not even be aware that the agent acted at all (Weitzenboeck, 2001)? Either we assume or not the possibility, in a near future, of any sort of legal personality for software agents, the truth is that we probably should not rely on a legal fiction of attribution of the acts of agents to humans and, at least, it must be considered the autonomous will of the agent for purposes of good faith, bad faith, error on declaration and divergences between will and declaration. And the fact that an agent acts on good or bad faith will surely be of the utmost importance for all those (software or humans) who have to deal with it. Trust will thus become an unavoidable question for agents contracting.

TRUST AND SMART CONTRACTS

Trust is intimately related to beliefs. "Trust is a belief an agent has that the other party will do what it says it will (being honest and reliable)" (Ramchurm et.al, 2004). As (Rotolo et.al, 2005) put it "agent x thinks that agent y not only is able to do certain actions but that y is willing to do what x needs" (formalization of a "Normative version" of Good Faith)

We can distinguish different levels of trust: the individual level ("an agent has some beliefs about the honesty or reciprocities nature of its interaction partners"), the community level (an agent must comply with certain standards of behaviour) and the system level ("the actors in the system are forced to be trustworthy by the rules of encounter (i.e. protocols and mechanisms) that regulate the system".

At the system level it will assume the most relevance special protocols made in "such a way that they prevent agents from manipulating each other (e.g. through lies or collusion) so as to satisfy their selfish interests" (Ramchurm et.al, 2004).

At this system level it will be interesting to focus our attention in the figure of "smart contracts" which are seen as a "set of promises, specified in digital form, including protocols in which the parties perform on these promises" (Szabo, 1996). These contracts are really program codes imposing by itself an enforcement of the contract (the "terms of the contract are enforced by the logic of the program's execution", turning the breach of the contract, at least, quite expensive) (Miller & Stiegler, 2003). Indeed, one of the most relevant and difficult issues about inter-systemic electronic contracting is the one related to enforcement. Enforcement may be seen at two different levels, "publicly, through the court system, and privately, largely through reputation" (Friedman, 2000). The perspective of smart contracts tries to escape these difficulties - "Instead of enforcement, the contract creates an inescapable arrangement" (Miller & Stiegler, 2003).

Smart contracts can thus enhance the trust in electronic contracting. An interesting idea of this model is to use contracts as games. Games have rules which have to be followed in order for the game to be played. This is the upcoming of a new and much more reliable form of "adherence contract", in which the contract is seen as an electronic game, managed or arbitrated by a board manager, which does not itself play the game but only allows the parties to make legal moves. And of course the board manager may be either a human or a software agent. Here, the contract may contain contractual clauses embedded in the software "in such a way to make breach of contract expensive (if desired, sometimes prohibitively so) for the breacher" (Szabo, 1996). In this model, trust is enhanced "by virtue of the different constraints imposed by the system" (Ramchurm et.al, 2004).

As far as electronic contracting is concerned we may well consider that "public enforcement will work less well and private enforcement better than for contracts in real space at present". In cyberspace, reputation will turn to be a key issue and trusted third parties or Networks of Trust (widely trusted intermediary institutions or entities) must play an important role. Trust at the system level is based upon different possibilities, that is to say that it might be dependent on special interaction protocols (as is the case with the referred smart contracts), reputation mechanisms and security mechanisms. Reputation mechanisms are thus unavoidable to be considered as instruments required to foster the trustworthiness of electronic interactions (as it was referred already in our previous work.

As far as security mechanisms are intended, we must refer the importance of authentication by trusted third parties, that is to say that information about the actors in the system specially delivered by trusted third parties may lead participants (human or software) to act upon what they think is trustable information. That is a special domain for trust and security in electronic relationships – here, as it happens with electronic signatures and

time-stamp, the intervention of a trusted third party will be determinant for establishing participant's trust. Of course, this by itself will not be enough to "ensure that agents act and interact honestly and reliably towards each other. They will only represent a barrier against agents that are not allowed in the system".

In the end, trust will be highly dependent on the existence of social networks and on the traceability of past interactions among the agents in the community. This will be a fundamental issue for the existence of virtual organizations and of assuring a minimum reliability for the intervention of agents in it.

CONCLUSION

Autonomy is a main advantage of software agents since they will act without any human intervention. At this stage we can talk of intelligent inter-systemic contracting. Yet, the autonomy of software agents brings along several issues concerning their behaviour and the legal consequences of it. One important issue to be considered is the one related to the legal consideration of software agents and the possibility of legal personification. Another relevant aspect has to do with participation of software agents in commercial on-line companies and virtual enterprises. The fact is that we have to consider software agents operating without the direct intervention of human beings. And this brings us to another important issue that has to be considered: trust in an individual, community and system level. At the community level, it must be considered that autonomous agents may act with good faith or bad faith, may comply or not with certain standards of behaviour. In this sense it is important to understand if software agents comply with social or legal norms. Upon the activities and behaviour of software agents engaging in business, it will be built a certain "image" of the agent and trust will be a mandatory requirement for commercial dealings. Trust may also be considered at the systemic level. And here, it may become quite interesting to consider the issue of smart contracts as a way of enhancing trust and of achieving enforcement in electronic contracting.

ACKNOWLEDGMENT

The work described in this paper is included in TIARAC - Telematics and Artificial Intelligence in Alternative Conflict Resolution Project (PTDC/JUR/71354/2006), which is a research project supported by FCT (Science & Technology Foundation), Portugal.

REFERENCES

Allen, T., & Widdison, R. (1996). Can Computer Make Contracts? *Harvard Journal of Law & Technology, 9*(1).

Almeida, C. (2000). *Contratos*. Coimbra: Almedina. (in Portuguese)

Andrade, F., Novais, P., Machado, J., & Neves, J. (2007). Contracting Agents: legal personality and representation. *Artificial Intelligence and Law, 15*(4). doi:10.1007/s10506-007-9046-0

Andrade, F., Novais, P., Machado, J., & Neves, J. (2008). Software agents in Virtual Organizatiosns: Good Faith and Trust. In Camarinha-Matos, L., & Picard, W. (Eds.), *Pervasive Collaborative Networks*. Springer-Verlag. doi:10.1007/978-0-387-84837-2_40

Andrade, M. D. (1974). *Teoria Geral da Relação Jurídica* (Vol. 1). Coimbra Editora. (in Portuguese)

Antunes Varela, J. M. (1973). *Das Obrigações em Geral*. Almedina. (in Portuguese)

Ball, G., & Breese, J. (2000). Emotion and Personality in a Conversational Agent. In Cassel, J., Sullivan, J., Prevost, S., & Churchill, E. (Eds.), *Embodied Conversational Agents*. Cambridge, MA: MIT Press.

Barbagalo, E. (2001). *Contratos Eletrônicos*. São Paulo: Editora Saraiva. (in Portuguese)

Barfield, W. (2005). Issues of law for software agents within virtual environments. *Presence (Cambridge, Mass.), 14*(6). doi:10.1162/105474605775196607

Binmore, K. (1992). *Fun and Games: A Text on Game Theory*. D. C. Heath and Company.

Boella, G., van der Torre, L., & Verhagen, H. (2008). Introduction to the special issue on normative multiagent systems. *Autonomous Agents and Multi-Agent Systems, 17*, 1–10. doi:10.1007/s10458-008-9047-8

Brazier, F., Kubbe, O., Oskamp, A., & Wijngaards, N. (2002). Are Law abiding agents realistic? In *Proceedings of the workshop on the Law of Electronic Agents (LEA 2002), CIRSFID, University of Bologna* (pp. 151-155).

Dignum, F. (2001). *Agents, markets, institutions, and protocols* (pp. 98–114). The European AgentLink Perspective.

Elias, L., & Gerard, J. (1991). *Formation of the contract by Electronic Data Interchange*. Commission of the European Communities.

Felliu, S. (2003). *Intelligent Agents and Consumer Protection*. Retrieved from http://www.eclip.org/documentsII/elecagents/consumer_protection.pdf

Fernandes, L. (1996). Teoria Geral do Direito Civil (Vols. 1 & 2, 2nd ed.) Lex, Lisboa (in Portuguese).

Friedman, D. (2000). *Contracts in cyberspace*. American Law and Economics Association meeting.

Gentili, A. (2000). L'inefficacia del contratto telematico. In "Rivista di Diritto Civile", Anno XLVI –, Parte I, Padova-Cedam.

Gonçalves, C. (1929). *Tratado de Direito Civil – em comentário ao Código Civil Português* (*Vol. 1*). Coimbra Editora. (in Portuguese)

Guttman, R. H., Moukas, A. G., & Maes, P. (1998). Agent-mediated electronic commerce: A survey. *The Knowledge Engineering Review*, *13*(2), 147–159. doi:10.1017/S0269888998002082

Jennings, N. & Wooldridge, M. (1996, January). Software Agents. *IEEE Review*.

Lerouge, J. F. (2003). The use of electronic agents questioned under contractual law. Suggested solutions on a European and American level. *The John Marshall Journal of Computer & Information Law*, *18*(2), 403–433.

Lima, F., & Varela, J. (1987). *Código Civil Anotado* (*Vol. 1*). Coimbra Editora Limitada. (in Portuguese)

Miglio, F., Onida, T., Romano, F., & Santoro, S. (2003). *Electronic agents and the law of agency*. Retrieved from http://www.cirfid.unibo.it/~lea-02/pp/DemiglioOnidaRomanoSantoro.pdf, visited 8/9/2003

Miller, M., & Stiegler, M. (2003). *The digital path: smart contracts and the third world. Markets, Information and Communication. Austrian Perspectives on the Internet Economy*. Routledge.

Pacheco, O., & Carmo, J. (2003). A Role Based Model for the Normative Specification of Organized Collective Agency and Agents Interaction. *Autonomous Agents and Multi-Agent Systems*, *6*(2), 145–184. doi:10.1023/A:1021884118023

Ramchurn, S. D., Huynh, D., & Jennings, N. (2004). Trust in multiagent systems. *The Knowledge Engineering Review*, *19*(1), 1–25. doi:10.1017/S0269888904000116

Rotolo, A., Sartor, G., & Smith, C. (2005). Formalization of a 'Normative Version' of Good Faith. In A. Oskamp & C. Cevenini (Eds.), *Proc. LEA 2005*. Nijmegen: Wolf Legal Publishers.

Russel, S., & Norvig, P. (2003). *Artificial Intelligence: A modern approach* (2nd ed.). Prentice-Hall.

Sartor, G. (2002). Agents in Cyberlaw. In *Proceedings of the Workshop on the Law of Electronic Agents* (LEA 2002) and "Gli agenti software: nuovi sogetti del ciberdiritto?" Retrieved from http://www.cirfid.unibo.it/~sartor/sartorpapers/gsartor2002_agenti_software.pdf

Szabo, N. (1996). *Smart contracts: building blocks for digital markets*. Retrieved from http://szabo.best.vwh.net/smart.contracts.2.html

Teubner, G. (2001). *Das Recht hybrider Netzwerke*. ZHR.

Thoumyre, L. (1999). L'échange des consentements dans le commerce électronique. *Lex Electronica, 5*(1).

Weitzenboeck, E. (2001). Electronic Agents and the formation of contracts. *International Journal of Law and Information Technology*, *9*(3), 204–234. doi:10.1093/ijlit/9.3.204

Wettig, S., & Zehendner, E. (2003). The Electronic Agent: A Legal Personality under German Law? In A. Oskamp & E. Weitzenböck (Eds.), *Proceedings of the Law and Electronic Agents workshop (LEA'03)*.

Wooldrige, M. (2002). *An Introduction to MultiAgent Systems*. John Wiley & Sons.

Chapter 13

Between Scylla and Charybdis:
The Balance between Copyright, Digital Rights Management and Freedom of Expression

Pedro Pina
Consultant, Portugal

ABSTRACT

As a reaction to the challenges of digitization, recent developments of international copyright law are characterized not only by its strengthening and proliferation but also by the protection of technological protection measures against circumvention acts. Consequently, in the digital context, copyright is being deconstructed and converted into a mere access right to legally and technologically protected information. Considering that copyright must represent a compromise between holders and users interests, the desired balance has been lost to the disadvantage of the users, potentially harming fundamental and human rights such as freedom of expression and freedom of access to information. In the present chapter, the author describes the conflict between copyright and freedom of expression, how the classic compromise achieved by the conflict's internalization within copyright law and the provision of copyright exemptions may no longer exist and how the users tend to find legal protection externally, outside copyright law.

INTRODUCTION

Until recently, it would cause wonder to say that copyright law could conflict with freedom of expression, since historically they had coexisted peaceably. Nevertheless, today, with the emergence of the knowledge economy based on creative digital contents, the tension between both rights is becoming increasingly clear.

DOI: 10.4018/978-1-61520-975-0.ch013

Freedom of expression is a fundamental human right that currently is not regarded only as a shield against government censorship (Birnhack, 2006, p. 64). Its scope of protection has been expanding since some private entities have gained the power to restrict others' speech and access to information.

That is precisely what has been happening in the field of digital copyright. In fact, recent developments of copyright law reveal a tendency to its global strengthening and to the recognition of self-help systems based on technological protection measures (TPM). As digital content and, in general, immaterial goods can easily be used or appropriated by others, to protect the creative economy the rights' holders needed to go beyond copyright's traditional field by expanding its object of protection and the powers granted to holders to control unauthorized utilizations. Since, traditionally, the enforcement of copyright was merely reactive, the infringements committed in the digital world seemed to remain unpunished, which caused substantial damages to copyright holders. In the digital environment, freedom of access to information and rights over informational and copyrighted contents have become realities in tension, and technology was seen as the adequate response to guarantee the holders' rights by promoting digital rights management (DRM) systems. In fact, DRM systems based on TPM allow the author or the rights' holders to digitally control access to copyright protected works (or even to unprotected works); to restrict unauthorized reproduction and other usages of works or to identify the users. Copyright law combined with self-help technological systems has adapted to become the adequate instrument to legally create scarcity and to restore the lost balance between holders and users' interests.

However, reality showed how the self-help systems can negatively affect the public domain and users' fundamental rights or freedoms like privacy or freedom of expression. In the latter case, by transforming the users' rights or freedoms into a mere access right to digitally private-controlled works, the use of TPM and DRM and the may have serious implications in usages that that in traditional copyright law were admitted. Accessing digital information for educational, scientific, artistic or other creative purposes, amongst other usages, may today rely more on the will of the rights´ holder, expressed by the terms of a contract celebrated with the end user, rather than on public interest oriented legal provisions.

Consequently, this privatization of the control of the access to digital information may lead to a context where freedom of information and expression can be undermined since creative speech based on (or influenced by) a restricted access work no longer relies only on the will of its creator, but depends on a contractual relation established with the rights' holders.

In the present chapter, I discuss the relationship between digital copyright and freedom of expression. I will start by describing the traditional balance between copyright and freedom of expression that was achieved inside copyright law itself and how digital technology has been challenging it. I will then explain how recent developments of copyright law may jeopardize freedom of expression and freedom of access to information and how the traditional internalized balance is being lost, leaving space to a model where freedom of expression tends to be considered an external limitation on copyright.

BACKGROUND

Traditionally, both in the common law copyright system and in the *droit d'auteur* system, despite their different bases and principles, copyright has been idealized as an engine for (or a means of) freedom of expression by granting the holder the exclusive right to use and to explore his original work, therefore providing him a reward for his labour.

That normative construction never meant that there was no inherent conflict between copyright and freedom of expression. In fact, to assign the holder the exclusive right to explore or to determine the terms by which a third person can exploit the former's work means that the copyrighted creative expression cannot be freely used by others without adequate authorization. The legal mechanisms that were created to protect copyrighted works can then be characterized as a restriction to freedom of expression functionally planned as an instrument to promote cultural, artistic and scientific creation, or, in other words, freedom of creative expression.

Regardless of the fact that the conflict between freedom of expression and copyright is congenital, it still constitutes, according to Nimmer (1970, pp. 1180-1181), "a largely ignored paradox". The main reason for the lack of debate may rely on the success of the conflict's internalization, thus placed within the boundaries of copyright law. Internal balance between the authors' or the holders' rights on the one side and public interest and fundamental freedoms on the other was achieved mainly by anticipating (1) objective limitations defining copyright itself based on the idea-expression dichotomy, as copyright is vested in the original expression of one idea, not in the idea itself, (2) temporal limitations, as copyright protection is time-bounded, which means that, once it has exceeded its term, the work enters into the public domain, (3) exemptions that allow free usages of copyrighted works like fair use/fair dealing in common law copyright systems or, in the continental European systems, the statutory exemptions listed in the Copyright Acts, that normally are related to citation, parody, educational or private non-commercial uses. Those are the main reasons why copyright, despite the conflict, "spares freedom of expression" (Jehoram, 2004, p. 276).

The careful balance that was kept for decades was jeopardized with the emergence of new informational and digital technologies.

These technologies allow users to make perfect digital copies of copyrighted works in a large scale and to globally disseminate them through the Internet.

It is clearly evident that technology has always been an essential factor for copyright regulation. Indeed, as the object of intellectual property consists in immaterial goods, its exteriorization can only be achieved by a physical *medium* that will evolve according to the technology available. This means that the *corpus mysticum*, i.e., the copyrighted creative expression, can be revealed

by the *corpus mechanicum* that technology permits. Without regulation, new technology allows an enormous, global and uncontrolled flow of information and digitized content, including copyrighted works.

The balance between the rights holders' interests and the public interest has greatly diminished, to the disadvantage of the formers. If digital electronic communications enlarge the market globally and create new economic horizons for authors or right's holders, they lead also, by their technological nature, principally in the case of the Internet, to the unauthorized use of works with apparent impunity, because it is difficult to control the flow of global information whose contents are protected.

In an unregulated digital environment, the economic nature of information and its content as a public, non-rivaled and non-excludable good becomes clear. As Boyle (1997) notes, the so-called digital libertarians built a Holy Trinity of Internet technology embodied in the technology of the *medium*, the geographical distribution of its users and the nature of its content, which made them believe that all their digital actions would be immune to state regulation or any other, as they acted in an alternative world of freedom and anonymity. Economically speaking, the positive externalities created by the free flow of copyrighted content information would increase disproportionately in this virtual world. Declared independent, the cyberspace would be a space devoid of heteronymous regulation and, therefore, traditional concepts of property and government were inapplicable. As a consequence, many of the consumers of digital works may act as free riders, choosing neither to pay nor to contribute for the production of the benefits. Actually, this is a traditional copyright's problem: each time technology promotes freer flows of information, whether we are referring to the invention of the printing press, audio or video-recorders or the internet, copyright always had to adapt to the new forms of usages and infractions. The current problem, however, is quantitative, considering the magnitude of uncontrolled, unauthorized and globally disseminated illegal utilizations. Moreover, the judiciary structures were not prepared to assure the enforcement of copyright in a digital world: courts' jurisdiction and competence are territorially confined and limited by national sovereignty. Mere reactive and localized state protection, by itself, has become inefficient and inadequate to face massive and transborder copyright infringements.

Thereby, the right's holders started to develop self-help systems based on TPM which are, basically, digital and electronic mechanisms created as means to control access to digitized information, its reproduction and other usages or even to identify the users.

According to Bygrave (2003, pp. 420-421), the basic functions of technology based DRM, which can involve, inter alia, steganography, encryption and various electronic agents,

"are envisaged as follows: (i) controlling access to copyright works (and possibly other information products); (ii) restricting unauthorised reproduction (and possibly other usage) of such works; (iii) identifying the works, the relevant right–holders (and possibly the conditions for authorised usage of the works); and (iv) protecting the authenticity of the latter identification data".

DRM systems using those technological protection measures started proliferating and were combined more with the provisions of contract and liability law rather than copyright law. One who wants to have access to informational content should contract the provider, assuming liability for damages resulting from unauthorized access or usage, regarding the contractual terms. In a world where public protection of copyright seemed anachronistic, it appeared that "the answer to the machine is in the machine" (Clark, 1996, p. 139).

At the same time, public reaction to the copyright's *de facto* loss of balance was characterized by the strengthening of international copyright law and by the recognition of the previously mentioned self-help systems based on technological protection measures, punishing acts of circumvention. As a result, it is correct to conclude that

"copyright owners have three levels of cumulative protection: the first is the legal protection by copyright. The second level is the technical protection of works through measures protection techniques. The third level is the new legal protection against circumvention of technological protection measures introduced by the WIPO Treaties" (Werra, 2001, p. 77)

Notwithstanding this attempt to recover the copyright's lost balance, self-help technology based systems can also contribute to the loss, in an opposite way, to the disadvantage of the users. As technology itself is neutral, it can only blindly block the access or the utilization of digitized works. Indeed, technology doesn't distinguish if a work is under copyright protection or not, or if the user is acting under free or fair use exemption. Furthermore, in European copyright law, as it will be explained below, free utilizations of copyrighted works are exhaustively listed and subjected to the "three-step test" and, in the case of digital usages, the limitations are less compared to those in the analogical world.

The proposed solutions unreasonably restrict the possibilities of free digital usages, principally when these consist of the creation of new works or in the exercise of fundamental rights or freedoms.

As Ascensão (2008, p. 55) incisively emphasises, "[i]t is an historical constant that when internal limitations are missing, external limitations emerge". That idea reflects the growing recognition of external limitations on copyright as the expansion of this branch of law has put it in collision with other fundamental rights of similar or greater importance. If, in the past, copyright law held internally the balance between divergent rights and interests, the current digital systems "may override copyright's escape valves – the idea-expression dichotomy, fair use, statutory exemptions – which are as much a part of copyright as are the exclusive right's themselves" (Goldstein, 2003, p. 170).

One of the fundamental rights or freedoms that can be overridden by current copyright's strengthening and proliferation is precisely freedom of speech. It is unquestionable that copyright will only be consistent with freedom of speech "when it exists to encourage the creation and distribution of more speech" (Chemerinsky, 2002, 97). However, current extended copyright protection may harm the exercise of freedom of expression as it may obstruct disproportionally access to digitized information.

A HUMAN RIGHTS FRAMEWORK FOR COPYRIGHT

Freedom of expression and information is a human right guaranteed by Article 19 of the Universal Declaration of Human Rights (UDHR). Under this article protection, freedom of expression and information includes the freedom to hold opinions without interference and to seek, receive and impart information and ideas through any media and regardless of frontiers.

The European Convention on Human Rights also protects freedom of expression and information in its Article 10, but expressly declares that

"the exercise of these freedoms, since it carries with it duties and responsibilities, may be subject to such formalities, conditions, restrictions or penalties as are prescribed by law and are necessary in a democratic society, in the interests of national security, territorial integrity or public safety, for the prevention of disorder or crime, for the protection of health or morals, for the protection of the reputation or rights of others, for preventing the disclosure of information received in confidence,

or for maintaining the authority and impartiality of the judiciary".

In fact, freedom of expression and information is not an absolute right, since it can be constrained when it collides with rights of similar dignity. That is precisely the case of copyright.

Currently, copyright is tended to be recognized as a human right.

In Article 27 of the UDHR, after being proclaimed that "[e]veryone has the right freely to participate in the cultural life of the community, to enjoy the arts and to share in scientific advancement and its benefits", it is granted by § 2 that "[e]veryone has the right to the protection of the moral and material interests resulting from any scientific, literary or artistic production of which he is the author". Similarly, the International Covenant on Economic, Social and Cultural Rights provides in its article 15, § 1, that the

"States Parties recognize the right of everyone: (a) To take part in cultural life; (b) To enjoy the benefits of scientific progress and its applications; (c) To benefit from the protection of the moral and material interests resulting from any scientific, literary or artistic production of which he is the author".

There is no direct reference to copyright or intellectual property in the European Convention of Human Rights (ECHR). However, in the *Anheuser-Busch Inc. v. Portugal* (case no. 73049/01) decision, the European Court of Human Rights considered that such matters are under protection of that convention as the propriety clause embodied in Article 1 of the First Protocol is applicable to intellectual property as such.

After a close reading, it can be concluded that none of the mentioned provisions defines the content of copyright's protection: whether, amongst other possible models, the authors' or rights holders' interests must be protected by assigning them an exclusive private right or by giving them a direct public reward for their works.

Actually, the option for the exclusive right's model was only taken in specifically oriented copyright normative instruments. That option is clearly drawn in Article 1, Section 8, Cl. 8, of the Constitution of the United States of America – the first to recognize copyright –, according to which the "Congress shall have power [...] to promote the progress of science and useful arts, by securing for limited times to authors and inventors the exclusive right to their respective writings and discoveries". But even in the bodies of copyright law that are not founded in the classic common law utilitarian perspective, the holder's right to exclusive economic exploitation of copyrighted works is considered the core of the granted protection.

At the international level, the exclusive holders' right is provided in the Berne Convention for the Protection of Literary and Artistic Works, in the Universal Copyright Convention, as revised at Paris on July 24, 1971. Consequently, the exclusive right had to be foreseen by each contracting state's national legislation. Although these legal instruments recognize copyright as a right attached to the author's personality, they also foresee the instrumentality of economic exclusive rights as an incentive to artistic or scientific creation. Indeed, the justification for qualifying copyright as a human right is the author's unique personality. The freedoms of thinking and creating are realities that each person has and that can differentiate him/her from others. That means that the special human rights' protection granted to copyright's holders shall be restricted only to the matters where a potential infringement can affect the author's personality and the control of works' unauthorized usages by others. According to Torremans (2004), the

"Human rights framework in which copyright is placed does [...] put in place a number of imperative guidelines: copyright must be consistent with the understanding of human dignity in the various human rights instruments and the norms defined therein; copyright related to science must promote scientific progress and access to its benefits; copyright regimes must respect the freedom indispensable for scientific research and creative activity; copyright regimes must encourage the development of international contacts and cooperation in the scientific and cultural fields" (p. 8).

COPYRIGHT AS AN INSTRUMENT TO LOCK-UP ACCESS TO INFORMATION

The problem today relies on the fact that copyright legislation is being used as one of the most relevant instruments to control access to the information that was flowing freely through the Internet. And that occurs even when, according to traditional legal standards, information's content wasn't copyrightable and therefore protected. In fact, whether we talk about works that have entered into the public domain or works lacking the requisites of creativity and originality, copyright law was used to control user's access to those works. If it is acceptable the conclusion according to which copyright law is a part of information law, it is not correct, however, to say that all the means to control access to digitized information may be under copyright's law protection. Providing to internet users the access to digitized information has an economic value. The relevant question is to know which branch of law is the most adequate to protect the investor against unauthorized access when a relevant part of the digital information has not a copyrightable content. Obviously, as copyright law ensured the holder exclusive exploitation rights, it constituted a desirable framework to the providers. The digital industry started lobbying and achieved its purposes by obtaining legal recognition and protection, within extended copyright law, of new realities like software or data bases. The fact that the right over data bases is qualified as a *sui generis* right reflects perfectly the expansion of copyright law to realities that were strange to it until recently. Where is the continuity between the author's personality and the data base that he has created? Where is the originality or the creativity in the mere compilation of facts? This means that what it matters today is not the creative work but the intellectual commodity regardless of its nature (Ascensão, 2006, p. 163).

The most controversial legal instruments that extended copyright protection in an user's freedom-unfriendly way were the Digital Millennium Copyright Act (DMCA), in the United States of America, and the Directive 2001/29/EC of the European Parliament and of the Council of 22 May 2001 on the harmonisation of certain aspects of copyright and related rights in the information society, also known as the InfoSoc Directive. Both instruments - not disregarding that a Directive needs to be transposed to state members' national legislations - were enacted to implement in the respective territories the World Intellectual Property Organization (WIPO) Copyright Treaty and the WIPO Performances and Phonograms Treaty.

According to Article 11 of the WIPO Copyright Treaty,

"Contracting Parties shall provide adequate legal protection and effective legal remedies against the circumvention of effective technological measures that are used by authors in connection with the exercise of their rights under this Treaty or the Berne Convention and that restrict acts, in respect of their works, which are not authorized by the authors concerned or permitted by law".

The DMCA and the InfoSoc Directive provide that protection by forbidding (1) the circumvention of effective technological access control measures (§ 1201(a)(1), Section 103, 17 U.S.C, and Article 6, no. 1, of the InfoSoc Directive), (2) the production and the distribution of circumvention equipments (§ 1201(a)(2), Section 103, 17 U.S.C, and Article 6, no. 2, of the InfoSoc Directive), and (3), only in the case of the European Directive, the circum-

vention of copy protection measures (Article 6, no. 3, of the InfoSoc Directive). Furthermore, infringements can constitute a criminal offense (§ 1204, Section 103, 17 U.S.C, and Article 8, no. 1, of the InfoSoc Directive).

In this context, the problem that arises is the compatibility of exemptions – especially those related to the exercise of freedom of expression and information – with the mentioned right's holders-friendly provisions.

It is true that both DMCA and InfoSoc Directive establish exceptions and admit a short number of legal circumventions. Nevertheless, the foreseen exceptions have been criticized as they are extremely narrow or ambiguous, closed-listed and copyright-centric (Samuelson, 2000, pp 4-8). As any fair use circumvention exemption was explicitly predicted, user's rights were impoverished. In fact, even when a usage could be considered fair, it still remained the question if fair use allows the user to circumvent technological protection measures so that he can access to the digitized work. Considering that owning a circumvention tool is itself a felony under DMCA, it is irrelevant whether the user uses it to circumvent DRM technology with a fair use purpose or not. Therefore, if the Article 11 of the WIPO Copyright Treaty provision obliged member states to protect DRM technologies that restrict acts which are not authorized by the authors concerned or permitted by law and that fair use is legally recognized, "a statutory prohibition on circumventing DRM that hinders fair use goes well beyond the requirements" of the Treaty (Armstrong, 2006, p. 67). That's why it's correct to say that with the mentioned regulatory provisions we are moving away from copyright to what is being called as *paracopyright*. DRM technology is a blind system that doesn't distinguish copyright protected works from works entered into the public domain or fair use from unfair use of copyrighted works. As a corollary, in the United States Copyright law, balance between digital copyright and freedom of expression is endangered.

The InfoSoc Directive lists, in Article 5, no. 2, the following mandatory exceptions to reproduction rights, to the right of communication to the public of works and to the right of making available to the public other subject-matter:

(a) *in respect of reproductions on paper or any similar medium, effected by the use of any kind of photographic technique or by some other process having similar effects, with the exception of sheet music, provided that the rightholders receive fair compensation;*

(b) *in respect of reproductions on any medium made by a natural person for private use and for ends that are neither directly nor indirectly commercial, on condition that the rightholders receive fair compensation which takes account of the application or non-application of technological measures referred to in Article 6 to the work or subject-matter concerned;*

(c) *in respect of specific acts of reproduction made by publicly accessible libraries, educational establishments or museums, or by archives, which are not for direct or indirect economic or commercial advantage;*

(d) *in respect of ephemeral recordings of works made by broadcasting organisations by means of their own facilities and for their own broadcasts; the preservation of these recordings in official archives may, on the grounds of their exceptional documentary character, be permitted;*

(e) *in respect of reproductions of broadcasts made by social institutions pursuing non-commercial purposes, such as hospitals or prisons, on condition that the rightholders receive fair compensation.*

Moreover, in Article 5, no.3, the directive foresees some facultative exceptions that Member States may provide for the following cases:

(a) *use for the sole purpose of illustration for teaching or scientific research, as long as the source, including the author's name, is indicated, unless this turns out to be impossible and to the extent justified by the non-commercial purpose to be achieved;*

(b) *uses, for the benefit of people with a disability, which are directly related to the disability and of a non-commercial nature, to the extent required by the specific disability;*

(c) *reproduction by the press, communication to the public or making available of published articles on current economic, political or religious topics or of broadcast works or other subject-matter of the same character, in cases where such use is not expressly reserved, and as long as the source, including the author's name, is indicated, or use of works or other subject-matter in connection with the reporting of current events, to the extent justified by the informatory purpose and as long as the source, including the author's name, is indicated, unless this turns out to be impossible;*

(d) *quotations for purposes such as criticism or review, provided that they relate to a work or other subject-matter which has already been lawfully made available to the public, that, unless this turns out to be impossible, the source, including the author's name, is indicated, and that their use is in accordance with fair practice, and to the extent required by the specific purpose;*

(e) *use for the purposes of public security or to ensure the proper performance or reporting of administrative, parliamentary or judicial proceedings;*

(f) *use of political speeches as well as extracts of public lectures or similar works or subject-matter to the extent justified by the informatory purpose and provided that the source, including the author's name, is indicated, except where this turns out to be impossible;*

207

(g)   *use during religious celebrations or official celebrations organised by a public authority;*

(h)   *use of works, such as works of architecture or sculpture, made to be located permanently in public places;*

(i)   *incidental inclusion of a work or other subject-matter in other material;*

(j)   *use for the purpose of advertising the public exhibition or sale of artistic works, to the extent necessary to promote the event, excluding any other commercial use;*

(k)   *use for the purpose of caricature, parody or pastiche;*

(l)   *use in connection with the demonstration or repair of equipment;*

(m)   *use of an artistic work in the form of a building or a drawing or plan of a building for the purposes of reconstructing the building;*

(n)   *use by communication or making available, for the purpose of research or private study, to individual members of the public by dedicated terminals on the premises of establishments referred to in paragraph 2(c) of works and other subject-matter not subject to purchase or licensing terms which are contained in their collections;*

(o)   *use in certain other cases of minor importance where exceptions or limitations already exist under national law, provided that they only concern analogue uses and do not affect the free circulation of goods and services within the Community, without prejudice to the other exceptions and limitations contained in this Article.*

The exhaustive list is, thereafter, redundantly subjected to the "three-step test", according to which limitations and exceptions shall only be applied in certain special cases which do not conflict with a normal exploitation of the work or other subject-matter and do not unreasonably prejudice the legitimate interests of the right´s holder. Originally predicted in the Berne Convention, where it appeared as a sort of general clause of internal limitations, as no descriptive list was foreseen, the "three-step test" now works as a limit to the limitations, strongly closing the possibilities of free usages of a copyrighted work.

The case gets worst when we talk about exceptions to anti-circumventions provided in Article 6, no. 4. Surprisingly, if, on the one hand, according to this provision, it must be ensured that

"rightholders make available to the beneficiary of an exception or limitation [...] the means of benefiting from that exception or limitation, to the extent necessary to benefit from that exception or limitation and where that beneficiary has legal access to the protected work or subject-matter concerned",

As Ascensão (2008, p. 63) warns, "amongst the sacrificed limitations is the quotation right! That's to say that the most important limitation, the one imposed by the necessity of cultural and social dialogue, ceases to exist online".

But the InfoSoc Directive goes further beyond the exposed, as it allows right´s holders to restrict the number of reproductions made under a legally recognized exception. This means that the InfoSoc Directive chose to deflect, moving toward market oriented contract law, rather than keeping public interest concerned copyright law as the relevant scenario.

Internal limitations on copyright were not all preserved in a digital environment, which take us to the discussion of whether freedom of expression as an external limitation can trump over digital copyright or not.

FREEDOM OF EXPRESSION AS AN EXTERNAL LIMITATION ON COPYRIGHT

Technology combined with contract law has unbalanced the interests in conflict inside Copyright law. Can those who get placed in a disadvantage position – the users who want to access to an electronically fenced work –invoke the direct application of freedom of expression? Is horizontal application of that fundamental right, without the intermediation of internal limitations, defensible?

The new expanded digital copyright laws don't seem to have internal place for the recognition of some traditional freedoms.

Nevertheless, the recognition of external safeguards, like freedom of expression, guaranteed, amongst others, by the First Amendment to the Constitution of the United States of America or Article 10 of the ECHR, is still meagre.

One of the most relevant decisions by the Supreme Court of the United States on the matter of the interface Copyright/Freedom of expression, in a pre-digital era where the balance was kept, was the *Harper & Row Publishers, Inc. v. Nation Enterprises*. According to the court, "copyright ultimately server to further First Amendment purposes by providing a financial incentive for creative speech, but the fact remains that in order to provide that incentive for some speech, other speech is restrained" (*Harper & Row, Publishers, Inc. v. Nation Enterprises*, 1985). In the *Eldred v. Ashcroft* (2003) decision, the Supreme Court held that courts must "construe copyright's internal safeguards to accommodate First Amendment concerns". However, the Supreme Court rejected the argument according to which first Amendment "should have a role in deciding copyright cases" (Birnhack, 2004, p. 38).

The recognition of an independent first amendment defence, free from the fair use doctrine, has deserved some reluctance from courts.

In the *Universal City Studios v. Reimerdes* (2001) decision, DMCA anti-circumventions provisions were tested for the first time. Fair use and freedom of expression defences were used by the defendants that have published links in a magazine to the DeCSS, a computer program that circumvented the DVD's encryption software programme called CSS. The 2.nd Circuit Court considered that regardless of the fact that with DeCSS fair use of DVD movies could be done, the defendants were only barred from trafficking anti-circumventions devices.

Furthermore, extending protection beyond copyright law, the courts have been finding that end user license agreements preventing commercial use of a database are enforceable although the facts contained in the database are not protected by copyright under the idea/expression dichotomy (Besek & Laben, 2006, p. 26).

In conclusion, in the United States of America there is no room for a direct First Amendment defence in cases of copyright infringement.

The internal perspective on admitted limitations or exceptions in Europe is also the prevalent. As Guibault states,

"statutory limitations on the exercise of exclusive rights are already the result of the balance of interests, carefully drawn by the legislator to encourage both creation and dissemination of new material. The protections of fundamental freedoms, of public interest matters, and of public domain material forms an integral part of the balance and, as a consequence, these notions should not be invoked a second time when interpreting statutory copyright limitations" (1998, p. 1)

Nevertheless, some courts started timidly to adopt the external perspective although limited to exceptional cases. According to Hugenholtz (2001), one of the most preeminent copyright scholars in Europe, in France,

"the Paris Court reminded that Article 10 ECHR is superior to national law, including the law of copyright, and then went on to conclude that, in the light of Article 10, the right of the public to be informed of important cultural events should prevail over the interests of the copyright owner" (pp. 357-358).

In the *Scientology* case, the Dutch Court of Appeal decided that, despite the inexistence of a quotation right, it was allowed to make available on a website large parts of copyrighted documents of the church considering the public interest in discussing the cult (Hugenholtz, 2004). The Dutch Supreme Court confirmed in the *Dior v. Evora* decision that, in principle, the use of copyrights may conflict with Article 10 ECHR (Hugenholtz, 2001, pp. 357). One other important decision is the one related to the *Anne Frank Fond v. B.V. Het Parool* case. The defendant, a dutch newspaper, published without the plaintiff's authorization, five missing pages of Anne Frank's diary. Despite of the fact that the appeal court denied the defendant's arguments, it still considered that freedom of expressions concerns could override copyright. *In casu*, that couldn't happen as the nature of the newspaper publication was commercial. As Birnhack astutely emphasizes,

"[I]t was an external view: copyright (interpreted on the background assumption of a proprietary view) vs. free speech, where the source is found to be outside the realm of copyright law. Free speech concerns were not forced into copyright law, but gained an independent position" (2004, p. 24).

A landmark on British copyright jurisprudence is the *Ashdown v Telegraph Group Ltd.* decision, in which the Court of Appeal decided that, from the moment Human Rights Act is in force, there is the clearest public interest in giving effect to the right of freedom of expression in those rare cases where this right trumps the rights conferred by the Copyright Act. Though exceptional, external perspective was then recognized as admissible. This cannot mean however that freedom of expression will always override copyright. As Angelopoulos states, "human rights have not been called into the copyright domain in order to expunge authors' rights" (2008, p. 353).

Notwithstanding the mentioned decisions, for the generality of the cases, the internal has revealed itself leading to reasonable solutions. But the shift that is embodied in the *Ashdown* deci-

sion may in fact have a prospective influence in future decisions, as in copyright laws are starting to have less room for users and public interests.

RECASTING THE BALANCE: FUTURE TRENDS

The recognition of external limitations is an important step to be taken in the quest for the rediscovery of balance on copyright. Still, it is not enough as it can only work in a reactive manner. For all the stakeholders, security is an important factor. That's to say that if external limitations are a last resort safeguard, it is inside the boundaries of copyright law that the balance must be recovered end redesigned.

Freedom of expression and information is not the only right endangered with copyright's law strengthening. Consumer's rights, privacy rights, antitrust issues, *inter alia*, are some of the matters that can today demand a proper answer from copyright and DRM based paracopyright law.

By expanding the holder's rights and narrowing the exceptions, copyright law is, today, too much privatized. As Ghosh states,

"[w]hile deregulation of traditional natural monopolies leads to the strengthening of private property rights, reforming intellectual property leads to the limiting of private rights and the recognition of public interest and public values in intellectual property" (2006, p. 4).

Non commercial use levies (Netanel, 2002), market based solutions, public rewards, compulsory licenses (Farchy, 2004), coded copyright management systems (Burk & Cohen, 2001), complementary between peer-to-peer technologies and copyright protection devices (Mazziotti, 2008), Creative Commons Licenses or General Public Licenses are some of the numerous proposed solutions to the recognition of public interest in copyright that go from hetero-regulation to self-regulation mechanisms. They are all worthy of generalized debate.

Copyright will survive the digital challenge: it is a human right that must be respected. Therefore, it cannot be used as a mere tool to protect investments. Other branches of law, like unfair competition law, are able to do it. The recognition of copyright as a human right is related to the promotion of the self-development of the person and that is the main reason why freedom of expression cannot, in theory, override it.

Therefore, to recast the balance of copyright in a human rights framework doesn't mean that only the users' interests deserve to be attended. Copyright and freedom of expression shall enhance and mutual respect each other.

In the current context, the balance has to be achieved through a combination of law and technology. Co-regulation mechanisms may be the start of the solution. If, on the one hand, fair use by design DRM mechanisms will have to be generated, on the other hand, law will have to open itself to reasonable user friendly solutions. Institutionally, regulatory agencies that can provide provisional administrative decisions on the fairness of the circumvention of technological devices and on the access to digitized information may be created. This a solution similar to the ones proposed by Burk and Cohen (2001) and Mazziotti (2008) and to the one that was foreseen in Article 221 of the Portuguese Copyright Act, according to which the right's holders that use TPM are obliged to deposit in an administrative authority the means that allow the access to the work. One who wants to circumvent the TPM for legally recognized free utilizations purposes may ask that authority to give him access to those means.

Nevertheless, it is still too early to be certain of the right way to restore public values within copyright law. The discussion is launched.

As the sailors passing through the Strait of Messina, who had to avoid Scylla and Charybdis, the two sea monsters located in each side of the channel, balance between holders' and users' rights

and interests must be recovered so that copyright, without the disadvantage of any of its stakeholders, can reach its real purposes: progress of art and science, protection and free dissemination of creative expression and cultural diversity.

REFERENCES

Angelopoulos, C. J. (2008). Freedom of expression and copyright: the double balancing act. *Intellectual Property Quarterly, 3*, 328–353.

Armstrong, T. K. (2006). Digital Rights Management and the Process of Fair Use. *Harvard Journal of Law & Technology*, 20. Retrieved April 29, 2009, from http://ssrn.com/abstract=885371

Ascensão, J. de Oliveira (2006). Propriedade Intelectual e Internet. In Direito da Sociedade da Informação, VI, 145-165.

Ascensão, J. de Oliveira (2008). Sociedade da informação e liberdade de expressão. In Direito da Sociedade da Informação, VII, 51-73.

Besek, J., & Laben, L. (2006). *U.S. Response to Questionnaire on Copyright and Freedom of Expression*. ALAI Study Days, Barcelona, Retrieved April 29, 2009, from http://www.aladda.org/docs/06Barcelona/Quest_USA_en.pdf

Birnhack, M. D. (2004). Copyrighting speech: a trans-atlantic view. In Torremans, P. (Ed.), *Copyright and human rights: freedom of expression, intellectual property, privacy* (pp. 37–62). Kluwer Law International.

Birnhack, M. D. (2006). More or Better? Shaping the Public Domain. In Guibault, L., & Hugenholtz, P. B. (Eds.), *The future of the public domain: identifying the commons in information law* (pp. 59–86). Kluwer Law International.

Boyle, J. (1997). *Foucault In Cyberspace: Surveillance, Sovereignty, and Hard-Wired Censors*. Retrieved April 29, 2009, from http://www.law.duke.edu/boylesite/foucault.htm

Burk, D. L., & Cohen, J. E. (2001). Fair Use Infrastructure for Copyright Management Systems. *Harvard Journal of Law and Technology, 15,* 41-83. Georgetown Public Law Research Paper No. 239731. Retrieved April 29, 2009, from http://ssrn.com/abstract=1007079

Bygrave, L. A. (2003). Digital Rights Management and Privacy. In Becker, E. (Eds.), *Digital Rights Management - Technological, Economic, Legal and Political Aspects* (pp. 418–446). New York: Springer.

Chemerinsky, E. (2002). Balancing Copyright Protections and Freedom of Speech: Why the Copyright Extension Act is Unconstitutional. *Loyola of Los Angeles Law Review, 36,* 83–97.

Clark, C. (1996). The Answer to the Machine is in the Machine. In Bernt Hugenholtz, P. (Ed.), *The Future of Copyright in a Digital Environment.* The Hague: Kluwer Law International.

de Werra, J. (2001). Le regime juridique des mesures techniques de protection des oeuvres selon les Traités de l'OMPI, le Digital Millennium Copyright Act, les Directives Européennes et d'autres legislations (Japon, Australie). *Revue Internationale du Droit d'Auteur, 189,* 66–213.

Eldred v. Ashcroft, 537 U.S. 186 (2003).

Farchy, J. (2004). *Seeking alternative economic solutions for combating piracy.* Retrieved April 29, 2009, from http://www.serci.org/2004/farchy.pdf

Ghosh, S. (2003). *Deprivatizing Copyright.* Retrieved April 29, 2009, from http://ssrn.com/abstract=443600.

Ghosh, S. (2006). *Decoding and Recoding Natural Monopoly, Deregulation, and Intellectual Property.* Retrieved April 29, 2009, from http://ssrn.com/abstract=935145.

Goldstein, P. (2003). *Copyright's highway: from Gutenberg to the celestial jukebox.* Stanford University Press.

Guibault, L. (1998), *Limitations Found Outside of Copyright Law – General Report.* ALAI Studies Days, Cambridge. Retrieved April 29, 2009, from http://www.ivir.nl/publications/guibault/VUL5BOVT.doc

Harper & Row, Publishers, Inc. v. Nation Enterprises, 471 U.S. 539 (1985).

Hugenholtz, P. B. (2001). Copyright and Freedom of Expression in Europe. In Dreyfuss, C. R., Zimmerman, D. L., & First, H. (Eds.), *Expanding the boundaries of intellectual property. Innovation policy for the knowledge society* (pp. 343–363). Oxford University Press.

Hugenholtz, P. B. (2004). *The balance of interests in copyright law.* Max Planck Institute for Intellectual Property, Competition and Tax Law. Retrieved April 29, 2009, from http://www.ip.mpg.de/ww/en/pub/research/publikationen/online_publikationen/3__externe_beschr_nkungen_exte.cfm?#hugenholtz

Jehoram, H. C. (2004). Copyright and freedom of expression, abuse of rights and standard chicanery: American and Dutch approaches. *European Intellectual Property Review, 26*(7), 275–279.

Mazziotti, G. (2008). *EU digital copyright law and the end-user.* Springer.

Netanel, N. W. (2003). Impose a Noncommercial Use Levy to Allow Free Peer-to-Peer File Sharing. *Harvard Journal of Law & Technology, 17,* 1–83.

Nimmer, M. (1970). Does Copyright Abridge the First Amendment Guarantees of Free Speech and Press? *University of California Law Review, 17.*

Samuelson, P. (2000). *Towards More Sensible Anti-circumvention Regulations.* Retrieved April 29, 2009, from http://people.ischool.berkeley.edu/~pam/papers/fincrypt2.pdf

Torremans, P. (2004). Copyright as a human right. In *Copyright and human rights: freedom of expression, intellectual property, privacy* (pp. 1–20). Kluwer Law International.

Universal City Studios v. Reimerdes 273 F.3d 429 (2d Cir. 2001).

214

Chapter 14
Analysis of Benefits and Risks of E-Commerce:
Practical Study of Spanish SME

Beatriz Sainz de Abajo
University of Valladolid, Spain

Isabel de la Torre Díez
University of Valladolid, Spain

Miguel López-Coronado
University of Valladolid, Spain

ABSTRACT

The objective of this chapter is the study of the art of e-commerce, analyzing the different existing commercial models in the market such as Business to Business (B2B), Business to Consumers (B2C), Business to Business to Consumers (B2B2C), Consumers to Business (C2B), Business to Employee (B2E), Administration to Business/Consumers/Administration (A2/B/C/A), Consumers to Consumers (C2C), Peer to Peer (P2P), Mobile to Business (M2B) and Small Office Home Office (SOHO) amongst others, the level of implementation in the work place as well as the level of acceptation in society and the regulatory framework for the development of the activity. After this study, the central theme will be one of carrying out a study of the pros and cons that e-commerce brings to the client and to the company. Moreover, a study is carried out of the implementation of e-commerce in a Small and Medium Enterprise (SME), analyzing the technological possibilities and the market of the company which is the object of the study, as well as the associated barriers and risks.

INTRODUCTION

Technological advances have led to a change in the way people live their lives and the way they conduct their business. Internet has brought about the globalisation of products and services and has

consolidated itself to become the ideal platform for the development of Small and Medium Enterprises (SMEs).

With the arrival of the internet, one can talk about a "before" and an "after", given that thanks to the internet and e-commerce we have taken a major leap forward in the way that not only

DOI: 10.4018/978-1-61520-975-0.ch014

companies but also companies and their clients interact. We have gone from a situation where communication was contained to one where it is freely available, where anyone with access can participate, without needing to be part of a group or having to know personally those with whom one is communicating.

The incorporation of the Information and Communication Technologies (ICT) in the banking sector has changed the traditional definition of a product, merchant and client, giving way to those who know how to bank on the internet. This new financial system has created a new way of selling, taken up by those companies who wish to reach potential clients across the world.

Research has shown that Small and Medium-sized Enterprises are rapidly adopting the Internet and e-commerce. However, there is little systematic research into how such companies are adopting this new technology (Daniel *et al.*, 2002).

Many new business have been created, and many others consolidated, which have had to adapt to take advantage of the potential that e-commerce offers them. However, in order to stand out in this business, a good sales strategy is of primary importance, also a product which is easy to send and does not need direct contact with the seller, as well as a strategy that promotes the website as much in "virtual" media as in traditional ones. Not taking into account one or more of these points can lead to the commercial failure from which the "dot.coms" suffer.

Security, which is a theme which bothers most clients, can be solved thanks to encryption systems, digital signatures and different security protocol up to the point where one is insured, all of which is much safer than leaving your credit card in the hands of the waiter that takes your money in a restaurant.

The objective is the study of the art of e-commerce, analyzing the different existing commercial models in the market such as Business to Business (B2B), Business to Consumers (B2C), Business to Business to Consumers (B2B2C), Consumers to Business (C2B), Business to Employee (B2E), Administration to Business/Consumers/Administration (A2/B/C/A), Consumers to Consumers (C2C), Peer to Peer (P2P), Mobile to Business (M2B) and Small Office Home Office (SOHO) amongst others, the level of implementation in the work place as well as the level of acceptation in society and the regulatory framework for the development of the activity.

After the study of the art of e-commerce, the central theme will be one of carrying out a study of the pros and cons that e-commerce brings to the client and to the company.

On the practical side, a study is carried out of the implementation of e-commerce in an SME, analyzing the technological possibilities and the market of the company which is the object of the study, as well as the associated barriers and risks.

DEFINITION

Is e-business the same thing as e-commerce? No.

E-business is the application of Internet-based technologies for conducting business. It includes eCommerce (i.e., the actual transaction activities) as well as other business-oriented applications such as logistics, order entry, information sharing, and transmission of information between exchange partners (Vlosky & Westbrook, 2002).

Whilst the former looks to improve efficiency and reduce production costs which form a part of the business, e-commerce is centred in the sale of products and finding customers, this being just a small part of e-business.

According to the different perspectives, e-commerce can be defined in different ways. A fairly complete definition comes not from considering it as a technology, but rather as a tool for improving the exchange of goods, services or information.

As well as the Internet, it is possible to offer e-commerce through other technologies, such as mobile phones, the fax, credit cards, Electronic Data Interchange (EDI), etc. But if we refer to e-commerce as an application which supports this type of business, it can be defined as a Web portal where goods are presented using multimedia (photos, music, images) and where the buyers and sellers can interact.

E-COMMERCE CATEGORIES

Companies, employees, consumers and public administration are those who take part in electronic commerce, although not necessarily at the same time.

According to who is involved, a classification of the different models of existing e-commerce may be established.

- **B2B:** concerns commercial operations between two or more companies.
- **B2C:** commercial operations between a company and the end-user.
- **B2B2C:** an electronic commerce model which groups categories B2B and B2C.
- **C2B:** commercial interactions between groups of consumers and the company.
- **B2E:** commercial exchanges between the company and its own employees.
- **A2/B/C/A:** exchanges between public administration and companies, citizens or the public sector.
- **C2C:** mercantile relations between two consumers.
- **P2P:** communication between end-users with the aim of exchanging information and/or files.
- **M2B:** the commercial exchange of goods or services using mobile devices.
- **SOHO:** associated with small home-grown businesses, outside of the business world.

Having laid out the various different categories into which electronic commerce can be grouped, it remains to detail briefly each one.

B2B

With the explosive growth of the number of transactions conducted via electronic channels, there is a pressing need for the development of intelligent support tools to improve the degree and sophistication of automation for eCommerce. With reference to the BBT business model, negotiation is one of key steps for B2B eCommerce (Lau, 2007).

Companies identify their partners and interact with them using electronic means. Amongst the benefits which come from using this system figure reduced costs as a consequence of the reduced margins of the suppliers, an increase in cooperation between companies, a lowering of the cost of transactions and the investment in promotion thanks to the use of a medium with world-wide impact.

The following classification covers the various models of B2B business.

Virtual Shop

Using one's own web page to offer information about the company, a catalogue of products and tools to make the sales transaction easier. An e-catalogue can be defined as the electronic presentation of information about the products and/or services of an organisation. While other applications can provide similar services, e-catalogues provide a range and effectiveness of service that exceeds the capability of any competing application, such as physical or CD catalogues (García *et al.*, 2002)

In addition, restricted areas are often included for those companies involved as well as applications which follow the activity of the client with the aim of procuring customer loyalty.

The infrastructure needed to set up a virtual shop involves the integration of the ICT tool in the web portal of the company. The companies which opt for this type of system are generally from the technology sector which has a virtual shop integrated into the web portal, e.g. Symantec (http://shop.symantecstore.com), *Telefónica* (http://www.telefonicaonline.com) or e-pages, a company which offers solutions for e-commerce (http://www.epages.eu/es/)

E-Procurement

This consists of the association of companies in order to buy products or services needed for their activity. It improves the internal and external communication of the organization and monitors the entire supply process of a company. It provides Internet based instantaneous updated information available only to authorized users.

Both the supplier and the client require internet access and the same running systems to allow for the electronic exchange of information (EDI, XML, ASCII) in order to show the internal data in graphic form through a web page.

E-Marketplace

E-marketplaces are web sites which allow for the interaction between a large number of companies, clients and suppliers in one meeting place.

Depending on the type of companies involved, the marketplaces can be classified into two types: horizontal and vertical. In the horizontal marketplace the participating companies are from different industrial sectors or communities. In the case of the vertical marketplace, the organizations belong to the same sector. Equally such virtual markets can be classified according to the possibilities of association (Roselló, 2001). In this case there are two distinct types: public, where participation is subject to complying with a series of established requirements known to the user; or private, where a group of companies sets up web space, limiting access to a number of authorized participants.

B2C

This category on many occasions resembles the generic concept of electronic commerce. The setting up, hosting and maintenance of a B2C platform is not expensive which makes this type of e-commerce attractive for both small and large businesses.

Different models exist depending on where the chain of value is found.

Virtual Shop Window

This is a space where products or services offered by the company are presented without the possibility of making a transaction. It allows the company to make its products known in the internet. An example of this would be *Zara* (www.zara.com), in its early days, where it was merely showing its products.

Virtual Shop

This is a space on the Web where companies present their products or services which may then be bought online, either through an auction or tradition sale. An example of this type of practice would be Buy (www.buy.com). There are companies that operate exclusively on the Internet and do not have physical establishments, such as Amazon. There are equally sites solely found on the Internet known as *bit sellers*, whose business is the sale and distribution of digital products. One such example would be the AppStore of Apple. Other companies on the other hand have physical establishments as well as virtual sites where they offer their products. Of these there are many examples, such as *El Corte Inglés* (www.elcorteingles.es), *La Casa del Libro* (www.casadellibro.es), etc.

Shopping Mall

This consists of a grouping of virtual shops from different sectors which come together in the same web space. This is somewhat similar to the e-Marketplace in the category B2B. Examples of this type in the Internet would be *Tiendanet,* etc.

Auctions

This is a B2C model where the seller marks the product with an initial price, in general very advantageous for the buyer, and from this point on bids is made, the product going to the best bidder. The organization which runs the platform acts as an intermediary, putting in contact potential buyers and sellers through the web site. This type of model has been very successful thanks to the interesting prices of the products offered through this type of platform, compared with the price of the same products found in physical establishments. Amongst the most notable examples of this model found in the net are *Ebay* (www.ebay.com) and *Ibazar* (www.ibazar.es).

Reverse Auction

The buyers make final offers for a specific product, and the managing agent of the virtual site undertakes to send them to the producing companies. It is a system where the clients fix the price that they are prepared to pay and where the companies sell their products or services below the real price in order to be able to place them in the market and in this way reduce loses. One of the notable virtual sites in the Net which works in this way is Priceline.

Search Agent

This is a virtual site which carries out a comparative search with the aim of presenting the final customer the most competitive price for the product in the market, as well as saving the consumer time. Examples of this: Atrapalo (www.atrapalo.com) or Lastminute (www.lastminute.com) basically orientated in the leisure market.

Meta-Intermediary

This is a virtual site run by a third person who unites buyers and sellers, facilitating exchange and guaranteeing security and the quality of the purchases.

Portals

These are virtual spaces which try to be the entrance to the Internet of the greatest number of users possible, offering chat, mail, news or free software downloads, etc. Getting a large user audience allows them to make money through advertising. The best examples of this would be Google (www.google.com), YouTube (www.youtube.com), Terra (www.terra.es), etc.

Classifieds

Consists basically in transferring the classifieds from the newspapers to a digital format. The key to success of this type of site is to get high user participation. Of this there are many successful examples: Segundamano (www.segundamano.es), LoQUo (www.loquo.com), Mundoanuncio (www.mundoanuncio.com), Milanuncios (www.milanuncios.com), Clasificados.es (www.clasificados.es), etc.

B2B2C

This is a type of electronic commerce which groups together B2B and B2C. It is an integration of the two businesses in the same platform, allowing clients and suppliers to interact in the same platform, without them negotiating directly. It unites the phenomenon of supply, typical of the B2B businesses and the sale of products to end users, typical of B2C businesses.

B2B2C is also sometimes used to define those markets known as "diagonal markets" in the Internet, those online platforms that deal with commercial transactions between companies as well as those between companies and final consumers. The producers or wholesalers set up a differentiation of prices and commercial conditions according to whether it involves a purchase by a distributor or retailer (other business) or a final consumer / citizen.

C2B

This is the commercial relationship between the end user and a company, in which the client instigates the relationship and fixes the conditions of sale with the companies.

Consumers may come together to increase buying power and negotiate with the companies.

This generally works in the same way as the auction sites in which specific offers are made to an auction house. Money is made by charging the seller a percentage of the sales as well as the purchaser for using the service.

Using the web, the consumers can also control the transactions with the companies, instead of being controlled. For example, on Priceline. com the customers can offer prices for airplane tickets, hotel rooms, car hire and even mortgages and leave the company to decide if they want to accept the offer or not.

We can find numerous examples of this type of business based on C2B: Priceline (www.priceline. com), Christie´s (www.christies.com), Skyauction (www.skyauction.com), etc.

B2E

This is the commercial relationship which is set up between a company and its own employees. In this way the company benefits from an interesting form of business where is makes commercial margin from the sale of products and generates income from publishing publicity banners. At the same time, the employees have access to products at interesting prices and attractive sales conditions, such as financing.

The aim is to reduce administrative processing time and costs. For the worker this implies a considerable saving in time, permanent access to information, the obtaining of services and personalized products online. All of which is integrated using the web, accessible both from work and home. The B2E platforms give, through an intranet, all the information of the company and provide the workers with products and services with added value, taking into account their condition as employees and consumers.

One of the companies which opted for promoting this type of platform within its corporate intranet was Microsoft with the setting up of the application Intranets MS Market, which registers a large volume of transactions on the part of the employees.

A2/B/C/A

This is the relationship established by public administration with companies, people and other administrations by digital means, principally the Internet. In this way there is a saving of both time and money for companies and individuals when they are required to undertake administrative paperwork. In the same way it allows the State to form a part of digital commercial activity as a regulator, promoter or user. An example of state initiative in this area is the web page *Agencia Tributaria Española* (www.agenciatributaria.es), where companies and citizens are able to interact with the Administration in a more flexible way. The increase in usage and also in the confidence of the population in electronic commerce in general is also reflected in this category, increasing the number of tax declarations presented using the Internet.

Three sub-categories can be highlighted:

- **Administration to Business (A2B):** This is the commerce between companies and governmental organizations. Publication of administrative regulations; electronic exchange of, and payment of taxes, etc.

- **Administration to Consumer (A2C):** These are transactions between citizens and governmental organizations. The consultation of legal paperwork, the payment of taxes, application for inclusion in the electoral roll, obtaining of certificates, public information pertaining to taxation.
- **Administration to Administration (A2A):** This refers to the transactions between governmental organizations. Transfer of information, funds, etc.

C2C

This category of electronic commerce refers to private transactions between end-users, where the consumers themselves act as buyers or sellers of goods or services without having to deal with intermediaries.

This commercial exchange can take place using various different models or platforms:

Auction

This is the same model seen in the category B2C where those taking part are exclusively end-users who bid for products using a virtual site which functions as a mediator. Known examples are: Ebay, Ibazar, Mercadolibre (www.mercadolibre.es).

P2P

Consists of the exchange of digital products between end-users using P2P networks.

P2P

Allows the communication between two people without the need for intermediaries. Broadly speaking, a computing network between equals refers to a network which does not have either clients or fixed servers, rather a series of nodes which behave simultaneously as clients and servers in relation to the other nodes on the Web.

The Peer to Peer relationship is found in the following examples:

- **Ares, LimeWire:** The exchange and search for files. Perhaps this is the most widespread application of this type of network.
- **Napster:** Two servers communicate and exchange music.
- **Bit Torrent:** Since 2006 an increasing number of European and American companies, such as Warner Bros or the BBC, started to see P2P as an alternative to the conventional distribution of films and television programs, offering a part of their content through technologies such as BitTorrent.
- **Skype:** Internet telephone systems.

We are almost never going to come across P2P as a model of electronic commerce, rather as one of a network in which someone is able to be both server and client at the same time.

M2B

M2B was born out of the mobile internet environment (telephones, PDA, Ipod, Iphone, etc.), using the telephone and other mobile devices for commercial activities, boosting the sales of many products, above all ring tones, games, images, music and videos.

Even though effectively there is no purchase of a product or service, the search for the product or service that one wants to buy, the consultation, the comparison of prices and delivery are commercial activities which fall into mobile commerce and are transactions which, without the mobile element, would be different.

M-commerce is a new sales channel that can be used by all companies, whatever their size.

A brief categorization of the diverse uses of m-commerce can be made:

- **Localization (GPS):** Localization of people in real time, interactive street plans and city guides, localization of floats of vehicles, localization of services (chemists, petrol stations, etc.), traffic information, etc.
- **Electronic commerce:** Personalized services (cinema tickets, shows, etc.).
- **Web surfing and multimedia:** Internet using the mobile device, the download of music, video.
- **Email.**
- **Entertainment and leisure:** Receipt of information about premières, cultural and sporting events, news, etc.
- **Games:** Videogames, on-line interactive games.
- **Banking:** Carrying out banking operations in a secure way, consulting accounts.

For companies:

- **Access to a database:** access to corporate and commercial databases (customer information, sales figures, etc.).
- Internet connection, email.
- Intranet connection.
- Connection to virtual private networks (VPN).
- Remote connection.

A recent survey carried out in the UK between 18th and 22nd September 2008 for Lightspeed Research based on an online panel (997 cases corresponding to regular users of mobile telephones) summarized that 50% of those surveyed had accessed the Web through their mobile, the most active segments being men (57%) and those between the age ranges 18 to 24 (77%) and 25 to 34 (74%).

What were the reasons given by those surveyed who did not connect to the Web using their mobile? Basically three: not interested (36%), too expensive (29%) or did not have the right mobile phone (24%). This reflects the need to increase promotion and the services offered through mobiles, the reduction and simplification of tariffs (for example a single fixed tariff) and the popularization of new generation phones.

The main uses of mobile internet are: email (47%), news (37%), sporting results (33%), social networks (31%), the weather (29%), entertainment (24%), tourism (20%).

Examples of this type of business are:

- **Movifun Shopping:** launched by *Ideas del Sur de Argentina* (production of the TV presenter Marcelo Tinelli) and having Visa as its strategic ally (Meaños, 2006).
- **Personal Shop** (strategic alliance between the supermarket Jumbo and Personal) (http://www.telecompersonal.com.ar/personas/mipersonal/shop.htm).
- **DoCoMo in Japan:** the Japanese company NTT DoCoMo, the first telephone operator in the world to offer commercial services with third generation mobile phones (UMTS). Its product I-Mode, a very small cell phone with a multi-colour screen the size of a credit card and especially designed for surfing the Web. 25% of the Japanese population has their own I-Mode. This mobile phone has increased the profits of NTT DoCoMo to such an extent that the income from services alone represents 85% of the turnover.
- **Mobipay in Spain** (http://www.mobipay.es): Mobipay is a company set up in 2001 with a 50% participation on the part of the banks and the remaining 50% telephone operators. With Mobipay one is able to pay in settings such as the taxi, the Internet, recharge the prepaid card of any mobile, make bets (the lottery), donations or sub-

scriptions to magazines, etc. It also allows one to pay for purchases from vending machines, parking in regulated zones and tickets on urban buses.

- *PAYM8* **in Africa** (http://wwwpaym8. co.za/): PAYM8 is an international company with operations in South Africa, Botswana, Kenya and Namibia. Set up in 2001, it created an alliance with the telecommunications company Radiospoor and latterly with the American company Cardinal Commerce to create a platform of mobile payments which would support different technologies (SMS, STK, USSD, WAP, etc.). Currently they are registered as authorizers of transactions for VISA and MASTERCARD. (Darin, 2008)

SOHO

This is associated with the category of business with one to ten employees. Bigger companies, which do not have this type of division of labour, are often called small- or medium-sized companies.

In the United States alone, one of the leading countries in this field, in 27.4% of households someone is doing some sort of outwork, according to the investigation "US Residential Telecommunications Survey," undertaken for the consultancy firm IDC in 1999.

Each day there are more small companies who ask themselves, somewhat confused and discouraged, when they read the Internet sales figures of larger companies, why they are not getting a part of the profits generated by the Internet. William Nothdruft makes the valid point that the main barrier is found within the companies themselves, not in the external markets. (Nothdruft, 1992) Electronic commerce puts into the hands of the SMEs and SOHO a low cost medium for developing exports, getting in contact directly with end consumers in all the different corners of the Earth.

In order to be able to benefit from this powerful commercial weapon the only things they need are knowledge, dedication and perseverance.

STUDY OF THE BENEFITS AND RISKS OF E-COMMERCE

Internet has had a crucial role in the development of electronic commerce, and so it is that many of the advantages and disadvantages of e-commerce are derived from the nature of the web itself. Amongst other things, it allows a company to present itself and its products through the medium of a website which operates 24 hours a day, seven days a week, allowing the users to buy in a more effective way, particularly because they are able to use the web to find suppliers and look for opportunities in the auction sites and those of second-hand goods. Companies can place orders, make transactions and payments to suppliers and distributors in a cheaper and quicker fashion, setting up extranets with their partners and intranets to ease communication between workers, as well as between themselves and head office. Equally companies have the possibility of promoting their products across a much broader geographical area, globally even, with the added benefit of being able to segment the market by personalizing offers, services and messages, making use of the Internet as a communication channel.

Many leaders have spoken of the virtues of the Internet as a platform for communication, buying and selling. Amongst them representatives of the world of commerce such as Jack Welch (former CEO of General Electric), John Chambers (official advisor to Cisco) as well as Bill Gates, who considers the Internet indispensable for all businesses: "The Internet is not simply another sales channel: In the future businesses with operate through a digital nervous system" (Ortiz, 2008).

Here are three examples of major companies who used the Internet before most, reducing costs substantially: Dell, who sends personalized offers for computers through the web, has grown at twice the industry average and is currently the leader in the sales of personal computers in the United States; General Electric has saved hundreds of millions of dollars of its budget by setting up a system of supply through the web; lastly Oracle has saved billions of dollar in the running costs using systems based on the Internet (Dell Computer, 2009).

ANALYSIS OF THE BENEFITS OF ELECTRONIC COMMERCE

Extensive literature review revealed a number of factors or attributes that either act as drivers or barriers of e-commerce success (Quaddus & Xu, 2007; Daniel & Grimshaw, 2002; Tan et al., 2009; Fillis & Wagner, 2005). No company is unaware that the Internet is a profitable business. Those businesses or companies which do not have a website lose money, although there are exceptions which will be looked at later, given that the Internet is not appropriate for certain types of products or services.

Benefits for the Supplier and the Client

Having seen individually the benefits for the client and the supplier, let us look at those which are common to both:

- Unlimited geographical localization.
- Increase in competitivity with the apparition of new online companies. The barriers to accessing markets, existing as well as new ones, are brought down, especially for SMEs (small- and medium-sized companies) given that the investment risk is low compared to traditional forms of commerce.
- New channels of distribution and sales are set up, eliminating intermediaries.

- It encourages interactivity and communication.
- It improves customer service given that the queries of customers, suppliers and distributors can be dealt with directly, which leads to a relationship based on confidence. Thanks to Internet it is possible to reply via email to questions any users might have.
- Increase in the market.
- One of the collateral advantages of electronic commerce is the arrival of the digital economy, which is a sector which includes goods and services whose development, production, sale or delivery depend critically on digital technologies.
- Globalization.

Electronic commerce does not signify solely the purchase of things through the Web, rather the possibility of setting up a line of stable commerce and achieve, using electronic means, an entire mercantile management which includes offers, orders and negotiations; in general everything which forms a part of daily mercantile life far from the electronic environment, as well as the concomitant problems (Roselló, 2001).

ANALYSIS OF THE RISKS AND INCONVENIENCES OF ELECTRONIC COMMERCE

The list of disadvantages is less important, although that is not to say less numerous or significant.

Inconveniences for the Company and the Client

- The vulnerabilities in the security of the Web affect not only customers but also suppliers who offer their goods using electronic commerce. In principle, there are already various technical media to ensure that purchases through the Web are as secure as those made traditionally. Despite this, no-one is able to assure us that a company is completely safe from the possible attacks of computer experts (Almasy & Rick, 2000).

- Certain legal and fiscal uncertainties exist relating to electronic commerce. These aspects are centred above all in knowing which legislation applies and in which region, taking into account that clients may come from a multitude of countries. As far as taxation is concerned, there is a consensus which exists between the European Union and the United States to avoid discrimination between electronic and traditional commerce. In particular it involves avoiding the creation of taxes specific to this new form of commerce. So that the electronic market can be truly global, it needs to create a legal environment which adequately resolves aspects such as the legal validity of commercial documents in electronic form, intellectual property rights, copyrights or proof of the identity of the parties involved in the transaction (Hagel & Armstrong, 1999).

- On-line commerce does not work for all companies neither for all products, given that some need to be touched or examined first (Conklin & Tapp, 2000).

- When one wants to put in place an electronic commerce solution an exhaustive analysis needs to be carried out, a complete business plan drawn up and a correct definition of the product and the target client. When these aspects are not taken into account, this leads to a lack of confidence in the customers and a poor image for the supplier, and may possibly lead to the end of relations between both parties in this particular case (Podlas, 2000).

ANALYSIS OF THE BENEFITS AND RISKS OF E-COMMERCE USING REAL CASES

Having looked at the potential advantages and risks that electronic commerce can bring to both clients and suppliers, let us look at a few established examples.

Amongst those companies using e-commerce to save money, encourage customer loyalty by being pioneers in the sector, offer customer service and supply without time limits and through this technology extend their influence without geographical constraints, three stand out:

Dell Computer

The makers of Dell Computer are a pioneering example of direct sales to both individuals and companies which has achieved one of the best rates of growth compared to other competitors in this sector, thanks to being the first producers to sell directly to the client, thus saving costs. With Dell, the client designs the type of computer he wants to his specifications and places his order by telephone or over the Web. Starting to assemble the computer once the order has been confirmed, in such a way avoiding stocking models that in no time become obsolete, a maximum of 36 hours passes between the order being received and the product leaving the factory to be distributed. The other advantage of e-commerce for Dell is the speed with which they are paid, converting the order into cash in 24 hours (Downes & Mui, 1999).

Amazon

Amazon challenged the traditional bookshops from the Web with a very high level of innovation and quality. They initiated an aggressive policy of pricing and created a new generation of services, such as the creation of sales recommendations based on the preferences of the customers possibly sharing the same tastes and interests (Amazon, 2009).

Faced with the economic potential of Barnes and Noble (www.barnesandnoble.com), Amazon has the advantage which comes from knowing how to anticipate. It has generated confidence, is well known and with a database of clients who have provided their email addresses so that they may be kept up to date about new releases.

American Family Life Assurance Company (AFLAC)

How is it that AFLAC (www.aflac.com), a company based in Georgia, has been able to triumph in a characteristically closed foreign market? Carrying out the main part of its business online has allowed the company to close contracts on products and process claims without the costly intervention of agents and claim processors, saving more than half the cost.

Amongst those companies whose failure in e-commerce is owed principally to poor management leading to poor knowledge and the use of the wrong marketing strategy, the following stand out.

Boo.com

The administrators of Boo.com set out with limited knowledge of the Internet as a channel of communication and sales. Testimony to this is the layout of the webspace with the use of a bewildering number of useless multimedia resources for the majority of users who still access the Internet using the Basic Telephone Network and which were lost in a site with little intuition and poor navigability. It was the first European company in failing. Nowadays, Boo is a new type of travel site that puts everything you need in one place (Boo.com, 2009).

KBKids.com

The case of the toy industry in the Internet has certain special characteristics, being populated by a high number of general brands in a niche market excessively large at the time of its explosion.

The game plan in certain successful Web sites has been in relying on recognized off-line brands, a question of confidence by the user in a large number of occasions, who can associate the electronic purchase with a physical outlet as in the case of ToyRUs.com. (http://www.toyrus.com).

However, no one determining factor is synonymous with the guarantee of success as in such case as KBKids.com (the web shop of KB Toys and previously known as Kay Bee Toys) who were not able to transfer sales to an electronic platform.

CASE STUDY

Introduction

The SMEs have an important role in the economy of our country, making up 99% of the fabric of Spanish business.

They are companies normally directed at niche markets where the competition still does not have a huge presence in the Internet. Therefore good strategic planning can guarantee a higher rate of success in these types of organizations. Often the sector of small- and medium-sized business lacks sufficient resources to carry out this strategic planning. And a good strategy is what is needed in order to triumph in e-commerce.

The following steps are essential to the formulation of a commercial strategy applicable to electronic business (see Figure 1).

These steps are explained briefly:

- Within the definition of the business of the company, the catalogue of products orientated towards the new digital environment which they wish to enter must be defined,

Figure 1. Steps to the formulation of a commercial strategy

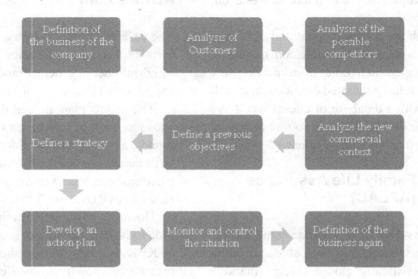

and answers must be found as to how to sell and how to give service.

- In the analysis of customers, the study must be centred in analyzing the different types of customers which the SME already has at the time of deciding to undertake the digital business.

- Analysis of the possible competitors that the company may come across in the development of the digital business. In order to know better this second group of competitors an adequate strategy would involve searching for the companies in the same sector using search engines. One needs to know their products, how they arrive with the public and their services of added value in the Internet. Certain profitable strategies may be copied and the possible vulnerabilities exploited to obtain a competitive advantage.

- The next step is to analyse the new commercial context (Internet). The two aspects which a company must take into account with respect to the nature of the Internet are immediacy (any time delay suffered in the sales process may lead to the loss of the client), and confidence (this is the principal warhorse in today's electronic commerce).

- The company must identify those previous objectives which dictated the prior development of its digital business and these must be revised and redefined every so often. The said concrete objectives are found within some of the strategies for growth identified by the Ansoff matrix.

- Define a strategy to make the most of the opportunities offered by the Internet and attack the possible vulnerabilities of the competitors.

- The strategy will involve an action plan that will define: the name of the domain, the structure and content of the electronic sales site, the techniques of e-marketing and the definition of services of added value associated with the Internet. Within the action plan, not only should aspects of the business be included, but also the processes necessary to carry out electronic commerce.

- The two ultimate points of the action plan are the hosting of the digital sales point and its creation, both developed by a specialized third-party.

- Finally, periodically the company must monitor and control the situation of the digital business, keeping an eye on the state of the initial objectives set out.

One must also be on guard, even though the digital business is successful and the goals set out are being achieved quickly.

The "time to market" must be minimized: the company has to reduce as much as possible the time lapse between the idea of the new product and the moment in which it is available to be invoiced and offered to the public (Smith & Merritt, 2002). The objective is clear: "be the first".

With regards to the design and development of the commercial platform, it is useful if the company implementing the application is conscious of the following points:

- Attractive design and easy navigation for the end-user.
- Easy purchasing process.
- Development orientated to getting a good positioning with the search engines in the Internet, as it is laid out in the section on e-marketing.
- Integration with the back-office.
- Presentation of information about the activity of the company and compliance with the regulatory framework, especially with respect to the treatment of customer data.
- Implementation of the commercial platform in such a way that it is easy to update by the company itself with all the new products in the business.

PERSPECTIVE OF THE COMPANY REQUIRING THE SITE

The following feature amongst the main demands or preoccupations that a self-employed person puts forward at the time of setting up an electronic commerce platform:

- Have available a dynamic platform in order to be able to update it in an easy way without having to call upon the help of the company creating the site.
- Have the possibility of making a payment both off- and on-line using a credit card. The security of payments is not seen as a great risk by SMEs, feeling as they do backed up by a banking firm.
- Concerning security, what bothers the company more is the information that an employee may be able to take out of the business.
- How to reach the customer through the Web.

PERSPECTIVE OF THE COMPANY SETTING UP THE SITE

It is vital to undertake a methodological study of the company, customers and competitors, in order to be able to define a strategy and various objectives t be achieved through the digital business. It is not always this way, given the difficulties in being able to pay for this sort of study. Where the SME is interested and is able to pay for such a business plan, a small scale consultancy is carried out. This will be based on a methodology developed by the company developing the site using experience gleaned from previous site developments. As a consequence a dossier of preliminary questions is generated which is presented to the client and serves as a means of identifying weak points and the objectives to be achieved.

A second area to be looked at is that of the set up of the computing tools with the SME for the development of electronic commerce. The needs of a small company (where the management of the physical business is carried out independently from the virtual business) are not the same as those

Figure 2. Infrastructure for applications

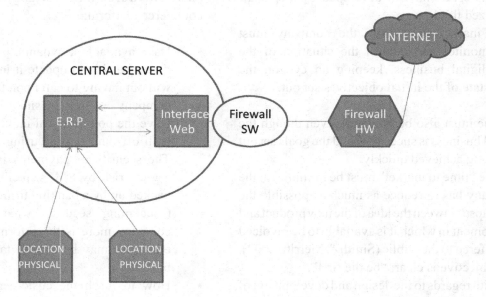

of a medium-sized business conscious of the importance of setting up a centralized management for both the physical and virtual parts of the business. Because of this, one of their main worries is how to achieve an efficient logistical control of the supply of those products sold through the different channels of distribution.

With respect to the software used, it is convenient to also talk about the techniques of e-marketing put in place for electronic sales in the SME sector. These types of digital strategies are not greatly sought after by these companies, given that electronic commerce is a phenomenon with which they are just starting to experiment. The techniques used tend to make up a small part of the total sum destined for technological investment by the SME.

Having analysed the software, one must describe and revise the infrastructure on which the applications will be mounted. Figure 2 shows this infrastructure.

The general plan consists of setting the site up in a central server housed within the company connected to the Internet, to which both personnel

situated in different physical locations and the company's customers have access.

Concerning the connection to the Internet, it is normally a double system involving access using ADSL and cable whose in-put and out-put is balanced using a physical firewall, with a two-fold objective:

- Ensure the availability of the service in case one of the two networks should fail.
- Obtaining high upload speed, using the load swing achieved at input, without having recourse to a symmetrical connection.

SECURITY MEASURES

- Implementation of a firewall at the interface with the Internet charged with filtering all the incoming traffic, in this way blocking all unwanted connections.
- Setting up of a software firewall in the central serve in order to have a second, more restrictive filter of the incoming connections to the server.

Table 1. Investment made by the SMEs in the implementation of e-commerce

	Product	Associated investment
SW	Sales interface and tailor made management program	≈ 3000 €
	ERP (implementation and parameterization with a license for 5 concurrent users)	≈ 10000 €
	ERP link with sales interface	≈ 5000 €
HW	Server (purchase, implementation, and UPS)	≈ 3000 €

- Installation of an antivirus.
- Implementation of a data conservation safeguard with various levels of redundancy.

Generally speaking, the investment made by the SMEs in the implementation of electronic commerce is as follows (see Table 1).

CASE STUDY: CASABLANCA VIDEO

To begin with, the established infrastructure in the Web resolved the problem of renting but did not adequately control the sale of products.

There are two clearly differentiated phases. On one hand everything to do with Web commerce and on the other the management of the physical business (see Figure 3).

PHASE 1: ELECTRONIC SALES

First the requirements of the customer are analysed and then a solution is offered to the client which resolves the most important functionality for their business at a cost adapted to the client, leaving clear the possible defects of the implementation and making it understood that these are areas for future improvement.

The quote from the company setting up the site is as follows in Figure 4.

Below are detailed the components of the infrastructure:

- Server HP ML 350.
  - Windows Operating System 2003 server.
  - Windows Firewall.
  - Web Server: IIS (Internet Information Server).
  - Access database.
  - Data storage in RAID 1.
- Communications infrastructure.
  - Signal Swing + Internet Firewall.
  - Internet networks working in parallel.
    - ADSL.
    - Cable.

Both the Web interface and the management of the same are housed within the same server.

The customers of Casablanca access the Web page of the video club where they come across the following. Figure 5 shows the Web page of Casablanca video club.

Offered at a glance in the first page are the most attractive new releases, the sale of films and video games as well as film rental, even though it is not possible to rent online. The Web is also used to publicize offers and discounts. The user who wishes to make a purchase online accesses the Web interface through a login-password which travels to the server without being encrypted (Figure 6).

If the authentication of the user is successful, he is then ready to make a purchase over the Web. In order to do this an SSL connection exists with the banking organizations, so that sensitive customer data travels securely to the banks, who then collect the money. The payments are made using a credit

Figure 3. Casablanca Video

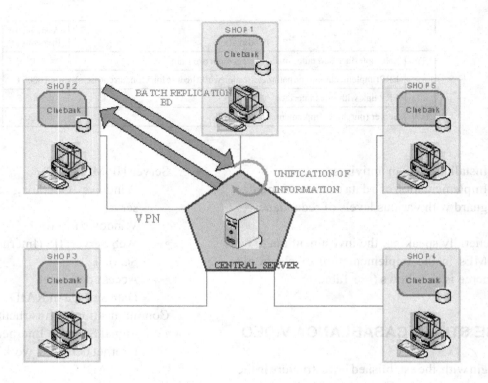

Figure 4. Quote from the company setting up

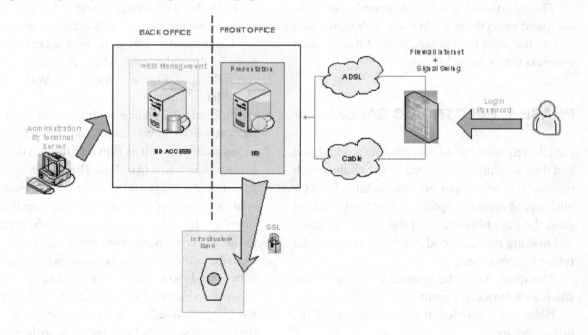

Figure 5. Web page of the Casablanca video club of the province of León (Casablanca, 2009)

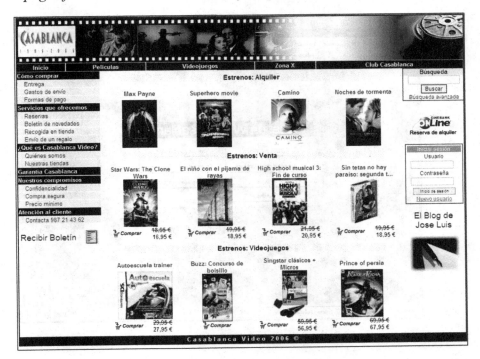

card. In this way, Casablanca does not deal with delicate customer information, thus relieving them of any problem relating to data privacy.

What is more, this virtual interface allows certain e-marketing mechanisms to be put in place, such as subscription to a newsletter. This newsletter is based in an HTML template which is distributed to the clients using an Outlook distribution list, which grows as customers express a desire to receive it through a Web-based form, where they indicate their name and email address.

The Web interface is connected and is fed by an Access database which is both simple and functional and which is administered by tailor-made management software. Through this program the Casablanca managers can update films, prices, publish offers on the Web, etc.

This tailor-made management software is as follows (see Figure 7). Moreover, it can be used to update the products offered through the Web (Figure 8).

Figure 6. Online access the Web interface (Casablanca, 2009)

Through this same software various administrative tasks can be carried out on the Web, such as the publication of offers and news (Figure 9).

As well as this Web-based database there are also Cinebank's own distributed databases. Cinebank (www.cinebank.com) updates its databases

Figure 7. Management software (Casablanca, 2009)

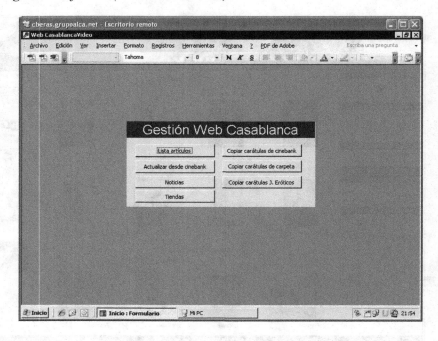

with head office twice a day, as it did prior to the implementation of the e-commerce project.

The Casablanca network is connected to the Internet using two different operator networks: one ADSL and on cable. These networks always function in parallel, the requests moving backwards and forward between both, which doubles the upload speed. Should a fault occur with one of the operators, all the requests can be channelled through the remaining live network.

Concerning security, the infrastructure also relies on a software-based firewall (Windows firewall) set up in their own server next to the other additional firewall which not only blocks undesirable connections but also acts as a swinging element between the two communication networks.

There are two hard disks in RAID 1 in the server. An exact copy (mirror) of all the information is created, which exponentially increases the reliability compared to just one disk. The read rate is more or less doubled, given that two different pieces of information in two different disks can be read simultaneously.

The hard disk is divided into three partitions or Windows units. Unit C houses the operating system, unit D the information and E is used to store the backups. Copies of each of the units C, D and E are made daily and with the same frequency this backup information is exported to an external hard disk via Universal Serial Bus (USB). This external disk is replaced weekly, so that if a disaster occurs the range of the possible loss would be a maximum of one week.

Thus, the entire infrastructure of the network of Casablanca cashiers together with its central server is as follows in Figure 10. This solution brings various advantages for the customer:

- Reduction in hardware costs due to having just one server.
- Automatic update of information thanks to having the two parts, management and Web, residing in the same machine (this

Figure 8. Products offered through the Web Casablanca video (Casablanca, 2009)

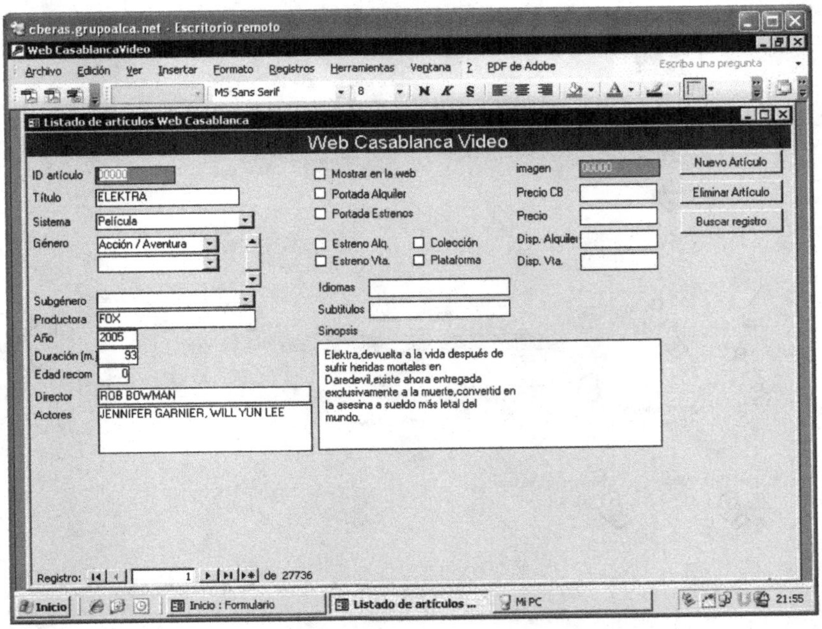

Figure 9. Publication of news in the Web Casablanca video (Casablanca, 2009)

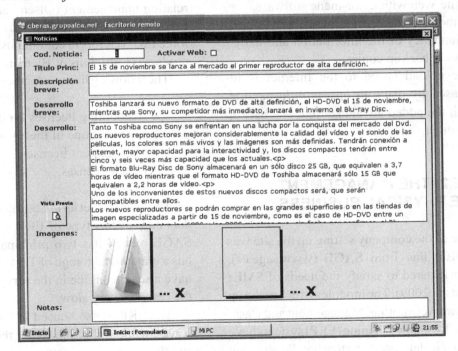

Figure 10. Entire infrastructure of the network of Casablanca cashiers

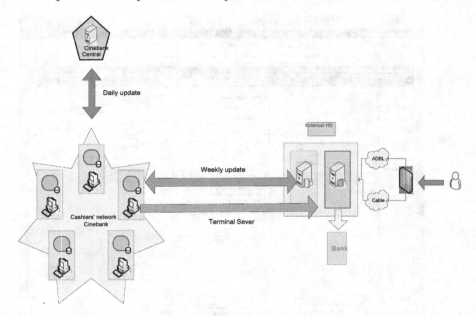

avoids the transfer of information between two different infrastructures).

- Eases the management and administration of the Web with tailor-made software.
- Without a huge investment, they obtain redundancy of the information and daily / weekly backup copies.
- The upload speed to the Internet is increased by using to operators in parallel, with the added advantage that one backup the other.

PHASE 2: THE MANAGEMENT OF THE PHYSICAL BUSINESS

The quote of the company setting up the site was the ERP100 line from SAGE (www.sage.es), an ERP orientated to satisfy the needs of SMEs (Karimi et al., 2009). The modules which make up this ERP are Accounting, Management and Cash. Enterprise Resource Planning (ERP) systems have grown from isolated systems that handle planning based on incoming orders and the component structure of the various products, to systems with ambitions to embrace the total functioning of the company including vendor and customer relation management (Olsen and Saetre, 2007). E-commerce developments and requirements will force ERP vendors to continuously innovate their products (Luttighuis & Biemans, 1999).

The following licenses for the software are sold:

- 4 Accounting licenses for concurrent users (only using one of these).
- 4 Management licenses.
- 10 Cash licenses.

The database set up in Casablanca is the default data base of this type of ERP: CBase, owner of SAGE, which has two principal limitations: it has a maximum storage of 1.5 Gb and it does not have a search engine in the server, which makes the searches very slow.

The ERP is also housed in the same ML 350 server, without this signifying that the ERP part and the e-commerce part are integrated.

Figure 11. Different routes in the infrastructure of Casablanca network

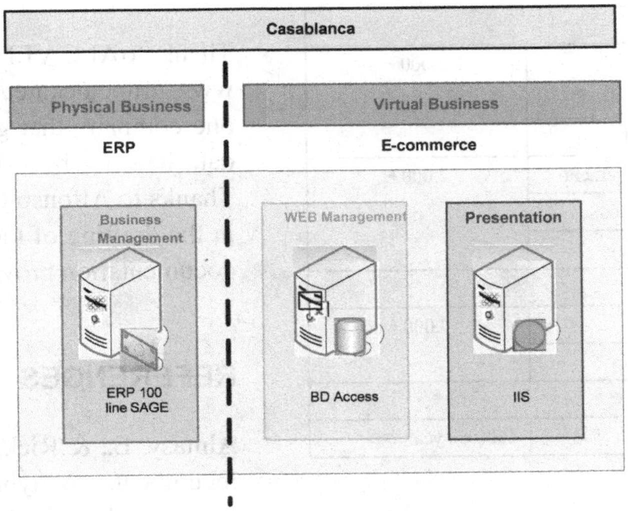

Consequently, at the end of this second phase of the project, the infrastructure of Casablanca is as follows: the same business which looks to integrate its virtual shop with the physical one and manage the two through different routes (Figure 11).

Once the two phases of the project have been dealt with, Casablanca negotiates a follow-on support contract with ALCA T.I.C., with a response time of 4 hours. (www.grupoalca.net). This support contract includes:

- Hardware.
- Software: ERP, management and Web interface.
- Database: ERP and Access.

The contract is annual and only covers telephone support and software updates.

Casablanca relies on a double conversion UPS which on the one hand completely isolates the server from electronic problems, including power cuts, brief drops and surges in tension, peaks, etc. as well as correcting the anti-noise signal or the distortion signal and finally detects low battery in the server, and if this should drop below 20%

of its capacity, requests an orderly shutdown of the server's processes.

PROJECT COSTS

The total cost of both phases of the project as well as the follow-on support is resumed as shown in Table 2.

FUTURE AVENUES

This type of SME, which has taken an important step at the moment of adapting its business to e-commerce in order to obtain the obvious advantages which it offers, is able to continue making improvements, assuming the company continues to make a profit.

The following are amongst the improvements that the business "Casablanca Video" could introduce:

- The integration of the virtual and physical businesses.

Table 2. Project Costs

Phase I		
HW	Server	3.000 €
	SO	
	Firewall	
SW	Software management	2.000 €
	Web interface	
	Consultancy	
Phase II		
SW	Licenses	9.000 €
	Consultancy	
Maintenance		
Support contract		4000 € / year

- They could toy with the possibility of having a highly available infrastructure by adding a second server.
- When the ERP starts to become scarce, the client could think about the possibility of migrating to SQL.
- Put into practice e-marketing, as well as improving the marketing practices already in place.

CONCLUSION

It is complicated trying to predict what the impact of the crisis will be on the technological sector. The reduction by companies in investment in research and development could affect the telecommunications sector, but it is possible that e-commerce itself could benefit if companies reduce costs, redirect and globalize the business thanks to electronic commerce. Another factor is the increasing in the number of users that access the Internet which compensates for the reduction in the average spend per user in times of crisis.

ACKNOWLEDGMENT

Thanks to ALCA T.I.C. of the group ALCA (http://www.grupoalca.net/) for providing the data of one company that gives support to, and whose data had not been possible to study this case. Thanks to Alfonso Castro, who has participated in the drafting of the designs of the figures and documentation provided to develop this chapter.

REFERENCES

Almasy, E., & Rick, W. (2000). E-venge of the incumbents: A hybrid model for the Internet economy. *Ivey Business Journal, 64*(5), 5–16.

Amazon Web page (2009). Retrieved March 26, 2009 from http://www.amazon.com

Boo.com Web page (2009). Retrieved March 25, 2009 from http://www.boo.com

Casablanca Web page (2009). Retrieved March 10, 2009 from www.casablancavideo.com

Conklin, D.W. & Tapp, L. (2000). The creative Web: A new model for managing innovation. *Ivey Business Journal, 64*(5).

Daniel, E., Wilson, H., & Myers, A. (2002). Adoption of E-commerce by SMEs in the UK. *International Small Business Journal, 20*(3), 253–270. doi:10.1177/0266242602203002

Daniel, E. M., & Grimshaw, D. J. (2002). An exploratory comparison of electronic commerce adoption in large and small enterprises. *Journal of Information Technology, 17*(3), 133–147. doi:10.1080/0268396022000018409

Darin, S. (2008). M-Commerce: compras con el Celular. Retrieved March 26, 2009 from http://www.villesnumeriques.org/rvn/bc_doc.nsf/0/20 e937de41b0bd79c12573c4006e4cfc/$File/Commerce_por_celular.doc

Dell Computer Web page (2009). Retrieved March 10, 2009 from http://www.dell.com

Downes, L., & Mui, C. (1999). *Aplicaciones Asesinas: Estrategias digitales para dominar el mercado*. Barcelona: Granica.

Fillis, I., & Wagner, B. (2005). E-business development - An exploratory investigation of the small firm. *International Small Business Journal*, *23*(6), 604–634. doi:10.1177/0266242605057655

García, F. J., et al. (2002) An Adaptive e-Commerce System Definition. In *Proceedings of the Second International Conference on Adaptive Hypermedia and Adaptive Web-Based Systems* (LNCS 2347, pp. 505-509).

Hagel, J., & Armstrong, A. G. (1999). *Negocios rentables a través de Internet*. Barcelona: Paidós.

Karimi, J., Somers, T. M., & Bhattacherjee, A. (2009). The Role of ERP Implementation in Enabling Digital Options: A Theoretical and Empirical Analysis. *International Journal of Electronic Commerce*, *13*(3), 7–42. doi:10.2753/JEC1086-4415130301

Lau, R. Y. K. (2007). Towards a web services and intelligent agents-based negotiation system for B2B eCommerce. *Electronic Commerce Research and Applications*, *6*(3), 260–273. doi:10.1016/j.elerap.2006.06.007

Luttighuis, P. O., & Biemans, F. (1999). ERP in the e-commerce era. Foundation's 2nd USP Roundtable ERP and Beyond, Utrecht.

Meaños, F. (2006).Un shopping en el bolsillo. Publicación semanal de Editorial Perfil S.A. N° 148. Retrieved March 26, 2009 from http://www.fortuna.uol.com.ar/edicion_0148/management/nota_01.htm

Nothdurft, W. E. (1992). *Going Global: How Europe Helps Small Firms Export*. Brookings Institution Press.

Olsen, K. A., & Saetre, P. (2007). IT for niche companies: is an ERP system the solution? *Information Systems Journal*, *17*(1), 37–58. doi:10.1111/j.1365-2575.2006.00229.x

Ortiz, T. (2008). *Curso de Comercio Electrónico*. Retrieved March 26, 2009 from http://www.scribd.com/doc/96477/fundamentos-del-comercio-electronico

Podlas, K. (2000). Global commerce or global liability? How e -commerce can lead to suit in foreign courts or under foreign law. *The Mid – Atlantic. The Journal of Business*, *36*(2), 89–101.

Quaddus, M., & Xu, J. (2007). Adoption of e-Commerce: A decision theoretic framework and an illustrative application. In *Proceedings of 10th International Conference on Computer and Information Technology (ICCIT 2007)* (pp. 292-297).

Roselló, R. (2001). *El Comercio Electrónico y la Protección de los Consumidores*. Barcelona: España. Editorial Cedecs.

Smith, P. G., & Merritt, G. M. (2002). *Proactive Risk Management*. Productivity Press.

Tan, K. S., Chong, S. C., Lin, B. S., & Eze, U. C. (2009). Internet-based ICT adoption: evidence from Malaysian SMEs. *Industrial Management & Data Systems*, *109*(1-2), 224–244. doi:10.1108/02635570910930118

Vlosky, R. P., & Westbrook, T. (2002). E-business exchange between homecenter buyers and wood products suppliers. *Forest Products Journal*, *52*(1), 38–43.

ACRONYMS

ADSL: Asymetric Digital Subscriber Line
A2B/C/A: Administration To Business/Consumers/Administration
ASCII: American Standard Code for Information Interchange

B2B: Business To Business
B2B2C: Business To Business To Consumers
B2C: Business To Consumers
B2E: Business To Employee
C2B: Consumers To Business
C2C: Consumers To Consumers
CEO: Chief Executive Officer
DB: Database
ERP: Enterprise Resource Planning
GPS: Global Positioning System
HW: Hardware
ICT: Information and Communication Technology
IIS: Internet Information Server

M2B: Mobile To Business
P2P: Peer To Peer
SML: Small and Medium Enterprises
SQL: Structured Query Language
SOHO: Small Office Home Office
SSL: Secure Sockets Layer
SW: Software
XML: Extensible Markup Language
UMTS: Universal Mobile Telecommunications System
UPS: Uninterruptible Power Supply
USB: Universal Serial Bus
VPN: Virtual Private Network
WAP: Wireless Application Protocol

Section 2
Policies, Models, Frameworks and Rules

Chapter 15
Data Security Legislative as Data Shredding Mill

Jaroslav Král
Charles University, Czech Republic

Michal Žemlička
Charles University, Czech Republic

ABSTRACT

Business intelligence is the most powerful part of enterprise information systems (ERP). It is shown that the absence of the counterpart of business intelligence in e-government called civic intelligence (CI) has important negative consequence that are probably more severe than the absence of business intelligence for enterprises. Missing CI threatens the prosperity of countries and nations as it has crucial negative effects on social processes like the quality of education, health-care research, and research and control of economic processes. Data security of CI is an issue. Current practices of data security are to a high degree equivalent to virtual massive data shredding. It is a big obstacle for the development of CI. An architecture of CI allowing satisfactory level of data security is proposed together with organizational and legislative preconditions of CI. The barriers of CI are analyzed.

INTRODUCTION

It is known that the applications of IT in enterprises (e.g. Enterprise Resource planning, ERP) are in many aspects substantially different from the applications in the organizations of any state (compare e-government systems). Enterprises are the example of the organizations with machine bureaucracy, the states are organizations with professional bureaucracy. It has substantial ef-

fects on the ways IT is used. The differences are in aims, responsibilities, processes, and contexts (e.g. limitations imposed by legislative or by the attitudes of public). We will discuss mainly the case of e-government – the most important case of professional bureaucracy.

The properties of the organizations with professional bureaucracy like the systems of e-government imply that the management of IT projects is not powerful enough, the visions are not clear depending on changing power of competing social groups, and moreover often

DOI: 10.4018/978-1-61520-975-0.ch015

not oriented enough to serve crucial needs of the entire country properly.

There are many adverse effects of this "state of art". The most important effects seem to be the effects of the prevailing data security practices implying that e-government system does not provide enough capabilities beyond operation level. The data security practices ban in fact the use of social data outside operations. For example, e-government systems do not provide powerful tools for the monitoring and prediction of economic processes. They moreover provide almost no information needed for the evaluating of the government measures in education and health-care. The current economic crisis manifests the fatal consequences of such a situation. Let us discuss prospective ways to change it.

MISSING CIVIC CONTROL INTELLIGENCE

The extent of the use of data collected in e-government is very limited by laws, current practices, and especially prevailing prejudices of public. The prejudices are based now on technically quite possible solution enabling Big Eye of Big Brother in the sense of Orwell's "1984" novel and in sense of many essays and articles written in the last years.

Some cautions are clearly legitimate here. The problem is the extent and the form of the applied measures, processes, and laws. The main snag is the overemphasis on the data accessibility.

It is very easy to apply the measure forbidding the access to the data without any assessment of its cost and consequences. It is quite different to assure their legitimate use and their data security.

It is well-know that the business intelligence is in long terms the most valuable part of information systems (ERP). The business intelligence (BI) is the precondition of well-chosen enterprise business strategy and of the optimization of business processes. It is well visible if we need to apply higher levels of capability maturity model (CMM,

Chrissis et al, 2003). The counterpart of business intelligence in e-government and in general in country control should be something like civic intelligence (CI) or society intelligence. There is (at least in some countries) in fact none now.

The absence of proper civic intelligence must have for countries similar consequences similar to the consequences known to exist for the enterprises not using business intelligence (BI). The consequences typically are: Improper processes and limited possibilities to improve them, limited availability of information allowing assessment of long term-consequences of political decisions, repeating erroneous decisions, and so on.

CI could provide tools enhancing some liberal arts by the methods common for sciences. In other words, the arts can be more based on experiments and on more objective analyses of social processes and of society in general. It can enable a better prediction of coming economical recessions and crises. It can be the most important effect of civic intelligence.

CIVIC INTELLIGENCE AND EDUCATION

A good education system is the crucial precondition of the prosperity of nations. Let us discuss the importance and technical issue of civic intelligence on the evaluation of the quality of educational systems. The norm ISO 9000:2005 defines the quality as:

The quality of something can be determined by comparing a set of inherent characteristics with a set of requirements. If those inherent characteristics meet all requirements, high or excellent quality is achieved. If those characteristics do not meet all requirements, a low or poor level of quality is achieved.

- Quality is, therefore, a question of degree. As a result, the central quality question is: How well does this set of inherent characteristics comply with this set of requirements? In short, the quality of something depends on a set of inherent characteristics and a set of requirements and how well the former complies with the latter.

- According to this definition, quality is a relative concept. By linking quality to requirements, ISO 9000 argues that the quality of something cannot be established in a vacuum.
- Quality is always relative to a set of requirements.

Quality of education depends therefore on the aims and needs of users and the users are different. The users can be the parents of a pupil choosing a best school for their child. Users can be officers or heads of different institutions, enterprises, or state majorities. It follows that an information system over appropriate personal data on education must be developed to provide the possibility to query data in various ways.

It is not difficult to see that the data must be sensitive (personal). The above discussed "practice" of data security implies that the needed data are often by law inaccessible, often intentionally destroyed. The result is that there in fact no information systems on education quality exist.

There is therefore no civic intelligence on education quality. The assessment of the quality of education is then object of rumors and the education processes are object of ill-founded "reforms". These problems are especially severe for post-communistic as well as for many developing countries. But the consequences e.g. for the U.S.A. are also critical. Compare the following citations published in (Spellings, 2006):

The Congress hereby finds and declares that the security of the Nation requires the fullest development of the mental resources and technical skills of its young men and women. - National Defense Education Act of 1958

The inadequacies of our systems of research and education pose a greater threat to U.S. national security over the next quarter-century than any potential conventional war that we might imagine. - U.S. Commission on National Security/21st Century (Hart-Rudman Commission), 2001

We must improve the way we teach math in our elementary schools. It's not just about helping younger students develop strong arithmetic skills; it's about planting the seeds of higher-order thinking for later in life. - Secretary Margaret Spellings, 2006

These citations indicate that the development in the education system of the U.S.A. can hardly be considered that it has been developing progressively. Worse enough is that that there is coming fall of U.S. car industry, growing lag of skilled analysts, scientists, engineers, and other skilled professionals (Jamieson, 2007; Manpower, 2005). The complains on the quality of science, technology, engineering, and mathematics (STEM) education appeared in several papers in the Science journal (Bhattacharjee, 2007; Mervis, 2007 and 2008).

The quality of STEM education is permanently felt to be unsatisfactory, even falling down. It was one of the main arguments of the forecasts of current crisis published several years ago (Pírko, 2004)[1].

It is, however, open whether any information system on education can change the situation. On the other hand it seems that if there is no such information system, the quality of education systems can be easily threaten and it will have no good prospects. So the existence of such a system is a necessary precondition for the positive changes in education.

Any such information system on education must use life-long data on individuals collected. A secure solution is based on observation that the majority of information on education system being of interest is publishable (not sensitive). The main points of the solutions are the following:

1. The needed data, personal ones inclusive, are collected, maintained, and safeguarded by an accredited institution and the data are made available for the generation of publishable information.

2. The personal identifiers (keys) are encoded using techniques like public key protocols and only the encoded forms of them are stored and used[2].

3. The information needed by users is generated from the data and it is assured that only public information is produced:

   a. if the data are provided via a database, the data queries must have publishable answer;

   b. in other cases the output of queries and the outputs of applications generating information are accredited and off-line as well as on-line tested whether the generated information is publishable;

   c. answers/outputs are logged and the users must not use any information obtained by them that is not public or not allowed to be accessible by the querying body.

CIVIC INTELLIGENCE AND RESEARCH

Assume that there is a system described above and that it can collect data from various sources. Then it is possible to enhance the quality research and the research in arts. The data and information provided by CI can be used to measure the validity of theories or to predict future changes. It can then have following effects on education:

- Testing of the effects of new education principles and processes (e.g. Waldorf education process);

- Testing the effects of the reduction of STEM education;

- Reasons for falling interests in STEM;

- Effects of scholarship in the looking for and development of talents as a crucial effect of entire education system;

- Support of any proper education as a precondition of prosperity of individual, institutions, and nations;

- Trends in requirements of enterprises on educational profiles;

- Etc.

Many social services, especially macroeconomics, must be mainly speculative as there is a little chance to do experiments. In the case when the information system supporting CI of above type is available, we can partly test the validity of the economic theories using historical data in CI. The data corresponding to a time moment T_0 can be used as the input of a system computing the predictions of the data values for a time $T_1 > T_0$. The system implements the models provided by the theory. The results can be compared with the known data for T_1.

There are quite simple but very useful applications. For example the prediction of rating agencies can be compared with real developments or people can apply some learning systems to develop good rating procedures. There is a (little) chance that we can detect warning signs in the economy.

The applications in health-care in CI can provide such function as epidemy outbreak control, sources of diseases, and so on. In research the following problem can be solved: The quality of medical research is often limited by the insufficient size of the data collections used for applied statistical inference. The size of the collections is often less than 10. Properly collected and used CI data on the health care activities can help in everyday health care practice. It can be used in the research of e.g. effects of the long-term applications of drugs, etc. In some cases CI can help well here. Similar opportunities exist for many liberal arts.

We can object that the society economy is changing and that such a simulation is of a limited use. It is partly true but it is nevertheless usually better than the mere speculative processes and models. Note that the data on economic processes can be hopefully used to predict recessions and to make the decisions of government better founded. The CI can support and speed up health care research like the effectiveness of drugs, trends in disease occurrence, etc.

TECHNICAL SOLUTIONS AND BARRIERS OF CI

Let us now discuss the possible implementation of CI in details.

1. In order to be able to link the data collections belonging to a given subject (i.e. to a person or to an institution) the subject (personal) ID is used and maintained. In some countries the existing personal/subject identifiers can be used. In countries where no identifiers neither exist by virtue of office nor it is in fact generally used a procedure enabling to "generate" the identifier must be used. The needed identifier can be assigned for the first occurrence of data associated with the given subject S. At the further occurrences of the data belonging to S the S must be identified by a procedure inspired by real-world processes (it can therefore imply human involvement) and then the identifier can be inserted. Note that the process can fail without spoiling the functions of CI provided that the failures are not too frequent.

2. The data used in CI related to a subject are stored and maintained by accredited bodies only. The data maintained by an accredited body B on an object or subject X are saved in a virtual data store D. The public functions over D produce publishable information only. It follows that the information must not provide any way to disclose sensitive information.

3. The data store D is filled from various (hopefully all) sources.

4. B formulates the policies and rules enabling to use sensitive data to produce publishable information. The policies include the rules from 3. B can accept applications or APIs producing the information and accredits them for use after it have viewed or tested them that they cannot produce information that is not publishable.

5. The users must be aware that the use of unpublishable information cannot be used without authorization and an unauthorized use can be punished.

6. Majorities imposing limitations on the data use must be able to show that it does not reduce the accessibility of related publishable information. It implies technical solutions discussed below.

7. The data resources (owners) implicitly provide their data to CI unless they explicitly forbid it. It is a solution known from healthcare in some countries. It is good when the subject not forbidding the use of the data is rewarded in an appropriate way.

A possible architecture of a system supporting CI is shown in Figure 1.

BANS WITHOUT RESPONSIBILITY

Current data security practices in e-government and elsewhere is mainly based on the reduction of data accessibility. One reason (and maybe the main one) is that there are powerful punishing procedures applicable in the case of any data leak. On the other hand there are no effective ways to affect subjects causing that publishable information is inaccessible due to inaccessibility of the data in CI. It in fact implies that if data leak is punishable the information inaccessibility is not.

Figure 1. The architecture of a system supporting civic intelligence

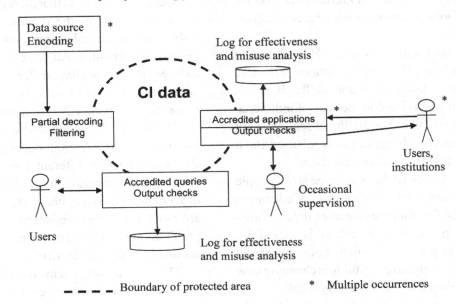

Under these conditions the practice will always tend to prefer data inaccessibility.

If we need to change such a situation, we must have tools to get an evidence that a publishable information can be generated from existing data. The only known way of achieving it is to make data definitions (metadata) of the data in the CI public.

In this case anybody can use the metadata to show how publishable information can be generated from the data in CI and to start procedure to avoid obstacles in information accessibility.

The requirement that none sensitive information can be provided by CI usually implies that the information must be generated in the form of an aggregate data (e.g. sample means) over data bodies being large enough. It can/should be partly tested by automated means.

The fact that the metadata are known increases the chance that the data will be misused e.g. by a hacker. We believe that such a danger is not too important as getting access to the data is typically followed by the obtaining the metadata. The metadata can be often mined from the data themselves. The danger of data misuse can be reduced by the anonymization techniques described above. It deserves further study.

OBSTACLES OF CI

The implementation of CI is quite complicated technical problem. The used data are stored in various information systems of different state institutions and offices. It is well-known that it is very difficult to assure a good formal quality of such data, formats, duplications, accessibility and so on. But technical problems are not any bottleneck of the solution now, i.e. they are no main barrier of CI.

We have stated that CI should have similar properties and similar rules as business intelligence. We must, however, take into account that business intelligence (BI) provides almost no outputs being against the interests of many people. The situation of CI is in this respect substantially different. There is a lot of individuals, institutions, groups and institutions, and lobbies the interests of which can be threaten by the information accessible via CI. We have no reliable data on the demand of jobs of various types (e.g. engineering or business).

Let us start with education. The outputs of CI can disclose education institutions providing unsatisfactory knowledge and skills. It is not welcome in general and in the case of individual schools in particular. The quality of schools is not easy to judge now. It can be easily misused and it can be a hidden weapon of objections.

Another reason of the resistance is the people pursuing various "modernizations" of education misusing the fact that the effects of their reforms cannot be properly assessed. It is especially dangerous in post-communistic countries as the tradition is broken and everything is changing now and the feedback is therefore very weak.

We have pointed out that CI can provide background and basis for the research in the area of social arts and sciences. It can be against interests of powerful bodies like various agencies giving assessment of institutions and people. There can be ideological prejudices and political objections.

Health-care (medicine) research is the background of highly profitable drug industry. The obstacles here are caused by strong regulations on health data. There can be no interests to make health-care research cheaper and therefore affordable for smaller firms. A necessary precondition is the rule that anonymized private health-care data can be used unless it is explicitly forbidden by the person.

If we take into account the power of lobbies in modern societies, we must conclude that the legislative enabling a powerful CI is very difficult not only to construct but also to start with its construction.

MOST IMPORTANT TECHNICAL ISSUES

Technical issues are now not the main challenge of any CI project. It unfortunately does not mean that they are easy to solve.

We have pointed out that there must be process enabling to support the request of computable public information what implies that the metadata should be accessible. An issue is when semantically equivalent data have different structures. We sometimes will need to obtain data with similar semantic (compare, e.g., semantic web search)

The main issue is the data quality (compare Pipino et al, 2002). Various data sources can store duplicated data in different formats sometimes with different mistakes like misprints, different order of items, missing items, etc. Such problems are well known from e-government systems. The problems are amplified by the necessity to generate missing subject identifiers.

There can be snags in the technical accessibility of data from some sources. The system should use powerful encoding and decoding procedures that can have too strong hardware requirements.

The amount of data can be too large, so the expenses of CI can be too high. It can impose limits on the use of modern data formats, e.g., on the use of XML databases. It can imply to use hardware platforms of specific properties.

There can be traps in input data cleansing and output information supervision. Some phenomena must be investigated using sample research techniques, compare e.g. sample research of personal agencies.

CONCLUSION

Business intelligence is the main tool for strategic planning in enterprises. The basis of the activities of enterprises is technology, engineering, science, and mathematics, often using experiments. Civic intelligence can be for government, as well as for society as a whole used in such activities like education system assessment, health-care research and control, and so on.

Civic engineering has the potential to support and maintain a long-term prosperity and sustainable development of a society. It can support and empower the enhancement of research methods of arts and science with possible substantial benefits for countries.

CI can open new perspectives for the research of liberal arts like macro-economy, pedagogy, health-care, and social processes in general. It can be used as a tool enabling a shorter feedback in political and economical processes and for proper decision making.

We can conclude that there are strong indications that the development of CI can provide a competitive advantage of countries and nations. Such an opportunity is not easy to meet as there are powerful groups and lobbies being against the application of the CI. The avoidance of this resistance as well as the technical problems of the implementation of CI will be a topic of future study. The steps towards CI should be the following:

1. Weakening/avoidance of the prejudices of the public blocking in fact the steps towards CI. An example is the fear of the personal identifiers and similar constructs.
2. The change of the attitude of majorities and state bodies from rejecting the CI towards the will not to limit it unless there are strong well-founded reasons for it.
3. Development of proper legislative enabling the implementation of CI:
   a. founding the certification activities and establishing needed procedures;
   b. changing the data treatment activities, especially formulating the rule that citizens have the right to have access to any publishable information and nobody is entitled to prevent it.
4. Gradual research and solution of technical issues and the development of hardware platform and software systems for CI.
5. The use of CI (hopefully).

It cannot be achieved without the strong collaboration of different subjects, especially without the involvement of industry together with academia and lawyers. The turbulences in economy might to pursue all the parties. There are still many research issues to be solved in IT, laws, statistics, etc.

ACKNOWLEDGMENT

This research was partially supported by the Program "Information Society" under project 1ET100300517 and by the Czech Science Foundation by the grant number 201/09/0983.

REFERENCES

Bhattacharjee, Y. (2007). New questions push for more degrees. *Science, 318*, 1052. doi:10.1126/science.318.5853.1052

Chrissis, M. B., Konrad, M., & Shrum, A. (2003). *CMMI: Guidelines for Process Integration and Product Improvement*. Boston, MA: Addison Wesley.

International Organization for Standardization. (2005). *ISO 9000:2005 Quality management systems – fundamentals and vocabulary*. Available from http://www.iso.org/iso/catalogue_detail?csnumber=42180.

Jamieson, L. (2007, Spring). Engineering education in a changing world. *The Bridge*.

Manpower (2005). *Confronting the coming talent crunch: What's next?* Retrieved from http://www.manpower.com/mpcom/files?name=Talent_Shortage_Whitepaper_Global_Final.pdf.

Mervis, J. (2007). Congress passes massive measure to support research and education. *Science, 317*(5839), 736–737. doi:10.1126/science.317.5839.736

Mervis, J. (2008). A new bottom line for school science. *Science, 319*(5866), 1030–1033. doi:10.1126/science.319.5866.1030

Pipino, L., Lee, Y. W., & Wang, R. Y. (2002). Data quality assessment. *Communications of the ACM, 45*(4), 211–218. doi:10.1145/505248.506010

Pírko, Š. (2004). Největší medvědí trh od roku 1929 před námi... (in Czech: The biggest bear market since 1929 ahead …). Retrieved April 10, 2009, from http://colosseum.cz/pdf_analyzy/200405_us-stocks.pdf.

Spellings, M. (2006). *Answering the challenge of a changing world.*

ENDNOTES

1   Main argument was that so called winter season of Kondratieff wave was approaching and that the phenomena typical for the winter are amplified by snags in education and that countries allowing STEM education decay will in long term loss their current positions and power. Compare Grandfather Education Report http://home.att.net/~mwhodges/education.htm. The analysis was inspired by several publications that appeared in the U.S.A. and Canada.

2   In some countries like the U.S.A. no generally accessible personal identifiers exist. In this case the CI must use techniques able to provide personal ID. The techniques will have to require human involvement when an ID is associated with a data piece.

Chapter 16
Collaborative Practices in Computer–Aided Academic Research

J. Leng
University of Manchester, UK

Wes Sharrock
University of Manchester, UK

ABSTRACT

This chapter focuses on sharing information through global communication systems in the context of computer-aided academic research: more specifically, on cross-disciplinary research primarily involving collaborations between natural scientists and colleagues in computational science. Our interest lies in the visualization and high performance computing (HPC) communities, branches of computational science providing enhanced ways of organising, analysing and presenting materials, models and results of research in other disciplines.

INTRODUCTION

We are interested in what constitutes 'best practice' for sharing data and developing softwares in cross-disciplinary research involving academics from (primarily, but not exclusively) natural sciences collaborating with colleagues in computational science. Computational science has existed since computers have in what used to be termed scientific computing, but as this practice diffuses into non-scientific disciplines that name does not fit so we term it computer-aided academic research.

Many collaborations involve software development and hence software engineering. Since the 1990's there have been several attempts to define 'best practice' in software engineering: the IEEE Computer Society has developed a number of software engineering standards (Moore, 2005; Pfleeger et al 2005) and the IEEE-CS/ACM has created a Software Engineering Code of Ethics and Professional Practice (ACM & IEEE, 2009; Abran et al, 2004; Thyler & Dorfman, a2006; Thyler & Dorfman, b2006; IEEE Computer Society, 2009). However within UK scientific research researchers increasingly advocate open-source practices for developing and sharing software and data. There are also growing demands from

DOI: 10.4018/978-1-61520-975-0.ch016

those who manage funding and assessment of the national research budget to encourage as 'best practice' the adoption of professional software engineering standards. There are issues as to how accreditation of software engineering will interact with open-source approaches and also how they will impact on established conventions for evaluating academic achievements. Changes in measuring success will alter how careers are shaped and will further impact the form of collaboration between disciplines featuring significantly different standards of disciplinary achievement and professional success (as with natural and computational sciences).

BACKGROUND

Computational Science

"Computational Science and Engineering (CSE) is interdisciplinary by nature and is relative newcomer on the academic scene. There are few degree programs in CSE and few university departments dedicated to this field; consequently, there is a scarcity of objective data on the state of the discipline in the UK", EPSRC & DFG (2005, p3). Computational science enables a new third means of discovery in the natural sciences in addition to experimentation/observation and theory. Computation, often in the form of simulation, is used to explore complex systems that can only be experimented on or observed in a limited fashion due to cost or technological difficulties. Computational models are usually based on mathematical models embodying theoretical understanding from the discipline and where possible results should be validated against observational/experimental data. With a valid computational model 'virtual experiments' can produce new findings. As computers become more prevalent and powerful computational science can utilize desk-top machines as well as HPC for more than simulation (e.g., statistical analyses) which is why we have termed

this activity 'computer-aided research'. Over time the techniques used in computational science have broadened and ever more academic disciplines use computers as research tools. While social scientists are still not great users of academic HPC services there is an Economic and Social Research Council (ESRC) initiative to encourage growth through the development of e-Social Science.

Many different disciplinary communities are involved in computational science and often must collaborate to produce meaningful results. Other communities (such as vendors or service providers) are stakeholders in these activities though not normally active in the collaboration

Collaborative Communities

- Academic researchers from any domain of science
- Applied mathematics experts
  - Numerical methods
  - Statistics
- HPC experts
  - Electrical engineering/computer science experts (hardware technologies)
- Visualization experts
  - Computer science (computer graphics, display technologies, HCI)
  - Applied mathematics (statistics, image processing)
  - Visual arts (graphics design, art)

Other Stakeholder Communities

- HPC service providers
- Systems Administrators
- Network providers
- Hardware vendors
- Software vendors

The UK eScience Initiative

Initially the UK eScience provided a variety of distributed computing resources to academic users with only one authentication. Later, it came to mean something different (see the *Case Studies* section). The technological ideas for the initiative came from the HPC and computational science communities. In retrospect it is most noted for its contribution to enabling interdisciplinary research.

"The UK, through its Interdisciplinary Research Collaborations (IRCs) and e-Science programmes, has made great strides in interdisciplinary research and in some areas this is attracting new talent into the ICT community. Both programmes have brought together groups that did not traditionally collaborate." - EPSRC (2006, p1).

Technologies for Sharing Data

The utilities given here are tools that aid collaborative practices, data sharing and/or software development although an explanation of HPC, a technology primarily used to create data, is included.

High Performance Computing

The definition of HPC changes with technology because HPC utilizes the latest technologies. Such computational resources are cutting edge demanding the highest levels of speed, cache, I/O or number of processors, allowing research problems to be approached that could not be tackled any other way. Some research groups can afford HPC resources but most high end academic HPC resources are expensive and tend to be delivered through national or even international services.

There are two classes of HPC users; those that use existing software for 'virtual experiments' and those developing their own software to address particular research questions. Both involve computational scientists but feature different practices and requirements. HPC is necessary for large problems such as modeling climate change or designing air flow over a new car. However transferring a software from a serial form running on a desk-top machine can be very difficult because of differences in hardware, calling for an efficient parallelisation strategy that can integrate into the software, and revision of numerical method (the core of the algorithm) and adaptation between the tools that work in serial environments and those available on parallel machines.

Systems Administration

If users are working on the same machine then data can be shared as long as the machine is administered to allow that. User permissions, groups and shared directories can be used to allow collaborating users to copy and move data into individual accounts.

Good systems administration requires all users have the best possible experience, which involves the machine being appropriately configured, software kept up to date, security patches installed in a timely fashion, new accounts quickly created, user accounts backed up regularly and the machine closely monitored so that issues slowing it down are resolved. Poor or inadequately funded systems administration means the users have a poor experience and risks security problems that result in data/softwares being 'lost' or 'stolen'.

Security

Computer security should include protection of the physical machine and information stored on it from theft, corruption or natural disaster while keeping the computational resource and data accessible to legitimate users. Any computer attached to a network or with multiple users needs an information security policy. Security measures range from providing back-up power supplies, restricting access to the machine room, monitoring network activity, checking the identity of new users, and creating regular data back-ups to monitoring user's login locations. Strict security measures may restrict users physical and cyber activities, e.g. the policy of changing the user password every month is good security but unpopular with users who may have many passwords to remember.

Archived Files

In Unix these are tar files, in windows zip files and in Java jar files. There are other types of archived files. An achieve file holds the directory structure and the files within as a single file. These archived files use compression to make the resulting file smaller than all the original files together.

Archived files are easier to move to a different location on the same machine or between machines, easy to distribute to others and often used to distribute software. However version control is not part of the format so it is the onus of the user to create archived files with consistent and meaningful names.

Tapes and Drives

Originally computers could not permanently store large amounts of data. Data was once input through punch cards while output/results were displayed on the screen. A screen allows sharing data but most people require that data be preserved in some way (perhaps as a screen dump) so that they can remember and represent their results to others.

Nowadays data can be saved to a drive or tape and transferred between machines. These devices present security hazards, if a hacker has access to the physical machine or the network on which it runs they may install inappropriate software or 'steal' data. Storage technology has changed massively over time and the capacity of the devices increased exponentially - hard drives, floppy drives, CD, DVD, flash drives and blu-ray discs.

Data stored on disc or tape is not as rapidly accessed as data held in memory. Software optimization strategies aim to keep as much relevant information as possible in memory. Specialist machines use special hardware systems to speedup data access from disc and tape and improve the 'I/O bottleneck'. Systems backups are often kept on tape and require the systems administrator to retrieve.

Documentation

Documentation and textual forms of user support take different forms. At the lowest level textual comments are embedded in the software and can only be read by those reading the software. The README files and manuals accompanying software explain how to compile, configure and run that software. Automated systems can document all the functions within in a software/library and identify the arguments for each function, as Java does through JavaDocs. Training courses can be delivered in person or over the internet and these add 'how to' information to the somewhat dry comments and documentation. 'How to' training manuals are also called 'cook books'. Forums and support wikis allow developers and users to discuss issues associated with the software. Since these discussions are open, once a problem is solved all users can access the solution, reducing the effort burden on the developer who otherwise receives emails for each individual issue each time a user has a problem.

Programmers and their managers tend to prefer software developers spending time developing software rather than documenting it. Documentation is often produced by different people to those developing software and typically the documentation cycle lags behind the development cycle.

Screens

Except for the first stored memory computers, where the screen was the memory and the display device, screens are used for the temporary information displays. Early screens were small, monochromatic and used vector graphics. Now large, they display information in colour pixel-based graphics. Screen size is important for single users and collaboration. Often several screens are tiled or in some cases a projector is used to increase the 'display real estate'. The adoption of colour screens means that colour encoded information is cheaper to display electronically.

Printers

People dislike reading long documents onscreen although changing screen technologies are improving this. Printers were originally designed to handle text files but users wish to print text in more 'readable' format and add diagrams and images so printers have adapted too. Print-out can be taken anywhere and probably has a longer storage time than digital formats that are prone to change.

FTP

FTP (File Transfer Protocol) allows the transfer of data between machines. It can be used through the command line, web pages or standalone (GUI based) tools. FTP can be made secure thus allowing the encryption of the data.

Email

Files attached to emails and sent to collaborators allow the 'owner' of the files to control who receives which version, in the first instance. It is relatively easy to transfer small files this way but large files may block inboxes or even, if large enough, block the email servers.

Data Repositories

Data and software can be held in repositories that for small datasets the users can access by internet such as data held by the European Bioinformatics Institute. Large dataset users, such as the Visible Human Project data, may need to register to receive hard copies of the data by post. Data repositories are often administered by paid personnel who check the data is 'clean' and 'sensible', even rejecting some data.

Version Control Software

CVS and Subversion are varieties of version control software. Subversion is newer, with slightly improved functionality, allowing for changes in directory structure unlike CVS. User interfaces to these has, like FTP, evolved from a command line utility to a web page download and now to GUI standalone tools that check file versions in or out from the same machine or from different machines.

Many open-source projects allow user access to CVS or Subversion software archives for those who wish to develop the software or eliminate bugs. These are more useful but more complex to use than archive files.

Software Development Tools

Tools supporting software development and optimization processes - Computer-Assisted Software Engineering (CASE) tools - are not explicitly designed for collaboration but their correct use improves productivity and quality. Knowledge of and correct use of these tools is considered to be 'best practice' (Abran et al, 2004; Thyler & Dorfman, a2005; Thyler & Dorfman, b2005; Wilson, 2005; Wilson, 2006). Unfortunately these tools tend not to work on HPC machines, and further tools are necessary on the more complex HPC architectures. These may be expensive and soon outdated by changing hardware, especially at a time when there is a paradigm shift in hardware such as the introduction of multi-core processors because the single CPU-chip is at its physical limit.

Automated Software Validation Systems

Software can be automatically validated and checked by systems such as Buildbot. These automate the compile/test cycle required by most software projects to validate software changes. By running the builds on a variety of platforms, developers who do not own facilities to test their changes everywhere at least soon know whether they have broken the build. Validation systems must be configured correctly to make them worthwhile. If configured too tightly issues of style may be highlighted and programmers may spend time on these rather than genuine validation issues. This is more likely to be a problem where large software is being tested for the first time rather than software that has been developed from the start using these systems.

Visualization and Virtual Reality

Visualization uses computer graphics to make information easier to understand. Scientific visualization was the first use of visualization. In this form visualizations were used to allow scientists developing physically-based simulations to examine results visually. Visualization software can produce images and animations that users may share in an informal way or formally in peer reviewed academic papers.

Visualization and virtual reality environments allow multiple users to explore data as a collaborating group.

Computational science is often criticised for poor use of visualization. There are many reasons for this but one is that those developing 'simulation' software do not also develop visualization software, resulting in two separate communities with different interests.

Computational Steering

Computational steering allows the scientist to interact with research software as it executes, normally using visualization. Thus research softwares can be used to explore the solution spaces of the computational model interactively so the software can run more effectively. Computational steering experiments are uncommon, relying on the collaboration of many specialists from systems administrators, to visualizers, to domain specific

researchers and possibly computational steering and HPC experts too. Small research software running on a desk top machine may output results to a graphical scene at run-time but this is much more difficult to do on remote HPC machines. Computational steering really relates to distributed computing environments where the research software runs on one machine, the visualization on another and the user may view that through another system.

Web Services and the Grid

Web services allow multiple users to distribute a resource (computational or data) in a task specific way over the web. These tasks may be specific to a particular academic discipline or may be applicable to types of data/applications relevant to several disciplines. These are problem solving environments, a label originally taken from HPC. The grid provides an almost unlimited computational resource, similar to the electric grid, where the complexities are hidden from the user behind web services. However such usability comes at the cost of flexibility and users lose functionality.

THE OPEN-SOURCE PHILOSOPHY

The open-source philosophy was formulated to regulate sharing software through licensing. It is sometimes referred to as free software but this can be confusing as the word 'free' comes from the Unix community where it means software distributed in source form that can be freely modified and redistributed. It does not refer to zero-cost software (free software, 2003). Also 'free' does not necessarily mean that the creator gives away all rights, hence the importance of licensing, with GNU licenses and creative commons (CC) the best known open-source licenses (Open Source Initiative, 2009). Yet again, the 'free software movement' is sometimes differentiated from 'open-source' on the grounds that the first has a predominantly moral concern with maximizing sharing and communality, whilst the latter has more pragmatic motivations relating to more efficient and effective ways of developing robust software by enabling potentially global participation in solving development problems (Erlich & Aviv, 2007).

This philosophy has evolved to include other electronic data/information and is promoted by the Open Access Movement and P2P. "However, there are also crucial distinctions that need to be made and understood, among the movements for (1) Free/Open-source software, (2) Open Access (to peer-reviewed research), (3) Open Data, (4) Creative Commons licensing, and (5) Wikipedia-style collective writing. The crucial distinctions revolve mostly around (a) the fundamental difference between author giveaway vs. non-giveaway and (b) the functional differences between the re-use needs for peer-reviewed research article texts on the one hand, and data, software and other kinds of digital content on the other" - (Harnad, 2008). The CC family of licenses designed by Lawrence Lessig allows creators to specify uses they would like to restrict and allow for their work (attribution, commercial re-use, personal re-use, etc.). CC applies to all digital media: text, video, audio, software, data. In an academic environment attribution is likely to be the most important as academic reward is based on impact and that can only be traced if the creator is credited (Harnad, 2004).

While the license gives terms on the use of the work it does not regulate the process or organizational form of creation and distribution. Many open-source projects involve (1), Volunteer association (2), Collectivist organization (3), Voluntary hierarchy which together can lead to a prevalence of conflict in deliberative procedures (O'Niel, 2009). Apart from the impracticality of having the provision and maintenance of software and data vital to large research communities dependent only on voluntary (spare time) software creators releasing software into a managed environment where the software can be validated and kept up to date is more valuable and can potentially reduce conflict.

The open-release of software existed before the open-source philosophy existed. UK Research councils have sometimes enforced the practice, as in the early 1970's the UK Science research council insisted software produced by its funded projects be openly released, but in 1979 lifted this requirement. Currently policy in the UK is not uniform across research councils; Biotechnology and Biological Sciences Research Council (BBSRC) requires release of software while Engineering and Physical Sciences Research Council (EPSRC) does not.

PROFESSIONAL CODES, STANDARDS AND PROFESSIONAL DEVELOPMENT

Professional codes and standards are defined by professional bodies so that the practices of their members are coherent. Professional bodies in computing have followed other mature professions in creating a professional development path for software engineering. Mature professions have a developmental path that includes (McConnell & Tripp, 2005):

- **Initial professional education:** probably a degree
- **Accreditation:** oversight body approves qualifications
- **Skills development:** work experience through apprenticeship
- **Certification:** voluntary examinations
- **Licensing:** mandatory examination
- **Professional development:** continual retraining, is especially important in roles where technology changes
- **Professional Societies:** for the exchange of knowledge
- **Code of Ethics:** to encourage responsible behaviour

It is worth looking at some elements in more detail.

Codes of Ethics

The legally minimum acceptable practices of a professional could have undesirable results (Dakin, 2005). Ethics are not necessarily legally enforceable (except by professional bodies) but guide practices for the 'good'. The IEEE/ACM Joint Code of ethics of Software Engineering comes in short and long versions (ACM & IEEE, 2009).

Standards

Standards such as the ISO standards clarify what should be included in particular procedures and methodologies. Standards relevant to computational science cover software engineering, software design and procurement and are ideally determined by consensually validated norms for reasonable conduct and have to accommodate variability in practice: "standards are important not because they represent 'best practice' but because they represent good enough practice" (Moore, 2005, p88). Software Engineering Standards benefit the buyer and seller of software and computing services. Software Engineering is not a matured profession and the technology is changing so that standards are difficult for the professional bodies to integrate (Moore, 2005), for software development enterprises to choose amongst (Pfleeger et al, 2005) and achieve consistent terminology for all stakeholders (Singh, 2005).

Accreditation and Professional Development

Professional accreditation schemes relevant to practitioners of computational science are based around software development. These schemes tend to be based on the notion that software development should be a certified/licensed activity similar to medicine, accountancy and engineering. Certified professions define 'best practice' and discipline those not abiding by their standards. It can also be used to guarantee the quality of work or insure that work against failure (Dakin, 2005).

Education and training schemes are different. Education is intended to improve knowledge while training improves skills. Education teaches how to investigate problems so that the 'best solution' can be identified, a sound approach no matter what the state of technology and as such is not so important to continue throughout a career. Training teaches skill and should be "specific, timely and results oriented" (Shafer, 2005, p386). Skills depend on technology and job role and therefore training should be continually updated over an engineer's career.

The IEEE Computer Society's Certified Software Development Professional (CSDP) program for professional development (IEEE Computer Society, 2009) is used by some universities as an accreditation standard for their undergraduate studies in computing. It is based on materials developed in the Software Engineering Body of Knowledge (SWEBOK). The SWEBOK was completed in the 1990's (Abran et al, 2004) so updated materials are in book form (Thyler & Dorfman, a2005; Thyler & Dorfman, b2005). These materials explain that software engineering traditionally did not fit easily into the computer science educational program (Parnas, 2005; Tockey, 2005), there are few graduate or undergraduate courses (Gibbs, 2005) and that there is little consensus over what skills are required (Tockey, 2005) hence the need for the SWEBOK and the CSPD.

CASE STUDIES

Here we review a number of models currently in use for the sharing of electronic data gathered for the purpose of academic research.

1. The Met Office, a UK government body for weather forecasting and atmospheric research has complex software. The Unified Model is the one most used by academics funded through the National Centre for Atmospheric Science (NCAS). There are 3 classes of users of the Unified Model: (1) researchers (2) operations users and (3) commercial users. Each class has a different licensing system. Researchers must submit an abstract of their research for review so the license can be tailored to individual circumstances. Operational users are meteorological institutes in other countries having collaboration agreements with the Met Office, which includes an operational and research license, and possibly an agreed programme of research and development work, aimed at waiving the standard annual license fee. Commercial users pay for their licenses which are negotiated and issued individually. All licensed users have access to support via the same web site but different research programs, collaborative agreements and support contracts probably result in other support being available. NCAS is a component of the Natural Environment Research Council (NERC) and was set up in 2002 as a distributed collaborative centre providing the UK with national capability in atmospheric science research and technology. The 130 staff, who are distributed across 19 organisations (15 of which are universities), have an annual budget to carry out both research and support. They provide 2 services (atmospheric modelling and atmospheric data services) and access to the softwares and data are regulated, some for the data by open-source. The complexity of the software and data mean that support is necessary and many tools are available. The web site shows 1152 technical publications, 2 knowledge exchange networks and 16 joint research activities/campaigns.

The Joint Climate Research Programme (JCRP), launched in March 2009, is a Met Office/NERC initiative to strengthen the UK's world-leading reputation in climate science through projects on adaptation to the effects of climate change which focus on developing new tools, increasing collaboration and filling gaps in research on climate and weather forecasting. By comparison, the ParaFEM parallel numerical library (Smith & Griffiths, 2004) for finite elements analysis is a voluntary distributed collaboration amongst academic researchers and their graduate students which have developed some spin offs into commercial use, some are open-source while some are not. It was originated in the late 1970's, converted into Fortran for the book *Programming the Finite Element Method* (Smith & Griffiths, 1980), released on punch cards and associated with training courses at the Rutherford Appleton Laboratories (CLRC). Its development and maintenance has been an opportunistic byproduct of funded research activities, improved, maintained and developed by graduates becoming familiar with it through their postgraduate research and continuing to use and support it in subsequent employment. ParaFEM is a self-recruiting operation, where use involves contact with the current developers which create new collaborations with adopting users. New users can access the latest version after the possibility of important publications being drawn from it has been exhausted so as to protect the developers' interests. However whist it is possible to have this simple security with new users, it is not so easy with other academic rivals using closed-source software. It is possible to track the provenance of open-source software by the use of text-mining and plagiarism algorithms but it is not possible to do this for closed-source software. This applies mainly to use amongst academic users, and where the software has been adopted for commercial purposes or incorporated into the 'national library' of software held at CLRC and NAG (Numerical Analysis Group, a non-profit company) as SERC and NAG/SERC only limited additional functionality has been subsequently included.

2. The Visible Human Project has developed since 1989 with the aim 'to build a digital image library of volumetric data representing complete, normal adult male and female anatomy' (http://www.nlm.nih.gov/pubs/factsheets/visible_human.html), going public in 1994 with a 15Gb dataset of 'the Visible Human Male', followed in 1995 with the 40Gb 'Visible Human Female'. 20,000 licenses have been issued for 48 countries, and its website records 20 software developments for viewing medical images, 25 products, 3 international mirror sites and 21 tools (some of which are open-source), 4 conferences and 912 publications between 1987 and 2007. The data is large so distribution has not taken the form of web services. Its real value seems to be facilitating cross-disciplinary research and collaboration by acting as a contact point for interested parties.

3. The European Bioinformatics Institute, a European community funded project to resource microbiological science and disseminate research technologies to industry is part of the European Molecular Biology Laboratory (EMBL), which is distributed in four sites across Europe in addition to the EBI itself. It is a repository for biological data and collects relevant data 'wherever practicable'. These data sets are not proprietary to the institute which facilitates download of all of them (claiming 2.5 million website hits per day). This contrasts with the Visible Human in managing constantly changing data sources, and also in having much more proactive involvement in the research community e.g. promoting standards and

languages. Its research role is to facilitate interdisciplinary work across the EMBL's sites (with 5 mirror sites across the world), accommodating its own research groups, supported by service teams. Its web services give the research community unregulated access to data (10Tb).

4. The development of web journals, wikis and blogs are opening up research. Results and discussions, not just papers, are going online making these instantly accessible to a global audience. Academic papers tend to report positive results but through these forums negative results can be presented too. The use of these Web 2.0 tools could develop into a new way of conducting research, currently called Science 2.0 (Waldrop, 2008). Some interesting examples include www.plsone.org, www.3quarksdialy.com, wwwopenwetware.org, www.webcitation.org, network.nature.com and www.sciencecommons.org. While the acceptance of open-access publications is strong (Harnad et al, 2004) Science 2.0 less likely to be as it is opening up the research processes that are currently closed. The debate over Science 2.0 is to do with how necessary is the secrecy gained by having a closed system? How much does a researcher need to keep their ideas or processes secure from their colleagues or the wider world?

5. The eScience initiative was initially funded by the then Department of Trade and Industry (DTI) to increase transfer of innovation from academia to business. eScience has focused on (a) digital data, all issues from collection to provision through web services (b) the vast levels of computation now available so that any computational problem seems tractable (c) cross-disciplinary collaboration, first, made easy through virtual collaborative environments so that the 'best' people could be put together in teams rather than using people in the same geographical location

and second, allowing computer scientists to collaborate with those in other disciplines to produce software solutions for particular research problems/questions. Many software applications funded through eSceince were only designed to act as proof of concept so never suited the aim of the DTI and most were not open-source. Some projects were treated more as cross-disciplinary software development projects and created applications to aid particular concerns such as mammography. A separate eScience initiative was set up for each disciplinary area through their respective research councils and little consensus exists between the disciplinary branches of eScience on what is important.

HOW TO CULTIVATE 'BEST PRACTICE'

The Appeal of Established Codes and Standards

To increase the dependability of software, changes are made not only to technology and techniques supporting software development, but also to standardize and upgrade the activities of the developers themselves through disseminating 'best practice'. Naturally, it is tempting to adopt and adapt existing codes and standards for software engineering, but the important existing codes and standards are developed mainly to regulate 'industrial' software development rather than academic research.

UK Academic Success

Whilst academic research – especially but not only – in the natural sciences is increasingly a collective and cross-disciplinary activity, within UK universities the imperatives of academic success remain centred on assessment of individual achievement (with consequent difficulties in acknowledging, let alone precisely evaluating, individual contributions to team and cross-disciplinary activity). The focus on individual achievement was maintained and strengthened through the dependence of University research funding on the rating of individual performance through the Research Assessment Exercise (RAE) although paradoxically the trend is that research grants are awarded less often to individuals but increasingly to research teams whether collaborating within the same institution or across different ones.

The RAE is a formal exercise periodically conducted by the UK research councils to rate the success of particular UK academic researchers and research departments. The RAE assesses the publications and the amount of resources held in terms of the monetary value of project grant awards and for resourcing equipment such as HPC machines. However the assessment only judges the research output for the primary discipline and what lies within and outside that discipline is only determined at the time of assessment. A good rating in the RAE increases the prestige of the researcher and of the department and university. The RAE evaluation of individual and departmental rankings determines the subsequent distribution of research funding awarded from central government funding. A discussion of the RAE for computer science is available from (UKCRC, 2006). The UK Computing Research Committee (UKCRC) are a recognized body that formally examines and comments on UK computing research funding and practices. The RAE in 2008 was largely based on publication which depends on peer review. The next review is planned to use scientometrics but as the plans for that RAE are not yet released it is difficult to predict the possible impact of such changes.

Research councils also conduct international reviews of particular disciplines to assess how UK research rates globally. Such reviews are strategic, normally conducted by an international panel, do not rank researchers or universities, but publish much information in a freely available long report. Relevant reviews include those for HPC (EPSRC & DFG, 2005), information and communications technology (EPSRC, 2006), mathematics (EPSRC & CMS, 2004) and engineering (EPSRC & The Royal Academy of Engineering, 2004).

All forms of academic success effectively depend on peer assessment. The process is governed by procedures prescribed by Research Councils or the organizers of academic journals and conferences. Currently the effectiveness of both the principles and procedures organizing the process of peer review are being debated. The RCUK (Research Councils UK) is reassessing peer review for the allocation of grants; the principals of the process are given as guidelines (Niven, 2009). The problems is discussed in (UKCRC, 2007; UKCRC, 2006). The current reappraisal of peer review seems motivated by cost considerations as the UK research councils have altered their funding model to full economic costing but exclude time spent on peer review which is unpaid (and largely unrecognized in RAE assessments). The RAE has meant that academics are less willing to undertake public service activities such as peer reviewing. A report on the motivation for the review is available from the BBSRC (2006) while the results of a recent survey are given by EPSRC (2009). This survey shows that those who responded are generally happy with the process but that there are issues to do with objectivity, anonymity and interdisciplinary.

Attention here focuses mainly on the position of the computational participants in computer-aided research, and so the importance of the RAE and the underlying peer review mechanism is considered relative to the difficulties such participants have in fitting into that system of evaluation such that

"As a whole, it was observed that the level of integration of computational science with computer science in the UK has not yet reached the highest international standards. Perhaps due in some measure to present funding practices,

many research groups in the UK appeared to be deficient in adapting to modern programming practices, anticipating the need for data management and visualization, and developing interoperable software and algorithm environments", EPSRC & DFG (2005, p4). The responsibility of teaching these practices is ambivalent not just within the UK but globally as discussed in the subsections *Accreditation and Professional Development* and *Attempts To Initiate a Structure to Develop 'Best Practice'*.

THE IMPACT OF ACADEMIC ORGANISATION ON COLLECTING AND SHARING DATA

There are three kinds of development: provision of 'public' computational infrastructures to facilitate the development of computational science, support services and 'home-grown' software developed primarily for the needs of specific projects.

Provision of Infrastructure

Infrastructure for large supercomputers includes the network connecting the academic to the computational resource (low band width connecting the academic and the supercomputer will be a bottleneck for generating or loading large quantities of data); a guaranteed electrical supply which may include backup generators; space in a machine room secured from physical attack or theft (necessary for insurance) as well as air-conditioning (water cooled and air cooled machines require different air-conditioning) and support staff needing physical access to monitor and repair machines. Often the role of the systems administrator is seen as infrastructure as the systems administrator keeps the machine running smoothly, maintains security policies and keeps software updated.

The scope of what counts as infrastructure is wide, depending on the size of the supercomputer and the resources available to the academic with funding for the computational resource. National network and computational resources are funded in holistic ways where the infrastructure is included in the funding (through competitive tendering) while funding for a local computational resource will depend on existing local infrastructures and what is applied for. The software to enable the computational research to be conducted is mainly developed by the disciplinary academics but some projects involve computer scientists or those supporting computational science either as funded researchers belonging to the collaborative group or as support. The computational specialist is not generally a permanent part of the research team.

Provision of Support

Both HPC and visualization are academic disciplines and support activities. While HPC is seen as an activity that requires focused support, hence the need for national academic services which does not generally include visualization support, the place of visualization is more complex. Local support for both visualization and HPC depends on the priorities of the universities that must fund them. This funding goes through trends and currently several UK universities are setting up services which may include computational resources, virtual environments and academic support personnel which boosts the output of research academics but is costly. While HPC is fairly bound to computational science visualization is more diffuse as it can apply to any data used for any human purpose. Thus currently visualization is more of an academic discipline than HPC and the visualization community is not particularly focused on computational science.

UK Research Funding for Software Development

Until recently software development could not be openly part of research funding applications. It is still not considered a bona fide research activity but a new stream funds software development. Software development can be a species of 'dirty work' for research scientists, so those committed to computational science can be marginalised within the structures of these disciplines.

Where software development is necessary, it is done 'unofficially' within funded research so that development is often tied tightly to the research project's specific needs , developed to the adequacy for those purposes and no further; not fully tested or documented. When software is released and commercialised either for academic or full commercial use the software tends to stay limited to existing functionality. Perhaps the attempt to create large repositories of software may bind the functionality to the technologies on which it was developed and to the creator's understanding at that time, as resourcing revision for numerous softwares whist maintaining backward compatibility is an overhead beyond the repository's reach.

Funding for computational solutions structures through the eScience initiative has been organised separately for different disciplines. Some software is developed as proof of concept and designed only for that purpose while others have had a development team where the software is designed and developed responsively i.e. not only to meet specific needs of disciplines but also bridge the difference between software development and research cultures (the approach best fitted to a client vendor model of development).

With 'home-grown' software there can be problems of possessiveness, especially when personally developed (possibly learning software skills to develop it), making for a reluctance to share, alter or use alternatives. Someone else may well benefit from or even publically identify faults in software that has had research results accepted by the developer's peers (it is easier to criticise something than create it). This possessiveness can apply even between different sites involved in joint projects. Nonetheless, the 'open-source' philosophy is one that is attracts many academics (for ideological, as well as practical reasons as this altruistic attitude can save others the effort of developing software and attract researchers with similar interests to the one who releases software). There is evidence that 'open' publication is being recognised and supported within academia (Harnad et al, 2004).

Some hope recognition may extend to software too but research publications remain key elements of academic output and are better understood than software. How to incorporate 'giving away' software into the reward and progression structure of academic careers should be addressed if those administrating research wish to encourage this sharing.

Issues that affect collaboration between research disciplines and computational specialists:

(a) Conflicts between proficient and/or optimised computational solutions and acceptability of outputs to the disciplinary research community where the latter's interest is in the results, not computational format.

(b) Conflicts between the criteria for career recognition between collaborating parties –

  (1) all publishable research potential must be extracted by all parties before software or data is released so each must know and respect each other's goals

  (2) all partners in the collaboration need recognition (while application of HPC and visualization may be novel to a particular discipline the solutions may not seem novel to the HPC or visualization communities).

(c) Problems placing the computational specialists within a research project – UK national HPC services have until the most recent one, HECToR, had a centralised support group but after consultation with the PIs who used the services the model was changed to a distributed one, the computational specialist acting as a travelling consultant, moving

every few months. It makes sense that the PI of a project would like the computational specialist in the team (probably permanently if there is funding). Unfortunately there are not many computational specialists and these roving support posts were difficult to fill.

(d) Division of credit for achievements between collaborators is a problem for teams that are all academic, however the criteria for success is different for service groups. CLRC put a request in their software that prints during runtime that publications produced with its use acknowledge the software to enable figures of use for research publication (impact) to be reported to funders.

UK ACADEMIC SOFTWARE DEVELOPMENT PRACTICES

The interest of research administrators in professional codes and standards is understandable, since these appear to contain ready-made correctives to the variability of software knowledge and development skills, but in this section we review aspects of software development in academic research which make such standardized solutions unsuitable, at least as yet.

Software is developed by UK academics as part of various research projects. These softwares are designed to answer specific research questions which may be a part of a long or short term research strategy. Answering research questions is not a recognized part of formal software engineering practices. The closest that it comes to a recognizable element of software engineering is as requirements capture or feature development. The formal models rely on requirements capture for the software design step (often as a means of attempting to stabilize requirements in a way that enables a contractual relationship between designer and customer). Research questions change over time depending on issues internal to the collaborative group and external because of the explorative, creative and competitive nature of research.

In the case of a collaboration involving a computer scientist specializing in distributed systems architecture and data structures, a computational civil engineer who has a stable numerical library designed to answer research questions for civil engineering, and a visualizer specializing in real-time distributed visualization. Each works at a different institution, to get funding each must identify novel research in their respective area of expertise (although their joint goal is a single proof of concept for a distributed rapid virtual prototyping system) and for their work to count they must each publish in their recognized field, where collaborative publications will probably not count significantly. The project fits the characteristics suitable to agile methods:

1. uncertain or volatile requirements
2. less than 50 responsible and motivated developers
3. a customer who understands and will get involved (Fowler, 2000).

Agile methods are applied and soon it is realized the network over which the system will run is overly restrictive on performance. The engineer can publish by increasing the functionality of the numerical library that already exists but had hoped that this project would produce visualization functionality necessary for future research. However, the visualizer is aware that similar systems have already been published in the visualization community for similar application areas e.g., automotive engineering and what is really novel is the system design not the functionality that the engineer wants. The computer scientist's originality involves using new web technologies to achieve proof of concept without need for a working system.

In this example agile methods adapt to the team's evolving needs but with limited success because there is no clear client or product. This is a

software/research dilemma: is the project delivering a software product or research output(s)? The engineer's wish for a product gives him a 'client' role and in the commercial world he would have a contract involving penalties. However Research Councils see participants as equal and expect each to publish in their own areas of expertise. The team fractures and 3 separate products are produced which brings academic success to all. Universities are not producing commercial products (despite governmental and funding council pressure to move in that direction) but are at the other end of the research innovation pipeline so methodologies to do with product release and support are unlikely to be of use.

Researcher's requirements for software are specific and pragmatic which means that they need to develop software to meet those (often rapidly evolving) requirements, and usually have little motivation (or resources) to develop software or its quality beyond the level of their needs, especially when the scientific research funding treats software development as an unfunded overhead. Research councils until recently have not funded projects involving software development since this is not deemed a research activity. This implies that software does not have a research value but that only the running of the software delivers research value, as though software already exists to answer all possible/important research questions. The assumption that enough software is available may work for some HPC communities but does not apply to areas such as global climate change or systems biology where the research questions and ideas are less well understood and where new software is need to make these questions answerable.

Recognition of an individual's contribution to the development of software is relevant both to the assessment of academic achievement and to the exploitation of intellectual property rights. Intellectual property can be held in many forms. Software is relatively new and so the laws are still adapting (Scully, 2005). Ideas embedded in software such as algorithms have a different status as intellectual property to the source code which is covered by copyright. Just as the intellectual property laws have not clearly identified where novelty and innovation lies within traditional frameworks of legal protections (i.e., whether it is within software and/or the use of that software on a particular physical device) so too is it for those that collaborate in and fund computational science. Thus running software created by disciplinary experts to produce novel results counts as research whilst the software combining a number of algorithms, data structures, input and output file formats and a validation of the numerical methods and results of running the software to resolve the relevant disciplinary research questions does not. Inconsistency is seen as software does have a commercial value and so even though the research councils may not be keen to fund software development the DTI and universities offer encouragements to license software and turn it into commercial products. Ironically, then the encoding of research questions within text in the form of a paper or any academic publication can be seen as research output (providing it passes peer review) but text encoding those same research questions in a programming language as software is not.

The nature of academic research projects compounds the difficulties in identifying individual contributions to the project's achievements, and especially of software developed. Groups of researchers working together to produce software often work informally with respect to the design and documentation of software, the participants change over time as involved research students come and go, collaborations form and break, and funding is gained or runs out. Nor are the researchers within a project all equally focused on common goals and may branch the software development onto an independent path.

ATTEMPTS TO INITIATE A STRUCTURE TO DEVELOP ACADEMIC 'BEST PRACTICE'

Because, in the judgment of the International Review of HPC

"The culture of best practices software engineering has not percolated effectively into the UK scientific community." – EPSRC & DFG (2005, p7)

The need to find ways of raising the scientific community's performance in international comparisons/competition ensures an interest on the part of administrators in encouraging the development of such a 'best practice culture', which will at least reduce the extent to which computational science collaborations involve reinventing the wheel, slowly and perhaps painfully developing software capabilities that are already available but unknown. In this section we look at some ways of making advanced software available:

The paper "Where's the Real Bottleneck in Scientific Computing?" by Wilson (2006) gives a good discussion of the problems. His online course in Software Carpentry (Wilson, 2005) aims to teach the tools and their use. Since 2001 Edinburgh has run a studentship that tries to address these problems before the EPSRC funded a number of studentships (EPCC, 2009). The CLRC have a software engineering programme focused on tools and dissemination in the aim of improving adoption (Greenough, 2009).

Research councils dislike dictating to academics how to conduct their research - academics are under their own individual pressures which include peer review. They prefer to raise awareness, disseminate and fund educational programs.

Newsletters and Technical Reports

The national HPC services have an obligation to encourage the most efficient use of their computational resources. As HPC architectures and related technologies change continually this requires exploring the impact of those changes on computational methods and software development practices. The results of these investigations need to be communicated to the user community in timely and open fashions. Technical reports are released on the web allowing users to assess the importance of technology's changes quickly while newsletters announce the release of technical reports and other changes to the service in a more journalistic fashion.

Studentships and On-the-Job Training

"The UK funding agencies have instituted High End Computing Studentships that provide four year funding, including one year equivalent of training in the computational sciences over the four years for M.Sc.-Ph.D. students enrolled in this program. In Warwick and Edinburgh, students work on computational science modules and thus obtain additional training. Even though small in scale (about ten students per year), this was found to be a good mechanism for interdisciplinary training by several consortia. The Integrated Biology group evolved computational life science modules where they trained students for six weeks. This program was widely subscribed to and regarded as a success by life science trainees. Several of the groups, however, had no formal training mechanism for their students and relied on the studentship training. The Materials Chemistry and UKCP consortia desired more extensive training for their students, but were limited by the three-year degree constraints. There was a paucity of students in some consortia, where shortage of students despite the presence of resources was a barrier for research productivity. To some extent this reflects the culture of education and training in UK institutions The Panel also were told that the difficulty of obtaining UK funding for nondomestic students imposes constraints on attracting the best talent." - EPSRC & DFG (2005, p7). These studentships have now been discontinued because of a lack of interest from students.

New users to computational methods and/or HPC tend to be relatively flexible to their approach although they may be restricted by their skills whereas long term users will have legacy softwares (and possibly researchers) that will limit the flexibility of their working practices. Mentoring researchers at an early point in a project can improve adoption of HPC and visualization.

Project Funding

These projects look at current and future technologies and disseminate via newsletters, training and technical reports what constitutes 'best practice'. Recently the research councils have started to fund projects aimed at software development and that encourage 'best practice'.

FUTURE TRENDS

The main developments that are already underway and are affecting computer-aided academic research and are likely to continue to impact on these are (a) the short and long term development of both cross- and multi-disciplinary teams (b) computational science's dependence on data sharing (c) open-source software development and (d) the bypass of traditional peer review through open-access publication. These developments will be affected by the existing structure of recognition in academic research but will also increasingly create pressures to change to recognize the increasingly team-based, cross- and multi-disciplinary character of research that will likely develop even further from increasingly open-sharing amongst researchers through the web. Web 2.0 will magnify sharing, making virtual communities and data available not only in vastly greater quantities but in much more detailed and refined forms that, in the past, only the closest collaborators could share.

Open-source, often without pecuniary motivation and invoking a communal spirit has significant appeal within university research where many have distaste for commerce. Those same researchers are also deeply involved in the individualized system of assessment, accepting the idea of a fair exchange between effort and achievement on the one hand and community recognition on the other, which can inhibit the readiness to make data or software available at an early stage, as well as create reluctance to invest effort specifically in improving data and software for ease of use by interested parties (especially if those parties are competing peers) who will benefit from the unrecognized effort invested in collecting the data and developing the software. This, as partly explained, affects not just the readiness to engage in the public collaboration of open-source but even relations within collaborative teams, especially where relations between research discipline and computational specialists are concerned.

Though there are resistances to open-source, undoubtedly ways will be sought to make it compatible with the 'effort bargain' governing academic research. In the short term, the current trend will continue where the relationship is informal and therefore indirectly beneficial to official academic recognition, as when open-release of software is associated with the developers name so as to create contact with others in related fields and to build the developer's research networks.

Open-access publication is most readily compatible with the existing structure of academic research and is advocated by Harnad as a realization of what it is that academic researchers require, namely, 'uptake, usage, application and impact'(2004, p2). The immediacy with which a paper can be archived on line contrasts with the long gestation period of publication through established peer review, with open-access providing a more telling form of 'peer review' since the paper is likely to be read, cited, and drawn upon by those who have an interest in the research. Open-access data is relatively well accepted as is

shown by the ESRC insisting on the open-release of data from all funded projects and data repositories such as the Visible Human and the EBI. Software is still integrating into the practices of academia as it has been more recently introduced into academic research than either publications or data. The importance of software for answering specific research questions will have to be more directly recognized by funding bodies if sharing is to involve/produce high quality software, for whilst it is accepted that open-data and publications should be managed by non-academic professionals, currently this is only so for a limited amount of software developed to run in HPC environments or for specific research campaigns. There is of course a difference between, on the one hand, individual researchers releasing software at the end of a project, and, on the other, the creation of open-source software to support the activities of research communities. With the former it is reasonable that the future maintenance of the software will depend on voluntary effort while with the latter voluntary effort is not a sufficiently secure source for development and maintenance.

The same tensions between concerns for priority and recognition as against the possibilities of freely and usefully pooling information amongst interested parties are to be found in the idea of 'open-research'. Openness is pushed still further back into the research processes, regarding blogs and wikis as ways of sharing information over the unfolding course of research projects that would, previously, be preserved only in private personal records. It encourages the documentation and sharing of materials (e.g., the practicalities of operating research protocols) that would not previously have been recorded. There are questions as to how far the sharing should go, whether blogs and wikis are primarily for sharing within a collaborative research project or whether they should be available quite openly.

CONCLUSION

We have pointed to some difficulties in optimizing the capacity of computational disciplines to contribute to the development of academic research owing to the fact that the research discipline interests and requirements tend to predominate over those of software development per se.

1. The professional codes for software development are not readily applicable because such codes often presuppose a professional-client model whereas academic software development involves no 'customer' or equivalent. This problem is compounded by cross-disciplinary software development where more than one discipline is involved in developing software and each must resolve different research questions. However much is clearly very appropriate, the most obvious example is the use of CASE and other automated or semi-automated tools for the development, validation and optimization of software. A more in depth study is needed to determine fully what is applicable.

2. On-going training and professional development is an important feature of any career involving software development. Accreditation programs such as the one described from the IEEE are sensible. However many come to computational science not from an 'accredited degree' but as Ph.D. students having graduated in a discipline other than computer science thus the learning curve of taking on a Ph.D., familiarizing themselves with software development 'best practices' and the additional knowledge required by the specialism of computational science is just too great.

3. Many research disciplines would benefit from software tailored to their research questions. Many issues will have to be overcome to make this possible. The problem can be divided into four activities software creation, improvement, maintenance and access and each activity can be facilitated by academics or academic support personnel, or both.

4. Interdisciplinary research is a separate but often related issue. There is currently funding for interdisciplinary research but still there is reluctance. Conditions that favour long term and short term collaboration differ because long term collaboration is a continuing situation where trust, working practices and funding are already established. However for both long and short term collaboration a change in the national research assessment so that the whole team is motivated to solve one main research problem would be beneficial.

5. Finally, the increasing enthusiasm, both ideologically and pragmatically motivated, for sharing which is expressed by promotion of open-source, open-access and open-data as well as cross-disciplinary research has the associated risk of giving away the returns from one's work as well as one's recognition and rights in intellectual property. We can envisage four solutions to these insecurities which are to follow (a) the open-source model of licensing each data type but these do not protect the collation of data of that is part of science 2.0; (b) the existing practice of some universities, creating collaborative agreements between institutions, but these don't easily relate to individual conduct and situations; (c) the commercial precedent of non-disclosure agreements, though these do not comfortably accommodate the diverse requirements of different disciplines in inter-disciplinary collaboration requiring multiple agreements, one for each disciplinary and/ or institutional team and (d) the example of professional codes of conduct which focus on individual's responsibility, but would nonetheless require considerable collaborative effort to create and institutionalise.

ACKNOWLEDGMENT

The authors would like to thank Mike Ashworth, Peter Halfpenny, Lee Margetts, Mike Pettipher, Ian Smith and the anonymous reviewer for their insights.

REFERENCES

Abran, A., Bourque, P., Dupuis, R., Moore, J. W., & Tripp, L. L. (2004). *Guide to the Software Engineering Body of Knowledge – SWEBOK* (2004 edition). Piscataway, NJ: IEEE Press. Retrieved April 11, 2009 from http://www.swebok.org

ACM & IEEE. (2009). *Software Engineering Code of Ethics and Professional Practice*. Retrieved April 11, 2009 from http://www.acm.org/about/se-code

BBSRC. (2006). *Efficiency and Effectiveness of Peer Review Project*. Retrieved April 14, 2009 from http://www.bbsrc.ac.uk/organisation/structures/council/2006/0610_peer_review.pdf

Dakin, K. (2005). Are Developers Morally Challenged? In R. H. Thyler & M. Dorfman (Eds.) Software Engineering Volume 1: The Development Processes (3rd ed.). IEEE Computer Society.

EPCC. (2009). *MSc in High Performance Computing*. Retrieved April 14, from http://www.ukhec.ac.uk/publications/ukhec_issue3.pdf

EPSRC. (2006). *International Perceptions of the UK Research Base in Information and Communications Technologies*. Retrieved April 5, 2009 from http://www.epsrc.ac.uk/AboutEPSRC/IntRevs/2006ICTIR/Report.htm

EPSRC. (2009). *Results of EPSRC Peer Review Survey*. Retrieved April 14, 2009 from http://www.epsrc.ac.uk/CMSWeb/Downloads/Other/PeerReviewSurveyReport.pdf

EPSRC & CMS. (2004). *An International Review of UK Research in Mathematics*. Retrieved April 13, 2009 from http://www.epsrc.ac.uk/AboutEPSRC/IntRevs/2003MathsIR/default.htm

EPSRC & the Deutsche Forschungsgemeinschaft (DFG). (2005). *International Review of Research Using High Performance Computing in the UK*. Retrieved June 28, 2009 from http://www.epsrc.ac.uk/CMSWeb/Downloads/Other/HPCInternationalReviewReport.pdf

EPSRC & The Royal Academy of Engineering. (2004). *The Wealth of a Nation: An Evaluation of Engineering Research in the United Kingdom*. Retrieved April 5, 2009 from http://www.epsrc.ac.uk/AboutEPSRC/IntRevs/2004EngIR/InternationalReviewData.htm

Erlich, Z., & Aviv, R. (2007). Open source software: strengths and weaknesses. In St Amant, K., & Still, B. (Eds.), *Handbook of Research on Open Source Software* (pp. 184–196). Hershey, PA: Information Science Reference.

Fowler, M. (2000). *The New Methodology* (Original). Retrieved April 14, from http://www.martinfowler.com/articles/newMethodologyOriginal.html#ShouldYouGoLight

Free Software. (2003). *Free Software* (Open Source). Retrieved April 14, 2009 from http://www.free-soft.org/

Gibbs, W. W. (2005). Software's Chronic Crisis. In R. H. Thyler & M. Dorfman (Eds.) Software Engineering Volume 1: The Development Processes (3rd Ed.). IEEE Computer Society.

Greenough, C. (2009). *Software engineering*. Retrieved April 14, 2009 from http://www.cse.scitech.ac.uk/seg/

Harnad, S. (2004). Apercus of WOS Meeting: Making Ends Meet in the Creative Commons. *American-Scientist-Open-Access-Forum*. Retrieved April 14, 2009 from http://users.ecs.soton.ac.uk/harnad/Hypermail/Amsci/3758.html

Harnad, S. (2008). Open Access, Free/Open Software, Open Data, and Creative Commons Commonalities and Distinctions. *Free Software Free Society Conference on Freedom in Computing, Development and Culture*. Retrieved April 14, 2009 from http://fsfs.in/schedule/events/61.en.html

Harnad, S., Brody, T., Vallieres, F., Carr, L., Hitchcock, S., Gingras, Y., et al. (2004). The green and the gold roads to Open Access. *Nature Web Focus*. Retrieved April 16, 2009 from http://www.nature.com/nature/focus/accessdebate/21.html

IEEE. Computer Society (2009). *IEEE CS Certification Programs*. Retrieved April 11, 2009 from http://www2.computer.org/portal/web/getcertified

McConnell, S., & Tripp, L. (2005). Professional Software Engineering: Fact or Fiction. In R.H. Thyler & M. Dorfman (Eds.), Software Engineering Volume 1: The Development Processes (3rd Ed.). IEEE Computer Society.

Moore, J. W. (2005). An Integrated Collection of Software Engineering Standards. In R.H. Thyler & M. Dorfman (Eds.), Software Engineering Volume 1: The Development Processes (3rd Ed.). IEEE Computer Society.

Niven, D. (2009). *Peer Review Principles, EPSRC*. Retrieved April 14, 2009 from http://www.epsrc.ac.uk/ResearchFunding/ReviewingProposals/Principles.htm

O'Neil, M. (2009). *The Social Impact of Online Tribal Bureaucracy*. Paper presented at the Fourth Oekonux Conference, University of Manchester, UK 27-29 MARCH 2009.

Open Source Initiative. (2009). *Open Source Licenses*. Retrieved April 14, 2009 from http://www.opensource.org/licenses

Parnas, D. L. (2005). Software Engineering Programs Are Not Computer Science Programs. In R.H. Thyler & M. Dorfman (Eds.), Software Engineering Volume 2: The Supporting Processes (3rd Ed.). IEEE Computer Society.

Pfleeger, S. L., Fenton, N., & Page, S. (2005). Evaluating Software Engineering Standards. In R. H. Thyler & M. Dorfman (Eds.), Software Engineering Volume 2: The Supporting Processes (3rd Ed.). IEEE Computer Society.

Scully, J. (2005). Software and the Law. In R. H. Thyler & M. Dorfman (Eds.), Software Engineering Volume 1: The Development Processes (3rd Ed.). IEEE Computer Society.

Shafer, P. S. (2005). Planning an Effective Training Program. In R. H. Thyler & M. Dorfman (Eds.), Software Engineering Volume 2: The Supporting Processes (3rd Ed.). IEEE Computer Society.

Singh, R. (2005). The Software Life Cycle Processes Standard. In R.H. Thyler & M. Dorfman (Eds.), Software Engineering Volume 2: The Supporting Processes (3rd Ed.). IEEE Computer Society.

Smith, I. M., & Griffiths, V. (1980). *Programming the Finite Element Method* (1st ed.). Wiley.

Smith, I. M., & Griffiths, V. (2004). *Programming the Finite Element Method* (4th ed.). Wiley.

Thyler, R. H., & Dorfman, M. (Eds.). (a2005). Software Engineering Volume 1: The Development Processes (3rd Ed.). IEEE Computer Society.

Thyler, R. H., & Dorfman, M. (Eds.). (b2005). Software Engineering Volume 2: The Supporting Processes (3rd ed.). IEEE Computer Society.

Tockey, S. (2005). Recommended Skills and Knowledge for Software Engineers. In R. H. Thyler & M. Dorfman (Eds.), Software Engineering Volume 1: The Development Processes (3rd Ed.). IEEE Computer Society.

UKCRC. (2006). *UK Universities Computing Research UKCRC Submission to the EPSRC International Review*. Retrieved April 5, 2009 from http://www.ukcrc.org.uk/resource/reports/ukcrc_part_a.pdf

UKCRC. (2007). *Response by UKCRC to RCUK Consultation on Efficiency and Effectiveness of Peer Review*. Retrieved April 14, 2009 from http://www.ukcrc.org.uk/resource/reports/2007-01.pdf

Waldrop, M. M. (2008). Science 2.0. *Scientific American*, *298*(5). doi:10.1038/scientificamerican0508-68

Wilson, G. (2005). *Software Carpentary*. Python Software Foundation. Retrieved April 13, 2009 from http://www.swc.scipy.org/

Wilson, G. (2006). Where's the Real Bottleneck in Scientific Computing? *American Scientist*, *94*(1), 5. doi:.doi:10.1511/2006.1.5

Chapter 17
Designing Appropriate Frameworks, Models, Strategies and Solutions

Pawan Chhabra
Infosys, India

Chetan Jagatkishore Kothari
Infosys, India

Subhadip Sarkar
Infosys, India

ABSTRACT

In recent times, the focus of innovation is increasingly moving beyond the centralized R&D programs of large firms to more of a collaborative innovation. This is true even in the Information Communication Technology (ICT) industries. With this approach in mind, the technical strategy has to be laid down to design appropriate architectural models that act as key foundations of building large software systems without compromising on access rights, privacy, confidentiality, ethics, policies, IP, etc. A platform that can enable researchers to share their views, ideas, thoughts or products in seamless manner is the need of the hour. This chapter examines the ways and means of creating a standard model which focuses on well proven software design practices to leverage full potential of open innovation platform; while focusing upon the evolution of IP trends and without compromising on access rights, privacy, confidentiality, ethics, policies, IP, etc.

INTRODUCTION

The ever changing trends in economic situations over the past decade demands that businesses identify means to reduce cost and increase efficiency and productivity at every level of organization supported by technology infrastructure. This is driving the trends of fusion of ideas, software, technologies and research, and it has become essential to resolve the issues of laws, rights and privacy attached to it by applying right technology principles and rules in the business infrastructure. This has also driven a new shift in the focus, to

DOI: 10.4018/978-1-61520-975-0.ch017

Figure 1. Progression of the chapter

have appropriate models, Frameworks and strategies that would govern these trends.

To win competitive advantage, servicing clients more effectively and efficiently and to maximize revenue by new techniques and business models, industry leaders are taking new technology research initiatives. Open Innovation, a new paradigm, is one of these key steps for creating and profiting from technology. In the field of information and communication, a number of innovations point the way to improved customer satisfaction and simplification of business processes, helping bringing down operational and maintenance cost. The demand of Innovation and rightful approach are bringing a new difference in software engineering equation.

The information technology (IT) and related service industry is achieving unprecedented level of new ideas either business or technology. Customers are the direct beneficiaries in terms of efficient and effective choice, and novel products or services. Innovation has become the great enabler and catalyst for the driving forces in organizations. Technology companies that can generate innovative services to reach to customers faster need to thrive. With no Innovation in their business plan, companies are at high risk of getting supplanted by the companies who has. Companies must formulate their expansion strategy on the basis of innovative products and service that

customer may find compelling to generate steady financial gain.

Driving business success through Innovation and to exploit other organizational assets under the union of laws, rights and ethics to ICT needs suitable software setups that affirm the ideas of collaborations. This chapter points out the facts about, collaboration of knowledge, information, software systems, & products represents the fundamental shift in the way businesses are done. Modular business has to be aligned with module Frameworks and Architectures and still the confidentiality must be maintained. The real knowledge of domain and technology must be under the boundaries of organization.

The chapter emphasizes upon factors that protect privacy, confidentiality and build confidence that are the key enablers to bring openness and global trade improve their relationships with ICTs.

Existing Trends

The section below highlights some of the existing trends of Innovation being followed in the past but has to be changed with the nature of business in an enterprise; Innovation needs to be defined in a customary way aligning with the business growth to realize its full potential as basis of progress. This requires collaboration, mixture of ideas and information across people and it is very essential to examine and analyze the role of moral responsibilities and ethics and realize it through proper techniques both locally and globally. Ideas and information has to be freed to all sides covered with patent and other Intellectual Property (IP) laws. One needs to protect information from arbitrary copying, unethical distribution of information and use it appropriately. An enterprise has to share their information and products with researchers, academics, or even competitors. The idea has to be aligned with a robust IT infrastructure that is agile and keep evolving with the nature of business. It needs thought process that is based upon laws, ethics, politics and social policies, to be governed across the enterprise and partners.

Currently evolved internet and related technologies have given companies new ways to harvest the talent of innovators that are working outside the walls of organization. Today, in all kinds of companies, retail, automotive, IT services and others are routinely involving customers, suppliers, partners and competitors to shape up their product line. It is very essential to give substantial control to outsiders that work together in the network. But this control has to be supported by protective layer of IP [1] to safeguard the interests. Distribution of Innovation through a governance mechanism will reduce the company cost and usher innovative products. But this is not enough. With a global distribution framework that is needed to share knowledge, it is equally important that, the product, that company wants to innovate, itself is flexible to adapt new ideas and supported technology backbone to align with business models. Software infrastructure has to built and designed in such a way that they could easily adapt new business strategies for faster ROI [2]. Rigid software can increase the cost to integrate and innovate many folds. This could hurt the idea of Innovation. And, the policy makers has to find ways to align market policies, IP-regulations, Innovation policies and business ethics in line with the idea of rapid changing needs of the enterprises.

Earlier, it was a perception among researchers that ideas must be originated from within enterprise and it should be kept secret till the researchers obtained success in commercialization. Software was designed, modeled to help client deliver the business solution as a closed source entity. The efforts were made to design such business processes with no external knowledge and partnerships by keeping their discoveries highly secret; and it was made sure that there is no technology idea implemented to promote sharing of knowledge to outside world. Software products were designed and modeled with no exposed interfaces that could lead to any enhancement from third party. IP regulations, policies, ethics and rights are enterprise level only in this culture. But due to relentless growth of networking through ICT, Innovation is crossing the boundaries of centralized R&D [3] labs to outside bodies of experts, researchers, students, partners, or even rival firms. This is because companies have realized that Innovation cannot be done secretly and more importantly cannot be kept as a secret because the pressure is for faster Innovation and quick launch of services or products.

The next section gives an idea about the background of the Open Innovation paradigm that is the need of the hour in today's business scenario and that has to be supported by right architectural solutions in building software systems.

BACKGROUND

"The term Open Innovation was coined by Henry Chesbrough in his 2003 book by the same name (Open Innovation: The New Imperative for Creating and Profiting from Technology, Harvard Business School Press, 2003)". "Chesbrough defines Open Innovation as a paradigm that assumes firms can and should use external ideas as well as internal ideas, and internal and external paths to market, as the firms look to advance their technology". For this article we define Open Innovation more narrowly as the process a company uses to connect with the global world of researchers and Innovation communities to source new In-

Figure 2. Types of innovation

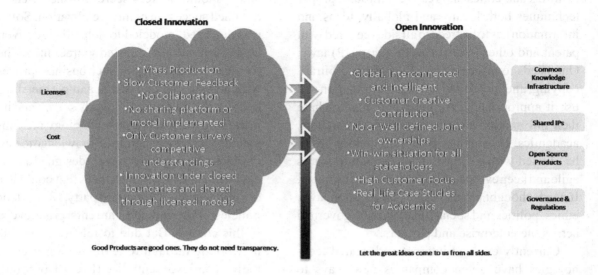

novation and knowledge. Open Innovation is not something that an organization outsources their product development or research. Outsourcing is moving the research and product development function out of the company by using an external business partner or supplier to supply this business function at low cost. This may entail moving staff from one firm's payroll to another or eliminating the firm's research and product development staff entirely. In this section, authors endorse idea of Open Innovation and points out that, business leaders have realized that their organization cannot rely on their own information and research. They have to collaborate, meet up, and integrate to overcome new business challenges. Parallel IT analysts has to find an approach to have a platform to share ideas from all sides; and design appropriate software engineering practices and models that makes products flexible enough to adapt changes at least cost without arbitrary distribution of the logics and source code.

As cited by experts in Open Innovation, the process of Open Innovation is focused on uncovering new ideas, reducing risk, increasing speed, and leveraging scarce resources (De Jong, J.P.J.,

W. Vanhaverbeke, T. Kalvet & H. Chesbrough, 2008). It is the process of explorations, and findings for novel thoughts processes and knowledge globally. It is about lowering risk by combining internal knowledge with a better understanding of what is "out there" and speeding up the Innovation process by integrating information from someone who might have already explored the area or a technology; or who may be farther along on the development path. Finally, it is about leveraging existing research and product development staff versus outsourcing them.

But in the scenarios of working across boundaries, enterprises, and in collaboration with research institutes, suppliers, customers, and even competitors; new tools and models has to be formulated to see changes throughout the enterprise. The major challenge lies in designing the technology Frameworks in such a manner so as to achieve the goal of Open Innovation without compromising on laws, ethics, politics, social policies and more importantly Intellectual Property. The next section focuses upon the trends of Collaborative Innovation in ICT industry and the growth of IP, technology ideas and the challenges that needs to be overcome to adopt Open Innovation culture in a holistic way.

COLLABORATIVE INNOVATIONS IN ICT

The Open Innovation fundamentally emphasize the importance of integrating a wide range of intellectual assets, knowledge, innovations of a company with that of customers, competitors, academics, and firms in related or unrelated industries (West & Gallagher, 2006). In addition, it focuses on commercializing these assets or knowledge in such a manner so as to enable all the partners to leverage and exploit its IPs and the IPs that are jointly created and generated.

Business leaders are finding new ways to increase their revenue. This has been more prominent when economy is seeing downturn which has shift focus that drove the business entities finding new profitable locations and economic sense. These models are well supported by advent of new technologies, internet, semantics web etc. where information is virtually transmitted irrespective of the location through communication technologies. Similarly Frameworks, models and solutions are made Open Source in which an idea patented by an organizations is given to a common pool or given unlimited licenses to anybody, where whole researchers, practitioners, leaders, and engineers can contribute and generate new concepts. The recent success of companies like Red Hat which have adopted Open Source model shows that it is a viable option. Red Hat for example is making significant revenue by offering complimentary services with easy to use installation assistant, documentation, and support along with free distribution of Linux.

Eclipse, an Open Source development environment by IBM is a common example that advocates the idea of Open Innovation and the all competitors can contribute to this Open Innovation network (West & Gallagher, 2006). All the competitors have contributed to enhancing features of eclipse and then have made significant revenue by commercializing their Integrated Development Environment built using base Eclipse Platform. But creation of knowledge assets, products and services by integrating with the partners, customers, competitors with no compromise on protection or rights, privacy, and reputation is still in its earliest stages.

Like other knowledgeable assets, software service sector also start recognizing the growing need of IP. Open Innovation has provided a platform to exploit various Open Source software like Linux Operating Systems, Apache Web Servers, Firefox Browser and many more (West & Gallagher, 2006). This is one area where one can directly donate a piece of software and invite to collaborate. Generating ideas, Frameworks, Architectures, building vertical solutions (like a banking, asset management system etc.) and taking these to partnered companies, individuals, rival, researchers, academics or universities to collaborate and help mature them to generate revenue, is the need in the industry to focus on key growth area and faster delivery to customers. But how should firms share their IP? How to lay down certain boundaries to protect the trust and value? These among others are questions that need to be answered more clearly.

Challenges

Although, companies have realized the importance of Open Innovation and their implications for future growth and sustainability, there are many issues that companies need to look into in much greater detail in order to foster the culture of Open Innovation or Collaborative Innovation. It is mainly because Open Innovation deals with leveraging or using Intellectual Property and assets of others and at the same time offering ones own IPs and assets to others. Therefore, the external framework drivers such as competition policies, IPR [4] rules and laws, government policies, ethics among others should be handled with extreme care and proper due diligence has to be done prior to such a collaborative arrangements. It is because these drivers ultimately have many direct or indirect implications for determining the success of Open Innovation.

As mentioned above, Government plays a vital role in the overall system through its various policies such as financial policies, IPR laws, competition policies, antitrust rules among others. Therefore, if the companies can play a role in predicting these policies well in advance then designing the framework for Open Innovation is easier and quicker. Also, if industry has a role to play while these policies are designed and implemented then the future roadblock and bottlenecks can be resolved easily. By way of example, "designing competition policy that does not preclude co-operation is an important challenge for policy makers, especially in industries where excessive competition can slow Innovation" International Chamber of Commerce (2008).

Therefore, though it is important for the government and the industry to work together in designing the laws and policies, it is also vital for the companies to design their Frameworks, Architecture and models in such a manner to accommodate the policies and rules. Furthermore, it is important for architects to keep the design elements flexible to accommodate the ever changing laws and policies without compromising the proprietary elements of the business models in an Open Innovation scenario. The main challenges in integrating the ideas of Open Innovation into the business Architecture are:

1. How to design a platform to exploit IP for companies benefits, with right kind of security in place.
2. How to use external ideas for internal growth without violating any law, ethics, policies and trust.

3. Keep the technology ideas in privacy to build right Frameworks and scalable and secure models.
4. How to motivate others to contribute (West & Gallagher, 2006)?
5. Change in the mindset of the people, Train them to co-create.
6. How to maximize the returns to internal Innovation?
7. How to bring agility that acts as a catalyst for change to be more proactive in continuous meetings with all stakeholders and focus on better delivery to customers.
8. How to build and designing appropriate systems that is usable to all kind of set of people even with varying physical and sensory capabilities.

The new ideas cannot be joined forces without reliance of supported IT solution, a holistic adoption by employees, vendors, partners or stakeholders that has been foregrounded above. To address these challenges companies are coming up with IP initiatives, conducting trainings, and adopting new trends that can be great differentiators in the success and failure of culture of Open Innovation. Let us understand the emerging trends of IP in the culture of collaboration and Innovation which has been playing an important role in protecting the investment in building the Frameworks and solutions.

EMERGING TRENDS OF INTELLECTUAL PROPERTY (IP): A KEY STRATEGY TO DESIGN SOLUTION

"Why we need protection when I want to share my solution/product/idea to the world? Do I really need to design my products and solutions appropriately?" – We will see here. Earlier, Open Innovation was meant for large organizations. However, due to the good effects of globalization

Figure 3. Driving forces for designing appropriate frameworks

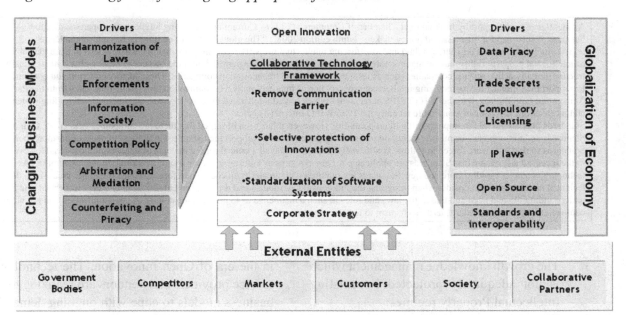

and advancement of science and technologies, even smaller companies and more importantly, SME's [5]are participating, and concentrating of generating revenues and even building their Frameworks and models in such a manner so as to promote the culture of Open Innovation or Collaborative Innovation. This in turn will surely bring in the aspect and complications with respect to IP. We look into these matters in more detail in the subsequent sections to follow.

IP has been an essential part of the software industry especially under the environment of Collaborative Innovation (Granstrand, O, 2003). Over the last few decades, Open Innovation has been the enabler of producing open-source products and services such as the Linux operating system, Apache products, and the JBoss server among others. Further, Open Innovation and the complexities of ever changing business models demonstrate that the dynamism of IT environment and how the overall competitiveness of enhanced. Therefore, if the technology architects locks his mindset in specific technology mandates then it essentially creates a roadblock to Open Innova-

tion. Hence, a mix of reasonable and objective criteria is recommended without compromising proprietary rights over there IPs in order to foster the culture of Open Innovation. It is crucial to have a centralized and appropriate model to provide governance of IP and laws to the entire system to cover the risk of copying and pasting the knowledge asset.

The Figure 3 as describes the various drivers and external entities which are forcing the companies to adopt and invent newer technology Frameworks; models and strategies for Open Innovation and several external forces influence them. Some of them are mentioned below. These external forces change the IP landscape and influence the possible impact on their evolution and exploitation in an Open Innovation scenario:

1. Market forces of commoditization, industrialization and globalization;
2. The rapid and ever changing technologies and infrastructure;

Table 1. Why 'standards' while creating technical architecture?

As mentioned in the report by International Chamber of Commerce (2008). "Current and emerging intellectual property issues for business: A roadmap for business and policy makers. Ninth edition 2008", "The global nature of commerce has added challenges to registering (in the case of registered rights) and to enforcing intellectual property rights in every country where goods that are the subject of intellectual property rights may be manufactured and widely sold without the permission of the owners of those rights. This is equally true for globally active service companies such as insurance, banks and transportation companies. These factors underpin and continue to support the rationale for harmonizing intellectual property norms internationally. Harmonization through treaties dates from the Paris Convention (1883) through to the WTO TRIPS agreement - which linked intellectual property rights to the international trading system and its sanctions mechanism – and more recently the 1996 WIPO Internet Treaties"

Standards play a vital role in implementing interoperability. However, it has been observed that there are companies who create their own Standards and through various means (including pressurizing government to support their standard activities) to drive or promote their Standards so that others are forced to follow. Traditionally, Standards played a crucial role in the area of telecommunications. However, in the recent times, we see that Standards are applicable for any domains or industry and play a significant role in interoperability. As technology changes rapidly, more and new Standards are required with greater frequency. Therefore, standard is another area which the technical architect should consider when designing the Frameworks or models and the government should play a very important role in understanding the real need and makes the laws and rules in such a manner so as to promote the culture of open innovation and not block companies from using Standards as a mechanism to foster innovation.

3. The growth knowledge management which is not adequately protected by existing Intellectual Property regimes;
4. The current complexities in Intellectual Property laws and rules;
5. The era of service innovations.

The following sections describes some of the best practices in IP management for enabling Open Innovation while keeping in mind economic, social, political and technological developments. This would govern the scope and visibility of the services and products to other vendors, partners or researchers while creating a technical model of the IT enabled solutions and products.

BEST PRACTICES IN IP MANAGEMENT FOR ENABLING OPEN INNOVATION

Global economic condition and the dollar depreciation are forcing the ICT companies to re-align the various components of the IT service ecosystems. Market forces of commoditization, miniaturization, industrialization and globalization are converging fast to accelerate this re-alignments. In this changing atmosphere, the "strategic IP" management has more relevance than past, especially in the era of Open Innovation. The technology service providers and vendors are realizing their business models to cope with ongoing demands of the buyers and the ever changing government policies, laws etc. For example, when a service in provided to customer through a product, the product may be proprietary. However, the service element should be made available to people so that new opportunities are created around that product in terms of allowing new service players to exploit newer opportunities. In addition, one can add controllers or software in such a manner so that it promotes Open Innovation and at the same time allows others to contribute to the Innovation to foster the culture of Collaborative Innovation.

a. Harmonization

There should be a harmonization of rules and laws across geographies in terms of first to invent or first to file. We feel that the rule should be first to file because this will enable inventors to file invention when it is matured. Today, due to some countries having the rule of first to invent, file patent applications where the inventions are not matured and hence cannot be enforced because what is filed is quite different to what goes for commercialization. In doing so, there is a huge fence of Patents or patent applications surrounding the Innovation, which prohibits or hinders Open Innovation.

The next aspect is on some differences between geographies still exists with respect to the patent norms in area of Innovation. An example is the difference between the European and US approaches to the patentability of computer software. Governments and corporate should ensure complete compliance with TRIPS and other WTO obligations when legislating on these issues so that there are no barriers that are created for fostering Open Innovation. In addition to this, there should be a harmonized way of granting patent rights to the owners without having any regional or national constraints.

The statutes of most countries include compulsory licensing and government use under some special conditions. However, the use of the same has been limited. Government should be stricter in implementing compulsory license to increase more Open Innovation. In addition to this, there must be consensus among nations on IP protection. The lack of realization to other national rights and systems may result uncertainty. These areas need to be harmonized across the globe to foster Open Innovation.

b. Strengthening Copyright Protection

In the era of web services and collaborations, copyright laws needs to be strengthened because this will be more complicated in future. The copyright laws needs to be harmonized and should also be enforceable. In addition, the moral rights of the creators should be respected, especially by Innovation community. Their ideas should not be unduly manipulated in the digital-networked environment under the Open Innovation environment.

In the age of ever-evolving technologies, copyright will play a very key role for technologists and will always challenge the researchers to determine new methods to protect and foster Open Innovation. The copyright owners will have to design new and innovative technical measures to regulate misuse of their copyrighted work. In addition, the owners will be forced to collaborate with clients and sometimes even with competitors to ensure that their work is not exploited by others without proper permissions from the owner. Further, the government should work closely with industries to promote and create platforms and support systems to enable companies enforce action against any such infringements. The copyright law should look at the nature of the work being copied with its purpose, the amount and substantiality of the copying and whether or not a copy was available at a reasonable time and at an ordinary commercial price and most importantly, the market impact of copying.

Furthermore, if the next generation systems and models are made modularized and over it a standardized interface is created, then it is better to distinctly determine the ownership of the IP during any collaboration. In addition, there should be harmonization of Copyrights laws which will enable owners to protect all kinds of information repositories including non – original ones.

c. Counterfeiting and Piracy

Another important aspect of IP is piracy and counterfeiting of software. This has become a great threat to most of the countries and also a threat to employees, which has resulted in substantial job losses in various sectors of industry. However, recently companies have joined hands to work towards combating piracy and counterfeiting. Many companies or group of companies have been working closely with law agencies and governments to investigate, analyse and prosecute the stealing of IP. However, in an Open Innovation culture, more sectors and government bodies should come together to work more closely in combating with this situation. In addition, the government should also play a vital role in creating awareness and enforcing the laws so as to promote the culture of Open Innovation.

d. Open Source

This is a class of software that is developed by one or more individuals and is licensed to others in such a manner that others will have access to the software and can use the same under certain terms and conditions as per the Open Source license agreement. It should be borne in mind that Open Source software need not mean that it is open for any type of exploitation. People have been using Open Source software and also contributing to Open Source since a long time. Open Source has created a very good platform for Collaborative Innovation. In addition, companies have also integrated Open Source software with their proprietary software as a small unit of functionality to an enterprise level IT solutions or a business process. Companies, Vendors have been leveraging Open Source components to their products whenever it makes sense to them. Some of these have even started Reuse Initiatives across organizations to save cost in staggering economy situations. For example, logging Open Source framework by apache has been integrated by many Open Source or commercial vendors in their products. This has created lot of debates among companies and Open Source lobbies. However, companies should continue to use Open Source along with proprietary IPs in such a manner so that they do not violate other's IP and at the same time respect the idea of Open Source and contribute effectively. It should be borne in mind that when Open Source software and proprietary software are combined, the commercialization of the software (Combined) may be governed by the Open Source software license and if one tries to patent the combined software, it may not be enforceable. It is important to note that Government should play a vital role in this initiative and should help the companies understand the pros and cons of using a mix of Open Source with proprietary IPs both in products and services and should allow flexibility to companies, which in turn will promote the culture of Open Innovation.

e. Public Disclosure

Public disclosure is a vital part of any Open Innovation, especially when the collaboration is with universities. Universities tend to make the results public via conference proceedings or journal publications. This is also regarded as one of the critical measure of success of any research activity for universities. Industries, however, prefer to patent the outcome of a research activity prior to public disclosure. Many universities now have an Intellectual Property Office that takes care of protecting any IPR that arises out of a research activity since those have a potential for strong earnings and funding of further research.

Public disclosure includes any form of public dissemination of information. Per the prevailing laws in most of the countries (excluding the United States), any disclosure of a new concept or technology prior to protecting it as a patent application would make that disclosure un patentable. The US allows a one year grace period to file a patent application after it has been disclosed to the public. However, most of the other major countries do not allow such an exception. This is because the US Patent and Trademark Office (USPTO) laws allows a "first to invent" policy whereas the rest of the world follows a "first to file" policy. The safest way forward for any technology aiming to be applied globally is to be invented first and filed first.

Apart from using Patents as a protection mechanism, it must be realized that there are better and cheaper mechanisms of protection a new technology. These include maintaining it as a trade secret, or making a technical publication. The objectives and reasons for each of these mechanisms vary and need to be carefully understood prior to arriving at a decision. When designing a technology framework, the architect needs to bear in mind that the design should be built in such a way so that all the aspects of protection (Patents, Trade Secrets etc) can be segregated in such a manner which will not restrict Open Innovation and at the same time the core technology can be shared without the possibility of misuse of the IP.

f. Ownership of Patent Rights

This is another important aspect of any collaborative research work. The question of who owns what does not really surface until one or both the parties realize a valuable application of the technology.

In order to understand and appreciate the subsequent section, it would be good to familiarize with certain terminologies used. Background IP (BIP) is referred as to any IP (whether it is Patent, Patent application, Trade secret, Copyrights, Know how, Trademarks etc) that is brought and owned by the respective collaborator and pooled together for achieving the common goal. BIP is by nature are not available for free use by the other party except for the collaboration purpose and only against relevant clauses and conditions of the collaborative agreement. Foreground IP (FIP) is the IP that is be generated by the collaboration, which generally comes out as a derivative work on the BIPs and which may be used as agreed upon by either collaborators.

In any collaborative agreement, all BIP (and the rights associated with it) pertinent to the collaboration need to be clearly identified and stated.

The next aspect to the ownership rights is to do with assignee for patent applications that are filed for one or more of the FIP. The decision to file should be mutually decided and should be based on a pre determined parameters as agreed by all the parties.

g. Transfer of Rights During M&A

This is one such issue which gets missed out in most of the collaborative agreement. It is always recommended to specify a separate clause mentioning the protocol to be adopted for the transfer of rights during any merger or acquisition. Typically, the agreement does not change with M&A transaction and all the rights belonging to the industry partner gets transferred to the new entity and he is obligated to follow all the clauses and terms of the agreement. There is no negotiation applicable at a later date. This point needs to be mentioned in the agreement and the same should be reflected in the design of Frameworks.

h. Confidentiality / Confidential Information

Confidentiality is another very important subject of dispute, which is mentioned in mostly all agreements. Patents often represent only a part of a technology, for example, an early prototypical embodiment of an invention. The remainder, such as secrets and know-how, are protected under most legal regimes as Trade Secrets or as confidential information. The term trade secret refers to information that is maintained in secrecy and has commercial value. In addition, the research conducted under a contract may result in the creation of new confidential information. The person who possesses confidential information can only prevent others from disclosing it, for example, to a competitor, if a confidential relationship exists between the person and the party to whom the information was initially disclosed. One of the best ways of ensuring this protection from disclosure is through a contract. In other words, Patents and Trade Secrets are not contradictory but actually highly complementary and mutually reinforcing.

As mentioned above, though this clause is mentioned in detail in almost all agreements, the following section emphasis on certain key parameters to look into. Confidentiality should include for all background IPs of both the parties as well as for foreground IPs and the rights should be explicitly different.

The confidentiality agreement should specify a time limit during which the information is to be kept confidential. Typical time limits are between two and five years after the end of the collaboration or from the point the information is generated.

The scope of what is held to be confidential should be well defined and understood. It should not be too broad to prevent publication and the use of evolving research. Moreover, since what should be kept confidential will depend on how the information is to be used; no single definition will apply well in all cases. The contractual supplying dealing with confidentialities should make clear to others, whom the information may be disclosed. The second aspect is that of Indemnity, wherein, both parties undertake to have done the detailed due diligence of their respective BIPs so as to not infringe on others IP and both parties will have to indemnify the other party during any litigation.

i. Commercialization and Exploitation of IP

This aspect of any collaborative research is perhaps one of the most critical elements for any research work, where the commercial rights are shared and the rights for exploitation of IP lies with both the parties. Though, typically, this aspect does not get covered in any research agreement, but as we discuss the issues, one will appreciate the importance of having at least a Memorandum of understanding (MoU), where the key points are articulated for clarity. The subsequent section highlights some of the key pointers.

Some of the drivers for unsuccessful commercialization of FIPs are:

1. Failure to define shared market opportunities: Research collaboration without an agreed joint product roadmap often lead into relationships tainted by jealously and mistrust. Therefore, it is recommended to have a detailed plan with regard to marketing and commercialization plan and identify the stakeholders for each of the activity.

2. Lack of agreement and investment strategies for exploitation of IPs: Sometimes, insufficient budgeting for sales incentives, marketing funds, and sales engineering time

jeopardize the commercialization plan. In addition, pricing decisions and time to go to market may cannibalize the relationship between partners in a collaborative research initiative.

3. Lack of ownership and segregation of responsibilities and identification of stakeholders for various activities regarding commercialization of IP: Typically, the partners fight for ownership of key functionality and the ambiguity in the ownership may delay time-to-market, sidetrack resources, and hamper existing sales efforts.

These IP practices would be key differentiator in assuring compliance, protection and recovery which otherwise can be costlier to the enterprises. In order to build a firm and reliable partnership in any Collaborative Innovation, it is essential to build a governance model and operating model for commercialization in business and IT strategy. Below section brings out some of the key technical strategies, products, architectural thoughts that enable the software systems, applications and products supporting Open Innovation paradigm.

CREATING APPROPRIATE ARCHITECTURAL BUILDING BLOCKS: FRAMEWORKS, MODELS, TOOLS AND STRATEGIES

As we have in above sections, the degree, extent and even existence of issue related to ethics, laws, policies and rights poses a great risk to Open Innovation and so the business growth. The environment of openness and co-create has to be backed up by a thoughtful software Architecture, design model and platforms.

Enterprises are seeing tremendous opportunities in Innovation but they are still struggling to define a cost effective mean to collaborate and innovate. IT budgets are squeezed in the economy turmoil and CTOs [6] are find hard time to convince

Table 2. What is a software architecture and and architecture principles that can impact business?

A software Architecture is structure or set of structures of an application, system or computing solutions that comprises software components, relationships of these components, and their orchestration to create an output. A robust Architecture which is a backbone of the system defines; how a software systems is built, used or modeled with reference to data, hardware, software systems, rules, people, processes, business functions, budget and so on? While defining Architecture for a large enterprise, it is very essential to address business and stakeholders interests. It must align with the business goals and parameters of growth. Some of the important aspects that needs to be taken are while defining an Architecture of IT infrastructure to align with today's business scenarios are:

• A **flexible and modular** approach that offers the required functions with protection and abstraction of the proprietary ideas should be the part of Architecture cycle. Awareness about IP policies and induction of required trainings has to be part of business plan to protect the business interests of the organization.

• An infrastructure has to be there to implement the idea of open innovation. The internet and new **social networking** technologies are offering new platforms to researchers and knowledge bearers to interact with unprecedented level of richness. Some of the open innovation companies are drawing the attention of their customers to participate in product development process to be more agile.

• It should be based upon **rich internet technologies** to motivate users, researchers, partners to participate and collaborate.

• Architecture should also define a model to software components like Frameworks, business functional points, User Interaction solutions etc. that account the varying capabilities of users to ensure that it can be used people with visual, hearing or any cognitive disabilities. It can be used by elderly or temporarily disabled and with not disability at all. Information is accessible to all section of the users. **Everybody can participate**.

• Architecture should be **extensible** and capable to integrate upward or downward and to scale it to any level of information repositories on the web, intranet, legacy systems or web services.

• **Automation,** with not manual intervention in the development life cycle, should be part of strategy to reach to market faster and respond to changes. Architecture should adapt automation to the maximum like integration of information can be automated; software development and reviews can be automated etc. A back-office system should be in place whenever and wherever needed.

to management on transformation. Moreover, customer is no longer a service consumer or a passive recipient. They want to participate in co creating of values and services.

IT team of an organization must be equipped with the knowledge of business and market objectives and be ready to transform or adopt new technology platforms. Cost must be measured while designing and transformation, and an incremental approach must be followed to see return of investment at every step. This should be realized by platform based approach that provides a basic infrastructure to build business solutions. IT team must be integrated and centralized to realize this development process. They need to follow these principles that must be realized in the software systems to align with the Open Innovation business objectives:

• **Remove Communication Barriers**: A social Networking infrastructure that is leveraged to build a Collaborative Innovation, a platform where everybody can contribute and create together.

• **Protecting Innovations:** Architecture strategies and principals which should be capable of embracing the new and innovative ideas that are aligning with business objectives to co-innovate the products. It focuses upon designing software and IT systems in such a way that the core idea of implementation is never revealed and protected with practices of IP as described in above section.

• **For All:** Designing Software Systems as per ISO (International Organization for Standardization) that is easier to use for the elderly, the disabled - and everyone else, similar to rules drafted by W3C for web site accessibility (OUT-LAW.com, 2008).

Based upon above three principles, this section helps finding out some of the key strategies to build large software systems in an appropriate manner that is key to business success and can be protected by legal process i.e. IP laws. To harness the real potential of Open Innovation, the section draws the significance of the need to well defined Architecture model and sharing platform.

This model defines the governance process of integration of knowledgeable assets by different partners and researchers. It also defines the appropriate technologies and choosing right kind of Frameworks to deliver an integrated powerful product to avoid free riding over other's ideas and knowledge.

a. Building More and More Values

The ideas of technology community and researchers never get past to conceptual stage. It had been lying within a common set of team unless supported by a common platform and software technologies. Web 2.0 recently offers a mix of technologies, Frameworks, and platform to take these ideas forward to the outer world, and acts as a catalyst to Open Innovation. This social networking technology landscape has brought Open Innovation to everyone, not just handful of entrepreneurs and investors. It helps providing a platform that tries to bring all related parties together that could build a great application or a business idea.

REALIZATION OF COLLABORATION THROUGH WEB 2.0

As the nature of Innovation has changed to become more open and collaborative, enterprises should make more of their IP available to others while they continued to be a leader in proprietary Innovation. By sharing technological inventions with the public at large, development in that area is encouraged so that Collaborative Innovations can be created upon which higher levels of Innovation can take place. IT infrastructure of an enterprise has to create a Collaborative Innovation based on concepts of Web 2.0 to assist in the generation and development of new ideas and Innovation through Open Innovation and Collaboration. This Platform can be leveraged for the successful commercialization of existing ideas, Innovation, technology,

Patents, Intellectual Property, expertise and know-how for building innovative solution, incubating and deploying such solutions. It should provide a true Innovation network which collaboratively share the information, ideas and develop innovative IPs, then proliferate the knowledgably asset throughout network.

We should design appropriate framework based on Web 2.0 Principles which provides architectural building blocks required to build such platform. Collaborative Innovation should provide mechanism to

- Provide mechanism to contextualize platform content and behavior based on the operating context of the user for data privacy and security
- Create community around enterprises, research institutions, academic institutions, Student Community, Startups, and Venture Capitalist etc.
- Create and browse profile of community. Provide ability to invite user group/communities group from profile page and send messages from profile page
- Share point of view, new ideas by uploading contents – documents, audio files, flash demos and publish papers on the site etc
- Collaborate through wikis, blobs, chat engines etc to brainstorm on new ideas, understand proposed Innovation and work together as a team to innovate new solutions. Unified Communication mechanisms like instant messenger, chat, web conference will help connect people in real time.
- Ability to add/delete/update blog, wiki pages, search pages for areas of interest for ideation and show search results in terms of tag clouds
- Provide mechanism to rate the ideas, provide feedback on ideas, prototype uploaded by different communities and provide various monetization strategies to motivate communities

- Development Infrastructure to perform prototype for innovative validation
- Commercialize Patents. Technology, ideas etc

Web 2.0 Realization Platform – This platform provides a holistic view of the system across all portfolios of an enterprise It is compendium of Frameworks, models, tools, documentation, repositories, training materials, workshops etc. that business solutions or a team can leverage. This platform should provide following architectural building blocks to build a Collaborative Innovation – (Details of each of these technology is out of scope of this chapter)

- User Experience Capabilities to enrich end user experience and facilitates faster decision making. This includes enriched presentation using rich UI[7], dashboard and information aggregation using mashups.
- User Assistance Capabilities include search for wiki/blog pages, discussion forum contents, information syndication using RSS, ATOM to assist users.
- Collaboration Capabilities like discussion forums, wikis, blobs, chat, web conferences instant messenger etc.
- User Participation Capabilities like Profile Creation, Communities around profile, upload and create contents
- User Content Management Capabilities to approve, manage, modify and publish the content through Content Management Solution
- Analytics to mine user participation and derive business benefits
- Event Manager Capabilities and Foundation Capabilities to provide flexible Architecture required to realize the system.

Earlier days, customers wait for the prototype of the solutions. When prototype cycle is over, customer provides feedback and the prototype goes through various iterations from customers to solutions provider. After a long time, product hits the market and both get the benefit. The Web 2.0 platform helps customers share their knowledge and expectations at very earlier stages resulting enhanced version of products or services at much lesser cost and time to deliver a real values. Collaborative Innovation acts as a backbone to provide an infrastructure for everybody – researchers, partners, students, knowledge workers etc. – can contribute to deliver a comprehensive innovative product that is much more than customer can expect.

b. Defining Models and Strategies Achieving Protection and Reduce Cost

It is very essential for enterprises to establish a thought process that impact their technology growth as a part of their organization goal, to be competitive. Models, Concepts or Proof of concepts need to be formally defined, and established, and communicated to all stakeholders. But if collaboration is part of the strategy, legal and IP is equally relevant to companies to formulate strategies not only to build enterprise level software infrastructure but also to protect their investment. Else, there are chances even if there are ideas and policies in place, NDA (Non- Disclosure Agreement) are formulated; that internal ideas are leaked out anonymously and the idea of Open Innovation get dissolved. An appropriate strategy is built to integrate arsenal of cross enterprises knowledge. This section defines architectural strategies to define appropriate techniques to realize Open Innovation and overcome those challenges. Architecture with rightful strategies and techniques can improve the confidence of business and technology stakeholders, and IP Officers to leverage Open Innovation without the fear of access rights, privacy, loosing confidentiality, reputations, and law and governance models. With right software engineering practices in adopting Open Innovation help enterprises to use this collaborative approach to achieve faster and effective growth. Below listed are few of the important points that surely needs not be forgotten -

Architectural Modeling

Software Infrastructure in an enterprise should be built thinking about Innovation that is happening. The architectural strategies and principles should be capable of embracing the new and innovative ideas that are aligning with business objectives. Software systems must be able to easily distributable and able integrate at well defined functional points with no impact to existing or collaborative efforts.

- Distributed Architecture to model Systems
- Enterprises should architect their system in such a way that it results in separation of concerns for different roles involved in building system so that communities while co-creating solution can partition their task and work on it effectively.
- Enterprises should build their IP based on sound design principles like Service Oriented Architecture which enables enterprises to create loosely coupled solution and foster Collaborative Innovation by integrating third-party products and solutions.
- Enterprise should design their system with a modular, plug-in Architecture for fostering future Collaborative Innovation. For examples the core pieces of software in Eclipse project were designed with a modular, plug-in Architecture which allowed for a reliable scaling of the process through growth of the development community. As

a result 30 sub-projects are being developed in parallel, which form essential or optional components of the Eclipse software platform

- While designing system, the design interfaces between tasks should play a vital role in making the partitioning functional so that the Innovation project is successfully completed. As cited by Dr Virginia Acha1 (2006), such innovative project should provide component tasks and task interfaces specified, implicitly or explicitly, so that all would fit and work together to form the total project when combined.
- Enterprise should build their IP leveraging Open Standards and should be interoperable to meet future requirements. Enterprises should leverage Open Source and at the same time should create value over and above Open Source to build closed IP.
- Right Obfuscation Techniques - Enterprises should leverage right obfuscation techniques to obfuscate binaries so that when they share their IP with external world, their IP is protected. Enterprises should integrate Obfuscation libraries as part of build process, so that when they take release of their IP, source code of IP is compiled into binaries which is obfuscated by obfuscation libraries
- Enterprises should use appropriate licensing strategy to protect their system. Licensing strategy should enable the features to be licensed individually. Licensing strategy should provide mechanism to generate license file and validate information at the run time when the system has been used.
- Abstraction – Enterprises should follow interface based design while building their IP. Interface based approach enables IP code to be extensible to incorporate ideas

incubated while innovating with external world using Collaborative Innovation.

- Security Framework – Enterprise should leverage Security Framework to
  - Authenticate user and authorize user against his role for sharing appropriate content with end user. When partners and other community's members get involved in developing system in collaboration environment, it is risky to expose complete system design and code to all the members. To mitigate risk, it is recommended to create role-based control so each partner/ community member could only access the IP it needed. Business decisions should be made as to the IP required by each partner, and then each team member should be assigned one or more products in one or more roles, each role having access to specific types of artifact.
  - Find vulnerabilities and take the necessary steps to eliminate them, making the system a more secure environment for its users.
- Hosting On Premise Systems – One of the ways to protect IP is to allow external world to asses and evaluate IP by hosting it on On-Demand model so that IP does not need to be shared with external world for co-creating ideas and solution.
- Multi-tenant Architecture – Enterprises should design, build and deploy their system with multi-tenancy in mind so that system can support multiple tenants to reduce cost and derive business value from Collaborative Innovation

c. Reachable to Users with Special Needs

This has been an upcoming area in usability of the technology in the universities, researchers,

and engineers. The industry technology leaders like IBM, Apple etc. have been working together with academia to create solution in this space. New Technology specification ISO/TS 16071, 'Ergonomics of human-system interaction – Guidance on accessibility for human computer interfaces ' provides road map to design such software systems that are accessible through supporting tools like screen readers, Braille Displays etc. For example if you can increase the font, size, contrast or overall visibility of screen displays as a part of software product design, it can help people with visual problems. As per legal obligation under the UK's Disability Discrimination Act of 1995, web sites should be accessible to the disabled (OUT-LAW. com, 2008).

Software systems must be enabled with "Speech System Transformation" module for the disabled. This helps disabled gaining educational and professional knowledge to greater extent. Many countries are coming up with ethics and definition of WWW guidelines and have provided very useful applications suited to specific disabilities and these have won appreciations from experts all over the world as well as various technology vendors laboratories. This also needs to internationalize and not be limited to only one language.

Multilingual editors based software systems can handle the language barriers and can create a new world of openness (Acharya Multilingual Computing for Literacy and Education Software for the Visually Handicapped, 2006).

FUTURE TRENDS

In future, business will find new dimensions to achieve more revenue. Enterprises would look more towards Open Innovations by finding new ways to collaborate, partnerships with different bodies of knowledge. World would continue to shrink with new advancements in accessing World Wide Web and growing number of users every minute. The road ahead is about evolution of creation and collaboration of ideas, innovating new business models, partnering across geographies and exploring new dimension to provide maximum benefits to customer with least cost; creating awareness of laws, ethics and rights. ICT will continue to play an important role to play in relating laws, ethics, social norms and legal bodies to the technology and then to business. Conceptual advances have been the driving force behind progress of information technologies and related laws, ethics and policies. This in turn relies upon creativity and ability to continue to capture new markets, production of new insights and ideas. However, the ever changing laws, ethics, social policies and more particularly IP laws will force the technological architects to continuously re-design and re-invent appropriate models, Frameworks and build strategies in line with these external drivers. These have to be supported with adoption of new business models, and Open Innovation paradigms.

There has been a big movement in Open Innovation towards customer Innovation engagement. Engaging with a diverse cross-section of customers on Innovation can help them with wider business challenges and can help embed suppliers in their culture, to better understand their pressures and add value as partners. In the new business model, as cited by C.K.Prahalad, Innovation trend will shift from a product-centric view of Innovation to Co-creation of a personalized experience. Co-creation here is important because here both company and consumer are jointly problem solvers. This will help us to realize a co-created, virtualized experience real value instead of a product-centric real value. More optimized search algorithms are needed to share and contribute knowledge that is focused to bring real value to the business. IP, Laws and Legal norms have to be formulated in a strong manner to provide strong security fundamentals.

This will enable enterprises to operate at the higher level of Open Innovation, differences between internal and external development will disappear as shared resources become interchangeable; shared IP ownership will become an enabler to faster product introduction and new product and service innovations will increasingly drive new perspectives on business Innovation

CONCLUSION

As enterprise systems continue to grow with business expansion and complexity, ICT departments are struggling to find better ways to meet the business goals while providing legal boundaries to protect the internal investments. Business growth has to be supported by technologies and technology infrastructure in and outside of enterprise. Built on strong Architecture foundation, software systems can be molded to align with the business objectives as and when required.

Business leaders who understand the power of collaboration demands this kind of flexibility to IT and the same time, they want to protect their investment, software assets, and knowledge artifacts. Globally accepted ICT laws, protections, rights and fair practices break new grounds in creating greater impact in optimally usage of technology. Intellectual Property (IP) rights have to be formulated and to be known by all – employees, vendors, partners, academia, etc. – in an enterprise or research bodies. It is a key enabler of greater Innovation and interoperability in the IT marketplace. In the new world of Open Innovation, IP's power to exclude is increasingly being replaced by its ability to serve as the currency or the "glue" for literally dozens of new business models and collaborations between competitors. In order to maximize Innovation, interoperability, competition, and economic growth, governments should establish strong IP protection Frameworks and avoid regulatory approaches and procurement decisions that waive IP rights or mandate particular technologies or business/licensing models to the exclusion of others. The chapter has provided the key points on IP that has been proven to act as a key fundamental in the world of build, share, collect ideas, innovate and reach to consumers with the best of breed solutions and products.

With economic ups and downs, and with the pressure to create good quality software systems that can be flexible enough and work with all, IT departments must follow guidelines to build appropriate Frameworks, models, strategies and solutions In this chapter, we have showcased the need and concept of Innovation in today's world and how a software can designed that can form an infrastructure so that everybody can share and collaborate. The chapter also pointed out the key strategies on the basis of which a software system can be designed to support the idea of integrations and innovations.

REFERENCES

Acha, V. (2006). *Open by Design: The role of Design in Open Innovation*. Paper presented at Science & Innovation Analysis Unit at the Department of Trade and Industry (now the Department for Innovation, Universities and Skills). Retrieved April 10, 2009, from http://www.dius.gov.uk/reports_and_publications/~/media/publications/O/Openbydesign

Acharya. (2009). *Multilingual Computing for Literacy and Education Software for the Visually Handicapped.* Retrieved March 20, 2009 from http://acharya.iitm.ac.in/disabilities/tts.php

Backer, D. K., Lopez-Bassols, V., & Marinez, C. (2008). *Open Innovation in a Global Perspective – What do existing Data tell us?* Paper presented at Statistical Analysis of Science, Technology and Industry DSTI/DOC(2008)4. Retrieved March 17, 2009 from http://www.oecd.org/dataoecd/25/38/41885837.pdf

Backer. D., K. & Cervantes, M. (2008). *OECD Business Symposium on Open Innovation.* Paper presented in Global Networks, Copenhagen, Denmark, 2008. Retrieved March 20, 2009 from http://www.oecd.org/document/48/0,3343,en_2649_34273_39858608_1_1_1_1,00.html

Burn, M. (1999). *A new paradigm for access: the implications of current copyright law reform initiatives.* Presented at the Australian Society of Archivists Annual Conference, Brisbane, Queensland. Retrieved March 20, 2009 from http://www-prod.nla.gov.au/openpublish/index.php/nlasp/article/viewArticle/1106/1369

Calster, G. V. (2008). Risk Regulation, EU Law and Emerging Technologies: Smother or Smooth? *Journal of NanoEthics, 2*(1), 61-71. Retrieved February 03, 2009 from http://www.springerlink.com/content/q14jn1284r4585gg/

Chesbrough, H. W. (in press). *Open Innovation: The New Imperative for Creating and Profiting from Technology.* Harvard Business School Press.

Consulting, D. (2001). *Collaborative Knowledge Networks: Driving Workforce Performance through Web-Enabled Communities.* A Viewpoint by Deloitte Consulting and Deloitte & Touche. Retrieved March 20, 2009 from http://www.ickn.org/documents/eview.pdf

De Jong, J. P. J., Vanhaverbeke, W., Kalvet, T., & Chesbrough, H. (2008). *Policies for Open Innovation: Theory, Framework and Cases.* Research project funded by VISION Era-Net, Helsinki: Finland. Retrieved March 25, 2009 from http://www.eurosfaire.prd.fr/7pc/doc/1246020063_oipaf_final_report_2008.pdf

Fredberg, T., Elmquist, M., & Ollila, S. (2008). *Managing Open Innovation -Present Findings and Future Directions* (VINNOVA Report VR 2008:02). VINNOVA - Verket för Innovationssystem/Swedish Governmental Agency for Innovation Systems. Retrieved February 20, 2009 from http://www.openinnovation.eu/download/vr-08-02.pdf

Gloor, A. P., Heckman, C., & Makedon, F. (2004). *Ethical Issues in Collaborative Innovation Networks.* Paper presented at MIT Center for Collective Intelligence. Retrieved April 03, 2009 from http://ccs.mit.edu/pgloor%20papers/COIN4Ethicomp.pdf

Gloor, P. Laubacher, R., Dynes, S., Zhao, Y. (2003). *Visualization of Communication Patterns in Collaborative Innovation Networks: Analysis of some W3C working groups*. Paper presented at Innovative Collaborative Knowledge Networks. Retrieved February 03, 2009 from http://www. ickn.org/documents/visualization_of_communication.pdf

Goolsby, K. (2008, November). Innovation and Economy: Trends Impacting Initial Stages of Outsourcing. *Outsourcing Journal*. Retrieved February 3, 2009 from http://www.outsourcingjournal.com/nov2008-trends.html

Granstrand, O. (2003). *Innovation and Intellectual Property*. Preliminary 3rd Draft of the paper presented at the Concluding Roundtable Discussion on IPR at the DRUID Summer Conference on Creating, Sharing and transferring knowledge. The role of Geography, Institutions and Organizations, Copenhagen. Retrieved April 03, 2009 from http://www.druid.dk/conferences/summer2003/Papers/GRANDSTRAND.pdf

Hansen, M., & Nohria, N. (2004). How to Build Collaborative Advantage, SMR. *MIT Sloan Management Review*. Retrieved April 03, 2009 from http://sloanreview.mit.edu/the-magazine/files/pdfs/46105SxW.pdf

Innovaro. (2006). *Innovation briefing 2006*, Retrieved April 17, 2009 from http://www.innovaro.com/inno_updates/Innovation%20Briefing%2007-06.pdf

International Chamber of Commerce. (2008). *Current and emerging Intellectual Property issues for business: A roadmap for business and policy makers* (9th ed.). Retrieved April 03, 2009 from http://www.iccwbo.org/uploadedFiles/ICC/policy/intellectual_property/pages/IP_Roadmap-2005(1).pdf

OUT-LAW. (2008). *Designing software for the disabled - ISO guidelines*. News from Out-laws IT and e-commerce legal help from international law firm Pinsent Masons. Retrieved March 20, 2009 from http://www.out-law.com/page-3625.

Prahalad, C. K., & Ramaswamy, V. (in press). *The Future of Competition: Co-Creating Unique Value with Customers*. Boston. *Harvard Business Press*.

Santos, D., Doz, Y., & Williamson, P. (2004). Is Your Innovation Process Global. *MIT Sloan Management Review*. Retrieved April 03, 2009 from http://sloanreview.mit.edu

Schacht, W. (2000). *Industrial Competitiveness and Technological Advancement: Debate Over Government Policy*. Report from CRS Issue Brief for Congress, Resources, Science, and Industry Division. Retrieved April 03, 2009 from http://fas.org/sgp/crs/misc/RL33528.pdf.

Sojyo, I. (2009). *IP and Management Strategies in the Era of Open Innovation*. Report on the International Patent Licensing Seminar 2009. Retrieved March 17, 2009 from http://www.ryutu.inpit.go.jp/seminar_a/2009/pdf/B1_e.pdf

Tsilas., L., N. (2007). Enabling Open Innovation and Interoperability: Recommendations for Policy-Makers. In *Proceedings of the 1st international conference on Theory and practice of electronic governance*. ACM International Conference Proceeding Series, Vol. 232.

Vanderburg, H. W. (2007). Technology and the Law: Who Rules? *Bulletin of Science Technology Society 2007, 27*, 322; DOI: 10.1177/0270467607302688: General Article: Published by SAGE at University from Toronto, Retrieved April 17, 2009 from http://www.sage-publications.com, http://bst.sagepub.com/cgi/content/abstract/27/4/322

Walden, A. E. (2005). Intellectual Property Rights and Cannibalization in Information Technology Outsourcing Contracts. *Journal of MIS Quarterly, 29*(4), 699-720. Retrieved March 25, 2009 from http://www.misq.org/archivist/vol/no29/Issue4/Walden.html

West, J., & Gallagher, S. (2004). Challenges of Open Innovation: The Paradox of Firm Investment in Open Source Software. *R&D Management, 36*(3). Retrieved April 03, 2009 from http://www.cob.sjsu.edu/opensource/research/

ENDNOTES

[1] Intellectual Property
[2] Return on Investment
[3] Research and Development
[4] Intellectual Property Rights
[5] Small and Medium Enterprises
[6] Chief Technology Officer
[7] User Interaction

Chapter 18
International Transfers of Personal Data:
A UK Law Perspective

Sam De Silva
Taylor Walton LLP, UK

ABSTRACT

Developments in technology and the global nature of business means that personal information about individuals in the UK may often be processed overseas, frequently without the explicit knowledge or consent of those individuals. This raises issues such as the security of such data, who may have access to it and for what purposes and what rights the individual may have to object. The Data Protection Act 1998 provides a standard of protection for personal data, including personal data that is being transferred outside of the UK. This chapter will focus on how a UK data controller (the organisation that controls how and why personal data is processed and is therefore legally responsible for compliance) can fulfill its business and operational requirements in transferring personal data outside the EEA, whilst ensuring legal compliance.

INTRODUCTION

Businesses increasingly operate on an international basis both internally with global group structures and externally with networks of customers and suppliers. This is facilitated by the Internet and information communication technologies which allow the quick and easy transmission of data across national boundaries, and technologies that allow the increasingly complex and cheap

collection, storage, use and disclosure of data. The combination of these factors means that personal information about individuals in the UK may often be processed overseas, frequently without the explicit knowledge or consent of those individuals. This raises issues such as the security of such data, who may have access to it and for what purposes and what rights the individual may have to object.

Europe has a long history of data protection and has traditionally been seen as having a higher standard than the rest of the world. European

DOI: 10.4018/978-1-61520-975-0.ch018

data protection legislation therefore builds in a standard of protection for personal data that is being transferred outside of the UK. In the UK this protection comes from the Data Protection Act 1998 (the "DPA"), primarily the eighth data protection principle in that Act.

This chapter will address the position in the UK by reference to the DPA, principally the eighth data protection principle. The chapter will then focus on how a UK data controller (the organisation that controls how and why personal data is processed and is therefore legally responsible for compliance) can fulfil its business and operational requirements in transferring personal data outside the EEA, whilst ensuring legal compliance including options such as:

- relying on the findings of adequacy by the European Commission;
- relying on the EU/US Safe Harbor deal;
- using the EU model clauses;
- using Binding Corporate Rules; and
- relying on one of the exemptions in Schedule 4 of the DPA.

This chapter is based on the law as at 1 July 2009.

UK DATA PROTECTION

The law which governs the processing of personal data in the United Kingdom is DPA. The DPA implemented Council Directive 46/1995/EC on the Protection of Individuals With Regard to the Processing of Personal Data and on the Free Movement of such Data Within the European Member States (the "Directive").

The purpose of the Directive and of the DPA is to set the rules for the processing of personal data, the data protection principles, and to give the subject individuals rights in relation to their information and how it is held and used.

In essence the DPA states that the data controller has a duty to comply with the eighth data protection principle (set out in Part 1 of Schedule 1 to the DPA). The eighth data protection principle (see below) is of direct relevance to the international transfer of personal data.

However, it should be noted that other principles and provisions of the DPA are relevant when looking at international transfers of personal data. For example, the first data protection principle requires a data controller to provide information to individuals about the processing of personal data about them. This can include telling people that information about them will go overseas. The seventh data protection principle requires appropriate technical and organisational security measures to be in place to protect data, including ensuring the reliability of staff and having written contracts in place with any data processors (suppliers/providers acting on behalf of a data controller in processing personal information). Compliance with the DPA should be considered as a whole. Although other principles of the DPA are relevant to international transfers, this chapter focuses on the eighth data protection principle.

TRANSFERS INTO THE UK

This chapter addresses transfers of personal data from the UK, but in a global business UK data controllers may also receive personal data from overseas. Some issues to consider in this scenario include:

- Is the UK entity only acting as a data processor on behalf of the overseas entity? If so, the overseas entity may wish to impose contractual obligations on the UK entity but, if the UK entity has no right to use the data for its own purposes, it will not become a UK data controller with compliance obligations.

- If the UK entity will use the data in its own right, is the overseas entity complying with the laws of its own country? Are there any restrictions on transfer from that country? Whilst this may not directly affect the UK data controller, it is possible that it will not be obtaining the data fairly and lawfully under the DPA if it is aware that this is in breach of overseas legislation.
- Similarly, will the UK data controller be using the data in a way compatible to the purposes for which it was originally collected? Again, it may be considered unfair under the DPA to use the data for purposes not anticipated by the subject individuals.

EIGHTH DATA PROTECTION PRINCIPLE

The eighth data protection principle states that:

Personal data shall not be transferred to a country or territory outside the European Economic Area unless that country or territory ensures an adequate level of protection for the rights and freedoms of data subjects in relation to the processing of personal data. (Paragraph 8, Part I, Schedule 1, DPA)

Transfers of personal data to a country outside the EEA (the 25 EU member states plus Iceland, Liechtenstein & Norway), otherwise known as a "third country" are therefore prohibited, unless:

- there is an adequate level of protection for the data subjects' rights and freedoms;
- the parties have put in place appropriate safeguards; or
- one of the exemptions set out in Schedule 4 of the DPA applies.

Prior to considering in detail how the DPA regulates international transfers of personal data,

it is useful to consider some of the key definitions used in the DPA.

KEY DEFINITIONS

Personal Data

The DPA applies only to "personal data".

Section 1(1) of the DPA defines "personal data" as:

data which relate to a living individual who can be identified:

(a) from those data, or
(b) from those data and other information which is in the possession of, or is likely to come into the possession of, the data controller,

and includes any expression of opinion about the individual and any indication of the intentions of the data controller or any other person in respect of the individual.

One of the key cases on personal data is the Court of Appeal decision in *Durant v Financial Services Authority* [2003] EWCA Civ 1746. In this case the Court emphasised that there are two elements comprising the definition of "personal data". The Court said that in addition to showing that the individual can be identified by the information, it must also be:

- shown that the information "relates" to the individual; and
- found to do so in a way which might affect his privacy, whether in his personal or family life, business or professional capacity.

Further, the information should have the data subject as its focus rather than some other person with whom he may have been involved or some transaction or event in which he may have had an interest; for example, as in this case, an investigation into some other person's or body's conduct that he may have instigated. In short, it is information that affects his privacy, whether in his personal or family life, business or professional capacity.

In *Durant*, the Court held that the Financial Services Authority's (FSA) investigation of Mr Durant's complaint against Barclays Bank was such an event and therefore the information held could not amount to personal data even though Mr Durant was named in it. Guidance from the Commissioner following the *Durant* case provides that an individual's name will be "personal data" where it appears together with other information about the named individual such as address, telephone number or information regarding his hobbies (ICO Technical Guidance: The Durant case and its impact on the interpretation of the Data Protection 1998, 2006).

The Court of Appeal's narrow interpretation of the meaning of "personal data" in *Durant* is significant as its effect is to make the obligations under the DPA easier to fulfil. As such, the decision was welcomed by HR departments as well as by organisations that typically hold large amounts of personal data, such as banks and insurance companies, on individuals other than staff.

Mr Durant sought leave to appeal the decision of the Court of Appeal in his case but the UK House of Lords refused this in November 2005 (House of Lords Minutes of Proceedings 29 November 2005)

In July 2004, the European Commission issued a "letter of formal notice" to the UK government identifying at least five areas of concern over the UK's implementation of the Directive. Although the letter was not published, it is understood that one area of concern is over the UK's narrow interpretation of "personal data" (Out-Law News, 15 July 2004).

In June 2007, the EC Article 29 Data Protection Working Party ("Working Party"), an independent advisory body on data protection and privacy established by Article 29 of the Directive adopted an opinion on the concept of personal data. The opinion attempts to summarise:

- the "common understanding of the concept of personal data" in the EU member states;
- the situations in which national data protection legislation should be applied; and
- how it should be applied.

The opinion analyses the four main elements which make up the concept of personal data and adopts a wide interpretation particularly in relation to the question of when the information "relates" to an individual. The Working Party opines that to establish this, one of three elements should be present:

- **Content:** The information is given about a particular person, regardless of any purpose on the part of the data controller or a third party, or the impact of that information on the data subject. The opinion gives two examples of such information: the results of a medical analysis (which relate to the patient), and the information contained in an RFID tag (which relates to the holder of the identity document).
- **Purpose:** The data is used, or is likely to be used, to evaluate, treat in a certain way or influence the status or behaviour of an individual. For example, a call log of a telephone call made inside a company office can be used to provide information about the maker and the recipient of the call (for instance, to check what time cleaning staff leave their workplace, if they are supposed to confirm by phone at what time they lock the premises).
- **Result:** The use of the data is likely to have an impact on a certain person's rights and interests, for example information generated by a satellite location system and then used by a taxi company, which is intended primarily to improve waiting times and

fuel efficiency but which also permits the company to monitor the performance of taxi drivers, whether they respect the speed limits, seek appropriate itineraries, and so on.

The opinion makes it clear that information may "relate" to an individual even if it does not focus on him or her.

Although the Working Party's opinion is not binding, it provides a basis for the interpretation of the Directive by data controllers and national data protection authorities. In this respect, the Working Party's rather wide interpretation of the "second element" stands in clear contrast to the restrictive construction adopted by the Court of Appeal in *Durant*. Although the Working Party's definition would not necessarily have meant that Mr Durant would have been successful in his claim against the FSA, it presented cause for concern for UK data controllers as its likely effect would be to make their obligations under the DPA more difficult to fulfil.

In August 2007, the Commissioner issued a Technical Guidance Note on what constitutes personal data for the purposes of the DPA (the "2007 Guidance") which seeks to reconcile the *Durant* decision with the Working Party's opinion.

According to the 2007 Guidance, information is only likely to constitute "personal data" under the DPA if:

- A living individual can be identified either from the information alone, or with other information which is in the possession of the data controller, or is likely to come into its possession. In cases where it is not immediately obvious whether a person can be identified, the question of whether or not the person is nonetheless identifiable will depend on the means the data controller is likely to reasonably use to identify that person.

- The information "relates to" the person in his personal or family life, business or profession. This is the case when it is either "obviously about" that person or if it is "linked to" that person so that it provides particular information about him or her.
- The information is used to inform or influence actions or decisions affecting that person.
- The information focuses or concentrates on the individual as its central theme rather than on some other person, or some object, transaction or event.
- The information impacts, or has the potential to impact, on an individual, whether in a personal, family, business or professional capacity.

While attempting to reconcile the Court of Appeal's findings in the *Durant* case and the Working Party's opinion on the concept of personal data, it is clear that the Information Commissioner has largely followed the approach taken by the Working Party.

The DPA applies only to data which relates to individuals and so will not apply to data relating to companies or other legal entities. However, the processing of, for example, the contact details of individuals within a company may be covered by the DPA.

Data

Section 1(1) of the DPA defines "data" as

- information which:
- (a) is being processed by means of equipment operating automatically in response to instructions given for that purpose,
- (b) is recorded with the intention that it should be processed by means of such equipment,

- (c) is recorded as part of a relevant filing system or with the intention that it should form part of a relevant filing system, or
- (d) does not fall within paragraph (a), (b) or (c) but forms part of an accessible record.

The DPA therefore can apply to automated data, such as that held on a computer. It also extends to certain manual records, and the obligations in this respect are discussed in more detail below (under the heading "Relevant filing system").

In January 2009, the ICO issued a Technical Guidance Note on what constitutes "data" for the purposes of the DPA (the "2009 Guidance Note"). The 2009 Guidance Note is in the form of a flowchart of numbered questions, which aims to help data protection practitioners determine whether information falls within any of the four categories of data covered by the DPA:

- automatically processed data;
- data forming part of a relevant filing system;
- data forming part of an accessible record; and
- data recorded by a public authority. It looks in particular at the meaning of a "relevant filing system" and considers, among other things, different ways in which filing systems may be structured.

Relevant Filing System

The DPA also applies to information recorded in a "relevant filing system". Section 1(1) of the DPA defines "relevant filing system" as:

any set of information relating to individuals to the extent that, although the information is not processed by means of equipment operating automatically in response to instructions given for that purpose, the set is structured, either by reference to individuals or by reference to criteria relating to individuals, in such a way that specific information relating to a particular individual is readily accessible.

This means that the DPA will apply to certain types of manual data contained in structured personnel files, card indexes and microfiches as well as to data held on a computer. There may be a large number of any such files within an organisation. The definition will extend, for example, to records kept by individual employees (such as managers) on their own files except to the extent that these are kept for purely personal use (for example, friends' contact details).

In *Durant* the Courts gave a very narrow interpretation to the term "relevant filing system". In that case, Mr Durant sought and was refused access to manual records concerning an investigation by the FSA into a complaint made by Mr Durant against Barclays Bank. The court of first instance held that the information did not come within the DPA since, although the documents were filed in a divider under the claimant's name, they were organised in date order rather than by any specific criteria relating to him (*Durant v Financial Services* Authority (unreported) Edmonton County Court, 2002). This decision, which adopted a restrictive interpretation of the DPA, was upheld by the Court of Appeal. It therefore operates to limit the categories of manual records that might conceivably have fallen within the scope of the data protection regime to those "of sufficient sophistication to provide the same or similar ready accessibility as a computerised filing system".

The 2007 Guidance issued by the Information Commissioner following *Durant* is helpful in clarifying that the content of manual records must either be sub-divided so as to allow the searcher to go straight to the correct category and retrieve the information requested without a manual search, or indexed so as to allow a searcher to go directly to the relevant pages. For example, if employee files are stored alphabetically by name, and the information on the files is stored in random or even chronological order regardless of subject matter, this would not amount to a relevant filing system as the searcher would have to leaf through the file to find specific information. However, if the files were indexed or sub-divided into categories (for example, sickness, absence, and contact details) enabling quick access to specific information, then they are likely to constitute a relevant filing system. In other words, the DPA will not apply if time needs to be spent leafing through the file for the information sought. The current view of the Information Commissioner is that the majority of manual files are therefore unlikely to fall within the DPA.

Data Controller

All of the obligations under the DPA fall upon the "data controller". Section 1(1) of the DPA defines "data controller" as:

the person who (either alone or jointly or in common with other persons) determines the purposes for which and the manner in which any personal data is, or is to be, processed.

For example, a company will be the controller of the data processed relating to its employees or customers. An entity may be a data controller even if the information concerned is held by a third party (for example, where payroll administration is outsourced to a third party) and there may be more than one data controller in respect of the same data (for example, companies in the same group which use the same data for different purposes).

Data Subject

This is defined as any individual about whom personal data is processed. Typically, data subjects will include customers (including those dealing with companies via the internet), individuals on contact lists or marketing databases, employees, contractors, suppliers and consultants.

Processing

The DPA imposes obligations on those who "process" personal data. "Processing" is very broadly defined to include obtaining, recording, holding, using, disclosing or erasing data (section 1(1) of the DPA). In effect, any activity involving personal data will fall within its scope.

In *Campbell v MGN* [2003] 1 All ER 224, the Court of Appeal held that where a data controller had processed data at one stage, for example, by storing it on a computer, further dissemination of the material in hard-copy form by the data controller would also form part of the processing and fall within the scope of the DPA. More generally, the Court said that the Directive and the DPA defined processing as "any operation or set of operations". It noted that this could include "obtaining the information" at one end of the process and "using the information" at the other end. The court said that while neither activity in itself could sensibly amount to processing, if that activity was carried on by a data controller and was linked to the automated processing of the data, it could see no reason why the entire set of operations should not fall within the scope of the DPA.

Transfer or Transit

The eighth data protection principle applies only to an actual transfer of personal data to a third country. It does not apply if the data simply passes through a country on the way to a final destination in the EEA, unless some substantive processing takes place in that third country *en route*. In the context of the electronic transmission of data, this means that even though personal data may be routed through a third country on its journey from the UK to another EEA country, this "mere transit" through a non-EEA country does not bring the transfer within the scope of the eighth principle.

This issue was considered by the European Court of Justice in the case of *Bodil Lindqvist v Kammaraklagaren* (Case C-101/01), when Mrs

Lindqvist, an active member of her local church in Sweden, set up an internet home page as part of a computer course and chose to create a site giving information to church parishioners. The site included names, telephone numbers and references to hobbies and jobs held by Mrs Lindqvist and her fellow parishioners.

Whilst the Court held that posting information on a website did constitute the processing of personal data as covered by the data protection legislation, it found that this did not constitute an overseas transfer of such personal data, where the site was hosted by a national ISP. It reasoned that the Directive could not be construed as intending the expression "transfer of data to a third country" to cover the loading of data onto an internet page, even though this resulted in data being made accessible to persons in other countries.

However, in the 2007 Guidance, the Information Commissioner has suggested that the intention of the person uploading the data is an important consideration and that in practice as data are often loaded onto the internet with the intention that they will be accessed across the world there will usually be a transfer and the *Lindqvist* principle will not apply. In Mrs Lindqvist's case this did not affect her as she had no intention that the information would be accessed overseas, it was a local initiative. But, though the legal position is unclear, for most global organisations, they do intend their websites to be accessed by anyone anywhere in the world and if they post personal data it is more likely that they are intentionally making a transfer overseas and eighth data protection principle applies.

The eighth data protection principle will apply to a transfer of data which is not held as personal data for the purposes of the DPA in the UK, but which is intended to be held as personal data after the transfer (for example, notes of an interview which are sent to another country by telephone or fax with the intention that they be entered into a computer).

OPTIONS FOR COMPLIANCE WITH EIGHTH DATA PROTECTION PRINCIPLE

Once it is established that there is a transfer of personal data from a UK data controller to a country outside the EEA, the next steps are to look at how that transfer can be made legally.

The Information Commissioner has made it clear that the onus is on the data controller to ensure that it complies with the eighth data protection principle in relation to any international transfer of personal data. In 1999, the Information Commissioner published a legal guidance document on the eighth data protection principle and international data transfer to assist data controllers in achieving this aim. A revised guidance document titled *The Eighth Data Protection Principle and International Data Transfers* was published in June 2006 which takes account of a number of developments within the EU and at domestic level (the "Guidance on International Data Transfers").

In the Guidance on International Data Transfers the recommendation is that the processing of personal data should be kept to a minimum and that data controllers should consider if it is possible for them to achieve their objective without such processing (for example, by anonymising the data). Where data transfers are unavoidable, the Guidance on International Data Transfers outlines a "good-practice approach", suggesting that the data controller should follow a four-step procedure in order to establish whether or not a cross-border transfer complies with the DPA:

- **Step 1:** The data controller should consider whether there will be a transfer of personal data to a third country.
- **Step 2:** The data controller should consider whether the third country and the circumstances surrounding the transfer ensure that an adequate level of protection

will be given to that data (for example, because the European Commission has made a finding of adequacy).

- **Step 3:** The data controller should consider whether the parties have or can put into place adequate safeguards to protect the data (for instance, by entering into model clauses or establishing binding corporate rules).
- **Step 4:** The data controller should consider if any of the other derogations to the eighth principle specified in the DPA apply (such as the consent of the data subject to the transfer).

In practice, a data controller will usually seek to rely either on a Community finding of adequacy or on one of the exemptions in Schedule 4 of the DPA. The author considers that a data controller will only be tempted to establish adequacy himself ("adequacy test") in cases where it is easy to establish that the transfer is being made to a country which can ensure an adequate level of protection or where the data controller is for some reason prevented from relying on one of the exemptions.

In the original guidance issued in 1999, the Information Commissioner made it clear that he did not consider the avoidance of the adequacy test to be good practice in terms of data protection and he expressed the view that such an approach may be more likely to lead to a breach of the data protection principles. In the Guidance on International Data Transfers he has taken a more practical approach and has acknowledged the fact that, because the adequacy test is complex, and because there is a risk that the data controller may wrongly evaluate the circumstances of the transfer, many data controllers are reluctant to take on the burden of applying this test where easier and less time-consuming methods are available.

FINDINGS OF ADEQUACY

Once the data controller has established that the way in which it processes the data constitutes a transfer of personal data to a third country, it must decide whether or not the third country ensures an adequate level of protection of that personal data. This decision will normally be based on either a Community finding of adequacy or a positive outcome when applying the adequacy test.

COMMUNITY FINDINGS OF ADEQUACY

Paragraph 15, Part II, Schedule 1 of the DPA provides that where the European Commission makes a finding that a country outside the EEA (or "third country") does, or does not, ensure an adequate level of protection within the meaning of Article 25(2) of the Directive, any question as to whether an adequate level of protection is met in relation to the transfer of any personal data to that country shall be determined in accordance with that finding.

As at the time of writing, findings of adequacy have been made in relation to Switzerland, Hungary, Canada (subject to certain conditions), Argentina, Guernsey and the Isle of Man. This means that transfers to these countries will comply with the eighth data protection principle. A list of "adequate" countries is published on the *Europa* website.

ADEQUACY TEST

It is always open to a data controller to assess adequacy on its own. However in the author's experience this process can be complex, time consuming and expensive and gives no guarantees that the transfer will comply with the eighth data protection principle.

An assessment of adequacy should be used only as a last resort, where there is no Community finding of adequacy (see above) or where one of the exemptions to the eighth data protection principle (set out below under the heading "Exemptions in Schedule 4 of the DPA") cannot be established.

In paragraph 13, Part II, Schedule 1 of the DPA, an "adequate level of protection" is one which is "adequate in all the circumstances of the case, having regard in particular to:

(a) the nature of the personal data;

(b) the country or territory of origin of the information contained in the data;

(c) the country or territory of final destination of that information;

(d) the purposes for which and period during which the data is intended to be processed;

(e) the law in force in the country or territory in question;

(f) the international obligations of that country or territory;

(g) any relevant codes of conduct or other rules which are enforceable in that country or territory (whether generally or by arrangement in particular cases); and

(h) any security measures taken in respect of the data in that country or territory."

In the Guidance on International Data Transfers, the Information Commissioner refers to criteria (a) to (d) and (h) as the "general adequacy criteria" and to criteria (f) and (g) as the "legal adequacy criteria."

General Adequacy Criteria

In the Guidance on International Data Transfers, the Information Commissioner has made it clear that the general adequacy criteria should be assessed by the data exporter in every case, as they relate to facts that are within the knowledge and to a certain extent, the control of the data exporter.

Nature of the Personal Data

Certain personal data are so widely available to the public that their transfer to a third country is of little consequence to the rights of the data subject (for example, personal details of sports stars or media personalities). Conversely, the transfer of previously unknown or sensitive personal data may have a considerable impact on the rights of the data subject, especially if that third country lacks the relevant regulatory protection for such data.

Country or Territory of Origin

If the data being transferred were originally obtained in a country outside the EEA, the data subject may have different expectations as to the level of protection that will be afforded to the data than if the data had been obtained in the EEA.

Country or Territory of Final Destination

If it is known that there will be a further transfer of the data to another country, the data protection regime of that country must also be considered.

Purposes for which the Data is Being Processed

Some purposes may pose a higher risk than others, for example wide use of data for marketing contact.

Period for which the Data is Being Processed

The longer the period of processing, the more likely it is that any deficiencies in the data protection regime of that country will be exposed.

Security Measures Taken in Respect of the Data in the Third Country

It may be possible to ensure security of the data by means of technical measures (for example, encryption) or the adoption of security management practices similar to those set out in ISO 27000, ISO 27001 and any other information security standards in the ISO 27000 series.

Legal Adequacy Criteria

This involves an analysis of the following in relation to the country to which data is being transferred:

- the law in force;
- the international obligations; and
- any codes of conduct or other enforceable rules.

As such matters are outside the control of both the data exporter and the data importer, the Information Commissioner recognises that it would be inappropriate, difficult, time-consuming and costly for exporting controllers to consider such "legal adequacy criteria" exhaustively in the case of every transfer to a non-EEA country. However, the data controller is expected to carry out an analysis of the "legal adequacy criteria" where it envisages greater involvement in the processing of the data in the third country after the transfer, for example, if it is proposing to set up a permanent operation in that country and anticipates making regular, large-scale transfers to that country.

At the same time, even in cases where the data controller does not conduct an exhaustive analysis of the legal adequacy criteria, the Information Commissioner expects it to be able to recognise countries where there would be danger of prejudice because of, for example, instability in the third country at the time of the transfer. In such cases, the Information Commissioner has made it clear that he expects the data controller to recognise that situation and to err on the side of caution in relation to any transfer.

SAFE HARBOR

Overview

In 2001 the US Department of Commerce and the European Commission approved the Safe Harbor scheme which sets out a framework of data protection standards which allow the free flow of personal data from EEA data controllers to the US organisations which have joined the scheme.

US companies that adhere to the Safe Harbor data protection standards, principles and procedures will be deemed to provide an adequate level of protection which satisfies, in UK terms, the requirements of the eighth data protection principle.

Benefits

For international companies with subsidiaries or trading partners in the US and the EEA the Safe Harbor scheme is designed to reduce the administrative burden of complying with the DPA and to ensure that data flows to Europe are uninterrupted. However, due to the limited take up, it is questionable whether this has been achieved in practice.

Scope

The Safe Harbor scheme applies only to the transfer of personal data from a data controller in the UK to a data controller in the US. It does not apply to transfers of personal data from a UK data controller to a US data processor that processes personal data in the US or the EEA, nor is the scheme applicable where data is obtained directly from individuals via a website.

At present, US businesses in sectors such as telecommunications and financial services are not able to take advantage of the scheme.

Requirements

In order to be eligible to join the Safe Harbor scheme, a US organisation must be subject to an independent statutory body which can protect personal privacy effectively and has jurisdiction to investigate complaints. The Federal Trade Commission (FTC) and the Department of Transportation (DOT) are such statutory bodies recognised by the European Commission. For example, air carriers may participate as they are subject to the jurisdiction of the DOT. Voluntary compliance, monitored by the FTC, therefore allows, for example, the transfer of customer details from a US company's European offices or subsidiaries into the US.

To qualify for the Safe Harbor scheme, a US organisation has three options. It can:

- develop its own self-regulatory privacy policy which conforms to the Safe Harbor requirements; or
- join a self-regulatory privacy programme which adheres to the requirements, organised by firms such as VeriSign and TRUSTe; or
- be subject to a statutory or other body of law or rule which effectively achieves the same standards.

Organisations must commit to a data protection and privacy notice which complies with all seven Safe Harbor principles, set out below.

Principles

The Safe Harbor scheme establishes seven principles which are broadly equivalent to the standards established by the principles of the DPA. The Safe Harbor Principles are:

- **Notice:** giving individuals notice of the purposes for which their data are collected, notice of the third parties to whom the data may be disclosed, information to enable the individuals to contact the organisation for enquiries or complaints and the means offered for limiting use and disclosure.
- **Choice:** offering individuals the choice of opting out of disclosure to third parties and the choice of whether or not to allow the organisation to use the data for purposes other than those for which they were originally collected. An opt-in approach is required if sensitive data are involved.
- **Onward transfers:** data may be disclosed only to third parties who either subscribe to the Safe Harbor Principles, or who are subject to the DPA, or who enter into a written agreement to provide the equivalent level of privacy protection.
- **Access:** providing the individual with access to his data and giving him/her the right to have the information corrected upon request, unless the burden or expense of doing so is disproportionate or would violate the rights of another individual.
- **Security:** taking reasonable precautions to protect personal data from loss or misuse and from unauthorised access, disclosure, alteration and destruction.
- **Data integrity:** ensuring that data are accurate, up-to-date, relevant and reliable for their intended use.
- **Enforcement:** providing effective enforcement mechanisms and dispute resolution procedures.

Although the Safe Harbor Principles are broadly equivalent to the principles in the DPA, there are some key differences. For example the seventh data protection principle requires "appropriate" security measures whereas the Safe Harbor Principles requires "reasonable" precautions, which is not necessarily as high a standard.

Once a US organisation has established a privacy policy which declares its compliance with Safe Harbor principles and has decided to participate in the Safe Harbor scheme, it must self-certify its compliance in writing with the US Department of Commerce. This can be achieved by a letter which sets out certain information including details of the organisation's activities in relation to the data collected and a description of its privacy policy. The Department of Commerce will maintain and make public a list of those self-certified organisations and their self-certification letters.

Enforcement

The Safe Harbor Principles require that an organisation's policy is enforceable. How does the law apply to ensure that those who self-certify do not merely pay lip-service to data protection principles? There are several ways in which enforcement can be achieved.

Once on the Safe Harbor register the organisation must self-certify annually. It does this by verifying its compliance with the principles by means of internal or external audits. At least once a year a statement must be signed by a corporate officer or other authorised representative of the organisation, to the effect that the organisation has conducted an assessment which verifies the organisation's compliance. This statement must then be made available upon request or whenever the organisation's compliance is being investigated.

An organisation's privacy policy must specify:

- the statutory body which has jurisdiction to hear complaints against it;
- the names of any privacy programs of which it is a member; and
- the independent dispute resolution mechanism by which complaints may be investigated.

This ensures that any member of the public can find out where to address complaints. The dispute resolution mechanism can be provided by private sector self-regulatory bodies such as TRUSTe, through legal or regulatory supervisory

authorities or by committing to co-operate with data protection authorities in the EEA. The US organisation must also be able to remedy problems arising out of a failure to comply with the Safe Harbor Principles.

Sanctions for non-compliance include publicising non-compliance, deletion of data, compensation and injunctive orders. If the recourse mechanism provided is a private sector dispute self-regulating body, then any failure to comply with its ruling must be notified to either the courts, the FTC or DOT (as appropriate) and in every case of persistent failure to comply with the Safe Harbor Principles, to the Department of Commerce.

The FTC and DOT are committed to taking action against companies who fail to live up to their self-certified privacy policies. Under the Federal Trade Commission Act 1914 (FTCA), "unfair or deceptive acts or practices in or affecting commerce" are illegal and the FTC is empowered to take action to prevent them. If an organisation signs up to the Safe Harbor Principles and then fails to comply, it has misrepresented its practice on the treatment of personal information.

After a formal hearing the FTC may impose sanctions for breach of the FTCA. Sanctions available to the FTC to stop processing include cease and desist orders, restraining orders and injunctions.

Non-compliance with such an order attracts a further penalty of $12,000 for each day of the period of non-compliance.

ADEQUATE SAFEGUARDS

Even if a data exporter is not using adequacy to justify an international transfer, the transfer will still be legitimate if it can be shown that the parties have put in place adequate safeguards, such as:

- the model clauses; or
- binding corporate rules.

MODEL CLAUSES

What are the Model Clauses?

Under Article 26(4) of the Directive, the European Commission has the right to decide that certain standard contractual clauses offer sufficient safeguards for the protection of the privacy and fundamental rights and freedoms of individuals, as required by the Directive.

What do the Model Clauses Contain?

The model clauses cover the following issues:

- data processing obligations of both the transferor data controller and the transferee data controller/data processor;
- rights of data subjects, in particular the right to compensation if damage is suffered;
- joint and several liability of the data exporter and data importer; and
- dealing with data protection authorities.

In essence the clauses require data importers and exporters to warrant and undertake that they have complied with data protection standards which meet the requirements of the DPA in respect of the data. Prior to the development of the Revised Controller to Controller Model Clauses (see below), the data importer and data exporter must accept liability to data subjects for breach of those standards, with cross indemnities to ensure that the one responsible for the actual breach meets the cost of the breach. Either party can be sued by data subjects for a breach of the contract, regardless of who is at fault.

The obligations on the data importer based outside the EEA are more onerous. The importer has to agree to limit the processing to what is agreed in the contract.

Understandably, organisations have concerns about using the model clauses in a commercial transaction as they are not particularly user-friendly but they are often the simplest option if the data exporter can persuade the overseas organisation to sign up to them.

Model Clauses: Transfer from Controller to Processor

The European Commission adopted a Decision (2002/16/EC) of 27 December 2001 on standard contractual clauses for the transfer of personal data to third countries under the Directive (OJ 2002 L6/52). This Decision contained model contract clauses for use by data controllers established in the EU when transferring data to data processors in countries outside the EEA (the "Controller to Processor Model Clauses"). The Decision lays down the minimum information that the parties must specify in the contract dealing with the transfer.

The standard clauses address not only the issues arising in the context of the eighth data protection principle, but also the requirements imposed on data processors by the seventh data protection principle. This seventh data protection principle requires the data controller to ensure that appropriate technical and organisational measures are taken against unauthorised or unlawful processing of personal data and against accidental loss or destruction of, or damage to, personal data (Paragraph 7, Part I, Schedule 1 of the DPA).

Under Paragraphs 11 and 12, Part II, Schedule 1 of the DPA, where the data controller uses a data processor:

- the data controller must ensure that the chosen data processor provides sufficient guarantees in respect of the technical and organisational security measures governing the processing to be carried out, and it must take reasonable steps to ensure compliance with those measures; and
- the processing must be carried out under a written contract under which the data processor is to act only on instructions from

the data controller and which requires the data processor to comply with obligations equivalent to those imposed on a data controller by the seventh data protection principle.

Model Clauses: Transfers from Controller to Controller

In 2001, the Commission adopted Decision 2001/497/EC of 15 June 2001 on standard contractual clauses for the transfer of personal data to third countries under the Directive (OJ 2001 L181/19), which set out model contract clauses intended to provide adequate safeguards for personal data transferred by data controllers established in the EU to data controllers in countries outside the EEA (the "2001 Controller to Controller Model Clauses").

Under the 2001 Controller to Controller Model Clauses, the data exporter and importer agree to process data in accordance with certain standards and they confer upon data subjects the right to enforce the contract as third parties. The Information Commissioner has authorised transfers made using these standard clauses as being made in a manner which ensures adequate safeguards for the rights and freedoms of data subjects.

In the absence of a Community finding of adequacy, the consent of the data subject or the application of one of the other exemptions in Schedule 4 of the DPA, the model clauses are widely seen as the only reliable way of ensuring compliance with the eighth data protection principle.

However, following calls by the International Chamber of Commerce (ICC) and others for the introduction of less onerous model clauses, the European Commission adopted a decision which amended its earlier decision by adding a new set of standard contractual clauses (the "Revised Controller to Controller Model Clauses") which it also regards as providing adequate safeguards in respect of the transfer of data outside the EEA (Commission Decision 2004/915/EC of 27 De-

cember 2004 amending Decision 2001/497/EC as regards the introduction of an alternative set of standard contractual clauses for the transfer of personal data to third countries, OJ 2004 L385/74).

The new Decision provides that data controllers may choose to use either the 2001 Controller to Controller Model Clauses or Revised Controller to Controller Model Clauses, but they cannot amend the clauses or "mix and match" them by combining clauses from the two different sets.

The key difference between the Revised Controller to Controller Model Clauses and the 2001 Controller to Controller Model Clauses relates to the apportionment of liability to third party data subjects as between the data exporter and the data importer. The 2001 Controller to Controller Model Clauses provide that the data exporter and the data importer agree that "they will be jointly and severally liable for damage to the data subject resulting from any violation..." of specified obligations of either the exporter or the importer under the contract containing the model clauses.

This was seen as unattractive by business groups, and the Revised Controller to Controller Model Clauses dispense with the principle of joint and several liability, replacing it with a regime under which, broadly:

- the data exporter and the data importer are liable to data subjects only for breach of their own contractual obligations;
- a data subject can proceed directly against a data exporter who has failed to use reasonable efforts to check that the data importer is able to satisfy its legal obligations under the contract (this is backed up by a broader right on the part of data exporters to gain access to data importers' records in order to audit compliance with their obligations under the contract);
- a data exporter assumes a greater responsibility for resolving data subjects' complaints by being required, in cases involving allegations of breach by the data

importer, to take appropriate action to enforce the data subject's rights against the data importer, and only if the data exporter fails to take such action within a reasonable period (normally a month) may the data subject then enforce his rights directly against the data importer.

Other differences between the Revised Controller to Controller Model Clauses and the 2001 Controller to Controller Model Clauses include:

- **Individuals' Rights:** in the Revised Controller to Controller Model Clauses, in most situations, individuals can enforce their data protection rights only against the party responsible for the data protection breach;
- *Obligations*: the obligations placed on exporting and importing parties are generally more flexible. For example, the ability to hold back confidential information when providing copies of the contracts to the individuals;
- **Contractual flexibility:** contracts can be modified to include additional transfers or changes to existing transfer processes;
- **Termination:** exporting companies are given greater scope for terminating agreements; and
- **Drafting clarity:** use of more explicitly-worded clauses and less reliance on cross-references to statutory sources.

Information Commissioner's Authorisations

The Information Commissioner has issued authorisations under section 54(6) of the DPA in relation to:

- the Controller to Processor Model Clauses on 8 March 2003;

- the 2001 Controller to Controller Model Clauses on 21 December 2001; and
- the Revised Controller to Controller Model Clauses on 27 May 2005,

providing that, for the purpose of paragraph 9 of Schedule 4 to the DPA, the eighth data principle does not apply where the transfer has been made using any of the model clauses. This means that an exporting data controller who uses these model clauses does not need to make a separate assessment of adequacy in relation to the transfer.

How can the Model Clauses be Incorporated?

The method of incorporation is identical in both data controller to data controller transfers, and data controller to data processor transfers. Parties can:

- use the model contracts word for word as standalone contracts as they are and only complete the blanks;
- as per the option above and include further commercial terms in the body of the contract, provided that the further commercial terms do not contradict the model contract;
- incorporate the model contract into a wider commercial agreement, either word for word or with minimal changes that are necessary to enable the model contract to fit into the context of the wider commercial agreement; or
- incorporate the model contract into a wider commercial agreement by making detailed reference to the EU Commission Decisions adopting the model data transfer contracts.

It should be noted that the Information Commissioner advises that, if the wordings in the model contracts are changed (even without altering the intended meaning or effect of any clause), the transfer will not be one authorised by the Information Commissioner (Guidance on the Use of Model Contract Clauses - data controllers established in the EU to data processors in countries outside the EU, 2003). Instead, with such changes, the use of the clauses could be used in presenting a case to the Information Commissioner that the transfer is made in circumstances where there are appropriate safeguards in place.

Model Clauses: An Assessment

In the author's experience the following issues have arisen with the model clauses, which somewhat question the effectiveness of using the model clauses:

- It is a time consuming activity to agree individual contracts for each transfer or set of transfers, particularly within multinational organisations transferring personal data between upwards of one hundred group companies. Also, each contract needs registering with the relevant national data protection authority. Then they need updating as company structures and processing activities change.
- The above is further complicated where there are internal EEA country differences in national and provincial laws requiring individual tailoring.
- The difficulty for an EEA data subject to determine if his/her rights are being breached or not by a third party.
- Ensuring the data importer is complying with the contract terms, even when there are no data subject complaints requires active management and policing of the contract by the data controller, especially if there are no penalties for non-compliance. Performance criteria can be built into associated contract schedules but these may not trap misuse of the data, or onward transfers, in breach of the contract terms. Instead the liability would rest with the data controller, who would then need to recover any losses in a separate legal action against the recipient. Such indirect liability may not be a deterrent.
- Hence, regular external verification of the importers data use and processing is needed, such as periodic audits carried out by a standards body, or specialist auditing firms.
- Enforcing the contract remotely may also be difficult logistically, even with an agreed EEA jurisdiction. Associated local enforcement may also be required, for example in the case of criminal activities by data processor employees, given local culture and speed of law enforcement.
- The difficulty of "remote" supervision by the data exporter's data protection authority is evident from the volume of data transfer contracts, and the staffing levels and current workloads in Information Commissioners' offices. These cast doubt on the feasibility and practicality of their acting in a truly supervisory, inspection or arbitration role, in a third country dispute. Reliance on commissioners under model contracts or assisting on offshore-related complaints may not be practical.
- Monitoring for "overriding law" disclosure to the third country authorities, which would breach the EU Convention on Human Rights may be problematic. Notification to the exporting data controller is proposed, but this may not occur.

BINDING CORPORATE RULES

Where a transfer is carried out by a UK-established company to other members of its group in different jurisdictions, the transfer will comply with the eighth data protection principle if it is governed by a set of legally enforceable corporate rules that have been approved by the Information Commissioner.

The Working Party has adopted *Working Document: Transfers of personal data to third countries: Applying Article 26 (2) of the EU Data Protection Directive to Binding Corporate Rules for International Data Transfers*, 11639/02/EN WP 74 ("Working Document WP74") which includes a model checklist for companies applying for approval of their binding corporate rules (BCRs), and has introduced procedures for selecting a lead data protection authority to approve applications to multiple authorities. Working Document WP74 includes a checklist of information which should be supplied to a data protection authority when a corporate group is applying for approval of its BCRs.

In summary, the recommendations in Working Document WP74 require that:

- The corporate rules must comply with the content principles, for example, purpose limitation, data quality & proportionality, transparency and security.

- The corporate rules are not merely a general statement but as tailor-made data protection rules and safeguards within the company's actual business processes and around each third country data transfer.

- The corporate rules must be binding in practice through measures adopted by the parent company board and propagated downwards throughout the organisation, ensuring awareness, implementation and commitment in all offices worldwide; including training programmes, clear practical employee and subcontractor guidance and disciplinary measures. The author's opinion is that verification of compliance can only be by regular audits by compliance managers and/or external auditors reporting to the parent board in the first place and thence the Information Commissioner periodically.

- The corporate rules must be binding in law on companies, employees, subcontractors and external third parties. Legal enforceability, liability and jurisdiction must all be clearly defined to ease practical redress for all data subjects via contractual third-party rights. Third party rights should be at least equivalent to those in the model clauses.

- The legal redress should be achieved group-wide through a single EEA jurisdiction (for example, a department in the UK head office) to which all complaints from all countries in the Group are sent, with sufficient funds to pay fines, organise alternative dispute resolution, co-operate with the relevant Information Commissioners and ensure compliance.

- A mechanism is present for recording and reporting changes to the rules as and when business activities change.

The checklist in Working Document WP74 sets out a detailed list of questions which should be dealt with in an application for approval, including:

- How have the rules been made legally binding on the applicant company, other companies in its group, employees and subcontractors?

- How can individuals enforce the BCRs against companies in the group?

- What are the applicant company's data protection audit procedures?

- What type or types of data are covered by the BCRs; for what purposes are the data being processed and to what extent are they being transferred between jurisdictions?

- What internal data protection safeguards are in place and how are these reflected in the BCRs?

- What procedures are in place for keeping the data protection authorities and other members of the group of companies informed about changes to the BCRs?

The ICC has issued detailed guidance on the drafting and implementation of BCRs (ICC Report on Binding Corporate Rules for International Transfers of Personal Data, 2004). In addition, an ICC Task Force on Privacy and the Protection of Personal Data has published a *Standard Application for Approval of Binding Corporate Rules for the Transfer of Personal Data outside the EU (to be used in all EU Member States)* (the "Application Form") which is based on the checklist in Working Document WP74.

The Application Form was adapted by the Working Party and can be used for approval of BCRs in all EU member states (Recommendation 1/2007 on the Standard Application for Approval of Binding Corporate Rules for the Transfer of Personal Data, 2007). Although use of the Application Form is not mandatory for applications to the Information Commissioner, it follows the checklist adopted previously by the Working Party, so companies who use it can be certain that they are following all the necessary requirements as set out in the checklist.

In addition, in June 2008, the Working Party also adopted a number of documents on BCRs:

- *Working Document Setting up a framework for the structure of Binding Corporate Rules*, 1271-00-01/08/EN WP154 that provides companies with an outline for the structure and content of BCRs in line with Working Party requirements. The document is not a model BCR and companies are warned that data protection authorities will not accept a copy of the framework. Instead, companies are expected to tailor the framework according to their particular circumstances.
- A table in *Working Document setting up a table with the elements and principles to be found in Binding Corporate Rules*, 1271-00-00/08/EN WP153 which, among other things, clarifies the necessary content of BCRs and distinguishes the details which

must be included in BCRs from the information which must be presented as part of a BCRs application.

- A set of frequently asked questions on BCRs in *Working Document on Frequently Asked Questions (FAQs) related to Binding Corporate Rules*, 1271-02-02/08/EN WP155 rev.03.

The BCR approach is likely to be more attractive to organisations with a significant multinational presence than the use of standard contractual terms, since it relieves UK companies of the need to negotiate such terms individually with each of their overseas affiliates. With the adoption of the checklist in Working Document WP 74, some of the practical problems preventing companies from using BCRs have been addressed. Whereas before the BCRs had to be approved by the data protection authority in each EU territory from which the organisation intended to transfer data overseas, the introduction of a "lead authority" responsible for dealing with the application for approval of BCRs is expected to simplify the process considerably. This should make this alternative more attractive to many international organisations. Companies should note, however, that if they transfer data from more than one EEA member state, they will still have to comply with any additional national requirements of such member states, such as notification or administrative formalities.

Summary on the Effectiveness of BCRs

The initial workload for developing BCRs and hurdles to overcome with data protection authorities are significant. If only certain types of data transfers require BCRs, then model contracts may be an easier option than developing and implementing corporate rules and structures across the globe. An assessment is required first. Implementation of BCRs requires the following extensive, resource-hungry and costly actions worldwide:

- **To verify the corporate rules comply with content principles** will involve significant review effort. Given the scale involved, few data processing authorities would be willing to dedicate time to verify these, except by using external reviewers.

- **To verify that the companies in the group are bound by those rules in practice** will require regular internal or external audits, reporting to the parent board and follow-up actions. This is effectively self-regulation. If a company neglected the enforcement of the rules, for example by turning focus elsewhere, reducing budgets for compliance activities, the rules would cease to be binding in practice relatively quickly.

- **To ensure that companies are bound in law** is the critical element in ensuring success, otherwise it is effectively a voluntary code. Since the main instruments to this are internal contracts backed by intra-group agreements, memorandums or unilateral undertakings, (and these will differ from country to country), it may be more cost-effective to employ these directly for the protection of discrete export data flows, than to use them to bind companies to carry out a range of corporate rules.

- **To ensure employees are bound in law** is critical to ensuring successful corporate practices. However attempts to bind employee practices to contracts of employment with disciplinary procedures have proved difficult to enforce. Current employment protection and collective agreements could make this challenging.

- **To ensure subcontractors are bound** is an unlikely requirement since most of any size are likely to be data processors with existing contracts, which therefore cannot be replaced by BCRs. Such subcontractors can stay satisfactorily controlled by contracts although there may need to be changes to allow 'linkage' to BCR processes.

EXEMPTIONS IN SCHEDULE 4 OF THE DPA

The eighth data protection principle does not apply in certain limited circumstances (Schedule 4 of the DPA), including where:

- The individual has consented to the transfer. For the purpose of obtaining an informed consent, the Information Commissioner has stated that the data controller should inform the data subject of the reasons for the transfer and, as far as possible, name the countries to which the data will be transferred. He should also bring any particular risks to the data subject's attention. Since it is the individual concerned who must consent, a company may not consent on behalf of its staff or customers. If the nature of the transfer changes, further consents may be required.

- The transfer is necessary to perform a contract with the individual, or to take steps at his request with a view to entering into a contract with him. This will include employment contracts. A transfer will be "necessary" in these circumstances where it is required to perform a contract (such as where a UK seller of goods passes names and addresses to its overseas manufacturer for the purpose of delivery), but not where it is due to the structure of the data controller's business (for example, where a data controller chooses to locate any of its data processing operations outside the UK). In other words, the condition is satisfied if the transfer is absolutely necessary for the performance of the contract and not merely convenient for the controller. This exemption might not cover, therefore, the transfer of data as part of the overseas outsourcing of the data controller's operations.

- The transfer is necessary for reasons of substantial public interest (such as crime prevention or detection). For example, the Immigration and Asylum Act 1998 provides that, in certain situations, the transfer of personal identification data by the Secretary of State under that Act is a transfer necessary for reasons of substantial public interest.

- The transfer is necessary for the purpose of, or in connection with, any legal proceedings (including prospective legal proceedings), for obtaining legal advice or otherwise for establishing, exercising or defending legal rights. The legal proceedings do not necessarily have to involve the data controller or the data subject.

- The transfer is necessary to protect the vital interests of the individual (that is, a life-or-death situation). The Information Commissioner gives as an example the transfer of medical records where an individual has been in a serious accident abroad.

- The transfer is made on terms which are of a kind approved by the Information Commissioner as ensuring adequate safeguards for the rights and freedoms of data subjects, or the transfer has been authorised by the Information Commissioner as being made in such a manner as to ensure adequate safeguards for the rights and freedoms of data subjects.

FAILURE TO COMPLY WITH THE EIGHTH DATA PROTECTION PRINCIPLE

Sending personal data to a third party in a country outside the EEA which does not provide the data subject with an adequate level of data protection is a breach of the eighth data protection principle.

Enforcement

Breach of the eighth data protection principle is not in itself a criminal offence. However, the Information Commissioner has the power to issue an enforcement notice, which will require the data controller to comply with the principle, or refrain from making the offending transfer, within a specified period. Failure to comply with an enforcement notice is a criminal offence (section 47, DPA), although data controllers receiving such a notice may appeal to the Information Tribunal, a non-judicial body made up of representatives of interest groups. Appeals from the Information Tribunal may be made to the High Court on points of law (section 49(6), DPA).

Prosecution and Penalties

Proceedings for criminal offences can be brought by the Information Commissioner or by the Director of Public Prosecutions. Offenders are liable to a fine of a maximum of £5,000 if convicted summarily in a magistrate's court, and an unlimited fine if convicted on indictment in a Crown Court (section 60, DPA).

Directors and other officers of companies who have committed offences under the DPA may also be liable to prosecution. Where a company has committed an offence and it is proved to have been committed with the consent or connivance of, or due to any neglect on the part of, the officer concerned, that person will be guilty of the offence, in addition to the company itself (section 61, DPA). The same applies to the members of a company in respect of a company that is managed by its members.

Civil Proceedings

A data controller may also face civil proceedings: any data subject suffering damage or damage and distress (but not distress alone) as a result of a data controller's failure to comply with the principles has a right to sue for damages under the DPA (section 13, DPA).

SUMMARY AND OVERALL RECOMMENDATIONS

Once it is established that there is a transfer of personal data from the UK, the next step is to look at the grounds for making the transfer.

This section gives a summary of the key ways in which compliance for overseas transfers can be achieved:

- **Findings of adequacy by the European Commission:** The European Commission undertakes a process of investigating the data protection legislation of certain countries outside the EEA. Its conclusions as to whether countries outside the EEA ensure an adequate level of protection are published on its website. Therefore a transfer to one of these countries is acceptable under the eighth data protection principle, although compliance with the other principles must still be considered.

- **The EU/US Safe Harbor deal:** Although the European Commission does not consider the national data protection legislation of the USA to be adequate, it has reached a deal that will allow a finding of adequacy if organisations in the USA sign up to a self-regulatory scheme known as Safe Harbor. This may be an option for companies transferring to a US head office or using a US supplier that has signed up to the Safe Harbor principles (although it should be noted that the take up in the US has been slow).

- **Model clauses:** A transfer of data from a data controller in the EEA to a data controller in a third country is permitted if that transfer is made in accordance with standard contractual clauses which the European Commission has decided offer sufficient safeguards. This is often the route used in outsourcing offshore deals.

- **Binding Corporate Rules:** A company code of practice, or set of BCRs, may be accepted by EU regulators as an adequate basis for transfer but can be time consuming to implement across a global organisation. This is discussed further below.

- **The adequacy test:** In the absence of any other option, it is always open to an organisation to determine for itself that the transfer it wishes to make will provide adequate safeguards. The Information Commissioner has recommended that such an assessment of adequacy should include an examination of a number of stated criteria applicable to the transfer ("the adequacy test"). However in the author's experience this process can be complex, time consuming and expensive and gives no guarantees that the transfer with comply with the eighth data protection principle.

- **Reliance on one of the Exemptions in Schedule 4 of the DPA:** The most likely exemptions an organisation is likely to rely on are:

  (1) **Consent:** However, before following this route an organisation should consider carefully whether it is the most appropriate option. For example, what would happen if an individual did not consent or subsequently withdraws their consent? Consent must be unambiguous, freely given, specific and informed. For business critical transfers consent is not really an option and organisations will need to rely on one of the other options, bearing in mind that there may still be a need to tell people about the transfer, even if their consent is not obtained.

313

(2) **Transfers necessary for the conclusion of a contract between an individual and the data controller:** In some cases, the nature of the relationship between the data controller and the individual may imply that a transfer of data is necessary for contract fulfilment. For example, if an individual books a holiday in Sri Lanka through a UK travel agency, it is implicit in that relationship that the travel agent may need to transfer information about the individual to the Sri Lankan airlines, hotels, tour operators. However, "necessary" should be something more than just convenient or cost efficient. This option is unlikely to apply where an employer wants to transfer employee data to an overseas head office as this is not going to be strictly necessary for fulfilment of the employment contract.

REFERENCES

Article, E. C. 29 Working Party (2007). (Opinion 4/2007 on the concept of personal data). Retrieved on June 30, 2009 from http://ec.europa.eu/justice_home/fsj/privacy/docs/wpdocs/2007/wp136_en.pdf

Article 29 Working Party. (2003, June 3). Working Document: Transfers of personal data to third countries: Applying Article 26(2) of the EU Data Protection Directive to Binding Corporate Rules for International Data Transfers, 11639/02/EN WP 74. Retrieved on June 30, 2009 from http://ec.europa.eu/justice_home/fsj/privacy/docs/wpdocs/2003/wp74_en.pdf

Article 29 Working Party (2007, January 10). Recommendation 1/2007 on the Standard application for approval of binding corporate rules for the transfer of personal data. Retrieved on June 30, 2009 from http://ec.europa.eu/justice_home/fsj/privacy/docs/wpdocs/2007/wp133_en.doc

Article 29 Working Party (2008, June 24). Working Document Setting up a framework for the structure of Binding Corporate Rules, 1271-00-01/08/EN WP 154. Retrieved on June 30, 2009 from http://ec.europa.eu/justice_home/fsj/privacy/docs/wpdocs/2008/wp154_en.pdf

Article 29 Working Party. (2008, June 24). Working Document setting up a table with the elements and principles to be found in Binding Corporate Rules, 1271-00-00/08/EN WP 153. Retrieved on June 30, 2009 from http://ec.europa.eu/justice_home/fsj/privacy/docs/wpdocs/2008/wp153_en.pdf

Article 29 Working Party. Working Document on Frequently Asked Questions (FAQs) related to Binding Corporate Rules, 1271-02-02/08/EN WP 155 rev.03, 21 January 2009. Retrieved on June 30, 2009 from http://ec.europa.eu/justice_home/fsj/privacy/docs/wpdocs/2008/wp155_en.pdf

Bodil Lindqvist v Kammaraklagaren (Case C-101/01)

Campbell v MGN (2003) 1 All ER 224

Decision 2001/497/EC of 15 June 2001 on standard contractual clauses for the transfer of personal data to third countries under the Directive (OJ 2001 L181/19). Retrieved on June 30, 2009 from http://eur-lex.europa.eu/LexUriServ/LexUriServ.do?uri=OJ:L:2001:181:0019:0031:EN:PDF

Decision (2002/16/EC) of 27 December 2001 on standard contractual clauses for the transfer of personal data to third countries under the Directive (OJ 2002 L6/52). Retrieved on June 30, 2009 from http://eur-lex.europa.eu/LexUriServ/LexUriServ.do?uri=OJ:L:2002:006:0052:0062:EN:PDF

Decision 2004/915/EC of 27 December 2004 amending Decision 2001/497/EC as regards the introduction of an alternative set of standard contractual clauses for the transfer of personal data to third countries (OJ 2004 L385/74). Retrieved on June 30, 2009 from http://eur-lex.europa.eu/LexUriServ/LexUriServ.do?uri=OJ:L:2004:385:0074:0084:EN:PDF

Durant v Financial Services Authority (2003). EWCA Civ 1746

Durant v Financial Services Authority (unreported) (2002). Edmonton County Court

European Commission suggests UK's Data Protection Act is deficient (2004, July 15). *OUT-LAW News*. Retrieved on June 30, 2009 from http://www.out-law.com/page-4717

House of Lords. Minutes of proceedings, 29 November 2005. Retrieved on June 30 2009 from http://www.publications.parliament.uk/pa/ld200506/minutes/051129/ldminute.htm

ICC Task Force on Privacy and Protection of Personal Data. (2004, October 28). ICC report on binding corporate rules for international transfers of personal data. Retrieved on June 30, 2009 from http://www.iccwbo.org/home/ebitt/FINAL_ICC_BCRs_report.pdf

ICC Task Force on Privacy and the Protection of Personal Data. (2006, July 5). Standard application for approval of binding corporate rules for the transfer of personal data outside the EU (to be used in all EU member states). Retrieved on June 30, 2009 from http://www.iccwbo.org/uploadedFiles/ICC/policy/e-business/pages/Standard_Application_for_Approval_of_BCRs.pdf

ICO. (2003). Technical Guidance. International transfers/Transborder Data Flows - Guidance on the Use of Model Contract Clauses – data controllers established in the EU to data processors in countries outside the EU. Retrieved on June 30 2009 from http://www.ico.gov.uk/upload/documents/library/data_protection/practical_application/model_contracts_for_data_processors_processing_personal_information_on_their_behalf001001.pdf

ICO. (2006, February 27). Technical Guidance. The "Durant" case and its impact on the interpretation of the Data Protection 1998. Retrieved on June 30 2009 from http://www.ico.gov.uk/upload/documents/library/data_protection/detailed_specialist_guides/the_durant_case_and_its_impact_on_the_interpretation_of_the_data_protection_act.pdf

ICO. (2006, June 30). Technical Guidance. The Eighth Data Protection Principle and international data transfers. Retrieved on June 30 2009 from http://www.ico.gov.uk/upload/documents/library/data_protection/detailed_specialist_guides/international_transfers_legal_guidance_v3.0_171208.pdf

ICO. (2007, August 21). Technical Guidance. Determining what is personal data. Retrieved on June 30 2009 from http://www.ico.gov.uk/upload/documents/library/data_protection/detailed_specialist_guides/personal_data_flowchart_v1_with_preface001.pdf

ICO. (2009, January 28). Technical Guidance. Determining what information is 'data' for the purposes of the DPA. Retrieved on June 30 2009 from http://www.ico.gov.uk/upload/documents/library/data_protection/detailed_specialist_guides/what_is_data_for_the_purposes_of_the_dpa.pdf

Chapter 19
Restricted Access and Blocking Websites, Internet Regulations and Turkey Practices

Murat Erdal
Istanbul University, Turkey

Gulşah Ekiz
Galatasaray University, Turkey

Selim Aksin
Turkey Telecommunication Council, Turkey

Necmi Murat Güngör
Turkey Telecommunication Council, Turkey

ABSTRACT

In Turkey, access blocking to websites by judicial orders has especially come into spotlight with the blocking of globally renowned websites such as www.youtube.com and www.wordpress.com. After the police operations in 2006 concentrating on internet child pornography, the need for legal provisions to regulate internet has started to be widely discussed and Law No. 5651 on the Regulation of Publications on the Internet and Suppression of Crimes Committed by means of Such Publications was enacted on 25 May, 2007. This law has generally defined the actors related to internet and has regulated the access blocking in the scheme of suppression of the crimes listed below. Telecommunications Communication Presidency is entitled to the enforcement of the law that has come into effect as of 23 October 2007. This work aims to trace the short history of access blocking and try to assess the subject in the light of cases from the applications in Turkey.

INTRODUCTION

It is historically the peculiarity of new technology that it presents itself as a fact to the legislator long before the law seizes it. Internet has for a long time grown and thrived without engaging with the law, the virtual community that it had created was rather governed by *sui generis* regulation mechanisms. Is it possible to say that the

DOI: 10.4018/978-1-61520-975-0.ch019

legislator, the lawyer and the politician should remain silent to a technological revolution that is as important as the invention of printing press back in the day that links millions of people in the world, has become one of the major platforms of commerce and created a free flow of information? (de Fillon F., 1997) Clearly, the general principles of law were challenged by this new technology, which transcends national borders and cannot be governed by any public or private authority.

As a matter of fact, as of today, a number of States around the world have made efforts to block or delimit Internet access. Some states have blocked access entirely, rendering justifications like "protecting public from destructive thoughts" or "national security and integrity". Some states, only the ISPs that are under the guidance of the political power are allowed to operate and hence the inhabitants of that state can use the Internet within the frame that is approved by the government. Another limitation method is to register all the users in a system that allows the government to trace their every activity online (Reporters Sans Frontières, 1999).

The first Internet connection in Turkey was established in 12 April 1993 in Middle East Technical University and has developed widely ever since. According to www.internetworldstats.com, 26 million people use Internet in Turkey as of December 2008, which make up 35% of the population and 6.8% of the European users (http://www.internetworldstats.com/stats4.htm, 2009). Almost half of the Turkish Internet users are between age 15 and 24.(Mestçi, 2005) The expansion of Internet usage is also encouraged by the State as it is stated in the 8th five-year (2001-2005) development plan: "Internet access capacity will be elevated to the level that necessitates the international developments... the necessary legal and institutional regulations within the frame of international rules and standards will be made to provide information security." (DPT, 2009)

STATE INTERFERENCE TO CYBERSPACE IN TURKEY

In Turkey, state interference to Internet content has started with cases about crimes committed through the medium of Internet and continued with access blocking to websites by judicial orders. This has especially come into spotlight with the blocking of globally renowned websites such as www.youtube.com and www.wordpress.com in the recent years. Yet, Turkish Parliament had started regulating the Internet content in 2001 and the judiciary intervened hitherto within the frame of general provisions regulating expression and intellectual property.

During the period of absence of regulation governing the Internet, the courts have compared the position of a forum moderator to that of a newspaper editor, treating Internet related criminal cases like ordinary mass media cases for the application of the highly controversial article 159 of the previous Turkish Criminal Code (article 301 in the current Turkish Criminal Code, with slight changes) which makes it illegal to insult Turkey, the Turkish ethnicity, or Turkish government institutions. Court of Cessation reversed this ruling because of an amendment made to the article 159 and in some civil cases openly announced that claims made to get web pages taken-down or blocked should be rejected since there was no law governing the Internet (Akdeniz & Altıparmak, 2008). However the counterview is also argued in the Turkish doctrine for the crimes committed through the medium of the Internet. According to this view, when the possible means through which the crimes may be committed are defined, expressions like "all means of mass communication, all types of publication" are used and consequently the acts realized through the mass communication means that will appear in the future are also included in the scope of the regulation. (Öngören, 2000; Sınar, 2000)

The former President of Turkey, Ahmet Necdet Sezer also grounded his veto to the parliamentary bill proposed in 2001 which proposed to govern Internet according to the Press Code on the argument that the nature of Internet broadcasting differs than the written press. Nonetheless, the amendment made to the Press Code in May 2002 (with Law No. 4676) envisaged that the provisions of the Press Code concerning pecuniary and non-pecuniary damages arising from publishing lies, defamatory statements and similar acts would apply also to the Internet (Akdeniz & Altıparmak, 2008).

Until May 2007, there have been many cases of website access blocking in Turkey. An important number of these were obtained by MUYAP, the Turkish Phonographic Industry Society, starting from 2005, against the intellectual property infringements of the artists that the Society represents. The others mainly concerned insult against Turkish identity, terrorist propaganda, defamation and gambling. The highly controversial blocking access to YouTube at domain level in March 2007 was because of a video clip, which included defamatory statements about the founder of the Turkish Republic Mustafa Kemal Atatürk (Akdeniz & Altıparmak, 2008).

After the police operations in 2006 concentrating on Internet child pornography, the need for legal provisions to regulate Internet has started to be broadly discussed. The Prime Minister Recep Tayyip Erdoğan expressed the government's stance in the matter: "Come, let's fight against the virtual gangs that make Internet into arms, drugs and sexual deviance. Let's start a clean Internet campaign. We have concentrated our efforts as the government to establish the legal infrastructure. You, the internet service providers, content providers, users and Internet café owners, parents, teachers, journalists and the non-governmental organizations, join this campaign. Let's decontaminate the Internet. Let's make it into a safe area, a clean source of information and communication for our children."(Erdoğan, 2007)

The legal infrastructure that the Prime Minister was referring to was the draft bill prepared by the Ministry of Transportation which was enacted with little discussion on 4 May 2007 and promulgated on 22 May 2007 as the Law No. 5651 entitled "Regulation of Publications on the Internet and Suppression of Crimes Committed by means of Such Publication". (While some provisions (article 9) came into force immediately, other provisions such as those related to article 8 came into force on 23 November, 2007.) Both the statements of the Minister of Transportation and the explanatory memorandum of the Law underlines that the aim of the legislation is to fulfill the duty to protect the families, children and youth in accordance with the articles 41 (Protection of Family) and 58 (Protection of Youth) of the Constitution (TBMM, 2008). It should be also noted that German Tele Services Law and Convention on Cyber crime were taken into consideration while Law No. 5651 was prepared.

LAW NO. 5651

The first article of the Law No. 5651 entitled "Purpose and Scope" is as follows: "The purpose and the scope of this law is to regulate the principals and procedures related to the liability of the content providers, hosting providers, internet service providers and collective usage providers and suppression of certain crimes committed on the internet, through content, hosting and service providers."

It is clear from this article and the articles that follow that the Law foresees criminal responsibility as well as administrative and civil liability for the content providers, hosting providers, Internet service providers and collective usage providers when they do not comply with certain obligations (Figure 1).

Figure 1. Process Management of Law 5651. (Source: Turkey Telecommunication Council, 2009)

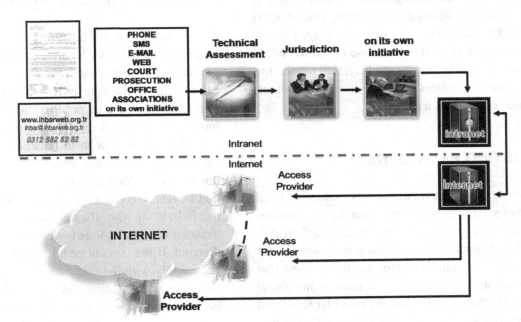

CONTENT PROVIDERS

The second article of the Law No. 5651 defines the content provider as "the natural or legal persons who produce, modify or provide any type of information or data that is presented to the users on the Internet". In this context, the content provider could be the person who prepares the content of a certain website or in forums a person who has the ability to put up or modify the messages written by other people (Sınar, 2001). Art. 4 states that the content provider is responsible for every type of content that he provides but will be responsible for the content that belongs to another person that he channels within the frame of general provisions only if it is clear from the presentation that he also embraces the certain content and intends the users to have access to it. Additionally, according to the Regulation issued in the Official Gazette Number: 26680, October 24, 2007 Wednesday on the rules and procedures set forth for issuance of operating certificate by the telecommunications authority to the access providers, content provider as well as

the hosting and internet service providers has the obligation to make available up-to-date information whose composition will be specified with an implementing regulation that allows the users on the Internet to identify them. Content providers who do not comply with this obligation faces an administrative fine given by the Telecommunications Communication Presidency with the amount between 2000 and 10000 Turkish Liras (approximately 1000 to 5000 euros).

COLLECTIVE USAGE PROVIDERS

This term is defined as "the persons who provide the facilities to use the Internet to other persons in a certain place for certain time" in Art. 2. This provision aims to cover the "Internet café owners" and according Art. 7, collective usage providers acting for commercial purposes have to obtain authorization from the civilian authority which will also inform the Telecommunications Communication Presidency and be responsible for supervision. The infringement of this obligation is penalized with an administrative fine of 3000 to 15000 Turkish Liras. Collective usage providers, regardless of their purpose (commercial or non-commercial) have the obligation to take the necessary measures to block access to content, which constitutes a crime.

HOSTING PROVIDERS

Hosting providers are defined as "natural or legal persons who provide and operate the systems which harbor the content and services" in Art. 2. According to Art. 5, Hosting providers do not have the obligation to monitor the content that it hosts and to ascertain that there is no illegal activity. However, the hosting provider is obliged to remove the content, when he is notified within the frame of Art. 8 and 9, which will be discussed subsequently, to the extent, which it is technically possible.

SERVICE PROVIDERS

In addition to the obligations of the hosting providers, service providers have to preserve the traffic information specified in the implementing regulation for a certain time that will be again specified in the implementing regulation (which shall be between 6 months and 2 years), to assure the accuracy, integrity and the confidentiality of this information and notify the Telecommunications Communication Presidency, content providers and its clients at least 3 months before it ceases activity and to deliver the traffic information to the Telecommunications Communication Presidency within the frame of procedures specified in the implementing regulation. Infringement of these obligations is penalized with an administrative fine of 10000 to 50000 Turkish Liras.

CIVIL LAW ASPECT OF LAW 5651

Article 9, brings a civil law provision which gives a right to individuals who alleges that their rights violated to ask the content provider, if cannot be reached to the hosting provider to remove the related content and to publish the reply that he has prepared for a week. The content of hosting provider complies with the demand in the two days which follow his notification. If he does not comply with the demand, it is considered that he has rejected it. If the demand is rejected the individual who alleges that his rights were violated invokes a judge to decide to execute the demand. If the content or hosting provider does not comply with the decision of the judge in the two days which follow his notification, he will be penalized with imprisonment from 6 months to two years. It should be noted that this article does not provide for blocking orders, instead the courts can only order the removal of the infringing content.

ACCESS BLOCKING AS A PROVISION OF LAW 5651

As we have mentioned, Law No. 5651 makes it an obligation to remove content and to block access in the existence of adequate suspicion that one of crimes that are listed in Art. 8 has occurred. The crimes that are listed are encouragement and incitement of suicide (article 84), sexual exploitation and abuse of children (article 103(1)), facilitation of the use of drugs (article 190), provision of dangerous substances for health (article 194), obscenity (article 226), prostitution (article 227), provision of means for gambling (article 228) and crimes committed against Atatürk (Law No. 5816, dated 25/7/1951). Lastly, betting websites and websites which enable users to play games of chance through the Internet with regards to football and other sports were included in the scope of the regulation (Table 1).

Table 1. Restricted website case examples in Turkey (related to Law No. 5651)

Type of the Website Which Is in the Scope of the Regulation	Jurisdiction - on its own initiative - Notification	City	Domain Name
Encouragement and incitement of suicide	----	----	-----
Sexual exploitation and abuse of children	on its own initiative - Notification	----	http://lolitas.alfasex.info/?1920 http://www.candy-teenies.com http://www.iwant18.com http://www.thehun.com http://reality-young.info http://www.hissetbeni.com/liseli-etek-alti.htm
Facilitation of the use of drugs and Provision of dangerous substances for health	Jurisdiction	Antalya	http://elephantos.com
Obscenity	Jurisdiction	Eskişehir Istanbul	http://www.youporn.com. http://www.gulcenneti.com
Prostitution	Jurisdiction	----	http://www travestiyiz.net http://www escorttravestiler.com
Provision of means for gambling	Jurisdiction	----	http://www glaxybetting.com http://www glaxybet.net http://www oyunagir.com http://www turkscore.com http://www.superbahis.com
Crimes committed against Atatürk	Jurisdiction	Sivas Denizli	208.65.153.251 --youtube.com 208.65.153.253 --youtube.com 208.65.153.238 --youtube.com http://www.slide.com http://www.tagged.com
Betting websites and websites which enable users to play games of chance	Jurisdiction	-----	http://www.glaxybetting.com http://www.glaxybet.net http://www.oyunagir.com http://www.turkscore.com http://www.hititbetcom
Terror campaign	Jurisdiction	Ankara	http://www.susaningulleri.net http://www.mucadeleci.com http://www.kiyamlardurmaz.com http://www.sehitlerkervani.com http://www.mustazaflar.com

Noncompliance with the order of access blocking will be penalized with imprisonment from six months to two years for the responsibles of hosting and service providers.

The measure of access blocking is highly controversial because of several reasons. First of all, it does not serve the purpose that is put forward by the legislator as a precautionary measure to suppress crime. Secondly the way the order is given and the authorities that have the capacity to give them do not comply with the principles of a democratic State. Thirdly, because of the first two reasons stated, access blocking orders delimit the freedom of expression in a way which is not compatible with the European Convention on Human Rights.

Art. 8 describes access blocking as precautionary measure in addition to the ones that are listed in Criminal Procedure Act. However, access blocking differs from these measures, since the ones in the Criminal Procedure Act, according to Akdeniz/Altıparmak "...aim to secure the

Figure 2. The main page of official website of telecommunications communication presidency, including related form pages to report in the existence of adequate suspicion that one of crimes that are listed in Art. 8 Has Occurred.

prosecution of criminals as well as the execution of the final judgments. They intend to keep the accused present and to reach the evidence of keep the evidence intact during prosecution and/or trial. On the other hand... blocking a website does not prevent the removal of evidence. Neither does it secure the presence of the accused. In other words, the measure envisaged under Law No. 5651 aims to prevent the continuous effects of a particular violation." Access blocking also differs from the police powers since "... those measures continue for a very short while. If the impugned act also constitutes a crime under criminal law, the prosecutor usually investigates the allegations. ... even if it is provisional, the measure adopted pursuant to article 8 applies for a very long time, in some cases indefinitely... More importantly some administrative blocking orders (with regards to foreign websites) issued by the Presidency are never brought to the attention of the Public Prosecutor. (Akdeniz & Altıparmak, 2008)

According to Art. 8, access blocking orders are given by a judge at the prosecution stage, by the Court during trial and by the Telecommunications Communication Presidency, *ex officio*, if the content or host providers are situated outside of Turkey and if it considers that there is adequate suspicion for the existence of sexual exploitation and abuse of children and obscenity even if the content and host providers are situated in Turkey (in this case the Presidency has to get its decision approved by a judge). Telecommunications Communication Presidency is an administrative body established in 2005 within the Telecommunications Authority which is an autonomous entity related to Ministry of Transportation. The Presidency is responsible for the surveillance of communications and execution of interception of communications warrants subject to Laws No. 2559, 2803, 2937 and 5271 (TİB, 2009). According to Art. 10 of the Law No. 5651, the Presidency has established a hotline to report potentially illegal content and activity subject to Art. 8 (Figure 2).

This capacity of the Presidency is found to be contrary to the separation of powers: "…the Law enables the Telecommunications Communication Presidency to determine whether there exists sufficient suspicion that the content of an impugned website constitutes a listed crime subject to article 8. Such a determination is a judicial activity and cannot be transferred to an administrative body... Although under Regulations 3, this decision shall be taken to a judge for the websites located in Turkey, no such requirement is envisaged for the websites based outside the Turkish jurisdiction. No doubt, recourse to judiciary is available upon blocking decisions according to article 8(12) of the Law. The law also provides that if the Presidency can establish the identities of those who are responsible for the content subject to the blocking orders the Presidency would request the Chief Public Prosecutor's Office to prosecute the perpetrators. However, considering that the Presidency does not inform the websites located outside the Turkish jurisdiction about its blocking decision and that generally websites located outside the jurisdiction have no legal representation in Turkey, the chances of getting a fair trial against the decisions of the Presidency is dim…". If the Presidency can establish the identities of those who are responsible for the content subject to the blocking orders the Presidency would request the Chief Public Prosecutor's Office to prosecute the perpetrators. This approach is evidently problematic, because all criminal allegations should be brought to the attention of Public Prosecutor's Office. It is not the duty of the Presidency to identify criminals. Furthermore, as explained above since the decision taken by the Presidency is quasi-judicial, all of them should be subject to judicial scrutiny." (Akdeniz & Altıparmak, 2008)

With the support of Turkish Ministry of Education, Information Technologies and Communications Council and Turkish Ministry of Transportation, an organizational web site "guvenliweb. org.tr (secureweb.org.tr) has been established (Figure 3). The mission of this website is to make the public but especially children, families and educators conscious of internet world which has been rapidly becoming widespread in every fields of our life. Within this context, while benefiting from internet, to form awareness about the possible dangers that come into our house, school and office and to foster the necessary cares.

This website also give reports about the number of Notification / Complaints, Number of Notificated Domain Names in Categorical Crimes and Restricted Web Site Statistics in Turkey (Table 2).

ACCESS BLOCKING WITHIN THE FRAME OF LAW NO. 5846

Access blocking is a legal remedy for intellectual property infringements provided under supplemental article 4 of the Law No. 5846 on Intellectual & Artistic Works (Table 3).

This provision was introduced in March 2004 and provides a two-stage approach. Initially the law requires the hosting companies, content providers, or access providers to take down the infringing article from their servers upon "notice" given to them by the right holders. The providers need to take action within 72hrs. If the allegedly infringing content is not taken down or there is no response from the providers, the right holders can ask the Public Prosecutor to provide for a blocking order, and the blocking order is executed within 72hrs.

CONCLUSION AND FUTURE TRENDS

Consequently, it is possible to conclude that access blocking orders can be obtained in three ways under Turkish law: temporary injunctions in the frame of general provisions, access blocking orders under Law No. 5651 and access blocking orders under Law No. 5846. With the clear problems on the legal context, it is hard to say that this kind

Figure 3. The main page of guvenliweb.org.tr.

Table 2. Number of notification / complaints, number of notificated domain names in categorical crimes and restricted web site statistics in turkey. (Source: http://www.guvenliweb.org.tr (updated 13.4.2009))

Number of Notification / Complaints	68.960
Number of Notificated Domain Names in Categorical Crimes:	17.047
Total Number of Restricted Web Site	1.874 (jurisdiction: 354, on its own initiative: 1.520)
Restricted Web Site Statistics Turkey (13.4.2009)	

Table 3. Restricted Website Cases in Turkey, Related to Law No. 5846

Type of the Website Which Is in the Scope of the Regulation	Access condition	Domain Name
Improper e-commerce and personal benefit	Restricted access	http://www. gelmp3indir.com
Improper e-commerce and personal benefit	Open	http://www.blogspot.com
Improper e-commerce and personal benefit	Open	http://www.alibaba.com

of limitation of freedom expression, being a human right protected by the European Convention on Human Rights will be able to pass the 3-part test (whether the interference is prescribed by law; whether the aim of the limitation is legitimate; whether the limitation is "necessary in a democratic society) required by the international jurisprudence.

Regulation of the Internet should be considered in the frame of new policies which are designed to provide protection from illegal and harmful Internet content wheras deliberations and decisions need to be transparent and democratic. Respect to freedom of speech and privacy of communication should also be taken into consideration.

Nevertheless, Law No. 5651 has closed a very important gap in Turkey and is the first substantive and seperate bill concerning Internet content regulation. Even though it has some contraversies, it is considered necessary. It is unexceptional that new regulations have problems in their application in the first years and the regulation will be improved with its application. It is also foreseen that the implementing regulations of the Law No. 5651 will be slightly modified when the Law No. 5809 (Law on Electronic Communications) concerning the infrastructure, network and services in electronic communications enters into force.

REFERENCES

Akdeniz, Y., & Altıparmak, K. (2008). *Internet: Restricted Access A Critical Assessment of Internet Content Regulation and Censorship in Turkey*. Retrieved January 10, 2009, from http://www.cyber-rights.org/reports/internet_restricted_bw.pdf.

Bilgi Teknolojileri ve Koordinasyon Dairesi Başkanlığı Web Sitesi (BTK). (n.d.). Information and Communication Technologies Authority Web Site. Retrieved April 5, 2009, from http://www.tk.gov.tr/Kurum_Hakkinda/Kurulus.htm.

de Fillon, F. (1997). *A.F.D.I.T. sous la direction de De Bellefonds. Internet Saisi Par le Droit*. Editions des Parques.

Erdoğan, T. (2007). Prime Minister Recep Tayyip Erdoğan's Addressing to the Nation, 30/01/2007. Retrieved April 06, 2009, from http://www.akparti.org.tr/haber.asp?haber_id=15449

Mestçi, A. (2005). Turkey Internet Report. Retrieved February 18, 2009, from www.internethaftasi.org.tr/hafta06/docs/turkiye-internet-raporu.pdf

Öngören, G. (2000). İnternet Yayıncılığında Hukuki Sorunlar. İnternet ve Hukuk Forumu'na Sunulan Yayınlanmamış Tebliğ, 14/04/2000, İstanbul.

Reporters Sans Frontières (RSF). (1999, August 9). *Press Release*. internetworldstats.com Web site (n.d.). Retrieved March 15, 2009, from http://www.internetworldstats.com/stats4.htm

Secure Web Portal. (2009). Retrieved April 12, 2009, from http://www.guvenliweb.org.tr

Sınar, H. (2000), İnternetin Ortaya Çıkardığı Hukuki Sorunlara Bir Ceza Hukuku Yaklaşımı. MHB – Yılmaz Altuğ'a Armağan, Yıl:17-18, İstanbul.

Sınar, H. (2001). *İnternet ve Ceza Hukuku*. İstanbul: Beta Yayınları.

Sitesi, D. P. T. W. (DPT) (n.d.). T.R. Prime Ministry State Planning Organization Web Site. Retrieved March 03, 2009, from http://ekutup.dpt.gov.tr/plan/plan8.pdf

Telekomünikasyon İletişim Başkanlığı (TİB). (2009). Telecommunication Council Web site. Retrieved March 22, 2009, from http://www.tib.gov.tr/baskanlik_gorevleri.html

Türkiye Büyük Millet Meclisi (TBMM). (n.d.). The Grand National Assembly of Turkey Web Site. Retrieved March 22, 2009, http://www.tbmm.gov.tr/sirasayi/donem22/yil01/ss1397m.htm

Section 3
Protection of Privacy and Trust

Chapter 20
Hardware Secure Access to Servers and Applications

J. A. Álvarez Bermejo
Universidad de Almería, Spain

J. A. López Ramos
Universidad de Almería, Spain

F. Gálvez Sánchez
Universidad de Almería, Spain

ABSTRACT

In this work, we propose a powerful yet inexpensive method for protecting and discriminating unauthorized accesses to sensible digital information (or even to the entire system) via common and conventional tools such as USB devices. The result of this work allows that the access to servers or the execution and access to specific data, take place only under a controlled and defined scenario.

INTRODUCTION

Current legislation at every country provides means to regulate the use and control of digital information (an useful standard to ensure a certain structured information security risk assessment can be found under the norm ISO/IEC 27002), specifically if its character compromises the private sphere or intimacy of persons. Operating systems provides standard protection methods, but nothing can be done to protect the data if the use of the operating system is not adequate (uncontrolled software installation may produce data stealing via Trojans, etc.). In addition, one may

consider how security is at hand of everybody. Abelson, Ledeen & Lewis (2008) underlined two unexpected behaviours experienced in the new digital era we are now living in (1) people give up their privacy too easily, and in the process may give up third party's privacy, and (2) little brother is watching, even non-experienced kids may run scripts to attack your data. Cryptography plays an important role offering privacy nowadays although few users employ it.

In this chapter we propose a system for granting secure access to stored data and even to applications that deal with them, based on a protocol of sharing secrets. The aim of this software is to avoid unauthorized uses of programs and their related data or even a whole system. Operating systems

DOI: 10.4018/978-1-61520-975-0.ch020

are in charge of protecting us from intrusions and our software will be responsible of converting the stolen information into a useless chunk of bits.

Restricted access to information stored in a system is turned into an issue of truly vital importance in certain circumstances. When access to such information is a privilege of only one person then it is usual that this information is encrypted using a symmetric cryptosystem, where the secret key is a property of the owner of the information. PGP (http://www.pgpi.org/) is a protocol that can be used to that end. However a problem arises when protected data should be accessible for a group of people and not only for a unique user. In that case, making copies of the key used to protect the information and giving them to authorized people is something that decreases the level of security in a significant way. *Secret sharing schemes come to the rescue in such scenario* (Menezes, A., 1996; Schneier, B., 2003). These algorithms are protocols that allow the sharing of the key used to protect the information in such a way that the original key can be recovered from a minimum number (maybe all) of the shares and, even if a lesser number keys are present such shares does not reveal any information about the shared key. Another issue of interest regarding the security scheme is one that has to do with length of the key. Keys used for any cryptosystem and thus, also the shares, are excessively long to be memorized which makes necessary providing any storing method, making the key susceptible of being stolen.

In this chapter we present an implementation that provides a security system based in USB devices for protecting data and applications on information systems, this can be carried out in an individual, shared or hierarchical way, also preventing the key or any sharing from being stolen was a desired objective. Section 2 will introduce the foundations of the cryptography used. Section 3 will show a roadmap of the decisions taken for choosing the Operating System where the software was to be deployed in, the language to build the

software, the way of using the USB device in order to use the secret sharing, etc. Section 4 will show the implementation details, how we dealt with big numbers. Section 5 will show the conclusions and issues to be improved.

2 BACKGROUND: CRYPTOGRAPHIC AND SECURITY BASIS

Secret keys used in cryptographic protocols give raise to several practical problems concerning key generation, storing and distribution. The most efficient solution to these is to keep the key in a unique and safe place, known only by its owner. However, in this way we have the risk that the information protected by the key becomes completely inaccessible if the owner loses it. Additionally, in many practical cases we need to distribute the key between the members of a group in such a way that it cannot be recovered without the cooperation of a minimal number of such persons. This scheme is especially suitable in the case that the secret is a responsibility of a group and not only a unique person due to the high level of privacy required (Lederman, 2004; Peterson, 2005; Tang, 2008).

Likewise, in some situations it could be necessary that the recovering of a determined secret key must be done in absence of its direct responsible, i.e. a key can be recovered by its owner or determined hierarchical groups chosen by him/her to this end. This can be done making that some of the shares of the key have a preferential role to others (Menezes, van Oorscht & Vanstone, 1996).

Key Generation

One of the initial problems to solve is the generation of the secret key, since it is clear, the fortress of our system lays on the security of the key. One possible solution to this is to use a hash algorithm such as MD5 (Menezes, 1996; Schneier, 2003). MD5 generates a hexadecimal 128 digits value in function of an initial value called seed. We have to take into account that the value of key should be as randomized as possible and, in order to generate different secrets each time, we use, jointly with a key phrase or word that can be changed at any moment, a mark of time given for a real time clock (with precision up to milliseconds, for example). The output of MD5 will be the secret S that we will use as our secret key in our system.

Once we have generated the value of the secret S, the next step is the distribution of such secret in as many parts as the final user of the application requires.

Secret Sharing

The aim of our application is, as noted above, to block a system by means of a secret key that is distributed between a group of authorized participants. In first place we have to know, on one hand, the total number of shares of the secret key that we want to create and, on the other hand, the minimal number of such shares needed to recover the key. This information will be given by the end user of the application.

Let us assume that we have decided the number of shares needed to recover the key and suppose that this number is k. Then we generate k-2 random numbers that, jointly the secret key S, will determine a polynomial of degree k-1, p(x), where the independent term is precisely S. Then we create the shares given by pairs of values (a,p(a)), where p(a) denotes the evaluation of p(x) in a. Since any polynomial of degree k-1 is determined by the interpolation of k points in the plane, the recovering of p(x) can only be done by the use of k shares (a,p(a)), i.e., the threshold of authorized shares required by our system. What we are doing in fact is to use the Shamir's threshold scheme for sharing secrets (Menezes, 1996; Schneier, 2003).

Two aspects to take into account of this method are the possibility of creating or eliminating shares dynamically without affecting the others or modifying the value of the shared secret.

Let us give finally some remarks on the implementation. As noted before, to create the shares of the secret S we only have to evaluate the generated polynomial whose independent term is S. We can do this in an efficient way by using the FFT algorithm (cf Chapter 21 of Childs' book). The reconstruction process is nothing else but an interpolation algorithm which can be considered, in some way, also an evaluation process and so we can also use FFT to recover the polynomial p(x) from the shares (a,p(a)), and so, the secret key S. From the point of view of Coding Theory, Shamir's threshold scheme can be considered as a particular case of codification with a Reed-Solomon code and such codes can be implemented in an efficient form using the FFT (Blahout, 1984; McEliece, 1981).

3 ISSUES, CONTROVERSIES, PROBLEMS: CONSIDERATIONS FOR BUILDING THE SYSTEM

Controlling who accesses the data is almost a solved problem; one can implement security policies inside the operating system, and so on. But controlling how the data is to be used turns out to be a much more complex issue. It is necessary to have a tool or an application that hinders the access to the system unless a minimum number of valid shares are introduced. In this section we present our proposed solution to this issue. This section establishes the design decisions and the problems encountered (and how they were solved) when planning the development of this tool.

Our application is divided in two separate parts: a *key generator* and an *agent*. The agent is in charge of locking/unlocking system/data access regarding the absence/presence of the keys. Basically, the key generator has to develop four tasks, listed below.

1. Getting the necessary parameters given by the user.

2. Generating the shares in function of the introduced parameters.
3. Storing the data in the Operating System.
4. Storing the shares into the authorized USB devices.

The first two tasks are related to what we have exposed until the moment, applying Shamir's threshold method. The two other tasks depend on the selected Operating System / language.

Preventing that an attacker gets the polynomial used to generate the shares would avoid compromising our security system. However, the security of our application lays on the fact that the polynomial used is not stored at any place. It disappears once the shares have been generated. We only have to know the value of the secret given by such polynomial. This value has to be stored in some place accessible by the System. This is what the third task is in charge of (storing in a place secured by the operating system). Once the system is blocked, to release the lock, it is necessary to get the polynomial used at the beginning. This is only possible by collecting the minimum number of shares specified by the user at the first step of our protocol. In order to maintain the shares stored in separated places, it is required to have a versatile system. This is what the last task that our *Key Generator* should do: segregating the shares, storing them in different storage devices –USB devices-. On the other hand, our *Agent* must block any attempt of accessing the system until the required shares are gathered and checked against the Operating System's protected key. Once the system is blocked, it will not be possible to execute any task or action on it. The system is, therefore, isolated in the absence of the required shares.

Once the application is briefly described, and prior to the reveal the implementation details, it is necessary to describe all the decisions we went through. These decisions may help to understand the implementation.

3.1 The Operating System Election

We shall start the design considerations by dissecting the decision of the platform we should build our security system on, due to the inherent importance of the OS regarding integral security on a computer. There is a key paragraph in the book from Howard & Leblanc (2003) that we are going to quote in order to underline how important is to care about the limits between applications and data:

"The principle of least privilege states that you should give a user the ability to do what he needs to do and nothing more. Properly defining the boundary between your application binaries and user data will also make your application easier to secure."

One of the critical issues regarding system's protection is the Operating System that manages its resources. Microsoft's Operating Systems, whether those installed in conventional desktops or those running on server platforms, are characterized by leaving almost none of the vast operational possibilities offered by an OS on the user's shoulders. On the other hand, Linux/Unix based OS allow users to take decisions of extreme importance (only recommended for five-star wizards), decisions ranging from *which modules should the OS load as a part of the kernel* to *replacing the TCP/IP stack for a particular communications module implementation.*

Windows XP can be considered to be one of the most stable OS from Microsoft ever. Recent attempts from Microsoft to evolve in the OS market (Windows Vista) did not succeeded as expected, the reason why could be found in the new strategies adopted that considered Vista's kernel as part of the dotNet framework. Vista is supported by a kernel whose functionality is clearly based on the dotNet platform. Integrating this platform as part of the OS core is considered to be the most aggressive turn adopted from Microsoft, for shifting the legacy Operating System into a modular approximation (as Linux / Unix OS). This new bet is based on an abstraction layer that offers a common execution environment (CLR) to all languages property of the giant of Seattle. Because of this, Vista is dangerously supported by a modular virtual machine that acts as its own kernel. Windows Vista is a system that succeeds in protecting from intrusions (and malware). Its modular Linux-like kernel, allows implementing layered security policies as advised in Smith & Komar (2005) work. Thus, any OS service is provided via this virtual machine. Executable programs have also to follow the guidelines imposed by the specifications that define this virtual machine, which means that executable programs are easily submitted to reverse engineering techniques. On the other hand, Vista also allows native executable programs to run and request OS services but these programs will not receive the same attentions from the OS that a program compiled for the virtual machine (which is part of the OS itself), the performance is, therefore, negatively affected.

3.1.1 Accessing Hardware Resources from NTVDM: Maybe not a Security Issue

Windows Vista still incorporates the old and well known 16 bits DEBUG program. It is supposed that accesses to hardware resources should be filtered by the OS (especially because this implies accessing to restricted memory addresses). If an ms-dos console (ntvdm process) is started, then, within it the DEBUG program can be run. To change the pointer to the data segment register, it will suffice to type RDS and press intro. Simply change it to B800 and, we will be indicating the OS to point into that address, which is the video memory buffer, where all the characters that will be shown on the screen are stored. To write any string (for instance, 1 2 3 4), it is enough to type the following: F 0 1000 A D. What we are doing

is forcing the repetition of a given byte pattern (0xAD) in the video memory buffer.

3.1.2 Reverse Engineering

An important aspect of the security system that we implemented is the strength of the executables. For this reason, and because we consider Vista as a yet immature Operating System, Windows XP was adopted as the preferred Operating System. Moreover, the number of XP Operating Systems in production is very high. In fact, as abovementioned, the main disadvantage found in Vista is that the specification of the virtual machine that it is based on (CLR – framework dotNet) is public and therefore the executable programs (based assemblies for that virtual architecture) may be easily reverted to expose their source code, situation that should be avoided at any expense. Exposing the source code can reveal exploitable defects of your code that could result in a severe security flaw (Howard & Leblanc, 2005). The best example to show the weakness of these assemblies can be found in a software product named *dotNet reflector* which can be downloaded with no charge from http://www.red-gate.com/products/reflector/. Given the abovementioned considerations, the election of Windows XP as a platform to develop our security system is justified.

3.2 The Language Choice: ¿Bytecode or Native?

When selecting a programming language we should choose the one that interact the best as possible with the target Operating System.

In June 2000, Microsoft presented the *dotNet* framework as a platform (as we stated before it really is a virtual machine) that provides a "language independent" environment where applications could be developed (mainly for Windows OS) and interoperate in a secure and easy way. The *dotNet* platform has been shown as an efficient alternative to the platform designed by Sun Microsystems,

J2EE, and introduced to developers of distributed applications as the most intelligent choice. This offer to distributed applications developers is evident, given the extensive support that dotNet offers for the developing of Web services and Web applications.

The set of aggregated components designed for dotNet are called *dotNet framework* and is composed of the CLR, a hierarchy of libraries of classes and support for different types of applications, including legacy client–server applications, Web applications and Web services. Moreover, dotNet offers database access libraries and XML management predefined libraries, being XML for this platform an interoperation standard. The CLR is part of the framework dotNet core. It is in charge of providing an abstraction layer between dotNet "bytecode" (known as Intermediate Language or IL) and the hardware platform it is executed on (for instance, x86 architectures and compatibles). This abstraction layer, equivalent to the Java virtual machine – JVM – in the J2SE environment, has serious issues regarding security and development of applications. In essence the CLR avoids the developer to face low level details of the target platform when writing applications, being the CLR itself the only one that can, on behalf of the developer, access to the memory and directly manage pointers, in brief it abstracts hardware. In addition, the code developed for the dotNet framework is executed under certain configurable security "roles", depending if the code is tagged as "trusted" code and on its source (Intranet, Internet, etc.). So the programmer has no direct access to the native management of the memory. Any compiler that generates code for the dotNet platform has to generate it in an intermediate language, IL, which is bound to a specification (CLS). The obtained IL will be translated to native code using JUST-IN-TIME strategies, so the time overhead due to this intermediate layer is almost inappreciable.

3.2.1 Is dotNet a More Secure Platform than J2SE/Java?

Doubtlessly, the dotNet framework is an execution environment much more controlled than the standard environment offered by Windows OS. This does not mean that the dotNet framework lacks security flaws. In fact there are plenty of security issues waiting for the dotNet developer. It is fair to underline that the dotNet framework was designed with all security issues that Java suffered, in mind. It can be said that dotNet learnt from the errors that Java had at its beginnings, but this can be also self-defeating since it has not initiated the development from scratch as Java did and this lack of experience can be also a reason for mistrust.

Certainly, even in the case that the dotNet framework was the most secure platform ever, the last word is to be said by the developer, he/she is the only one responsible of the potential risks that could compromise the security of the application. It is the developer who in plenty of cases ignores the basic principles of secure programming. Two instructive readings that every developer should have on-the-shelf are the books from Howard & Leblanc (2003) and from McConnell (2004). In the case of the dotNet platform, all the security is relied on the Operating System (XP shared it among the system and the native executable format). The CLR does no offer protection against faulty code containing programming errors or that unnecessarily exposes private or compromising information.

Security in the dotNet platform is further compromised with keywords like "unsafe" that allow third party components (note that these components may have explicit references to memory o native memory/resources management) to be considered as managed code (code able to run on the CLR). Unsafe keyword is an interesting keyword from the security point of view. Let us suppose that a Web application manages the request and entry of data from users with a module/component developed using C# (managed code). After processing this information, inputs are transmitted to an "unmanaged code" that accesses to the shared memory of a certain third party component. This component is in charge of communicating with corporative servers. Under this scenario it could be possible that the code executed under the unmanaged section boundaries had errors. Therefore, it could be possible for a user to cause a runtime error in the application or even worse, it could be possible for the user to execute arbitrary code. For this reason, the unsafe keyword should be avoided whenever it is possible since it cancels all the security walls that the framework and the CLR offer to the applications.

When developing code that is to be executed at the client-side it is important to remember that the user could manipulate and interrupt the execution independently that this code has been developed using Java, any of the languages for the dotNet framework or in a language that could be compiled to native code (C++ / C, etc.). With patience and time, the code could be submitted to techniques such as the reverse engineering, techniques that would show relevant details. For this reason it is recommended not to forget to apply as most secure codification techniques as possible together with the adoption of programming habits like not including sensible information as passwords in executable files.

Java bytecodes as well as dotNet IL assemblies can be easily reversed using reverse engineering techniques, of course, easier than when using native executables in a native platform. This is due to the fact that dotNet and Java have an intermediate abstraction layer that relies on an easy and clear specification. Thus, the understanding of the executables for these platforms (there exist tools such as dotfuscator designed for hindering these practices) is easier than trying to "decompile" the native executables (i.e., those executables that will be executed directly using the instructions from the processors' ISA).

To conclude this section, we could state that the dotNet framework offers many enhancements concerning security and improvements to facilitate the development of distributed applications. Although the J2SE development platform is much more mature when compared to the dotNet framework, there are a number of advantages when executing IL managed code, in addition, the CLR has learnt from the attacks against Java, avoiding plenty of the attacks known up-to-date. However, it is important to remember that faults and errors introduced by developers are undetectable and perhaps, attackers are more interested in exploiting these implementations errors and accessing the company data rather than getting access to the server where the application is being executed.

The choice of our execution environment was formed by Windows XP due to the abovementioned security considerations. XP also provides an interesting API to access certain advanced functionality offered by the Operating System. Therefore, the ability to use this API is important for deploying our security system. The choice of the programming language is, therefore, conditioned to provide facilities for accessing the mentioned APIs. The choice of a native language, given the security considerations for the dotNet framework (or Java platform) is the best option. dotNet was discarded because even with the obfuscation techniques, the system could be easily compromised. Therefore, for the development of our application, the language of our choice was Visual Basic 6.0. One of the key points for choosing Visual Basic 6.0 was the fact that it is pretty integrated with the Operating System (therefore its API can be accessed easily), another point was that in compiles to native (check to disable the p-code option).

3.3 USB and MiniSD Cards: The Storage Solution for our Share

USB devices have been used mainly as storage devices. The reason for this are two: (1) it is a fast

Figure 1. Internal description for a common USB Pen-Drive unit

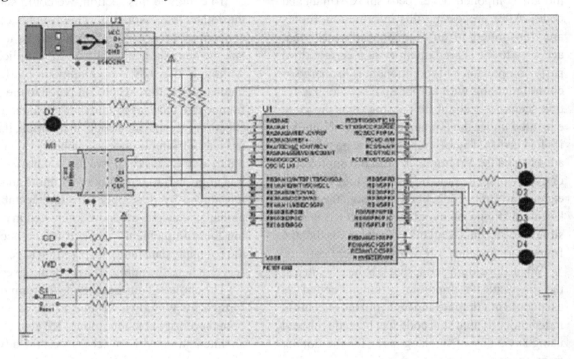

and flexible interface, and (2) devices that uses this protocol can be auto-fed devices, because USB wires transports data and power. This last characteristic allows the existence of small storage devices, known as "pen-drives". Figure 1 shows an internal scheme of one of these devices. *The figure was taken from the* **ISIS design suite**, *property of* **Lab Center Electronics**. There we can observe the NAND-flash card that serves as storage for the keys. The write / read controller (where further security extensions could be implemented by means of drivers that could hinder accesses to the shares by blocking the reads under certain conditions), and the USB interface that carries out the two differential lines of data and power.

The PIC that usually incorporates pen-drives is an intelligent circuit that has a small program capable of interpreting orders coming from the data lines that are given by the USB connection. This PIC is in charge of sending the precise orders to the SD memory to store the BYTES that the PIC

sends or read the BYTES that the PIC asks for. Thus it can be used to extend our security system.

Once that we selected the OS to develop our solution, the language that we will use and which hardware will give support to the shares, we are ready to talk about the implementations details of the software. Section 4, will be devoted to this issue.

4 SOLUTIONS AND RECOMMENDATIONS: IMPLEMENTATION OF THE SECURITY SYSTEM

One of the main characteristics of our software is that the system is only accessible when the required shares, that each authorized person owns, are gathered. This means that accesses to the system should be blocked unless all the required shares are provided to the Security System. An advanced blocking scheme was developed to implement the cited limitations; the security system needs, therefore, to block special keys shortcuts such as the WinKey, disabling the Windows' Start button, hiding the task bar, minimizing all the windows (Winkey + M), disabling the "Administrator Tasks" window and blocking accesses to the Windows Register. The Windows Register is an especial area secured by the OS that keeps key values for the OS itself and for certain user and system applications.

Our system is divided into two separated parts. On one hand, a *Key Generator* was developed, this generator implements mathematical functions that provides all the support and flexibility necessary to use Shamir's threshold methods. On the other hand, an *Agent* was also developed. This *Agent* will be in charge of blocking the system or any other chosen program while the keys, created by the *Key Generator*, are missing.

The Security System divides its scope into two important areas. Firstly, the mathematical area, for facing everything related to the generation of the key and shares and, secondly, the hardware side, that is in charge of providing support in reading and writing to and from USB storage devices, blocking the OS and offering means for interacting with the Windows Register; that although this second area it is not truly hardware related but it deals with low-level functions contained the Windows API. The Security System implementation also needed to be complemented with support provided by third party libraries.

One of the most important problems that arose when using Visual Basic 6.0 was its built-in limitations when working with big numbers (lengthy numbers). In general, no language has any data types to internally represent huge numbers, but they implement classes or specific libraries to emulate the numbers and their arithmetic operations. An example is the BigInteger library (http://java.sun.com/) implemented for the Java language and virtual machine. Diving into details for each one of the third party libraries used escapes from the scope of this chapter, instead, we kindly

recommend to the reader to review the books collection and webs referred in the bibliography. Next, we provide a brief description of the third party libraries used.

- Library SysNagra.dll for dealing with big numbers.
- Library EventVB.dll for facing the interaction with the keyboard and the Mouse.
- Windows API for interacting with the Windows Register.
- Windows API for interacting with USB devices.
- Other functions implemented by ourselves.

As abovementioned, Visual Basic 6.0 lacks data types that can internally represent lengthy (big) numbers. This is not completely true. It does have a sort of data type that can be used for trickily storing big numbers: the String type. Its use allowed us to work with numbers with even more than 100 digits. This means that the only way of working with big numbers is to store and treat them as Strings -another reason for choosing VB 6.0, because the dotNet languages suffers from immutable Strings, byte arrays should be used instead, see Howard & Leblanc (2003)-. This implies that all mathematical operations as addition or subtraction, should be implemented from scratch. Since Visual Basic 6.0 does not support these operations for Strings, these and other operations, much more complex are what SysNagra. dll deals with. Its general workings are exposed:

First, it gets two Strings, each one with arbitrary length numbers. Then, strings are treated in arithmetic operations as usual, but simply considering the actual numbers implicated in the operation (one digit from each string) and ignoring the rest of the characters (digits), without caring about the length. Each character is converted into a digit and operated with its peer "digit" in the other string.

Furthermore, to accelerate the calculus, the operations are carried out in binary. First a number of an arbitrary length is introduced and converted into a string. Then, using a function from this library, we store this value in a register and transform it into binary. Then the desired operation is carried out and the result is converted again from binary to a string to view the result. Specifying if numbers (the string) are decimal or hexadecimal is necessary since binary conversions differs, being the hexadecimal conversions faster than the decimal one, for obvious reasons. The library implements the following algorithms: AES, DES, 3DES, IDEA, SHA1, CRC16 and CRC32, LRC.

In order to be able to provide consistency to our security system it is not enough to have an "unbreakable" key. We need to eliminate all other ways of accessing the system that are not considered within our application. It is not useful to have a secure key if we could avoid the security restrictions by simply invoking the "Tasks Administrator" (CTRL+ALT+DEL shortcut) and then kill the processes that are part of the Security System. Therefore it is necessary, to disable all functionalities related to the keyboard and mouse. This way the user-OS interactions are truly limited and he/she cannot send key combinations to get the responses from the OS.

Without entering in deep implementations details, we can underline that the general form in which the library EventVB.dll (that contains tens of classes with different functionalities and that we use only a few) acts is to detect that an event has been produced by pressing a key and, if the code of that key matches with the key that we want to control, instead of executing the expected action, another action is executed, in this case, ignoring the key. Thus, basically, if we want to avoid the option that an attacker could kill our processes or avoid it without using the authorized keys, we simply need to tell the keyboard to ignore those key interruptions. Therefore, the reason why we use this library is that, allowing the blocking of

those keys events that could interfere with the correct working of our security system. So, capturing the action of the following key combinations, ALT+F4 (which causes the focused application to be closed), CTRL+ESC (the Windows Menu), ALT+TAB (switching applications) and the Winkey that launches the initial menu is a mandatory task.

4.1 Agent Implementation

The *Agent* is a program whose mission is to work in a transparent manner (backgrounded as an operating service or resident task). Figure 2 pretends to describe briefly using a flow diagram how this *agent* works.

The first time that the service is started, the *agent* blocks the system. The condition for releasing the lock or for maintaining it, is checked when USB devices are inserted. As it is shown in the flow scheme depicted in Figure 2, this condition is evaluated each certain period of time (as the current USB implementations are not interrupt-driven, trusting on events/OS signals, may negatively affect the effectiveness of the security system). With the forthcoming USB 3.0 protocol specifications, our system will be able to use interruptions for triggering blocking/unblocking without needing to manage events or using the, always annoying, polling techniques.

Once the insertion of keys is initiated, the *agent* has to start the module for Checking Inserted Keys. This module is prepared to receive a number of keys (this information is stored in the OS register and the agents takes it into consideration). The module, Check Inserted Keys has to wait the insertion of a minimum number of pre-established shares. Once the condition is satisfied, this means that all inserted keys are valid, the secret will be recovered and validated. The secret is a value stored in the Windows Register. Storing information in the register is an extended practice in Microsoft Operating Systems. The register is a hierarchical database that allows storing configuration values,

Figure 2. Brief flow diagram for depicting how the agent works

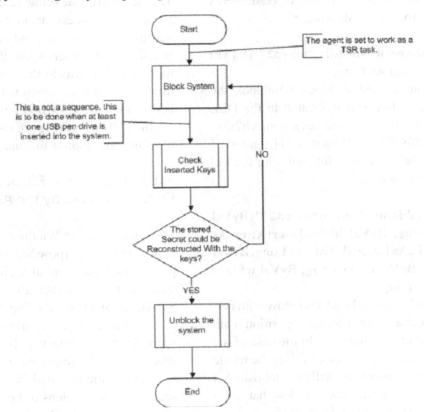

licences, etc. for applications and the OS itself. Its utility is evident and its sensibility is high. Operating Systems offer high security in accessing the register (check section 4.4 some security considerations to be applied in the Operating System-The Windows Register). After checking if the secret recovered gives a valid key, the agent will unblock the system or maintain it blocked, otherwise.

4.1.1 APIs Used to Implement the Agent

DLLs used to implement the *Agent* were user32.dll and kernel32.dll. Next, a relation of the functions used from each DLL to block / unblock the system is presented.

Function BlockInput Lib "user32" (ByVal fBlockIt As Long) As Long
Function located inside the DLL user32, and it has been supported since the OS version Windows 2000 / Windows 98. Its mission is to block events coming from the keyboard and mouse whenever the parameter fBlockIt is true. The most important characteristic of this function is that the thread of execution that initiated the blocking is the only one authorized to unblocking the events. Therefore only the *Agent* will be able to unblock them.

Function GetDriveType Lib "kernel32" Alias "GetDriveTypeA" (ByVal nDrive As String) As Long
This function, extracted from the library kernel32.dll allows identifying if a disk drive, identified by the Operating System is a fixed unit, extractable,

USB, etc. This function is used to read shares exclusively from the USB units.

Function ShowCursor Lib "user32" (ByVal bShow As Long) As Long

This function is used to block / unblock the pointer of the Mouse. It is located in the DLL user32.dll. In [http://www.devx.com/vb2the-max/Door/18897?cat=1680&type=1] a group of functions to be invoked to interact with the I/O subsystem can be found.

Function SetWindowPos Lib "user32"" (ByVal hwnd As Long, ByVal hWndInsertAfter As Long, ByVal x As Long, ByVal y As Long, ByVal cx As Long, ByVal cy As Long, ByVal wFlags As Long) As Long

This function is used to build a window with certain dimensions and in a predefined position (with respect to the other windows). In the case of the agent, its window will be placed filling the whole screen and its Z-coordinate will be established at 0, in such a way that any other window that could be opened remains behind the Agent's.

Function FindWindow Lib "user32" Alias "FindWindowA" (ByVal lpClassName As String, ByVal lpWindowName As String) As Long

This function is used for the *Agent* to identify the window that is over all the others. Evidently the *Agent* has to check that the window on top of the rest is its own windows and no other application's window that could reveal sensible information.

Function ShowWindow Lib "user32" (ByVal hwnd As Long, ByVal nCmdShow As Long) As Long

This function is used to allow the *Agent* to determine the state of visualization of all the windows.

Sub Sleep Lib "kernel32" (ByVal dwMilliseconds As Long)

This function inside kernel32.dll is used to activate / deactivate a process/thread in sleep state (does not waste CPU cycles except when they're awakened or activated, then the process / thread accomplishes its task and returns to the sleepy stated). It was used to provide the *Agent* with the capability of being in the system without disturbing, only using the CPU when keys are inserted, or when the blocking condition is to change.

4.1.2 Detail of the Block / Unblock Functions Used by the Agent

The agent uses the Windows Register, as noted above. For this purpose we have used the advapi32.dll (advanced api dll). This dynamic library contains functions that allow accessing to the System Register for reading / writing values in it. Evidently advapi only allows accesses granted according to the security policies in use. It is here where arises the importance of considering the recommendations stated in section 4.4, (Some security considerations to be applied in the Operating System-The Windows Register).

Following figures will help to illustrate the blocking and unblocking process driven by the agent. Figures are taken from the online resource in (Alvarez, J.A, & Lopez, J.A, & Galvez, F., 2009). Initially, as Figure 3 shows, the whole system is blocked avoiding any kind of interaction. The agent blocks it until all keys are inserted.

In Figure 4, the first key (which is stored in a common USB pen drive) is inserted, the agent recognizes it as a valid key and proceed to inform that there are still more keys to be inserted to unlock the system.

Figure 5 shows how the system unlocks after the minimum set of required keys are inserted, and all are valid. Once the agent gets all the keys, the agent builds and checks the secret. If keys are valid, the secret is valid as well, so the system is unlocked.

Once the system is unlocked, it can be locked back again by simply clicking on the tray icon

Table 1.

Block()	Unblock()
BlockInput True ' Hide desktop icons (desktop window) Dim Hwd As Long Dim rtn As Long Hwd = FindWindow("Progman", vbNullString) rtn = ShowWindow(Hwd, SW_HIDE) ' Hide task bar Hwd = FindWindow("Shell_traywnd", vbNullString) rtn = ShowWindow(Hwd, SW_HIDE) ' Minimize windows (Win+M) keybd_event VK_LWIN, 0, 0, 0 keybd_event Asc("M"), 0, 0, 0 keybd_event VK_LWIN, 0, KEYEVENTF_KEYUP, 0 Call SetWindowPos(Me.hwnd, -1, 0, 0, 0, 0, 3) 'Disable task's manager CallSaveDWSetting("Microsoft", "Windows\CurrentVersion\Policies\System", "DisableTaskMgr", 1, HKEY_CURRENT_USER)	BlockInput False ' Show icons (desktop window) Dim Hwd As Long Dim rtn As Long Hwd = FindWindow("Progman", vbNullString) rtn = ShowWindow(Hwd, SW_RESTORE) ' show task bar Hwd = FindWindow("Shell_traywnd", vbNullString) rtn = ShowWindow(Hwd, SW_RESTORE) ' Enable task manager Call SaveDWSetting("Microsoft", "Windows\CurrentVersion\Policies\System", "DisableTaskMgr", 0, HKEY_CURRENT_USER)

Figure 3. System blocked by the agent

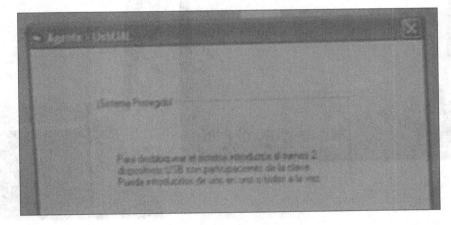

that represents to the security application agent. Doing this, the system will be blocked until all keys are inserted again.

4.2 Implementation of the Key Generator

The Key Generator is the kernel of the whole system and it is in charge of creating the secret, the shares and storing them in a safe place inside the Windows register. In the election of the method for storing they keys, MD5 was selected and on how to share the secret Shamir's threshold scheme was the chosen and we implemented the process to build the shares and recover the secret using the Fast Fourier Transform (FFT), method that relies the real efficiency of the system proposed.

To implement this system a series of procedures were needed, such as selecting the number of shares that were to be created, selecting the minimum number of shares needed to recover the secret, generating randomized numbers when

Figure 4. After inserting 1 of 2 keys. System informs that another key should be inserted

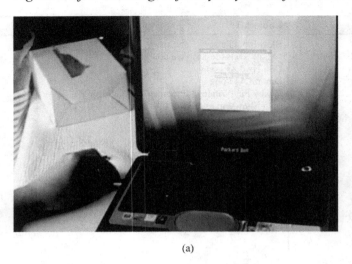

(a)

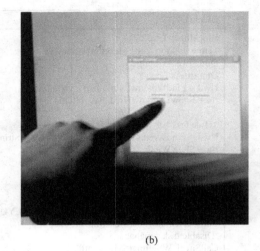

(b)

Figure 5. Inserting 2 of 2 keys and unlocking the system

(a)

(b)

required, generating a prime number bigger that one given and establishing a secret in a numerical form.

Figure 6 shows a flow diagram depicting the operation of the key generator. The objective of this is to distribute a secret S into n shares in such a way that any $t \geq n$ shares could recover the secret while the use of a less number of shares than t does not allow to get any information about

S. Procedures based on this idea are called (n,t)-threshold methods.

APIs used in the implementation of the generator are limited to the use of advapi.dll for accessing the Register and the use of the library SisNagra.dll to deal with big numbers. This library uses Strings to implement numbers that are not represented internally for obvious reasons regarding the range of representation. Therefore, the use of Strings has

Figure 6. Flow diagram depicting how the Key Generator works

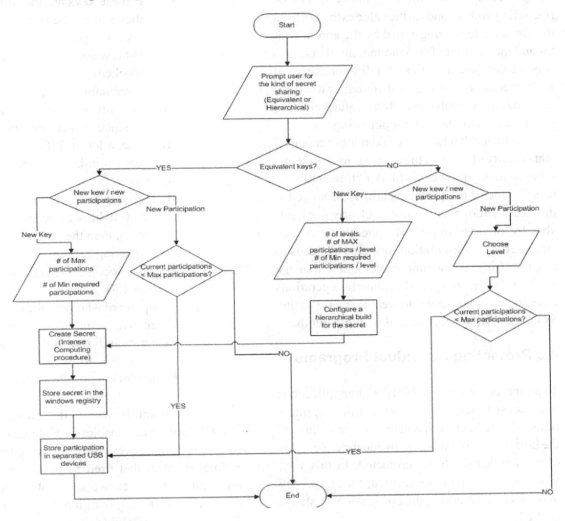

to be optimum and secure in the chosen Operating System and language. This is the reason because of Visual Basic 6.0 was chosen as a programming language. As stated before strings in thedotNet framework are not secure, being necessary the use of byte arrays instead of strings.

4.2.1 Secret Generation: Treatment of Big Numbers

The secret S is the fundamental value that finally will check and probe if the collecting of a certain number of shares is coming from authorized users and, therefore, will grant the access to the system. The secret value of S can be any number that we want to transmit, but, in order to make it more secure, we have opted for generating it automatically using the MD5 algorithm. The reason for this comes from the necessity of having a key as inviolable as possible to external attacks and since we need that the secret S has no explicit value and so it will be good to generate a random value. MD5 is capable of generating any value of 128 hexadecimal digits from any text chain.

In order to randomize as much as possible the input for the MD5 algorithm, the resulting text string is going to be built using the system clock (including milliseconds in the value extracted from the clock), a text string typed by the administrator and the product of two random numbers. This way we get the generation of a different string at each execution and thus a different value of S, minimizing the probability that an attacker could generate exactly the same input string.

One factor that has to be taken into account is that security of many of the cryptographic systems is based in big numbers to hinder "force brute attacks". One of the problems still to be solved is the treatment of such numbers, clearly not treatable by obvious questions concerning storage and internal representation format. This leads to employ strings as the unique medium to manage the key. Evidently special arithmetic operations have to be implemented to treat this case [using SysNagra.dll] in order to deal with big numbers.

4.3 Protecting Individual Programs

To protect certain executable files like applications that access to databases, entertainment applications, browsers, etc... it will be enough to "inject" the binary code of the *Agent* inside the executable of the application to be protected. In this way, when such program is executed, the *Agent* will make its task gathering the corresponding shares of the key.

The insertion of our security system in conventional executables is carried out by means of executable binding techniques. To do so we can select any of the binders which are freely available on the Internet. Some binder examples are Spider Binder, Afx, file-joiner which can be used to inject the *Agent* into any executable. In this way when attempting to run a protected executable:

- In the computer where the secret is stored:
  - The process of keys request is initiated when attempting to execute the program.

- If these keys are introduced and they satisfy the conditions, then access is granted.
- Otherwise, the system is blocked.
  - If the executable is opened to attempt to apply reverse engineering techniques, since it was compiled to native code, a lot of difficulties derived from the optimized compilation will be found.
  - If the Register of the Operating System is to be accessed by unauthorised users, then the policies in use for the Operating System for granting or rejecting accesses will be applied (see Section 4.4).
- In the computer of who stole the executable.
  - There will be no secret stored in its Register and thus the system will never be able to recover it, resulting in the blocking of the system.

At this point is where the characteristic (IL+CLR) of the executables for Vista are insecure. In this technique we intended (using the same technology than that used for building Trojans are created) to inject two segments of text and convert them into only one global segment of text. This technique is flexible since it is not needed to know the original source code of the executable to be protected. Once the code of the *Agent* is injected in the executables to be protected, these will not be able to start their execution unless the USB containing the shares have not been inserted previously. See Figure 7.

4.4. Security Considerations: The Windows Register

The security system that is introduced in this chapter can be completed with security policies of the operative system. The authors recommend

Figure 7. Using our agent to protect a single exe instead of the whole system.

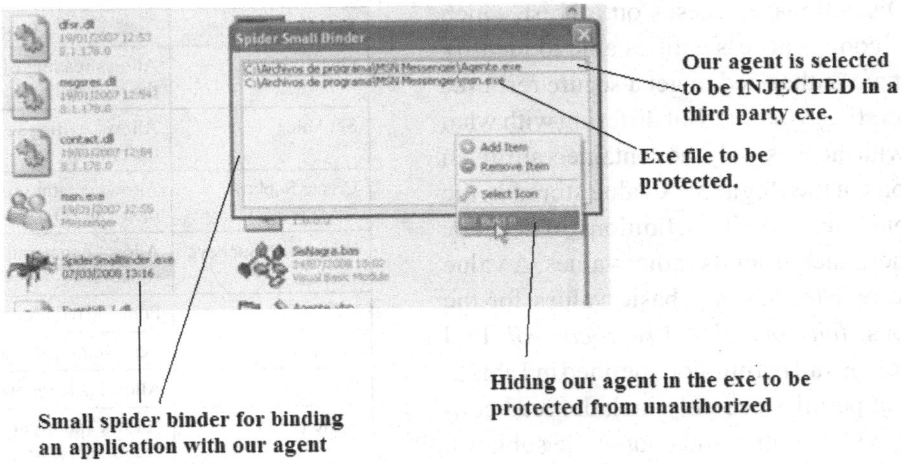

Our agent is selected to be INJECTED in a third party exe.

Exe file to be protected.

Small spider binder for binding an application with our agent

Hiding our agent in the exe to be protected from unauthorized

an active reading of the work from Smith&Komar (2005), concretely chapter 4 entitled *Configuring Authentification for Microsoft Windows*.

The place where our system stores sensible information is the Register. The Register is, as noted before, a dynamic and hierarchical database that contains values of variables used by the Operating System and by applications. Since the Register is available from the moment in which the Operating System is loaded, the applications can make their data persistent with only writing / reading from the Register (an example of this is that our software writes / reads from the register by using advapi.dll). The place where to keep the information is not arbitrary. The Register has six entry points clearly differenced and with different levels of protection.

- HKEY_CURRENT_USER stores information about the profile of the users actually active in the system. The information about all possible users of the system is in HKEY_USERS
- HKEY_USERS persistent information for all users of the system. HKEY_CLASSES_ROOT contains information of association between types of files and programs that

open them as well as information about the register of components COM in the system.

- **HKEY_LOCAL_MACHINE** Useful information for the configuration of the operative system and applications. Here is where we have decided to store our values.
- HKEY_CURRENT_CONFIG Current profile of the hardware that is usually stored in a persistent way in HKLM\SYSTEM\CurrentControlSet\Hardware Profiles\Current.
- HKEY_PERFORMANCE_DATA Contains information about performance counters of the system.

This way, when we use administrative tools to change the configuration of any service or application, the registered changes are stored directly in the register. If the changes are applied by us without administrative tools, the effect is not immediate, a reboot is usually required. In this case we have to restart the system in order to these changes are applied (or at least restart the session).

Given the importance of the register of the Operating System, it is indispensable to know how to apply licences and restrictions in an adequate manner. As well as it happens with files stored in NTFS partitions, the Register is protected by DACLs Discretionary Access Control List, which is a list of control access entities able to identify users that are authorized to get a secure resource in the Operating System). But differing with what happens with the files, only the containers are given permissions in the Register. A value stored in the register only acquires its definitions of security via an inheritance from its father values. A value inside the register has two basic values for the permissions: *full control* and *read control*. Full control includes all permissions defined in Table 2.

Reading permissions only include: read control, query value, notify and enumerate subkeys. Recommended practices to be adopted regarding the Register, the following actions are encouraged:

1. Assign to each key the minimum privilege as possible.
2. Assign permissions in the highest point as possible in the hierarchy.
3. Assign permissions to secure groups and not only users: in this way, the model of security can be scalable and flexible, allowing the addition or removal of users in an easy way without having to review assignation policies.

5 CONCLUSIONS AND FUTURE IMPROVEMENTS

We have provided a flexible and yet powerful security system for protecting applications or Information Systems from unauthorized accesses. This system is susceptible of improvements and enhancements especially those related to the new specification for the USB 3.0 interface that will report immediate benefits to our security system. On one hand the new USB specifications 3.0 will allow transfer rates of information to be increased in a factor of ten. On the other hand, the current USB 2.0 specification works with as a protocol bus, which forces the security system to check the stack of protocols of the Operating System looking

Table 2.

Permission	Description
Query Value	Allows reading of a value of the key of the register.
Set Value	Allows writing in the value of a key of the register.
Create Subkey	Allows creating subkeys (and modifying their values).
Enumerate Subkeys	Allows enumerating the keys and their subkeys.
Notify	Forces to require notifications of changes.
Create Link	Reserved for the operative system
Delete	Allows deleting the key
Write DACL	Allows modifying the list DACL that grants access to the resource.
Write Owner	Allows altering the owner of the value of the key.
Read Control	Allows reading the SACL.

for the insertion of new devices that could contain the key, or extend the implementation in order to add the detection mechanism based on the events triggered by the Operating System. However, USB 3.0 uses a protocol based on interruptions, which will make possible to install our protection system inside the vector of interruptions of the system which will result in accelerated device detection.

In addition, the using specific drivers for the PIC/controller of the USB may increase the security of the system since the reading of the key is only allowed in blocked servers / blocked applications.

We kindly request the reader to check how the system works, in (Alvarez, J.A, & Lopez, J.A, & Galvez, F., 2009) the online resource can be visited.

REFERENCES

Abelson, H., Ledeen, K., & Lewis, H. (2008). *Blown to Bits: Your Life, Liberty, and Happiness after the Digital Explosion*. Addison Wesley.

Alvarez, J. A., Lopez, J. A., & Galvez, F. (2009). *Demonstration of the system*. http://www.ace.ual.es/~jaberme/ict_law/

Anton, A. I., et al. 2. Financial privacy policies and the need for standardization. *Security & Privacy, 2,* 36-45.

Blahut, R. E. (1984, February). A Universal Reed-Solomon Decoder. *IBM Journal of Research and Development, 28.*

Childs, L. N. (1997). *A concrete introduction to Higher Algebra*. Springer.

Howard, M., & Leblanc, D. (2003). *Writing Secure Code* (2nd ed.). Microsoft Press.

Lederman, R. (2004). The Medical Privacy Rule: Can Hospitals Comply Using Current Health Information Systems? In *Proceedings of the 17th IEEE Symposium on Computer-Based Medical Systems.*

McConnel, S. (2004). *Code Complete* (2nd ed.). Redmon, WA: Microsoft Press.

McEliece, R. J., & Sarwate, D. V. (1981). On Sharing Secrets and Reed-Solomon Codes. *Communications of the ACM, 24.*

Menezes, A., van Oorscht, P., & Vanstone, S. (1996). *Handbook of Applied Cryptography.* CRC Press.

Peterson, M. G. E. (2005, January). Privacy, Public Safety, and Medical Research. *Journal of Medical Systems, 29*(1), 81–90. doi:10.1007/s10916-005-1106-y

Schneier, B. (2003). *Practical Cryptography.* Wiley & Sons.

Smith, B., & Komar, B. (2005). *Microsoft Windows Security.* Microsoft Press.

Tang, X. (2008, March). *Frontiers of Law in China: Vol 3. Personal health care and medical treatment information and protection of privacy right* (pp. 408-422).

The BigInteger Library of Java. (n.d.). http://java.sun.com/j2se/1.4.2/docs/api/java/math/BigInteger.html

The International PGP Home Page. (n.d.). http://www.pgpi.org/

(n.d.). The SysNagra.dll. *The Library*. http://sis-nagra.webcindario.com/LibreriaSisNagra.html.

Chapter 21
Ensuring Users' Rights to Privacy, Confidence and Reputation in the Online Learning Environment:
What Should Instructors Do to Protect Their Students' Privacy?

Louis B. Swartz
Robert Morris University, USA

Michele T. Cole
Robert Morris University, USA

David A. Lovejoy
Robert Morris University, USA

ABSTRACT

There is no clear right to privacy, confidence, and reputation in United States case law or in legislation for students in the online environment. While some privacy interests are protected under a variety of legal theories, none expressly applies to online education. This study examines pertinent issues concerning the privacy rights of students while engaged in online learning. A survey of students using online tools in their courses demonstrated a widespread belief that their communications were private. A second survey of business law instructors using online tools revealed a lack of awareness of the potential for abuse by third parties able to access users' information. Survey results were inconclusive with regard to the existence of policies and procedures within the institutions with regard to protecting users' privacy rights in online instruction. Survey respondents made several recommendations for action to mediate the lack of existing protections for privacy in online learning.

DOI: 10.4018/978-1-61520-975-0.ch021

INTRODUCTION

What are the rights to privacy, confidence and reputation as they apply to online instruction? While a person's right to privacy has been recognized in several forums, the right to confidence or trust, and the right to reputation are less discussed. The United States Supreme Court has recognized a right to privacy emanating from the First, Fifth and Fourteenth Amendments. In Commonwealth countries, the right to privacy can be protected under the equitable doctrine of breach of confidence. Member nations of the Council of Europe accord a right to privacy under Article 8 of the European Convention for the Protection of Human Rights and Fundamental Freedoms.

However, what do the rights to privacy, confidence and reputation mean in the educational context; specifically, what do the rights to privacy, confidence and reputation mean in an online classroom environment? More importantly, how do instructors ensure that those rights are protected? Are instructors building safeguards into their courses to protect users' rights? Are university policies in place to support instructors' efforts? Are the instructors aware of, and using, those policies?

To date, research has focused on how best to use the online platform to facilitate learning, with limited attention given as to how online instruction might impact the students' rights to privacy, confidence, and reputation. Francis (2002) noted that online courses bring into play a new set of instructional factors and variables. We argue that chief among these is the matter of online security without which online learning may be constrained.

As the use of information communication technologies in education continues to grow, and as access to information broadens, institutions and their instructors need to find ways to ensure students' rights to privacy, confidence, and reputation in the online learning environment. It is not that the need to protect students' rights is new, but rather that the potential for violation of those

rights has increased with expanding internet usage. Technology opens up the world to students and students to the world in ways that educators and policy-makers had not thought possible a decade ago, confirming that the information highway is, if you will, a two-way street.

The focus of this chapter is on: (1) U.S. case law relative to privacy in cyber-space and the Family Education Rights and Privacy Act of 1974 (FERPA); (2) expectation of privacy in an online setting and what students believe about the privacy of their communications online; (3) what educational online platforms are doing to advise users of privacy issues; (4) what institutions of higher education are currently doing to ensure students' rights to privacy, confidence and reputation in online learning programs; (5) what instructors are doing to protect students' privacy, confidence and reputation in their courses; and (6) suggestions as to what steps institutions might take to effect policies and procedures to ensure users the rights to privacy, confidence and reputation in online learning programs.

BACKGROUND

Rights to Privacy, Confidence, and Reputation

Sandler (1997) defines "privacy" as an expectation that personal information disclosed in a private place that if known, would cause distress to a reasonable person, will not be disclosed to a third party. Personal information is a broad concept that encompasses facts, photos, videos, and opinions. The "right to privacy" as a separate and distinct entitlement is an emerging right (Sandler) which has been protected under various legal theories including the equitable doctrine of breach of confidentiality. Reputation is generally protected under the umbrella of legal theories protecting an individual's right to privacy as a property interest. For the purposes of this chapter, the rights to confidence and to reputation are considered integral to the right of privacy.

In the United States, recognition and development of the right to privacy has developed incrementally through case law and legal commentary. Although Judge Cooley is said to have coined the phrase, "to be let alone" in 1888 as a statement of a right to privacy, it was not until the publication of Warren and Brandeis' Harvard Law Review article in 1890 that privacy as a separate legal doctrine was considered by American courts. Prior to their article which chronicled a series of cases in which relief was granted on the basis of defamation, a particular property right, implied contract, or breach of confidence, American courts had not expressly recognized a right to privacy. Warren and Brandeis argued that the series of decisions they had reviewed were really based on a broader principle, which should be recognized as a separate right (Prosser, 1971). Nonetheless, it remains the case that privacy or the right to be let alone, may be violated when there is a reasonable public interest in the individual's activities, such as when suspected terrorism is used as the basis for wiretapping.

While the U.S. Constitution does not contain an express right to privacy, privacy interests have been protected under the First, Fourth and Fifth Amendments to the Constitution. The Fourteenth Amendment has been interpreted as providing a right to personal autonomy. The decisions in *Griswold v. Connecticut* (1965) and in *Roe v. Wade* (1973) particularly rested on a constitutional right of privacy. This right generally is confined to marriage, family, procreation, motherhood, and child rearing (LII b, 2009).

Similar constitutionally derived protections exist in Canada, particularly under section 8 of the Charter, which establishes a right to protection from unreasonable searches and seizure. The critical factor is the expectation of privacy. With regard to privacy in an online environment, Steeves (2008) reviewed the Supreme Court of Canada's position on reasonable expectations of privacy and

the adequacy of protection in the online environment and found it wanting. She argues that the legal test is out of step with modern technology and people's online experiences.

In the United States, a Constitutional right of privacy has been developing along with statutory limitations on access to personal information. Federal legislation in this area seeks to protect the consumer from unauthorized use of personal information, such as the Fair Credit Reporting Act of 1970, the Privacy Act of 1974, the Family Education Rights and Privacy Act of 1974, the Right to Financial Privacy Act of 1978, the Privacy Protection Act of 1980, the Cable Communications Policy Act of 1984, the Electronic Communications Privacy Act of 1986, the Video Privacy Protection Act of 1988, the Telephone Consumer Protection Act of 1991, the Driver's Privacy Protection Act of 1994, the Communications Assistance for Law Enforcement Act of 1994, the Telecommunications Act of 1996, the Health Insurance Portability and Accountability Act of 1996, the Children's Online Privacy Protection Act of 1998, and the Financial Modernization Act of 1999, also known as the Gramm-Leach-Bliley Act (LII a, 2009).

Richardson (2002), writing about a right to privacy for Australia, notes that the English accession to the European Convention on Human Rights opened the door for Commonwealth countries to recognize a right to privacy similar to that enjoyed by European countries. Prior to that, rather than a reliance on a right to privacy, in Australia and the United Kingdom, privacy interests had been protected under the equitable doctrine of breach of confidence. With the accession to the Convention, courts in the United Kingdom and in Australia began to consider privacy interests protected under the equitable doctrine of breach of confidence as *rights* (Richardson, 2002). Richardson notes that the multiple references in *Australian Broadcasting Corporation v Lenah Game Meats Pty Ltd* to personal autonomy as the reason why privacy interests should be protected might be construed as the emergence of an Australian right to privacy. Yet she concludes that in both the United Kingdom and Australia, while the discussion of privacy rights has been important in recognizing that personal autonomy is the basis of the protection, it remains unclear what the scope of the protection would be. Until then courts continue to rely on the doctrine of breach of confidence to protect privacy interests (See, *Minister for Immigration and Citizenship v Kumar* (2009)).

Other examples of differing privacy statutes include New Zealand's Privacy Act of 1993, which regulates the collection, use, and transfer of personal information in the public and private sectors. The Act guarantees access to personal information held by agencies to individuals. It incorporates twelve privacy principles from Australia's Privacy Act of 1988 (Discussion paper 2, 1999). Canada has proposed a model privacy code (CSA Model Code for the Protection of Personal Information) that incorporates ten interrelated principles; accountability, identifying purposes, consent, limiting collection, limiting use, disclosure and retention, accuracy, safeguards, openness, individual access and challenging (Canadian Standards Association, 2009).

Online Privacy Protections

In a report to Congress in 1999, Stevens acknowledged that successful internet and e-commerce depended upon the resolution of the very issues that concerns this chapter, that is, the privacy of online personal information. Should the law recognize a right to information privacy (an individual's rightful control of the terms and uses of personal information) for online transactions? As stated elsewhere and reinforced in the report is the fact that in the United States there is no comprehensive protection in law for personal information collected in the public and private sectors. While personal information collected by the federal government has some protection in

federal law, the only protection for online personal information collected by others is found in the Children's Online Privacy Protection Act of 1998.

Threats to privacy interests found in the disclosure of personal information are the result of burgeoning technology, widespread internet usage for social as well as commercial purposes, and usage by marketers and advertisers of information posted on websites and released in the commercial context. The result has been the publication of an enormous amount of personal data on finances and credit, health and medical issues, taxes, employment histories, business transactions, proprietary information and customer profiles. All of this information is of use to the information industry, such as government agencies, direct marketers, reference services and consumer reporting agencies (Stevens, 1999).

The Federal Trade Commission's 1999 report on self-regulatory initiatives of commercial websites found that the majority of sites collected vast amounts of personal information from consumers, but for the most part, did not employ fair information practices. There are more protections in place in the European Union. The EU's Directive on the Protection of Personal Data, effective in 1998, comprises a general framework of data protection packages for processing personal data (Stevens, 1999). In the end, however, online privacy protection relies on what Stevens refers to as a patchwork of federal laws.

Online Education

In their report *Staying the Course: Online Education in the United States, 2008,* Allen & Seaman (2008) note that online enrollments continue to outpace the growth in overall higher education enrollment. According to the available evidence, growth in online enrollments will continue to outpace enrollment in onground courses. At the start of the academic year in 2007, they report that over 20% of all students in higher education were taking at least one online course, an increase of 12% over 2006. The report demonstrates that growth in online education is occurring across disciplines, in public and private-for-profit and private nonprofit institutions and at all levels, from the associate degree to the doctoral/research level.

Course delivery methods vary in different institutions but for the purposes of this chapter, the Allen & Seaman classifications are being used. Traditional courses are those with no online technology used, a face-to face environment in which content is delivered verbally or in written format. Web-facilitated courses are those that use web-based technology to facilitate an otherwise face-to-face course. For example, the instructor may use a course management system (CMS), a web page, or platform to post syllabi and assignments. The proportion of the online content is less than 29% in web-facilitated courses. The third type is the blended/hybrid course in which 30-79% of the course is online, blending face-to-face delivery with online instruction. Blended or hybrid courses typically use online discussions and few face-to–face meetings. Those courses that are 80-100% online are considered "Online" courses. Most if not all of the content is delivered online.

The exponential growth of online education forms the basis for Storey & Tebes' (2008) research into protecting users' rights to privacy. They focused on the institution's responsibility to the instructor and his or her right to privacy in the conduct of online courses. Their emphasis was on the development and adoption of a universal ethical model that could be applied to participants' privacy issues.

Lin, Korba, Yee, Shih, and Lin (2004) note that while there has been considerable attention paid to developing instructional tools for online education, little attention has been paid to ensuring security and privacy for users. The literature that has focused on ensuring security and privacy has dealt with legislative requirements, user trust/confidence issues, and design concerns.

Wallace (2007) notes that the use of online instructional methods has grown consistently, thus, online teaching is no longer on the fringe, nor can users be considered first adopters. Her research examined the connection (or disconnection) between online course delivery and institutional policies and found "Despite the growth in use of educational technologies, universities often reflect an institutional assumption that instructors, students and instruction are on campus. As a result, existing policies often fail to provide guidelines for online teaching and learning activities" (p. 88). Wallace notes that in Canada, privacy legislation has caused universities to examine their procedures for balancing the institution's academic and research needs with students' privacy rights. The result has been that some universities are starting to use release forms in order to keep prior course discussions and online contributions; informing students how third parties may use their work; and telling students who has access to the course website. She suggests that release policies be required to inform students of the option to withhold permission and still participate in the course. Wallace would include all modes of communication in the policy such as e-mail, video and video conferencing (p. 95).

A series of training guides (Quick Guides) on online teaching and learning published by the Australian National Training Authority is an exception to the general rule. In the 2003 *Privacy issues in online teaching and learning,* the authors describe what privacy law covers and establish which organizations are bound to the ten national privacy principles because of it. The Guide includes recommendations on the collection and use of students' personal information. It also presents several issues of concern with regard to online instruction surrounding the use of otherwise effective pedagogical techniques, such as asking students to share personal information. The list includes group pressure, technical infrastructure issues, using photographs of people, distributing and publishing e-mail addresses, making records of e-mail and chat rooms available, and records of student enrollment.

The Applicable Law

Students attending institutions of higher education in the United States that receive funding from the Department of Education have some privacy protection afforded by the Family Education Rights and Privacy Act (FERPA). FERPA is a Federal law that applies to educational agencies and institutions that receive funding under a program administered by the U. S. Department of Education. The statute is found in Title 20, United States Code, section 1232g *et seq.* and the Department's regulations are found at 34 Code of Federal Regulations, Part 99.

Under FERPA, schools must generally allow students who are 18 years or over, or attending a postsecondary institution:

- access to their education records
- an opportunity to seek to have the records amended
- some control over the disclosure of information from the records

However, FERPA coverage is limited to student education records. Privacy of student communications, whether online or in the classroom is not expressly covered by statute in the United States. The United States Constitution does not contain the word "privacy". However, courts have consistently held that it is the essence of the Bill of Rights and thus a guaranteed right.

The authors have encountered a dearth of case law on the issue of student expectation of privacy in the classroom and other educational settings. It is generally held that a student in a secondary or primary school is not afforded the same protections from search and seizure as the general population, and it might be expected that such limitations would, by analogy, extend to student expectations of privacy in classroom settings in post-secondary education. To date, the issue of what rights do students have in the online learning environment has not been brought before any court. With regard to a defendant's expectation of privacy, at least one court has held that a student who connects his computer to a university network does not thereby "extinguish his legitimate, objectively reasonable privacy expectations" even though he was engaged in criminal activity (United States v. Heckenamp, 2007).

Courts have narrowly limited FERPA's application to educational records, and have specifically held that activities in a classroom are not "educational records" subject to FERPA (Falvo v. Owasso Independent School District, 2002*).* Thus, having students grade each other's papers is not a FERPA violation because the grades, not yet having been entered in a grade book, are not educational records. In the same year as *Falvo v. Owassa,* the Supreme Court held in *Gonzaga University v. Doe* (2002) that the individual has no right of action under FERPA and so could not seek to enforce the law or remedy a violation of the statute's provisions. The court in *United States v. Miami University* (2002) did hold that the federal government did have standing to sue under FERPA and held that disciplinary records were covered as educational records under the statute (Shiley, 2003).

Whether other classroom activities, such as discussion or question and answer sessions, are subject to FERPA is a question that has not been answered by any court. It is the authors' opinion that such activities are not subject to FERPA. However, on-line activities, such as chat rooms or threaded discussions, are not a direct analogy to in-person classroom activities. Classroom discussions and other activities (including those that are taped), by their nature, are not easily communicated to the world at large, whereas on-line activities can be instantaneously emailed, blogged, twittered and posted to the entire on-line world. Does a student have an appreciation of this difference, and do institutions need to warn students of it?

How to protect a student's right to privacy when engaged in internet activity is difficult both to communicate to students and to ensure on their behalf. There are a number of online postings regarding this issue, such as the following:

The right to privacy in Internet activity is a serious issue facing society. Some Internet users wish to shield their identities, while participating in frank discussions about sensitive topics. Others fulfill fantasies and harmlessly role-play under the cover of a false identity in chat rooms, MUDs or the IRC. However, there are the eternal "bad apples", and on the Internet, they are the people who use anonymous servers as more than a way to avoid responsibility for controversial remarks. Cases of harassment and abuse have become increasingly frequent, aided by a cloak of anonymity. There are also problems with frauds and scam artists who elude law enforcement authorities through anonymous mailings and postings. Other users are concerned about the proliferation of information on the Internet. Databases of court records are now available free over the World Wide Web. Since no formal law exists within cyberspace, Internet users can find recourse only through the applicable laws of their own government. (Internet Attorney, Introduction, 2009)

The above conclusion holds particularly true with online instruction. There are no U.S. statutes or case law which these authors could find that govern or set forth guidelines as to how to protect the privacy, confidence and reputation expected by students. Therefore, it is the responsibility of the individual institutions of higher education, their instructors, and the educational online platforms which they use to provide this protection.

Expectation of Privacy

In the United States, the "expectation of privacy" typically arises in criminal cases where a court determines if governmental action was a violation of the Fourth Amendment protection against "unreasonable searches and seizures". The Pennsylvania Superior Court, for instance,

has held that in general, in a criminal case to have a reasonable expectation of privacy, one must intend to exclude others and must exhibit that intent (Commonwealth v. Hunter, 2008). Such a standard clearly does not apply in a classroom setting, where educational recitation and question and answer sessions take place every day.

Although students have a reduced right to privacy in the classroom, their right is not reduced to zero. In the case of *Doe v Little Rock School District* (2004), the court had to decide whether the practice of the Little Rock School District that subjects secondary public school students to random, suspicionless searches of their persons and belongings by school officials is unconstitutional. It concluded that such searches violate the students' Fourth Amendment rights because they unreasonably invade their legitimate expectations of privacy.

In an Illinois case about teachers' rights to privacy, where the school district had installed audiovisual recording equipment in their classrooms, the court held that the Fourth Amendment does not protect teachers or other school staff members in relation to public areas of the building, such as classrooms and hallways and other openly shared settings, including school buses. *Plock v. Bd. of Educ. of Freeport Sch. Dist. No. 145* (2007).

Orin S Kerr, in his 2007 Stanford Law Review article, *Four Models of Fourth Amendment Protection*, concludes that the Fourth Amendment protects reasonable expectations of privacy, but that the Supreme Court has refused to provide a consistent explanation for what makes an expectation of privacy *reasonable*. The Court's refusal has disappointed scholars and frustrated students for four decades.

In a case involving the right of the New Jersey Department of Education to withhold the results of a study of alternative education, the New Jersey Supreme Court has held that deliberative work requires an expectation of privacy to allow for the efficient, unrestrained development of thoughts and their frank examination (*C.M. v.*

Board of Educ. of Union County Regional High School Dist., 2005). Thus, a student might have an expectation of privacy in the process of writing a research paper for example, but not in reading the same paper to the class.

There is no reasonable expectation of privacy in directory information, defined under the regulations promulgated pursuant to FERPA as information contained in an education record of a student that would not generally be considered harmful or an invasion of privacy if disclosed, including, but not limited to, the student's name, address, telephone listing, electronic mail address, photograph, date and place of birth, major field of study, dates of attendance, grade level, enrollment status, participation in officially recognized activities and sports, weight and height of members of athletic teams, degrees, honors and awards received, and the most recent education agency or institution attended.

For the most part, as Wallace (2002) notes, institutional policies on disclosure and security of students' academic records, do not address disclosure and security in an online setting. Some universities have begun to ask students taking online courses to sign release forms at the beginning of the course. The releases would apply to keeping the student's online work for a specified time period, would inform students if and how their online discussions could be used for research, and who could access their discussions in the course.

Students' Expectation of Privacy in the Online Environment

The authors surveyed their spring 2009 classes, three undergraduate and one graduate class, regarding the students' beliefs about the privacy of their communications in the online environment. There were one hundred sixty-two students in the four classes. The survey was anonymous. Students in all of the undergraduate classes were offered bonus points to respond to the survey.

Survey Results

Over a three-day period, one hundred fifteen responses were received for a participation rate of 71%. More than 95% thought that their e-mails were private; seventy-one percent expected that their online communications with the course instructor would be private. When asked if the student knew if the university or the student's department had a privacy policy, 43% thought the university did have a policy (none was aware of a departmental policy). Of those who were aware of a university policy, 55% said that they had read it. Sixty-two percent were not aware that others in the institution, such as web managers, administrators or those associated with the online platform could access the information they posted. Seventy-nine percent did not know that the information posted online could be used for marketing purposes by the online platform. Yet 77% had been asked to share personal information, 83% had been asked to share e-mail addresses, and more than 62% had been asked to share contact information beyond e-mail addresses.

Independent samples t-tests were run on the six parts of question three, asking if the student had an expectation of privacy when using any of the online tools such as, chat rooms, student lounges, e-mail, discussion boards, drop boxes, or other tools. There were no statistically significant differences between the two largest grouping variables, students who taken only traditional courses and those who had taken both online and onland courses. T-tests were also run on question four, asking if the student had taken courses in which other students' work was made available, and on question seven, asking if in any course, the student had had access to other students' grades. For parts of both questions, there were statistically significant differences at the .005 level with regard to the availability of student work, and access to student evaluations, when using the same grouping variables.

Forty-seven students provided comments and recommendations such as:

- "Everything online should be confidential,"
- "don't share information that you do not want others to have,"
- "make student personal information unavailable, and posts to blackboard forums anonymous and not allow other students to view it."
- "Policy review should occur and students should sign a confidentiality agreement. At any time, information cannot be kept confidential, students should be informed,"
- "enhancing the privacy policies, and having a printed copy in each classroom."
- "Make sure students are informed of policies and methods to protect themselves."

Gross & Acquisti (2005), in their survey of 4,000 university students using online social networks, found that students were willing to provide vast amounts of personal information without much concern for the risks to privacy. Because so few students actually used the privacy protections available, the authors concluded that student users exposed themselves to a variety of physical and cyber risks and made it easy for third parties to create profiles of their behaviors.

Privacy Policies of Educational Online Platforms

Blackboard, a popular online instructional platform that is utilized by instructors at several U.S. universities, publishes a privacy policy on its online site at http://www.blackboard.com. Within that policy, it states: "Blackboard automatically logs IP addresses, session sources, and other data which tracks users' access to the Services. We access these logs for sales and marketing purposes as well as system performance monitoring." (Blackboard, 2009)

eCollege, another online educational platform and a competitor of Blackboard, also publishes a privacy policy on its online site. Within its policy, it states:

By registering with or contacting us through the eCollege website, you agree that any information or comments you provide may be shared between eCollege, its affiliated companies and partners, and used without restriction to contact you and to improve or market our products and services. (eCollege, ¶ 1, 2009)

However, unless the instructor advises the students about the instructional platform's policies and of similar applications, the students are unlikely to be aware that they exist. Is it incumbent upon the platform, the university, or the instructor make sure the students are aware of such policies? The question might then become how effective such notice could be given the amount of information presented now in the lengthy terms of agreement that accompany certain web documents as prerequisites to downloading.

Privacy Policies of Institutions of Higher Education

A number of universities have attempted to address the issue of privacy in the online classroom. They have recognized a concern for their students' privacy, published policy statements and made guidelines for use in web teaching available to instructors. Dartmouth College in New Hampshire is an example of one such university. In *Privacy in the online classroom*, Horton observes of the Dartmouth privacy policy:

One of the benefits of Web publishing is that you can make something as visible and accessible as a billboard, but only to a select audience. Although privacy seems to run counter to the philosophy of the Web - all information for all comers - in many instances, you may not want your Web-

based materials to be world-accessible. When considering privacy issues for your course Web site, first determine whether you have a need for restricting access to your materials. If so, evaluate the different restriction methods to determine which best accommodates your needs, and find out which ones are in use at your institution. (Horton, ¶¶ 1-2, 2002)

There are practical reasons to limit access, despite the advantages to the students of the wide publication of their work possible on the web. Limiting access only to users in the course may allow the instructor to better tailor material. Limiting access also protects users' work from misappropriation. Knowing that the course is open only to classmates and the instructor might encourage fuller participation (Horton, 2002), although if the Gross & Acquisti (2005) study is any guide, most students are not hesitant to participate in unsecured sites.

For the University of Sydney Faculty of Health Sciences, three principles in online educational website management are paramount: notice, choice, and security. Because students need to know how privacy issues are addressed in each website, the University makes its privacy policy readily accessible from each website from its homepage. Students and users are told what sort of information could be collected, who would collect it and for what purpose, how anonymity would be insured, how to consent and what the consequences of not consenting would be and where to locate the University/Faculty privacy policy. In specified instances, users may refuse to allow information to be collected or used. It is the Faculty's responsibility to insure that how data is collected and stored is secure (Faculty of Health Sciences, 2004).

The Department of Management, Marketing, & Information Management/E-Commerce at Jacksonville State University privacy policy clearly states what and when personal identifying information (PII) of a student may be used by the

institution. For example, PII voluntarily provided to the Department is collected so that student needs may be better served. That information also may be used for legitimate academic purposes, such as research and for promotional purposes as well as to improve course offerings and the Department's web sites. The policy statement explicitly states that it is not the policy to share student's personal identifying information with third parties outside of the College of Commerce and Business Administration. The policy statement also advises students that those outside of the Department may access what they do post in a public area of the Web site (Thomas, 2009).

Notwithstanding the fact that some universities are providing warnings to their students concerning privacy in online teaching, a crucial question still remains: Is there or should there be a responsibility and an effort by instructors, at the course level, to adopt privacy policies to be communicated to their students in a syllabus, or by way of announcements or email, prior to the commencement of an online course.

Instructors' Perspective on Students' Right to Privacy

The authors conducted a survey of instructors of online business law courses in the United States to determine what is being done now to protect students' rights and what the expectations for privacy are in an online course from the instructor's perspective. Participants were drawn from the membership of the Academy of Legal Studies in Business (ALSB).

Using Vovici, a web-based survey tool[1], data was gathered on current practices with regard to the use of synchronous and asynchronous teaching tools, chat rooms, faculty and student "lounges", e-mail, discussion boards, drop boxes, grading forums, etc. Open-ended questions on experiences with privacy violations, and recommendations for safeguards captured qualitative data. Results were transferred from Vovici into SPSS (statistical analysis software). Analysis was both quantitative and qualitative.

The preface to the survey, "Protecting Users' Rights to Privacy in Online Instruction", explains the significance of the study and asks for recommendations for the field.

Survey Results

Eighty-five responses to the survey were received. Twenty-seven (31.8%) respondents taught both online and onland courses, three (3.5%) taught only online and two (2.4%) used hybrid or online components in the classroom. Eighty-three instructors or 97.6% of the respondents used e-mail. With regard to the online instructional tools, forty-four (51.8%) used threaded discussions or discussion boards, both of which are online features. Twenty-six (30.6%) used the drop box feature. Fifteen instructors chose "other". Sample responses in this category included downloaded materials onto course website, online quizzes, assignments posted in Blackboard, video conferencing, live audio with moderated text window, blogs, grade book, syllabus and resource forums.

With regard to sharing student work with others, the majority of the responses were negative. Forty-eight (57.1%) said "never". However, twenty-one (25%) responded "sometimes". Six instructors chose "other" without really answering the question, but instead offered caveats, such as "very rarely", "with permission or advance notice", "samples from prior semesters", "after those works have been graded". Only one respondent said "only with express student permission". Two of those who selected "other" indicated that the discussion areas were open and that posting in the thread is voluntary.

Thirty-four instructors (40%) asked students to share personal information. Six (7.1%) asked students to post or make available photos. Twelve (10.6%) asked the students to keep the information shared confidential. Comments added in "other" pointed to the voluntary nature of the postings.

Yet fifty-five (66.5%) of the instructors did not advise students that others at the institution could access the information that the students posted online. Eleven (13.1%) did inform their students that others had access to their postings. Seventeen (20.2%) said the question did not apply, possibly because those instructors did not teach online and/or viewed "e-mail" as outside the scope of the question.

When instructors were asked if their institutions had a privacy policy, fifty-seven (67.1%) said yes; twenty-six (30.6%) did not know. When the institution or department did have a privacy policy, in fourteen (28.1%) cases, instructors did advise the students of it. However, the majority or forty-three (50.6%) did not advise students of the policy. Fifty-nine instructors (70.2%) did not advise users of the online platform's privacy policy, possibly because the instructor was unaware of it.

Requirements of the policies around privacy of student records (FERPA in the United States, FOIP in Alberta, Canada) were better known. Fifty-nine instructors (69.4%) were familiar with the policies, twenty-one (24.7%) were not.

Some suggestions were made in response to the question, "What recommendations do you have for protecting users' privacy rights in online instruction? In the classroom?" Such as:

- Better education of student rights for all those who may have an opportunity to view student users' private items.
- Regular faculty/staff training.
- All privacy rights begin with the concept of "reasonable expectation." As everything that takes place in the classroom, and nearly everything that is shared in an online class, is viewed by several dozen people, there is no "reasonable expectation" of privacy in such cases, and consequently no privacy rights. Grades and other personal records are absolutely protected by FERPA, but peer grading does not violate that statute.
- Not use the program that allows students to

upload their course-related productions to the university server and then allow third parties to access the information. Severely restrict access to all online course materials, such as eCourses, with some built-in device that tracks at least the identity of persons who access the source, when and for how long.

- Participation in an on-line community, including a class, should entail informed consent and waiver of privacy rights to the extent that they would preclude having the community in the first place. Unless technology can provide a hacker proof equivalent of Rawls' "original position/veil of ignorance" …
- Syllabus notice for students to not share employer or other organization's information without permission.
- Use of passwords, limited access.
- Stress confidentiality in syllabus, before class assignments and class discussions that draw on professional and personal experience.
- Tell students that anything in a computer can be gotten out by someone who knows how to do it. Protect self even in disposing of a computer.

Independent samples t-tests were run on questions three through six which asked instructors whether they made student work available to others in the course, if they asked students to share personal information, if they required students to evaluate other students and if students had access to other students' grades. Comparing the two largest groups of instructors, those who taught in the classroom (fifty-two) and those who taught in both formats (twenty-seven), there were statistically significant differences with regard to question three, do you make student work, e.g., essays or projects, available to others in the course? ; and two parts of question four, do you ask students to: share information about themselves, post or make available photos of themselves. Means for question three were 1.46 and .78; for question four, the means were .23 and .70, and .02 and .15. Significance (2-tailed) for question three was .038. For question four, significance (2-tailed) was .000 and .024.

Sharing student work, such as essays or projects, with other students was higher in the classroom setting than in the online environment. As might be expected, the sharing of students' personal information and photos was higher online than in the classroom. There were no other statistically significant differences between the classroom and online uses of student information.

Using the same grouping variables, instructors who taught in the classroom and those who taught both onland and online, independent samples t-tests were run on question seven asking about the use of copyright material in courses being taught. There were no statistically significant differences between the two groups. Usage of copyrighted material was equivalent in both settings. With regard to whether instructors advised their students that third parties could access their personal information once placed online, there was a statistically significant difference between the two groups at the .001 level.

FUTURE TRENDS

Online education is expected to continue to grow, to meet the demands of a more diverse workforce in need of continuing education, working adults seeking undergraduate and graduate degrees, people in the military unable to take traditional classroom coursework, students with disabilities, learners in rural communities, and students for whom online education better suits their learning styles as well as those who prefer the convenience of distance learning. Technology will continue to link people together and facilitate access to information, all types of information. As it does, the limited protections afforded currently by various statutes will be inadequate to protect users in an online environment.

In her article on the effectiveness of different web-based tools for reaching students to strengthen their reading and writing skills in the age of the internet, Imperatore (2009) comments that in using web-based instructional tools, teachers are forced to face issues of student safety and privacy. She suggests that one way to address these concerns is to use blog and wiki services designed with classrooms in mind. For example, by using a free wiki service, Webpaint, instructors may eliminate advertisements and provides varying levels of privacy to insure that unauthorized users cannot access the wiki.

She notes that certain education-focused blogging services, such as Gaggle, also offer options for protecting students engaged in online activities. With Gaggle, users' e-mails can be monitored by school personnel for inappropriate content. Blog security settings can be set by the instructor to prohibit unauthorized access, hide e-mail addresses, and block offensive content. Whether tools such as Webpaint and Gaggle would also work in a university environment is not certain, however.

The Electronic Privacy Information Center (EPIC) publishes an online guide to privacy tools found at http://epic.org/privacy/tools.html. The guide is designed for the individual user with an emphasis on practical applications. Categories of privacy tools include "snoop proof email", "anonymous remailers", "surf anonymously", "html filters", "cookie busters", "voice privacy", "email and file privacy", "secure instant messaging", "web encryption", "telnet encryption", "disk encryption", "disk/file erasing programs", "privacy policy generators", "password security", and "firewalls". Additional resources are listed there as well.

The solution for protecting students' personal information and ensuring their privacy rights will need to be on an institutional level. Obviously, institutions have access to more powerful and comprehensive applications than do individual

users. Nor can we be certain that individual applications would not interfere with other instructional applications in the online learning environment.

CONCLUSION

This chapter has focused on the need for privacy protections for users of online learning platforms. Surveys of students in online programs as well as those enrolled in traditional classroom courses revealed an erroneous view among most of the students of the degree to which their use of e-mail and online course tools were protected from third-party observation and use. A survey of instructors of business law courses who used web-based instructional tools demonstrated more awareness of a lack of privacy when participating in internet activities, but also a general lack of course policies to inform students of the openness of their communications. In both surveys, participants were asked if they knew if the institution had a privacy policy and if they believed the institution did have a privacy policy, had they read it. More than 40% of the students and 60% of the instructors thought there was a policy; approximately half of the students had read it or were made aware of the policy by their instructors.

The Family Education Rights and Privacy Act of 1974 (FERPA) provides no privacy protections for users in online instructional programs beyond that included in the Act for the security of educational records. FERPA coverage is also limited in scope and by the enforcement options in the statute (Shiley, 2003).

Privacy policies were posted on the websites for the instructional platforms (Blackboard and eCollege) used at one institution. These were lengthy, as are many included on commercial websites. It would be difficult to say if users of any website actually read and understand the policy statements. It might be that the user's need or desire to access the site's information, product, or service is of more concern than the potential misappropriation of the user's personal information.

In the United States, protections for internet users, commercial as well as educational, have developed differently than they have in Europe. In the U.S., there is no convention or statute comparable to the Council of Europe's Convention for the Protection of Human Rights and Fundamental Freedoms. Instead, there are a number of statutes that provide protection for personal information in specific situations. To date, the authors have found no U.S. case law on the rights of users' to privacy in online education.

Litigation that has been brought has concerned criminal defense strategies, search and seizure cases, commercial fraud, and of course, identity theft. Traditionally, privacy rights (the right to seclusion, to one's name, to personal information, to reputation) have been enforced under tort[2] actions, such as trespass, defamation, intentional infliction of emotional distress.

Recommendations on how to protect users' personal information from unauthorized publication from the students and instructors who were surveyed were limited to making users aware that their information was not protected (and not worrying about it) and not using the online tools that could not make information secure. We suggest that these are understandable but unrealistic solutions.

In 2009, the Obama administration announced the creation of a White House office of cybersecurity citing threats to the nation's information, economic and security networks. In his remarks, President Obama said, "It's about the privacy and economic security of American families." (Text, May 29, 2009). Appointed in December, 2009, Howard A. Schmidt, Special Assistant to the President and Cybersecurity Coordinator is responsible for cybersecurity policy coordination and integration, ensuring that agency budgets reflect those policies and coordination of any necessary response to cyber attack. His task is to focus on the means to secure the privacy of data

critical to the national security and economy of the United States (NSC, 2010). The new security measures will not be designed to interfere with how businesses protect their data. But, the Administration has recognized the need for technology fields to gain attention in educational institutions, "…we will begin a national campaign to promote cybersecurity awareness and digital literacy from our boardrooms to our classrooms…" (Text, May 29, 2009). Privacy protections in online educational forums may follow. One step the Obama Administration has said it will not take is the monitoring of private sector networks or Internet traffic to protect the personal privacy and civil liberties of Americans. This tension between individual liberty and national security can be seen in President Obama's remarks introducing the new cyber-security initiative.

On the policy level, striking a balance between individual rights and the state's rights almost certainly preclude a comprehensive ban on access to information. At this time, with the exception of the *Children's Online Privacy Protection Act* (COPPA) which gives parents control over the types and uses of information on their children collected by third parties in the private sector, it seems unlikely that legislation limiting commercial access would pass constitutional tests in the United States.

It seems clear that with regard to protecting users' rights to privacy in online courses, instructors and institutions need to engage in a serious conversation about the need to protect users. On the institutional level, this would require a review of technology and development of guidelines and policies. What should instructors do to protect their students' rights to privacy in the current environment? Instructors should familiarize themselves with their institutional and departmental policies and protections for users in online learning; communicate those policies to their students (in their syllabi, postings, announcements in class and online); alert students to the openness of electronic communications, e-mail, discussion boards, chat rooms, Facebook, etc; and provide guidelines for online exchanges in the course.

As the use of the internet continues multiply and change or, at the very least expand the methods which university instructors use in teaching both online and in the classroom, institutions as well as instructors will be forced to perfect policies to protect their students' rights to privacy, confidence and reputation.

It is clear from this research, as well as the research of others, on the subject of the online teaching environment along with its online learning tools and activities, there will be a greater demand for online instruction in the years to come. In this litigious society, both universities and their instructors would be well advised to pay the utmost attention to the issues addressed in this chapter and develop viable policies and procedures, not only for the sake of their students, but to insulate themselves from potential liability.

REFERENCES

Allen, I. E., & Seaman, J. (2008). *Staying the course: Online education in the United States, 2008*. Needham, MA: Babson Survey Research Group & the Sloan Consortium.

Australian Broadcasting Corporation v Lenah Game Meats Pty Ltd (2001). HCA63.

Backroad Connections Pty Ltd. (2003). *Privacy issues in online teaching and learning (Version 1.00). Australian Flexible Learning Framework Quick Guide series*. Australian National Training Authority.

Blackboard (2009). *Privacy policy*. http://www.blackboard.com/Footer/Privacy-Policy.aspx.

Cable Communications Policy Act, 47 U.S.C. § 521 (1984).

Canadian Standards Association. (2009). *Privacy code*. Retrieved April 12, 2009 from http://www.csa.ca/standards/privacy/code/

Children's Online Privacy Reporting Act, 15 U.S.C. §§ 6501-6506 (1998).

C.M. v. Board of Educ. of Union County Regional High School Dist. (2005). 128 Fed.Appx. 876 C.A.3 (N.J.).

Commonwealth v. Hunter, 963 A.2d 545, 533 (Pa. Super. 2008).

Communications Assistance for Law Enforcement Act, 47 U.S.C. §§ 1001-1021 (1994).

Convention for the Protection of Human Rights and Fundamental Freedoms as amended by Protocol No.11. Rome, 4.XI. 1950. Retrieved Nov. 25, 2008 from http://conventions.coe.int/treaty/EN/Treaties/

Council of Europe. (2003). Convention for the protection of human rights and fundamental freedoms as amended by protocol No.11 with protocol nos. 1,4,6,7,12 and 13.

Doe v Little Rock School District, 380 F.3d 349 (Eighth Circuit, 2004).

Driver's Privacy Protection Act. 18 U.S.C. § 2721 et. seq. (1994). eCollege (2009). Retrieved April 17, 2009 from http://www.ecollege.com/Privacy_Policy.learn

Electronic Communications Privacy Act, 18 U.S.C. § 2510 (1986).

Faculty of Health Sciences, University of Sydney. (2004). Teaching and learning on-line: Privacy management. Retrieved April 17, 2009 from http://www.fhs.usyd.edu.au/staff/acad_docs/tlprivacy.pdf

Fair Credit Reporting Act, 15 U.S.C. § 1681 et seq. (1970).

Falvo v. Owasso Independent School District, 122 S. Ct. 934 (2002).

Family Education Rights and Privacy Act (FERPA), 20 U.S.C. § 1232g (1974).

Financial Modernization Act, 15 U.S.C. § 6803 (1999).

Francis, D. (2002). Privacy and anonymity: Perceptions and expectations of online students. In G. Richards (Ed.), *Proceedings of World Conference on E-learning in Corporate, Government, Healthcare, and Higher Education 2002* (pp. 1473-1476).

Gonzaga University v. Doe, 122 S.Ct. 2268 (2002).

Griswold v. Connecticut, 381 U.S. 479 (1965).

Gross, R., & Acquisti, A. (2005). Information revelation and privacy in online social networks. *Workshop on Privacy in the Electronic Society (WPES)*. Retrieved April 17, 2009 from http://www.heinz.cmu.edu/~acquisti/papers/privacy-facebook-gross-acquisti.pdf.

Health Insurance Portability and Accountability Act, 42 U.S.C. § 290dd-2 (1996).

Horton, S. (2002). Privacy in the online classroom. *Web Teaching Guide*. Retrieved April 17, 2009 from http://www.dartmouth.edu/~webteach/articles/restrict.

Imperatore, C. (2009). Wikis and blogs: Your keys to student collaboration & engagement. *Techniques*, *84*(3), 30.

Internet Attorney. (2009). *Internet privacy law*. Retrieved April 17, 2009 from http://www.netatty.com/privacy/privacy.html.

Kerr, O. S. (2007). Four models of fourth amendment protection. *Stanford Law Review*, *60*(2), 503.

Legal Information Institute. (2009). *Consumer privacy guide*. Cornell University Law School. Retrieved April 10, 2009 from http://topics.law.cornell.edu/wex/personal_Information

Legal Information Institute. (2009). *Privacy*. Cornell University Law School. Retrieved April 10, 2009 from http://topics.law.cornell.edu/wex/personal_Information

Lin, N. H., Korba, L., Yee, G., Shih, T. K., & Lin, H. W. (2004). Security and privacy technologies for distance education applications. In *Proceedings of the 18th International Conference on Advanced Information Networking and Application*.

Minister for Immigration and Citizenship v Kumar (2009) S473/2008.

National Security Council. (2010). Cybersecurity. Retrieved May 10, 2010 from http//www.whitehouse.gov/cybersecurity.

New Zealand Privacy Commissioner. (1999). *Discussion paper 2: Information Privacy principles*. Retrieved April 12, 2009 from http://www.cdt.org/privacy/eudirective.

Plock v. Bd. of Educ. of Freeport Sch. Dist. No. 145, 545 F. Supp. 2d 755 (N.D. Ill. 2007).

Privacy Act, 5 U.S.C. § 552a (1974).

Privacy Protection Act, 42 U.S.C. § 2000aa et seq. (1980).

Prosser, W. L. (1971). Handbook of the law of torts: Chapter 20 §117 right of privacy (4th ed.). St. Paul, MN: West Publishing Co.

Richardson, M. (2002). Whither breach of confidence: A right of privacy for Australia? *Melborne University Law Review*. Retrieved Nov. 25, 2008 from http://www.austlii.edu.au/au/journals/MULR/2002.

Right to Financial Privacy Act, 12 U.S.C. 3401 et seq. (1978).

Roe v. Wade, 410 U.S. 113 (1973).

Sandler, R. B. (1997). Privacy law in the USA. Retrieved April 10, 2009 from http://www.rbs2.com/privacy.htm

Sanger, D. E., & Markoff, J. (2009, May 30). Obama outlines coordinated cyber-security plan. *New York Times*. Retrieved June 6, 2009 from http://www.nytimes.com/2009/05/30/us/politics/30cyber.html

Shiley, C. S. (2003). *Putting the rights into the Family Education Rights and Privacy Act: Enforcement and the private right of action.* Unpublished Thesis. Massachusetts Institute of Technology.

Steeves, V. (2008). If the Supreme Court were on facebook: Evaluating the reasonable expectation of privacy test from a social perspective. *Canadian Journal of Criminology and Criminal Justice, 50*(3), 331–347. doi:10.3138/cjccj.50.3.331

Stevens, G. M. (1999). *Online privacy protection: Issues and developments.* National Library for the Environment. CRS Report: RL30322. Retrieved April 11, 2009 from http://digital.library.unt.edu/govdocs/crs/permalink/meta-crs-895:1

Storey, V. A., & Tebes, M. L. (2008). Instructor's privacy in distance (online) teaching: Where do you draw the line? *Online Journal of Distance Learning Administration XI* (II). Retrieved April 8, 2009 from http://www.westga.edu/distance/ojdla/summer112/storey112.html

Telecommunications Act, 47 U.S.C. §§ 153, 255. § 153 (1996).

Telephone Consumer Protection Act, 47 U.S.C. § 227 (1991).

Text: Obama's remarks on cyber-security. (2009). *New York Times.* Retrieved June 6, 2009 from http://www.nytimes.com/2009/05/29/us/politics/29obama.text.html

Thomas, J. L. (2009). Online, teaching, & academic research privacy policy. Retrieved from http://www.ccba.jsu.edu/Thomas/PrivacyPolicy.doc

United States v. Heckenamp, 482 F3d 1142, Ninth Circuit (2007).

United States v. Miami University, 294 F. 3d 797 (2002)

Video Privacy Protection Act, 18 U.S.C. § 2710 (1988).

Wallace, L. (2007). Online teaching and university policy: Investigating the disconnect. *Journal of Distance Education, 22*(1) 87-100. Retrieved April 6, 2009 from http://www.jofde.ca/index.php/jde/article/viewFile/58/471.

Warren, S.D. & Brandeis, L.D. (1890). The right to privacy. *Harvard Law Review, 4*(5), 193-220. Posted February 8, 1999. Retrieved April 10, 2009.

ENDNOTES

[1]   Vovici is a company that focuses on Enterprise Feedback Management (EFM), providing comprehensive survey software, panel management and online community solutions.

[2]   Prosser (1971) defines a tort as a civil wrong, other than breach of contract, for which a court will provide a remedy in the form of an action for damages.

Chapter 22
Legislation–Aware Privacy Protection in Passive Network Monitoring

Georgios V. Lioudakis
National Technical University of Athens, Greece

Francesca Gaudino
Baker & McKenzie, Italy

Elisa Boschi
Hitachi Europe, France

Giuseppe Bianchi
University of Rome Tor Vergata, Italy

Dimitra I. Kaklamani
National Technical University of Athens, Greece

Iakovos S. Venieris
National Technical University of Athens, Greece

ABSTRACT

Passive network monitoring is very useful for the operation, maintenance, control and protection of communication networks, while in certain cases it provides the authorities with the means for law enforcement. Nevertheless, the flip side of monitoring activities is that they are natively surrounded by serious privacy implications and, therefore, they are subject to data protection legislation. This chapter's objective is the investigation of the challenges related to privacy protection in passive network monitoring, based on a joint technical and regulatory analysis of the associated issues. After introducing the issue and its special characteristics, the chapter provides background knowledge regarding the corresponding legal and regulatory framework, as well as some related work. It then delves into the description of the legal and regulatory requirements that govern network monitoring systems, before providing an overview of a reference monitoring system, which has been designed with these requirements in mind.

DOI: 10.4018/978-1-61520-975-0.ch022

INTRODUCTION

"On the Internet, nobody knows you are a dog" according to the famous Pat Steiner cartoon in The New Yorker in 1993, which has been very frequently cited in order to emphasize the potential for anonymity and privacy that the Internet was supposed to offer. However, the reality seems to be rather different and, among the several threats to personal privacy caused by the emerging Information and Communication Technologies, activities related to passive network monitoring hold an outstanding position. While extremely useful and important for purposes such as network operation, management, planning and maintenance, security protection (e.g., in terms of intrusion detection and prevention), scientific research based on real traffic traces, as well as law enforcement, network monitoring not only may lead to privacy violations but it is also surrounded by legal implications (see e.g., Sicker, Ohm & Grunwald, 2007). Indeed, as electronic communications increasingly proliferate in everyday life, privacy with all its facets is increasingly considered as a quality attribute of paramount importance. More than a century after the seminal essay identifying that privacy as a fundamental human right was endangered by technological advances (Warren & Brandeis, 1890), never before in history citizens have been more concerned about their personal privacy and the threats posed by emerging technologies (Gallup Organization, 2008) and, in this context, violations related to passive network monitoring and communications' surveillance have started hitting the headlines and feed the citizens' concerns. There are numerous documented mishaps; for instance, consider the U.S. National Security Agency's warrantless wiretapping, secretly authorized by the Bush Administration (Risen & Lichtblau, 2005), or the major contemporary wiretapping scandal, that took place recently in Greece (Prevelakis & Spinellis, 2007).

As the privacy domain is increasingly becoming a legislated area, the activities bound to passive network monitoring have been the focus of several legal and regulatory initiatives worldwide. In addition, they constitute the subject of regulations that target at leveraging network monitoring in order to increase public security; such regulations often contradict with the requirement for privacy, imposing provisions for communications' surveillance and data collection and retention and compromising the common expectation for privacy when communicating electronically. In that respect, legislation can have repercussions far beyond privacy concerns and can even damage governments' reputation, as has been recently the case with the Swedish New Signal Surveillance Act law (Economist, 2008).

This chapter investigates the issue of privacy protection in the context of passive network monitoring from a joint regulatory and technical viewpoint. The next three sections provide some background information regarding, respectively, passive network monitoring and the entailed privacy concerns and challenges, some related work and the applicable legislation. Based on the latter and focusing on the European legislation that comprises the most mature framework worldwide, the chapter continues with the thorough description of the corresponding legal and regulatory requirements that should characterize a monitoring system. Before concluding, the chapter provides the overview of an innovative generic passive network monitoring system that has been conceived on the basis of the legislation and follows engineering practices that reflect the underlying requirements.

PASSIVE NETWORK MONITORING

Opposed to active monitoring that involves the injection of test packets in the network and the consequent measurement of their qualitative characteristics, the approach for communications network monitoring referred to as passive concerns the inspection of the actual network traffic using special software and/or hardware equipment. Enabling factors for the recent surge of passive network monitoring have been the availability of high-performance capturing devices, such as network probing cards, and storage systems of large capacity, as well as the development of intelligent methods for traffic analysis and knowledge inference.

The domain of passive network monitoring applicability is quite broad. It is crucial for the effective operation and management of communication networks, since it enables the real-time acquisition of essential information and the identification, among other, of performance bottlenecks, while the offline analysis of the resulting traces is very useful for network planning and the accounting and billing of network services. In this context, passive network monitoring can additionally serve for the validation of Service Level Agreements and generally for the observation and fine-tuning of parameters related to quality of service. With respect to security and protection of networks, it constitutes the fundamental basis for Intrusion / Anomaly Detection Systems (IDS/ADS) which trigger alarms and set up countermeasures in reaction to events, such as network intrusions, denial-of-service attacks and worm infections. In addition, the data traces that constitute the result of passive network monitoring are very useful for the research community that investigates the fields mentioned above, as well as other network-related research domains. Last but not least, passive network monitoring provides the means for the implementation of several obligations mandated by the law; these include the retention of certain data for ensuring their availability if needed for the investigation, detection and prosecution of serious crimes, as well as the performance of lawful interception.

Intuitively, since passive network monitoring depends by default on the collection and processing of information, it raises issues related to the protection of personal data. Even more, passive network monitoring activities are in particular interesting

compared to other domains (e.g., e-commerce), as far as privacy protection is concerned, for a number of reasons:

- Privacy-sensitive information is not limited to the payload of the network packets, i.e., the content of the monitored communications. In fact, this case could be even considered as trivial from a privacy protection point of view, since the confidentiality of the content can be adequately achieved by using strong end-to-end encryption. The focus of passive network monitoring is on the collection of so-called context data (Zugenmaier & Claessens, 2007). Lioudakis et al. (2007) have characterized such data as "semi-active", in the sense that data collection occurs transparently for the user; this type of transparent, implicit collection tends to raise greater privacy concerns than those initiated by the user (Cranor, 2004).

- While the various protocols' headers already reveal much information (e.g., a visited web-site or the peers of a VoIP call), a huge amount of personal information can be further extracted from their processing, even if they have been anonymised. Literature has shown that once a flow can be examined in isolation, fingerprinting techniques allow to derive personal information from as little as the basic statistics (i.e., packet sizes and inter-arrival times correlation) of the delivered packets (Bissias et al., 2005; Crotti et al., 2006; Hintz, 2002). Danezis (2002) and Sun et al. (2002) have demonstrated that SSL/TLS does not resist statistical traffic analysis, while meaningful data can be finally extracted even from "unsuspicious" header fields, such as the IP ID alone (Bellovin, 2002).

- The passive network monitoring activities, as well as the underlying categories of data, have been subject of specific regulations, as it will be described later. Additionally, in many countries, independent data and communication protection authorities regulate and audit privacy protection in communications.

- Finally, passive network monitoring deals with very high data rates that exceed the order of Gbps; thus, any mechanisms deployed for privacy preservation should be able to cope with such stringent requirements.

RELATED WORK

Several approaches have been proposed for privacy protection of data traces generated in the context of passive network monitoring activities, most of them targeting the anonymisation of the traffic. Although frameworks such as the ones proposed by Koukis et al. (2006) and Pang et al. (2006) are aimed to be quite generic, a significant drawback is that they base on quite "static" anonymisation policies specification; in all cases, the policies that will regulate the execution of the underlying anonymisation Application Programming Interfaces must be defined in an explicit manner. Additionally, although they work well for applications using previously collected traffic data (e.g., billing services or applications devised for Internet research based on packet traces), they are not applicable to applications' domains that demand real-time data, such as intrusion detection systems.

Any privacy violation certainly includes illicit access to personal data and, intuitively, access control constitutes a fundamental aspect of privacy protection. There are several approaches for privacy-aware access control, comprising now a quite mature research area. A milestone in the area has been the concept of Hippocratic Databases (Agrawal et al., 2002). Nevertheless, since they target stored data and make use of database

tables for their operation, this approach, as well as other database-oriented ones (Bertino, Byun & Li, 2005), can not be suitable for real-time monitoring systems.

The provision of the automation of the privacy policies enforcement has been the focus of several approaches, including the ones proposed by IBM (Ashley et al., 2003; Backes, Pfitzmann & Schunter, 2003), OASIS (2004) and Hewlett Packard (Casassa Mont, 2005; Casassa Mont & Thyne, 2006), the concept of Purpose Based Access Control (Byun, Bertino & Li, 2005) and the family of Privacy aware Role Based Access Control Models (P-RBAC) (Ni et al., 2007). All these frameworks enhance traditional Role-Based Access Control (RBAC) models (Ferraiolo et al., 2001) with additional, privacy-related aspects, such as the purpose for data collection and the automation of retention periods' enforcement, in order to put in place privacy-aware access control. Recently, some similar approaches with the additional feature of being grounded on a semantic basis have been proposed by Finin et al. (2008), Noorollahi Ravari et al. (2008) and Lioudakis et al. (2008). However, all these approaches are not suitable for the case of passive network monitoring, because on the one hand they have not been designed for meeting the stringent performance requirements of passive network monitoring, while on the other hand they do not incorporate the mechanisms for traffic anonymisation.

OVERVIEW OF THE LEGAL AND REGULATORY FRAMEWORK

The design of a network monitoring system cannot be considered as a purely technical activity, as it clearly has a considerable societal impact (in terms of both its implications on privacy and in terms on its consequences on public security). Moreover, public policies and regulatory requirements do affect to a significant extent the technical requirements of such a system. Therefore, the provision of an overview of the underlying legal and regulatory framework is deemed necessary.

In this section, the focus is on the legislation of the European Union, since it comprises the most representative, influential and mature approach worldwide, that seems to pull a general framework and has been characterized as an "engine of a global regime" (Birnhack, 2008). For some insights in the frameworks of the U.S. and other countries, the reader is referred to the essays of Solove (2006) and Sicker, Ohm & Grunwald (2007).

Data Protection and Passive Network Monitoring

Privacy is recognized as a fundamental human right by the Universal Declaration of Human Rights of the United Nations (1948), as well as the Charter of Fundamental Rights of the European Union (European Parliament, Council & Commission, 2000). It is protected by relevant legislation in all the democratic countries throughout the world.

A significant milestone in the privacy literature has been the codification of the fundamental privacy principles by the Organization for Economic Co-operation and Development (1980), as this codification lays out the basis for the protection of privacy. The OECD principles are reflected in the European Directive 95/46/EC (European Parliament and Council, 1995), "*on the protection of individuals with regard to the processing of personal data and on the free movement of such data*". The Directive 95/46/EC enforces a high standard of data protection and constitutes the most influential piece of privacy legislation worldwide, affecting many countries outside Europe in enacting similar laws.

Under Article 2, the Directive 95/46/EC defines personal data as "*any information relating to an identified or identifiable natural person ('data subject'); an identifiable person is one who can be identified, directly or indirectly, in particular by reference to an identification number or to one or more factors specific to his physical, physiologi-*

cal, mental, economic, cultural or social identity". This definition stresses on the explicit reference to indirect identification data, implying any information that may lead to the identification of the data subject through association with other available information (thus indirectly), that may be held by any third party. With respect to communications' context data, the definition has been further elaborated in a subsequent document from the Article 29 Data Protection Working Party (2007), which has concluded that "*... unless the Internet Service Provider is in a position to distinguish with absolute certainty that the data correspond to users that cannot be identified, it will have to treat all IP information as personal data to be on the safe side*". Therefore, data gathered through passive monitoring may be considered as personal data, subject to the data protection legislation.

The Directive 95/46 EC is further particularized and complemented with reference to the electronic communication sector by the Directive 2002/58/EC (European Parliament and Council, 2002), which imposes explicit obligations and sets specific limits on the processing of users' personal data by network and service providers in order to protect the privacy of the users of communications services and networks. It has granted a specific and high degree of protection to traffic and location data, imposing strict limits and requirements to their processing due to their peculiar nature. Indeed, traffic data allow knowing user's activities and behavior and defining the user's personality; traffic data allow the user's localization and tracking. Combined traffic and location data enable to build user's profile enriched with geographical information, thus resulting in a significant encroaching into the individual's personal life and in invasive surveillance. Moreover and as has been described above, the amount of data that may be gathered through communications network traffic analysis is potentially indefinite; from a privacy law perspective, the amount of data processed raises privacy concerns, since the application of data mining algorithms and specific elaboration techniques gives the possibility to build precise users' profiles.

Concluding the relation between passive network monitoring and personal data protection legislation, it should be stressed that network monitoring i) involves the gathering of information which constitutes 'personal data' under the meaning of the Directive 95/46/EC; ii) represents an activity that poses serious risks to the individual's right to data protection and freedoms, and iii) data processing activities performed while monitoring traffic should be carried out in line with the set of rules and limitations provided by data protection legislation.

Passive Network Monitoring and Public Security

On the other hand, the design of a network monitoring system is complicated by the need to additionally satisfy public security and safety constraints. Traffic logging was fostered by governmental entities as a means to protect the citizens' safety by facilitating the trace-back of malicious or criminal network users. In Europe, data retention obligations were translated into concrete regulations with the Directive 2006/24/EC (European Parliament and Council, 2006), which mandates the preemptive storage of communications' context data.

In addition to the provisions regarding data retention, there exist specific regulations with respect to the lawful interception of communications. In the U.S., the Federal Wiretap Act has been enacted already in 1968 and since then has been adapted in order to include modern communication systems (Monnat & Ethen, 2004). In the European Union, the Resolution on the Lawful Interception of Telecommunications (Council of the European Union, 1996) has explicitly recognized the requirement for the availability of the lawful interception means to the law enforcement agencies.

Nowadays to intercept telephone and Internet communications and to monitor the activities performed over the Internet is perceived as a need to ensure public security and also to prevent especially serious crimes such as terrorism. To this end, within the European Union member states have adopted different regulations whose aim is providing security for citizens, while at the same time limiting the monitoring and interception activities within specific boundaries in order to respect the privacy and rights of citizens. Even though this is a difficult balance to be reached, legislation has tried to avoid excessive encroaching within the lives of persons, but the always new and more invasive technical solutions offered by the market have made this task more difficult to achieve, since the law is not always able to follow the technical developments. The general principle followed is that encroaching into private life of citizens is allowed only when there is an overriding public interest, that is, to provide security to citizens and to investigate on specific crimes that trigger significant alert.

LEGAL AND REGULATORY REQUIREMENTS FOR MONITORING SYSTEMS

From the analysis of the legal and regulatory framework, certain requirements can be described that should characterize a passive network monitoring system. The basis for the following overview of the main regulatory requirements has been the European framework since, as aforementioned, it comprises the basis for many jurisdictions worldwide; nevertheless, it is stressed that similar requirements are derived by the jurisdictions of other countries.

Lawfulness of Data Processing

A monitoring system should be able to evaluate the lawfulness of each request for personal data with applicable laws and regulations. In practice, the system should be structured in a way that enables assessing the legitimacy of a request of access to data submitted by the different components of the system. The lawfulness of a given data processing activity should be evaluated against the type of collected information and the purposes for which it was collected, taking into account not only the legislation ruling on privacy and data security, but more generally of all applicable laws and regulations. It follows that the system should be configurable with a set of data types and purposes deemed to be lawful and, for these specified and pre-identified data types and purposes, the system should allow the processing of the personal data.

All such configuration of the system with respect to the lawfulness of stated processing purposes must be done by persons who are competent both in the means used to configure the system and in the applicable legal context.

Any request that is not specifically determined to be lawful according to the set of lawful purposes must be denied. If the request is concerned with a certain kind of network monitoring on the basis of the specific purpose of said monitoring activity, the system should be able to apply the other mandatory legal requirements. For example, the use of data in anonymous or identifiable form would be permitted or not permitted depending upon the specific monitoring function to be carried out.

Purposes for Which Data are Processed

A monitoring system should provide the means for identifying the purpose of each request, in order to comply with the "purpose principle". In practice, the system should function so that it allows the collection and processing of personal data only when said activities are carried out for specified, explicit and legitimate purposes. In addition, the system should prohibit that personal data collected for some specific and legitimate purposes are used for other purposes, incompatible with those for which the data have been originally collected.

The purpose principle also implies that the controller should act transparently. This means that the controller should specify and make explicit to the data subjects the reasons why the personal data are used. To this purpose, the system should allow a certain kind of communication with end users in order to make them explicit the purposes for which their personal data are being gathered and processed or, alternatively, the system should provide technical features that allow kind of negotiation with the party submitting the personal data processing request and, during said negotiation process, the system should be able to verify that the requesting party has complied with the aforementioned requirement towards the data subjects.

Necessity, Adequacy, and Proportionality of the Data Processed

A monitoring system should operate according to the so named "proportionality principle", which requires that the personal data of the end users may be gathered and processed only to the extent that they are adequate, relevant and not excessive if compared with the monitoring function for which are collected by the system.

The system in practice should be able to determine the amount of personal data that may be processed within a specific monitoring function and the type of data may be processed within the same function. For example, if the monitoring is aimed at producing statistical figures, the data may be processed in anonymous form and there is no need of using information that may identify the data subjects.

Processing activities may be performed only on data that are functional and necessary to the specific purpose that it is sought by the monitoring function. The system should automatically delete or make anonymous any data that are redundant or no longer needed for a specific monitoring function.

Quality of the Data Processed

A monitoring system should ensure that the data processed are correct, exact and updated. Moreover, the system should be able to perform corrective actions in order to delete or correct inaccurate data and to delete or update data that are outdated or redundant.

In addition to these corrective remedies, the system should also allow periodic audits on the personal data that it stores, so as to verify the legitimacy of said data.

Minimal Use of Personal Identification Data

A monitoring system should minimize to the extent possible the use of identification and personal data only when this is a prerequisite to the specific monitoring function that is to be performed.

When a given monitoring result may be achieved without personal identification data, the system should be able to use anonymous data or alternatively to allow the identification of the data subject only under specific circumstances, for example in case of mandatory data retention obligations under the Directive 2006/24/EC.

Storage of Personal Data

A monitoring system should keep personal data in an identifiable form only for the time that it is strictly necessary to the specific monitoring function that is carried out. Personal data that are redundant or no longer needed should be deleted or anonymised. As noted above, periodic audits on the data stored by the system should be performed, together with functions that perform automated deletion or anonymisation of redundant or unneeded data.

Data Retention

A monitoring system should comply with the requirements set forth by applicable data retention regulations. This implies that the system should store the specific data that are subject to the data retention regulations for the time periods specified under the applicable regulatory framework. Moreover, the system should disclose the data only to the law enforcement authorities that are specifically designated and authorized under applicable legislation.

It should be stressed that compliance with data retention law requirements implies additionally that the system should fulfill specific and mandatory security requirements to be applied for the storage of the data and relevant access. For example, the data stored for data retention purposes should be kept logically separated from the other data stored by the system.

Access Limitation

A monitoring system should authenticate all users of the system, should provide different levels of access to the stored data and should provide for the logging of all access to the stored data in order to detect attempted or successful unauthorized access. These levels of access should be granted based on the authentication of individual users, the need to know associated with each individual user's role, as well as the types of data to be accessed. For example it may be the case that a specific user profile allows the access and consultation of the data, but does not allow the modification or deletion of the data.

Information to and Rights of the Data Subject

With regard to the requirements relating to providing to the data subjects adequate information on the purposes, conditions and features of the data processing, as well as to the requirements relating to offering to the data subjects the possibility to obtain information on their data and to actively intervene on the data processing enforcing privacy rights such as the rights to access data, ask for data updating, integration, deletion and others, the core of the matter is that these requirements may be fulfilled only by the entity having direct contact with the data subjects. The scenario would change according to the entity that performs the monitoring. In case the network provider itself performs monitoring on its customers, the provider should comply with applicable legislation with regard to information to the data subjects and enforcement of their privacy rights. In case the monitoring is performed by an entity having no direct contact with users, these requirements should be addressed by negotiation between the network provider and the entity that intends to perform the monitoring. The subset of mandatory information that the data subject should receive varies across different jurisdictions, so it is important that the system allows a high degree of flexibility. In general terms, the data subjects should be informed about the following issues: the purposes and the methods of the data processing; the extent of data communication and/or data diffusion; the mandatory or optional nature of providing his/her personal data and the consequences that he/she may undergo in case of refusal to provide personal data; the contact details of the entities in charge of the data processing acting as data controller and data processor.

As to the privacy rights of the data subjects, we may recall for example that the data subject should be provided with the possibility to access his/her personal data, to ask for specific information about the processing of his/her personal data, to ask for his/her personal data to be integrated, updated, rectified, deleted or transformed in an anonymous form. The data subject should also be enabled to block the processing of his/her personal data in case of breach of applicable laws and to object the processing of his/her personal data for legitimate reasons.

Consent of the Data Subject

For compliance with the consent requirements, please refer to the above comments. The monitoring system should guarantee that, when required by applicable data protection legislation, the data subject's consent to the data processing is requested and obtained and that the data processing is further performed according to the preferences expressed by the data subject.

The data subject should be enabled to revoke at any time the consent previously granted (even temporarily in case of location and traffic data processed for the performance of value added communications services).

Moreover, it is also important that the consent bears the features as described under applicable data protection legislation, notably the consent of the data subject should be free (in the sense that it should be given by the data subject without being forced to do so); express (that is, there should be some kind of material evidence that the data subject provided the consent); written (this usually applies to the processing of sensitive data and it depends on the specific circumstance and on the applicable privacy legislation); specific (notably the consent should be provided by the data subject with regard to a specifically identified data processing activity); and informed (which implies that the data subject prior to giving his/her consent has been provided with the mandatory set of information on the applicable data processing as requested under relevant regulatory framework).

Data Security Measures

A monitoring system should adopt appropriate technical and organizational measures with the purpose of protecting the personal data that are collected and processed against the risks of accidental or unlawful destruction, accidental loss, alteration, unauthorized disclosure or access, in particular where the processing involves the transmission of data over a network, as well as against any other unlawful possible data processing operation or set of operations.

Taking into account the technical state of the art and the economic efforts in terms of implementation, the security measures that are applied should be able to ensure an adequate level of security. The adequacy should be assessed having regard to the risks represented by the nature of the personal data to be protected and the processing operations to be performed.

Under some data protection national legislations, there may be specific lists of mandatory security measures to be implemented; any deployment of the system subject to these laws must implement these measures.

With specific focus on the area of telecommunications services, it should be added that the security provisions are addressed not only to the service providers, but also to the network providers. In case security concerns occur in the network or for the performance of a given service, the data subject must be duly informed about said concerns.

Special Categories of Data

A monitoring system should guarantee that the processing of special categories of data (for example, but not limited to, traffic or other location data, sensitive and judicial data) is performed in compliance with the specific requirements that the applicable data protection legislation sets forth for said categories of data.

For the processing of traffic data and location data, which are of particular interest for passive network monitoring, the Directive 2002/58/EC requires that the data subject should be provided with some information that supplements the usual set of mandatory information to be given to the data subject when his/her personal data are collected. Indeed, for the processing of location and traffic data, the data subject should be specifically informed with regard to the type of location and traffic data that are to be processed,

the purposes of the processing (which should be very detailed and clear), the intended duration of the data processing and (for location data) whether the data are to be transmitted to a third party for the purpose of providing the service requested by the data subject. Moreover, for the processing of traffic and location data, the consent of the data subject is requested, even in the case where the processing is functional to performance of services required by the data subject, while in contrast the circumstance that the processing is necessary to offer to the data subject a service that the same has requested represents a general exemption from the need to obtain the data subject's consent prior to starting the data processing activities. For these requirements relating to information to the data subjects and consent of the data subjects, please further refer to the sections above.

The Directive 2002/58/EC also imposes specific security requirements for the processing of traffic and location data. For instance, the access to said data and their processing should be restricted to persons acting under the authority of the provider of the public communications network or publicly available communications service, or of the third party providing the value added service, while it must be restricted to what is necessary for the purposes of providing the value added service.

Lastly, there are also limitations applying to the purposes for which said special categories of personal data may be processed. For example, sensitive data usually cannot be used for activities such as profiling and building of pattern behaviors and individuals' profiles.

Overall, the monitoring system should implement the tighter security measures and limitations set forth by applicable data protection legislation, in terms of application of the requested security measures and compliance with the limitations imposed for the processing of the special categories of personal data (for example with regard to the limitations imposed on the purposes for which said data may be collected and processed).

Coordination with Competent Data Protection Authority

A monitoring system should monitor compliance with the notification requirement and with the provisions of the authorizations of the competent Data Protection Authorities, as ruled under applicable data protection legislation. Moreover, the system should allow communications between the system and the competent Data Protection Authorities in order to validate and verify that the notification and/or authorization requirements have been duly complied with.

This kind of interaction with the competent Data Protection Authorities may result in a kind of alert that the system submits to the referenced Authorities, in order to notify them that a certain data processing activity, which is subject to notification and/or authorization requirements, is being performed. Verification of compliance with notification and/or authorization requirements may also be considered within the negotiation process between the system and the entities asking access to the personal data stored within the system. Then it would be up to the competent Data Protection Authority to verify accomplishments of the due legal conditions.

Supervision and Sanctions

A monitoring system should provide the competent Data Protection Authorities with the means for supervising and controlling all actions of personal data collection and processing. This function is very important, as it often happens that the competent Data Protection Authorities encounter difficulties in auditing the processing of personal data carried out through technical means and over the Internet; this is due to the peculiar nature of the technical means deployed, that allow the hiding of the data processing activities performed.

The system would not act as an enforcement authority, since it would lack the necessary competence; instead it should provide information to the competent Data Protection Authorities, so that they can perform the necessary verifications and impose the sanctions in cases of breaches of the applicable data protection legislation.

This activity of providing of information should be structured as a communication channel, specified by an accepted technical standard or by agreement, between components of the monitoring system and the competent Data Protection Authorities, so that the system provides the aforementioned Authorities with a log of data processing activities performed.

Communications Confidentiality and Lawful Interception

A monitoring system should be structured consistent with the protection of the confidentiality of communications over the monitored networks. Indeed, the European Union legislation prohibits the listening, tapping, storage or other kinds of interception or surveillance of communications and the related traffic data, unless the user has given consent and such surveillance is technically necessary to provide the data subject with the requested communication service.

Therefore, the monitoring system should guarantee confidentiality in the communications, but should also be able of complying with the lawful interception requests coming from the competent public authorities. The system should support the strict legal requirements posed as preconditions for the interception. Interception is allowed only when it is necessary, appropriate and proportionate to safeguard public interests such as national security, defense, public security, and the prevention, investigation, detection and prosecution of criminal offences or of unauthorized use of electronic communications systems.

The monitoring system should therefore provide the competent public authorities with the means to perform interception in accordance with the applicable requirements and under the defined conditions. The necessary "hooks" for the lawful interception should under no circumstance become available to other not authorized third parties. Moreover, according to applicable legal framework, the system should allow the transmission of the relevant personal data in a robustly secure way and as requested by the legitimate addresses of the data communications. The personal data should usually be immediately and definitively deleted after they are communicated to the competent authorities. There may be an agreement between the system and the competent national public authorities as to the means of retention and communication of the personal data representing the subject matter of the interception.

Flexibility and Adaptability of Legal Compliance Provisions

Finally, the domain of privacy protection has been characterized as a "regulatory jungle" (Pletscher, 2005). Given the complexity of the legal environment in which a monitoring system operates, the different legal requirements across different jurisdictions and the nature of the law to change from time to time, the system's design should to the extent possible be flexible and adaptable with respect to all the provisions described in this section. Specifically, the system should encode as much of these provisions in dynamic policies.

PRIVACY-PRESERVING PASSIVE NETWORK MONITORING

"The machine is the problem: the solution is in the machine" according to Poullet (2006) and, following this principle, this section describes the architecture and engineering practices that should characterize a privacy-preserving passive network monitoring system. The proposed framework has been conceived on the basis of the afore-described legal and regulatory requirements and its aim is to put limitations on the undisciplined information flows from the network to the monitoring applica-

tions that lead in excessive and non-proportional information acquisition.

Conceptually, the problem of technically enforcing privacy protection in this context can be seen as the provision of the means to effectively control access to monitoring data and monitoring results such that only the data and/or monitoring results strictly necessary to the operation of a monitoring task are becoming available to that task. This paradigm highlights some key engineering principles for the privacy-preserving monitoring system under consideration, which are the following:

- Protection of the data as soon as they are captured, i.e., already on the online monitoring probes.
- Provision of a comprehensive mechanism for the control of the access and processing of the collected data.
- Separation of duties and dual control of the action related to data processing; in other words, decoupling of the entities in charge of enforcing data protection and in charge of running monitoring applications.
- To the greatest possible extent, execution of the privacy-sensitive parts of the monitoring applications' logic inside the system, in order for the disclosure of the corresponding data to be avoided.

The reference system architecture is sketched in Figure 1. Unlike traditional architectures, that are typically monolithic, the system is comprised of three separate subsystems that are administratively independent: the Front-End, the Back-End and the Privacy-Preserving Controller (PPC). Goal of the former is to capture network traffic and to isolate, extract and protect traffic data which are consequently delivered for further processing to the Back-End. Goal of the Back-End is to mediate between the information source (i.e., the Front-End) and the monitoring applications, enforcing control on how the latter are granted access to the

Figure 1. Reference system architecture

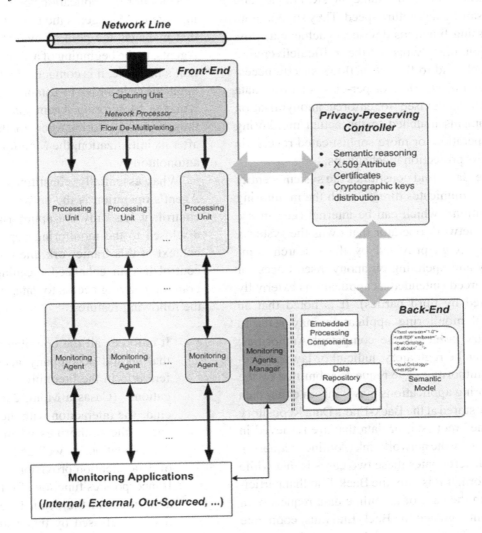

data in a privacy-aware manner. Additionally, it plays the role of the "information warehouse", for the cases when the retention of data is needed. These two components define in essence two different stages in the data lifecycle: raw collection on the one hand and storage, processing and potential disclosure, on the other. Finally, the PPC is not directly involved into the monitoring process, but implements administrative duties.

Data processing within the Front-End is enforced at two stages. First, the traffic flows are classified according to the canonical 5-tuple at the

Capturing Unit at wire speed. The Capturing Unit is implemented by means of a hardware network processor for meeting the stringent performance requirements imposed by the high rates of packets' arrival. After their classification, the flows are de-multiplexed and delivered to several Processing Units. Each Processing Unit is dedicated to act as the interface to a specific Back-End Monitoring Agent and execute the processing, filtering and protection mechanisms demanded to tailor their output to the strict needs of the Back-End monitoring task. The Processing Units are not necessarily implemented over the same physical device and at the same data capture speed. They support both processing functions devised to achieve a) flow isolation, namely restrict the traffic delivered to the Back-End to the set of flows strictly necessary, and b) per-flow or per-class-of-flows data protection, devised to enforce anonymisation mechanisms matched to the actual monitoring task operation, or more sophisticated reversible per-flow protection mechanisms.

The Back-End constitutes the system's entity that communicates directly with the monitoring applications, which can be internal (i.e., in use by the network operator that owns the system), external (e.g., provided by the research community and operating on anonymised traces) or out-sourced (intended as applications externally deployed by third parties). It is noted that an external monitoring application may refer to the entry point for the competent Authorities; these can be regulatory, judicial or law enforcement Authorities. The requests submitted by the monitoring applications may concern either data already stored at the Back-End's Data Repository ("offline" requests) or data that are retrieved in real-time by the network link ("online" requests). What differentiates these two cases is that while in the former it is only the Back-End that participates, in the case of an online data request both the Front-End and the Back-End must cooperate in order for the request to be served; in essence, the offline scenario constitutes a sub-case of the online one.

As illustrated in Figure 1, the fundamental components of the Back-End are the Monitoring Agents. A Monitoring Agent is in charge of mediating between a monitoring application and the Processing Unit of the Front-End which provides the data stream that is the subject of a monitoring application's execution. That is, a Monitoring Agent is the peer entity of a Front-End Processing Unit on the one hand and of the monitoring application on the other. It is a stateful component that is initialized when the execution of a monitoring application begins. The Monitoring Agents Manager is the Back-End component that manages the pool of available Monitoring Agents. In the beginning of a monitoring application's lifecycle, it is contacted by the monitoring application in order to establish an association with the Monitoring Agent that will constitute the serving Monitoring Agent for this application; after its initialization, the Monitoring Agent acts autonomously.

What essentially constitutes a Monitoring Agent's operation is the enforcement of access control; it lets only the appropriate data to be disclosed to the monitoring application. In the context of this framework, the notion of access control has an enhanced meaning; apart from granting/denying access to data, it encompasses the following features:

- It enforces all the complementary actions that should accompany access, often referred to in the literature as "privacy obligations" (Casassa Mont, 2004). These include the interaction with the data subjects and/or the Authorities when mandated by the legislation, as well as the enforcement of data retention provisions.
- It incorporates functions for the automated adjustment of the detail level of any data that are released by the system, based on the underlying contextual parameters. That is, constitutes an integral part of the access control procedure.

In that respect, the Back-End incorporates a rich library of software tools, referred to as Embedded Processing Components, which take care of the corresponding actions.

As derived from the requirements presented in the previous section, the semantics of the data, the underlying collection and processing purposes, as well as the entities involved, play a fundamental role for the determination of the procedures subject of which the data will be and, consequently, the behavior of the monitoring system. In that respect, the system is grounded on a semantic model, implemented by means of an ontology (Noy & McGuinness, 2001). The semantic model integrates all the aspects related to the intelligence of the system, in terms of taking decisions regarding data handling, including:

- The purpose of a monitoring task (e.g., SLA enforcement, intrusion detection, traffic profiling, accounting and billing, etc.).
- The specific traffic information required to accomplish that purpose (e.g., information explicitly present in the observed packets such as header fields, payload sections, or derived from one or more functions performed on the observed packets).
- The entity running the monitoring task (a system administrator, a division in the operator's organization, the public research community, etc);
- The "privacy context" in which the information is collected and processed, including legal obligations, temporal constrains and mutual exclusions between data types.

The semantic model is implemented by means of an OWL ontology (World Wide Web Consortium, 2004), exploiting the expressive power of the formalisms used to describe the underlying concepts. The ontology specifies hierarchical graphs with well-defined inheritance relationships for all the contextual information; on top of this rich in semantics basis, the access control rules are specified. The implementation details of the semantic ontology are out of the scope of this chapter; nevertheless, Figure 2 illustrates an example of an access control rule, stating that *"for purposes related to QoS provision by means of queue classification, an actor holding the role of Network Administrator may have read access to the Differentiated Services Code Point (DSCP) of a traffic flow. However, no modification is allowed, while such data should not be retained by the corresponding systems. This rule is not inherited to the descendants of the specified data, service or role, while it doesn't override the privacy preferences of the data subject, if any"*.

For every access decision, semantic reasoning upon the semantic knowledge base results in the specification of the necessary actions (e.g., execution of a series of Embedded Processing Components) that should be performed in order for the request to be served. In order to improve the performance of the reasoning procedure, as well as to enable the enforcement of access control

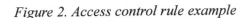

Figure 2. Access control rule example

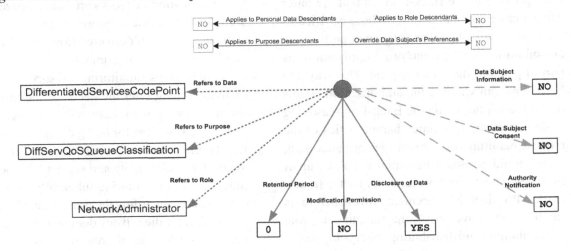

also between the Front-End and the Back-End (i.e., what data the former will release to the latter), the described framework adopts a two-phase reasoning procedure. The two phases concern, respectively, the execution of "static" and "dynamic" control; the former enforces the rules that are *a priori* applicable, grounded on the data, role and purpose semantics, while the latter evaluates the real-time "privacy context" for the adaptation of the access control procedures to the particular conditions underlying a request. Indeed, to what concerns the role- and purpose-based part of the access control decision, the corresponding reasoning can take place "offline", since the underlying parameters are static as long as the associations between roles and actors remain unchanged.

The entity performing the offline part of reasoning is the last high-level component of the reference architecture, namely the Privacy-Preserving Controller (PPC). Among the administrative tasks of the PPC is the creation and maintenance of the semantic model. In that respect, the PPC executes in an offline manner the static part of reasoning and proceeds with the generation of X.509 Attribute Certificates (International Telecommunication Union, 2005) that reflect the outcome. The certificates describe not only the data that should be disclosed by the Back-End to the monitoring application, but also the corresponding raw data that the Front-End must provide to the Back-End, so that the latter can generate the final data set. These certificates are made available to the interested parties and are submitted by the monitoring applications as part of performing a data request. This way, the Front-End can validate the authorization claims of the Back-End, while the Back-End reasoning is limited to the real-time characteristics of the request, resulting in enormous performance gain.

It should be noted here that the PPC, apart from being the Source of Authority for the framework's Privilege Management Infrastructure as summarized above, holds the fundamental role of maintaining and distributing the cryptographic keys used within the framework. This becomes especially important for the cases when some cryptographic data protection measures that have been applied by the Front-End must be reversed by the Back-End or the monitoring application (e.g., in some case of law enforcement).

Finally, it must be mentioned here that for the implementation of the two primary data paths of the architecture, i.e., the data plane connection between the Front-End and the Back-End and the data export connection between the Back-End and the monitoring applications, the IP Flow Information Export (IPFIX) protocol (RFC5101, 2008) has been selected. This is because this protocol meets all of the requirements of the data paths: they should be oriented toward common types of traffic data and flexible enough to transport diverse types of traffic data, as well as derived information, while they should be based upon defined or de facto standards in order to facilitate both the substitution of components within a measurement ecosystem and to ensure the widest possible utility of the exported data. Additionally, there are some recent efforts for the standardization of IPFIX-specific anonymisation techniques (Boschi & Trammell, 2009).

CONCLUSION

Communication networks are characterized by a significant increase in terms of capacity, traffic volume, number of delivered flows and diffusion capillarity. At the same time, the technologies for communications' monitoring and surveillance are evolving, along with the needs of the providers for monitoring their networks for operational purposes, as well as for being compliant with the legislation that leverages network monitoring as a means for public safety and security. At the same time, network monitoring inherently raises serious concerns regarding the protection of personal data and, since the privacy domain is increasingly becoming a legislated area, there is a need for bridging the contradictory underlying requirements. Overall, the issue of protecting privacy in the context of passive network monitoring is very challenging; it essentially concerns how to balance the needs for law enforcement, information usability and privacy assurance.

To face the issues, network monitoring architectures should be rethought so as to incorporate privacy preservation in their design and make the legal and regulatory provisions an integral part of their operational and functional procedures. In that respect, this chapter has investigated the issue from a dual perspective; the legal and regulatory on the one hand and the technical on the other. It has provided an analysis of the legal and regulatory requirements, stemming from the domains of both personal data protection and public safety and security.

With the legal and regulatory provisions, as well as the associated technical challenges in mind, the chapter additionally described an innovative privacy-preserving network monitoring system that aims at breaking new ground regarding compliance with the legislation. In fact, the described system does not only take into account the corresponding provisions; it has been conceived on the basis of the legislation and constitutes the result of collaborative work between lawyers and engineers. The described system creates a "wall" in the flow of personal data between the network link and the monitoring applications that consume traffic data with the introduction of a two-tier approach: a Front-End tier is devised to protect the collected data as soon as they are gathered, while a Back-End middleware tier caters for the disclosure of data to the monitoring applications in a legislation-aware manner.

REFERENCES

Agrawal, R., Kiernan, J., Srikant, R., & Xu, Y. (2002). Hippocratic Databases. In *Proceedings of the 28th International Conference on Very Large Data Bases (VLDB '02)*.

Article 29 Data Protection Working Party (2007). *Opinion 4/2007 on the Concept of Personal Data*. Retrieved June 25, 2009, from http://ec.europa.eu/justice_home/fsj/privacy/docs/wpdocs/2007/wp136_en.pdf

Ashley, P., Hada, S., Karjoth, G., Powers, C., & Schunter, M. (2003). *Enterprise Privacy Authorization Language (EPAL 1.2)*. Retrieved June 25, 2009, from http://www.zurich.ibm.com/security/enterprise-privacy/epal/Specification/index.html

Backes, M., Pfitzmann, B., & Schunter, M. (2003). A Toolkit for Managing Enterprise Privacy Policies. In G. Goos, J. Hartmanis, & J. van Leeuwen (Eds.), *Proceedings of the 8th European Symposium on Research in Computer Security* (LNCS 2808, pp. 162-180). Berlin, Germany: Springer-Verlag.

Bellovin, S. M. (2002). A Technique for Counting NATted Hosts. In *IMW '02: Proceedings of the 2nd ACM SIGCOMM Workshop on Internet Measurement* (pp. 267-272). New York: ACM.

Bertino, E., Byun, J., & Li, N. (2005). Privacy-Preserving Database Systems. In A. Aldini, R. Gorrieri, & F. Martinelli (Eds.), Foundations of Security Analysis and Design III (LNCS 3665, pp. 178-206). Berlin, Germany: Springer-Verlag.

Birnhack, M. D. (2008). The EU Data Protection Directive: An Engine of a Global Regime. *Computer Law & Security Report, 24*(6), 508–520. doi:10.1016/j.clsr.2008.09.001

Bissias, G. D., Liberatore, M., Jensen, D., & Levine, B. N. (2006). Privacy Vulnerabilities in Encrypted HTTP Streams. In G. Danezis, & D. Martin (Eds.), *Proceedings of the 5th Workshop on Privacy Enhancing Technologies* (LNCS 3856, pp. 1-11). Berlin, Germany: Springer-Verlag.

Boschi, E., & Trammel, B. (2009). *IP Flow Anonymisation Support*, internet-draft, publication as RFC expected within 2010. Retrieved June 25, 2009, from http://tools.ietf.org/html/draft-boschi-ipfix-anon-03

Byun, J.-W., Bertino, E., & Li, N. (2005). Purpose Based Access Control of Complex Data for Privacy Protection. In *Proceedings of the 10th ACM Symposium on Access Control Models and Technologies* (pp. 102-110). New York: ACM.

Casassa Mont, M. (2004). Dealing with Privacy Obligations: Important Aspects and Technical Approaches. In S. Fischer-Hübner, S. Furnell, & C. Lambrinoudakis (Eds.) Trust and Privacy in Digital Business (LNCS 4083, pp. 1-10). Berlin, Germany: Springer-Verlag.

Casassa Mont, M., & Thyne, R. (2006). A Systemic Approach to Automate Privacy Policy Enforcement in Enterprises. In G. Danezis, & P. Golle (Eds.) *Proceedings of the 6th Workshop on Privacy Enhancing Technologies* (LNCS 4258, pp. 118-134). Berlin, Germany: Springer-Verlag.

Claise, B. (Ed.). (2008). *Specification of the IP Flow Information Export (IPFIX) Protocol for the Exchange of IP Traffic Flow Information* (RFC 5101). Retrieved June 25, 2009, from http://tools.ietf.org/html/rfc5101

Council of the European Union (1996). Council Resolution of 17 January 1995 on the lawful interception of telecommunications. *Official Journal of the European Communities, C* 329, 1-6.

Cranor, L. F. (2004). I Didn't Buy It for Myself. In Karat, C.-M., Blom, J. O., & Karat, J. (Eds.), *Designing Personalized User Experiences in E-Commerce* (pp. 57–73). Norwell, MA: Kluwer Academic Publishers. doi:10.1007/1-4020-2148-8_5

Crotti, M., Gringoli, F., Pelosato, P., & Salgarelli, L. (2006). A Statistical Approach to IP-Level Classification of Network Traffic. In *Proceedings of the 2006 IEEE International Conference on Communications* (Vol. 1, pp. 170-176).

Danezis, G. (2002). *Traffic Analysis of the TLS Protocol and its Suitability for Providing Privacy Properties (Internal Report)*. Cambridge, UK: University of Cambridge.

Economist (2008), *Surveillance sweep: A new surveillance law causes a rumpus in Sweden.* Retrieved June 25, 2009, from http://www.economist.com/agenda/displaystory.cfm?story_id=11778941

European Parliament, Council, & Commission (2000). Charter of Fundamental Rights of the European Union. *Official Journal of the European Communities, C* 364, 1-22.

European Parliament and Council (1995). Directive 95/46/EC of the European Parliament and of the Council on the protection of individuals with regard to the processing of personal data and on the free movement of such data. *Official Journal of the European Communities, L* 281, 31-50.

European Parliament and Council (2002). Directive 2002/58/EC of the European Parliament and of the Council concerning the processing of personal data and the protection of privacy in the electronic communications sector (Directive on privacy and electronic communications). *Official Journal of the European Communities, L* 201, 37-47.

European Parliament and Council (2006). Directive 2006/24/EC of the European Parliament and of the Council of 15 March 2006 on the retention of data generated or processed in connection with the provision of publicly available electronic communications services or of public communications networks and amending Directive 2002/58/EC. *Official Journal of the European Communities, L* 105, 54-63.

Ferraiolo, D. F., Sandhu, R., Gavrila, S., Kuhn, R. D., & Chandramouli, R. (2001). Proposed NIST Standard for Role-Based Access Control. *ACM Transactions on Information and System Security, 4*(3), 224–274. doi:10.1145/501978.501980

Finin, T., Joshi, A., Kagal, L., Niu, J., Sandhu, R., Winsborough, W., & Thuraisingham, B. (2008). ROWLBAC: representing Role Based Access Control in OWL. In *Proceedings of the 13th ACM Symposium on Access Control Models and Technologies* (pp. 73-82). New York: ACM.

Gallup Organization. (2008). *Data protection in the European Union: Citizens' perceptions – Analytical Report (Flash Eurobarometer 225)*, Retrieved June 25, 2009, http://ec.europa.eu / public_opinion/flash/fl_225_en.pdf

Hintz, A. (2002). Fingerprinting Websites Using Traffic Analysis. In R. Dingledine, & P. Syverson (Eds.), *Proceedings of the 2nd Workshop on Privacy Enhancing Technologies* (LNCS 2482, pp. 171-178). Berlin, Germany: Springer-Verlag.

International Telecommunication Union. (2005). *Information technology – Open Systems Interconnection – The Directory: Public-key and Attribute Certificate Frameworks, ITU-T Recommendation X.509*. Retrieved June 25, 2009, from http://www.itu.int/rec/T-REC-X.509-200508-I

Koukis, D., Antonatos, S., Antoniades, D., Markatos, E. P., & Trimintzios, P. (2006). A Generic Anonymization Framework for Network Traffic. In *Proceedings of the 2006 IEEE International Conference on Communications* (Vol. 5, pp. 2302-2309).

Lioudakis, G. V., Koutsoloukas, E. A., Dellas, N., Kapitsaki, G. M., Kaklamani, D. I., & Venieris, I. S. (2008). A Semantic Framework for Privacy-Aware Access Control. In M. Ganzha, M. Paprzycki, & T. Pełech-Pilichowski (Eds.), *Proceedings of the International Multiconference on Computer Science and Information Technology* (pp. 813-820). Los Alamitos, CA: IEEE Computer Society Press.

Lioudakis, G. V., Koutsoloukas, E. A., Dellas, N., Tselikas, N., Kapellaki, S., & Prezerakos, G. N. (2007). A Middleware Architecture for Privacy Protection. *Computer Networks, 51*(16), 4679–4696. doi:10.1016/j.comnet.2007.06.010

Monnat, D. E., & Ethen, A. L. (2004). A Primer on the Federal Wiretap Act and Its Fourth Amendment Framework. *Journal of the Kansas Trial Lawyers Association, 28*(1), 12–15.

Ni, Q., Trombetta, A., Bertino, E., & Lobo, J. (2007). Privacy Aware Role Based Access Control. In *Proceedings of the 12th ACM Symposium on Access Control Models and Technologies* (pp. 41-50). New York: ACM.

Noorollahi Ravari, A., Amini, M., & Jalili, R. (2008). A Semantic Aware Access Control Model with Real Time Constraints on History of Accesses. In M. Ganzha, M. Paprzycki, & T. Pełech-Pilichowski (Eds.), *Proceedings of the International Multiconference on Computer Science and Information Technology* (pp. 827-836). Los Alamitos, CA: IEEE Computer Society Press.

Noy, N. F., & McGuinness, D. L. (2001). *Ontology Development 101: A Guide to Creating Your First Ontology* (Technical Report SMI-2001-0880). Stanford, CA: University of Stanford, Knowledge Systems Laboratory.

Organization for Economic Co-operation and Development – OECD. (1980). *Guidelines on the Protection of Privacy and Transborder Flows of Personal Data*. Retrieved June 25, 2009, from http://www.oecd.org /document/18/0,3343,en_2649_34255_1815186_1_1_1_1,00.html

Organization for the Advancement of Structured Information Standards – OASIS. (2004). *OASIS eXtensible Access Control Markup Language (XACML) TC*. Retrieved June 25, 2009, from http://www.oasis-open.org/committees/xacml/

Pang, R., Allman, M., Paxson, V., & Lee, J. (2006). The Devil and Packet Trace Anonymization. *ACM SIGCOMM Computer Communication Review, 36*(1), 29–38. doi:10.1145/1111322.1111330

Pletscher, T. (2005, September). *Companies and the Regulatory Jungle*. Intervention at the 27th International Conference of Data Protection and Privacy Commissioners, Monteux, Switzerland.

Poulllet, Y. (2006). The Directive 95/46/EC: Ten Years After. *Computer Law & Security Report, 22*(3), 206–217. doi:10.1016/j.clsr.2006.03.004

Prevelakis, V., & Spinellis, D. (2007). The Athens Affair. *IEEE Spectrum, 44*(7), 26–33. doi:10.1109/MSPEC.2007.376605

Risen, J., & Lichtblau, E. (2005, December 16). Bush Lets U.S. Spy on Callers Without Courts. *The New York Times*. Retrieved June 25, 2009, from http://www.nytimes.com/2005/12/16/politics /16program.html?ei=5090&en=e32072d78 6623ac1&ex=1292389200

Sicker, D. C., Ohm, P., & Grunwald, D. (2007). Legal Issues Surrounding Monitoring During Network Research. In *IMC '07: Proceedings of the 7th ACM SIGCOMM Conference on Internet Measurement* (pp. 141-148). New York: ACM.

Solove, D. J. (2006). A Brief History of Information Privacy Law. In Wolf, C. (Ed.), *Proskauer on Privacy: A Guide to Privacy and Data Security Law in the Information Age* (pp. 1–46). New York: Practising Law Institute.

Sun, Q., Simon, D. R., Wang, Y.-M., Russell, W., Padmanabhan, V. N., & Qiu, L. (2002). Statistical Identification of Encrypted Web Browsing Traffic. In *Proceedings of the 2002 IEEE Symposium on Security and Privacy* (pp. 19-30).

United Nations. (1948). *Universal Declaration of Human Rights*. Retrieved June 25, 2009, from http://www.ohchr.org/EN/UDHR/Documents/60UDHR/bookleten.pdf

Warren, S. D., & Brandeis, L. D. (1890). The Right to Privacy. *Harvard Law Review, 4*(5), 193–220. doi:10.2307/1321160

World Wide Web Consortium. (2004). *Web Ontology Language (OWL)*. Retrieved June 25, 2009, from http://www.w3.org/2004/OWL/

Zugenmaier, A., & Claessens, J. (2007). Privacy in Electronic Communications. In Douligeris, C., & Serpanos, D. N. (Eds.), *Network Security: Current Status and Future Directions* (pp. 419–440). Piscataway, NJ: Wiley-Interscience & IEEE Press.

Section 4
Access Rights

Chapter 23
The Project of the Ancient Spanish Cartography E–Library:
Main Targets and Legal Challenges

P. Chías
University of Alcalá, Spain

T. Abad
University of Alcalá, Spain

E. Rivera
University of Alcalá, Spain

ABSTRACT

The Council of the European Union is developing some strategies about the European Digital Libraries considered as a common multilingual access point to Europe's digital cultural heritage. Our project of a digital cartographic database accessed through GIS looks for the integration of digital technologies with the cartographic heritage providing new approaches to, and new audiences for the history of cartography. The online presence of this cartographic material will be a rich source of raw material to be re-used in different sectors and for different purposes and technological developments; but we must also afford some legal challenges because digitisation presupposes making a copy, which can be problematic in view of intellectual property rights (IPR). As the transparency and clarification of the copyright status of works is very relevant to us, those legal challenges and their solutions will be the main subjects of this chapter.

INTRODUCTION

According to the strategies of the Council of the European Union about the European Digital Libraries (Commission, 2005) considered as a common multilingual access point to Europe's digital cultural heritage, and assuming that the

ancient maps and plans are important cultural materials, in the last decade several cartographic databases have been created to allow an efficient online accessibility.

These libraries are defined as organised collections of digital contents made available to the public, and are composed of analogue materials that have been digitised as well as of born digital

DOI: 10.4018/978-1-61520-975-0.ch023

materials. They must also follow several main strands as are:

- The online consultation, stressing the importance of exchanging information and publishing the results, in order to maximise the benefits that users can draw from the information (Council Conclusions, 2006).
- The preservation and storage of these digital collections to ensure that future generations can access the digital material, and to prevent losses of contents.

Maps represent an important part of the richness of Europe's history and its cultural and linguistic diversity, and can be increasingly accessed through local libraries websites based on open-access models settled on the principles of free, worldwide access to the information, following the trend of voluntary sharing.

Our project of a digital cartographic database accessed through GIS is related to, but distinctive from the history of cartography, and looks for the integration of digital technologies with the cartographic heritage providing new approaches to, and new audiences for the history of cartography (Chías & Abad, 2006).

To define the contents of our cartographic database we have decided to apply the ICA's Working Group broad definition of cartographic heritage as "anything of cultural value inherited from maps and accessible to a broad public community", as well as the wide sense concept of a cartographic document of Harvey (1980, p. 7) and Harley and Woodward (1987, vol. 1, p. xvi) that includes all kinds of maps, plans and charts at different scales (architectural, urban and territorial scales), as well as pictures and bird's-eye views (Kagan, 1986, pp. 18-26; De Seta, 1996), with no restrictions due to techniques, functions or origins.

As we must also restrict the temporal and the geographical subject of the contents of the cartographic databases, we firstly decided to include all historic documents drawn before 1900, mainly because along the 20th century the cartographic production and techniques have very much increased in many senses and its study should be carried separately. Secondly, the spatial restriction has been imposed to the search and we decided that the cartographic database should concern the actual Spanish territories and Latin America (Chías & Abad, 2008; 2008a).

Ancient cartography, as well as old pictures, drawings and photographs, has not been used traditionally as a reliable source of information about the history and the evolution of the land- and the townscape. Those graphic materials have been usually considered as 'second order' documents, mainly because of the difficulties that their interpretation can sometimes involve (Harley, 1968) due to the different conventions that are applied in each case by the cartographer.

But this is not the only reason why cartography is so seldom used in the historical searches; other problems, mainly related to the difficulties of their localisation and visualisation have to be considered.

Obviously, it is not easy to access to an original big size and small-scale map that is sometimes composed by several printed sheets; and it is also complicate to see properly the symbols present in the map and read its texts when it is imposed to handle a reduced hardcopy or a low resolution digital image.

Although we find it is not essential to have an exhaustive knowledge of the context of each map to get a meaningful interpretation of it (Skelton, 1965: 28; Andrews, 2005), it is necessary to achieve some basic specific concepts on the theory of the cartographic expression and design (about map projections, symbols or representation of relief, for instance), because the lack of them can difficult the right interpretation of the document and twist the results of the investigations (Vázquez Maure & Martín López, 1989, pp. 1-10).

Nowadays the "digital cartography and the history of cartography are not yet comfortable bedfellows" (Fleet, 2007, p. 102).

We have set up a geo-portal that will have an important role as aggregator for the common European access point, provided that it implement the right standards (Chías & Abad, 2008).

We have designed a methodology that applies the digital technologies to the history of cartography and helps to establish new relationships, provides an easy access to images to make analysis and comparisons, shows the map distribution on the different archives, and finally allows to reconstruct the historical landscapes and the history of the territory through old maps. This is one of the main targets of our project, but the final one is to diffuse the old cartographic treasures that compose a relevant part of the Spanish cultural heritage, nowadays still unknown to the public and even to a great number of specialists.

According to this, our methodology includes three main tables, that are the following:

- **'Cartography'**: contains all the registers concerning the cartographic documents and follows the ISBD Norms of cataloguing.
- **'Bibliography'**: includes the complete bibliographical references that appear in the field *Bibliography* of the table 'Cartography'.
- **'Libraries, Archives and Map Collections'**: is the table that includes the complete references of the collections that have been visited, and that appear just as an acronym in both *Collection* and *Signature* fields of the table 'Cartography'.

The design of the table 'Cartography' joins both the descriptive and the technical data about each document, joining the perspectives of the historian and the cartographer (Figure 1). As it can be seen, among the items that have been included are the following related to the problem of the copyright:

- **Collection and Signature (text):** the collection that preserves the document and the signature; the first one is quoted through an acronym and the second one is abbreviated according to the norms (its total extension can be consulted in the table 'Libraries, Archives and Museums'); if possible, it includes the link to other e-libraries or references.
- **Image (object/container field):** it is included a low resolution raster image in highly compressed jpg format of the cartographic document. By clicking on the image and depending on the conditions set by the right holder, it can be possible to display a high resolution one in a *tiff* format that allows to see the details and to read the texts. If the map is composed by several sheets, it is possible to see each one separately (and to compose it apart).

Some technical specifications about digitisation that have been used in the project are the following:

- The name of the image files: FFFXX_NNNNNNNN_T.EXT, where:
  - FFF: Archive ID, max. length 5 characters; provided by each archive.
  - XX: Internal ID of the collection; length 2 characters.
  - NNNNNNNN: File ID that includes a geographical reference (province); variable length from 1 to 20 characters, from A to Z or from a to z, without accent, includes (-) but not the rest of characters including (_), that is used to separate the different ID groups of the image.
  - T: image format on screen: V = illustration, T = 1/3 screen, P = full screen, 2 = high definition (2.000 x 3.000 pixels), 4 = high definition 4.000 x 6.000 pixels, H = high definition (more than 4.000 x 6.000 pixels).
  - EXT: extension of the format: JPG, GIF, TIFF, PCD...

Figure 1. The table cartography of the Ancient Spanish cartography e-Library, now accessible through the web page of the Instituto de Estudios Latinoamericanos (IELAT) of the University of Alcalá, Spain (www.ielat.es).

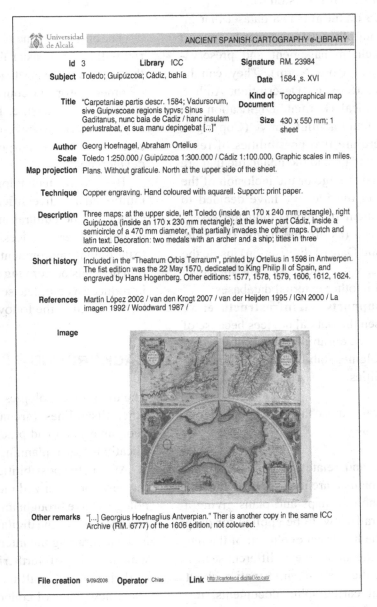

- Example for an image of the Biblioteca Nacional de España, BNEM_002348CR_V.jpg
- **Image formats:** open formats based upon norms and standards whose specifications are public. We have only considered both formats of preservation and diffusion when images are born digital material in the University of Alcalá, and can be diffused in a high definition version because there

are no copyright problems. We always indicate the file format, including the version (for example, TIFF version 6).

- **Image file metadata:** is a dataset that informs about other data in order to support their search, management and preservation (Dublin Core Norm). They can be descriptive (Subject, Description, Author, etc.), technical (Format, Digitisation options, etc.) and administrative (Copyright, etc.). There are two possibilities of relating the metadata and the image file that are the external storage or the inclusion of the metadata in the file. We have decided to combine them by maintaining the essential metadata (as are the image ID, Title, Archive and Date of digitisation) inside the digital file, while the rest of the metadata are stored in other external databases.
- **Storage supports and infrastructure:** we have chosen the optical devices because of their capacity, durability, reliability, accessibility, volume, stability, and cost, among other qualities.

In short we can expose the main targets of our e-Library as follows:

- To diffuse and relate the contents of the various Spanish archives to provide the study of the old maps and plans giving a broad overall view, to be applied for deep study of the historical evolution of the territory and the landscape at different scales.
- To enlarge the available information about the ancient cartographic documents, not only through the metadata of each image, but also with other contents that are located in particular or non digitised collections.
- To enlarge the possibilities of the traditional searches on the databases through the queries that are useful through the GIS tools, which include issues as metric and geometric accuracy.

- To use the new technologies to study and diffuse the cartographic heritage through Internet.

The online presence of this cartographic material will make it easier for citizens to appreciate their own culture heritage as well as the heritage of other European countries, and to use it for study, work or leisure. It will be a rich source of raw material to be re-used in different sectors and for different purposes and technological developments.

But as the technological development has multiplied and diversified the possibilities of accessing to the cultural materials, the traditional model of library services is not easily translatable to the digital environment, and as digital preservation depends on copying and migration, we have introduced a complete set of new issues that will be discussed in the following pages.

BACKGROUND

The digital technologies were formerly used by other disciplines (archaeology and historical geography) and had practical non-academic applications (town planning, librarianship).

Among the possibilities of the digital images, the new computerized methods and digital technologies have brought an explosion of the scope and potential of the digital cartography, allowing and encouraging the interaction with early maps with the aim of furthering our understanding of their content in all its aspects. But they also allow new ways of connecting early maps with other kinds of information, inviting us to use new forms of presentation and making easy a speedier transmission of images the world over. This is particularly interesting for the creation of the European Space of Information.

On the other hand, the digital cartography is not a loss, but a useful tool in the traditional scholar research (Fleet 2007, p. 100); but it must remain as a central theme of discussion the ways in which the digital technologies may be of particular value to historians of cartography, deepening on subjects as:

- How digital technologies are already providing access to early maps (and related materials) through a range of methods, including: improved reproduction, electronic facsimiles, websites, new forms of presentation and integration, and new forms of digital preservation and archiving (for instance, by using photogrammetric techniques in seaming together images of large maps to create more authentic facsimiles), dynamically integrating maps with other information using the web, applying new ways of visualising and presenting early mapping, and associating new metadata as structured summary information about a cartographic source to encode data on and about historical maps.
- Digital technologies that are unveiling new ways of understanding the content of early maps, allowing the digital analysis of map geometry and the use of digital transparency techniques focused on the cartometric analysis of early maps, the reassessment of the projections used in 15th and 16th nautical charts -based on a study of navigational practices, technologies and texts- or the use of precise methods and mathematics behind the transformations of old maps in various geo-referencing projects.
- How digital technologies and especially Geographic Information Systems (GIS) are enabling new ways of integrating early maps with other information making the 3-D visualisation more accessible, realistic and impressive, or combining historical maps and associated textual and numerical information to get a spatial analysis of agricultural productivity and its relationship with the landowners through integrating

cadastral and statistical information (as do the *Gregoriano Cadastre* (Orciani et al., 2007) and the old cadastral maps of Utrecht (Heere, 2006), both focused on a deep knowledge of the reconstruction of the old properties).

Technological developments have historically always had implications regarding regulatory framework for copyright and have been at the origin of the need for modification. The limitations of analogue technologies and offline platforms have governed the traditional legal framework that supports them.

But the paradigm of a traditional archive or library has changed radically since the e-Library concept has been introduced. Digitisation has transformed this traditional environment and has given rise to a potentially huge market of content.

First, we must distinguish between the maps that we have digitised and the use of images that have been digitised by the archives and libraries, or even the private owners of the maps.

On the other hand, individuals can make an unlimited number of more or less perfect copies of digital data at a little cost, and to distribute them world-wide at practically no additional cost increasing the risk of piracy.

In our collection of the ancient cartographic documents that we have digitised and stored in our databases, we have considered from the beginning not only the rights of the different archives and libraries were the originals are located, but also the possibilities offered to piracy.

THE COPYRIGHT ENVIRONMENT IN THE ONLINE WORLD

The EU Framework

The EU's Council of Ministers adopted on 9 April 2001 a Directive establishing pan-EU rules on copyright and related rights in the Information

Society, that secured the legitimate interests of users, consumers and the society at large, and harmonised the rights of reproduction, distribution, communication to the public, the legal protection of anti-copying devices and rights management systems (European Parliament, 2001). As far as no new concepts for the protection of intellectual property were needed, the current law on copyright and related rights was adapted and ammended to respond adequately to the new communication realities.

This Directive enabled the Community and its Member states to ratify the 1996 World Intellectual Property (WIPO) Treaties, the 'Internet Treaties'. Article 151 of the Treaty required the Community to take cultural aspects into account in its actions.

The copyright environment consists of three main aspects:

- Rights (what can be protected by copyright) and exceptions (e.g. copies for private use or for public libraries).
- Enforcement of rights (sanctions for making illegal copies and for trading in circumvention devices).
- And digital management of rights (DRM, exploiting the rights) (Directive 2001/29), what supposes the use the technology to describe and identify digital content protected by intellectual property rights, and which enforces usage rules set by right holders or prescribed by law for digital content.

The notion of 'digital rights' refers to copying and related rights in the digital environment, and those rights do not differ in principle from the rights that persist in analogue works.

In the particular case of the e-Libraries, the objective of a proper support for the dissemination of cultural heritage must not be achieved by sacrificing strict protection of rights or by tolerating illegal forms of distribution of the digitised materials.

About half of the Member States of the EU have implemented legislation that allows the active collection of web material (web harvesting) by selected institutions, and in most cases, the organisation responsible for harvesting being the national library. Access policies in relation to web-harvested material are generally restrictive, owing to considerations of intellectual property rights and privacy.

Under current EU-law and international agreements, material resulting from digitisation can only be made available online if it is in the public domain (in a narrow sense, refers to information resources which can be freely accessed and used by all, for example because copyrights have expired) or with the explicit consent of the right holders.

The legal framework in which the e-Libraries must be administered balances incentives to create and distribute content with mechanisms which ensure appropriate revenue through the exercise of intellectual property rights and at the same also serves the interest of the individual users by requiring access to copyright works for certain types of users.

Thus, the main rights granted to authors and other right holders are:

- The right of reproduction.
- The right of communication to the public including the right of making available.
- The right of distribution.

On the other hand, there are important differences between the author' copyright and the rights held by the different archives and libraries where the maps are actually located. The solutions that can be given in both cases will be exposed later.

Some E-Library Examples: Europeana, the Spanish AVANZA Plan, the World Digital Library

As we mentioned above, in September 2005, the European Commission launched the Digital Libraries initiative with the aim of making Europe's cultural and scientific heritage accessible online (Commission, 2005).

Europeana, the European Digital Library, opens new ways to of exploring Europe's cultural heritage by accessing to more than two million books, maps, recordings, photographs, archival documents, paintings and films from national libraries and cultural institutions of the EU's Member States. This portal contributes to improving the conditions for the online accessibility to Europe's cultural institutions (Reding, 2007; 2008).

In Spain the AVANZA plan for the development of the Information Society has started a first digitisation and online publishing programme for the 2006-2010 period, in accordance with the national standards in an OAI-PHM protocol compatible system.

Although the main Spanish cultural offices are making a strong effort to digitise the public collections of historical documents -which at the beginning of 2006 included 109 collections of Spanish libraries, the particular case of ancient maps carries up problems such as those posed by the different locations, techniques, sizes and preservation conditions, as well as the high costs that are delaying the prompt achievement of their diffusion. And we have to mention another issue related to the difficulties of finding those maps, for they are frequently embedded in other documents or inside bundles of old papers, and remain yet undiscovered.

Among those important initiatives we will emphasize the digital libraries created by the Biblioteca Nacional de España, the Institut Cartogràfic de Catalunya, the Instituto Geográfico Nacional and those of the Portal de Archivos Españoles (PARES) that is participating in the MICHAEL project; they not only show free low-resolution images of each map, but provide an accurate description of the document and the conditions of use.

At a global scale, the World Digital Library will be launched on April 21, 2009, with the aim of making available in Internet, free of charge and in multilingual format, significant materials from cultures around the world, including manuscripts and maps. The objectives are to promote international and inter-cultural understanding and awareness, provide resources to educators and contribute to scholarly research (World Digital Library, 2009).

PROBLEMS AND SOLUTIONS

The essential challenges that we have afforded during the development of the project are:

- Those that have impacted the pace and efficiency of digitisation:
  - **The financial challenges:** because digitisation is labour-intensive and costly, and as it is impossible to digitise all relevant material, choices have to be made on what is to be digitised and when.
  - **Organisational challenges:** a 'digitise once, distribute widely' strategy benefits all the organisations involved in digitisation projects; in this sense, ours not only shows the duplicate maps in the different collections, but allows to find the various stages of the plates, following the history of the different prints and editions of a map or the collections, and their origins.
  - **Technical challenges:** we have tried to improve digitisation techniques in order to make digitisation cost-efficient and affordable. To digitise the non-digitised funds we apply both the contact scanning and the non-contact photographic methods, trying to minimize distortion problems by digitising each sheet separately, although this process cannot eliminate other problems in the final assembly of the mosaic image.

- The legal challenges: digitisation presupposes making a copy, which could raise an issue in observance of intellectual property rights (IPR). Those legal challenges can be resumedas follows:
  - How we have considered the Directive 2001/29/EC on the harmonisation of certain aspects of copyright and related rights in the information society (European Parliament, 2001, p. 10), that foresees an exception for specific acts of reproduction by publicly accessible libraries, educational establishments, museums or archives.
  - The conditions under which we are able to offer an image of the maps that are yet unpublished or remain unknown in case of any legal obstacle.

The transparency and clarification of the copyright status of works is very relevant to us, and the protection of technological measures should ensure a secure environment for the provision of interactive on-demand services, in such a way that members of the public may access the cartographic heritage databases from a place and at a time individually chosen by them.

As a matter of fact, our digital library is in principle focused on public domain material, and as digital preservation implies copying and migration, it has always been considered in the light of IPR legislation: the digitised funds of other libraries are precisely quoted and respect the conditions that have been established for consulting the documents by the right holders; and we must neither set other supplementary caution that restricts the access to the different data sets, nor establish different access levels.

The Universities' Exception

The EU Member States must consider some exceptions or limitations for cases such as non-commercial educational and scientific purposes,

for the benefit of public institutions such as universities, libraries and archives; but they must be limited to certain special cases covered by the reproduction right, and should not cover uses made in the context of on-line delivery of protected works or other subject-matter. The exceptions to the use of the digital materials are limited to the sole purpose of illustration for teaching or scientific research, as long as the source, including the author's name and in our case the location of the cartographic material, is indicated (Commission Recommendation, 2008).

Teaching and research are essential targets of our e-Library, and thus the Code of Practice for our university and other related public research organisations concerning the management of intellectual property in knowledge transfer activities, has been designed on three main sets of principles:

- The basic set of the principles for an internal intellectual property (IP) policy, that each public research organisation should implement in order to effectively manage the intellectual property resulting for their own or collaborative activities in the field of research and development.
- The principles for a knowledge transfer policy, which complement those relating to the IP policy but focusing on the active transfer and exploitation of such intellectual property.
- And the principles regarding collaborative and contract research, including the private sector.

The basic set of IP principles include those focused on the promotion of the broad dissemination of research and development results (e.g. through open access publication).

Among the principles for a knowledge transfer policy and in order to promote the use of publicly funded research results and maximise their socio-economic impact, all kinds of possible spin-off or partnership exploitation mechanisms must be considered, selecting the most appropriate ones. On the other hand, it is necessary to develop and publicise a licensing policy, in order to harmonise practices within the university and ensuring fairness in all deals.

In our case, archival facilities for research results, such as Internet-based repositories, are developed with public funding in connection with open access policies.

The Problem of the Orphan Works

Orphan works are copyrighted works whose owners are difficult or even impossible to locate. This poses problems of rights clearance for digitisation and online accessibility of the material.

In general, little practical progress is reported about this problem and its solution, but is being considered together with other copyright related-issues within the digital libraries domain.

Actions at European level such as the ARROW project in which right holders and cultural institutions together address the creation of databases of orphan works, should be reinforced by national efforts.

Solutions

The main trends must be directed to identify barriers in the legislation to the online accessibility and subsequent use of cultural material that is in the public domain and take steps to remove them. But as partial solutions can be mentioned the following.

Watermarking of the digital images as an identification technique can be a solution because it can guarantee their integrity and authenticity. As an advantage, it allows the protection system to be incorporated for the first time into the 'fabric' of the content, rather than being added on as a separate information. In this case, if the map is copied, the watermark follows the copy.

This system is being already used by some Spanish cartographic e-Libraries such as the one of the Instituto Geográfico Nacional de España (IGN) in its MTN series 1:50.000, or the collection of the Centro de Información Cartográfica y Territorial de Extremadura. But we do not apply this solution because each map is adequately referenced through its signature and we also provide the links in case that the documents are included in other cartographic databases that can be accessed through Internet (see Figure 1).

Another solution is the Microsoft Digital Asset Server (DAS), a system client server based, with part of the software residing on the users computer, and the other at an Internet server at the e-Library site. The client software enables the user to download files at various levels of security. By logging on to the e-Library site, users are able to access the databases and to get new files.

This kind of solution has been successfully adapted to our platform, through measures as:

- The introduction of technological protection measures to prevent copying.
- We are already studying the possibility of setting a digital rights management system restricting the access to digital material, with the aim to ensure that IPR mechanisms maintain a balance between enabling access and use while respecting the rights of the creators.

The maps that are yet unpublished or remain unknown (for instance, those of the private collectors) if there is any legal obstacle that allows them to be shown, we offer a link to a high resolution image 1:1 that makes possible to see every detail and to read every name to analyse it properly.

The digital image can never change the integrity of the original map, and must be stored and presented to the public without changes, suppressions or additions.

About the Author's Copyright

The term of protection of copyright, originally ten years in the 19th century, is now seventy years after the death of the author. As it stands today the situation is heavily weighted in favour of the heirs of deceased authors (about three generations) and the holder of related rights.

These terms have become disproportionate in relation to the needs of the public and the creators themselves and they should be revised.

A very large number of maps and views are manuscripts or have been only published once, and will not be published again during the life of his/her heirs. And though many of them remained almost unknown to the public, they have nevertheless some value but quickly become inaccessible to potential users.

A long term extension of rights would, in practice, benefit only a relatively small number of potential users. Most permissive licenses will help to promote the dissemination and appropriation of works by users, and are fully in line with the objectives of the rapid diffusion of knowledge and technology.

Anyway, the case of existing cartographer's heirs is not relevant to our e-Library purposes.

The Archives' and Libraries' Exploitation Copyright

In this case it has been essential for us to obtain the rights for making the cartographic material available beyond national borders. An approach that limits access to digitised materials to users within a specific national territory runs counter to the basic idea of an e-Library.

In our case is quite frequent that images have a copyright holder that is the archive or library where images are located. Then we propose as a solution to set an agreement in advance with all of them, including always the complete quotation and signature, and in some exceptional cases, even their institutional logo.

It must be previewed the possibility of paying a symbolic reproduction fee to diffuse some digital images through the web.

Anyway we do not give the possibility of getting a digital copy of the copyrighted images, but just to see a reproduction on the screen as a part of the information obtained through the searches made by the user in the databases.

FUTURE TRENDS

To protect the interests of the right holders it is important to 'put knowledge into practice' by designing a broad base strategy to increase innovation of scientific enterprises by addressing their needs in the area of IPR usage and enforcement.

Our particular interest on the field of the IPR problem is to apply interoperable enabling tools and components for the controlled access, delivery and consumption of multimedia information over networks. At the present many 'Management-Projects' are being developed, with the aim of creating a generic model applicable to the different domains using technical means to provide control in respect of the use of copyrighted material stored and transmitted in digital form. Among them, the OCCAM Project is one of the latest, addressing the problem of open architectures and interfaces for online access to digital content with IPR protection and management.

It will be also interesting to promote the introduction of electronic exchange of information with the private collectors, to the greatest possible extent, keeping them always informed about the procedures relating to IPR enforcement.

CONCLUSION

The online distribution of cultural assets via the Internet, such as our Ancient Spanish Cartography e-Library, provides a tremendous opportunity for everyone to have access to culture and cultural diversity, and contributes to improving knowledge.

Nowadays the web-based digital resources are quite frequent as a way to preserve and diffuse the cartographic heritage as well as to access to the modern cartography (Zentai 2006; Livieratos 2008).

Under current EU-law and international agreements, material resulting from digitisation can only be made available online if it is in the public domain (in a narrow sense, refers to information resources which can be freely accessed and used by all, for example because copyrights have expired) or with the explicit consent of the right holders. The transparency and clarification of the copyright status of works is very relevant to us.

As a matter of fact, our digital library is in principle focused on public domain material, and as digital preservation implies copying and migration, it has always been considered in the light of IPR legislation (Commission, 2005): the digitised funds of other libraries are precisely quoted and respect the conditions that have been established for consulting the documents by the right holders; and we must neither set other supplementary caution that restrict the access to the different data sets, nor establish different access levels.

It is then indispensable to improve consumer information on the conditions for the use of content of the platform and on the restrictions applying to the use of technical measures to protect and manage rights.

REFERENCES

Andrews, J. H. (2005). Meaning, knowledge and power in the philosophy of maps. In Harley, J. B. (Ed.), *The new nature of maps. Essays in the history of cartography* (pp. 21–58). Baltimore, MD: The Johns Hopkins University Press.

Chías, P., & Abad, T. (2006). A GIS in Cultural Heritage based upon multiformat databases and hypermedia personalized queries. *ISPRS Archives, XXXVI-5*, 222–226.

Chías, P., & Abad, T. (2008). Visualising Ancient Maps as Cultural Heritage: A Relational Database of the Spanish Ancient Cartography. In *12th International Conference on Information Visualisation* (pp. 453-457).

Chías, P., & Abad, T. (2008a). Las vías de comunicación en la cartografía histórica de la cuenca del Duero: construcción del territorio y paisaje. *Ingeniería Civil, 149*, 79–91.

Commission of the European Communities. (2005). i2010: Digital Libraries. Brussels.

Commission Recommendation of 10 April 2008 on the management of intellectual property in knowledge transfer activities and Code of Practice for universities and other public research organisations, 2008/416/EC.

Council Conclusions of 20 November 2008 on the development of legal offers of online cultural and creative content and the prevention and combating of piracy in the digital environment, 2008/C 319/06.

Council Conclusions on the Digitisation and Online Accessibility of Cultural Material, and Digital Preservation, 2006/C 297/01.

De Seta, C. (1996). L'iconografia urbana in Europa dal XV al XVIII secolo. In *Cittá d'Europa. Iconografia e vedutismo dal XV al XIX secolo* (pp. 11–48). Napoli: Electa.

European Parliament and Council Directive 2001/29 of 22 May 2001 on the harmonisation of copyright and related rights in the Information Society. Copyright Directive.

Fleet, Ch. (2007). Digital Approaches to Cartographic Heritage: The Thessaloniki Workshop. *Imago Mundi, 59*(1), 100–104. doi:10.1080/03085690600997894

Harley, J. B. (1968). The evaluation of early maps: Towards a methodology. *Imago Mundi, 22*, 68–70.

Harley, J. B., & Woodward, D. (1987). Preface. In Harley, J. B., & Woodward, D. (Eds.), *The history of cartography: Cartography in prehistoric, ancient, and medieval Europe and the Mediterranean* (*Vol. 1*, pp. 15–21). Chicago, IL: The University of Chicago Press.

Harvey, P. D. A. (1980). *Topographical maps. Symbols, pictures and surveys*. London: Thames and Hudson.

Heere, E., 2006. The use of GIS with property maps. *e-Perimetron, 4*(1), 297-307.

Kagan, R. L. (1998). *Imágenes urbanas del mundo hispánico, 1493-1780*. Madrid: Eds. El Viso.

Livieratos, E. (Ed.). (2006). *Digital Approaches to Cartographic Heritage*. Thessaloniki: National Centre for Maps and Cartographic Heritage. Microsoft Digital Asset Server (DAS). Retrieved January 12, 2009 from http://www.microsoft.com/reader/das/default.htm

Orciani, M., Frazzica, V., Colosi, L., & Galletti, F. (2007). Gregoriano cadastre: transformation of old maps into Geographical Information System and their contribution in terms of acquisition, processing and communication of historical data. *e-Perimetron, 2*(2), 92-104.

Reding, V. (2007). Scientific Information in the Digital Age: How Accessible Should Publicly Funded Research Be? *Conference on Scientific Publishing in the European Research Area Access, Dissemination and Preservation in the Digital Age*. Brussels, European Commission for Information Society and Media.

Reding, V. (2008). La bibliothèque numérique européenne: du rêve à la réalité. *Forum d'Avignon 2008 – Culture, facteur de croissance*. Retrieved January 12, 2009 from http://ec.europa.eu/commission_barroso/reding/index_fr.htm

Skelton, R. A. (1965). *Looking at an early map*. Lawrence, KS: University of Kansas Library.

Vázquez Maure, F., & Martín López, J. (1989). *Lectura de mapas*. Madrid: Instituto Geográfico Nacional.

World Digital Library. (n.d.). Retrieved April 16, 2009 from http://worlddigitallibrary.org/project/English/index.html

Zentai, L. (2006). Preservation of modern cartographic products. *e-Perimetron, 4* (1), 308-313.

Chapter 24
Trusted Computing or Distributed Trust Management?

Michele Tomaiuolo
Università di Parma, Italy

ABSTRACT

Nowadays, in contrast with centralized or hierarchical certification authorities and directory of names, other solutions are gaining momentum. Federation of already deployed security systems is considered the key to build global security infrastructures. In this field, trust management systems can play an important role, being based on a totally distributed architecture. The idea of distributed trust management can be confronted with the concept of trusted computing. Though having a confusingly similar denomination, the different interpretation of trust in these systems drives to divergent consequences with respect to system architectures and access policies, but also to law, ethics, politics. While trusted computing systems assure copyright holders and media producers that the hosting system will respect the access restrictions they defined, trust management systems, instead, allow users to grant trust to other users or software agents for accessing local resources.

INTRODUCTION

A number of architectures and systems are being proposed as a ground for improved interoperability among diverse systems, mainly exploiting the idea of service-oriented architecture. Yet, some issues remain open. In fact, composition of services requires some delegation of goals and duties among partners. But these delegations cannot

come into effect, if they're not associated with a corresponding delegation of privileges, needed to access some resources and complete delegated tasks, or achieve desired goals.

The traditional approach for inter-domain security is based on centralized or hierarchical certification authorities and public directory of names. In contrast with this hierarchical approach, other solutions are possible, where the owner of local resources is considered as the ultimate source of trust about them, and he is provided

DOI: 10.4018/978-1-61520-975-0.ch024

with means to carefully administer the flow of delegated permissions. *Trust management* principles argue no a-priori trusted parties should be supposed to exist in the system, as this would imply some "obligated choice" of trust for the user, and without *choice*, there's no real *trust*. Moreover, the presence of some third party as a globally trusted entity implies that all systems participating in the global environment have to equally trust it.

Nowadays, new technologies, in the form of protocols and certificate representations, are gaining momentum. They allow a different approach toward security in global environments, an approach which paradoxically is founded on the concept of "locality". Federation of already deployed security systems is considered the key to build global security infrastructures. This way, users are not obliged to adopt some out of the box solution for their particular security issues, to rebuild the whole system or to make it dependent upon some global authority, for gaining interoperability with others.

Instead they're provided with means to manage the trust relations they build with other entities operating in the same, global environment. In the same manner as people collaborate in the real world, systems are being made interoperable in the virtual world. Cooperation and agreements among companies and institutions are making virtual organizations both a reality and a necessity. But they'll never spring into success if existing technologies will not match their needs.

This chapter will deal with trust management in open and decentralized environments. Up-to-date technologies like SAML, OpenID, XRI, XDI, XACML, Web Services protocols and extensions, will be analysed from the perspective of *peer to peer* networks, intended not only as a technology, but above all as a web of trust relationships, where parties interoperate directly, without reliance on any centralized directory or authority.

Securing access to the resources made available by the peers is a requirement to make peer to peer interoperation a more widespread paradigm. The secure management of trust relationships, the ability to precisely control the flow of delegated permissions to trusted entities, is a fundamental requirement to allow the composition of the more disparate services provided on the network.

This chapter will also analyse the fundamental differences between decentralized trust management, on the one hand, and digital rights management and trusted computing, on the other hand. The different interpretation of *trust* in these systems drives to divergent consequences with respect to system architectures and access policies, but also to law, ethics, politics. While *trusted systems* assure *copyright holders* and *media producers* that the hosting system will respect the access restrictions they defined, *trust management systems*, instead, allow *users* to grant trust to other users or software agents for accessing local resources.

The analysis will start from XrML and ODRL, two similar XML-based languages oriented to the management of digital rights for media content distribution. Both languages are oriented to the management of digital rights (DRM) for publishing and accessing media content, and can hardly fit different applications. In fact, these *Rights Expression Languages* resulted from efforts of businesses to protect digital material from reproduction and sharing. They just allow copyright owners to express restrictions about the usage of a resource, without being able to enforce by themselves the policies they convey. This can only happen on so-called "*trusted systems*". Support for DRM is being included into a growing number of devices and systems. The international legal framework is also paying attention to DRM systems. Many nations adhering to the World Intellectual Property Organization (WIPO) are implementing the 1996 WIPO Copyright Treaty (WCT), which requires to enact laws against DRM circumvention. The 1998 Digital Millennium Copyright Act (DMCA) in the USA and the 2001 European directive on copyright (EUCD) are two important examples.

BACKGROUND

Public-key cryptography is the basis for digital signature, and it is founded on public/private key pairs. The scalability of this technology is assured by the fact that only the private component of the public/private key pair must be protected, while the public component can be distributed on public networks, thus allowing interested parties to use security services.

The idea itself is as old as the paper of Diffie and Hellman, which in 1976 described, for the first time, a public key cryptographic algorithm (Diffie, Hellman, 1976).

Given a system of this kind, the problem of key distribution is vastly simplified. Each user generates a pair of inverse transformations, E and D, at his terminal. The deciphering transformation, D, must be kept secret, but in fact it does never need to be communicated on any channel. Instead the enciphering transformation, E, can be made public by placing it in a public directory along with the user's name and address. Anyone can then encrypt messages and send them to the user; no one can decipher messages but their intended recipients.

Before Diffie and Hellman published their algorithm, key distribution was a highly risky process. The revolutionary idea of public key cryptography was to greatly simplify this problem. But it was soon realized that, even if the public key can be distributed freely, some form of integrity must be assured to make it usable in security services. In fact, most security services require the public key to be associated with other information, and this binding must be protected. In particular, the user of the public key must be assured that:

- the public key, and the information associated to it, must be protected in its integrity against unnoticed tampering;
- the association between the public key and other information has been gathered in a trusted manner.

In fact, a data integrity mechanism is not sufficient, by itself, to guarantee that the binding between the public key and its owner (or any other information associated to it) has been verified in a trustworthy manner. Moreover, any implemented protection scheme should not affect the scalability of the overall public-key infrastructure. These goals are at the basis of each public-key infrastructure, and in particular they inspired the X.509 infrastructure (Housley, Polk & al., 2002).

Digital certificates were originally introduced to ensure the integrity of public keys, thus providing a scalable solution to the key distribution problem. Their primary function was to bind names to keys or keys to names.

Before continuing, however, it's worth spending some words about "digital certificates". First of all, the expression itself is not very precise, as it could include paper certificates after being digitized. Also, it's confusing, as it seems to suggest that security services can be enabled by presenting proper certificates. In reality, digital certificates, per se, don't provide any security, but can be used together with digital signatures to provide some additional information about the message sender. In contrast, digital signatures have an intrinsic meaning, at least demonstrating that the message sender has access to a particular private key.

The original idea of encapsulating the public key into a signed data structure before distributing it to its users can be traced back to 1978, when Loren Kohnfelder presented it in his bachelor's thesis in electrical engineering from MIT, entitled "Towards a Practical Public-Key Cryptosystem" (Kohnfelder, 1978). As the integrity of digital certificates can be guaranteed by their signature, they can be held and distributed by untrusted entities, thus in principle assuring the desired performance and scalability properties to the whole system.

Public-key communication works best when the encryption functions can reliably be shared among the communicants (by direct contact if possible). Yet when such a reliable exchange of functions (their parameters) is impossible, the next best thing is to trust a third party. Diffie and Hellman introduced a central authority known as the Public File. Thus, the idea of a trusted third party as a scalable and secure solution to the problem of key integrity is not very new. Actually, it has been around for three decades now.

A reasons for its failure to solve many real world problems can probably traced back to poorly designed standards for certificates and infrastructures, which make PKI difficult to deploy and to use, expensive, hardly interoperable, not matching real users needs and requirements. Peter Gutmann in (Guttman, 2004) collected a number of official statements about PKI in general, and about X.509 in particular. Those critical statements represent a quite widespread sentiment due to unclear and hardly understandable standards, but a deeper analysis take into account the very idea of a global directory of names. Even if they augment the standard with so-called *Proxy Certificates*, also some *grid computing* platforms like *Globus* rely on traditional PKI, namely *X.509* (Foster, Kesselman & Tuecke, 2001; Welch, Foster & al., 2004).

The following sections will deal with these issues and with the different approaches that could be adopted to overcome the limitation of current PKI, some of the proposed standards and their use for delegation of access rights among users. These solutions will then be confronted with proposed schemes for protection of copyrighted material in a distributed environment.

RETHINKING PKI

According to a number of proposals, including PolicyMaker (Blaze, Feigenbaum, Lacy, 1996), KeyNote (Blaze, Feigenbaum & al., 1999), Simple Distributed Security Infrastructure (SDSI) (Rivest, Lampson, 1996), Simple Public Key Infrastructure (SPKI) (Ellison, Frantz & al., 1999), the very foundation of digital certificates needs to be re-thought, trying to make them really useful in application scenarios. The main rationale is that

what computer applications need is not to get the real-life identity of keyholders, but to make decisions about them as users. Often these decisions are about whether to grant access to a protected resource or not.

In available PKI systems, these decisions should be taken on the basis of a keyholder's name. However, a keyholder's name does not make much sense to a computer application, other than use it as an index for a database. For this purpose, the only important thing is the name being unique, and being associated with the needed information. Given this reasoning, it is extremely unlikely that the given name by which we identify people could work on the Internet, as it will not be unique.

Moreover, since the explosion of the Internet, contact with person became often only digital, without ever encountering partners personally. In this cases, which are more and more common, there is no body of knowledge to associate with the name. Then trying to build an on-line, global database of facts and people is obviously unfeasible, since it will face privacy problems, as well as unwillingness of businesses to disclose sensible data about their employees and their contacts.

Instead, the revolution of SPKI is it empowers local entities to protect their own resources. They're the ultimate source of all trust relationships, and centralized "trusted" third parties are considered unnecessary (Khare & Rifkin, 1997). Relying on an external entity, and thus trusting it, should not be imposed by technical limitations, but it should be a choice founded on security considerations. There cannot be trust when there's no choice.

Authorization Certificate

In fact, security cannot be founded just on identity, or given names, but more appropriately on principals and authorization (Aura, 1998). In general, a principal is any entity that can be taken accountable for its own actions in the system, and in particular, principals could be simply thought as entities associated with public keys. The SPKI documentation goes even further, dealing with principals as they "are" public keys. This means that each principal must have its own public key, through which it can be identified, and each public key can be granted rights to access system resources.

The main concept in a trust management system, in fact, is authorization, and more precisely distributed authorization. Each entity in the system has the responsibility to protect its own resources, and it is the ultimate source of trust, being able to refuse or accept any request to access the resource.

On the other end, each entity can access some resources without being listed in a comprehensive Access Control List (ACL).

In fact, relying on local authorities and delegation, ACLs can be relegated to a marginal role, while a central role is played by authorization certificates. A basic authorization certificate defines a straight mapping: *authorization -> key*.

The complete structure of a certificate can be defined as a 5-tuple:

1. **issuer:** the public key (or an hash of it) representing the principal who signs the certificate;
2. **subject:** the public key (or, again, an hash, or a named key) representing the principal for whom the delegation is intended to; other types of subjects are allowed, but they can be always resolved to a public key; for example, a threshold subject can be used to indicate that k of n certificate chains must be resolved to a single subject (i.e. to a public key) to make the authorization valid;
3. **delegation:** a flag to allow or block further delegations;
4. **authorization:** an s-expression which is used to represent the actual permissions granted by the issuer to the subject through the certificate;
5. **validity:** the time interval during which the certificate is valid and the delegation holds.

Thus, through an authorization certificate, a manager of some resources can delegate a set of access rights to a trusted entity. This newly empowered principal can, on its turn, issue other certificates, granting a subset of its access rights to other entities. When finally requesting access to a resource, the whole certificate chain must be presented. Precise algorithms are presented in the SPKI proposal to combine certificates in a chain and to solve them to an authorization decision.

It can be easily noted that, in the whole process of delegation, identities and given names never appear. Keyholder names are certainly important, and careful identification is obviously a necessary condition before delegation can be granted. Otherwise principals (i.e. public keys) cannot be associated with the humans ultimately responsible for their actions.

But the interesting thing is that this association is never used in the authorization process, as in fact it is not necessary. The result is a radical simplification of the whole security infrastructure. Also, the whole system is much more flexible, allowing arbitrary delegation of permissions and anonymous communications (in the sense that user's identity is never communicated through the network). Above all, trust chains are made part of the system, being its real core, and they can be easily traced following the chains of authorization certificates issued by the involved principals.

Name Certificates

The Simple Digital Security Infrastructure (SDSI), which eventually became part of the SPKI proposal, showed that local names could not only be used on a local scale, but also in a global, Internet-wide, environment. In fact local names, defined by a principal, can be guaranteed to be unique and valid in their namespace, only. However local names can be made global, if they are prefixed with the public key (i.e. the principal) defining them.

A convention of SDSI is to give names defined in a certificate a default namespace, being the issuer of the certificate itself. Otherwise local names have always to be prefixed with a public key which disambiguates them. When used in this way, names become Fully Qualified SDSI Names. Compound names can be built by joining local names in a sequence. So, for example, *PK1's Joe's Bill* can be resolved to the principal named *Bill* by the principal named *Joe* by the principal (holding the public key) *PK1*.

Another type of SPKI certificates is defined for associating names with their intended meaning: name -> subject. A SPKI Name Certificate doesn't carry an authorization field but it carries a name. It is 4-tuple:

1. **issuer:** the public key (or an hash of it) representing the principal who signs the certificate;
2. **name:** a byte string;
3. **subject:** the intended meaning of the name; it can be a public key or another name;
4. **validity:** the time interval during which the certificate is valid and the delegation holds.

There's no limitation to the number of keys which can be made valid meanings for a name. So in the end, a SPKI name certificate defines a named groups of principals. Some authors (Li, 2000; Li, Grosof, 2000) interpret these named groups of principals as distributed roles.

Certificate Revocation

Validity conditions of certificates usually come in the form of time intervals, but other options are defined in the SPKI proposal, including on-line tests, certificate revocation lists (CRLs), revalidation and one-time use.

Some critics of X.509 (Gutmann, 2000) note that their management doesn't allow to obtain consistent results, making the evaluation of the validity of a certificate a non-deterministic process.

In SPKI, instead, the computation of authorization is always deterministic by design.

Three conditions are defined to use CRLs in SPKI:

1. the certificate must designate a key to sign the CRL and some locations to retrieve it;
2. the CRL must have validity dates set;
3. the validity intervals of CRLs must not intersect, i.e. a new CRL cannot be issued to replace a still valid one and without users expecting it.

It is suggested to use delta CRLs whenever possible. Under these conditions, a CRL is a completion of a certificate rather than an announcement to the world about a change of mind. Another possibility is to use revalidations, which in a sense are a positive version of CRLs. They are subject to the same conditions of CRL. Finally one-time revalidations allow a principal to issue one-shot delegations, which expire as soon as they're first used.

Anyway, in most cases revalidation can be avoided if short-lived certificates are issued. This requires a more careful administration of delegation, but, on the other side, it improves performance and makes the whole system better adhering the principle of least privilege (Saltzer & Schroeder, 1975). In SPKI, using short-lived certificates is possible, since delegation certificates are clearly distinguished from identity certificates and, usually, the information they convey has an intrinsic validity period, which is related to the time needed for the subject to complete the delegated task.

Logical Foundation

Several research works focused on giving the SPKI theory a logical foundation. In particular, in (Abadi, 1998) authors provide a generalized setting to study the problem of compound names for authorization decisions. In (Halpern & van der Meyden, 1999) the problem is restricted to

Figure 1. A chain of name certificates

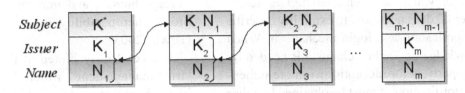

adhere SDSI names, only. However, in (Li & Grosof, 2000) it is proved that this logic does not capture the key features of SDSI, and an alternative solution is proposed. In particular, the conclusions that can be derived using the axioms of (Abadi, 1998; Halpern & van der Meyden, 1999) are not monotonic, i.e. a decision to allow access to a resource can be changed to a deny, if more certificates are provided. SDSI, instead, is monotonic by design, and this is a fundamental feature. In fact, in a distributed application, it's often difficult to guarantee that all relevant certificates have been collected.

Moreover, in (Li & Grosof, 2000), an interesting discussion deals with the importance of authorization certificates. Even recognizing that flexibility and granularity in permission handling are improved by authorization certificates, authors demonstrate that most use cases can be satisfied by using local names and name certificates, only. In their perspective, local names are the distributed counterpart of roles in role based access control (RBAC) frameworks. The following picture (Figure 1) shows how name certificates can be organized in a chain to link local roles, for delegation of access rights.

Like roles, local names can be used as a level of indirection between principals and permissions. Both a local name and a role represent at the same time a set of principals, as well as a set of permissions granted to those principals. But, while roles are usually defined in a centralized fashion by a system administrator, local names, instead, are fully decentralized. This way, they better scale to Internet-wide, peer-to-peer applica-

tions, without loosening in any way the principles of trust management.

CERTIFICATE FORMATS AND INTEROPERABILITY

One of the main objectives of new protocols and formats, often designed around XML and other web technologies, is an integrated environment, where systems built on different models and technologies can interoperate, both providing and accessing services.

For this purpose, it is also important to use security models which can enable a corresponding interoperability with regard to the management and delegation of privileges, allowing trusted partners to access protected resources even when their particular application is founded on different models and technologies.

OpenID, Xri, Xdi

OpenID (OpenID, 2007) is a decentralized digital identity system, in which any user's online identity is given by URL (such as for a blog or a home page) and can be verified by any server running the protocol. In its latest version, OpenID also supports *XRI* and *i-names* (Reed & McAlpin, 2005).

The main motivation for OpenID is to avoid Internet users, in particular users of blogs, wikis and forums, to create and manage a new account for every site they intend to contribute in. Instead, on OpenID enabled sites, users only need to provide their home url, so that the authentication process can be completed with their own identity provider. A limitation which has been often highlighted, is that OpenID does not allow to explicitly describe the authentication and login mechanism. When the knowledge of used mechanism is needed by a relying party, before accepting a remote authentication notification, it must be obtained by other means. This is the case of access to sensitive data, for example in the context of e-banking applications, which require the use of strong authentication mechanisms.

Probably, this limitation will be overcome by more mature versions of the standard. At the Internet Identity Workshop 2006, Pat Patterson from Sun Microsystems has shown a straight integration of OpenID and SAML, where users were authenticated after resolving their url to a SAML Identity Provider. In this case, SAML could be used to provide explicit information about authentication context. I-Name Single Sign-On (ISSO) is another proposal to join i-names and SAML for single sign-on.

Yet, the main problem is that, even if integrated with SAML, OpenID will remain focused on authentication, thus its usefulness and applicability will be confined to very simple application domains, where trust relationships are not built among users, with delegation of access rights, but instead based on federation of identity providers. However, in the generic context of service composition, above all in open peer to peer networks, identity information alone (especially if it is provided by some remote host) is not sufficient to take decisions whether to grant access to a local resource or a service, or not.

SAML Overview

Traditionally, the problem of identity management was considered equivalent to PKI, and in some sense it is. However, in practice, all efforts to deploy a X.509 infrastructure have fallen below expectations. Professionals share with users a widespread bad taste about PKI. PKI is expensive

and hard to manage, even harder to use for the average human, and implementations lack the broad interoperability the standards promised (Lewis, 2003).

We've already hinted at the trend towards "trust management", which deals with identity in a radical different way. Today, there's an opportunity for this trend to finally make its way to every day applications. Web services, while not being a solution to every problem as a lot of "technology evangelists" claim, are finally moving the focus to local resource management in a global – federated – environment, paving the way for a "trust management" infrastructure. Probably the success of peer-to-peer applications, as well as the potential of the Grid and of ubiquitous computing will eventually overcome the resistance of large businesses operating in the certification arena.

There's a concrete and widespread interest to avoid the deployment of a whole new security infrastructure, but to fully exploit and integrate existing and different security models and mechanisms, which have already been deployed. These vary according to the different degree of "sensibility" associated with the protected data and resources, and include plain-text username/ password pairs, Kerberos, X.509, KeyNote, SPKI and various "trust management" infrastructures.

The Security Assertion Markup Language (SAML), being standardized by OASIS, is an open, XML-based format to convey security information associated with a principal (Ragouzis, Hughes & al., 2008). While SAML allows to exploit digital signature and PKI technologies, its specifications are not about the deployment of some PKI, but about their use in a federated environment along with other technologies. The Liberty Alliance, for example, concentrates its work on SSO, to allow the use of services from different providers without repeating the login operations at every site.

The approach of SAML is radically different from X.509, above all as its specifications start from realistic use cases, which deal with problems that traditional, X.509 based, PKI was never able to solve. The lack of attention to real world cases is probably one of the main weaknesses of X.509. SAML and federated identity, instead, deal with the problem of system security following a bottom-up software engineering approach, taking into account already existing infrastructures.

Instead of defining, and imposing, a top down model, SAML and federated security enable already deployed systems to grow and join others, on the basis of precise and limited agreements. This way, the experience gained in the implementation and deployment of security infrastructures is not lost. On the contrary, it is the basis for the new generation of integrated security systems.

Moreover, SAML is based on XML, and so it easily integrates with Web-services and other XML based applications. It can leverage existing standards and protocols, like XML Digital Signature, XML Encryption, SOAP, WSDL and WS-Security.

SAML Specifications

The first version of SAML was standardized by OASIS in November 2002. Version 1.1 and 2.0 were released in the following years. Since its initial development, the definition of the requirements of SAML was driven by three use cases:

- web single sign-on (SSO),
- attribute-based authorization,
- web services security.

More scenarios were chosen, for each use case, to provide a detailed description of the involved interactions. From this analysis, a generic architecture emerged, to describe the various actors and their interactions.

SAML itself deals with three different kinds of assertions:

- authentication assertions,
- attribute assertions,
- authorization decision assertions.

Authorization decision assertions are a somehow "frozen" feature in current specifications, suggesting a better solution is to rely on other available standards for security policies, like XACML. A profile to integrate XACML authorization decisions into a SAML assertion has been standardized with SAML 2.0 (Anderson & Lockhart, 2004).

The generic structure of a SAML assertion is shown in the following example, which makes evident it is very similar to what is usually called a "digital certificate".

1. **<saml:Assertion** ID=*"Example-752cc 91237677a05f4a079a7dd718c2a"* IssueInstant=*"2006-11-10T11:00:00.000Z"* Version=*"2.0">*
2. **<saml:Issuer>**MD5:aU+xBe6Pi// bSbAZMMmXvw==**</saml:Issuer>**
3. **<ds:Signature>**<!—*Actual signature goes here* -->**</ds:Signature>**
4. **<saml:Subject>**
5. **<saml:NameID** NameQualifier=*"MD5:kX n8dsd9irpJm3/j6epdCQ=="*>
6. Researcher
7. **</saml:NameID>**
8. **</saml:Subject>**
9. **<saml:AttributeStatement>**
10. **<saml:Attribute** Name=*"NameID">*
11. **<saml:AttributeValue** xsi:type=*"xs:string">*
12. Colleague
13. **</saml:AttributeValue>**
14. **</saml:Attribute>**
15. **</saml:AttributeStatement>**
16. **<saml:Conditions** notOnOrAfter=*"2007- 06-30T12:00:00.000Z"* />
17. **</saml:Assertion>**

Like in every other certificate, an issuer attests some properties about a subject, digitally signing the document to prove its authenticity and to avoid tampering. Conditions can be added to limit the validity of the certificate. As usual, a time interval can be defined. Moreover, it can be limited to a particular audience or to a one-time use. Conditions can also be put on the use of the certificate by proxies who want to sign more assertions on its basis.

SAML from the "Trust Management" Perspective

Being designed to allow interoperability among very different security systems, SAML offers a variety of schemes to format security assertions. In particular, there are a number of possible ways to represent a subject, which also allow to keep away X.500 directories and DN names.

One interesting possibility is to use a SubjectConfirmation object to represent a subject directly by its public key, which resembles the basic idea of SPKI, where, at the end, principals "are" always public keys.

Thinking about the use of SAML as a representation of SPKI authorization certificates, it would be important to have access rights, or permissions, associated with the subject. This is best achieved through the integration of an XACML policy into a SAML assertion. The precise way to accomplish this is described in a separate profile.

But, apart from direct delegation of permissions, SPKI-like trust management frameworks can also be used to implement distributed RBAC access control systems, as discussed in (Li, 2000). For this purpose, local names are particularly important, as they allow each principal to manage its own name space, which, on the other hand, is also one of the foundations of "federated identity" and SAML.

In fact, while SAML allows the use of X.509 distinguished names, it also support a number of other heterogeneous naming schemes. In this sense, its reliance on XML for assertion encoding is not irrelevant, as it provides intrinsic extendibility through schemas and namespaces.

Assigning a local name to a public key, or to a set of public keys, is as simple as defining a role, as in SAML names, and roles, are not considered globally unique by design. And also assigning a named principal to a local name, or to a role, is perfectly possible. In particular, though not being foreseen in the specifications, it is perfectly possible to use SAML assertions to represent certificate in a chain like the one shown in Figure 1.

Of course, allowing interoperability with existing X.509 infrastructures is important, and in fact X.509 certificates can be used in conjunction with SAML assertions as a mean of authentication. Moreover, an X.500/LDAP attribute profile has been defined for the representation of X.500 names and attributes when expressed as SAML attributes.

Authentication Context

In reality, till now, the main application area of SAML has been federated identity and SSO, thus authentication. But authentication doesn't play a direct role in trust management system, as identity is kept out of the authorization process, and is used only if an out-of-band verification is requested, for example for legal use.

Anyway, SAML based authentication comes with some useful features, even from a trust management perspective. In fact, in (Ellison, Frantz & al., 1999) authors already noted that the whole X.509 PKI model was founded on not always valid basis, assuming the issuer has the ability to eventually decide the conditions under which the certificate must be considered valid, and the enabled uses of the public key. This has certainly a sense, since the issuer must be able to define the limits of its delegation. But the role of the final user was not acknowledged, though being the entity who eventually takes a risk by accepting the certificate. This aspect is particularly important in a business environment, for example.

Thus, if the relying party has to place some confidence in the certificate, it may need additional information about the assertion itself. SAML allows the authentication authority to specify which mechanisms, protocols, and processes were used for the authentication. The Authentication Context can include – but is not limited to – the actual method used for authentication (for example, face-to-face, online, shared secret). Much more details can be specified, allowing confidence in a certificate to be based on clearer basis than those allowed by ambiguous X.509 policies and related extensions.

XACML Overview

The eXtensible Access Control Markup Language (XACML) is a language for specifying role or attribute based access control policies. It is standardized by the OASIS group and, at the time of this writing, its latest release is 2.0 (Moses, 2005).

The following example shows a policy expressed through the XACML language. A read permission for the files in a folder (/home/mackdk/Music/) is granted to a role defined by a known principal (identified by the hash of its public key) in its namespace (MD5:Mf73k3kleAD3sf/53SGlk51d friends).

```
1.   <Policy PolicyId="policy:da08f
     500f4f6975eb6f6450cc8faa03f"
     RuleCombiningAlgId="deny-overrides">
2.   <Target>
3.   <Subjects><Subject>
4.   <SubjectMatch MatchId="string-equal">
5.   <AttributeValue DataType="string">
6.   MD5:Mf73k3kleAD3sf/53SGlk51d friends
7.   </AttributeValue>
8.   <SubjectAttributeDesignator... />
9.   </SubjectMatch>
```

```
10.  </Subject></Subjects>
11.  <Resources><Resource>
12.  <ResourceMatch
     MatchId="regexp-string-match">
13.  <AttributeValue DataType="string">
14.  /home/mackdk/Music/*
15.  </AttributeValue>
16.  <ResourceAttributeDesignator... />
17.  </ResourceMatch>
18.  </Resource></Resources>
19.  <Actions><Action>
20.  <ActionMatch MatchId="string-equal">
21.  <AttributeValue DataType="string">
22.  Read
23.  </AttributeValue>
24.  <ActionAttributeDesignator... />
25.  </ActionMatch>
26.  </Action></Actions>
27.  </Target>
28.  <Rule Effect="Permit" RuleId="policy:r
     ule:071392128297ef2"/>
29.  </Policy>
```

Its main components are:

- **Rule:** the basic element of each policies;
- **Policy:** A set of rules, together with the algorithms to combine them, the intended target and some conditions;
- **Policy set:** A set of policies, together with the algorithms to combine them, the intended target and some obligations.

In particular, each XACML rule is specified through its:

- **Target:** indicating the resources, the subjects, the actions and the environment to which the rule applies;
- **Effect:** can be Allow or Deny;
- **Condition:** can further refine the applicability of the rule.

XACML from the "Trust Management" Perspective

As described in the previous sections, trust management uses public keys as a direct mean to identify principals, and authorization certificates to allow delegation of access rights among principals. SAML defines some rudimentary structures to convey authorization decisions in assertions. However, these structure are not able convey all the information that can be represented using the XACML language. On the other hand, XACML lacks means to protect requests and responses of its Policy Enforcement Points (PEP). It is clear, and so it appeared to both the SAML and the XACML working groups, that the two languages were in many senses complementary, and thus a SAML profile of XACML was defined. It effectively makes the two languages work together in a seamless way (Anderson & Lockhart, 2004).

From the "trust management" perspective, the conjunction of SAML and XACML, in particular the inclusion of XACML policies and authorization decisions into SAML assertions, provides a rich environment for the delegation of access rights. From this point of view, the fact that logic foundations of the XACML language exist is very important, as they provide XACML with a clear semantic. The problem is to find algorithms through which the combination of permissions granted in a chain of certificates could be computed in a deterministic way, as it is already possible in SPKI.

In fact, even if the semantic of a XACML policy is logically sound, nevertheless subtle problems can appear when different policies, linked in a chain of delegation assertions, have to be merged.

One major problem is about monotonicity of authorization assertions, which cannot be guaranteed in the general case. Using XACML authorization decisions as SAML assertions, it is possible to assert that access to a particular resource is denied, instead of allowed. Though being a perfectly legal and meaningful concept, the denial of a permission (a "negative permission") is not desirable in decentralized environments. In this case, a service provider can never allow access, as it cannot be sure to possess all issued statements. On the other hand, the non-monotonicity of the system can also lead to attacks, as issued assertions can be prevented to reach the provider, this way leading it to take wrong authorization decisions.

Therefore, it is necessary to define a specific profile of SAML and XACML which could enable the secure delegation of permissions in decentralized environments. One of the first requirements is to make "negative permissions" illegal.

Threshold Subjects

In SPKI, threshold subjects are defined as a special kind of subjects, to be used only in authorization certificates. In (Li & Grosof, 2000) authors question the usefulness of this construct, arguing it is used as an alternative to simulate conjunction and disjunction of subjects. Moreover, they provide an intuitive meaning for threshold subjects when used in name certificates, also.

XACML does not support threshold subjects in its general case, but conjunction of multiple subjects is possible. In particular XACML allow the association of multiple subjects per access request, representing the multiple entities which are responsible for the request. For example, the request could originate from a user, but it could also be mediated by one or more middle agents, and also some computing devices could be taken into account, being represented, for example, by their IP address.

The XACML Multi-Role Permissions profile specifies a way to grant permissions only to principals playing several roles simultaneously. This kind of policy can be defined by using a single subject in its target, but adding multiple subject-match elements to it.

Moreover, a Role Assignment policy could be used to define which roles should be associated with which principals. Restrictions could be also specified about the possible combinations of roles, as to limit the total number of roles played by a principal. This way, the disjunction of some roles could also be imposed. However, this use could be complicated in decentralized environments, as it could invalidate the monotonicity of the system. Showing more credentials should never lead to obtaining fewer permissions.

TRUSTED SYSTEMS

The following part of this chapter will analyse the fundamental differences between decentralized trust management, on the one hand, and digital rights management and trusted computing, on the other hand. The analysis will start from XrML and ODRL, two similar XML-based languages oriented to the management of digital rights for media content distribution. The usage of so-called "trusted systems" and the application of international laws is necessary for actually enforcing the policies these languages allow to express.

XrML and ODRL

XrML and ODRL are two different proposals, both based on XML, which are making their way in the management of digital rights for media content distribution (XrML, 2002; Iannella, 2002). Both XrML and ODRL are based on previous works made at Xerox PARK, which resulted in the definition of the Digital Property Rights Language (DPRL, 1998), and many distinctions are simply linguistic, naming similar fields in a different way. The real difference lies in their intended domain. While XrML has a broader applicability, instead ODRL seems more oriented to the specific media publishing market. In fact it specifies media formats, resolutions and frame rates, while XrML doesn't. Both languages, under some restrictions, can be used to delegate access rights to other users, also.

Apart from their differences, however, both languages are oriented to the management of digital rights (DRM) for publishing and accessing media content, and can hardly fit different applications. Moreover, they're supported by few software applications, and virtually none in the public domain.

Trusted Computing Platforms

The various *Rights Expression Languages* resulted from efforts of businesses to protect digital material from reproduction and sharing. However all rights expression languages just allow copyright owners to express restrictions about the usage of a resource (for this reason, they're often referred to as *restrictions expression languages*), without being able to enforce by themselves the policies they convey. This can only happen on so-called "trusted systems". (Coyle, 2003)

DRM infrastructure is being included into a growing number of devices and systems, with the support of big ICT and content producers and distributors, including Adobe, Apple, Sony, Microsoft, Intel, AMD, just to cite a few.

One of the most important cases of DRM inclusion into widespread technologies is MPEG, the standard from the Moving Picture Experts Group for multimedia applications. The MPEG-21 version of the standard defines three technologies to deal with DRM: Intellectual Property Management and Protection (IPMP), Rights Expression Language, Rights Data Dictionary. Specifically, MPEG-21 defines a "Rights Expression Language" standard for sharing digital rights/permissions/restrictions for digital content from content creator to content consumer. The language is directly based on XrML, to which it adds a precise dictionary of terms and permissions for describing and accessing multimedia content. In MPEG-21, a digital item is defined as the fundamental unit of distribution and transaction, which users can interact with. Thus, MPEG-21 itself can be defined as a standardized technology for allowing users to access, exchange and manipulate digital items.

Another application area of DRM is the eBook market. Some new interest can be seen from the point of view of content availability, provided for example by the British Library and traditional publishers. But in general protected eBooks have found a quite strong resistance, both from users and authors. This has been due to unclear policies, on the one hand, and piracy concerns, on the other hand. The market is still fragmented, with different formats competing for affirmation, while Adobe PDF remains the de-facto standard for viewing and printing electronic documents. The reader software, available on a wide range of platforms, includes and implementation of DRM. However, the PDF DRM management has been proven quite weak, above all for its obfuscation method.

In reality, obfuscation is the Achille's heel of most DRM systems (Stamp, 2003). Obfuscation is necessary for the realization of DRM restrictions on common PCs and other open systems, to make reverse engineering more difficult and protect in some way the decryption function. But in traditional cryptography, obfuscation was always considered a poor solution, with uncertain resistance to attacks. Moreover, in open systems the decryption function (generally a cryptographic key) can be gathered by scanning the system memory at runtime.

To overcome this problem, content producers are encouraging laws against circumvention of DRM policies. But another parallel effort is directed toward the realization of so-called *trusted computing systems*, composed only of approved hardware and software components, which are verified to respect media access restrictions.

One of the largest projects in this field is the Next-Generation Secure Computing Base (NGSCB), Microsoft's security architecture for trusted computing, to be included in operating systems and hardware components of common PCs. It is composed by both software and hardware components and it is paradigmatic of the way copyright

holders can trust the DRM restrictions they impose will be effectively respected on users' systems.

NGSCB Architecture

The hardware parts of NGSCB are specified by the Trusted Computing Group (TCG) in the form of two main components: a cryptographic coprocessor, called the Trusted Platform Module (TPM), and curtailed memory support in the CPU. The TPM provides basic features including fast random number generation, symmetric and asymmetric cryptography, sealed cryptographic keys storage. This is the most peculiar and controversial feature of "trustworthy computing" systems, which makes keys impossible to modify, or even simply to retrieve, by everyone including the legitimate owner of the system. It is the basic element to allow remote attestation of hardware and software configurations of any enabled computer.

The unique cryptographic key of each TPM is generated and stored during its production. Afterwards, it's kept inside the module and never communicated outside. To use the key for encrypting or decrypting some data, this has to be passed to the TPM module. The operation will be performed only under certain circumstances. In particular it has to be managed by a trusted application and resulting data has not to be stored outside of curtained memory. This way, data is inaccessible to other code, also to the operating system itself.

Given the cryptographic capabilities of the TPM module, it can also be used to sign data, and the signature can be verified by the user of the local system or by any party who needs the attestation that the computer has not been manumitted and it's in a secure state. Obviously, apart from signature, the sealed key can be used to encrypt any data, which can afterwards be decrypted only using the same module.

The other main hardware component of the NGSCB architecture is the so called "curtained memory" feature. Data stored into this memory can only be read and modified by its owner process. This way, a trusted application can use the attestation capability of the platform to confirm the safe storage of its own data, and also its code can be protected from reverse engineering attempts.

Since the functionalities of the TPM module cannot be altered by anyone, including the owner of the system, some critics have argued that, this way, the owner would be deprived of the ultimate control over its system. An "Owner Override" feature has been proposed, to solve this problem. When imposing the owner override mode, the TPM would still protect its key, but it would allow to produce signature, encryption and decryption of arbitrary data, thus empowering the user to produce false attestations. While allowing users to hold ultimate control over their systems, the owner override feature would make the NGSCB architecture ineffective for DRM purposes.

The software components of NGSCB are also two: the Nexus kernel, a security component that is part of the Operating System, and Nexus Computing Agents (NCAs), trusted modules within NGSCB-enabled applications.

DRM is one of the main application area of trusted computing. It is not directly provided by the NGSCB, but it can be obtained by using the basic features provided by the platform, in particular attestation, curtained memory and sealed cryptographic key. In fact, DRM protected files can be encrypted in such a way that only trusted applications can access them, after attestation of full operation of the TPM, without alteration of the running code. In this case, some protected usage of the decryption key could be allowed for the trusted code. Various protection schemes and policies can be implemented, on the basis of the same feature set.

Attestation could be useful in corporate environments and large networks of computers, where it can be used to limit access to services made available on the network. Only unmodi-

fied nodes would be granted access to sensible data and services. This feature would be useful in network applications in general. For example, multiplayer online games could be secured from most cheating attempts, like alteration of network traffic, application code, drivers or other system components.

Legal Context

The diffusion of digital contents and DRM systems is accompanied by a certain development in the legal framework, too. Since the market of digital content has a global reach, also the legal updates are being discussed in international forums. The main international body in this field is the World Intellectual Property Organization (WIPO), which was created in 1967 and entered into force on April 26, 1970. Its aim is "to encourage creative activity, to promote the protection of intellectual property throughout the world". In 1974 it became a specialized agency of the United Nations and its headquarter is now in Geneva, Switzerland. WIPO currently has 184 member states and administers 24 international treaties. Most of UN members have already joined WIPO. The Bureaux Internationaux Réunis pour la Protection de la Propriété Intellectuelle (BIRPI) – which had been established in 1893 to administer the Berne Convention for the Protection of Literary and Artistic Works and the Paris Convention for the Protection of Industrial Property – can be considered a predecessor of WIPO.

In 1996 the WIPO Copyright Treaty (WCT) was approved. It is one of the main results of the international body and is being implemented by many of its members. It requires WIPO members to pass bills against the circumvention of DRM mechanisms. Among the main enactment of the treaty, there are the Digital Millennium Copyright Act (DMCA), passed in the USA in 1998, and the European directive on copyright (EUCD), passed in the EU in 2001.

The DMCA is the act which criminalizes the circumvention of DRM and other measures implemented to protect copyrighted material. The law is infringed by the very circumvention of DRM mechanisms, whether or not copyrighted material is actually accessed. The DMCA also increases the penalties for unauthorized access to copyrighted material through communication networks and the Internet in particular. It extends the reach of copyright, but it reduces the liability of service providers for copyright infringement by their users. After being passed by a unanimous vote in the U.S. Senate, the act was signed into law by President Bill Clinton on October 28, 1998.

The EUCD is a directive of the European Union which addresses the same issues as the DMCA. A separate directive, the Electronic Commerce Directive, addressed the exemption from liability (both direct and indirect) of Internet service providers. The Copyright Directive is also known as the Information Society Directive and officially is identified as the Directive 2001/29/EC of the European Parliament. It was enacted under the internal market provisions of the Treaty of Rome. Its execution requires separate legislation within each member state of the Union. Due to some vagueness of the EUCD directive, which does not deal with all cases, and public attention to copyright laws, the transposition has not been entirely linear, with six member states being taken to Court of Justice for failure to implement the directive in time.

Trusted Systems vs. Trust Management Systems

It's certainly important to note that *trusted systems* are radically different from *trust management systems*, in that the former assure *content owners* and *media producers* that the hosting system will respect the "rights" they defined (but from the point of view of users these rights are better defined as "restrictions"); instead, trust management system

allow *users* to grant trust to other users or software agents for accessing local resources.

According to various authors, the diffusion of trusted computing systems could lead to worrying scenarios (Walker, 2003; Anderson, 2003; Stallman, 2006; Schneier, 2002; O'Riordan, 2006). For examples, certain users could be locked out from accessing certain files or software products, on the basis of remote choices. This can be used by companies to acquire a competitive advantage, by requiring that only a particular application has to be used to open certain files. This would be possible if the files were to be encrypted by the application itself. The effect would be independent from the ability of other applications to handle a particular file format. But certain authors expressed even tougher preoccupations. In fact, the local enforcement of remote policies, once made possible, could be used not just for DRM control. It could also pave the way for social control and limitation of users abilities. This possibility could be directed to avoid criminal activities, for example. But it could also lead to plain censorship on political basis.

FUTURE TRENDS

Federated identities and security assertions are a novel technique to connect already existing security systems, without requiring to design and deploy a whole new one, which could hardly fit the extremely heterogeneous variety of goals and requirements the different applications have.

Particular attention deserve SAML and XACML, for their wide applicability, their intrinsic extensibility, and their XML grounding, which allows them to easily fit into the existing web-based applications, as well as into new systems based on web or grid services. Nowadays, SAML is used especially for SSO purposes. Some proposals show that, in the near future, SAML could be used together with OpenID, too.

But, in future, the usage of different SAML documents joined in chains could allow the management of trust relationships in a completely distributed environment. In this sense, SAML could become the standard format for expressing delegation of permissions and roles in a peer-to-peer fashion.

Other formats are proposed to specify the digital rights granted to a user for accessing a particular media content. Among the proposals, XrML and ODRL are two notable and similar examples. XrML, in particular, could become quite important, in future. In fact it is at the basis of the DRM system for the MPEG-21 format, for digital audio and video content.

The international legal framework is also paying increasing attention to DRM systems. Many nations are implementing the 1996 WIPO Copyright Treaty (WCT), as well as other acts to prevent the circumvention of DRM mechanisms. Apart from legal constraints, technical means are being designed to make this circumvention practically impossible for common users. NGSCB is one of the largest initiatives in this field.

CONCLUSION

While the traditional approach for inter-domain security is based on centralized or hierarchical certification authorities and public directory of names, new solutions are appearing. Trust management systems do not assume, a-priori, the existence of some trusted parties. In fact, this assumption would become an "obligated choice" of trust for the user, and without choice, there's no real trust. Moreover, the presence of some third party as a globally trusted entity implies that all systems participating in the global environment have to equally trust it. Instead, users should be provided with means to manage the trust relations they build with other entities operating in the same, global environment. In the same manner as people collaborate in the real world, systems will be made interoperable in the virtual world. A number of emerging technologies, including SAML and XACML, can enable this kind of solutions in the context of web services.

On the other hand, other XML-based languages are being defined for the management of digital rights (DRM), for publishing and accessing media content. XrML, ODRL and other Rights Expression Languages allow copyright owners to express restrictions about the usage of a resource. But the actual enforcement of such policies can only happen on the basis of widespread use of so-called "trusted systems", and of the application of international laws against DRM circumvention. The 1998 Digital Millennium Copyright Act (DMCA) in the USA and the 2001 European directive on copyright (EUCD) are two important examples.

This chapter analysed the fundamental differences between decentralized trust management, on the one hand, and digital rights management and trusted computing, on the other hand. At their core, trusted systems are radically different from trust management systems. While the former assure copyright holders and media producers that the hosting system will respect the access restrictions they defined, instead, trust management system allow users to grant trust to other users or software agents for accessing local resources. In this sense, the different interpretation of trust in these systems drives to divergent consequences with respect to system architectures and access policies, but also to law, ethics, politics.

REFERENCES

Abadi, M. (1998). On SDSI's Linkd Local Name Spaces. *Journal of Computer Security*, 6(1-2), 3–21.

Anderson, A., & Lockhart, H. (2004). SAML 2.0 profile of XACML. Retrieved April 20, 2009, from http://docs.oasis-open.org/xacml/access_control-xacml-2.0-saml_profile-spec-cd-02.pdf

Anderson, R. (2003). Trusted Computing Frequently Asked Questions. Version 1.1. Retrieved April 20, 2009, from http://www.cl.cam. ac.uk/~rja14/tcpa-faq.html

Aura, T. (1998). On the structure of delegation networks. In *Proc. 11th IEEE Computer Security Foundations Workshop* (pp. 14-26). IEEE Computer Society Press.

Blaze, M., Feigenbaum, J., Ioannidis, J., & Keromytis, A. (1999). The KeyNote Trust-Management System Version 2. IETF RFC 2704, September 1999. Retrieved April 20, 2009, from http://www. ietf.org/rfc/rfc2704.txt

Blaze, M., Feigenbaum, J., & Lacy, J. (1996). Decentralized trust management. In *Proc. of the 17th Symposium on Security and Privacy* (pp. 164-173). IEEE Computer Society Press.

Coyle, K. (2003, November). The Technology of Rights: Digital Rights Management. Retrieved April 20, 2009, from http://www.kcoyle.net/ drm_basics.pdf

Diffie, W., & Hellman, M. E. (1976). New directions in cryptography. *IEEE Transactions on Information Theory*, 22(6), 644–654. doi:10.1109/ TIT.1976.1055638

DPRL. (1998, November 13). The Digital Property Rights Language, Manual and Tutorial - XML Edition, Version 2.00. Retrieved April 20, 2009, from http://xml.coverpages.org/DPRLmanual-XML2.html

Ellison, C., Frantz, B., Lampson, B., Rivest, R., Thomas, B., & Ylonen, T. (1999, September). SPKI certificate theory. IETF RFC 2693. Retrieved April 20, 2009, from http://www.ietf.org/ rfc/rfc2693.txt

Foster, I., Kesselman, C., & Tuecke, S. (2001). The anatomy of the grid-enabling scalable virtual organizations. *International Journal of High Performance Computing Applications*, 15(3), 200–222. doi:10.1177/109434200101500302

Gutmann, P. (2000). X.509 Style Guide. Retrieved April 20, 2009, from http://www.cs.auckland. ac.nz/~pgut001/pubs/x509guide.txt

Gutmann, P. (2004). How to build a PKI that works. 3rd Annual PKI R&D Workshop. NIST, Gaithersburg MD. April 12-14, 2004.

Halpern, J., & van der Meyden, R. (1999). A Logic for SDSI's Linked Local Name Spaces. In *Proc. 12th IEEE Computer Security Foundations Workshop* (pp.111-122).

Housley, R., Polk, W., Ford, W., & Solo, D. (2002, April). Internet X.509 Public Key Infrastructure Certificate and CRL Profile. IETF RFC 3280. Retrieved April 20, 2009, from http://www.ietf. org/rfc/rfc3280.txt

Iannella, R. (2002). Open Digital Rights Language (ODRL), Version: 1.1. Retrieved April 20, 2009, from http://odrl.net/1.1/ODRL-11.pdf

Khare, R., & Rifkin, A. (1997). Weaving a web of trust. *World Wide Web Journal*, 2(3), 77–112.

Kohnfelder, L. (1978). Toward a Practical Public Cryptosystem. *Bachelor's thesis* (pp. 39-44). Dept. Electrical Engineering, MIT, Cambridge, Mass. Lewis, J. (2003, March 1). Reinventing PKI: Federated Identity and the Path to Practical Public Key Security. Retrieved April 20, 2009, from http://www.burtongroup.com/

Li, N. (2000). Local names in SPKI/SDSI. In *Proc. 13th IEEE Computer Security Foundations Workshop* (pp. 2-15). IEEE Computer Society Press.

Li, N., & Grosof, B. (2000). A practically implementable and tractable delegation logic. Proc. *2000 IEEE Symposium on Security and Privacy* (pp. 29-44). IEEE Computer Society Press.

Moses, T. (2005). eXtensible Access Control Markup Language (XACML) Version 2.0. Retrieved April 20, 2009, from http://docs.oasis-open.org/xacml/2.0/access_control-xacml-2.0-core-spec-os.pdf

O'Riordan, C. (2006, January). Transcript of Opening session of first international GPLv3 conference. Retrieved April 20, 2009, from http://www.ifso.ie/documents/gplv3-launch-2006-01-16.html

Open, I. D. (2007, December 5). OpenID Authentication 2.0. Retrieved April 20, 2009, from http://openid.net/specs/openid-authentication-2_0.html

Ragouzis, N., Hughes, J., Philpott, R., Maler, E., Madsen, P., & Scavo, T. (2008). Security Assertion Markup Language (SAML) V2.0 Technical Overview. Retrieved April 20, 2009, from http://www.oasis-open.org/committees/download.php/27819/sstc-saml-tech-overview-2.0-cd-02.pdf

Reed, D., & McAlpin, D. (2005). Extensible Resource Identifier (XRI) Syntax V2.0. Retrieved April 20, 2009, from http://www.oasis-open.org/committees/download.php/15377/xri-syntax-V2.0-cs.pdf

Rivest, R. L., & Lampson, B. (1996). SDSI - A Simple Distributed Security Infrastructure. September 15, 1996. Retrieved April 20, 2009, from http://people.csail.mit.edu/rivest/sdsi10.html

Saltzer, J. H., & Schroeder, M. D. (1975). The protection of information in computer systems. *Proceedings of the IEEE, 63*(9), 1278–1308. doi:10.1109/PROC.1975.9939

Schneier, B. (2002). Crypto-Gram Newsletter August 15, 2002. Retrieved April 20, 2009, from http://www.schneier.com/crypto-gram-0208.html

Stallman, R. M. (1997). The Right to Read. [from http://www.gnu.org/philosophy/right-to-read.html]. *Communications of the ACM, 40*(2), 85–87. Retrieved April 20, 2009. doi:10.1145/253671.253726

Stamp, M. (2003). Digital Rights Management: The Technology Behind The Hype. *Journal of Electronic Commerce Research, 4*(3), 102–112.

Walker, J. (2003). The Digital imprimatur: How big brother and big media can put the Internet genie back in the bottle. Retrieved April 20, 2009, from http://www.fourmilab.ch/documents/digital-imprimatur/

Welch, V., Foster, I., Kesselman, C., Mulmo, O., Pearlman, L., Tuecke, S., et al. (2004). X.509 Proxy Certificates for Dynamic Delegation. In *Proceedings of the 3rd Annual PKI R&D Workshop*. Gaithersburg MD: NIST Technical Publications.

XrML. (2002, March 8). XrML 2.0 Technical Overview Version 1.0. Retrieved April 20, 2009, from http://www.xrml.org/Reference/XrMLTechnicalOverviewV1.pdf

Chapter 25
Senior Web Accessibility:
Laws, Standards and Practices

Isabelle Motte
Facultés Universitaires Notre-Dame de la Paix, Belgium

Monique Noirhomme-Fraiture
Facultés Universitaires Notre-Dame de la Paix, Belgium

ABSTRACT

Web accessibility is a major question in present ICT legislation. An ageing population is a known phenomenon that makes older people become a specific interest group. In this chapter, we present the evolution encountered in laws and standards due to specific concern about older people. This publication is related to the works of the W3C WAI-AGE group. We specifically interest in the adaptations encountered in W3C accessibility guidelines (WCAG) while considering the difficulties related to ageing. We also propose some practical recommendations for web designers that want to develop websites targeting seniors. We finally give some perspectives about accessibility legislation and standards.

INTRODUCTION

A lot still has to be done to reach e-accessibility. However, legislation and standards are being formulated. These days, new laws apply in many countries concerning not only the accessibility for disabled persons but general accessibility for all persons. Seniors are one of the new target populations. We present in this chapter the laws, researches and standards that exist in the matter of senior web accessibility.

First of all, we present some analysis of world statistics showing that seniors constitute an important target group for the web services of tomorrow. A lot of studies show that the population pyramid is turning upside down. Seniors often encounter difficulties in mobility and are therefore highly interested in home services.

Therefore we propose a survey of the new laws concerning seniors' accessibility. A lot of countries already implement other accessibility rules in practical life (inclined plane,...). For web accessibility, standards are still being formulated and awareness has to be incited in every aspect of web site construction: authorities ordering and cre-

DOI: 10.4018/978-1-61520-975-0.ch025

Figure 1. Population previsions for European population

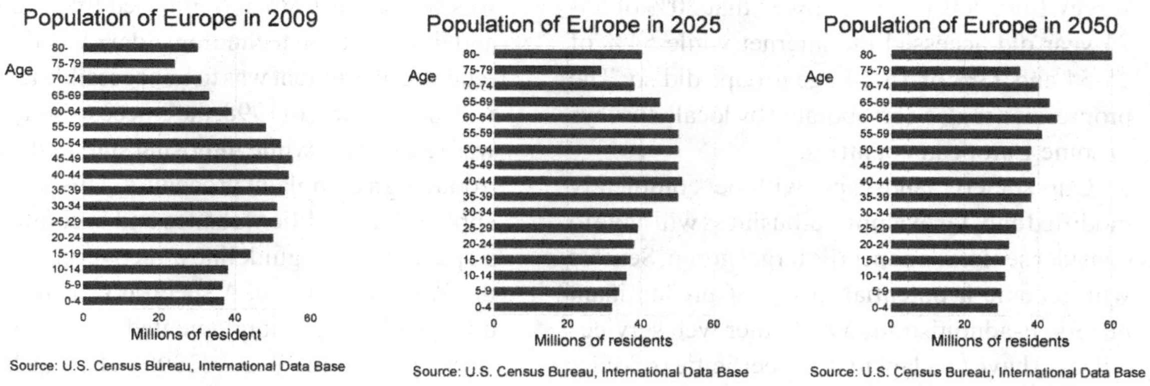

Population of Europe in 2009

Source: U.S. Census Bureau, International Data Base

Population of Europe in 2025

Source: U.S. Census Bureau, International Data Base

Population of Europe in 2050

Source: U.S. Census Bureau, International Data Base

ating web sites must mention accessibility in web site specifications, people filling the contents in content management systems have to be informed of the main rules to respect,... Web accessibility has to become a public preoccupation.

Next, we propose to review the literature about web accessibility difficulties of seniors. The problems encountered by seniors are due to sensory acuity decline: failing eyesight, hearing loss, motor skill depreciation, and cognitive decline.

We propose to analyze the World Wide Web Consortium (W3C) accessibility guidelines (WCAG) and to show how much they have been adapted from version WCAG 1.0 to version WCAG 2.0 in order to take care of seniors' difficulties. A special W3C group discussed that question, the WAI-AGE group, and we will study some of their works.

Finally, we summarize the seniors' web accessibility rules from the standpoint of web developers.

SOME POPULATION STATISTICS

The population ageing is a major challenge for the future. If we consider, for example, the population of Europe, previsions let us think that the age pyramid is turning upside down. We retrieved statistical previsions from U.S. Census Bureau IDB

(2009). Figure 1 presents the predicted evolution of European population along years.

Presently, young people (younger than 20) are as numerous as older persons (older than 65). In the year 2050, the number of seniors will be almost twice that of young people. This analysis could be constructed according to different prevision sources but would lead to the same conclusion for all developed countries. This phenomenon is generalized but follows a different rhythm depending on the countries.

We also want to emphasize the generalization of the internet usage throughout the world. According to Internet World Stats (2009), about one in two people uses the internet in Europe uses. Internet-user growth is impressive, especially in countries that currently present a lower penetration level. For example, in Albania, about 16% of the population uses the internet today. Looking back in time, we notice that the penetration rate was multiplied by more than 200 between 2000 and 2008! While for a country like Belgium, where more that 67% of population uses the internet, the penetration rate was multiplied by 2.5 over the same period.

Statistics presenting the internet use according to age also show that the elderly group specifically presents a progression. In America, the Pew internet (2009) study highlighted that from 2005 to 2009, the proportion of online 70-75 year olds had moved on from 26% to 45%. In Europe, the survey Eurostats (2006) showed that 20% of 55-74 year old accessed the internet while 54% of 25-54 and 73% of 16-24 age groups did so. The progression is also corroborated by locale surveys in some European countries.

Our society landscape will be completely modified and, for example, e-business will have to consider seniors as a specific target group. Seniors will become a potential group of predominant buyers. E-administration and other web services will also have to adapt to the specificities of older people.

SENIOR ACCESSIBILITY LEGISLATION

Accessibility legislation currently looks like a patchwork built of numerous components:

- actual laws on accessibility exist in some countries while these are not even considered in others;
- explicit reference to W3C WAI standards are sometimes given while specific guidelines are proposed by some counties;
- seniors are explicitly cited as an accessibility target group or are not directly considered.

In this section, we give an overview of the international situation on e-accessibility and specifically study the case of seniors. We considered the review of international accessibility legislation proposed by W3C group in W3C Policies (2006) and review of The Web Accessibility in Mind Group (2009).

United States of America has been interested in web accessibility for a long time and they proposed a specific law well-known as the Section 508. Section 508 is a part of the Rehabilitation Act of 1973, the last aiming at accessibility for

disabled persons. The first version of Section 508 was written in 1986 and imposed that electronic and information technology developed by the federal government was to be accessible to people with disabilities. In 1998, the e-accessibility policy was reinforced, while imposing standards and introducing a complaint procedure. This legislation applies to all public websites and is composed of a specific set of guidelines, recovering partially the W3C-WCAG1.0. A specific website on that question has been implemented to help web developers: section508.gov (2008). The legislation is already well implemented in practice but does not consider the seniors as specific population target.

Their neighbours in Canada followed almost the same direction: they propose a more recent legislation that explicitly refers to W3C-WCAG1.0. But they also forgot the special case of seniors. See Treasury Board of Canada Secretariat (2007) for more informations.

Australia has also specific legislation since 2000 that explicitly takes seniors into account. They also refer to W3C standardisation guidelines. Australian Human Right Commission (2000) gives a description of the applied policy.

In the same part of the globe, the New Zealand government already refers to WCAG2.0 in its policy (see Networking Government in New Zealand (2009)).

In Europe, the e-accessibility is in discussion since end 1999. At that moment, the Commission launched the *e*Europe initiative, an ambitious programme aimed at making information technologies accessible to all. In 2001, the Commission voted specific objectives to be met by the end of 2002: eEurope 2002. The objectives were to increase Internet connectivity in Europe, open up all communications networks to competition and encourage Internet use by placing emphasis on training and consumer protection. Disabled persons where cited as one of the priority target groups. The next step was approved in 2002 and gave the objectives to be reached for 2005. The eEurope 2005 action plan was aimed at translating the connectivity into increased economic productivity and improved quality and accessibility of services for all European citizens. Web accessibility was then imposed in the public administration sector with specific reference to W3C WAI standards. Now, the i2010 plan is being applied: Information Society and the media working towards growth and jobs. The purpose of this new, integrated policy is to encourage knowledge and innovation with a view to boosting growth and creating more better-quality jobs. One of the leading actions was to create an e-Inclusion program that is up to date and that specifically takes seniors into account: EC e-Inclusion program (2008). Certification schemes and standards for e-accessibility are under study.

Some countries, such as United Kingdom, France, Spain, Portugal, Italy Germany, Ireland, Switzerland, Denmark and Finland already propose an accessibility policy aimed at disabled persons. They sometimes refer to a specific set of guidelines, or explicitly refer to the W3C WCAG. This situation should evolve towards much more harmonisation according to the e-Inclusion action plan. The progress of e-accessibility in Europe may be observed on empirica & Work Research Center (2008).

The essentials of European policy may be consulted on Europa.eu (2009) and the above paragraphs have been inspired a lot from this reference.

In Asia, some countries already have accessibility policies such as India, Hong Kong and Japan.

It seems rather clear that accessibility has become an important preoccupation in industrialized countries. The older people are not always specifically mentioned but current debates lead us to think that it will arise. The standardization process is an important condition for implementation. In the next sections, we propose to present some adaptations in W3C standards with specific interest to the difficulties of seniors.

SENIORS WEB ACCESSIBILITY DIFFICULTIES: A LITERATURE REVIEW

Depending on the studies, the « seniors » category begins after 55, 60 or 65. The main difficulty in that group is that it is absolutely not homogeneous: each person is concerned by one or some of the difficulties we present.

This section has been written while summarizing the content of different studies about senior web accessibility difficulties. These studies are the following: Boucher A. (2007), De Redish, J. & Chisnell, D. (2004), Holt, B. (2000), Agelight LLC (2001), NIH & NLM (2002), Coyne, K.P. & Nielsen (2002), AARP (2005), Zaphiris, P., Kurniawan, S., & Ghiawadwala, M. (2007), Fidgeon, T. (2006), SOPRANO project HIC (2006), SOPRANO project SOC (2006) and W3C EOWG (2008). Main problems are reported in all surveys so that we do not mention the above list. When some specific difficulties are described, highlighted in few references, we cite the concerned sources.

The difficulties are presented in four sections organized according to the sensory changes encountered: vision, hearing, motor skill and cognition are affected. These are inspired from the literature review proposed by W3C EOWG (2008) and by SOPRANO project SOC (2006). The difficulties analysis has been leaded independently to the W3C research and some differences will be highlighted in the next section, devoted to senior accessibility guidelines.

Failing Eyesight

The Ageing Eye

Vision is the most common physiological change associated with aging. This section is structured according to Lighthouse International (2009).

Between 40 and 50, the loss of elasticity lens causes prebyopia, resulting in closely visual acuity deterioration. The near tasks such as reading fine prints become a difficulty. The lens of eye also becomes more yellow with age. This may affect the colour perceptions and contrast sensitivity. For example, it may become impossible to distinguish between blue and green colours. And it may become difficult to distinguish where an objects ends and where its background begins. As the eyes age, the pupil gets smaller, so that more light is needed to see well.

Older adults may also be concerned with some specific eye diseases. We shortly present the four main causes of age-related vision losses:

- Macular degeneration is a deterioration of central vision due to a retina worsening. It is one of the leading cause of blindness. According to University of Illinois Eye & Ear Infirmary (2007), approximately 10% of patients 66 to 74 years of age will have findings of macular degeneration. The prevalence increases to 30% in patients 75 to 85 years of age.
- Glaucoma is another aging eye disease. It is caused by progressive damage to the optic nerve resulting from high fluid pressure inside the eye. The main symptom of it is a loss of contrast resulting notably in difficulty for driving at night. When glaucoma progresses, it also may cause an irreversible loss of peripheral vision.
- Cataracts is a clouding of the lens that reduces visual acuity, producing an overall haze, loss of contrast and increased sensitivity to glare. Sperduto RD & Seigel D. (1980) proposed a population sample study in the United States. They found that age-related lenticular changes where ranging from 42% at ages 52 to 64 years to 91% at ages 75 to 85 years.
- Diabetic retinopathy is one of the complications of advanced or long-term diabetes. It is caused by leaking blood vessels that

damage the entire retina. The symptoms are distorted near vision and partial obstruction of parts of the visual field.

Difficulties on the Web

We saw that most seniors suffer from view troubles that can decline under several forms: closely visual acuity decline, colour perception modification, contrast sensibility decrease, light glare and visual field reduction.

We now present the associated difficulties they encounter while surfing on the web. These are numbered to allow us to refer to in the standardisation section.

1. **Actual difficulty in reading small size and special fonts.**

We saw that prebyopia is a normal eye deterioration with age. The problems for reading small fonts is therefore the most important. It affects all seniors with various intensity.

Some surveys (Holt, B. (2000), NIH & NLM (2002), Zaphiris, P., Kurniawan, S., & Ghiawadwala, M. (2007) and SOPRANO project SOC (2006)) reported that special fonts are also difficult to read. Agelight LLC (2001) and NIH & NLM (2002) noticed also problems for reading capitalized fonts. Justified text is also advised against seniors according to Holt, B. (2000), Agelight LLC (2001), NIH & NLM (2002), Zaphiris, P., Kurniawan, S., & Ghiawadwala, M. (2007), SOPRANO project HIC (2006) and SOPRANO project SOC (2006). Italic has to be avoided according to Holt, B. (2000). All studies recommend using Sans Sérif fonts that are easier to read.

2. **Difficulty in colour perception.**

The seniors' web lecture performances are affected by the background/text colour contrasts. This also concerns the composition of images and medias. This difficulty affects all seniors but when they are older.

3. **Difficulty to distinguish clickable elements.**

Due to presbyopia and to the different eye diseases, a lot of seniors meet with blurred effect in the center of visual field and/or reduction in visual field. They therefore experience problems to localize the navigation elements of the websites.

Due to the contrast deterioration, blue/black perception is affected and seniors are less efficient to detect links along the text. Contrasts problems also get them weaker in detecting interactive images.

4. **Difficulties to catch messages from animated elements.**

Static information is preferable for many seniors affected by visual problems. Movies and animations often perturbate the seniors' lecture.

Hearing Loss

ENT Considerations

Above 60 years, one in two persons suffers from hearing loss and for 20% of them, problems are not light (according to the UK survey from The Royal National Institute for Deaf People (1996)).

Difficulties on the Web

This difficulty is much less considered in the literature. De Redish, J. & Chisnell, D. (2004), SOPRANO project HIC (2006) and SOPRANO project SOC (2006), interested in the hearing difficulties. This results in the following point:

5. **Difficulty to catch message from audio resources.**

Audio feedback is fewer used in websites. It could be implemented to dub important visual messages. That is the reason why we add the following specific difficulty.

Motor Skill Diminishing

Medical Approach

The major cause of mobility problems of seniors is arthritis. Several forms of the disease exist, but they all consist in a damaging of the joints between the bones. The joints become stiff and painful, causing troubles in moving around. One of the most frequently affected joints is in the hands, so that the mouse use becomes a difficulty. After 65 years old, one in two persons encounters arthritis problems (according to Arthritis Foundation (2008) leading a survey in USA).

The Parkinson's disease is a degenerative disease of the central nervous system, impairing in particular motor skills. The four primary symptoms are trembling, rigidity of the limbs, slowness of movement and postural instability. As fast as it begins with light symptoms, it is not easy to estimate the proportion of seniors that are actually affected.

Difficulties on the Web

The seniors' mobility problem mainly reduces their ability to use the mouse. These may be summarized as follows:

6. **Difficulty to aim precisely with mouse.**

Trembling and rigidity of the limbs causes imprecision in mouse movement. This gets worse when vision acuity also weakens. This difficulty is reported in all surveys about senior web accessibility.

Cognitive Decline

Cognitive Impairments

A lot of studies show that the ability to perform mental operations changes with age. The mental abilities affected by ageing are essentially information processing, attention, memory, executive functioning, visiospatial abilities and language. The cognitive deterioration also varies a lot from one person to another. This section is inspired from Carmichael, A. (1999).

It is commonly admitted that seniors slower process information. Several physiological studies showed also that sensory function declines with ageing so that the older persons have to do more to process information. Perception is deteriorated and information treatment is slower.

Attention capacity also decreases especially while accomplishing several tasks at a time. Complex tasks also become challenging for the elderly. These differences in attention with age are related to difficulties in filtering relevant from irrelevant information. Irrelevant information treatment rally around much cognitive resources that may not be used to treat relevant information. Furthermore, irrelevant information treatment may lead to erroneous solution.

Getting older, memory deteriorates and especially episodic memory (see Nilsson, L-G. (2003)). This compound of long term memory allows us to remind lived events in context. These deficits may be related to impairments in the ability to refresh recently processed information (according to Johnson, M.K., Reeder, J.A., Raye, C.L., & Mitchell, K.J. (2002)).

While ageing, executive functioning also indicates impairments. The ability to make judgment and decision is therefore deteriorated. However, the older persons may make up for experience and affect. Executing tasks they are used to remains approachable.

Capacity to recognize and produce three-dimensional or two-dimensional objects also becomes difficult with age.

Finally, language abilities decline over age 70 as well for word retrieval as for word list generation.

Statistics about cognitive impairments are not easy to establish because difficulties arise progressively and are often detected while problems are already serious. According to Alzheimer Europe (2005), dementia, including Alzheimer's Disease, affects about one over five senior older than 85.

Difficulties on the Web

7. **Orientation difficulties.**

Due to memory deterioration, seniors tend to lose themselves virtually, with difficulties to find one's way in website after some clicks. This was noticed in all references about seniors' web difficulties.

8. **Difficulties to detect and use navigation mechanism.**

Cognitive fails also cause difficulties to detect navigation toolbar, to distinguish between primary and secondary navigation tool. The more links are proposed in the page, the more difficult it is to decide where to click.

9. **Difficulty to extract important message off a page.**

Seniors slower process information so that they trend to read the whole pages and are facing difficulties to extract important message off a page.

10. **Difficulty to use new web techniques.**

Today, a lot of seniors encounter difficulties while surfing the web because they are newbies.

This was reported in all accessibility studies. We could hope that these difficulties will disappear while time passes. But according to the discussion we had with seniors trainers, it seems that even people that already used the web encounter difficulties. It is actually accepted that cognitive decline diminishes adaptability ability. New tasks are more challenging for seniors.

THE W3C ACCESSIBILITY GUIDELINES ADAPTATIONS FOR SENIORS

The World Wide Web Consortium (W3C) develops interoperable technologies (specifications, guidelines, software, and tools) to lead the Web to its full potential. The Web Accessibility Initiative (WAI) works with organizations around the world to develop strategies, guidelines, and resources to help make the Web accessible to people with disabilities. We interested in a specific project focusing on senior accessibility: the WAI-AGE project.

WAI-AGE is a European Commission IST Specific Support Action with the goal of increasing accessibility of the Web for the seniors as well as for people with disabilities in European Union Member States. The project started in April 2007 and runs for 36 months.

The works of the WAI-AGE group may be consulted on the WAI-AGE project page http://www.w3.org/WAI/WAI-AGE/. One of the objectives was to analyse the WAI guidelines regarding the seniors' difficulties.

We present the adaptation from W3C WCAG 1.0 Recommendation (1999) to W3C WCAG 2.0 Recommendation (2008) related to the senior difficulties. It is important for reader to notice that adaptations from WCAG 1.0 to WCAG 2.0 not only rely on the work of the WAI-AGE group. Other modifications where implemented to make guidelines applicable to different web technologies, for making it more objectively testable, or

making it flexible for different situations. But in this section, we only focus on adaptations concerning the seniors' difficulties.

We will follow the presentation of the previous section and relate informations from our own review. They mainly agree with the recommendation comparison table of W3C WAI-AGE Group (2009). The WCAG 2.0 Citations are presented in boxes and WCAG 2.0 citations have grey background for clear presentation.

Vision

1. Actual Difficulty in Reading Small Size and Special Fonts

Several are concerned:

- **Use relative font size that may be enlarged.** Suggested in: Boucher A. (2007), Agelight LLC (2001), AARP (2005), Zaphiris, P., Kurniawan, S., & Ghiawadwala, M. (2007) and Fidgeon, T. (2006).
  - ○ **WCAG 1.0 Recommendation:**
    3.4   Use relative rather than absolute units in markup language attribute values and style sheet property values. [Priority 2]
  - ○ **WCAG 2.0 Recommendation:**
    1.4.4 Resize text: Except for captions and images of text, text can be resized without assistive technology up to 200 percent without loss of content or functionality. (Level AA)
- **Use sans sérif fonts and avoid special fonts.** Suggested in: Holt, B. (2000), Agelight LLC (2001), NIH & NLM (2002), AARP (2005), Zaphiris, P., Kurniawan, S., & Ghiawadwala, M. (2007), SOPRANO project HIC (2006) and SOPRANO project SOC (2006).

- ○ **WCAG 1.0 Recommendation:** Nil
- ○ **WCAG 0.2 Recommendation:** 1.4.8 Visual Presentation: For the visual presentation of blocks of text, a mechanism is available to achieve the following: (Level AAA)
  3. Text is not justified (aligned to both the left and the right margins).
  Remark: No specific W3C recommendation on sans serif fonts.
- **Produce well-spaced text to make reading easy.** Suggested in: Holt, B. (2000), Agelight LLC (2001), NIH & NLM (2002), AARP (2005), Zaphiris, P., Kurniawan, S., & Ghiawadwala, M. (2007),
  - ○ **WCAG 1.0 Recommendation:** Nil
  - ○ **WCAG 2.0 Recommendation:** 1.4.8 Visual Presentation: For the visual presentation of blocks of text, a mechanism is available to achieve the following: (Level AAA)
    2. Width is no more than 80 characters or glyphs (40 if CJK).
    4. Line spacing (leading) is at least space-and-a-half within paragraphs, and paragraph spacing is at least 1.5 times larger than the line spacing.
- **Avoid using text in images (except for logotypes).** Suggested in: Agelight LLC (2001) and AARP (2005)
  - ○ **WCAG 1.0 Recommendation:** 3.1 When an appropriate markup language exists, use markup rather than images to convey information. [Priority 2]
  - ○ **WCAG 2.0 Recommendation:** 1.4.5 Images of Text: If the technologies being used can achieve the visual presentation, text is used to convey information rather than images of text except for... (Level AA)
    1.4.9 Images of Text (No Exception): Images of text are only used for pure decoration or where a particular presentation of text is essential to the information being conveyed. (Level AAA)
    Note: Logotypes (text that is part of a logo or brand name) are considered essential.

2. Difficulty in Colour Perception

The proposed ameliorations are the following:

- **Make your site understandable without colour perceptions.** Suggested in: Boucher A. (2007), De Redish, J. & Chisnell, D. (2004), Holt, B. (2000), SOPRANO project HIC (2006) and SOPRANO project SOC (2006).
  - ○ **WCAG 1.0 Recommendation:** 2.1 Ensure that all information conveyed with colour is also available without colour, for example from context or markup. [Priority 1]
  - ○ **WCAG 2.0 Recommendation:** 1.4.1 Use of colour: colour is not used as the only visual means of conveying information, indicating an action, prompting a response, or distinguishing a visual element. (Level A)
- **Use dark text on light background.** Suggested in: Boucher A. (2007), Agelight LLC (2001), NIH & NLM (2002), AARP (2005), Zaphiris, P., Kurniawan, S., & Ghiawadwala, M. (2007), SOPRANO project HIC (2006) and SOPRANO project SOC (2006).
  - ○ **WCAG 1.0 Recommendation:** 2.2 Ensure that foreground and background colour combinations

provide sufficient contrast when viewed by someone having colour deficits or when viewed on a black and white screen. [Priority 2 for images, Priority 3 for text].

○ **WCAG 2.0 Recommendation:**

1.4.3 Contrast (Minimum): The visual presentation of text and images of text has a contrast ratio of at least 4.5:1, except for... (Level AA)

1.4.6 Contrast (Enhanced): The visual presentation of text and images of text has a contrast ratio of at least 7:1, except for... (Level AAA)

1.4.8 Visual Presentation: For the visual presentation of blocks of text, a mechanism is available to achieve the following: (Level AAA)

1. Foreground and background colours can be selected by the user.

3. Difficulty to Distinguish Clickable Elements

The W3C standards evolved essentially with the guidelines below:

- **Provide a clear label for text links.** Suggested in: Boucher A. (2007), AARP (2005), Zaphiris, P., Kurniawan, S., & Ghiawadwala, M. (2007), Fidgeon, T. (2006), NIH & NLM (2002) and SOPRANO project SOC (2006).

  ○ **WCAG 1.0 Recommendation:**

  13.1 Clearly identify the target of each link. [Priority 2]
  Link text should be meaningful enough to make sense when read out of context—either on its own or as part of a sequence of links. Link text should also be terse.

  ○ **WCAG 2.0 Recommendation:**

2.4.6 Headings and Labels: Headings and labels describe topic or purpose. (Level AA)

- **Avoid reactive images.** Suggested in: Boucher A. (2007), Agelight LLC (2001), NIH & NLM (2002) and SOPRANO project SOC (2006).

  ○ **WCAG 1.0 Recommendation:**

  3.1 When an appropriate markup language exists, use markup rather than images to convey information. [Priority 2]

  13.1 Clearly identify the target of each link. [Priority 2]

  ○ **WCAG 2.0 Recommendation:**

  1.1.1 Non-text Content: All non-text content that is presented to the user has a text alternative that serves the equivalent purpose, except for...(Level A)

  1.3.1 Info and Relationships: Information, structure, and relationships conveyed through presentation can be programmatically determined or are available in text. (Level A) 2.4.4 Link Purpose (In Context): The purpose of each link can be determined from the link text alone or from the link text together with its programmatically determined link context, except.... (Level A)

  2.4.9 Link Purpose (Link Only): A mechanism is available to allow the purpose of each link to be identified from link text alone, except... (Level AAA)

The WAI initiative does not take the following guideline into account, but it seems important to us:

- **Use (blue and) underlined font exclusively for links.** Suggested in: Boucher

A. (2007), De Redish, J. & Chisnell, D. (2004), Holt, B. (2000), Agelight LLC (2001), AARP (2005) and Fidgeon, T. (2006).

- ◦ **WCAG 1.0 Recommendation:** Nil
- ◦ **WCAG 2.0 Recommendation:** Nil

4. Difficulties to Catch Messages from Animated Elements

Changes in WCAG are following:

- **Have a text or audio equivalent for animated elements.** Suggested in: Boucher A. (2007), Holt, B. (2000), Agelight LLC (2001), NIH & NLM (2002), AARP (2005), Zaphiris, P., Kurniawan, S., & Ghiawadwala, M. (2007), SOPRANO project HIC (2006) and SOPRANO project SOC (2006).
  - ◦ **WCAG 1.0 Recommendation:**
    1.1 Provide a text equivalent for every non-text element (e.g., via "alt", "longdesc", or in element content). [Priority 1]
    1.3 Until user agents can automatically read aloud the text equivalent of a visual track, provide an auditory description of the important information of the visual track of a multimedia presentation. [Priority 1]
    1.4 For any time-based multimedia presentation (e.g., a movie or animation), synchronize equivalent alternatives (e.g., captions or auditory descriptions of the visual track) with the presentation. [Priority 1]
  - ◦ **WCAG 2.0 Recommendation:**
    1.1.1 Non-text Content: All non-text content that is presented to the user has a text alternative that serves the equivalent purpose, except for...(Level A)
    1.2.1 Audio-only and Video-only (Prerecorded): For prerecorded audio-only and prerecorded video-only media, the following are true, except when the audio or video is a media alternative for text and is clearly labeled as such: (Level A)
      1. Prerecorded Video-only: Either an alternative for time-based media or an audio track is provided that presents equivalent information for prerecorded video-only content.
    1.2.5 Audio Description (Prerecorded): Audio description is provided for all prerecorded video content in synchronized media. (Level AA)
    1.2.7 Extended Audio Description (Prerecorded): Where pauses in foreground audio are insufficient to allow audio descriptions to convey the sense of the video, extended audio description is provided for all prerecorded video content in synchronized media. (Level AAA)
    1.2.8 Media Alternative (Prerecorded): An alternative for time-based media is provided for all prerecorded synchronized media and for all prerecorded video-only media. (Level AAA)
- **Give user the ability to control the animated elements.** Suggested in: Boucher A. (2007), Holt, B. (2000), Agelight LLC (2001), NIH & NLM (2002), AARP (2005), Zaphiris, P., Kurniawan, S., & Ghiawadwala, M. (2007), SOPRANO project HIC (2006) and SOPRANO project SOC (2006).

○ **WCAG 1.0 Recommendation:**

7.3 Until user agents allow users to freeze moving content, avoid movement in pages. [Priority 2]

○ **WCAG 2.0 Recommendation:**

2.2.2 Pause, Stop, Hide: For moving, blinking, scrolling, or auto-updating information, all of the following are true: (Level A)

1. Moving, blinking, scrolling: For any moving, blinking or scrolling information that (1) starts automatically, (2) lasts more than five seconds, and (3) is presented in parallel with other content, there is a mechanism for the user to pause, stop, or hide it unless the movement, blinking, or scrolling is part of an activity where it is essential; and

2. Auto-updating: For any auto-updating information that (1) starts automatically and (2) is presented in parallel with other content, there is a mechanism for the user to pause, stop, or hide it or to control the frequency of the update unless the auto-updating is part of an activity where it is essential.

Hearing

5. Difficulty to Catch Message from Audio Resources

Specific guidelines about audio files are the following:

• **Provide text equivalent for audio content.** Suggested in: De Redish, J. & Chisnell, D. (2004), SOPRANO project HIC (2006) and SOPRANO project SOC (2006).

○ **WCAG 1.0 Recommendation:**

1.1 Provide a text equivalent for every non-text element (e.g., via "alt", "longdesc", or in element content). [Priority 1]

○ **WCAG 2.0 Recommendation:**

1.1.1 Non-text Content: All non-text content that is presented to the user has a text alternative that serves the equivalent purpose, except for...(Level A)

1.2.1 Audio-only and Video-only (Prerecorded): For prerecorded audio-only and prerecorded video-only media, the following are true, except when the audio or video is a media alternative for text and is clearly labeled as such: (Level A)

1. Prerecorded Audio-only: An alternative for time-based media is provided that presents equivalent information for prerecorded audio-only content.

1.2.2 Captions (Prerecorded): Captions are provided for all prerecorded audio content in synchronized media, except... (Level A)

1.2.3 Audio Description or Media Alternative (Prerecorded): An alternative for time-based media or audio description of the prerecorded video content is provided for synchronized media, except... (Level A)

1.2.4 Captions (Live): Captions are provided for all live audio content in synchronized media. (Level AA)

1.2.8 Media Alternative (Prerecorded): An alternative for time-based media is provided for all prerecorded synchronized media and for all prerecorded video-only media. (Level AAA)

1.2.9 Audio-only (Live): An alternative for time-based media that presents equivalent information for live audio-only content is provided. (Level AAA)

Motor Skill

6. Difficulty to Aim Precisely with Mouse

Recommendations concerning the mouse use are the following:

- **Use static menu.** Suggested in: Boucher A. (2007), De Redish, J. & Chisnell, D. (2004), Holt, B. (2000), Agelight LLC (2001), Coyne, K.P. & Nielsen, J. (2002), AARP (2005) and Zaphiris, P., Kurniawan, S., & Ghiawadwala, M. (2007).
  - ○ **WCAG 1.0 Recommendation:** Nil
  - ○ **WCAG 2.0 Recommendation:**
    3.2.1 On Focus: When any component receives focus, it does not initiate a change of context. (Level A)
    2.2.2 Pause, Stop, Hide: For moving, blinking, scrolling, or auto-updating information, all of the following are true: (Level A)
    1. Moving, blinking, scrolling: For any moving, blinking or scrolling information that (1) starts automatically, (2) lasts more than five seconds, and (3) is presented in parallel with other content, there is a mechanism for the user to pause, stop, or hide it unless the movement, blinking, or scrolling is part of an activity where it is essential;...
- **Avoid horizontal scrolling and make essential information visible with-**out **vertical scrolling.** Suggested in: De Redish, J. & Chisnell, D. (2004), Holt, B. (2000), Agelight LLC (2001), AARP (2005), Zaphiris, P., Kurniawan, S., & Ghiawadwala, M. (2007), Fidgeon, T. (2006) and SOPRANO project SOC (2006).
  - ○ **WCAG 1.0 Recommendation:**
    13.8 Place distinguishing information at the beginning of headings, paragraphs, lists, etc. [Priority 3]
  - ○ **WCAG 2.0 Recommendation:**
    2.2.2 Pause, Stop, Hide: For moving, blinking, scrolling, or auto-updating information, all of the following are true: (Level A) - Moving, blinking, scrolling: For any moving, blinking or scrolling information that (1) starts automatically, (2) lasts more than five seconds, and (3) is presented in parallel with other content, there is a mechanism for the user to pause, stop, or hide it unless the movement, blinking, or scrolling is part of an activity where it is essential;
    1.4.8 Visual Presentation: For the visual presentation of blocks of text, a mechanism is available to achieve the following: (Level AAA)
    5. Text can be resized without assistive technology up to 200 percent in a way that does not require the user to scroll horizontally to read a line of text on a full-screen window.
    Some recommendations have been reported in literature and have no explicit formulation in W3C guidelines:
- **Avoid scrolling lists in forms.** Suggested in: Boucher A. (2007), De Redish, J. & Chisnell, D. (2004), Holt, B. (2000), Agelight LLC (2001), Coyne, K.P.

& Nielsen, J. (2002), AARP (2005) and Zaphiris, P., Kurniawan, S., & Ghiawadwala, M. (2007).

- ◦ **WCAG 1.0 Recommendation:** Nil
- ◦ **WCAG 2.0 Recommendation:** Nil

- **Clearly separate clickable elements to avoid errors.** Suggested in: Boucher A. (2007), AARP (2005) and SOPRANO project HIC (2006)
  - ◦ **WCAG 1.0 Recommendation:**
    10.5 Until user agents (including assistive technologies) render adjacent links distinctly, include non-link, printable characters (surrounded by spaces) between adjacent links. [Priority 3]
  - ◦ **WCAG 2.0 Recommendation:** Nil
- **Make clickable area larger than button or text.** Suggested in: Boucher A. (2007), Holt, B. (2000), Agelight LLC (2001), AARP (2005), Zaphiris, P., Kurniawan, S., & Ghiawadwala, M. (2007) and SOPRANO project HIC (2006).

Cognition

7. Orientation Difficulties

W3C guidelines concerning orientation difficulties are numerous:

- **Propose a consistent navigation menu on each page.** Suggested in: Boucher A. (2007), De Redish, J. & Chisnell, D. (2004), Agelight LLC (2001), Zaphiris, P., Kurniawan, S., & Ghiawadwala, M. (2007) and SOPRANO project HIC (2006).
  - ◦ **WCAG 1.0 Recommendation:**
    13.4 Use navigation mechanisms in a consistent manner. [Priority 2]

13.5 Provide navigation bars to highlight and give access to the navigation mechanism. [Priority 3]

14.3 Create a style of presentation that is consistent across pages. [Priority 3]

- ◦ **WCAG 2.0 Recommendation:**
  3.2.3 Consistent Navigation: Navigational mechanisms that are repeated on multiple Web pages within a set of Web pages occur in the same relative order each time they are repeated, unless a change is initiated by the user. (Level AA)
  3.2.4 Consistent Identification: Components that have the same functionality within a set of Web pages are identified consistently. (Level AA)

- **Propose a breadcrumbs.** Suggested in: Boucher A. (2007), AARP (2005), Zaphiris, P., Kurniawan, S., & Ghiawadwala, M. (2007) and SOPRANO project HIC (2006).
  - ◦ **WCAG 1.0 Recommendation:** Nil
  - ◦ **WCAG 2.0 Recommendation:**
    2.4.8 Location: Information about the user's location within a set of Web pages is available. (Level AAA)
- **Propose a site map.** Suggested in: Holt, B. (2000), AARP (2005) and Zaphiris, P., Kurniawan, S., & Ghiawadwala, M. (2007)
  - ◦ **WCAG 1.0 Recommendation:**
    13.3 Provide information about the general layout of a site (e.g., a site map or table of contents). [Priority 2]
  - ◦ **WCAG 2.0 Recommendation:**
    2.4.5 Multiple Ways: More than one way is available to locate a Web page within a set of Web pages except where the Web Page is the

result of, or a step in, a process. (Level AA)

2.4.8 Location: Information about the user's location within a set of Web pages is available. (Level AAA)

- **Propose an efficient search engine.** Suggested in: Fidgeon, T. (2006)
  - ○ **WCAG 1.0 Recommendation:**
    13.7 If search functions are provided, enable different types of searches for different skill levels and preferences. [Priority 3]
  - ○ **WCAG 2.0 Recommendation:**
    2.4.5 Multiple Ways: More than one way is available to locate a Web page within a set of Web pages except where the Web Page is the result of, or a step in, a process. (Level AA)

- **Present visited links in a different colour (red)** Suggested in: Agelight LLC (2001), Coyne, K.P. & Nielsen, J. (2002), Zaphiris, P., Kurniawan, S., & Ghiawadwala, M. (2007), Fidgeon, T. (2006) and SOPRANO project HIC (2006).
  - ○ **WCAG 1.0 Recommendation:**
    Nil
  - ○ **WCAG 2.0 Recommendation:**
    2.4.8 Location: Information about the user's location within a set of Web pages is available. (Level AAA)

- **Avoid new window and new tab openings.** Suggested in: Agelight LLC (2001) and AARP (2005).
  - ○ **WCAG 1.0 Recommendation:**
    10.1 Until user agents allow users to turn off spawned windows, do not cause pop-ups or other windows to appear and do not change the current window without informing the user. [Priority 2]
  - ○ **WCAG 2.0 Recommendation:**
    Nil

3.2.2 On Input: Changing the setting of any user interface component does not automatically cause a change of context unless the user has been advised of the behavior before using the component. (Level A)

3.2.5 Change on Request: Changes of context are initiated only by user request or a mechanism is available to turn off such changes. (Level AAA)

8. Difficulties to Detect and Use Navigation Mechanism

Navigation and structure is an important concern for WAI initiative:

- **Use menu labels that are simple, exclusive and complementary.** Suggested in: Boucher A. (2007), AARP (2005), Zaphiris, P., Kurniawan, S., & Ghiawadwala, M. (2007) and SOPRANO project HIC (2006).
  - ○ **WCAG 1.0 Recommendation:**
    13.1 Clearly identify the target of each link. [Priority 2]
    12.4 Associate labels explicitly with their controls. [Priority 2]
  - ○ **WCAG 2.0 Recommendation:**
    2.4.6 Headings and Labels: Headings and labels describe topic or purpose. (Level AA)

We furthermore would like to add the principle below that has no direct equivalent in W3C standardisation:

- **Structure information with low level arborescence.** Suggested in: AARP (2005), Zaphiris, P., Kurniawan, S., & Ghiawadwala, M. (2007), SOPRANO project HIC (2006) and SOPRANO project SOC (2006).

9. Difficulty to Extract Important Message Off a Page

The concerned guideline is the following:

- **Make information structure visually clear on each page.** Suggested in: Boucher A. (2007), De Redish, J. & Chisnell, D. (2004), Holt, B. (2000), AARP (2005), Zaphiris, P., Kurniawan, S., & Ghiawadwala, M. (2007), Fidgeon, T. (2006), SOPRANO project HIC (2006) and SOPRANO project SOC (2006).
  - **WCAG 1.0 Recommendation:**
    - 3.5 Use header elements to convey document structure and use them according to specification. [Priority 2]
    - 6.1 Organize documents so they may be read without style sheets. For example, when an HTML document is rendered without associated style sheets, it must still be possible to read the document. [Priority 1]
    - 10.2 Until user agents support explicit associations between labels and form controls, for all form controls with implicitly associated labels, ensure that the label is properly positioned. [Priority 2]
    - 13.8 Place distinguishing information at the beginning of headings, paragraphs, lists, etc. [Priority 3]
  - **WCAG 2.0 Recommendation:**
    - 2.4.2 Page Titled: Web pages have titles that describe topic or purpose. (Level A)
    - 2.4.6 Headings and Labels: Headings and labels describe topic or purpose. (Level AA)
    - 2.4.10 Section Headings: Section headings are used to organize the content. (Level AAA)

10. Difficulty to Use New Web Techniques

- **Propose help and clear feedback for important actions and errors.** Suggested in: Holt, B. (2000), Agelight LLC (2001), Coyne, K.P. & Nielsen, J. (2002), AARP (2005), Zaphiris, P., Kurniawan, S., & Ghiawadwala, M. (2007), Fidgeon, T. (2006) and SOPRANO project SOC (2006).
  - **WCAG 1.0 Recommendation:**
    - 4.1 Clearly identify changes in the natural language of a document's text and any text equivalents (e.g., captions). [Priority 1]
    - 4.2 Specify the expansion of each abbreviation or acronym in a document where it first occurs. [Priority 3]
  - **WCAG 2.0 Recommendation:**
    - 3.3.1 Error Identification: If an input error is automatically detected, the item that is in error is identified and the error is described to the user in text. (Level A)
    - 3.3.2 Labels or Instructions: Labels or instructions are provided when content requires user input. (Level A)
    - 3.3.3 Error Suggestion: If an input error is automatically detected and suggestions for correction are known, then the suggestions are provided to the user, unless it would jeopardize the security or purpose of the content. (Level AA)
    - 3.3.4 Error Prevention (Legal, Financial, Data): For Web pages that cause legal commitments or financial transactions for the user to occur, that modify or delete user-controllable data in data

storage systems, or that submit user test responses, at least one of the following is true: (Level AA)

1. Reversible: Submissions are reversible.

2. Checked: Data entered by the user is checked for input errors and the user is provided an opportunity to correct them.

3. Confirmed: A mechanism is available for reviewing, confirming, and correcting information before finalizing the submission.

3.3.5 Help: Context-sensitive help is available. (Level AAA)

3.3.6 Error Prevention (All): For Web pages that require the user to submit information, at least one of the following is true: (Level AAA)

1. Reversible: Submissions are reversible.

2. Checked: Data entered by the user is checked for input errors and the user is provided an opportunity to correct them.

3. Confirmed: A mechanism is available for reviewing, confirming, and correcting information before finalizing the submission.

- **Use lower non technical vocabulary.** Suggested in: Boucher A. (2007), De Redish, J. & Chisnell, D. (2004), Holt, B. (2000), Agelight LLC (2001), NIH & NLM (2002), AARP (2005), SOPRANO project HIC (2006) and SOPRANO project SOC (2006).
  - ○ **WCAG 1.0 Recommendation:**
    14.1 Use the clearest and simplest language appropriate for a site's content. [Priority 1]
  - ○ **WCAG 2.0 Recommendation:**

3.1.3 Unusual Words: A mechanism is available for identifying specific definitions of words or phrases used in an unusual or restricted way, including idioms and jargon. (Level AAA)

3.1.4 Abbreviations: A mechanism for identifying the expanded form or meaning of abbreviations is available. (Level AAA)

3.1.5 Reading Level: When text requires reading ability more advanced than the lower secondary education level after removal of proper names and titles, supplemental content, or a version that does not require reading ability more advanced than the lower secondary education level, is available. (Level AAA)

- **Make your site usable without scripting language activated and do not ask for special plugin to be installed.** Suggested in: Boucher A. (2007), Fidgeon, T. (2006) and SOPRANO project SOC (2006).
  - ○ **WCAG 1.0 Recommendation:**
    6.3 Ensure that pages are usable when scripts, applets, or other programmatic objects are turned off or not supported. If this is not possible, provide equivalent information on an alternative accessible
  - ○ **WCAG 2.0 Recommendation:**
    Nil

Remark: These special concerns may evolve while tomorrow seniors will be much more common with the scripts and plugins but we think that new difficulties will arise while new web techniques will evolve.

The content presentation was already a preoccupation in WCAG 1.0 but has been reinforced in WCAG 2.0. The page structure has to be semantic (titles, headings, lists,...), well-spaced text is advised and images of text are explicitly banished. Colour contrasts guidelines have also been much perfected. Media equivalent where already needed for disabled persons and will also be beneficial for seniors. Moving and scrolling elements have been much pointed out in WCAG 2.0. Orientation and navigation questions also have been much more considered in WCAG 2.0. Finally the use of natural language has been much insisted upon.

However, some admitted advises have not been taken into account, such as the use of default sans serif font, of blue and underlined font for links and the importance to make main information accessible with low level arborescence.

The essential idea to retain from this section is that standards have to evolve. Populations and technologies are changing so that standards will always have to be adapted.

SENIOR WEB ACCESSIBILITY IN PRACTICE

We finally propose a technical section designed for web developers. We take back the recommendations formulated before and present some techniques to be used to respect the recommendations. Readers do not have to take this section as a normative standardization section. Our aim is to show the proposed rules do not ask for much technical adaptations. Further information about techniques for designing fully accessible web sites may be found in W3C WCAG 2.0 How to (2008). We do not consider in this chapter essential accessibility principles, such as ensuring website usability with assistive technologies.

Vision

1. Actual difficulty in reading small size and special fonts.
   - **Use relative font size that may be enlarged.** Relative font sizes are specified in percentage unit or em. Keywords such as small, large, xx-smal, etc. may also be used. Developers absolutely have to avoid specifying font size in pixels.
   - **Use sans sérif fonts and avoid special fonts.** Literature recommends to use sans sérif fonts and to use bold weight to emphasize text. Avoid specifically italics and other special fonts.
   - **Produce well-spaced text to make reading easy.** Set the default font line-height property to 150% to 200% and obtain a well-spaced text.
   - **Avoid using text in images (except for logotypes).** Present text information as text and especially avoid navigation buttons as images. Navigation elements better have to be presented as lists that may be organized horizontally setting property display to value inline. Some examples of CSS menu may be found notably on Alsacréations Menu (2009).
2. Difficulty in colour perception.
   - **Make your site understandable without colour perceptions.** Reinforce colours with special styles and avoid references to colours in text.
   - **Use dark text on light background.** A lot of applications may be used to measure the colour contrast ratio of web pages. We recommend putting the Colour Contrast Analyser Firefox Extension in the web developer toolbox. This gives you a rapid measure of the contrasts of each element. The W3C recommended values for contrast ratio is minimum 4.5:1 and preferably more than 7:1.
3. Difficulty to distinguish clickable elements.

○ **Provide a clear label for text links.** Avoid labelling links with non specific label such as « Click here ». The link label has to be sufficient to know the destination.

○ **Avoid reactive images.** Reactive elements have to be specific links or forms button. Other reactive elements will be skipped by seniors.

○ **Use (blue and) underlined font exclusively for links.** It is a convention to present link with underlined font. Blue colour is also generically used for links. Respect these conventions for senior accessibility. These properties may be specified in a stylesheet for a convenient presentation.

4. **Difficulties to catch messages from animated elements.**

○ **Have a text or audio equivalent for animated elements.** Vision and cognition problems associate to make animated elements a challenge for seniors. Give them the possibility to skip these without losing information.

○ **Give user the ability to control the animated elements.** Avoid auto-starting medias and animations. Autostart and autoplay tags have to be banished.

Hearing

5. Difficulty to catch message from audio ressources.

○ **Provide text equivalent for audio content.** Audio content should be dubbed by textual information to help seniors to catch message from audio resources.

Motor Skill

6. Difficulty to aim precisely with mouse.

○ **Use static menu.** Simply avoid all onrollover effects! Designers may think such sites to be technically too simple but as Jacob Nielsen says: « Priority to simplicity ».

○ **Avoid horizontal scrolling and make essential information visible without vertical scrolling.** Do not use layout presenting all blocks with specific width and height. Make sure content adapts to different screen resolutions and window size. Some site templates may be found on Alsacréations Templates (2008).

○ **Avoid scrolling lists in forms.** Especially long scrolling lists should be avoided. They cause difficulties to seniors but also to other users.

○ **Clearly separate clickable elements to avoid errors.** Put a margin around each interactive element so that seniors do not make a mistake click. This may be implemented in CSS for the consistency, using the property margin of the elements.

○ **Make clickable area larger than button or text.** The padding CSS property allows to enlarge the clickable area without having to enlarge the button image size. Webmasters also can enclose all interactive image buttons in a div block with specific style ensuring padding to be constant among the whole site.

Cognition

7. Orientation difficulties.

○ **Propose a consistent navigation menu on each page.** The content organization is one of the main success criterion for a site. Mind mapping or cards sorting may be used to achieve an efficient organization. Once this good job has been done, you have to design your navigation menu that has to be present on each page.

- **Propose a breadcrumbs.** In dynamic applications, each new page is linked to another trough a parent-child relation. This is directly used to generate a breadcrumbs on each page. In static development, this has to be handled manually. It is then essential to have well thought the site structure not to have to start this work again.

- **Propose a site map.** Interactive site map often help visitors but are much difficult to make accessible. A simple table of content showing the structure of the site is already a good solution to help seniors to orient in a site. This may be achieved automatically in dynamic websites and has to be implemented and updated manually in static web sites.

- **Propose an efficient search engine.** An efficient search engine looks in all pages of the site. It gives better results if a specific description or keywords are given for each page. It is also better if the search engine takes bad spelling errors into account. All of it suppose some dynamic interaction in the web site.

- **Present visited links in a different colour (red)** Designers only have to set the a tag CSS property visited to {colour:red}. And to change flown over links appearance, they simply have to assign a special style to hover property of the a tag.

- **Avoid new window and new tab opening.** When linking toward a new page, the best is to let visitor choosing what to do: opening in the same window, opening in a new window or opening in a new tab. To achieve that,

the target attribute of a tag has to be avoided. Remaining in the same window will help much older people that will be able to use the back button of the navigator to come back to a previous page.

8. Difficulties to detect and use navigation mechanism.

- **Use menu labels that are simple, exclusive and complementary.** An other much important point for the success of a website: the menu labels have to be clear. The difficulty is to find the right compromise between short and explicit description. Content managers also have to make the different labels complementary so that no ambiguity is possible between them. Finally, it is important to use the same label to point toward the same link. This will help many seniors and all visitors of the website. This may look like a puzzle but it is better for developers to have to solve a puzzle than for the visitors of the website

- **Structure information with low level arborescence.** Specifically seniors encounter cognition difficulties with high level arborescence structure. Regardless, if needed, it is better to ensure the most important information is in the low level links.

9. Difficulty to extract important message of a page. The concerned guideline is the following:

- **Make information structure visually clear on each page.** It is necessary to make an efficient use of the title and headings tags h1, h2, h7 to semantically structure the content. For seniors, it is important that each page has a descriptive heading in much larger font and a short description in large font. This helps them to decide if they need to read the all page or not.

10. Difficulty to use new web techniques.

○ **Propose help and clear feedback for important actions and errors.** The action encountered by each interactive button has to be announced. Clear feedback to each action has to be implemented, in case of success as in case of failure. For an online inscription, for example, it is recommended to give a confirmation by email. It is also better to propose a confirmation step allowing visitor to go back in process, for important actions. It is a good idea to suggest also visitors to print sensitive information they could forget, such as authentification information. User tests help a lot for error detection: actual users will make errors designers did not thought about. If seniors are a specific target public for a site, they have to be considered in the tests. That is the idea proposed by personas approach suggested in particular in Boucher A (2007) and AARP (2005).

○ **Use lower non technical vocabulary.** Technical vocabulary will turn seniors blocked or even scared on a web site. The W3C standards suggest to consider as reference language level the lower secondary education level. User tests can help evaluating the vocabulary is adapted.

○ **Make your site usable without scripting language activated and do not ask for special plugin to be installed.** Seniors are afraid of technical messages asking for them to install some plugin or application or to activate some scripting language. Sites have to be usable without spe-

cial artifice or at least give a clear and reassuring procedure to manage the technical operations. Developing a senior accessible website may seem quite complicated but the aim of this short technical section it to give some techniques than can easily implemented. We propose to analyze some web giants such as ebay or Google regarding the above guidelines. Reader will remark the rules we propose are essentially observed. These international groups specifically take care about accessibility question in their developments. We encourage to do the same and invite developers to read carefully the W3C WCAG 2.0 How to (2008) that presents all the principles and techniques to design fully accessible websites. In the previous section, we showed that guidelines had to evolve and we also encourage developers to consult regularly the adaptations of these guidelines at W3C WCAG 2.0 Latest.

CONCLUSION

In this chapter, we saw that the ageing population is a big challenge for the future. Web accessibility laws are being formulated since the beginning of the century. We presented the essential difficulties of seniors when using the internet. We also showed the evolution of the W3C standardization process on accessibility specifically regarding the seniors' needs. We finally gave some essential guidelines for developers considering seniors in their specific target group.

Evolving legislation is a slow process and the progression of standardization also takes a long time. It is clear that the movement toward (senior) web accessibility is gaining momentum.

The challenges for tomorrow will be to work on legislation implementation and on repression measures. Harmonization is also a question of much interest to lawyers. The importance to refer to standards should also be addressed: standards evolve in relation to techniques and changes in population. In countries that choose to refer to their self-made recommendations, who will be in charge of their evolution? For the accessibility standardization groups, the impending considerations for the future will be to adapt accessibility guidelines to new techniques developed for surfing the web. The harmonization of standards is also a key issue that will help much to implement accessibility: for the moment, web developers get confused when thinking about accessibility because numerous labels and recommendations exist, depending on the country, on the application type.

Finally, web accessibility has to become a public concern. Older persons have to know that they have the right to access websites with ease. They have to be aware of the procedure for complaining about an inaccessible web site. The web developers and web content managers have to become aware that seniors constitute an important target group for the web services of tomorrow. They also have to be trained to build accessible web pages. A global public campaign could raise the accessibility question. The older persons constitute an important group of interest that will hopefully aid in this progression.

REFERENCES

W3C EOWG (2008), *Web Accessibility for Older Users: A Literature review (Working Draft)*. W3C Education and Outreach Working Group. World Wide Web Consortium, (Massachusetts Institute of Technology, European Research Consortium for Informatics and Mathematics, Keio University). Retrieved May 25, 2008 from http://www.w3.org/TR/wai-age-literature/

W3C Policies (2006). Policies Relating to Web Accessibility. World Wide Web Consortium, (Massachusetts Institute of Technology, European Research Consortium for Informatics and Mathematics, Keio University). Retrieved April 9, 2009 from http://www.w3.org/WAI/Policy/

W3C WAI-AGE Group (2009). WAI Guidelines and older users: findings from a litterature review. [Editor's DRAFT - 11 March 2009]. World Wide Web Consortium, (Massachusetts Institute of Technology, European Research Consortium for Informatics and Mathematics, Keio University). Retrieved April 6, 2009 from http://www.w3.org/WAI/WAI-AGE/comparative.html

W3C WCAG 1.0 Recommendation (1999). Web Content Accessibility Guidelines 1.0 - W3C Recommendation 5-May-1999. World Wide Web Consortium, (Massachusetts Institute of Technology, European Research Consortium for Informatics and Mathematics, Keio University). Retrieved April 6, 2009 from http://www.w3.org/TR/1999/WAI-WEBCONTENT-19990505

W3C WCAG 2.0 How to (2008). Web Content Accessibility Guidelines (WCAG) 2.0 - How to Meet WCAG 2.0 - A customizable quick reference to Web Content Accessibility Guidelines 2.0 requirements (success criteria) and techniques. World Wide Web Consortium, (Massachusetts Institute of Technology, European Research Consortium for Informatics and Mathematics, Keio University). Retrieved April 6, 2009 from http://www.w3.org/WAI/WCAG20/quickref/

W3C WCAG 2.0 Latest. Web Content Accessibility Guidelines (WCAG) 2.0 – W3C Latest Recommendation. Copyright © World Wide Web Consortium, (Massachusetts Institute of Technology, European Research Consortium for Informatics and Mathematics, Keio University). Retrieved April 6, 2009 from http://www.w3.org/TR/WCAG20/

W3C WCAG 2.0 Recommendation (2008). Web Content Accessibility Guidelines (WCAG) 2.0 - W3C Recommendation 11 December 2008. World Wide Web Consortium, (Massachusetts Institute of Technology, European Research Consortium for Informatics and Mathematics, Keio University). Retrieved April 6, 2009 from http://www.w3.org/TR/2008/REC-WCAG20-20081211/

AARP. (2005). *Designing Web Sites for Older Adults: Heuristics.* Retrieved May 25, 2008 from http://www.aarp.org/olderwiserwired/oww-resources/designing_web_sites_for_older_adults_heuristics.html

Agelight, L. L. C. (2001). *Interface Design Guidelines for Users of all Ages.* Retrieved May 25, 2008 from http://www.agelight.com/webdocs/designguide.pdf

Alsacréations Menu. (2009). *Créer des menus simples en CSS.* Retrieved April 9, 2009 from http://www.alsacreations.com/tuto/lire/574-Creer-des-menus-simples-en-CSS.html

Alsacréations Templates. (2008). *Galerie des Gabarits.* Retrieved April 9, 2009 from http://www.alsacreations.com/static/gabarits/

Alzheimer Europe. (2005). *The Population of People with Dementia in Europe.* Retrieved March 11, 2009 from http://www.dementia-in-europe.eu/?lm2=HIXPJGBKGFTQ

Arthritis Foundation. (2008). *Arthritis Prevalence: A Nation in Pain.* Retrieved April 6, 2009 from http://www.arthritis.org/media/newsroom/media-kits/Arthritis_Prevalence.pdf

Australian Human Right Commission. (2000). *Accessibility of electronic commerce and new service and information technologies for older Australians and people with a disability.* Retrieved April 9, 2009 from http://www.hreoc.gov.au/disability_rights/inquiries/ecom/ecomrep.htm

Boucher, A. (2007). *Ergonomie web, pour des sites web efficaces* (pp. 207–209). Eyrolles.

Carmichael, A. (1999). *Style Guide for the design of interactive television services for elderly viewers.* Retrieved April 6, 2009 from http://www.computing.dundee.ac.uk/projects/UTOPIA/publications/Carmichael%20-%20DesignStyleGuideFinal.pdf

Coyne, K. P., & Nielsen, J. (2002) *Web Usability for Senior Citizens - design guidelines based on usability studies with people age 65 and older.* Nielsen Norman Group. Retrieved May 25, 2008 from http://www.useit.com/alertbox/seniors.html

De Redish, J., & Chisnell, D. (2004). *Designing Web Sites for Older Adults: A Review of Recent Literature.* Retrieved May 25, 2009 from http://assets.aarp.org/www.aarp.orog_/articles/research/oww/AARP-LitReview2004.pdf

EC e-Inclusion program (2008). *Europe's Information Society Thematical Portal – eInclusion Program.* Retrieved April 9, 2009 from http://ec.europa.eu/information_society/activities/einclusion/policy/ageing/index_en.htm

empirica & Work Research Center (2008). *MeAC - Measuring Progress of eAccessibility in Europe.* Retrieved April 9, 2009 from http://www.eaccessibility-progress.eu/

Europa.eu. (2009). *Activities of the European Union, Summaries of legislation, Information Society.* Retrieved April 10, 2009 from http://europa.eu/scadplus/leg/en/s21012.htm

Eurostats (2006). *Eurostat News Release. Internet usage in the EU25.* Retrieved April 6, 2009 from http://epp.eurostat.ec.europa.eu/pls/portal/docs/PAGE/PGP_PRD_CAT_PREREL/PGE_CAT_PREREL_YEAR_2006/PGE_CAT_PREREL_YEAR_2006_MONTH_11/4-10112006-EN-AP.PDF

Fidgeon, T. (2006) *Usability for Older Web Users.* Report from WebCredible Group, Retrieved May 25, 2008 from http://www.webcredible.co.uk/user-friendly-resources/web-usability/older-users.shtml

Holt, B. (2000). Creating Senior Friendly Websites. Issue Brief 1(4) Centre for Mediacare Education Retrieved May 25, 2009 from http://www.medicareed.org/PublicationFiles/V1N4.pdf

Internet World Stats. (2009). *World Internet Users and Population Stats.* Retrieved April 2, 2009 from http://www.internetworldstats.com/stats.htm

Johnson, M. K., Reeder, J. A., Raye, C. L., & Mitchell, K. J. (2002). Second thoughts versus second looks: An age-related deficit in selectively refreshing just-active information. *Psychological Science, 13,* 64–67. doi:10.1111/1467-9280.00411

Lighthouse International. (2009). *The Aging Eye.* Retrieved March 9, 2009, from http://www.lighthouse.org/medical/the-aging-eye/

Networking Government in New Zeland. (2009). *New Zealand Government Web Standards.* Retrieved April 9, 2009 from http://www.e.govt.nz/standards/web-guidelines

NIH & NLM. (2002). *Making Your Web Site Senior Friendly: A Checklist.* National Institute on Aging and National Library of Medicine. Retrieved May 25, 2008 from http://www.nlm.nih.gov/pubs/checklist.pdf

Nilsson, L.-G. (2003). Memory function in normal aging. *Acta Neurologica Scandinavica, 107*(Suppl. 179), 7–13. doi:10.1034/j.1600-0404.107.s179.5.x

Pew internet (2009). *Generational Differences in Online Activities.* Retrieved April 4, 2009 from http://www.pewinternet.org

Section508.gov. (2008). Retrieved April 9, 2009 from http://www.section508.gov

SOPRANO project HIC. (2006). *Review of HIC Concepts* (pp. 83-85). Retrieved May 25, 2008 from http://www.soprano-ip.org/ecportal.asp?id=226&nt=18&lang=1

SOPRANO project SOC. (2006) *Review of social & cultural aspects* (pp. 12-42). Retrieved May 25, 2008 from http://www.soprano-ip.org/ecportal.asp?id=226&nt=18&lang=1

Sperduto, R. D., & Seigel, D. (1980). Senile lens and senile macular changes in a population-based sample. *Am J Ophthalmol, 90*(1), 86-91. Retrieved on March 11, 2009 from http://www.ncbi.nlm.nih.gov/pubmed/7395962

The Royal National Institute for Deaf People. (1996). *Statistics on deafness.* Retrieved April 6, 2009 from http://www.rnid.org/html/info-factsheets-general-statistics-on-deafness.html

The Web Accessibility in Mind. (2009). *World laws.* Retrieved April 9, 2009 from http://www.webaim.org/articles/laws/world/

Treasury Board of Canada Secretariat. (2007). *Common Look and Feel for the Internet 2.0.* Retrieved April 9, 2009 from http://www.tbs-sct.gc.ca/clf2-nsi2/index-eng.asp

University of Illinois Eye & Ear Infirmary. (2007). *Macular Degeneration Info, The Eye Digest.* Retrieved March 10, 2009, from http://www.agingeye.net/maculardegen/maculardegeninformation.php

U.S. Census Bureau IDB. (2009). *International Data Base.* Retrieved March 1, 2009 from http://www.census.gov/ipc/www/idb/

Zaphiris, P., Kurniawan, S., & Ghiawadwala, M. (2007) A Systematic Approach to the Development of Research-Based Web Design Guidelines for Older People. *Universal Access in the Information Society Journal, 6*(1), 59-76, Retrieved from http://www.springerlink.com/content/087050g2771rj416/fulltext.pdf

Section 5
ICT Ethics

Chapter 26
E–Health at Home:
Legal, Privacy and Security Aspects

Juan José Andrés-Gutiérrez
Telefónica R&D, Spain

Esteban Pérez-Castrejón
Telefónica R&D, Spain

Ana Isabel Calvo-Alcalde
University of Valladolid, Spain

Jesús Vegas
University of Valladolid, Spain

Miguel Ángel González
University of Valladolid, Spain

ABSTRACT

This chapter describes the present situation of E-Health at home taking into account legal, privacy and security aspects. As a first step, some background and a general description of E-Health activities at home are presented. In order to have a general idea of the current status of this field, we analyze the general legal situation in terms of ICT for E-Health and several related issues on data mining privacy and information recovery aspects. The topics covered include the taxonomy for secondary uses of clinical data and a description of the role that controlled vocabularies play. Concerning the provision of E-Health at home, the chapter revises the current situation in the digital home evolution including topics on sensors and sanitary devices. Furthermore the challenge of digital identity at home and the differences between the domestic environment and the professional one are considered. Finally some ethical considerations under the "InfoEthics" concept and future lines of work are addressed.

INTRODUCTION

All over the world we are facing up to important problems regarding healthcare services. Due to the growth on the number of elderly and the changes in life styles the demand and cost of healthcare have increased. At the same time patients and families are asking for a better accessibility to healthcare outside hospitals, moving health provision into the

DOI: 10.4018/978-1-61520-975-0.ch026

patient's own homes. These challenges, along with a need for increased efficiency and quality-oriented care, have turned E-Health at home into one of the fastest growing areas of healthcare. E-Health can be seen on its own as a new concept of health provision. But health services are being offered more and more outside the traditional clinical environment due to a better quality of life for patients and the need to reduce costs.

In this context, most of the legal, privacy and security aspects when facing an E-Health at home service are inherited from the general telemedicine field. The objective of this chapter is to raise awareness of the importance of security and privacy aspects when transferring E-Health services to the personal environment. E-Health at home faces a double challenge and therefore a double change. The first one is the shift from direct face to face medicine to the distant provision of health services. That is the classic telemedicine physician to physician application like in radiology or teleconsultation. The second shift is a radical one, from a clinical and controlled scenario to the everyday patient environment.

Another important objective is to highlight the ethical aspects of E-Health at home such as informed consent and legitimate objectives. Most of the E-Health trials fail to become sustainable services because of organizational problems and, sometimes, also because of technical and economical ones. When transferring E-Health services to the personal environment the lack of an ethical and legal framework is not a new challenge but since patients are at home and do not have a direct access to their physician, there is a stronger need to preserve their privacy, consent and security rights. Every new initiative carried out in the field of E-Health at home should ideally take into account a well established ethical framework.

Finally this chapter aims to stimulate the scientific literature on the legal, privacy and security issues as a means to promote a true shift in E-Health services at home and personal digital environment.

BACKGROUND

E-Health is an emerging field, which arises from the intersection of health informatics and communications. E-Health refers to the use of modern information and communication technologies to meet the needs of citizens, patients, healthcare professionals, healthcare providers, and policy makers ("Ministerial Declaration," 2003). In a broader sense, the term includes not only technical development and new business models, but also a change in our way of thinking, and the compromise of enhancing health both locally and in the widest possible scope by means of information and communications technologies (Eysenbach, 2001). Regarding these considerations a huge amount of medical data is generated, stored, treated... and the medical traditional law must be adapted to this new situation.

E-Health services are being offered more and more outside the traditional clinical environment. As it is shown in **Figure 1**, the main reasons for this fact are a better quality of life, primarily for patients with a chronic condition, and the need to reduce costs when providing health services for the elderly. Very old people (aged over 80) are the fastest growing population group and this puts the health systems — the way they are designed today — under a strong pressure. Little by little this shift is placing patients' homes as the centre of the E-Health service provision.

When we refer to E-Health at home we emphasize the fact that the health service delivery is provided outside the traditional clinical environment. But most of the health services which are offered to a patient at home can be, and in many real situations they are, mobilized outside the home by means of flexible E-Health applications not tied to specific hardware or communication infrastructures. When travelling, working or being in contact with the community, the E-Health enables homes to remain the centre of the Personal Digital Environment. As a consequence services should be designed to be flexible because they

Figure 1. Evolution of E-health services provision

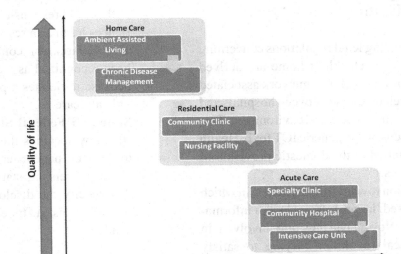

are not provided in a single user context or using a single user interface or physical device. This lack of fixed context puts extra pressure on the privacy and on the security aspects of the E-Health provision.

E-Health at home, is not just seeking to meet the needs in case of health crisis (due to an acute or chronic illness) or to detect situations of a decline in health, but rather seeking to motivate the development of habits that promote a healthy life. In this context, E-Health is included in the Ambient Assisted Living (AAL) concept whose paradigm offers a way to solve the challenges we are facing regarding our ageing societies. AAL is related to both Information and Communication Technologies (ICT) as well as legal and organizational innovations. In this context:

"AAL aims to prolong the time people can live in a decent way in their own home by increasing their autonomy and self-confidence, the discharge of monotonous everyday activities, to monitor and care for the elderly or ill person, to enhance the security and to save resources" (Steg, Strese, Loroff, Hull, & Schmidt, 2006).

Legal changes should face the challenges that E-Health at home creates. This legislation will focus at least on the security and privacy aspects that can be summarized in the four traditional areas related to information transfer security:

- **Authentication:** users (sender and receiver) have to provide their identity in a unique way.
- **Integrity:** ensure that the data has not been altered during the transmission and therefore accurately reflect the information sent. This includes the inability to change or corrupt data, either by accident or deliberately.
- **Privacy and access:** only the operations allowed to the user (read, erase, write...) on the accessed data must be carried out.
- **Non refusal:** the user who sent or entered the data will not be able to deny such access. There are sender and receiver non-refusal.

General Legal Analysis: ICT for E-Health

Most of the existing legal regulations concerning the provision of E-Health at home are derived from the general E-Health framework associated to traditional telemedicine between hospitals and not related to homes or personal environment. This section will focus on the generic ICT for E-Health that can be applied to the domestic provision of medical services.

The evolution towards digital issues, in which we are immersed, largely affects health information systems. Nowadays they are involved in a "technological revolution" trying to satisfy the growing quality demand from society. This technological evolution implies several changes in everything related to health provision. In this context, with a lot of different players involved, it is of vital importance to guarantee personal and health data privacy.

In the United States there are a series of state and federal statutes and common law rules mandatory for physicians aimed at protecting patient confidentiality. Potential threats to the patient confidentiality in telematic healthcare provision were the objective of federal regulations implemented in the U.S. under the Health Insurance Portability and Accountability Act of 1996 (HIPAA). Legal obligations to protect patient privacy and confidentiality are based on the state and federal statutes and the common law. The privacy rule implemented in 2003 under HIPAA establishes new confidentiality protections. (Moskop J.C., Marco C.A., Geiderman J.M., Derse A.R., 2005).

- **The Common Law Rules.** In addition to being responsible for the privacy, US courts have found the physicians responsible for unauthorized release of medical information through the concept of a fiduciary duty of confidentiality in the physician-patient relationship. Physicians who release personal information of a patient to third parties without proper justification will be held responsible if the patient experiences harm as a result of such disclosure. The violation of confidentiality has also been recognized as a crime of negligence, because it violates a professional standard of healthcare.

- **State and Federal Statutes.** A variety of state law specifies the general obligations to protect patient confidentiality. Many medical licensing statutes include clauses that specify the disclosure of medical information as a type of unprofessional conduct.

Moreover, federal regulations that came into effect in 2003 impose standards for health care confidentiality across the United States. These regulations, implemented under HIPAA, require providers to protect the confidentiality, integrity, and availability to patients of "individually identifiable personal health information" in any form, whether electronic, written, or oral. Personal health information includes information that relates to a person's physical or mental health, the provision of health care, or the payment for health care. The regulations apply to all health care organizations, including hospitals, physicians' offices, health care plans, employers, public health authorities, life insurers, clearinghouses, billing agencies, information systems, and "any person or organization who furnishes, bills or is paid for health care in the normal course of business." (US Department of Health, 2000) and (US Department of Health, 2004).

In Europe the main problem related to health provision is the lack of uniformity, standards and common regulation for all the countries that are part of the community. This lack of regulation is a technological barrier in to establish common technological standards that ensure medical information confidentiality for European citizens. The ongoing integration and consolidation of a common Europe takes into account multiple issues that need to be solved and it is clear that health regulations are one of the most important, as well as economic aspects. Unfortunately, some changes have started to happen in economy, education, and so on, but they are going at a slower pace in health issues. The establishment of a common framework (or the expansion of the current one) is a key factor for the whole European development ("ICT for better Healthcare in Europe," n. d.).

Legislation on eHealth matters is relatively new, dating from the 90s when they began to consider extending the existing legislation in relation to concepts of telemedicine and teleassistance. Nowadays there are still many open questions and legal issues.

A brief analysis of the current situation regarding European legislation will be addressed bellow. This legal analysis, related to E-Health, will be focused on studying European directives. A directive of the European Union is a legislative act stipulated by the Council of the European Union in which a mandatory collective decision is adopted by all member states. The directive does not impose the ways to achieve its decisions or results. The states will take the necessary measures in order to carry out the directive.

Prior to going into details about the European directives, there are other interesting documents which were used as a base for current directives like the following ones:

- The European Convention on Human Rights and Fundamental Freedoms held in Rome on November 1950 ("The European Convention", 1950). These topics are made explicit also when it's 8th article states that "everyone has the right to respect for his private and family life…there shall be no interference by a public authority with the exercise of this right except such as is in accordance with the law and is necessary in a democratic society…for the protection of health…". Fundamental rights were declared in this convention, which are part of the general principles of the European Community law. At the time of the convention, people were protected against fundamental rights infractions from the States or public entities. However, the protection against infractions from private entities is not clear and each state is in charge of legislating in order to provide this protection. The 8th article protects the right of privacy and forbids any interference in personal details from public entities. Health details are included, although there are exceptions where access to private details is allowed such as health protection cases or research of criminal activities.

- The treaty on European Union ("The treaty on European Union", 1992) establishes that the Union is based on freedom, democracy, respect to human rights and fundamental freedoms and state's rights.

- The Charter of Fundamental Rights of the European Union ("The Charter of Fundamental", 2000). The 8th article establishes the right to personal details protection, the rules to process personal details and the need of an independent authority to control the execution of laws.

- Guidelines of the Organization for Economic Co-operation and Development (OCDE) ("Organization for Economic"). The OCDE works on guidelines for security on networks and information systems pointing out that each player involved in the communication, is responsible for security.

- The legal regulations and international associations have established the importance of the correct use of personal data (Lawson, 2008). The Nuremberg code (1947) establishes "the voluntary consent of the human subject is absolutely essential". Soon after that, the Universal Declaration of Human Rights (1948) in its 27th and 12th articles stated, respectively, that "everyone has the right freely to participate in ...scientific advancement and its benefits" and "no one shall be subjected to arbitrary interference with his privacy...".

- The International Covenant on Civil and Political Rights (1966) ("The International Covenant on Civil", 1966) states that "no one shall be subjected to arbitrary or unlawful interference with his privacy..." and "no one shall be subjected without his free consent to medical or scientific experimentation" (articles 17 and 7, respectively).
- In the medical context, the World Medical Association, Helsinki Declaration (1964, as amended) ("Declaration of Helsinki", 2008 as amended): states that "the right of the subject to safeguard his integrity must always be respected. Every precaution should be taken to respect the privacy of the subject..." (1975) and "It is the duty of the physician in medical research to protect the life, health and privacy and dignity" (2000).
- Also, the World Medical Association, in its Statement on the Use of Computers in Medicine declares ("World Medical Association", 2006) "it is not a breach of confidentiality to release or transfer confidential health care information required for the purpose of conducting scientific research...provided the information released does not identify, directly or indirectly, any individual patient in any report of such research...or otherwise disclose patient identities in any manner..." (1973, amend.1983)
- More recently, the Council of Europe, Recommendation on the Use of Medical Data (1997); regarding Scientific Research (s.12) recommends the following:
  i. Whenever possible, use anonymous data
  ii. Where impossible (+ legit purposes), the research must have:

  - "free, express, informed consent" of data subject; or
  - defined project, important public interest, authorization of legally designated body, impractical to get consent, and data subject doesn't object; or
  - the research "is provided for by law and constitutes a necessary measure for public health reasons"

There are three main directives (*Directive 95/46/EC, Directive 2002/58/EC, Directive 2006/24/EC*) related to legal, privacy and security aspects that need to be taken into account when we specifically refer to E-Health. The main objective is the protection of the users focusing on the following axes:

- Protection of individuals with regards to the processing of personal details and the free movement of such details.
- Processing of personal data and the protection of privacy in the electronic communications sector.
- Retention of data generated or processed in connection with the provision of publicly available electronic communications services or of public communications networks.

These directives are briefly detailed below:

1. **Directive 95/46/EC** ("Directive 95/46/EC", 1995). Member States shall ensure individual rights to privacy regarding data processing. Also, member States may not restrict the free movement of persons for reasons related to data protection.(See Table 1).
2. **Directive 2002/58/EC** ("Directive 2002/58/EC", 2002). This directive harmonizes the provisions of the member States to ensure protection of civil liberties and privacy in

Table 1. Directive 95/46/EC

General principle	Application
The principles state that the treatment has to be fair and lawful, which must establish the purpose for which it is collected and will not be handled in a manner incompatible with those purposes	Informed consent, signed by the person concerned (patient or citizen)
They should be accurate and upgradeable	The person in charge of the treatment should provide the necessary mechanisms in order to update the data when they are changed or when it is proved that they are wrong
Conditions in order to process data	Due to the characteristics of the project, it will comply with the informed consent
The responsible person should provide enough information to the concerned one	This requirement, although it will not be applied in cases of research, could be met by the project in the informed consent
The person concerned has the right to access and correct his/her data	The supplier must provide the necessary tools in order to allow users to access their complete record
The person / organization in charge must establish the necessary measures to ensure data security and confidentiality	The supplier must provide the necessary security and confidentiality systems. This will probably be the most complicated point to be treated.
Obligation to notify the authority of control	The person / organization in charge must notify the requested information, as it is defined in article 19.

the treatment of personal data in electronic communications. It is applied in the provision of electronic communications services in public networks. This Directive addresses several more or less delicate issues, such as keeping data connections by the Member States for police surveillance (data retention), the sending of unsolicited e-mails, the use of cookies and the inclusion of personal data in public directories. (See Table 2).

3. **Directive 2006/24/EC** ("Directive 2006/24/ EC", 2006) related to the conservation of generated and treated data related to the provision of electronic communication services of public access or public communications networks. (See Table 3).

General Legal Analysis: Data Mining Privacy and Information Recovery in E-Health

This section will focus on generic data mining privacy and information recovery in E-Health associated to traditional Electronic Health Records and telemedicine. Like the previous section, this legal analysis is the framework that can be applied

to the domestic provision of medical services.

Data processing aspects, all the available techniques to achieve data integrity and its unambiguous meaning (such as controlled vocabularies and ontologies), data mining privacy and information recovery in E-Health are explored deeply in this chapter. Furthermore, the major points of the ethical, legal, and social issues in the management of medical information can be considered under different points of view (Cios & Moore, 2002).

Thousands of terabytes of information related to health and the associated health activities are generated annually in North America and Europe. However, these data are buried in heterogeneous databases, and scattered throughout the medical care establishment, without any common format or principles of organization. The corpus of human medical data potentially available for data mining is enormous. The question of patient information ownership is unsettled, and the object of recurrent, highly publicized lawsuits and congressional inquiries. There is an open question of data ownership in medical data mining. In legal theory, ownership is determined by who is entitled to sell a particular item of property (Moore & Berman, 2000). It is a fact that the data selling to third

Table 2. Directive 2002/58/EC

General principle	Application
It must ensure data security at a proper level according to the existing risks	The service provider must take the necessary and appropriate technical and management measures.
If there are some data security risks clients must be informed	Clients are informed of the risks with the informed consent
Data confidentiality must be ensured through public networks	The service provider must provide the necessary tools to ensure confidentiality
It is forbidden to listen, record, store and surveil communications without user's consent	The service provider must ensure that these activities do not happen
Stored traffic data must be removed or be anonymous when they are no longer needed	The supplier carries out this task and reports the types of processed traffic data
Location data may be used only if they are anonymous or with user's consent and only during the time needed to provide a value-added service	The provider needs the informed consent signed by the customer to get access to these data

Table 3. Directive 2006/24/EC

General principle	Application
Traffic and location data to identify the user are stored and will be only provided to the competent national authorities	The supplier of communications services is in charge of data storage and only provides them to the competent entities
Any data that can reveal the communication content can not be stored	The supplier is responsible for not storing this kind of information
The stored data will be of the same quality and will have the same security as the existing data. They must be protected from accidental destruction or illegal, accidental loss or modification. The data will be destroyed after the period of conservation	The services provider will take the technical and security measures to ensure these conditions

parties is considered unseemly, so the question of data ownership in medicine is right now in the ethical limelight.

One aspect in the E-Health field that contributes to increase physicians' concerns is "data mining". It is relevant in order to take precautions and be prepared for the possible lawsuits against physicians and other health-care providers. This aspect, especially relevant in the USA, is related to the planning of all medical actions providing a "defensive medicine", including unnecessary tests oriented to be used as a protecting tool for potential future lawsuits. This defensive attitude is also affecting the use of medical data mining causing relevant secondary effects. So, data mining in health recordings could be a useful tool to detect malpractices, which in many cases, are data-omission or data-transmission errors, not a negligent behaviour

An important aspect related to the privacy and security concerns of the medical data, is the patient identification concealment. This concealment must be irreversible as a general procedure in order to ensure confidentiality of the patient, and to avoid the possible effects in the physician-patient relationship that could produce a security incident revealing personal data. This is especially important if the data are going to be transferred via the Internet, due to the insecure nature of the network, in which case the identities must be hidden even for transfers within different units of a single medical institution. Just in some cases, the re-identification will be needed: first, to prevent accidental duplicated records of the same patient; second, to verify the correctness or to obtain additional information on specifics patients.

Identity protection of the patients can be done as follows: (1) anonymous data, whose identification was removed when the information was collected; (2) anonymized data, whose identification has been removed irrevocably; (3) de-identified data, whose identification has been encrypted or coded; and (4) identified data, possible only under the supervision of an institution and with the correspondent written informed consent of the patient.

Any use of patient data, specially those de-identified data, must be justified and approved by the appropriate institution, and must provide some benefits. An obstacle is using Internet as a channel to distribute data, and to make it accessible to the research community which may have legitimate reasons to access it, like for example a rare-disease interest group. There is a conflict between the public access and the frivolous use of public human data that must be resolved.

It's clear that sufficient attention is being paid to this issue in the different organizations and ambits, but a lack of specific rules and laws is patent.

In this field, it is necessary to highlight the effort made by the USA and the European Union in the development of a legal framework in which the protection of health information is covered. In the USA, the protection of personal health information has been regulated and a voluntary reporting system has been established to enhance the data available to assess and resolve patient safety and health care quality issues ("Health Information Privacy," n. d.).

Data Processing Aspects and Electronic Health Record (EHR)

Protection of patient records can be achieved by implementing security policies to control access, appropriate authorization before releasing the health data and by providing additional security measures to more sensitive data (Chilton, Berger, Melinkovich, Nelson, Rappo, Stoddard et al., 1999). The Electronic Health Records EHR form an integral part of the healthcare system, and it is imperative that EHRs are safe. EHRs have a variety of functionalities which include storage of health information and data, results management, order entry and management, decision support, electronic communication and connectivity, patient support, administrative processes and reporting and population management ("Institute of Medicine," 2003).

In the EU, the "The European Institute for Health Records", alias "The EuroRec Institute", encompasses directly or indirectly issues related to the development, implementation, and use of efficient, interoperable, and secure Health Records in the European context, notwithstanding a wider international perspective, and without prejudice against any predetermined area of knowledge or skills that might be necessary to address these issues. More particularly, though not exclusively, this concerns any Health Records, in whichever format (paper, magnetic, digitalized, electronic, and so on.), and applying any technology (the Internet, etc.), that allow the data and information to be processed by computers whenever relevant ("EuroRec Institute," n. d.).

Beyond the definition of EHR, it is important to recognize that it is not a unified concept but it is associated with the evolving capacity of the health information systems. The importance of physicians in the use of information systems using EHR to allow the development of decision-making systems has been discussed. The doctor is responsible for maintaining the information daily, due to the importance of medical information storage.

Through appropriate policies, this widespread use of ICT in health makes the data more secure and confidential than when data are hold in paper-based records (Barrows & Clayton, 1996). As it has been previously presented, Europe has established regulations to protect confidentiality of individually identifiable health information and security of computer systems that store and transmit patient information.

Taxonomy for Secondary Uses of Clinical Data

Keeping all health information stored is vital to obtain statistics and research the extent of new diseases, and so on. However these data can be used for different purposes and therefore require a categorization of their potential uses when the time comes to set policies and security access to that information.

The American Medical Informatics Association, AMIA, has been working for some time in the field of secondary use of clinical information that is the use of data for a purpose different from the original one. The last activity fulfilled so far has been a meeting in July 2007 by the working group on secondary uses of clinical data (Anonymous, 2007).

Below, there is a taxonomy for secondary uses of clinical data divided into four sections.

Secondary Uses of Clinical Data

Table 4 lists the possible secondary uses of clinical data according to the purpose of the objectives which may be objecting the exploitation of such data.

Influential Factors in the Use of Secondary Data Authorization

Table 5 is a list of influential factors faced to the definition of their policies of use.

Requirements Imposed on the Secondary Use of Clinical Data

Table 6 meets the requirements and restrictions that may be imposed for the use of secondary data.

Potential and Existing Data Sources for Secondary Use

Table 7 is a listing of possible data sources.

Controlled Vocabularies (CV)

Controlled vocabularies (CVs) are a form of organization of the extensive medical terminology used by professionals around the world. An estimate of this volume of terminology is always vague but, as an indicator, standard medical dictionaries include between 40,000 and 100,000 words.

Health professionals belong, at the same time, to the international scientific community and to some country where different languages are spoken. In each of these languages, the medical terminology uses precise and emotionally neutral words whose equivalent in other languages is often difficult to establish. Other problems are the existence of eponyms associated with people's names, acronyms and onomatopoeias. As in any other vocabulary there is also polysemy (different meanings for one word) and homonymy (words of different origin but with the same written form) but synonymy is much more frequent (different words with same meaning).

In general, controlled vocabularies or standardized classifications make use of a hierarchical structure where the more generic term (e.g. disease) is chained with other lower-level terms (e.g. heart disease). Also, each term of these structures is associated with internationally accepted abbreviations and synonyms. Examples of these classifications are ICD (International Classification of Diseases) and SNOMED (Standardized Nomenclature on Medicine).

From a legal perspective, the use of controlled vocabularies allows data integrity and unambiguous expression of a number of terms associated with medical diagnoses, treatments or other circumstances of medical practice. These classifications are particularly useful in the case of E-Health as there is an information retrieval system that maintains coded terms available for the clinical or ambulatory care use.

Table 4. Secondary uses of clinical data

Use	Purpose
1. Protect and enhance public health	
	• Enable and support biosurveillance
	1. Monitor and report vital statistics
	2. Monitor and report biometric demographics (e.g. weight, height, blood pressure, normal lab values)
	3. Identify, monitor, and report health and illness trends
	4. Identify, monitor, and report infectious diseases (e.g. culture, serology, DNA/RNA probe results)
	• Export data to health registries
	1. Cancer or rare disease registries
	2. Drug and device registries
	• Report toxic exposures (e.g. smoking, Agent Orange)
2. Develop security and confidentiality algorithms	
	• Develop and test de-identification routines
3. Conduct research	
	• Conduct clinical epidemiology and outcomes research
	• Assess health technology
	• Investigate disease risk predictors
	• Investigate treatment effectiveness
4. Create and maintain terminology and representation formalisms	
	• Development of terminology
5. Develop and apply decision support for health care providers	
	• Develop and test the efficacy of decision support algorithms
	• Develop order sets, rules, and alerts
6. Support quality of patient care	
	• Manage quality and outcomes
	• Manage staffing and resources
	• Develop and assess quality indicators
	• Support quality reporting (e.g. HEDIS)
7. Improve patient safety	
	• Conduct pharmacovigilance (post market drug and device surveillance)
	1. Detect and analyze adverse and sentinel events.
	2. Support risk profiling
	• Monitor and survey to prevent patient adverse events
8. Manage personal health	
	• Provide patient-specific feedback and assessments of progress towards health goals
	• Maintain personal health records
	• Provide links to knowledge resources based on personal health information
9. Educate and credential healthcare providers and assess training activities (e.g. types and outcomes of procedures)	

continued on following page

Table 4. continued

Use	Purpose
	• Log number of successful procedures
	• Log types of procedures performed
10. Analyze and Manage Finances	
	• Conduct automated billing, claims processing
	• Analyze activity-based charge capture, cost accounting
	• Develop predictive models of costs and accounting
11. Detect fraud and illicit activity	
	• Detect illegal and inappropriate activity (e.g., Medicare upcoding)
	• Report drug screen results to detect illegal drug use
12. Identify markets and promote sales	
	• Conduct market research
	• Target marketing at physicians
	• Target marketing at patients and families

Table 5. Influential factors in the use of secondary data authorization

Factor	Values
1. Identification Status	
	• Patient-identifiable data
	• De-identified data (HIPAA definition)
	• Anonymized data
	1. No possible linkage (alteration of PHI, precluding linkage)
	2. Relinkable data
	3. Linked with protected key (trusted third party)
2. Consent provided at the time of data collection	
	• No consent by the individual
	• Consent by the individual
	1. Broad and unspecified
	2. Time-limited consent
	3. Consented for partial, source specific use (e.g., no psychiatric data)
	4. Consented for the particular type of secondary use
3. Demographic representation	
	• Age
	• Race
	• Gender
	• SES
	• Insurance status

continued on following page

Table 5. continued

Factor	Values
4. Focus on a vulnerable population	
	• Prisoners
	• Pregnant women
	• Undocumented immigrants
5. Original collector and aggregator of the data	
	• Government
	• iHealth Plan
	• Other private entity
6. Proposed secondary user of the data	
	• Government agency
	• Academic institution
	• Private, not-for-profit entity
	• Private, for-profit entity
7. Funding source for secondary use	
	• Government agency
	• Academic institution
	• Private, not-for-profit entity
	• Private, for-profit entity
8. Financial compensation to data collector or data steward for providing data to a second party	
	• No compensation
	• Compensation
9. Beneficiary of secondary use	
	• Society
	• Researcher
	• Academic institution/medical center
	• Private, for-profit entity (e.g., financial gain)
10. Disclosure of secondary use	
	• Not disclosed publicly
	• Publicly disclosed
	1. Disclosure of results only
	2. Disclosure of research methods utilized
	3. Disclosure of analytic principles that guided the use of the data

In the E-Health home environment and, more broadly, in the personal digital environment, there is often a lack of information whereas that information is available to a doctor when seeing the patient in a medical centre. This makes the normalization of symptoms, diagnoses or episodes particularly important. That normalization is even more important in the case of patients who travel to other countries and their condition monitoring is carried out by professionals other than usual and they often speak different languages. A standard-

Table 6. Requirements imposed on the secondary use of clinical data

Requirements	Restriction
1. Required level of consent and authorization	
	• IRB evaluation not required
	• IRB evaluation required
	1. No consent by the individual required
	2. Consent by the individual required
2. Compensation of patients	
	• No compensation required
	• Compensation of individual patients required

Table 7. Existing and potential data sources for secondary use

Status	Data source
1. Public Use Datasets	
	• Medicare
	• Medicaid
	• CDC surveys (some Primary data use, e.g. NHANES)
2. Private Datasets	
	• Open-source data
	• Commercial use datasets (at patient level)
	1. Pharmacy benefit/claims manager
	2. Provider databases
	a. Individual providers
	b. Aggregated data from provider consortia
	• Consortium databases
	1. CaBIG
	2. CTSA recipients
	3. University Health Systems Consortium
	• Aggregated clinical repositories hosted by HIT vendors
	• Personal health records, including patient-entered data
	• Health Information Exchanges (RHIOs, etc)

ized nomenclature eliminates the ambiguity and greatly limits the liability for malpractice.

In this way, controlled vocabularies are useful in E-Health scenarios such as cross border provision of services including remote treatment and follow-up of chronic patients. From a legal point of view, it must be the responsibility of national authorities to ensure the safety of the patient in cross-border E-Health services particularly when the patient has no contact with the professional providing the service ("Health and," 2006).

The Provision of E-Health at Home

This section focuses on specific aspects of the provision of E-Health services at home. Furthermore, it presents a comparison between the professional and home domains, an overview of sanitary products at home regulations and, finally, some aspects of security levels and users' roles.

What is Happening in the Digital Home?

Nowadays the digital home or smart home has the capability of providing constant monitoring health services. The digital home can be seen as a number of technological areas that deal with different user needs like home health and telecare. Current homes must face an ever-growing number of consumer electronic devices that provide a lot of information which has to be managed in a secure way.

The digital home handles all domestic generated information in an easy way and observes everything happening in it. As a consequence, there is a potential risk of the digital home becoming a kind of big brother. Automatic tracking systems, fall motion detectors, monitoring cameras and other kind of intelligent devices raise obvious concerns about privacy. The misuse of this information may also involve risks in the integrity of patients. So, the awareness of information could drag the patient to vulnerability, humiliation, risk and discrimination.

Therefore it is necessary to have the acceptance of the patient before providing any health service within the home and the compliance to the confidentiality standards. Currently, there is the problem of Non-Compliance from the industry to these standards. The acceptance by the patient of the provision of services involves another problem in many cases, especially when dealing with elderly, because the user does not understand the fine print of contracts for the acceptance of these services.

It is a must to manage only a single personal health identity which is controlled by external auditors who have to be responsible for ensuring the integrity and security of such information. Without leaving behind user's obligations at the time of providing a service at home, the user is in charge of:

- Choosing or rejecting the provision of service.
- The primary and secondary use of his/her own personal data.
- The acceptance of sharing these data with third parties.
- The expiration time of the health information.

Regulations of Medical Devices for the Home

This section presents a review of the European regulations that affect product certifications at the home domain. These regulations guarantee the required quality levels for the products (devices such as biomedical sensors, terminals, and so on.). The main directives are the 2006/95/EC and the 2004/108/EC directives.

The Directive 93/44/EC draws the limits of the products:

1. **Health product:** A product is considered as a "health product" according to the definition presented in the directive 93/42/EC ("Council Directive 93/42/EEC", 1993): *"Any instrument, device, equipment, software, material or other item, used in isolation or in combination, with any accessory, included the software programs intended by its manufacturer to be specifically used for diagnostic and/or therapy and that are involved in its smooth-running, aimed by the manufacturer at being used in humans for diagnosis, prevention, monitoring, treatment or alleviation of disease".*

This directive clearly establishes that the product will be classified according to "its predicted purpose" but other industrial directives must be taken into account (without intending to be exhaustive directives like 73/23/EC, 93/68/EC, 89/336/EC, 93/68/EC, 89/392/EC, 90/384/EC, 91/263/EC and 89/686/EC).

Moreover, the CE marking, also known as CE mark, indicates the conformity of the product to the directive(s) that is (are) of application. Furthermore, in Europe the marketing and subsequent use of products without this mark is illegal. Also, directives require several minimum requirements for products evaluation and certification to get the CE mark.

Manufactures are required to offer the following guarantees:

- **Information Warranty:** There must be a technical documentation of the product. This document should include specifications, drawings, user manuals, technical assistance service manuals, labels and other related documents.
- **Security Warranty:** The equipment must be tested according to the normative of application.
- **Compliance Specifications Warranty:** Clinical evaluation and, where appropriate, clinical research for safety evaluation and product compliance with the specifications must be performed.
- **Quality Warranty:** The company must implement a quality assurance system according to EN ISO 13485 with the appropriate process to guarantee its correct implementation.
- **Conformity Assessment:** The process used by the manufacturer to ensure compliance with the essential requirements established in the directive that apply to their product is the "conformity assessment".
- **Quality System:** One of the necessary guarantees for product certification is the quality process. The industrial directives have taken the ISO 9000 series (EN 29000) as the quality framework. This se-

ries consists of specific rules for each type of supplier:

- ○ The ISO 9001 norm, establishes the quality system for companies according to design, development, production, installation, services, testing and final inspection.
- ○ For medical devices the norms EN ISO 13485 and EN ISO 13488 supplement the ISO 9001 norm about the particular requirements of medical devices.

European Household Products Regulation

Directive 2006/95/EC and Directive 2004/18/EC
Briefly the main objectives of the directives ("Directive 2004/18/EC", 2004) and ("Directive 2006/95/EC", 2006) are the following ones:

1. General conditions are (1) main characteristics on whose knowledge and observance its use depends will be included in the electrical material or in the enclosed note, (2) the brand will be clearly printed on the electrical equipment or on the packaging, (3) electrical equipment will be built allowing a safe connection and (4) electrical equipment should be designed so that the protection against the dangers will be assured, on condition that it is used according to its destination and its proper maintenance.

2. Protection against the related electrical equipment hazards. There will be technical measures, in order to (1) protect people and domestic animals against risks, (2) do not allow dangerous temperatures or radiation, (3) protect people, domestic animals and objects against the dangers of non-electrical problems and (4) a proper insulation system must be provided for the predicted use conditions.

3. Protection against the dangers caused by external influences on the electrical equipment. There will be technical measures in order to protect people, domestic animals and objects against (1) in the predicted mechanical demands, (2) in non-mechanical influences and (3) in the overload predicted conditions.

4. Describes the way electric or electronic apparatus behave (regarding electro magnetic aspects) in the presence of other equipment. The directive will be applied to all electrical and electronic equipments and to the equipment and installations that have electric or electronic components that can create electromagnetic disruptions or whose performance can be affected by these disturbances. The technical goal of this directive is double (1) to protect the radio spectrum against equipment interference and (2) to protect equipment from common interference.

Sensors and Sanitary Devices for the Digital Home

Data transmission from sensors at home to a remote center involves many potential points of failure in the secure information sending process. Thus, personal data encryption is essential to protect the user and to ensure that such data is sent with the knowledge and the consent of the patient to all the information systems. These systems are constantly monitoring their biometric signals for medical or diagnosis objectives in the home environment.

This new understanding of health contrasts with the traditional monitoring in patients who are used only as the subject for short-term monitoring. All of this involves changes in information processing because the information flow is radically different as the one in traditional monitoring in hospitals, as may be for example in an Intensive Care Unit, ICU.

Therefore it is necessary to ensure prevention of unauthorized data modifications, ensuring that only authorized and registered sensors can send information through the home network and this way avoid phishing attacks, etc.

Sensors are vulnerable to physical handling, which is not easy to prevent using the logic of the system. It is therefore important to use devices resistant to physical handling, but it is often very expensive and these aspects are usually neglected. Receiving information from sensors in the home network should therefore be guaranteed using tamper resistant devices. In order to do this, it is necessary to use devices implementing cryptographic systems for secure transmission of information.

The availability of information is another important aspect. It is difficult to ensure the availability of devices and sensors because users turn off the devices by themselves, and they often unconsciously make an improper use of them. This situation could be confused with a denial of service attack in which the device is not able to send the information.

Another related problem is the location of that information, given that the confidentiality of data must be ensured and only authorized persons have access to medical data. Also, these data should not be stored locally and otherwise they should be centralized with a single identity provider.

As an example, we have been using techniques such as MAC device address filtering and WEP encryption for transmission of data over the wireless home network (typically an 802.11bg network) so far today, but it has been proved an ineffective mechanism given the ease of spoofing. TIC must avoid this inconvenient providing real secure mechanism for home environment.

Health Provision: Domestic Environment vs. Professional Environment

The provision of health in residential environments has important differences from the centralized health care in hospital regarding privacy of information.

The information in hospitals is stored in the hospital's own systems such as RISC, PASC, HIS, etc. Although medical information, in the remote case, remains divided between patients' homes and hospitals. In any case all information obtained at a patient's home must travel through the network with the potential risks that involves.

Another problem is the heterogeneity of health service providers within the household. In this case, health care providers at home are numerous and may be public health, private insurers and other players in the health area. But the patient's health information must be unique to ensure, as far as possible, the integrity and security. It is therefore a need in the area known as "Identity Federation or Unique ID". This provides mechanisms for an organization to accept users that have already been authenticated in other health organization and to give them access without having to manage their identity and credentials again.

Currently, one of the biggest problems regarding the security of the user's medical information is the consideration of the third party providers as providers with independent functions and services. These providers require users to transfer their personal data and to be authenticated for each service. This process causes a significant decrease in information security.

The federated infrastructures largely solve this problem allowing a unique identity stored in an Identity Provider (IDP), which is accepted by one, or more, service providers (SP). The combination of one or more IdP's and one or more SP's is called a federation, and is characterized by a trust relationship among its members which allows the communication and validation of user data in a secure way.

The Digital Identity at Home Challenge

Digital identity is defined as the total set of attributes that correspond to a user distributed among different information systems (Windley, 2005). This information includes data of several kinds.

That is, for users' digital identity is the sum of all sensitive data of their person, such as, in this case, their medical data.

Nowadays, digital identity represents the ability to know and control the actors involved in the process of providing health care to different groups and thus better managing these services producing a more satisfactory result for all involved players. Nowadays, the problem created by the dispersion of all parts which form user's digital identity, is that the user is currently responsible for maintaining all this information in a coherent and consistent way.

Up to this date, one of the principal objectives of Internet security has been the Single Sign On (SSO), that is, the way that a user is authenticated only once in an organization's network and that identity is recognized by all systems. Single sign-on is defined by the Open Group as follows: "Single sign-on (SSO) is a mechanism whereby a single action of user authentication and authorization can permit a user to access all computers and systems where he has access permission, without the need to enter multiple passwords. Single sign-on reduces human error, a major component of systems failure and is therefore highly desirable but difficult to implement" ("The Open Group," n. d.). Within each organization there are systems that maintain their own users database and that require authentication for each user that needs access to such systems. It is necessary to minimize the different IDs (and credentials) that users have in order to access health services and once they have been authenticated in a specific system have access to the rest in which they are authorized.

Before the authentication by such techniques can be used, the user must have different ways of accessing all systems within a circle of trust, and must be previously authenticated on one of them. This is the federation process, and thanks to this, the identity provider and the service provider create a unique and secure identifier referring to the user in their communications. Therefore this is a key process for federated identity management.

The identification process at home is quite complex: missing similar interfaces to those used by a computer. In every human act there can be an implicit identification (using a mobile phone, etc.) or explicit (user / password, fingerprint, and so on). This is the classical problem providing this kind of services at home: how to ensure that the blood pressure measurement is from the person who says so? There is not an assessment by a professional of all the data taken by unattended applications.

People can be uniquely identified by traditional technological methods (what we know about these people, what you have, who you are) or through a professional agreement (e.g. videoconference). In the absence of unambiguous identification, this identification must be done only if the consequences of making decisions on the basis of a misidentification are not harmful for people or the community. This is an open point that is under investigation and there are several initiatives to create care protocols.

In Figure 2 a scenario using just one identity provider is shown.

This approach allows to use services in a local network and also enumerate the features and services provided by each service provider using just one identity provider which is in charge of storing user credentials and medical data through the following flow: (1) users are consuming one service provided by Service Provider 1; (2) Service Provider 1 redirects the request to the Identity Provider; (3) the Identity Provider deals with the user in order to assure his identity; (4) once checked his Identity Provider sends the user's medical data needed to Service Provider 1; (5) Service Provider 1 provides the specific services to the user, from now on the user is able to consume different services (by different providers) without having to be authenticated again and just with the data that the service provider needs in every moment.

Ethical Considerations

The application of E-Health at home is using new technologies for remote supporting of different groups (elderly, dependent, etc.), and in various use cases. In any of these scenarios, environmental parameters as well as personal and vital signs are being monitored. We must take into account that the involved individuals are particularly the vulnerable ones like elderly or subjects with some chronic disease.

In any E-Health project there is a patient-professional relationship that has been shifted from the traditional direct connection without intermediate elements to a direct or deferred connection but intermediated by distance, time and technology. This section introduces new aspects that need to be addressed. Some of these aspects involve this new relationship and others and the specific technological tools.

In this regard, the European Commission's European Group on Ethics ("EGE," 1999), raises the following ethical aspects related to the introduction of Information and Communication Technology (ICT) in health:

- The pervasiveness of a technology which is beyond comprehension for many people.
- The potential lack of transparency in the work of the health professionals and its effect on the physician-patient relationship.
- Difficulties to maintain privacy when third parties (including health administrations) may have an interest in access to information stored in computer systems.
- The complexity in ensuring the security of shared data related to health.
- The shortage of infrastructure in some regions and the lack of technological background in broad sectors of the population.

To these aspects we could add the unreliability of some technological solutions and the effect this unreliability may have on patient care. A possible

Figure 2. Scenario

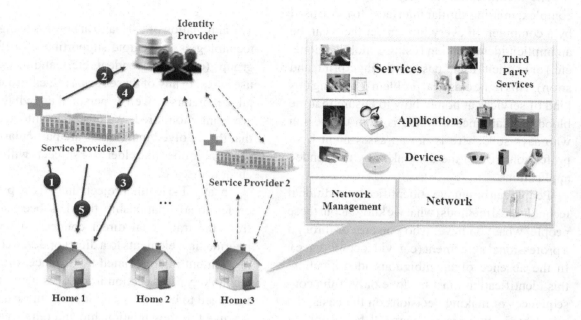

outcome could be the lack of care or bad medical decisions due to the lack of direct and reliable information.

As a result, the European Group on Ethics proposes the following principles for the health sector, in what is called "InfoEthics":

- **Privacy:** as an extension of the human right to respect of privacy.
- **Confidentiality:** all those eligible to use health data should have a duty of confidentiality equivalent to medical confidentiality.
- **Principle of "legitimate objectives":** all users of personal health data must demonstrate a legitimate purpose in their access.
- **Consent:** access to health data by legitimate users must require the explicit consent and informed consent of the owners of these data.
- **Security:** the security of ICT used in health is an ethical imperative for the fulfilment of some of the principles stated above. As a consequence, it is required to use encryp-

tion technologies, as well as all the security standards that apply to electronic data transmission.

- **Transparency:** the standardization of medical terms that reflects the actual medical facts is inherently necessary when applying ICT. Since many of the possible standards (clinical protocols, diagnostic codes, etc.) are not neutral when selecting specific values, these values should be subject to evaluation by independent bodies (ethics committees, patient organizations, etc).
- **Participation:** the citizen should have the right to participate in medical decision procedures. Citizens must have access to their electronic health records (EHR).
- **Education:** the citizen should be trained in the ethical and legal implications of ICT applied to health.

Another important issue, which is immersed in the above principles, is the usefulness of new technologies. New ICTs require a large investment, but the involved resources could be given a more socially profitable use. In this sense, any such E-Health at home project must include a cost-effectiveness analysis before its execution.

There is also the added difficulty of assessing the clinical effectiveness of the implementation of these technologies (Cornford & Klecun-Dabrowska, 2001). Methodologies of randomized trials are not appropriate for the evaluation of ICTs in health, and the cited authors seek to establish an evaluation framework for a home-care system based on videoconferencing. The issues that are important to establish indicators to evaluate results for E-Health at home are:

- Empower patients and their communities.
- Contribute to social cohesion.
- Democratize services and health structures.
- Reduce the social information gap.
- Reduce the alienation and depersonalization in the provision of health services.

Literature is scarce on this topic. In (Bjorneby, Topo, Cahill, Begley, Jones, Hagen et al., 2004) the authors reflect on the ethical standards applicable to the ENABLE project, which considers the use of technological support at home for people with dementia and their families. These authors note the absence in the literature of an ethical framework that provides support for this type of study and discuss about some of the principles mentioned above, namely: autonomy, beneficence and justice.

An important conclusion of this analysis is the need to raise a procedure of informed consent related to E-Health services at home. This is especially important when one considers the technological elements that are not error free and then can produce undesirable effects and the lack of direct relationship with the health professional.

Other authors, as in (Marziali, Serafini, & Mc-Cleary, 2005) and (Koch, 2006), have reviewed the existence of professional and ethical standards in scientific literature and the application of technology in home support programs for the elderly. The main conclusion from the analysis of all the documents reviewed is that ethical aspects are poorly reported. These studies also show the lack of ethical codes for such applications. In addition, most studies have focused on privacy and data security. However they don't take into account, other aspects such as ensuring that there is a good professional practice and minimizing the risks of using the technology. This ICT technology could malfunction and cause direct (injury) or indirect effects (wrong medical decisions due to design problems).

FUTURE TRENDS

The digital identity at home is a future aspect of E-Health at home evaluation that needs to be addressed. Care protocols are needed for cases in which the unambiguous identification of the person involved in the medical act is not possible.

A lot of research has been performed on home telehealth, but we lack an evaluation framework bearing in mind legal and ethical aspects, as well as organizational and technical ones. As a consequence, there is a need for more research on privacy and confidentiality issues, as well as legal and ethical topics (Koch, 2006).

E-Health at home faces a double challenge. The first one is the distance challenge such as in the classic telemedicine applications. The second shift is from a clinical and controlled scenario to the everyday patient environment. Most of the scientific literature is related to the first challenge although the second one is a more radical and deep change.

Related to the controlled vocabulary (CV) concept, the ontologies are formal representations of knowledge with definitions of concepts, their attributes and relations between them expressed in terms of axioms in some well-defined logic (Rubin, Shah, & Noy, 2007). Ontologies are becoming one of the centres of research on biomedical sciences in areas such as data exchange among applications and Natural Language Processing (NLP). But in spite of the wide attention these technologies are attracting, they will be a useful tool for patient safety but the quality assurance issues remain unclear. Some works (Dritsas, Gymnopoulos, Karyda, Balopoulos, Kokolakis, Lambrinoudakis et al., 2006) suggest they could be used as a method of knowledge acquisition through the process of developing secure E-Health applications. But as a matter of fact, the legal framework is not able nowadays to take into account the outcome CV or what ontologies could produce when they are applied to E-Health. In fact, there is not at the moment an ontology describing the ADL (Activities of Daily Living) at home or in the personal digital environment outside the clinical scenario. Useful information and initiatives in this field are grouped under the eHealth Ontology Project ("eHealth Ontology Project," n. d.).

CONCLUSION

E-Health has changed the traditional relationship between doctor and patient, as well as all roles involved in health care, to improve our quality of life, especially for those patients who do not have to be hospitalized due to the severity of their health condition. They are able to lead a normal life while their medical condition is being monitored and sometimes controlled by healthcare professionals from their homes. However, as the technologies evolve, the threats also grow in parallel and put the patient's privacy at risk. It is important to guarantee the security (in this context, protection of data integrity, availability, authenticity and confidentiality) and privacy (compliance with personal data protection regulations) of personal health data in order to achieve user's trust and acceptance of E-Health at home systems.

E-Health at home creates a new paradigm that requires an ethical framework which should include the present legislation, although these legal standards only reflect part of the new problems. The rules on privacy and data protection provide a set of regulations to be applied in all the technological developments involving the use of personal data. But we are confronting a broader legal and ethical challenge. E-Health at home involves a radical shift from a clinical and controlled scenario to the everyday patient environment and this is by far the deeper change we have to face.

REFERENCES

Anonymous, & the American Medical Informatics Association. (2007). *Secondary uses and re-uses of healthcare data: Taxonomy for policy formulation and planning*. Retrieved April 16, 2009, from http://www.amia.org/inside/initiatives/healthdata/2007/amiataxonomyncvhs.pdf.

Barrows, R. C., & Clayton, P. D. (1996). Privacy, confidentiality, and electronic medical records. [American Medical Informatics Association]. *Journal of the American Medical Informatics Association, 3*, 139–148.

Bjorneby, S., Topo, P., Cahill, S., Begley, E., Jones, K., & Hagen, I. (2004). Ethical considerations in the ENABLE Project. *Dementia (London), 3*, 297–312. doi:10.1177/1471301204045162

Chilton, L., Berger, J. E., Melinkovich, P., Nelson, R., Rappo, P. D., & Stoddard, J. (1999). Pediatric Practice Action Group and Task Force on Medical Informatics. Privacy protection of health information: patient rights and pediatrician responsibilities. *Pediatrics, 104*, 973–977.

Cios, K. J., & Moore, G. W. (2002). Uniqueness of medical data mining. *Artificial Intelligence in Medicine, 26*(1), 1–24. doi:10.1016/S0933-3657(02)00049-0

Cornford, T., & Klecun-Dabrowska, E. (2001). Ethical perspectives in evaluation of telehealth. *Cambridge Quarterly of Healthcare Ethics, 10*(2), 161–169. doi:10.1017/S0963180101002079

Council Directive 93/42/EEC of 14 June 1993. Retrieved June 15, 2009, from http://eur-lex.europa.eu/LexUriServ/LexUriServ.do?uri=CELEX:31993L0042:EN:HTML

Declaration of Helsinki (Sixth revision). (2008). Retrieved June 15, 2009, from http://www.wma.net/e/policy/pdf/17c.pdf

Directive 2002/58/EC of the European Parliament and of the Council of 12 July 2002. Retrieved June 15, 2009, from http://eur-lex.europa.eu/LexUriServ/LexUriServ.do?uri=CELEX:32002L0058:EN:HTML

Directive 2004/18/EC of the European Parliament and of the Council of 31 March 2004. Retrieved June 15, 2009, from http://eur-lex.europa.eu/LexUriServ/LexUriServ.do?uri=CELEX:32004L0018:EN:HTML

Directive 2006/24/EC of the European Parliament and of the Council of 15 March 2006. Retrieved June 15, 2009, from http://eur-lex.europa.eu/LexUriServ/LexUriServ.do?uri=CELEX:32006L0024:EN:HTML

Directive 2006/95/EC of the European Parliament and of the Council of 12 December 2006. Retrieved June 15, 2009, from http://eur-lex.europa.eu/LexUriServ/LexUriServ.do?uri=OJ:L:2006:374:0010:0019:EN:PDF

Directive 95/46/EC of the European Parliament and of the Council of 24 October 1995. Retrieved June 15, 2009, from http://eur-lex.europa.eu/LexUriServ/LexUriServ.do?uri=CELEX:31995L0046:EN:HTML

Dritsas, S., Gymnopoulos, L., Karyda, M., Balopoulos, T., Kokolakis, S., Lambrinoudakis, C., & Katsikas, S. (2006). A knowledge-based approach to security requirements for e-health applications. eJETA.org Special Issue.

eHealth Ontology Project. (n.d.). Retrieved December 20, 2008, from http://www.ehealthserver.com/ontology

European, E. G. E. Group in ethics in science and new technology. (1999). Ethical issues of health care in the information society. Retrieved December 7, 2008, from http://ec.europa.eu/european_group_ethics/docs/avis13_en.pdf

EuroRec Institute. (n.d.). European Institute for Health Records. Retrieved April 16, 2009, from http://www.eurorec.org/

Eysenbach, G. (2001). What is E-Health? *Journal of Medical Internet Research, 3*(2), 20. doi:10.2196/jmir.3.2.e20

Health and Consumer Protection Directorate-General. European Commission. (2006). Summary report of the responses to the consultation regarding "Community action on health services". Retrieved April 20, 2009, from http://ec.europa.eu/health/ph_overview/co_operation/healthcare/cross-border_healthcare_en.htm

Health Information Privacy. (n.d.) Retrieved April 12, 2009, from http://www.hhs.gov/ocr/privacy/index.html

ICT for better Healthcare in Europe. (n.d.). Retrieved June 9, 2009, from http://ec.europa.eu/information_society/activities/health/index_en.htm

Institute of Medicine. (2003). Committee on data standards for patient safety: board of health care services. Key capabilities of an electronic health record system: letter report. The National Academy of Sciences. Retrieved April 7, 2009, from http://www.iom.edu/report.asp?id=14391

Koch, S. (2006). Home telehealth—Current state and future trends. *International Journal of Medical Informatics, 75*(8), 565–576. doi:10.1016/j.ijmedinf.2005.09.002

Lawson, P. (2008). Privacy & Public Health: Ensuring Public Trust. *Electronic Health and Information Privacy Conference* (pp. 45-55).

Marziali, E., Serafini, J. M., & McCleary, L. (2005). A systematic review of practice standards and research ethics in technology-based home health care intervention programs for older adults. *Journal of Aging and Health, 17,* 679–696. doi:10.1177/0898264305281100

Ministerial Declaration. (2003). In the framework of the eHealth. 2003 conference. Retrieved December 7, 2008, from http://ec.europa.eu/information_society/eeurope/ehealth/conference/2003/doc/min_dec_22_may_03.pdf.

Moore, G. W., & Berman, J. J. (2000). Anatomic pathology data mining. In Cios, K. J. (Ed.), *Medical data mining and knowledge discovery* (pp. 61–108). Heidelberg: Springer.

Moskop, J. C., Marco, C. A., Geiderman, J. M., & Derse, A. R. (2005). From Hippocrates to HIPAA: Privacy and confidentiality in emergency medicine. I. Conceptual, moral and legal foundations. *Annals of Emergency Medicine, 45*(1), 53–59. doi:10.1016/j.annemergmed.2004.08.008

Organization for Economic Co-operation and Development. (n.d.). Retrieved June 15, 2009, from http://www.oecd.org

Rubin, D. L., Shah, N. H., & Noy, N. F. (2007). Biomedical ontologies: a functional perspective. *Briefings in Bioinformatics, 9*(1), 75–90. doi:10.1093/bib/bbm059

Steg, H., Strese, H., Loroff, C., Hull, J., & Schmidt, S. (2006). Europe Is Facing a Demographic Challenge. Ambient Assisted Living Offers Solutions. In the framework of The Ambient Assisted Living (AAL) Joint Programme. Retrieved March 10, 2009, from http://www.aal-europe.eu/.

The Charter of Fundamental Rights of the European Union. (2000). Retrieved June 15, 2009, from http://www.europarl.europa.eu/charter/default_en.htm

The European Convention on Human Rights. (1950). Retrieved June 15, 2009, from http://conventions.coe.int/treaty/en/Treaties/Html/005.htm

The International Covenant on Civil and Political Rights. (1966). Retrieved June 15, 2009, from http://www2.ohchr.org/english/law/ccpr.htm

The Open Group. single sign-on. Retrieved June 8, 2009, from http://www.opengroup.org/security/sso/.

The treaty on European Union. (1992). Retrieved June 8, 2009, from http://europa.eu/eur-lex/en/treaties/dat/EU_treaty.html

US Department of Health and Human Services, Office for Civil Rights. Standards for privacy of individually identifiable health information. (2000). Retrieved June 15, 2009, from http://www.ihs.gov/AdminMngrResources/PrivacyAct/pdf/combinedregtext.pdf

US Department of Health and Human Services, Office for Civil Rights. Summary of the HIPAA privacy rule. (2004). Retrieved June 15, 2009, from http://www.hhs.gov/ocr/privacy/hipaa/understanding/summary/privacysummary.pdf

Windley, P. (2005). *Digital Identity.* O'Reilly.

World Medical Association. World Medical Association statement on the use of computer in medicine [rescinded at the WMA General Assembly, Pilanesberg, South Africa, 2006]. Geneva (CH): WMA; 2006. Retrieved June 15, 2009, http://www.wma.net/e/policy/c9.htm

KEY TERMS AND DEFINITIONS

E-Health: This term refers to the use of electronic processes and communication in the provision of healthcare practises.

ICT: Information and Communication Technologies.

Ontology: A formal definition of a set of concepts within a domain and the relationships between them.

Digital Home: Refers to a number of home devices that are connected through a home network and exchange information. A digital home includes domotics, entertainment, Internet shared access as well as usability in the home.

Data mining: Refers to the process of extracting hidden patterns from data as a way to transform data into valuable information.

Controlled Vocabularies: A form of organization of extensive terminologies used by professionals. In general, controlled vocabularies or standardized classifications make use of a hierarchical structure where the more generic term is chained with other lower-level terms.

Infoethics: The principles of applying ethics in the field of ICT. The term includes concepts of privacy, confidentiality, consent, transparency, etc.

Directive: A directive of the European Union is a legislative act stipulated by the Council of the European Union in which a mandatory collective decision is adopted by all member states. The directive does not impose the ways to achieve its decisions or results. The states will take the necessary measures in order to carry out the directive.

Digital Identity: Digital identity is the part of digital technologies related to the means of providing an identity for people and things. Digital identity is a fundamental issue to provide trust to online transactions.

Chapter 27
Controlling Informational Society:
A Google Error Analysis!

Gonçalo Jorge Morais da Costa
De Montfort University, UK

Nuno Sotero Alves da Silva
De Montfort University, UK

Piotr Pawlak
Adam Mickiewicz University of Poznan, Poland

ABSTRACT

"Informational Society" is unceasingly discussed by all societies' quadrants. Nevertheless, in spite of illustrating the most recent progress of western societies the complexity to characterize it is well-known. In this societal evolution the "leading role" goes to information, as a polymorphic phenomenon and a polysemantic concept. Given such claim and the need for a multidimensional approach, the overall amount of information available online has reached an unparalleled level, and consequently search engines become exceptionally important. Search engines main stream literature has been debating the following perspectives: technology, user level of expertise and confidence, organizational impact, and just recently power issues. However, the trade-off between informational fluxes versus control has been disregarded. So, our intention is to discuss such gap, and for that, the overall structure of the chapter is: information, search engines, control and its dimensions, and exploit Google as a case study.

INTRODUCTION

The term "Information Society" or "Informational Society" emerges continuously in contemporary discussion. The intricacy to define it is well-known, but simultaneously, its content is somewhat clarified, when investigating the key features that characterize the most recent evolutionary stage of western societies: communication, interaction, automation, post-industrial, specialist, service, immaterial needs, postmodern, or learning society (Castells, 2000; Webster, 2006). However, Ives Courrier (2000) differentiates "Information society", and "Knowledge society". Nevertheless, the historical roots of this sociological debate lie on the

DOI: 10.4018/978-1-61520-975-0.ch027

work of Fritz Machlup (1962) and Peter Drucker (1969) to describe the changing economical paradigm. This work has been incessantly updated in order to demonstrate the economical, sociological, or even philosophical reconfigurations.

Given the introductory analysis an important question arises: how can "Information Society" or "Informational Society" be defined or characterized? During the World Summit on the Information Society in 2003, representatives of governments and civil society organizations from 175 countries declared that: "… common desire and commitment to build a people-centred, inclusive and development oriented Information Society, where everyone can create, access, utilize, and share information and knowledge, enabling individuals, communities and peoples to achieve their full potential in promoting their sustainable development and improving their quality of life" (World Summit on the Information Society, 2003, pp. 1). Plus, the European Commission describes it as: "the society currently being put into place, where low-cost information and data storage and transmission technologies are in general use. This generalization of information and data use is being accompanied by organizational, commercial, social and legal innovations that will profoundly change life both in the world of work and in society generally" (European Commission, 1997, pp. 15).

Therefore, it is understandable that governments or organizations, want to make sure that they are not left out of the opportunities associated with the information society (Lallana, 2004). However, before governments or organizations proceed to developing plans and strategies for the information society, it is important to investigate the underlying key feature of this paradigm: information. Information taxonomies are intrinsically bounded to the level of abstraction adopted, gather of requirements and desiderata orientating a theory (Shannon, 1948; Butler, 2001; Floridi, 2003; Kornai, 2008). As a consequence of computer networks the available information

increased exponentially, allowing that search engines become remarkably important.

A search engine is a program that sends a spider to "crawl" web pages, in order to extract links, and in return the information found on the page (Pinkerton, 1994). So far, search engines literature focuses its attention on the following perspectives: technology (Zien et al., 2006), user level of expertise and confidence (Teevan, Dumais & Horvitz, 2005), organizational impact (Wielki, 2008), and just recently power issues (Rieder, 2005).

However, the ethical impacts concerning informational fluxes versus control have been disregarded. In order to obtain a plausible answer concerning this theoretical gap, it is crucial to address control and its boundaries. Therefore, it is vital to perceive what technological means allow to control and monitor cyberspace (Glorioso, 2008), as well as, what ethical and legal dilemmas arise to society in case of overstated control (Jung, 2001). As a final remark, the authors will include Google as case study due to its remarkable excellence recognized through its market share, but also as a consequence of their personal experience using search engines, namely this.

BACKGROUND

Information

Etymologically information derives from "inform", which means "to give form to, put into form or shape" (Oxford English Dictionary, 2008). In fact, the earliest characterizing example of this concept in accordance to the Oxford English Dictionary arises in 1590, when Edmund Spense wrote in *The Faerie Queene* about "infinite shapes of creatures…informed in the mud". However, the ancient Greek word εἴδος ("eidos") denoted the ideal identity or essence of something in Plato's philosophy. So, metaphorically "information" represents not only a communication, but also a belief or a decision. Therefore, it is possible to describe information as a polymorphic phenomenon and a polysemantic concept so, as an *explicandum*, which can be clarified by some research disciplines, depending on the level of abstraction adopted, cluster of requirements and desiderata orientating a theory.

Given the nature of our argument, information will be approached by the following perceptions: mathematical, economical, biological, semantical, philosophical and ethical.

The complete absence of semantically content is bounded to Claude Shannon's theory (1948), in which information is related to uncertainty. Following Martin (1995), Shannon attempts to see information as a "thing" leading to a tangible analysis when compared to knowledge, which is rather intangible by nature (Rowley, 1998). Therefore, this tangible dimension of information implies a natural conclusion: information can be seen as a "commodity". According to Cash, MacFarlan & McKenney (1992), information can be seen as a raw material that will be used by a manufacture in the following production stage. This analogy illustrates the idea that information can be considerably different in accordance to its function or future function into the economical process.

Nevertheless, several authors illustrate information qualities as an economical resource (Jarvenpaa & Staples, 2001):

- **expandable:** because it increases with use;
- **compressible:** allowing to be summarized;
- **substitute:** information can substitute other resources;
- **transportable:** it is virtually instantaneous;
- **diffusive:** tending to leak from the straightjacket of secrecy and control, and the more it leaks the more there is; information is sharable, not exchangeable;
- **human:** it exists only through human perception.

For the biological consideration we plead Lange & Lapp (2007), nevertheless the work of Jonas Salk & Jonathan Salk (1981) is considered praxis. These authors defined three main eras of the universal evolution and increasing complexity. They outline three types of systems (or matter): physical, biological, being each of them characterised by new emergent and essential properties. The emergence of a new third system properly narrowly incident to new aspects (or types) of information, because in higher levels are important aspects of information from lower levels of physical systems (intrinsic property of systems).

Finally, the other three dimensions- semantical, philosophical and ethical- are intrinsically correlated with the metaphor of a precious fluid (Lakoff & Johnson, 1980). These authors related the features of ordinary liquids like water and to less tangible but nevertheless appealing notions like *chi*. Information can flow from a source to a recipient over a channel and it can be diluted, compressed, or stored in vessels of specific capacity, using a fluid metaphor to express it. Classical information theory provides a rational reconstruction of the fluid metaphor, with the bit as the fundamental volumetric unit from which other units such as channel capacity are derived by standard dimensional analysis. These informational fluids go far beyond mathematical representations, requiring a semantic analysis (Himma, 2005) or, philosophical (Floridi, 2005). Through the combination of these analyses Kornai (2008) illustrates that information as fluid engages the following characteristics: identity, sentience, volition, and reverence.

Search Engines

The exponential growth of informational fluxes in the digital age, lead to a critical issue: information retrieval. Web search is today one of the most challenging problems of the Internet, striving at providing users with the most relevant search results to their information needs (Finkelstein et al., 2002). The instrumental tool that allows such achievement is a search engine, which can be described as a database that defines the set of documents that can be searched by the search engine (Wang, Meng & Yu, 2000). Or, it is a two-directional gateway: from the information provider to the user and from the user to the information provider. A search engine determines which information provided by information provider can be found by the end-user, as well as, what information the end-user will ultimately find (Liddy, 2003). Moreover, search engines can be classified as general or specialized. Specialized search engines index data from a specific domain, as opposed to general search engines, which attempt to index a broad range of information (Min, 2004).

According to Introna & Nissenbaum (2000), only in United States in 2000 Internet users conducted 6.9 billion searches! This importance has been a subject of research (see Hoffman & Novak, 1998); however, only recently power issues have been addressed (Elseem, 2007).

Nevertheless, main stream literature seems only to perceive the following analytical dimensions:

- **search engine evaluation**: this taxonomy induces multiple criteria, as for instance evaluation using click through data, and a user model (Dupret, Murdock & Piwowarski, 2007). Wang & DeWitt (2004) debate computing page rank in a distributed Internet search system. Lakshminarayana (2009) investigates how search engines categorize web pages. Or, finally, if the search engine brand name influences search results (Bailey, Thomas & Hawking, 2007);

- **website indexing versus queries results**: a research conducted by Ding & Marchionini (1996), first pointed a small overlap between results retrieved by different Web search engines for the same queries. However, Lawrence & Giles (1998) have demonstrated that a search engines indexes no more than 16% of all Websites. In accordance to Search Engine Watch (2005), this is a result of millions of new pages are added every single day. Plus, web query characteristics may influence these results (Zien, Meyer & Tomlin, 2001);

- **queries taxonomies**: Broder (2002) developed a web search taxonomy that classifies the "need behind the query" into three classes: navigational, informational, and transactional. Navigational are tasks where the user's intent is to find a particular web page. Informational arise when the purpose is to find information about a topic that may reside on one or more web pages. Transactional search tasks reflect the desire of the user to perform an action. Moreover, Kang and Kim (2004) demonstrated that optimizing search engines based on implicit data about informational versus navigational search improved performance;

- **information retrieval**: focuses how users retrieve online information and assimilate it even across more diverse niches (Evans & Card, 2008), allowing to understand what web aids are necessary. Literature still engages the analysis of intelligent information seek (Perkowitz & Etzioni, 2000; Domingues et al., 2008) and ontology design based on the schemas of databases and collection of queries that encompasses users areas of interest (Kashyap, 1999);

- **linguistic possibilities**: search engines have evolved, however the use of non-western language characters is still a limitation. Therefore, some studies are trying to evaluate how a search engine deals with these characters (Sornlertlamvanich, Tongchim & Isahara, 2007);

- **cached content**: evaluate the existing cached content in search engines has been a growing concerning by societies, therefore some studies have been conducted regarding such subject (see for example: Anagnostopoulos, 2007);

- **sponsored search**: a whole new range of issues has evolved due to the use of sponsored search (Fain & Pedersen, 2006). For example, Jansen & Mullen (2008) provide an overview of the factors that have led to the development of these sponsored web search platforms;
- **user's profiling**: Teevan, Dumais & Horvitz (2005) point out the value of personalizing web search. Other studies attempt to determine the user's intent of using a web search engine (Jansen, Booth & Spink, 2007), or user's behaviour regarding their information need or formulating their queries (Machill et al., 2003), as well as a refined ontology for the informational needs of the users community, which is targeted (Kashyap, 1999). Moreover, Shen, Tan & Zhai (2006) exploit the relationship between personal search history and accuracy, which can be perceived as Internet search strategy (Ruvini, 2003). Finally, Agichtei et al. (2006) strive to predict web search results through learning user interaction models;
- **organizational impact:** similarly to the power and legal issues only recent become a topic under discussion (Wielki, 2008).

In conclusion, search engines are a vital tool regarding informational fluxes. Still, an ethical debate concerning related to control, transparency and legal issues has been neglected.

Informational Fluxes vs. Security

Information security is scarcely a novel conception, as well as the need to protect information, given how this concept forged mankind evolution. However, the "Information Society" translates a critical stage of protection concerning four key ele-

ments of informational flows (Bossi et al., 2004): availability, integrity, authenticity, confidentiality. While the idea of information security is certainly not new, the practice of information security has been and continues to be an evolving endeavour where in technological advances both help and hinder its progress. The advent of the information age, as a messenger of rapid and widespread digital computing and networking technologies, has fundamentally changed the practices concerning informational fluxes, adding a new dynamic to computer security (Seehusen & Stolen, 2008).

In the networked world or cyberspace (combination of the World Wide Web, Deep Web and other networks) informational fluxes are instantaneous, leading to a whole new range of security (computer virus, hacking, etc.) and ethical issues (privacy, intellectual property, transparency, equity, etc), because data is easily copied, transmitted, modified or destroyed. In March 2009, Internet had 1.596 billion users (Miniwatts Marketing Group, 2009) accessing through multiple technological platforms, leading to an important conclusion: even a minute percentage of people with malicious intent, constitute a substantial threat.

In 2002, the Organization for Economic Cooperation and Development (OECD) released the document *OECD Guidelines for the Security of Information Systems and Networks: Towards a Culture of Security* (Organization for Economic Cooperation and Development, 2002), with the intention to initiate a new international acceptance concerning information systems safeguard. In spite of this effort the drawbacks detected by Cuppens (2001) seem to continue (see Ganame et al., 2008); however, we need to recognize the effort of evolving technologies in order to minimize these risks. Therefore, the following step of our analysis is to debate the current available technologies that allow informational entities to preserve their informational fluxes, which can be categorized into:

- **human filtering**: our bodies will be the keys that give us access to the Internet (Bullinga, 2001);
- **machine filtering**: embraces hardware and software technological regarding informational fluxes and content (Patterson, Shepherd & Watters, 2000).

Biometrics is the use of technology to recognise individual human features such as fingerprints, retinas and hand prints. That is, a computer can be programmed to identify an individual by recognising each individual's thumbprint (Crowley, 2006). Such technology needs not only to protect the stored personal data that underpin biometric authentication, but also the biometric image that is unique to each individual. Enhanced protection can be gained by use of a mixture of security techniques.

The leading providers of informational fluxes, as for example Internet Service Providers (ISP's) or search engines, have at their disposal firewalls, anti-virus, and anti-spyware grids that allow to describe the behaviour of current viruses, spyware or other bad code which is circulating (Microsoft Corporation, 2009; Heise, 2009), establishing an appropriate securing mechanism through a security policy (Federal Office for Information Security in Germany, 2008).

Regarding content based filtering, *deep pack inspection technologies*, allowed a more effective analysis concerning data that is intercepted and analyzed (Glorioso, 2008). However the effectiveness of content filters is still discussable (Thornburgh & Lin, 2002), given two kinds of errors: blocking a page that should not be blocked, *overblocking*; and, failing to block a page that should be blocked, *underblocking* (Stark, 2007). Finally, the core technologies that allow content filtering are (Patterson, Shepherd & Watters, 2000):

- **site labels**: labelling refer to schemes to assign content related labels to Uniform Resources Locator (URL's) and/or specific Web pages. Once a label schema has been chosen by a service or a community, then a Platform for Internet Content Selection (PICS) is required to implement that schema for individual Web pages;
- **lists of appropriate or inappropriate sites**: most frequently used content control mechanism is the use of lists of acceptable and/or unacceptable URL's;
- **automated text analysis**: another way to analyze a Web site is to use software that scans the text of a site to determine the relevance or suitability of pages.

In conclusion, in spite of the positive evolution of these technologies it is urgent to understand, if they ethically comply with the admissible policy enforced by the automated system (Gan & Suel, 2007).

Information Control

Conceptualizing Control

Following the etymological roots of control, it is possible to acknowledge that is a "power" that directly determines a situation; a relation of constraint of one entity (thing or person or group) by another, or, the state that exists when one person or group has power over another (Online Etymological Dictionary, 2008).

The Perception of Security

In an explanatory meaning, security and its complement in diverse languages, reproduce the affairs between object (subject) and its environment. Nevertheless it is imperative that security is a normative, an emotionally loaded idea (Mesjasz, 2004). Any attempts to elaborate a complete definition of security are of course vain, given the broader and expanded meanings of such concept. In fact, typically security is categorized in:

- a traditional meaning- security as an attribute of state, absence of military conflict (Kaldor, 2007);
- a broader sense- referring directly to a phenomena occurring in international relations, or directly/indirectly caused by inter-state relations security as a public good (Buzan, 2003; Deudney, 2004);
- a universal sense (of a unit and of a social entity)- human security (Cahill & Melo, 2004; Nickel, 2007).

Moreover, considering an etymological discussion a double outlook appears: the Latin expression is *secures*, meaning safe or secure. Adding the noun *cura* (care), security becomes a quality or state of being secure, or as a freedom from danger. This is similar what Cycero claims: the absence of anxiety upon which the fulfilled life depends (Liotta, 2002). The following interpretation is bounded to the word *securus*, which initially referred to liberation from uneasiness, or a peaceful situation without any risks or threats. Nevertheless, the linguistic perception of security is often shaped by cultural elements leading to more interpretations (Morgenthau, 1960).

Given the nature of argument the authors will draw their attention to the universal sense of security. Our decision may seem awkward, namely given the United Nations (UN) (2008) report: the concept of security must change- from an exclusive stress on national security to a much greater stress on people's security, from security through armaments, human development, territorial security to food, employment and environmental security (United Nations, 2008); however, given the potential *Tragedy of Good Will* (Floridi, 2006) that computer networks configure (insecure or lack of integrity concerning personal data, absence of privacy, and other ethical issues), the argument seems perfectly justifiable. Plus, the authors plead the argument of Manunta (2000) that security in a philosophical sense entails into the sense of freedom due to perception, or awareness

of not existent "worries" or "dangerous", which computer networks seem to promote in user's, in spite of *Barbarians at the Gate* (Mierzejewska, 2008). Therefore, this "unintended ignorance" may provoke serious consequences!

Informational Fluxes vs. Control

Searching on the Web expands from a quick question to "progressive or composite", for which a lot of information is known to exist. Casual users simply cause a quick question; and, "usual" users understand the need for query syntax or, search engine construction features and operations, according to their potential interests and curiosity (Decker, 2008). Plus through the work of Pirolli & Card (1999), is possible to comprehend how user strategies and technologies for information seeking, gathering, and consumption interact concerning the environmental fluxes of information, leading to the following concepts as Furnas (1997) pleads:

- **information scent**: imperfect information at intermediary locations that is applied by the searcher to decide what paths should take in order to target information through a library or an on-line text database;
- **information diet**: information distributed by link descriptors, images, contextual clues, such as preceding headings, or by page arrangement.

Therefore, search engines try to provide users the information that satisfies their needs, however with the growing number of pages created every day their information retrieval process versus control become relevant. An example of this dilemma is illustrated in project WebWatcher, which encompasses an information agent that is tries interactively to deliver what information is sought. In fact, as the user navigates through the Web, the software utilizes its learned knowledge to recommend especially promising hyperlinks to the user by highlighting these links on the user's display (Armstrong et al., 1995).

Nonetheless, the level of exposure of search engines to possible malicious attacks, or other intended practices or content is extremely high (Fishkin & Pollard, 2007; Schlembach, 2008). These authors have demonstrated through studies that usually Hypertext Preprocessor (PHP) pages (responsible for delivering search results) are compromised in certain keywords due to malware; or, proxy abuses that are typical of rogue search engines. In that sense, metaphorically the authors address the work of Cao, Feito & Touchette (2009) regarding stochastically informational fluxes control, who claims that control theories have two types of ratchets: open-loop, and closed looped. The first group concerns the appliance of a rectifying potential independently state of the system to be controlled; and the second engages a rectification action on a system has an explicit dependence on that system's evolution in time. Moreover, Decker (2008) claims the search engines optimization tools are based on two key factors:

- **on-site**: refers to contents and formats applied within the websites;
- **off-site**: engages the mainly associated URL's concerning to their domain reputation/ranking value.

Due to previous arguments the level of invisible Web[1], high-quality information, is not available due to search engines technical limitations, or will not, due to deliberate choice add to their indices of Web pages (Sherman and Price, 2001). Therefore, invisibility is a dynamic attribute that search engines must acquire, or else, some serious controversies will arise from search engines (Gerhart, 2004): often articulate the richness and intensity of a topic; dramatize change; may induce a critical dissimilarity in life by shifting decisions; scientists, journalists, and intelligence analysts are professionally mandatory to deal with multiple

perceptions, evidences, authorities, and judgments on topics. In that sense, the authors agree with the arguments of Poullet (2009) concerning the two major trends that information society will face: the privatisation of cyberspace and, the global consequences of local actions and decision (for more details see section future trends).

A Organizational Approach

Human organizations are complex systems, which according to Kaufman (1995) are an organizational unit that it intends to preserve his identity and integrity, in order to guarantee its survival, being "forced" to interpret an amount of information greater than is processing capacity. Therefore, information security is an issue of tremendous concern to businesses worldwide (Whitman 2003), leading to a positive network externality (Kunreuther & Heal, 2002).

The management of information security should occur within all organizational levels (Gordon & Loeb, 2006), that is, expenditures for enterprise security have been distributed over tools, policies, technology, procedures and personnel to achieve the highest level of asset protection (Eloff & von Solms, 2000). However, top management has a different perspective and must answer the following question: what is the optimal enterprise-wide security budget that minimizes informational losses? So, "information" is an asset similar to other business assets.

The answer to this question establishes the budgetary boundaries for building a security capability and for acceptable losses, given the risk tolerances of decision makers (risk assessment analysis) (Anderson & Shain, 1991).

It involves modelling the costs of achieving various levels of best practice implementation in the presence of uncertain losses and establishes the optimal enterprise security budget using various decision criteria. The strategic management of security focuses on the competing demands for enterprise resources and their opportunity costs, and seeks to identify security benefits that justify related costs (Kwon et al., 2007). If there were no threats, security resources would not exist, costs would be lower, profits higher, and entities would have higher equity values.

According to Turban et al. (1996), risk is the likelihood that a threat materializes. Risk is to some degree unavoidable, so the organization must accept some degree of risk. Therefore, the attitudes and tolerances for risks are considerably different given context, individual decision maker, and degree of uncertainty (Finne, 2000), leading to a gap between managers and technicians (Bakari et al., 2007). They also can vary with the absolute magnitude of probable and expected (average) losses, or the chosen risk analytical method (Gordon et al., 2006).

A Societal Approach

The Internet was born in the aftermath of technological advancement, which was fundamental to the US defence system. Thus, with its advent it was strictly administered by the American Defence Advanced Research Projects Agency (later DARPA). Formally speaking, in 1990 the US army yielded ground to the National Science Foundation. From this moment on, the truly global expansion of the Internet began and it went hand in hand with privatization. In 1991, in prospect of the impending deregulation of the Internet by the US administration, the National Science Foundation (NSF) established the Internet Society (ISOC), a watchdog of the future global Web development. Furthermore, the ISOC intended to prop up various groups of specialists working on the Internet advancement. American IT specialists- Vinton G. Cerf & Robert E. Kahn (TCP/IP protocol inventors), who are considered the Internet founding fathers, took the helm of the organization. However, as the Web was becoming more and more international, the institution's ambiguous status (which, although autonomous, was in fact controlled by the US administration)

came into harsh criticism from governments from other countries, European ones in particular (Castells, 2001). Currently, the Internet Society is a US non-profit organization registered in the Washington city court with its branches scattered worldwide (in consequence, it is an international organization).

The Internet Corporation for Assigned Names and Numbers (ICANN) is yet another important organization, which shaped the Internet. For the purpose of a vast global representation, members of the Board come from various parts of the world. Yet, this perfect picture, where global Internet community appoints its representation by electronic ballot, is tarnished by lobbing of powerful groups and campaigns, which back up specific candidates. In the context of the prevalent influence of large corporations, a truly democratic operation in the ICANN formal structures is pure fiction. What is more, the organization is closely bound with the US Department of Commerce (Castells, 2001). As a result, the US is the main player in the ICANN, which from time to time is harshly criticized.

The World Wide Web Consortium (W3C) is another Web-shaping organization. It seeks to implement standard solutions in websites. The organization was established in 1994 by Tim Berners-Lee (WWW inventor). Its branches are scattered worldwide, but its headquarters are located in the US (with the Massachusetts Institute of Technology), in Europe, and in Japan. W3C currently affiliates over 500 organizations, companies, government agencies and universities from all parts of the world. The W3C publishes its recommendations, which however are not legally effective. Despite the fact, the organization is considered influential and must not be ignored. A company, or an organization, which wants to join the W3C "club" must pay annual membership fees, which are computed individually, depending on the candidate size (it seems logical to calculate higher fees for the more powerful members of the organization). The W3C members include organizations of various types, collages, universities, associations, companies of different size, among others, such giants as, for instance, Microsoft.

The discussion about the legal aspects of the Internet must touch upon the US IT security policy, as its regulations have exerted a tangible influence on the shape of the new medium. Indisputably, the US can be deemed a forerunner, when it comes to technological advancement, IT infrastructure, communication technology and connectivity. It can also be inferred that the US is the only country in the world with such a consistent and coherent IT security policy. It is largely based on cooperation between private and public entities. The idea stems from the American property structure. In the USA computer technology production is to a large extent private (Microsoft, IBM, HP, Compaq etc.) and the sector generates growing proceeds (Bogdat-Brzezinska & Gawrycki, 2003). For this world's top profitable business to operate safely, the company owners ensure that the high level security measures are applied. It is symbiotic, as it is a win-win situation for all parties involved.

The US ICT sector makes for a powerful lobby, which affects state policy in terms of government procurement, product licence protection. IT security policy constitutes a vital element of the entire national security policy. The US IT security is made up of legal acts, institutional regulations, political statements and numerous international activities, which, among others, seek to promote the global concept of cyber-defence (Bogdat-Brzezinska & Gawrycki, 2003) American technologies and democracy worldwide.

In the aftermath of the 9/11 attacks the US Congress adopted the "Patriot Act", which obliged Internet and ICT operators to monitor Web communication and provided federal services with access to private accounts and connections (therefore, the authorities are entitled to read e-mails, listen to and record telephone calls, etc.). On the premise that most of the Web operations "are transmitted" through systems located in the USA and that most

of the Internet operators and suppliers are based there, it appears plausible for the US administration to control (or at least to have a capacity to control) the Internet communication. The USA is actively involved in numerous international undertakings pertaining to the widely understood ICT issues. It promotes the UN concept of information society and, for instance, provides ICT infrastructure assistance to APEC countries.

When it comes to the US international policy, it seeks to gain an edge and to be streets ahead of its competitors aspiring to the role of global technological leaders. In consequence, it implements initiatives, which undermine the role of the European Union and Japan in this field. Bill Clinton's and George Bush's (National Information Infrastructure) administration documents featured the concept of information society. It disseminates establishment of information highways as a part of national information web infrastructure, which makes the Internet widely available, but still chargeable. A closer look at the American strategy corroborates the statement that the concept of information society is to work for the benefit of business beneficiaries and to secure the US technological advantage in the world (Bogdat-Brzezinska & Gawrycki, 2003).

Many scholars perceive the Internet as a tool, which puts liberal ideas into practice (in particular, when it comes to communication). It is a common belief that the global Web (its architecture and operation) best safeguards observance of liberal rules, as there is no questioning the "freedom of speech" (the right to freely speak of one's opinions in public and to respect the opinions), "freedom of information" and "freedom of communication". Liberalism largely emphasizes individual liberty and values rights of an individual higher than the rights of a community. It promotes unlimited liberty of citizens to take actions (which are properly regulated, though) in all areas of collective life. There is no denying that the US still prevails in shaping the Internet and that the

US capital controls a substantial part of the ICT sector. In consequence of the prevalence, the American mainstream viewpoints are transposed on the ICT space. "American liberalism" (also referred to as "modern liberalism"), which is focal for this chapter, appears to be the chief and the most vital viewpoint of this type. In some aspects it differs from traditional liberalism. In contrast to classic liberalism, it promotes a more significant role of state both in social and business life. Hence, it seems that this ideology predetermines the premises of the security policy, which allows various business entities to oversee the widely understood information.

It is becoming increasingly common to state that freedoms of information and communication are more and more frequently regulated. The different forms of constraints and control are factor-dependent. They depend on the institutional organization of the Internet, government activities of various states and actions of various business entities. The first factor was elaborated on in the paragraphs above. When it comes to factor two, it is best illustrated by the US authorities' control of electronic media transported into the States. Laptops and mobile devices are browsed through and correspondence and documents stored on them checked. The Echelon system is also a good example. This world's leading signal intelligence collection and analysis network makes it possible to control 90% of digital information sent worldwide. The totality of business sector is subsumed under factor three. It is of significance, as it was noted by Castells in *The Internet Galaxy*. He concluded that business is one of four elements, which shape the Internet culture, but is the element, when it comes to Web content input.

The final factor is multi-aspect and complex. It covers a wide spectrum of corporate activities: with monitoring employees' conduct to begin with and Web consumer behaviour control, to end with. Particular electronic communication technologies are increasingly subject to control (for instance, by aggressive patent assignment). All these actions are taken as corporate security policy measures (understood as information security, including confidential information protection) and ICT security actions. Confidential information protection refers to information considered confidential by legal acts effective in a given country and information perceived trade secret by specific entities. The scope of protected (controlled) information can be wide and different depending on a given entity. Nonetheless, there is no doubt that in every case personal data must be protected and personal databases should be created and processed in a way which allows the identity and individuality be protected. Detailed information availability must be specified (to whom, where, when, to what extent, for what purpose). It is also a common obligation to promptly destroy outdated data as well as information, the processing purpose of which was attained.

The obligation to control information under the adopted security policy is in fact well-grounded. However, the regulatory structure, which serves as the basis for pertinent regulations, is too comprehensive and incoherent (Foucalt, 1986). As a result, there are (numerous) cases of abuses or actions, which verge on legitimacy and ethical rules. The corporate intention to control the largest possible scope of cyberspace information is in conflict with liberal freedom of information, which is the foundation of ICT revolution mechanism. The freedom is best characterized by Tim Berners-Lee (2000) about the World Wide Web service that he invented: if this technology was my property, was under my control, so probably would never have been invented. The decision to make the Web an open system was necessary to make it widely available. We cannot propose to make it a public space and still have it under our control.

FOCUS: THE CASE OF GOOGLE

Why Debate Google

The choice concerning Google is justifiable by its amazing evolution as a company, being recognized worldwide through its market share, but namely due its unique search engine. In spite of using a possible Google´s inaccuracy concerning user´s security or profiling, the truth is that Google is the best search engine available.

The idea of Google as a company emerged in 1995 when Larry Page and Sergey Brin started a project during the University. Given their difficult to find a buyer or receive funding, David Filo, the founder of Yahoo!, advised them to grow the service themselves (Information Week, 2008). For that, they had the assistance of their families and friends and, Andy Bechtolsheim as a business angel (Google, 2009a).

Near the year 2000 Google´s popularity was already considerable due to its unique organizational philosophies, to the introduction of new products (Google toolbar or AdWords) and a partnership with Yahoo. Giving their continuous innovation process regarding products (Addwords, Algorithmic Search, etc.), as well as, its business model (see for example, Google AdSense, Froogue, G-mail, Google Groups, Chrome, Maps, Wi-Fi services, etc.) Google become the worldwide market leader (Eisenmann & Herman, 2006; Lastowka, 2007), which is related with the company mission: "Google´s mission is to organize the word´s information and make it universally accessible and useful" (Google, 2009b); and name, "Googol" is the mathematical term for a 1 followed by 100 zeros (...)" (Google, 2009b).

This leadership is easily perceived through the evolution of the market share analysis regarding two dimensions: organic search, and paid search. Following Sisson (2004), this analysis entails into the following criteria:

- **number of indexed pages:** measures in billions the number of indexed pages, including types of files (Word, Excel, PDF, etc.) within a determined time period;
- **search-referral percentage:** computes the percentage of visitor traffic. This can comprise paid keywords, unpaid search results, and even banner ads on the search portal's web site within a determined time period;
- **number of performed searches:** determines in billion the number of conducted searches within a determined time period;
- **search time hours:** calculates in billion the number of conducted searches within a determined time period;
- **paid search accounts:** quantify in percentage the existent online advertising in the major online advertisers within a determined time period.

According to Lipsman (2003) scores for indexed web pages Google represented 32% of the market, Yahoo 25% and MSN 19%. Also considering WebSideStory (2004) collected data, the leader in on-demand Web analytics is Google with a search referral percentage of nearly 41 percent, up from 35.99 percent on 2003. Second place player and previous leading search referral domain, Yahoo, posted 27.40 percent, against the 30.95 percent on 2003. The third placed was MSN with 19.57 percent.

Plus, following Bausch & Han (2006) report *Mega View Search*, searches on Google and Yahoo grew 41 percent and 47 percent, respectively, outpacing the overall search growth rate of 36 percent. Google's searches increased from 2.1 billion in March 2005 to 2.9 billion in March 2006, while in the same time period Yahoo's searches increased from 907.8 million to 1.3 billion. The number three ranked search provider, MSN, reported a 9 percent year-over-year growth in searches, from 0.592 billion to 0.643 billion.

Finally concerning paid search market, Google appears to have a market share of 70 percent, followed by Yahoo with a market share of 22 percent, and Microsoft with about 8 percent (SearchIgnite, 2008). However, including within the market other forms of online advertising would reduce Google's market share. Paid search accounts represents 41 percent of online advertising, but display advertising accounts for percent (Swisher, 2008). Google has only a 1.5 percentage share of display advertising. Display advertising, unlike paid search, is highly fragmented. Fox Interactive Media has the largest market share with 15.9 percent, followed by Yahoo with 10.5 percent, AOL with 5.8 percent, and finally Microsoft with 4.7 percent (Kawamoto, 2008).

This impressive growing has generated some critics and worries, namely under the analysis of US Anti-Trust Laws leading to the denial of Google and Yahoo agreement regarding advertising, because such partnership could represent around 70 to 80% of U.S. market share (see for example Lastowka, 2007; Hawker, 2008).

Google Search Engine

Google is well recognized, and it is possible that become even more widespread. The use of a search engine to detect information is vital, and traditionally, information search engine performance is measured along two dimensions: recall and precision. Recall is defined as the ratio involving the number of significant items retrieved and the overall amount of relevant items into the search space. Precision is acknowledged as the relation between the numeral relevant items retrieved and the total number of items (relevant and non-relevant) retrieved. In practice, there is an inverse correlation between recall and precision (Sullivan, 2002).

Google has tackled this challenge in a relatively unique way. Rather than pressing towards both perfect precision and recall, the engine's ranking technology, which uses link analysis to determine how important other sites on the Web deem a given item to be, enables Google to return quality results

"early on." While this solution functions in many circumstances (and is most effective when the information sought for is general and popular), it still cannot fully answer the problem of relevance. Google works best as a mode of online research when one already has an understanding of the contextual features of a certain research domain. As Sisson (2004) claims in his metaphor: "The Google search engine is like a blind person reading a book in Braile- anything that is graphical, spatial, or visual in nature is simply not seen" (pp. 12). Moreover, this dilemma is still enhanced when the search topic list involves non-western languages, like Arabic or Hebrew. However, it is also necessary to recognize Google's in overcoming this dilemma (Physorg, 2006).

At this point however, some important questions arise: how Google really work? Which are its technical features that allow presenting the informational choice? Can locate an existing ontology, which conforms to the user's requirements?

After the users introduce the query, Google's webserver post it to the *index servers*. The content of these servers is comparable to an index, which refers which pages possess the corresponding words of the query. The following step of the process is to retrieve the documents from the *doc's server*, leading to the results delivery (Google, 2009c). All this process relies on *Google File System* (*GFS*), which consists of a single master and many chunk servers. Each file is broken into large chunks, identified with chunk handles. When a user intends to read or write a segment of a file, it calculates the chunk index using the offset of the segment and the size of a chunk (Ghemawat, Gobioff & Leung, 2003). The idea of *GFS* is to gain high performance and fault tolerant system using inexpensive hardware that often fails. *GFS* is optimized for storing large files, appending large amounts of data to the end of the file and making large streaming reads and small random reads. The system also features atomic concurrent appending of records into a single file with minimal synchronization overhead.

And the technical features? Checking the company's website once again, the authors conclude that Google's search engine gathers more than 200 signals in order to achieve which pages are more important. After that, a hypertext-matching analysis is conducted (Google, 2009c). However, not all the technical features are presented due to intellectual property issues, as recognized throughout our research. So, a detailed analysis of the technical features is required for: *PageRank*, *Bombs*, and *Hypertext-Matching Analysis*.

Google describes *PageRank* as the uniquely democratic nature of the web by using its vast link structure as an indicator of an individual page's value (Google, 2009c). In essence, Google interprets a link from page A to page B as a vote, by page A, for page B. But, Google looks at more than the sheer volume of votes, or links a page receives; it also analyzes the page that casts the vote. Votes cast by pages that are themselves "important" weigh more heavily and help to make other pages "important" (Huang & Paturi, 2005). These authors still point out some important drawbacks concerning this feature: spam abusing, evaluating older versus new pages, and spoofing. Spam problems are related to the possibility of an advertiser could have multiple spam pages pointing out for such destination page, leading to an enhancement of the *PageRank*. The second drawback concerns that older pages are tendentially more ranked. Finally, spoofing refers that *PageRank* would increase for all pages that vote for (or link to) a page.

Google's bombs acknowledge the intended practices of the company to manipulate the ranking of particular pages, in results returned by its search engine. The concept is related to the Internet jargon of improve a page ranking often due to humorous or political intentions (Zeller, 2006). However, Hiler (2002) proposed a broader typology of *Google's bombs*: fun, personal promotion, commercial, justice, ideological, and political. Nevertheless, Bar-Ilan (2007) debates each category illustrating several examples, and tries to determine if such examples are *Google's bombs*.

Hypertext-Matching Analysis refers how the search engine analyzes pages content. This feature represents a combination of text, fonts, location, and even neighbouring to determine the most relevant results (Google, 2009c). So far, literature did not recognize any drawbacks concerning Google's technology.

And what about the feature to locate an existing ontology, which conforms to the user's requirements? For Google the answer is "yes!", through its AdSense or Conceptual Information Retrieval and Communication Architecture (CIRCA), which is based on a language independent, scalable ontology consisting of millions of words along with what the words mean, how the words are related concept (Paulen, 2009), or even through Google Web API (Zhang, Vasconcelos & Sleeman, 2004). Moreover, as pointed out in DuCharme (2004), it is possible to simply use the Google facility "filetype:" to limit the type of searching file. At a first glimpse, Google presents suitable online ontology resources however, after some experiments (basically focused on finding RDFs files); the results are not the intended. Plus, it is very hard to use Google to search for suitable ontological files.

Google Security Features

In this section, the security measures undertaken by Google concerning privacy and data integrity, network security and its features, content policy will be detailed.

According to the company (Google, 2008a):

- it is not required to users give personal contact or demographic information;
- it never trades or crafts available individual names, lists of users, or aggregate data to any third parties;

- only uses client user configuration information to deliver;
- it maintains all user-specific and email message information, including content, addresses, categorizations, and IP addresses strictly confidential;
- it commits that client data will be protected following the provisions in its standard client contract:
- security and compliance products include specific confidentiality provisions in every client contract;
- when handling security and compliance products transactions, Google not just creates a contractual commitment but as well an operational in order to preserve client data integrity based on international standards;
- commitment concerning confidentiality and data security is integral to the security and compliance products' architecture.

Still in accordance to the company (Google, 2008a), the network security is achieved through duplicated storage systems and operational flows, with high degree of fault tolerance level. The operating system runs on a commercial version of Linux, however adapted and modified by Google. Nevertheless which are the features concerning network security, and measures taken? Google Search Appliance relies on a firewall as the main protection against malicious hackers (I-node, 2005); however, FitzGerald (2008) that is possible to inject spam into Google Web history. Plus, Nielson, Fogarty & Wallach (2004) point out that personal search engine contained serious security flaws that would allow a third party to read the search result summaries that are embedded in normal Google web searches by the local search engine. In spite of these critics McMillan (2006), acknowledges that through an agreement with Websense, Google detected over 2.000 malicious Web sites just in one month. Beyond the firewall,

Delichatsios & Sonuyi (2005) resume the other measures: IP address recording and cookies.

Finally concerning content policy management, a deep content inspection using filters tries to enable security and regulatory violations to content. Policy options include the ability to block, quarantine, redirect, bounce, log, or even encrypt with *Google Message Encryption* (Google, 2008b). These filters combination is known as *Google's Giant Sandbox*, which started in March 2004. The sandbox filter appears to affect almost all new websites that were considered under the "probationer" category. In spite of appearing in the search results pages, if a website falls into such category it does not have immediate success (Daoust, 2009).

Reporting the Problem to Google

After debating Google's market share, its search engine, and its security features, it is time to introduce the key issue of our contribution. This matter is a consequence of Google long hour's usage, which can be bounded to the relationship between personal search history and accuracy (Shen, Tan & Zhai, 2006).

However, in order to allow a comprehensive recognition regarding the chapter focus, the authors will follow a four steps approach:

- **search question:** introduces an example concerning a possible search issue;
- **search process:** details how the search is conducted;
- **focus:** illustrates the input of our contribution;
- **reporting:** reports the communicational process between the authors and Google.

Consider a short search example concerning the debate of marketing and ethics. The following step is to perform the search; however previously to this, the strategy is to prepare a topic list with different combinations to allow an improved outcome. Note that, the combination will be achieved through "search within results" within Google search engine. During the process the aim is to perceive the first 50 web pages that, Google give as a result for each search group. In spite of the speed reading rate for each web page be extremely fast, leading to a 5 minutes average time period for the 50 results, the aim is to download information for future reading.

After 30 minutes (average time), Google presents a web page stating the following message: "We're sorry... but your query looks similar to automated requests from a computer virus or spyware application. To protect our users, we can't process your request right now. We'll restore your access as quickly as possible, so try again soon in the meantime, if you suspect that your computer or network has been infected, you might want to run a virus checker or spyware remover to make sure that your systems are free of viruses and other spurious software. We apologize for the inconvenience, and hope we'll see you again on Google." Given this scenario the co-author is inhibited to continue his search at least for a 2 hours time period.

Plus, the following ideas must be pointed out:

- the personal computer of the co-author is protected against viruses or spyware;
- the co-author used several other protected personal computers, and even universities computer networks, which possess a higher level of security, and the outcome was equal.

After conducting a search within the company's website (including newsgroups and blogs) (Google, 2009d), the authors concluded that until now this issue have been not reported. Therefore, the communicational process started through an e-mail contact in November 24, 2008, in which the whole process and consequences were de-

scribed (similar to this contribution). Google's answer was automatic acknowledging the e-mail acceptance, however imposing some conditions in order to continue the communicational process (see next section: Google's assumptions). Given no further contact by Google and with the problem still holding a phone call become a hypothesis! The main ideas of this contact are present also into the following section. Nevertheless, the key conclusion concerning it was that a similar e-mail should be submitted once again, which occurred in February 25, 2009. Until now, the feedback process engages the same results: Google's automatic response had recognized the e-mail, but no further contacts arise. Moreover, the characterized issue is still a reality!

Google's Assumptions

In order to comprehend Google's assumptions we need to approach three analytical dimensions, which are a combination of the communicational process (see previous section), and literature review:

- **search engines:** refers to the ethical dilemmas that search engine optimization imposes;
- **organizational:** acknowledges the ethical quandaries of organizational transparency;
- **reported issue:** the author's opinion concerning Google's perception of the reported issue and intended consequences.

The search engine optimization leads to ethical problems which usually are categorized into the main domains: the "white hats" that use "lawful" techniques to accomplish ranking; and, the "black hats" that employ more discussable practices (Hurlbert, 2004). According to Google Webmaster Guidelines (Google, 2006b) the concept "grey" defines the space between these domains, and follow the general rule-of-thumb of creating pages for the users, not for the search engine. Plus, these guidelines outline that "black hats" methods need to be avoided. However, the key ethical dilemmas do not arise from this discussion, but from the search engine design characteristics (*PageRank*) and its intended consequences for users (stakeholders). Can a zero *PageRank* have real effects on the commerce of a website which is dependent on traffic from search engines? (United States District Court, 2006a; 2006b) Or, a zero *PageRank* configures the same results from a "search"? (Caufield, 2006) Moreover, the inexistence of a regulatory body of practices concerning ethical standards complied by all market players' results into the serious dilemmas, and enhances a pessimistic view of the "Information Society".

To address organizational transparency we will follow Vaccaro and Madsen (2006) to demonstrate the ethical and economical forces that affect a company organizational transparency. Engaging a top-bottom analysis Google's mission can lead to the first level of discussion: it will be possible? How Google will handle with the ethical dilemmas described by James Caufield. This author argues that search engines bear excessive ethical burdens given their influence in people's every day options. As "gatekeepers to information on the Web", companies like Google face two dilemmas: people's trust and, the socio-political implications that derive from have access not to a private space but to public, open and democratic properties (Caufield, 2006). These dilemmas are enhanced when the following questions are attended: can informational fluxes be controlled? And, who controls search engines?

Regarding Google's corporate information, it seems to disregard some underlying issues concerning information transparency, because is obsessive about his products characteristics and functioning, which is of course is a natural phenomenon; however, it is difficult to search or address other ways of working with its products even into corporate blogs. Moreover, in spite of technical questions are bounded to a specific

technical service, which a very positive approach by Google and easily perceived in the corporate website; the truth is that for technical issues concerning the search engine does not exist any available contact, even performing a "search" within Google's help. Even, when contacting Google by phone the process is not transparent enough because who is contacting Google needs to know the person's name that you want to contact, or else the system gives as hypothesis the e-mails already presented in the website. So, in order to become a XXI century organization, transparency needs to bind to corporate values as a "mental state" (Costa, Prior and Rogerson, 2008).

For the reported issue our analysis will entail into two sub-dimensions: e-mails; and, phone call. Through the e-mails exchange it is possible to conclude that Google's assumes the importance of security issues, which is a positive sign; however, the automatic reply also claims that if a security problem was not being reported an answer will not be obtained, which had occurred. Moreover, during the phone contact two it was possible to understand that this issue is not related to security, and above all that until now this issue have been not reported by worldwide users.

Thus, an important question still remains: if it is not a security issue, then in what category it falls? Our personal believe given the previous arguments, and in some extent the critical work of Seth Finkelstein (2007), is that Google categorize it as a profiling issue. Profiling is a formal review or analysis of data, often in the form of a graph or table, representing distinctive features or characteristics of an object or a person's behaviour. Such process usually occurs through Technology Profile Inventory (TPI) (DeYoung & Spence, 2004), and it is possible to determine a hacker or spyware profile (Dantu et al., 2007). In this particular case, given the speed and the way search is conducted Google's assumes that the co-author has similar distinctive characteristics. As a consequence, productivity is seriously affect as well as equity, because an outlier's behaviour or non traditional corresponding ways to conduct a search are also affected due to these controls. So, given the previous arguments some questions remained answered: which are the real economical costs concerning productivity losses? What criteria Google's TPI engages? It is fair to profile these outliers as spammers or viruses? It is possible to achieve a more flexible profiling? For example, why not engage a learning ontology (Li, Du & Wang, 2005) for the profiling system, allowing that users create queries involving them and their personal believes or experiences for information retrieval without be considered outliers, as well as reflects the true informational needs of the user community.

FUTURE TRENDS

Search engines evolution will never rest in order to increase the quality and relevancy of the results, as well as, to diminish *PageRank* limitations, spam and viruses (Achte, 2006). A lot has changed over the years, and the future is sure to also deliver its plethora of surprises, but this growing role leads to even greater ethical dilemmas. Thus, the question is how to control their actions trough legal acts, and since Web 2.0 is becoming embedded into business models (European Parliament, 2002), the problem is enhancing. In spite of existing regulation, search engines are still largely "lost in law" or represent a policy vacuum.

Grimmelmann (2007) illustrates four broad areas of law that need to intervene:

- **intellectual property:** to what extent might search engines and hyperlinks infringe copyright laws? Beyond private copying, to what extent should other traditional exceptions to copyright apply in the digital environment? How to ensure that authors and other right holders are able to obtain proper remuneration for the exploitation of their material?;

- **free speech:** to what extent might search engines through their features allows free speech according to human rights conventions? Or, if it is possible to manipulate content?;

- **antitrust:** does the law and jurisdiction regarding to Internet activities different from other markets?;

- **openness (transparency) of search algorithms:** beyond traditional information, what information should be provided to stakeholders in order to guarantee transparency?

In addition, van Eijk (2007) points out privacy as another intervention. In spite of recognize the bound between freedom of expression and privacy, this author goes beyond that claim and acknowledges the need for a principle concerning a minimum of personal data that should be stored and processed, as well as the reason why it has been collected. Some critics may arise due to the Resolution on Privacy Protection and Search Engines; however, policy vacuums are still a reality. Moreover, the authors of this contribution still emphasise corporate responsibility regarding the liability of search engines in order to prevent issues similar to the reported one, which go further beyond Achte (2006) perception, so a truth organizational transparency occur.

Given such arguments, van Eijk (2009) recently presented a possible converged regulatory model for search engines with the following characteristics:

- **market power:** potentially pertinent as a basis for decision making concerning market regulation through several non-discriminatory, transparent and objective criteria;

- **relevant legal issues:** include "cloud computing", which in spite of produce efficiency concerning business, entails an absolute lack of transparency regarding the location of sensitive data. So, within the scope of good governance, risks must be clearly defined.

However, we follow Grimmelmann (2005) claim that is needed representatives from all groups, and not a single resolution. For that, the authors' proposal is to present a joint solution between World Trade Organization (WTO) and UN in order to obtain plausible results, and given the global influence of information. The framework should engage two fundamental dimensions:

- **research:** will investigate possible law limitations and policy vacuums;
- **operability:** will monitor law compliance of each search engine worldwide and by region.

Finally, the procedures for both dimensions follows UN operations by regions, however given cultural differences, as for example, Eurasia region should be divided into Europe and Asia. Besides that, Europe should so be separated into: Mediterranean Europe, Central Europe, Eastern Europe, and North European countries.

CONCLUSION

Google is undoubtedly the best search engine available in any technological platform (Schofield, 2006), which is recognized worldwide. In fact, the focus of this contribution is a consequence of the previous argument and co-authors personal usage due to its unique features. Nevertheless, Google's profiling is non flexible and needs to evolve in order to allow outliers with ethical behaviours too perform their searches without any problem. Thus, in spite of Google's argument that "democracy on the web works" (Google, 2006a), and that *PageRank* do not influence or manipulates search results, the truth is that the perception of organizational transparency is affected (O'Shea, 2003; Livingston, 2004).

Even if, we accept Zook (2005) case concerning Internet as the Schumpeterian power for "creative destruction", Google's search engine in some extent controls informational fluxes, imposing serious ethical and legal challenges. Moreover, such dilemmas are enhanced and become normative due to pervasive computing. Like Wellman (2001, pp. 2) stated, it is precisely when "technological changes get pervasive, familiar and boring that their impact on society is usually most felt" (2001, p. 2), namely network personalization. Therefore, a wide and multidisciplinary debate is necessary concerning search engines!

As a final remark, it is necessary to understand that locking down a network resumes a trade-off between flexibility and control. Wherever the line is draw, it is important to be aware that gray areas will exist. Plus, if users do not possess technical expertise, could undermine acceptable usage policies.

REFERENCES

Achte, S. V. (2006). *Future evolution of search.* Resource document. Internet Search Engine Database. Retrieved February 20, 2009, from http://www.isedb.com/db/articles/1559/1/Future-Evolution-of-Search-/Page1.html.

Agichtein, E., et al. (2006). Learning user interaction models for predicting web search result preferences. In *Proceedings of the 29th Annual International ACM SIGIR Conference on Research and Development in Information Retrieval* (pp. 3-10). Seattle, WA, USA.

Anagnostopoulos, I. (2007). Monitoring the evolution of cached content in Google and MSN. In *Proceedings of the 2007 International Conference on the World Wide Web* (pp. 1179-1180). May 8-12, Banff, Alberta, Canada. Retrieved January 22, 2009, from http://www2007.org/posters/poster993.pdf

Anderson, A., & Shain, M. (1991). Risk management. In Caelli, W., Longley, D., & Shain, M. (Eds.), *Information Security Handbook* (pp. 75–127). New York: Stockton Press.

Armstrong, R., et al. (1995). WebWatcher: A learning apprentice for the World Wide Web. In *AAI Spring Symposium on Information Gathering from Heterogeneous, Distributed Environments* (pp. 6-12). California: Stanford University, United States.

Bailey, P., Thomas, P., & Hawking, D. (2007). Does brandname influence perceived search result quality? Yahoo! Google, and WebKumara. In *Proceedings of the 12th Australasian Document Computing Symposium*. Retrieved March 7, 2009, from http://es.csiro.au/pubs/bailey-thomas-hawking-adcs2007.pdf.

Bakari, J. K. (2007). Bridging the gap between general management and technicians- A case study on ICT security in a developing country. *Computers & Security, 26*(1), 44–55. doi:10.1016/j.cose.2006.10.007

Bar-Ilan, J. (2007). Manipulating search engines algorithm: The case of Google. *Journal of Information. Communication & Ethics in Society, 5*(2/3), 155–166. doi:10.1108/14779960710837623

Barry, B., & Weaver, O. (2003). *Regions and powers: The structure of international security*. Cambridge: Cambridge University Press.

Bausch, S., & Han, L. (2006). *Nielsen//Net Ratings announces December US search engine rankings*. Resource document. NetRatings, Inc. Retrieved February 28, 2009, from http://www.nielsen-online.com/pr/pr_079123.pdf.

Berneers-Lee, T. (2000). *Weaving the Web: The original design and ultimate destiny of the World Wide Web*. New York: Collins Business.

Bogdat-Brzezinska, A., & Gawrycki, M. F. (2003). *Cyberterroryzm i problemy bezpieczenstwa informacyjnego we wspoczesnym swiecie. Fundacja Studiów Międzynarodowych*. Warszawa: Oficyna Wydawnicza ASPRA-JR.

Bossi, A. (2004). Unwinding in information flow security. *Electronic Notes in Theoretical Computer Science, 99*, 127–154. doi:10.1016/j.entcs.2004.02.006

Broder, A. Z. (2002). A taxonomy of Web search. *ACM SIGIR Forum, 36*(2), 3-10. Retrieved March 25, 2009, from http://www.sigir.org/forum/F2002/broder.pdf.

Bullinga, M. (2001). *In total self/control: Internet 2005-2010. Verschijningsjaar, Nederlands: Ten Hagen Stam Uitgevers*. Den Haag.

Butler, B. S. (2001). Membership size, communication activity and sustainability: A resource-based model of online social structures. *Information Systems Research, 12*(4), 346–362. doi:10.1287/isre.12.4.346.9703

Cahill, K., & Mello, S. V. (2004). *Human security for all: A tribute to Sergio Vieira de Mello*. New York: Fordham University Press.

Cao, F. J., Feito, A., & Touchette, H. (2009). Information and flux in a feedback controlled Brownian ratchet. *Physica A, 388*(1/2), 113–119. doi:10.1016/j.physa.2008.10.006

Cash, J. I., McFarlan, F. W., & McKenney, J. L. (1992). *Corporate information systems management- The issues facing senior executives* (3rd ed.). Homewood, Ill: Business One Irwin.

Castells, M. (2000). *The rise of the network society: The information age: economy, society and culture* (2nd ed., *Vol. 1*). Malden: Blackwell.

Castells, M. (2001). *The Internet galaxy: Reflections on the Internet, business, and society*. Oxford: Oxford University Press.

Caufield, J. (2006). The myth of automated meaning. *International Review of Information Ethics*, 5, 48–62.

Costa, G., Prior, M., & Rogerson, S. (2008). Will the evolution of ICT ethics engage organizational transparency? In Vaccaro, A., Horta, H., & Madsen, P. (Eds.), *Transparency, Information and Communication Technology- Social Responsibility and Accountability in Business and Education* (pp. 31–50). Virginia: Softbound.

Courrier, Y. (2000). Société de l'information et technologies. Report. *United Nations Educational, Scientific and Cultural Organization*. Retrieved April 5, 2009, from http://www.unesco.org/webworld/points_of_views/courrier_1.shtml.

Crowley, M. G. (2006). Cyber crime and biometric authentication- The problem of privacy versus protection of business assets. In *Proceedings of the 4th Australian Information Security Management Conference ECU - School of Computer and Information Science*. Perth: Edith Cowan University. Retrieved March 3, 2009, from http://scissec.scis. ecu.edu.au/conferences2008/proceedings/2006/aism/Crowley%20-%20Cyber%20crime%20 and%20biometric%20authentication%20the%20 problem%20of%20privacy%20versus%20protection%20of%20business%20assets.pdf.

Cuppens, F. (2001). Managing alerts in a multi-intrusion detection environment. In *Proceedings of 17th Annual Computer Security Applications Conference* 2001 (pp. 22-31). New Orleans, LO, USA.

Dantu, R. (2007). Classification of attributes and behaviour in risk management using Bayesian networks. In [New Brunswick, NJ: IEEE.]. *Proceedings of Intelligence and Security Informatics*, 2007, 71–74.

Daoust, M. (2009). *Google's Giant Sandbox.* Resource document. Netbiz. Retrieved March 17, 2009, from http://www.netzbiz.com/Pages. asp?PageName=GGS.

Decker, A. (2008). *Search engines- How trustworthy are they?* Resource document. Trend Micro Inc. Retrieved April 4, 2009, from http://us.trendmicro.com/imperia/md/content/us/pdf/threats/securitylibrary/avar_how_trustworthy_ are_search_engines.

Delichatsios, S. A., & Sonuyi, T. (2005). *Get to know Google ... Because they know you.* Resource document. Massachusetts Institute of Technology. Retrieved April 7, 2009, from http://groups.csail. mit.edu/mac/classes/6.805/student-papers/fall05-papers/google.pdf.

Deudney, D. (2004). Publius before Kant: Federal-Republican security and democratic peace. *European Journal of International Relations*, 10(3), 315–356. doi:10.1177/1354066104045540

DeYoung, C. G., & Spence, I. (2004). Profiling information technology users: En route to dynamic personalization. *Computers in Human Behavior*, 20(1), 55–65. doi:10.1016/S0747-5632(03)00045-1

Ding, W., & Marchionini, G. (1996). A comparative study of Web search service performance. In S. Hardin (Ed.), *Proceedings of the 59th Annual Meeting of the American Society for Information Science* (pp. 136-142). Medford, NJ: Information Today, Inc.

Domingues, M. A., et al. (2008). A platform to support web site adaptation and monitoring its effects: A case study. In P. Pu, D. Bridge, B. Mobasher & F. Ricci (Eds.), *Proceedings of the 2008 ACM Conference on Recommender Systems* (pp. 299-302). Lausanne: École Polytechnique Fédérale de Lausanne, Switzerland.

Drucker, P. F. (1969). *The age of discontinuity: Guidelines to our changing society*. London: Heinemann.

DuCharme, B. (2004). *Googling for XML*. Resource document. O'Reilly XML Web site. Retrieved April 8, 2009, from http://www.xml.com/pub/a/2004/02/11/googlexml.html.

Dupret, G. E., Murdock, V., & Piwowarski, B. (2007). Web search engine evaluation using click-through data and a user model. In *Proceeding of the Workshop on Query Log Analysis: Social and Technological Challenges (WWW '07)*. May 8, Alberta, Canada. Retrieved January 25, 2009, from http://www2007.org/workshops/paper_28.pdf.

Eisenmann, T. R., & Herman, K. (2006). *Google Inc*. Harvard: Harvard Business School Publishing.

Elgesem, D. (2008). Search engines and the problem of transparency. In Bynum, T. W., Murata, K., & Rogerson, S. (Eds.), *ETHICOMP 2007: Glocalisation- Bridging the Global Nature of Information and Communication Technology and the Local Nature of Human Beings* (pp. 150–157). Tokyo: Meiji University, Japan.

Eloff, M. M., & von Solms, S. H. (2000). Information security management: A hierarchical framework for various approaches. *Computers & Security*, *19*(3), 243–256. doi:10.1016/S0167-4048(00)88613-7

European Commission. (1997). Building the European information society for us all: Final policy report of the high-level group of experts. *Office for Official Publications of the European Community*. Resource document. Retrieved April 11, 2009, from http://meritbbs.unimaas.nl/publications/2-hleg.pdf.

European Parliament. (2002). *Directive 2002/21/EC of the European Parliament and of the Council of 7 March 2002 on a common regulatory framework for electronic communications networks and services*. Resource document. Europa. Retrieved March 14, 2009, from http://europa.eu/scadplus/leg/en/lvb/l24216a.htm.

Evans, B. M., & Card, S. K. (2008). Augmented information assimilation: Social and algorithmic web aids for the information long tail. In *Proceedings of the 26th Annual SIGCHI conference on Human Factors and Computing* (pp. 989-998). San Diego: University of California.

Fain, D. C., & Pedersen, J. O. (2006). Sponsored search: A brief history. *Bulletin of the American Society for Information Science and Technology*, *32*, 12–13. doi:10.1002/bult.1720320206

Federal Office for Information Security in Germany. (2008). *Secure information technology-for our society*. Resource document. Federal Office for Information Security in Germany. Retrieved on February 25, 2009, from http://www.bsi.bund.de/english/publications/annualreport/BSI_annual_report_2006-2007.pdf.

Finkelstein, L. (2002). Placing search in context: The concept revisited. *ACM Transactions on Information Systems*, *20*(1), 116–131. doi:10.1145/503104.503110

Finkelstein, S. (2007). *Google spam filtering gone bad*. Resource document. Retrieved April 7, 2009, from http://sethf.com/anticensorware/general/google-spam.php.

Finne, T. (2000). Information systems risk management: Key concepts and business processes. *Computers & Security*, *19*(3), 234–242. doi:10.1016/S0167-4048(00)88612-5

Fishkin, R., & Pollard, J. (2007). *Beginner's guide for search engine optimization*. Resource document. SEOMoz.Org. Retrieved April 5, 2009, from http://www.seomoz.org/article/beginners-guide-to-search-engine-optimization.

Fitzgerald, N. (2008). *Re: [Full-disclosure] Injecting spam into Google web history via I'm feeling lucky queries*. Resource document. Derkeiler. Retrieved April 5, 2009, from http://www.derkeiler.com/Mailing-Lists/Full-Disclosure/2008-04/msg00540.html.

Floridi, L. (2003). Information. In Floridi, L. (Ed.), *The Blackwell guide to the philosophy of computing and information* (pp. 40–61). Oxford, New York: Blackwell. doi:10.1111/b.9780631229193.2003.00006.x

Floridi, L. (2005). Semantic conceptions of information. Resource document. *Sanford Encyclopedia of Philosophy*. Retrieved April 5, 2009, from http://plato.stanford.edu/entries/information-semantic

Floridi, L. (2006). Information technologies and the tragedy of good will. *Ethics and Information Technology, 8*(4), 253–262. doi:10.1007/s10676-006-9110-6

Foucault, M. (1986). *Power/Knowledge: Selected interviews and other writings 1972-1977*. Sussex: The Harvester Press Limited.

Furnas, G. W. (1997). Effective view navigation. In *Proceedings of the SIGCHI conference on Human Factors and Computing* (pp. 367-374). Atlanta: University of Georgia, United States.

Gan, Q., & Suel, T. (2007). Improving Web spam classifiers using link structure. In *AIRWeb '07: Proceedings of the 3rd Int. Workshop on Advers. Inf. Retrieval on the Web* (pp. 17-20). Banff, Alberta, Canada. Retrieved February 10, 2009, from http://airweb.cse.lehigh.edu/2007/papers/paper_124.pdf.

Ganame, A. K., Bourgeois, J., Bidou, R., & Spies, F. (2008). A global security architecture for intrusion detection on computer networks. *Computers & Security, 27*, 30–47. doi:10.1016/j.cose.2008.03.004

Gerhart, S. L. (2004). Do web search engines suppress controversy? *First Monday, 9*(1). Retrieved April 2, 2009, from http://firstmonday.org/htbin/cgiwrap/bin/ojs/index.php/fm/article/view/1111/1031.

Ghemawat, S., Gobioff, H., & Leung, S. (2003). The Google file system. In *SOSP '03: Proceedings of the nineteenth ACM symposium on Operating systems principles* (pp. 29-43). New York: ACM Press.

Glorioso, A. (2008). Ethics on a chip? Some general remarks on DRM, Internet filtering and trusted computing. In T. W. Bynum, M. Calzarossa, I. Lotto & S. Rogerson (Eds.), ETHICOMP 2008: Living, Working and Learning Beyond Technology (pp. 287-297). Mantova: University of Pavia, Italy.

Google. (2006a). *Our philosophy*. Resource document. Google. Retrieved February 20, 2009, from http://www.google.com/intl/en/corporate/tenthings.html.

Google. (2006b). *Webmaster guidelines*. Resource document. Google. Retrieved April 4, 2009, from http://www.google.com/support/webmasters/bin/answer.py?answer=35769.

Google. (2008a). *Security backgrounder: for Google security and compliance products*. Resource document. Google. Retrieved April 5, 2009, from https://www.postini.com/legal/Security_Backgrounder2.pdf.

Google. (2008b). *Content policy management*. Resource document. Google. Retrieved March 17, 2009, from www.google.com/a/help/intl/nl/security/pdf/content_policy_management.pdf.

Google. (2009a). *Google milestones*. Resource document. Google. Retrieved February 23, 2009, from http://www.google.com/intl/en/corporate/history.html.

Google. (2009b). *Company overview*. Resource document. Google. Retrieved February 23, 2009, from http://www.google.com/corporate.

Google. (2009c). *Technology overview*. Resource document. Google. Retrieved February 22, 2009, from http://www.google.com/corporate/tech.html.

Google. (2009d). *Google blog*. Resource document. Google. Retrieved February 22, 2009, from http://googleblog.blogspot.com/.

Gordon, L. A., & Martin, P. L. (2006). Budgeting process for information security expenditures. *Communications of the ACM*, *49*(1), 121–125. doi:10.1145/1107458.1107465

Grimmelmann, J. (2005). *Regulating search?* Resource document. Yale Law School. Retrieved March 14, 2009, from http://james.grimmelmann.net/presentations/2005-12-03-search-engines.pdf.

Grimmelmann, J. (2007). *The structure of search engine law*. Resource document. *University of Iowa College of Law*. Retrieved April 4, 2009, from http://works.bepress.com/cgi/viewcontent.cgi?article=1012&context=james_grimmelmann.

Hawker, N. (2008). *The proposed Google-Yahoo alliance: An anti-trust white paper*. Washington: The American Anti-Trust Institute.

Heise Security. (2009). *Heise Security*. Resource document. Heise. Retrieved February 2, 2009, from http://www.heise.de/security/

Himma, K. E. (2005). Information and intellectual property protection: Evaluating the claim that information should be free. Resource document. *Berkeley Center for Law and Technology*. Retrieved April 5, 2009, from http://repositories.cdlib.org/bclt/lts/12.

Hoffman, D. L., & Novak, T. P. (1998). Bridging the racial divide on the Internet. *Science*, *280*(5362), 390–391. doi:10.1126/science.280.5362.390

Huang, R., & Paturi, R. (2005). *Analysis of the benefits and drawbacks of the PageRank algorithm*. Resource document. University of California. Retrieved February 8, 2009, from http://www.cse.ucsd.edu/~paturi/cse91/Presents/rhuang.pdf.

Hurlbert, W. (2004). *SEO ethics: Which hat to wear*. Resource document. Search Optimization. Retrieved April 4, 2009, from http://www.seochat.com/c/a/Search-Engine-Optimization-Help/SEO-Ethics-Which-Hat-To-Wear/.

I-node. (2005). *Security of the Google search appliances*. Resource document. I-node. Retrieved April 7, 2009, from http://www.i-node.it/documenti/GSA-physical-security.pdf.

Information Week. (2008). *The case of universal search: White paper*. Resource document. Information Week. Retrieved February 14, 2009, from http://www.informationweek.com/whitepaper/Internet/Search/the-case-for-universal-searc-wp1227642995192;jsessionid=0BRM2105ZCVD2QSNDLPCKHSCJUNN2JVN?articleID=50500003.

Introna, L. D., & Nissenbaum, H. (2000). Shaping the Web: Why the politics of search engines matter. *The Information Society*, *16*(3), 169–186. doi:10.1080/01972240050133634

Janse, B. J., & Mullen, T. (2008). Sponsored search: An overview of the concept, history, and technology. *International Journal of Electronic Business*, *6*(2), 114–131. doi:10.1504/IJEB.2008.018068

Jansen, B. J., Booth, D. E., & Spink, A. (2007). Determining the user intent of Web search engine queries. *WWW 2007*. May 8-12, Banff, Alberta, Canada. Retrieved March 3, 2009, from http://www2007.org/posters/poster989.pdf.

Jarvenpaa, S. L., & Staples, D. S. (2001). The use of collaborative media for information sharing: An exploratory study of determinants. *The Journal of Strategic Information Systems*, *18*(1), 151–183.

Jung, B. (2001). *Media, communication and electronic business*. Warsaw: Difin Publishing.

Kaldor, M. (2007). *Human security: Reflections on globalization and intervention*. Cambridge: Polity Press.

Kang, I.-H., & Kim, G. C. (2004). Integration of multiple evidences based on a query type for web search. *Information Processing and Management: An International Journal*, *40*(3), 459–478. doi:10.1016/S0306-4573(03)00053-0

Kashyap, V. (1999). Design and creation of ontologies for environmental information retrieval. In *Proceedings of the 12th Workshop on Knowledge Acquisition, Modelling and Management*. Alberta, Ontario, Canada. Retrieved April 3, 2009 from http://eprints.kfupm.edu.sa/34189/1/34189.pdf.

Kaufman, P. (1995). *New trading systems and methods*. London: Wiley.

Kawamoto, D. (2008). *Study: Fox Interactive tops digital display ad market*. Cnet News. Retrieved April 5, 2009, from http://news.cnet.com/8301-1023_3-10026578-93.html.

Kornai, A. (2008). On the proper definition of information. In T. W. Bynum, M. Calzarossa, I. Lotto & S. Rogerson (Eds.), ETHICOMP 2008: Living, Working and Learning Beyond Technology (pp. 488-495). Mantua: University of Pavia, Italy.

Kunreuther, H. C., & Heal, G. M. (2003). Interdependent security. *Journal of Risk and Uncertainty*, *26*(2/3), 231–249. doi:10.1023/A:1024119208153

Kwon, S. (2007). Common defects in information security management system of Korean companies. *Journal of Systems and Software*, *80*(10), 1631–1638. doi:10.1016/j.jss.2007.01.015

Lakoff, G., & Johnson, M. (1980). *Metaphors we live by*. Chicago, IL: University of Chicago Press.

Lakshminarayana, S. (2009). Categorization of web pages- Performance enhancement to search engine. *Knowledge-Based Systems*, *22*(1), 100–104. doi:10.1016/j.knosys.2008.07.006

Lallana, E. C. (2004). *An overview of ICT policies and e-strategies of select Asian economies*. New Delhi: APDIP.

Lange, J., & Lappe, M. (2007). The role of spatial and temporal information in biological motion perception. *Advances in Cognitive Psychology*, *3*(4), 419–428. doi:10.2478/v10053-008-0006-3

Lastowka, G. (2007). *Google's law*. Working Paper. Rutgers University. Retrieved February 20, 2009, from http://works.bepress.com/lastowka/4.

Lawrence, S., & Giles, C. L. (1998). Searching the World Wide Web. *Science*, *280*, 98–100. doi:10.1126/science.280.5360.98

Li, M., Du, X. Y., & Wang, S. (2005). Learning ontology from relational database. In D. S. Yeung, Z.-Q. Liu, X.-Z. Wang & H. Yan (Eds.), *Proceedings of the 4th International Conference on Machine Learning and Cybernetics* (pp. 3410-3415). Guangzhou: University of Guangzhou, China.

Liddy, E. D. (2003). Automating & evaluating metadata generation. *The Eighth Search Engine Meeting*. April 7-8. Boston, Massachusetts, USA.

Liotta, P. H. (2002). Boomerang effect: The converegence of national and human security. *Security Dialogue*, *33*(4), 473–488. doi:10.1177/0967010602033004007

Lipsman, A. (2003). *ComScore Media Metrix launches breakthrough system to track actual consumer search queries*. Resource document. Retrieved February 2, 2009, from http://www.comscore.com/press/release.asp?id=325.

Livingston, B. (2004). *Google grumbles*. Resource document. eWeek. Retrieved February 17, 2009, from www.eweek.com/article2/0,4149,1530367,00.asp.

Machill, M., et al. (2003). Wegweiser im netz: Qualität und nutzung von Suchmaschinen. In M. Machill & C. Welp (Eds.), Wegweiser im Netz (pp. 13-490). Gütersloh: Bertelsmann Stiftung.

Machlup, F. (1962). *The production and distribution of knowledge in the United States*. Princeton: Princeton University Press.

Manunta, G. (2000). Defining security. [Cranfield: Cranfield Security Centre.]. *Diogenes*, 1.

Martin, W. J. (1995). *The global information society. Brookfield, VT*. Aldershot: Aslib Gower.

McMillan, R. (2006). *Google's binary search helps identify malware*. Resource document. PC World. Retrieved March 17, 2009, from http://www.pcworld.com/article/126371/googles_binary_search_helps_identify_malware.html.

Mesjasz, C. (2004). *Security as a property of social systems*. Resource document. ISA Convention. Retrieved February 25, 2009, from http://www.allacademic.com/meta/p72561_index.html.

Microsoft Security Home Page. (2009). Microsoft Security. Resource document. Microsoft. Retrieved February 20, 2009, from http://www.microsoft.com/security/default.mspx.

Mierzejewska, B. (2008). Barbarians at the gate. In Wunderlinch, W., & Schimd, B. (Eds.), *Die Zukunft der Gutenberg-Galaxis* (pp. 99–116). Bern, Stuttgart, Wien: Haupt Verlag.

Min, P. (2004). *A 3D model search engine*. PhD Thesis. Computer Science. *Princeton University*. Retrieved March 3, 2009, from http://www.cs.princeton.edu/~min/publications/min04.pdf.

Miniwatts Marketing Group. (2009). *Internet world stats*. Resource document. Miniwatts Marketing Group. Retrieved January 5, 2009, from http://www.internetworldstats.com/stats.htm.

Morgenthau, H. J. (1960). *Politics among nations. The struggle for power and peace*. New York: Alfred A. Knopf.

Nickel, J. W. (2007). *Making sense of human rights*. Malden, Massachusetts: Blackwell Publishers.

Nielson, S., Fogarty, S. J., & Wallach, D. S. (2004). *Attacks on local searching tools*. Technical report. Department of Computer Science. Rice University. Retrieved March 17, 2009, from http://seclab.cs.rice.edu/pubs/gdesktop-tr-dec04.pdf.

O'Shea, D. C. (2003). The bloom is off the Google. *Optical Engineering (Redondo Beach, Calif.)*, *42*(4), 894. doi:10.1117/1.1569244

Online Etymology Dictionary. (2001). *Content*. Resource document. Online Etymology Dictionary. Retrieved January 1, 2009, from http://www.etymonline.com/index.php?l=c&p=24.

Organization for Economic Co-operation and Development. (2002). *OECD guidelines for the security of information systems and networks: Towards a culture of security*. Resource document. Retrieved February 2, 2009, from http://www.oecd.org/document/42/0,2340, en_2649_34255_15582250_1_1_1_1,00.html.

Oxford Dictionary. (2008). *Oxford English dictionary*. Oxford: Oxford University Press.

Patterson, C., Shepherd, M., & Watters, C. (2000). An ethical framework: mechanisms for user-enabled choice and normative claims. *INFOETHICS 2000*. Resource document. United Nations Educational Scientific and Cultural Organization, Paris. Retrieved March 8, 2009, from http://web-world.unesco.org/infoethics2000/report_151100.html#conley.

Paulen. A. (2009). Google Adsense Ontology. Resource document. *Enzine*. Retrieved April 5, 2009, from http://ezinearticles.com/?Google-Adsense-Ontology&id=290598.

Perkowitz, M., & Etzioni, O. (2000). Towards adaptive websites: Conceptual framework and case study. *Computer Networks*, *31*(11), 1245–1258. doi:10.1016/S1389-1286(99)00017-1

Physor. (2006). *Google buys a new search algorithm*. Resource document. Retrieved February 7, 2009, from http://www.physorg.com/news63882927.html.

Pinkerton, B. (1994). *Finding what people want: Experiences with the webcrawler*. The Second International WWW Conference Chicago, USA, October 17-20. Retrieved April 11, 2009, from http://www.webir.org/resources/phd/pinkerton_2000.pdf.

Pirolli, P., & Crad, S. K. (1999). Information foraging. *Psychological Review*, *106*, 643–675. doi:10.1037/0033-295X.106.4.643

Poullet, I. (2009). Data protection legislation: What is at stake for our society and democracy? *Computer Law & Security Report*, *25*(3), 211–226. doi:10.1016/j.clsr.2009.03.008

Rieder, B. (2005). Networked control: Search engines and the symmetry of confidence. *International Review of Information Ethics*, *3*(1), 26–32.

Rouvini, J.-D. (2003). Adapting to the user's internet search strategy on small devices. In L. Johnson & E. Andre (Eds.). *International Conference on Intelligent User Interfaces 2003* (pp. 284-286). Miami, Florida, USA.

Rowley, J. (1998). What is information? *Information Services & Use*, *18*(4), 243–254.

Salk, J., & Salk, J. D. (1981). *World populations and human values*. New York: Harper & Row Publishers.

Schlembach, I. (2008). *Reputation stat antivirus-software, URL-filter und blacklisting*. Resource document. SearchSecurity.de. Retrieved April 1, 2009, from http://www.searchsecurity.de/themenbereiche/plattformsicherheit/client-security/articles/120503/.

Schofield, J. (2006). *How does Google envisage the future?* Resource document. The Guardian. Retrieved March 17, 2009, from http://media.guardian.co.uk/newmedia/story/0,1726289,00.html.

SearchIgnite. (2008). *Potential impact of Google-Yahoo! Partnership & cost to marketers*. Resource document. Retrieved February 22, 2009, from http://www.searchignite.com/si/cm/tracking/trackredirect.aspx?siclientid=76&redirecturl.

Seehusen, F., & Stolen, K. (2008). *A method for model driven information flow security*. Report. University of Oslo, Norway. Retrieved March 3, 2009, from http://folk.uio.no/fredrise/publications/4.report-seehusen.pdf.

Shannon, C. E. (1948). A mathematical theory of communication. *The Bell System Technical Journal*, *27*, 379–423, 623–656.

Shen, X., Tan, B., & Zhai, C. (2006). Exploiting personal search history to improve search accuracy. In *Proceedings of 2006 ACM Conference on Research and Development on Information Retrieval- Personal Information Management Workshop (PIM'2006)* (pp. 94-97). Retrieved March 2, 2009, from http://pim.ischool.washington.edu/pim06/files/shen-paper.pdf.

Sherman, C., & Price, G. (2001). *The invisible Web*. Medford, NJ: Information Today, Inc.

Sisson, D. (2004). *Google secrets: How to get a top 10 ranking on the most important search engine in the world*. Redmond, WA: Blue Moose Webworks, Inc.

Sornlertlamvanich, V. Tongchim, S., & Isahara, H. (2007). Evaluation of Web search engines with Thai queries. In *Proceedings of Workshop on NTCIR-6 and EVIA-1, NII, National Center of Sciences* (pp. 17-21). Tokyo: Japan.

Stark, P. B. (2007). The effectiveness of Internet content filters. *A Journal of Law and Policy for the Information Society, 2*(3), 943-979.

Sullivan, D. (2002). *Google tops in search hours ratings*. Resource document. Search Engine Watch. Retrieved February 21, 2009, from http://searchenginewatch.com/sereport/article.php/2164801.

Sullivan, D. (2005). *Search engine sizes*. Resource document. Search Engine Watch. Retrieved March 25, 2009, from http://searchenginewatch.com/2156481.

Swisher, K. (2008). *Microsoft's trojan horse (also Google's): Display advertising*. Resource document. All Things Digital. Retrieved February 22, 2009, from http://kara.allthingsd.com/20080716/microsofts-trojan-horse-also-googles.

Teevan, J., Dumais, S. T., & Horvitz, E. E. (2005). Personalizing search via automated analysis of interests and activites. In *Proceedings of 28th Annual International ACM SIGIR Conference on Research and Development in Information Retrieval* (pp. 449-456). New York: ACM Press.

Teevan, J., Dumais, S. T., & Horvitz, E. (2005). Beyond the commons: Investigating the value of personalizing Web search. In *Proceedings of the Workshop on new Technologies for Personalized Information Access, part of the 10th International Conference on User Modelling (UM '05)* (pp. 84-92). Retrieved March 2, 2009, from http://research.microsoft.com/en-us/um/people/sdumais/pia2005-final.pdf.

Thornburgh, D., & Lin, H. S. (Eds.). (2002). *Youth, pornography and the Internet*. Washington, D.C.: National Academies Press.

Turban, E., McLean, E., & Wetherbe, J. (1996). *Information technology for management: Improving quality and productivity*. New York: John Wiley & Sons.

United Nations. (2008). Human development report 2007/2008. Report. *United Nations*. Retrieved January 5, 2009, from http://hdr.undp.org/en/media/HDR_20072008_EN_Complete.pdf.

United States District Court. (2006a). *Kinderstart.com LLC v. Google Inc. first amended complaint, C 06-2057 RS*. Resource document. United States District Court: Northern District of California. San Jose. Retrieved February 10, 2009, from http://docs.justia.com/cases/federal/district-courts/california/candce/5:2006cv02057/178063/3/0.pdf.

United States District Court. (2006b). *Kinderstart.com LLC v. Google Inc. judgement order, C 06-2057 JF (RS)*. Resource document. United States District Court: Northern District of California. San Jose Division. Retrieved February 10, 2009, from http://docs.justia.com/cases/federal/district-courts/california/candce/5:2006cv02057/178063/43/0.pdf.

Vaccaro, A., & Madsen, P. (2006). Firm information transparency: ethical questions into the information age. In Berleur, J., Numinen, M. I., & Impagliazzo, J. (Eds.), *Social Informatics: An Information Society for All? In Remembrance of Rob Kling* (pp. 145–156). Boston: Springer. doi:10.1007/978-0-387-37876-3_12

van Eijk, N. (2007). Search engines, the new bottleneck for content access. In *Proceedings of International Telecommunications Society ITS 19th European Regional Conference*, 2-5 September 2007. Istanbul, Turkey. Retrieved March 14, 2009, from http://www.itseurope.org/ITS%20CONF/istanbul2007/index.php?page=abstracts.

van Eijk, N. (2009). A converged regulatory model for search engines? *International. Magazine of the Society for Computers and Law*, *19*(6), 1–3.

Wang, W., Meng, W., & Yu, C. (2000). Concept hierarchy based text database categorization in a metasearch engine environment. In Q. Li, Z. M. Ozsoyoglu, R. Wagner, Y. Kambayashi & Y. Zhang (Eds.), *Proceedings of the First International Conference on Web Information Systems Engineering (WISE'00)* (Vol. 1, pp. 283-290). Hong Kong, China.

Wang, Y., & DeWitt, D. J. (2004). Computing PageRank in a distributed Internet search system. In *Proceedings of the 30th VLDB Conference* (pp. 420-431). August 29-September 3, Toronto, Ontario, Canada. Retrieved January 27, 2009, from http://www.vldb.org/conf/2004/RS11P1.PDF.

WebSideStory. (2004). *Google's search referral market share reaches an all-time high*. Resource document. Retrieved February 2, 2009, from http://www.websidestory.com/pressroom/press-releases.html.

Webster, F. (2006). *Theories of the information society* (3rd ed.). London: Routledge.

Wellman, B. (2001). Changing connectivity: A future history of Y2.03K. *Sociological Research Online, 4*(4). Retrieved January 21, 2009, from http://www.socresonline.org.uk/4/4/wellman.html.

Whitman, M. E. (2003). Enemy at the gate: Threats to information security. *Communications of the ACM, 46*(8), 91–95. doi:10.1145/859670.859675

Wielki, J. (2008). The impact of search engines on contemporary organizations- The social and ethical implications. In T. W. Bynum, M. Calzarossa, I. Lotto & S. Rogerson (Eds.), ETHICOMP 2008: Living, Working and Learning Beyond Technology (pp. 769-803). Mantova: University of Pavia, Italy.

World Summit on the Information Society. (2003). *Declaration of principles: Document WSIS-03/GENEVA/DOC/4-E, 12 December*. Resource document. International Telecommunications Union. Retrieved April 5, 2009, from http://www.itu.int/wsis/docs/geneva/official/dop.html.

Zeller, T. J. (2006). A new campaign tactic: manipulating Google data. Resource document. *The New York Times (Late Edition (East Coast))*, 20. Retrieved February 28, 2009, from http://www.nytimes.com/2006/10/26/us/politics/26googlebomb.html.

Zhang, Y., Vasconcelos, W., & Sleeman, D. (2004). Ontosearch: An ontology search engine. In M. Bramer, F. Coenen & T. Allen (Eds.9), *Proceedings of the 24th SGAI International Conference on Innovation Techniques and Applications of Artificial Intelligence* (pp. 58-69). Cambridge, United Kingdom.

Zien, J., et al. (2001). Web query characteristics and their implications on search engines. In *Proceedings of the 10th WWW International Conference*. May 1-5, Hong Kong, Hong Kong. Retrieved January 25, 2009, from http://www10.org/cdrom/posters/1077.pdf.

Zook, M. A. (2005). *The geography of the Internet industry venture capital, dot-coms, and local knowledge (Information Age Series)*. Oxford: Blackwell Publishing.

ENDNOTE

[1]   Deep Web or Dark Matter are also expressions for this concept

Compilation of References

2006/24/EC. (European Union Directive 2006/24/EC of March 2006 on the retention of data generated or processed in connection with the provision of publicly available electronic communications services or of public communication networks and amending Directive 2002/58/EC). *Official Journal of the European Union, L 105*, 56-63.

AARP. (2005). *Designing Web Sites for Older Adults: Heuristics.* Retrieved May 25, 2008 from http://www.aarp.org/olderwiserwired/oww-resources/designing_web_sites_for_older_adults_heuristics.html

Abadi, M. (1998). On SDSI's Linkd Local Name Spaces. *Journal of Computer Security, 6*(1-2), 3–21.

Abelson, H., Ledeen, K., & Lewis, H. (2008). *Blown to Bits: Your Life, Liberty, and Happiness after the Digital Explosion.* Addison Wesley.

Abramowicz, W., Stolarski, P., & Tomaszewski, T. (2007). Reasoning Using Polish Commercial Companies Code Ontology. In Lodder, A. R., & Mommers, L. (Eds.), *Legal Knowledge and Information Systems, JURIX 2007* (pp. 163–164). Amsterdam: IOS Press.

Abran, A., Bourque, P., Dupuis, R., Moore, J. W., & Tripp, L. L. (2004). *Guide to the Software Engineering Body of Knowledge – SWEBOK* (2004 edition). Piscataway, NJ: IEEE Press. Retrieved April 11, 2009 from http://www.swebok.org

Acha, V. (2006). *Open by Design: The role of Design in Open Innovation.* Paper presented at Science & Innovation Analysis Unit at the Department of Trade and Industry (now the Department for Innovation, Universities and Skills). Retrieved April 10, 2009, from http://www.dius.gov.uk/reports_and_publications/~/media/publications/O/Openbydesign

Acharya. (2009). *Multilingual Computing for Literacy and Education Software for the Visually Handicapped.* Retrieved March 20, 2009 from http://acharya.iitm.ac.in/disabilities/tts.php

Achte, S. V. (2006). *Future evolution of search.* Resource document. Internet Search Engine Database. Retrieved February 20, 2009, from http://www.isedb.com/db/articles/1559/1/Future-Evolution-of-Search-/Page1.html.

ACM & IEEE. (2009). *Software Engineering Code of Ethics and Professional Practice.* Retrieved April 11, 2009 from http://www.acm.org/about/se-code

Adams, A., & Sasse, A. (1999). Privacy issues in ubiquitous multimedia environments: Wake sleeping dogs, or let them lie? In *Proceedings of INTERACT'99*, Edinburgh (pp. 214-221).

Adams, A., & Sasse, A. (1999). Taming the wolf in sheep's clothing: privacy in multimedia communications. In *Proceedings of ACM Multimedia'99*, Orlando (pp. 101-107).

Adams, A., & Sasse, A. (2001). Privacy in multimedia communications: Protecting users, not just data. In Blandford, A., & Vanderdonkt, J. (Eds.), *People and Computers XV - Interaction without frontiers. Joint Proceedings of HCI2001* (pp. 49–64).

Agelight, L. L. C. (2001). *Interface Design Guidelines for Users of all Ages.* Retrieved May 25, 2008 from http://www.agelight.com/webdocs/designguide.pdf

Agichtein, E., et al. (2006). Learning user interaction models for predicting web search result preferences. In *Proceedings of the 29th Annual International ACM SIGIR Conference on Research and Development in Information Retrieval* (pp. 3-10). Seattle, WA, USA.

Akdeniz, Y., & Altıparmak, K. (2008). *Internet: Restricted Access A Critical Assessment of Internet Content Regulation and Censorship in Turkey.* Retrieved January 10, 2009, from http://www.cyber-rights.org/reports/internet_restricted_bw.pdf.

Alben, L. (1996). Quality of experience: defining the criteria for effective interaction design. *Interactions (New York, N.Y.), 3,* 11–15. doi:10.1145/235008.235010

Allen, I. E., & Seaman, J. (2008). *Staying the course: Online education in the United States, 2008.* Needham, MA: Babson Survey Research Group & the Sloan Consortium.

Allen, T., & Widdison, R. (1996). Can Computer Make Contracts? *Harvard Journal of Law & Technology, 9*(1).

Almasy, E., & Rick, W. (2000). E-venge of the incumbents: A hybrid model for the Internet economy. *Ivey Business Journal, 64*(5), 5–16.

Almeida, C. (2000). *Contratos.* Coimbra: Almedina. (in Portuguese)

Alsacréations Menu. (2009). *Créer des menus simples en CSS.* Retrieved April 9, 2009 from http://www.alsacreations.com/tuto/lire/574-Creer-des-menus-simples-en-CSS.html

Alsacréations Templates. (2008). *Galerie des Gabarits.* Retrieved April 9, 2009 from http://www.alsacreations.com/static/gabarits/

Alvarez, J. A., Lopez, J. A., & Galvez, F. (2009). *Demonstration of the system.* http://www.ace.ual.es/~jaberme/ict_law/

Alzheimer Europe. (2005). *The Population of People with Dementia in Europe.* Retrieved March 11, 2009 from http://www.dementia-in-europe.eu/?lm2=HIXPJGBKGFTQ

Amazon Web page (2009). Retrieved March 26, 2009 from http://www.amazon.com

American Medical Association. (2009). American Recovery And Reinvestment Act of 2009 (ARRA) [Electronic Version]. Retrieved March 5, 2009 from http://www.ama-assn.org/ama/pub/legislation-advocacy/current-topics-advocacy/hr1-stimulus-summary.shtml.

Anagnostopoulos, I. (2007). Monitoring the evolution of cached content in Google and MSN. In *Proceedings of the 2007 International Conference on the World Wide Web* (pp. 1179-1180). May 8-12, Banff, Alberta, Canada. Retrieved January 22, 2009, from http://www2007.org/posters/poster993.pdf

Andersen, B., & Striukova, L. (2001). *Where Value Resides: Classifying Measuring Intellectual Capital and Intangible Assets.* Birkbeck, University of London.

Anderson, A., & Lockhart, H. (2004). SAML 2.0 profile of XACML. Retrieved April 20, 2009, from http://docs.oasis-open.org/xacml/access_control-xacml-2.0-saml_profile-spec-cd-02.pdf

Anderson, A., & Shain, M. (1991). Risk management. In Caelli, W., Longley, D., & Shain, M. (Eds.), *Information Security Handbook* (pp. 75–127). New York: Stockton Press.

Anderson, R. (2003). Trusted Computing Frequently Asked Questions. Version 1.1. Retrieved April 20, 2009, from http://www.cl.cam.ac.uk/~rja14/tcpa-faq.html

Andrade, F., Novais, P., Machado, J., & Neves, J. (2007). Contracting Agents: legal personality and representation. *Artificial Intelligence and Law, 15*(4). doi:10.1007/s10506-007-9046-0

Andrade, F., Novais, P., Machado, J., & Neves, J. (2008). Software agents in Virtual Organizatiosns: Good Faith and Trust. In Camarinha-Matos, L., & Picard, W. (Eds.), *Pervasive Collaborative Networks.* Springer-Verlag. doi:10.1007/978-0-387-84837-2_40

Andrade, M. D. (1974). *Teoria Geral da Relação Jurídica* (*Vol. 1*). Coimbra Editora. (in Portuguese)

Andrejevic, M. (2007). iSpy: Surveillance and Power in the Interactive Era. Kansas: University of Kansas Press.

Andrews, J. H. (2005). Meaning, knowledge and power in the philosophy of maps. In Harley, J. B. (Ed.), *The new nature of maps. Essays in the history of cartography* (pp. 21–58). Baltimore, MD: The Johns Hopkins University Press.

Angelopoulos, C. J. (2008). Freedom of expression and copyright: the double balancing act. *Intellectual Property Quarterly, 3,* 328–353.

Anonymous, & the American Medical Informatics Association. (2007). *Secondary uses and re-uses of healthcare data: Taxonomy for policy formulation and planning.* Retrieved April 16, 2009, from http://www.amia.org/inside/initiatives/healthdata/2007/amiataxonomyncvhs.pdf.

Anton, A. I., et al. 2. Financial privacy policies and the need for standardization. *Security & Privacy, 2,* 36-45.

Antunes Varela, J. M. (1973). *Das Obrigações em Geral.* Almedina. (in Portuguese)

Areeda, P. (1990). Essential facilities: an epithet in need of limiting principles", *58 Antitrust L. J. 841.*

Armstrong, R., et al. (1995). WebWatcher: A learning apprentice for the World Wide Web. In *AAI Spring Symposium on Information Gathering from Heterogeneous, Distributed Environments* (pp. 6-12). California: Stanford University, United States.

Armstrong, T. K. (2006). Digital Rights Management and the Process of Fair Use. *Harvard Journal of Law & Technology, 20.* Retrieved April 29, 2009, from http://ssrn.com/abstract=885371

Arthritis Foundation. (2008). *Arthritis Prevalence: A Nation in Pain.* Retrieved April 6, 2009 from http://www.arthritis.org/media/newsroom/media-kits/Arthritis_Prevalence.pdf

Article 29 Working Party (2007, January 10). Recommendation 1/2007 on the Standard application for approval of binding corporate rules for the transfer of personal data. Retrieved on June 30, 2009 from http://ec.europa.eu/justice_home/fsj/privacy/docs/wpdocs/2007/wp133_en.doc

Article 29 Working Party (2008, June 24). Working Document Setting up a framework for the structure of Binding Corporate Rules, 1271-00-01/08/EN WP 154. Retrieved on June 30, 2009 from http://ec.europa.eu/justice_home/fsj/privacy/docs/wpdocs/2008/wp154_en.pdf

Article 29 Working Party. (2003, June 3). Working Document: Transfers of personal data to third countries: Applying Article 26(2) of the EU Data Protection Directive to Binding Corporate Rules for International Data Transfers, 11639/02/EN WP 74. Retrieved on June 30, 2009 from http://ec.europa.eu/justice_home/fsj/privacy/docs/wpdocs/2003/wp74_en.pdf

Article 29 Working Party. Working Document on Frequently Asked Questions (FAQs) related to Binding Corporate Rules, 1271-02-02/08/EN WP 155 rev.03, 21 January 2009. Retrieved on June 30, 2009 from http://ec.europa.eu/justice_home/fsj/privacy/docs/wpdocs/2008/wp155_en.pdf

Article, E. C. 29 Working Party (2007). (Opinion 4/2007 on the concept of personal data). Retrieved on June 30, 2009 from http://ec.europa.eu/justice_home/fsj/privacy/docs/wpdocs/2007/wp136_en.pdf

Ascensão, J. de Oliveira (2006). Propriedade Intelectual e Internet. In Direito da Sociedade da Informação, VI, 145-165.

Ascensão, J. de Oliveira (2008). Sociedade da informação e liberdade de expressão. In Direito da Sociedade da Informação, VII, 51-73.

Aura, T. (1998). On the structure of delegation networks. In *Proc. 11th IEEE Computer Security Foundations Workshop* (pp. 14-26). IEEE Computer Society Press.

Australian Broadcasting Corporation v Lenah Game Meats Pty Ltd (2001). HCA63.

Australian Human Right Commission. (2000). *Accessibility of electronic commerce and new service and information technologies for older Australians and people with a disability*. Retrieved April 9, 2009 from http://www.hreoc.gov.au/disability_rights/inquiries/ecom/ecomrep.htm

Autio, E., Sapienza, H. J., & Almeida, J. G. (2000). Effects of age at entry, knowledge intensity, and imitability on international growth. *Academy of Management Journal, 43*(5), 909–924. doi:10.2307/1556419

Backer, D. K., Lopez-Bassols, V., & Marinez, C. (2008). *Open Innovation in a Global Perspective – What do existing Data tell us?* Paper presented at Statistical Analysis of Science, Technology and Industry DSTI/DOC(2008)4. Retrieved March 17, 2009 from http://www.oecd.org/dataoecd/25/38/41885837.pdf

Backer. D., K. & Cervantes, M. (2008). *OECD Business Symposium on Open Innovation*. Paper presented in Global Networks, Copenhagen, Denmark, 2008. Retrieved March 20, 2009 from http://www.oecd.org/document/48/0,3343,en_2649_34273_39858608_1_1_1_1,00.html

Backroad Connections Pty Ltd. (2003). *Privacy issues in online teaching and learning (Version 1.00). Australian Flexible Learning Framework Quick Guide series*. Australian National Training Authority.

Bailey, P., Thomas, P., & Hawking, D. (2007). Does brandname influence perceived search result quality? Yahoo! Google, and WebKumara. In *Proceedings of the 12th Australasian Document Computing Symposium*. Retrieved March 7, 2009, from http://es.csiro.au/pubs/bailey-thomas-hawking-adcs2007.pdf.

Bakari, J. K. (2007). Bridging the gap between general management and technicians- A case study on ICT security in a developing country. *Computers & Security, 26*(1), 44–55. doi:10.1016/j.cose.2006.10.007

Ball, G., & Breese, J. (2000). Emotion and Personality in a Conversational Agent. In Cassel, J., Sullivan, J., Prevost, S., & Churchill, E. (Eds.), *Embodied Conversational Agents*. Cambridge, MA: MIT Press.

Barbagalo, E. (2001). *Contratos Eletrônicos*. São Paulo: Editora Saraiva. (in Portuguese)

Barfield, W. (2005). Issues of law for software agents within virtual environments. *Presence (Cambridge, Mass.), 14*(6). doi:10.1162/105474605775196607

Bar-Ilan, J. (2007). Manipulating search engines algorithm: The case of Google. *Journal of Information. Communication & Ethics in Society, 5*(2/3), 155–166. doi:10.1108/14779960710837623

Barrows, R. C., & Clayton, P. D. (1996). Privacy, confidentiality, and electronic medical records. [American Medical Informatics Association]. *Journal of the American Medical Informatics Association, 3*, 139–148.

Barry, B., & Weaver, O. (2003). *Regions and powers: The structure of international security*. Cambridge: Cambridge University Press.

Bausch, S., & Han, L. (2006). *Nielsen//Net Ratings announces December US search engine rankings*. Resource document. NetRatings, Inc. Retrieved February 28, 2009, from http://www.nielsen-online.com/pr/pr_079123.pdf.

BBSRC. (2006). *Efficiency and Effectiveness of Peer Review Project*. Retrieved April 14, 2009 from http://www.bbsrc.ac.uk/organisation/structures/council/2006/0610_peer_review.pdf

Beauregard, R., Younkin, A., Corriveau, P., Doherty, R., & Salskov, E. (2007). *Assessing the quality of user experience*. Intel Technology Journal.

Bellucci, E., Zeleznikow, J., & Lodder, A. R. (2004). Integrating artificial intelligence, argumentation and game theory to develop an Online Dispute Resolution Environment. In *Proceedings of the 16th IEEE International Conference*.

Bender, S., & Fish, A. (2000). The transfer of knowledge and the retention of expertise: the continuing need to global assignments. *Journal of Knowledge Management, 4*(2), 125–137. doi:10.1108/13673270010372251

Bennett, S. C. (2002). *Arbitration: Essential concepts*. ALM Publishing.

Bentham, J. (1995). *The Panopticon Writings*. London: Verso.

Berne (1886). Berne Convention for the Protection of Literary and Artistic Works.

Berneers-Lee, T. (2000). *Weaving the Web: The original design and ultimate destiny of the World Wide Web*. New York: Collins Business.

Berners-Lee, T., Hendler, J. & Lassila, O. (2001, May). The Semantic Web A new form of Web content that is meaningful to computers will unleash a revolution of new possibilities. *Scientific American*.

Berry, D., & Moss, G. (2005). *On the "Creative Commons": a critique of the commons without commonalty. Is the Creative Commons missing something?* Free Software Magazine.

Besek, J., & Laben, L. (2006). *U.S. Response to Questionnaire on Copyright and Freedom of Expression*. ALAI Study Days, Barcelona, Retrieved April 29, 2009, from http://www.aladda.org/docs/06Barcelona/Quest_USA_en.pdf

Bhattacharjee, Y. (2007). New questions push for more degrees. *Science, 318*, 1052. doi:10.1126/science.318.5853.1052

Bhusate, A., & Pitt, J. (2009). Pervasive Adaptation for Enhancing Quality of Experience. In *Proceedings 2nd PerAda Workshop on Pervasive Adaptation at the AISB Conventions*, Edinburgh. Retrieved from http://www.aisb.org.uk/convention/aisb09/Proceedings/PERADA/FILES/PittJ.pdf

Bhusate, A., Kamara, L., & Pitt, J. (2006). Enhancing the quality of experience in cultural heritage settings. Proc. 1st European Workshop Intelligent Technologies for Cultural Heritage Exploitation. *17th European Conf. on Artificial Intelligence* (pp. 1-13).

Bignami, F. (2007). Protecting Privacy against the Police in the European Union: The Data Retention Directive. *Duke Law School Science, Technology and Innovation Research Paper Series,* Research Paper No. 13.

Bilgi Teknolojileri ve Koordinasyon Dairesi Başkanlığı Web Sitesi (BTK). (n.d.). Information and Communication Technologies Authority Web Site. Retrieved April 5, 2009, from http://www.tk.gov.tr/Kurum_Hakkinda/Kurulus.htm.

Binmore, K. (1992). *Fun and Games: A Text on Game Theory*. D. C. Heath and Company.

Birch, D. (2005, June). *Opening a Branch in Narnia – You have no idea what is going on the virtual world*. Prepared for the 10th Annual Workshop on Economic Heterogeneous Interacting Agents at the Centre for Computational Finance and Economic Agents (CCFEA) and the University of Essex. Retrieved March 1, 2009, from http://digitaldebateblogs.typepad.com/digital_money/Birch_WEHIA.pdf

Birch, D. (2007). A new dawn for digital money. *E-finance & payments. Law & Policy, 1*(5).

Birch, D. (2007). Regulating virtual worlds: current and future issues. *E-Commerce. Law & Policy, 9*(1), 12–13.

Birch, D. (2007). Virtual Money: Money laundering in virtual worlds: risks and reality. *E-finance & payments. Law & Policy, 1*(7).

Birnhack, M. D. (2004). Copyrighting speech: a transatlantic view. In Torremans, P. (Ed.), *Copyright and human rights: freedom of expression, intellectual property, privacy* (pp. 37–62). Kluwer Law International.

Birnhack, M. D. (2006). More or Better? Shaping the Public Domain. In Guibault, L., & Hugenholtz, P. B. (Eds.), *The future of the public domain: identifying the commons in information law* (pp. 59–86). Kluwer Law International.

Bjorneby, S., Topo, P., Cahill, S., Begley, E., Jones, K., & Hagen, I. (2004). Ethical considerations in the ENABLE Project. *Dementia (London), 3*, 297–312. doi:10.1177/1471301204045162

Blackboard (2009). *Privacy policy*. http://www.blackboard.com/Footer/Privacy-Policy.aspx.

Blackburn, R. A. (1998). *Intellectual Property and the Small and Medium Enterprise*. London: Kingston University.

Blacker, F., Crumb, N., & Macdonald, S. (1998). Knowledge, organizations and competition. In Krogh, G., Roos, J., & Kleine, D. (Eds.), *Knowing in Firms: Understanding, managing, and measuring knowledge* (pp. 67–86). London: SAGE Publications Inc.

Blahut, R. E. (1984, February). A Universal Reed-Solomon Decoder. *IBM Journal of Research and Development, 28*.

Blaze, M., Feigenbaum, J., & Lacy, J. (1996). Decentralized trust management. In *Proc. of the 17th Symposium on Security and Privacy* (pp. 164-173). IEEE Computer Society Press.

Blaze, M., Feigenbaum, J., Ioannidis, J., & Keromytis, A. (1999). The KeyNote Trust-Management System Version 2. IETF RFC 2704, September 1999. Retrieved April 20, 2009, from http://www.ietf.org/rfc/rfc2704.txt

Bloodgood, J. M., & Salisbury, W. D. (2001). Understanding the influence of organizational change strategies on information technology and knowledge management strategies. *Decision Support Systems, 31*(1), 55–69. doi:10.1016/S0167-9236(00)00119-6

Boella, G., van der Torre, L., & Verhagen, H. (2008). Introduction to the special issue on normative multiagent systems. *Autonomous Agents and Multi-Agent Systems, 17*, 1–10. doi:10.1007/s10458-008-9047-8

Boer, A., Engers, T. v., & Winkels, R. (2003). *Using ontologies for comparing and harmonizing legislation* (pp. 60–69). ACM.

Bogdat-Brzezinska, A., & Gawrycki, M. F. (2003). *Cyberterroryzm i problemy bezpieczenstwa informacyjnego we wspoczesnym swiecie. Fundacja Studiów Międzynarodowych*. Warszawa: Oficyna Wydawnicza ASPRA-JR.

Bonczek, R. H., Holsapple, C. W., & Whinston, A. B. (1981). *Foundations of decision support systems*. Academic Press.

Bontas, E. P., Mochol, M., & Tolksdorf, R. (2005). *Case Studies on Ontology Reuse*.

Bontis, N. (2002). *World Congress on Intellectual Capital Readings*. Boston: Elsevier Butterworth Heinemann KMCI Press.

Bossi, A. (2004). Unwinding in information flow security. *Electronic Notes in Theoretical Computer Science, 99*, 127–154. doi:10.1016/j.entcs.2004.02.006

Boucher, A. (2007). *Ergonomie web, pour des sites web efficaces* (pp. 207–209). Eyrolles.

Bourcier, D. & de, M. D., Legrand, J. (2005). *Methodological perspectives for legal ontologies building: an interdisciplinary experience.* (pp. 240-241). ACM.

Boyle, J. (1997). *Foucault In Cyberspace: Surveillance, Sovereignty, and Hard-Wired Censors.* Retrieved April 29, 2009, from http://www.law.duke.edu/boylesite/foucault.htm

Braman, S. (2006). Tactical Memory: the Politics of Openness in the Construction of Memory. *First Monday, 11*(7). Retrieved from http://firstmonday.org/issues/issue11_7/braman/index.html.

Brazier, F., Kubbe, O., Oskamp, A., & Wijngaards, N. (2002). Are Law abiding agents realistic? In *Proceedings of the workshop on the Law of Electronic Agents (LEA 2002), CIRSFID, University of Bologna* (pp. 151-155).

Breuker, J., & Boer, A. Hoekstra R & van den Breg K. (2006). Developing content for LKIF: Ontologies and frameworks for legal reasoning. In T.M. van Engers (Ed.), Legal Knowledge and Information Systems. Jurix 2006. IOS Press.

Breuker, J., & Winkels, R. (2004). *Use and reuse of legal ontologies in knowledge engineering and information management.*

Brito, L., Novais, P., & Neves, J. (2003). The logic behind negotiation: from pre-argument reasoning to argument-based negotiation. In *Intelligent agent software engineering* (pp. 137–159). Hershey, PA: Idea Group Publishing.

Broder, A. Z. (2002). A taxonomy of Web search. *ACM SIGIR Forum, 36*(2), 3-10. Retrieved March 25, 2009, from http://www.sigir.org/forum/F2002/broder.pdf.

Brown, H., & Marriott, A. (1999). *ADR Principles and Practice*. Sweet and Maxwell.

Bullinga, M. (2001). *In total self/control: Internet 2005-2010. Verschijningsjaar, Nederlands: Ten Hagen Stam Uitgevers*. Den Haag.

Burk, D. L., & Cohen, J. E. (2001). Fair Use Infrastructure for Copyright Management Systems. *Harvard Journal of Law and Technology, 15*, 41-83. Georgetown Public Law Research Paper No. 239731. Retrieved April 29, 2009, from http://ssrn.com/abstract=1007079

Burn, M. (1999). *A new paradigm for access: the implications of current copyright law reform initiatives*. Presented at the Australian Society of Archivists Annual Conference, Brisbane, Queensland. Retrieved March 20, 2009 from http://www-prod.nla.gov.au/openpublish/index.php/nlasp/article/viewArticle/1106/1369

Butler, B. S. (2001). Membership size, communication activity and sustainability: A resource-based model of online social structures. *Information Systems Research, 12*(4), 346–362. doi:10.1287/isre.12.4.346.9703

Bygrave, L. A. (2003). Digital Rights Management and Privacy. In Becker, E. (Eds.), *Digital Rights Management - Technological, Economic, Legal and Political Aspects* (pp. 418–446). New York: Springer.

C.M. v. Board of Educ. of Union County Regional High School Dist. (2005). 128 Fed.Appx. 876 C.A.3 (N.J.).

Cable Communications Policy Act, 47 U.S.C. § 521 (1984).

Cahill, K., & Mello, S. V. (2004). *Human security for all: A tribute to Sergio Vieira de Mello*. New York: Fordham University Press.

Calster, G. V. (2008). Risk Regulation, EU Law and Emerging Technologies: Smother or Smooth? *Journal of NanoEthics, 2*(1), 61-71. Retrieved February 03, 2009 from http://www.springerlink.com/content/q14jn-1284r4585gg/

Camp, B. T. (2007). The Play's the Thing: A Theory of Taxing Virtual Worlds. *The Hastings Law Journal, 59*(1).

Campbell v MGN (2003) 1 All ER 224

Canadian Standards Association. (2009). *Privacy code*. Retrieved April 12, 2009 from http://www.csa.ca/standards/privacy/code/

Cantador, I., Fernández, M., & Castells, P. (2007). Improving Ontology Recommendation and Reuse in WebCORE by Collaborative Assessments. In *Proceedings of the 1st International Workshop on Social and Collaborative Construction of Structured Knowledge (CKC 2007), at the 16th International World Wide Web Conference (WWW 2007)*. Banff, Canada, May 2007. CEUR Workshop Proceedings, vol. 273.

Cao, F. J., Feito, A., & Touchette, H. (2009). Information and flux in a feedback controlled Brownian ratchet. *Physica A, 388*(1/2), 113–119. doi:10.1016/j.physa.2008.10.006

Carmichael, A. (1999). *Style Guide for the design of interactive television services for elderly viewers*. Retrieved April 6, 2009 from http://www.computing.dundee.ac.uk/projects/UTOPIA/publications/Carmichael%20-%20DesignStyleGuideFinal.pdf

Casablanca Web page (2009). Retrieved March 10, 2009 from www.casablancavideo.com

Casanova, J. M. (2006). E-Money: EU reform of the E-Money Directive: the current state. *E-finance & payments. Law & Policy, 1*(1).

Cash, J. I., McFarlan, F. W., & McKenney, J. L. (1992). *Corporate information systems management- The issues facing senior executives* (3rd ed.). Homewood, Ill: Business One Irwin.

Castells, M. (2000). *The rise of the network society: The information age: economy, society and culture* (2nd ed., Vol. 1). Malden: Blackwell.

Castells, M. (2001). *The Internet galaxy: Reflections on the Internet, business, and society*. Oxford: Oxford University Press.

Caufield, J. (2006). The myth of automated meaning. *International Review of Information Ethics, 5*, 48–62.

Chemerinsky, E. (2002). Balancing Copyright Protections and Freedom of Speech: Why the Copyright Extension Act is Unconstitutional. *Loyola of Los Angeles Law Review, 36*, 83–97.

Chesbrough, H. W. (in press). *Open Innovation: The New Imperative for Creating and Profiting from Technology.* Harvard Business School Press.

Chías, P., & Abad, T. (2006). A GIS in Cultural Heritage based upon multiformat databases and hypermedia personalized queries. *ISPRS Archives, XXXVI-5*, 222–226.

Chías, P., & Abad, T. (2008). Visualising Ancient Maps as Cultural Heritage: A Relational Database of the Spanish Ancient Cartography. In *12th International Conference on Information Visualisation* (pp. 453-457).

Chías, P., & Abad, T. (2008). Las vías de comunicación en la cartografía histórica de la cuenca del Duero: construcción del territorio y paisaje. *Ingeniería Civil, 149*, 79–91.

Children's Online Privacy Reporting Act, 15 U.S.C. §§ 6501-6506 (1998).

Childs, L. N. (1997). *A concrete introduction to Higher Algebra.* Springer.

Chilton, L., Berger, J. E., Melinkovich, P., Nelson, R., Rappo, P. D., & Stoddard, J. (1999). Pediatric Practice Action Group and Task Force on Medical Informatics. Privacy protection of health information: patient rights and pediatrician responsibilities. *Pediatrics, 104*, 973–977.

Choo, C. W. (1996). The Knowing Organization: How organizations use information to construct meaning, create knowledge and make decisions. *International Journal of Information Management, 16*(5), 329–340. doi:10.1016/0268-4012(96)00020-5

Chrissis, M. B., Konrad, M., & Shrum, A. (2003). *CMMI: Guidelines for Process Integration and Product Improvement.* Boston, MA: Addison Wesley.

Cios, K. J., & Moore, G. W. (2002). Uniqueness of medical data mining. *Artificial Intelligence in Medicine, 26*(1), 1–24. doi:10.1016/S0933-3657(02)00049-0

Clark, C. (1996). The Answer to the Machine is in the Machine. In Bernt Hugenholtz, P. (Ed.), *The Future of Copyright in a Digital Environment.* The Hague: Kluwer Law International.

Cohen, J., & Lemley, M. (2001). Patent Scope and Innovation in the software industry. [from http://www.law.georgetown.edu/Faculty/jec/softwarepatentscope.pdf]. *California Law Review, 89*(1), 1–57. Retrieved on June 10, 2009. doi:10.2307/3481172

Coleman, R., & Fishlock, D. (1999). Conclusions and Proposals for Action Arising from the Intellectual Property Research Programme. The Department of Trade and Industry and the Intellectual Property Institute. London: Economics & Social Research Council (ESRC).

Commission of the European Communities. (2005). i2010: Digital Libraries. Brussels.

Commission of the European Communities. (2006). Commission Staff Working Document on the Review of the E-Money Directive (2000/46/EC). *SEC(2006) 1049.* Retrieved April 2, 2009, from http://ec.europa.eu/internal_market/bank/docs/e-money/working-document_en.pdf

Commission Recommendation of 10 April 2008 on the management of intellectual property in knowledge transfer activities and Code of Practice for universities and other public research organisations, 2008/416/EC.

Communications Assistance for Law Enforcement Act, 47 U.S.C. §§ 1001-1021 (1994).

Conklin, D.W. & Tapp, L. (2000). The creative Web: A new model for managing innovation. *Ivey Business Journal, 64*(5).

Consulting, D. (2001). *Collaborative Knowledge Networks: Driving Workforce Performance through Web-Enabled Communities.* A Viewpoint by Deloitte Consulting and Deloitte & Touche. Retrieved March 20, 2009 from http://www.ickn.org/documents/eview.pdf

Convention for the Protection of Human Rights and Fundamental Freedoms as amended by Protocol No.11. Rome, 4.XI. 1950. Retrieved Nov. 25, 2008 from http://conventions.coe.int/treaty/EN/Treaties/

Corcho, O., Fernández-López, M., & Gómez-Pérez, A. (2003). Methodologies, tools and languages for building ontologies. Where is their meeting point? *Data & Knowledge Engineering, 46*(1), 41–64. doi:10.1016/S0169-023X(02)00195-7

Cornford, T., & Klecun-Dabrowska, E. (2001). Ethical perspectives in evaluation of telehealth. *Cambridge Quarterly of Healthcare Ethics, 10*(2), 161–169. doi:10.1017/S0963180101002079

Costa, G., Prior, M., & Rogerson, S. (2008). Will the evolution of ICT ethics engage organizational transparency? In Vaccaro, A., Horta, H., & Madsen, P. (Eds.), *Transparency, Information and Communication Technology- Social Responsibility and Accountability in Business and Education* (pp. 31–50). Virginia: Softbound.

Council Conclusions of 20 November 2008 on the development of legal offers of online cultural and creative content and the prevention and combating of piracy in the digital environment, 2008/C 319/06.

Council Conclusions on the Digitisation and Online Accessibility of Cultural Material, and Digital Preservation, 2006/C 297/01.

Council Directive 2006/112/EC of 28 November 2006 on the common system of value added tax.

Council Directive 2006/138/EC of 19 December 2006 amending Directive 2006/112/EC on the common system of value added tax as regards the period of application of the value added tax arrangements applicable to radio and television broadcasting services and certain electronically supplied services.

Council Directive 93/13/EEC of 5 April 1993 on unfair terms in consumer contracts.

Council Directive 93/42/EEC of 14 June 1993. Retrieved June 15, 2009, from http://eur-lex.europa.eu/LexUriServ/LexUriServ.do?uri=CELEX:31993L0042:EN:HTML

Council of Europe. (2003). Convention for the protection of human rights and fundamental freedoms as amended by protocol No.11 with protocol nos. 1,4,6,7,12 and 13.

Courrier, Y. (2000). Société de l'information et technologies. Report. *United Nations Educational, Scientific and Cultural Organization*. Retrieved April 5, 2009, from http://www.unesco.org/webworld/points_of_views/courrier_1.shtml.

Cowan, R. & Harison, E. (2001). Intellectual property rights in a knowledge-based economy. *MERIT- Infonomics research Memorandum series*, 2001-027.

Coyle, K. (2003, November). The Technology of Rights: Digital Rights Management. Retrieved April 20, 2009, from http://www.kcoyle.net/drm_basics.pdf

Coyne, K. P., & Nielsen, J. (2002) *Web Usability for Senior Citizens - design guidelines based on usability studies with people age 65 and older*. Nielsen Norman Group. Retrieved May 25, 2008 from http://www.useit.com/alertbox/seniors.html

Craig, W. J. (2001). *Taxation of E-Commerce – Fiscal regulation of the Internet*. Tolley LexisNexis.

Crowley, M. G. (2006). Cyber crime and biometric authentication- The problem of privacy versus protection of business assets. In *Proceedings of the 4th Australian Information Security Management Conference ECU - School of Computer and Information Science*. Perth: Edith Cowan University. Retrieved March 3, 2009, from http://scissec.scis.ecu.edu.au/conferences2008/proceedings/2006/aism/Crowley%20-%20Cyber%20crime%20and%20biometric%20authentication%20the%20problem%20of%20privacy%20versus%20protection%20of%20business%20assets.pdf.

Cuppens, F. (2001). Managing alerts in a multi-intrusion detection environment. In *Proceedings of 17th Annual Computer Security Applications Conference* 2001 (pp. 22-31). New Orleans, LO, USA.

Curry, M. R. (2004). The Profiler's Question and the Treacherous Traveler: Narratives of Belonging in Commercial Aviation. *Surveillance & Society, 1*(4), 475–499.

Dakin, K. (2005). Are Developers Morally Challenged? In R. H. Thyler & M. Dorfman (Eds.) Software Engineering Volume 1: The Development Processes (3rd ed.). IEEE Computer Society.

Damianou, N., Dulay, N., Lupu, E. & Sloman, M. (2001). The Ponder policy specification language. *POLICY01*, 18-38.

Daniel, E. M., & Grimshaw, D. J. (2002). An exploratory comparison of electronic commerce adoption in large and small enterprises. *Journal of Information Technology, 17*(3), 133–147. doi:10.1080/0268396022000018409

Daniel, E., Wilson, H., & Myers, A. (2002). Adoption of E-commerce by SMEs in the UK. *International Small Business Journal, 20*(3), 253–270. doi:10.1177/0266242602203002

Dantu, R. (2007). Classification of attributes and behaviour in risk management using Bayesian networks. In [New Brunswick, NJ: IEEE.]. *Proceedings of Intelligence and Security Informatics, 2007*, 71–74.

Daoust, M. (2009). *Google's Giant Sandbox.* Resource document. Netbiz. Retrieved March 17, 2009, from http://www.netzbiz.com/Pages.asp?PageName=GGS.

Darin, S. (2008). M-Commerce: compras con el Celular. Retrieved March 26, 2009 from http://www.villesnumeriques.org/rvn/bc_doc.nsf/0/20e937de41b0bd79c12573c4006e4cfc/$File/Commerce_por_celular.doc

Davara, M. A. (2008). *Manual de Derecho Informático.* Spain: Thomson-Aranzandi.

Davenport, T. H., & Prusak, L. (1998). *Working knowledge: How organizations manage what they know.* Boston: Harvard Business School Press.

Davies, G., & Trigg, G. (2006). Being Data Retentive: A Knee Jerk Reaction. *Communications Law, 11*(1), 18–21.

de Bruijn, J., Martın-Recuerda, F., Manov, D. & Ehrig, M. (2003). *D4.2.1 State-of-the-art survey on Ontology Merging and Aligning.*

de Fillon, F. (1997). *A.F.D.I.T. sous la direction de De Bellefonds. Internet Saisi Par le Droit.* Editions des Parques.

de Hoekstra, S., Winkels, R., Maat, R., & Kollar, E. (2008). MetaVex: Regulation Drafting meets the Semantic Web. In *Computable Models of the Law. Languages, Dialogues, Games, Ontologies* (LNCS 4884). Fitterer, R., Greiner, U. & Stroh, F. (2008). Towards Facilitated Reuse of Ontology Results from European Research Projects – a Case Study. In *Proceedings of the 16th European Conference on Information Systems (ECIS).*

De Jong, J. P. J., Vanhaverbeke, W., Kalvet, T., & Chesbrough, H. (2008). *Policies for Open Innovation: Theory, Framework and Cases.* Research project funded by VISION Era-Net, Helsinki: Finland. Retrieved March 25, 2009 from http://www.eurosfaire.prd.fr/7pc/doc/1246020063_oipaf_final_report_2008.pdf

De Redish, J., & Chisnell, D. (2004). *Designing Web Sites for Older Adults: A Review of Recent Literature.* Retrieved May 25, 2009 from http://assets.aarp.org/www.aarp.orog_/articles/research/oww/AARP-LitReview2004.pdf

De Seta, C. (1996). L'iconografia urbana in Europa dal XV al XVIII secolo. In *Città d'Europa. Iconografia e vedutismo dal XV al XIX secolo* (pp. 11–48). Napoli: Electa.

de Werra, J. (2001). Le regime juridique des mesures techniques de protection des oeuvres selon les Traités de l'OMPI, le Digital Millennium Copyright Act, les Directives Européennes et d'autres legislations (Japon, Australie). *Revue Internationale du Droit d'Auteur, 189*, 66–213.

Decision (2002/16/EC) of 27 December 2001 on standard contractual clauses for the transfer of personal data to third countries under the Directive (OJ 2002 L6/52). Retrieved on June 30, 2009 from http://eur-lex.europa.eu/LexUriServ/LexUriServ.do?uri=OJ:L:2002:006:0052:0062:EN:PDF

Decision 2001/497/EC of 15 June 2001 on standard contractual clauses for the transfer of personal data to third countries under the Directive (OJ 2001 L181/19). Retrieved on June 30, 2009 from http://eur-lex.europa.eu/LexUriServ/LexUriServ.do?uri=OJ:L:2001:181:0019:0031:EN:PDF

Decision 2004/915/EC of 27 December 2004 amending Decision 2001/497/EC as regards the introduction of an alternative set of standard contractual clauses for the transfer of personal data to third countries (OJ 2004 L385/74). Retrieved on June 30, 2009 from http://eur-lex.europa.eu/LexUriServ/LexUriServ.do?uri=OJ:L:2004:385:0074:0084:EN:PDF

Decker, A. (2008). *Search engines- How trustworthy are they?* Resource document. Trend Micro Inc. Retrieved April 4, 2009, from http://us.trendmicro.com/imperia/md/content/us/pdf/threats/securitylibrary/avar_how_trustworthy_are_search_engines.

Declaration of Helsinki (Sixth revision). (2008). Retrieved June 15, 2009, from http://www.wma.net/e/policy/pdf/17c.pdf

Delichatsios, S. A., & Sonuyi, T. (2005). *Get to know Google... Because they know you.* Resource document. Massachusetts Institute of Technology. Retrieved April 7, 2009, from http://groups.csail.mit.edu/mac/classes/6.805/student-papers/fall05-papers/google.pdf.

Dell Computer Web page (2009). Retrieved March 10, 2009 from http://www.dell.com

Despres, S., & Szulman, S. (2004). Construction of a Legal Ontology from a European Community Legislative Text. In *Legal Knowledge and Information Systems. Jurix 2004: The Seventeenth Annual Conference* (pp. 79-88).

Deudney, D. (2004). Publius before Kant: Federal-Republican security and democratic peace. *European Journal of International Relations, 10*(3), 315–356. doi:10.1177/1354066104045540

DeYoung, C. G., & Spence, I. (2004). Profiling information technology users: En route to dynamic personalization. *Computers in Human Behavior, 20*(1), 55–65. doi:10.1016/S0747-5632(03)00045-1

DG Internal Market. (2004). Application of the E-money Directive to mobile operators. Retrieved April 2, 2009, from http://ec.europa.eu/internal_market/bank/docs/e-money/2004-05-consultation_en.pdf

Díez Estella, F. (2003, Apr-Jun). La doctrina del abuso en los mercados conexos: del "monopoly leveraging" a las "essential facilities." *Revista de Derecho Mercantil, 248*.

Díez Estella, F. (2003, Mar-Apr). Los objetivos del Derecho antitrust. *Gaceta Jurídica de la Unión Europea y de la Competencia, 224*.

Díez Estella, F. (2006). Abusos mediante precios: los precios excesivos. In Pons, M. (Ed.), *El abuso de posición de dominio*. Fundación Rafael del Pino.

Díez Estella, F., & Baches, S. (2006, Apr-Jun). La aplicación del derecho "antitrust" al ejercicio unilateral de los derechos de propiedad intelectual e industrial: el estado de la cuestión en la Unión Europea y en los EE.UU. *Revista de Derecho Mercantil, 260*.

Diffie, W., & Hellman, M. E. (1976). New directions in cryptography. *IEEE Transactions on Information Theory, 22*(6), 644–654. doi:10.1109/TIT.1976.1055638

Dignum, F. (2001). *Agents, markets, institutions, and protocols* (pp. 98–114). The European AgentLink Perspective.

Ding, W., & Marchionini, G. (1996). A comparative study of Web search service performance. In S. Hardin (Ed.), *Proceedings of the 59th Annual Meeting of the American Society for Information Science* (pp. 136-142). Medford, NJ: Information Today, Inc.

Ding, Y., Lonsdale, D., Embley, D. W., & Xu, L. (2007). *Generating ontologies via language components and ontology reuse*.

Directive 2002/58/EC of the European Parliament and of the Council of 12 July 2002. Retrieved June 15, 2009, from http://eur-lex.europa.eu/LexUriServ/LexUriServ.do?uri=CELEX:32002L0058:EN:HTML

Directive 2004/18/EC of the European Parliament and of the Council of 31 March 2004. Retrieved June 15, 2009, from http://eur-lex.europa.eu/LexUriServ/LexUriServ. do?uri=CELEX:32004L0018:EN:HTML

Directive 2006/24/EC of the European Parliament and of the Council of 15 March 2006. Retrieved June 15, 2009, from http://eur-lex.europa.eu/LexUriServ/LexUriServ. do?uri=CELEX:32006L0024:EN:HTML

Directive 2006/95/EC of the European Parliament and of the Council of 12 December 2006. Retrieved June 15, 2009, from http://eur-lex.europa.eu/LexUriServ/ LexUriServ.do?uri=OJ:L:2006:374:0010:0019:EN:PDF

Directive 95/46/EC of the European Parliament and of the Council of 24 October 1995 on the protection of individuals with regard to the processing of personal data and on the free movement of such data. Retrieved on April 9, 2009 from http://www.cdt.org/privacy/eudirective/ EU_Directive_.html.

Doherty, B. (2001). Just What are Essential Facilities? *CMLR, 38.*

Domingues, M. A., et al. (2008). A platform to support web site adaptation and monitoring its effects: A case study. In P. Pu, D. Bridge, B. Mobasher & F. Ricci (Eds.), *Proceedings of the 2008 ACM Conference on Recommender Systems* (pp. 299-302). Lausanne: École Polytechnique Fédérale de Lausanne, Switzerland.

Doran, P. (2006). *Ontology reuse via ontology modularisation.*

Dougherty, C., Lastowka, G. (2007). Copyright: Copyright issues in virtual economies. *E-Commerce Law & Policy, 9*(5).

Dowe, D. L., & Hajek, A. R. (1997). A computational extension to the Turing Test [Tech. Rep. #97/322]. Dept Computer Science, Monash University, Melbourne. France Presse. (2008, July). Spain's Telecinco wins lawsuit against YouTube. Inquirer.net. Godin, S. (2007). Please don't buy this book. Seth Godin Blog.

Downes, L., & Mui, C. (1999). *Aplicaciones Asesinas: Estrategias digitales para dominar el mercado.* Barcelona: Granica.

DPRL. (1998, November 13). The Digital Property Rights Language, Manual and Tutorial - XML Edition, Version 2.00. Retrieved April 20, 2009, from http://xml.coverpages.org/DPRLmanual-XML2.html

Dritsas, S., Gymnopoulos, L., Karyda, M., Balopoulos, T., Kokolakis, S., Lambrinoudakis, C., & Katsikas, S. (2006). A knowledge-based approach to security requirements for e-health applications. eJETA.org Special Issue.

Driver's Privacy Protection Act. 18 U.S.C. § 2721 et. seq. (1994). eCollege (2009). Retrieved April 17, 2009 from http://www.ecollege.com/Privacy_Policy.learn

Drucker, P. F. (1969). *The age of discontinuity: Guidelines to our changing society.* London: Heinemann.

DuCharme, B. (2004). *Googling for XML.* Resource document. O'Reilly XML Web site. Retrieved April 8, 2009, from http://www.xml.com/pub/a/2004/02/11/ googlexml.html.

Dupret, G. E., Murdock, V., & Piwowarski, B. (2007). Web search engine evaluation using click-through data and a user model. In *Proceeding of the Workshop on Query Log Analysis: Social and Technological Challenges (WWW '07).* May 8, Alberta, Canada. Retrieved January 25, 2009, from http://www2007.org/workshops/ paper_28.pdf.

EC e-Inclusion program (2008). *Europe's Information Society Thematical Portal – eInclusion Program.* Retrieved April 9, 2009 from http://ec.europa.eu/information_society/activities/einclusion/policy/ageing/index_en.htm

Eden, S. (2005). VAT on Electronic Services Directive 2002/38/EC – Amending VAT Law for Electronic Transactions: A Simple Choice for a Simple Tax? In Edwards, L. (Ed.), *The New Legal Framework for E-Commerce in Europe* (pp. 203–238). Oxford: Hart Publishing.

Eecke, P. V., & Truyens, M. (2008). Recent Events in EU Internet Law. *Journal of Internet Law, 11*(12), 32–34.

eHealth Ontology Project. (n.d.). Retrieved December 20, 2008, from http://www.ehealthserver.com/ontology

Eisenmann, T. R., & Herman, K. (2006). *Google Inc.* Harvard: Harvard Business School Publishing.

Eldred v. Ashcroft, 537 U.S. 186 (2003).

Electronic Communications Privacy Act, 18 U.S.C. § 2510 (1986).

Elgesem, D. (2008). Search engines and the problem of transparency. In Bynum, T. W., Murata, K., & Rogerson, S. (Eds.), *ETHICOMP 2007: Glocalisation- Bridging the Global Nature of Information and Communication Technology and the Local Nature of Human Beings* (pp. 150–157). Tokyo: Meiji University, Japan.

Elias, L., & Gerard, J. (1991). *Formation of the contract by Electronic Data Interchange.* Commission of the European Communities.

Ellison, C., Frantz, B., Lampson, B., Rivest, R., Thomas, B., & Ylonen, T. (1999, September). SPKI certificate theory. IETF RFC 2693. Retrieved April 20, 2009, from http://www.ietf.org/rfc/rfc2693.txt

Eloff, M. M., & von Solms, S. H. (2000). Information security management: A hierarchical framework for various approaches. *Computers & Security, 19*(3), 243–256. doi:10.1016/S0167-4048(00)88613-7

empirica & Work Research Center (2008*). MeAC - Measuring Progress of eAccessibility in Europe.* Retrieved April 9, 2009 from http://www.eaccessibility-progress.eu/

EPCC. (2009). *MSc in High Performance Computing.* Retrieved April 14, from http://www.ukhec.ac.uk/publications/ukhec_issue3.pdf

EPSRC & CMS. (2004). *An International Review of UK Research in Mathematics.* Retrieved April 13, 2009 from http://www.epsrc.ac.uk/AboutEPSRC/IntRevs/2003MathsIR/default.htm

EPSRC & the Deutsche Forschungsgemeinschaft (DFG). (2005). *International Review of Research Using High Performance Computing in the UK.* Retrieved June 28, 2009 from http://www.epsrc.ac.uk/CMSWeb/Downloads/Other/HPCInternationalReviewReport.pdf

EPSRC & The Royal Academy of Engineering. (2004). *The Wealth of a Nation: An Evaluation of Engineering Research in the United Kingdom.* Retrieved April 5, 2009 from http://www.epsrc.ac.uk/AboutEPSRC/IntRevs/2004EngIR/InternationalReviewData.htm

EPSRC. (2006). *International Perceptions of the UK Research Base in Information and Communications Technologies.* Retrieved April 5, 2009 from http://www.epsrc.ac.uk/AboutEPSRC/IntRevs/2006ICTIR/Report.htm

EPSRC. (2009). *Results of EPSRC Peer Review Survey.* Retrieved April 14, 2009 from http://www.epsrc.ac.uk/CMSWeb/Downloads/Other/PeerReviewSurveyReport.pdf

Erdoğan, T. (2007). Prime Minister Recep Tayyip Erdoğan's Addressing to the Nation, 30/01/2007. Retrieved April 06, 2009, from http://www.akparti.org.tr/haber.asp?haber_id=15449

Erlich, Z., & Aviv, R. (2007). Open source software: strengths and weaknesses. In St Amant, K., & Still, B. (Eds.), *Handbook of Research on Open Source Software* (pp. 184–196). Hershey, PA: Information Science Reference.

Ess, C. (2006). Ethical pluralism and global information ethics. *Ethics and Information Technology, 8*(4), 215–226. doi:10.1007/s10676-006-9113-3

EU(2004). Directive 2004/48/EC of the European Parliament and of the Council of 29 April 2004 on the enforcement of intellectual property rights.

EurLex. (n.d.). *Council Directive 91/250/EEC of 14 May-1991 on the legal protection of computer programs.* Retrieved on June 10, 2009, from http://eur-lex.europa.eu/smartapi/cgi/sga_doc?smartapi!celexapi!prod!CELEXnumdoc&numdoc=31991L0250&model=guichett&lg=en

Europa.eu. (2009). *Activities of the European Union, Summaries of legislation, Information Society.* Retrieved April 10, 2009 from http://europa.eu/scadplus/leg/en/s21012.htm

European Commission suggests UK's Data Protection Act is deficient (2004, July 15). *OUT-LAW News.* Retrieved on June 30, 2009 from http://www.out-law.com/page-4717

European Commission. (1997). Building the European information society for us all: Final policy report of the high-level group of experts. *Office for Official Publications of the European Community.* Resource document. Retrieved April 11, 2009, from http://meritbbs.unimaas.nl/publications/2-hleg.pdf.

European Parliament and Council Directive 2001/29 of 22 May 2001 on the harmonisation of copyright and related rights in the Information Society. Copyright Directive.

European Parliament. (2002). *Directive 2002/21/EC of the European Parliament and of the Council of 7 March 2002 on a common regulatory framework for electronic communications networks and services.* Resource document. Europa. Retrieved March 14, 2009, from http://europa.eu/scadplus/leg/en/lvb/l24216a.htm.

European Patent Office. (n.d.) Convention on the Grant Of European Patents (European Patent Convention). Retrieved on June 12, 2009, from http://www.epo.org/patents/law/legal-texts/html/epc/1973/e/ma1.html

European, E. G. E. Group in ethics in science and new technology. (1999). Ethical issues of health care in the information society. Retrieved December 7, 2008, from http://ec.europa.eu/european_group_ethics/docs/avis13_en.pdf

EuroRec Institute. (n.d.). European Institute for Health Records. Retrieved April 16, 2009, from http://www.eurorec.org/

Eurostats (2006). *Eurostat News Release. Internet usage in the EU25.* Retrieved April 6, 2009 from http://epp.eurostat.ec.europa.eu/pls/portal/docs/PAGE/PGP_PRD_CAT_PREREL/PGE_CAT_PREREL_YEAR_2006/PGE_CAT_PREREL_YEAR_2006_MONTH_11/4-10112006-EN-AP.PDF

Evans, B. M., & Card, S. K. (2008). Augmented information assimilation: Social and algorithmic web aids for the information long tail. In *Proceedings of the 26th Annual SIGCHI conference on Human Factors and Computing* (pp. 989-998). San Diego: University of California.

Eysenbach, G. (2001). What is E-Health? *Journal of Medical Internet Research, 3*(2), 20. doi:10.2196/jmir.3.2.e20

Faculty of Health Sciences, University of Sydney. (2004). Teaching and learning on-line: Privacy management. Retrieved April 17, 2009 from http://www.fhs.usyd.edu.au/staff/acad_docs/tlprivacy.pdf

Fain, D. C., & Pedersen, J. O. (2006). Sponsored search: A brief history. *Bulletin of the American Society for Information Science and Technology, 32*, 12–13. doi:10.1002/bult.1720320206

Fair Credit Reporting Act, 15 U.S.C. § 1681 et seq. (1970).

Fairfield, J. (2005). Virtual Property. *Boston University Law Review 85,* 1047; Indiana Legal Studies Research Paper Number 35. Retrieved March 1, 2009, from http://ssrn.com/abstract=807966

Family Education Rights and Privacy Act (FERPA), 20 U.S.C. § 1232g (1974).

Faramarz, D. (2001). E-business e-commerce evolution: Perspective and strategy. *Managerial Finance, 27*(7), 16–18. doi:10.1108/03074350110767268

Farchy, J. (2004). *Seeking alternative economic solutions for combating piracy.* Retrieved April 29, 2009, from http://www.serci.org/2004/farchy.pdf

Federal Office for Information Security in Germany. (2008). *Secure information technology- for our society.* Resource document. Federal Office for Information Security in Germany. Retrieved on February 25, 2009, from http://www.bsi.bund.de/english/publications/annualreport/BSI_annual_report_2006-2007.pdf.

Federal Trade Commission Protecting America's Consumers. (2004). Retrieved on March 22, 2007 from http://www.theiia.org/chapters/index.cfm/view.resources/cid/90.

Federal Trade Commission Protecting America's Consumers. (2005). Retrieved on March 22, 2007 from http://www.ftc.gov/privacy/privacyinitiatives/promises.htm

Feiler, L. (2008). *The Data Retention Directive*. European and International Technology Law Seminar: Intellectual Property Rights, Information Technology Law, Biotechnology Law. Retrieved from www.rechtsprobleme.at/doks/feiler-DataRetentionDirective.pdf

Felliu, S. (2003). *Intelligent Agents and Consumer Protection*. Retrieved from http://www.eclip.org/documentsII/elecagents/consumer_protection.pdf

Fernandes, L. (1996). Teoria Geral do Direito Civil (Vols. 1 & 2, 2nd ed.) Lex, Lisboa (in Portuguese).

Feste, K. A. (1991). *Plans for peace*. Greenwood Publishing Group.

Fidgeon, T. (2006) *Usability for Older Web Users*. Report from WebCredible Group, Retrieved May 25, 2008 from http://www.webcredible.co.uk/user-friendly-resources/web-usability/older-users.shtml

Fifth Annual BSA and IDC Global Software Piracy Study. (2008). Crime Statistics: Software piracy rate (most recent) by country. Retrieved from http://www.nationmaster.com/graph/cri_sof_pir_rat-crime-software-piracy-rate

Fillis, I., & Wagner, B. (2005). E-business development - An exploratory investigation of the small firm. *International Small Business Journal, 23*(6), 604–634. doi:10.1177/0266242605057655

Financial Modernization Act, 15 U.S.C. § 6803 (1999).

Fine, F. (2002). NDC / IMS: A Logical Application of Essential Facilities Doctrine. *European Competition Law Review, 23*(9).

Finkelstein, L. (2002). Placing search in context: The concept revisited. *ACM Transactions on Information Systems, 20*(1), 116–131. doi:10.1145/503104.503110

Finkelstein, S. (2007). *Google spam filtering gone bad*. Resource document. Retrieved April 7, 2009, from http://sethf.com/anticensorware/general/google-spam.php.

Finne, T. (2000). Information systems risk management: Key concepts and business processes. *Computers & Security, 19*(3), 234–242. doi:10.1016/S0167-4048(00)88612-5

Fishkin, R., & Pollard, J. (2007). *Beginner's guide for search engine optimization*. Resource document. SEOMoz.Org. Retrieved April 5, 2009, from http://www.seomoz.org/article/beginners-guide-to-search-engine-optimization.

Fitzgerald, N. (2008). *Re: [Full-disclosure] Injecting spam into Google web history via I'm feeling lucky queries*. Resource document. Derkeiler. Retrieved April 5, 2009, from http://www.derkeiler.com/Mailing-Lists/Full-Disclosure/2008-04/msg00540.html.

Fleet, Ch. (2007). Digital Approaches to Cartographic Heritage: The Thessaloniki Workshop. *Imago Mundi, 59*(1), 100–104. doi:10.1080/03085690600997894

Floridi, L. (2003). Information. In Floridi, L. (Ed.), *The Blackwell guide to the philosophy of computing and information* (pp. 40–61). Oxford, New York: Blackwell. doi:10.1111/b.9780631229193.2003.00006.x

Floridi, L. (2005). Semantic conceptions of information. Resource document. *Sanford Encyclopedia of Philosophy*. Retrieved April 5, 2009, from http://plato.stanford.edu/entries/information-semantic

Floridi, L. (2006). Information technologies and the tragedy of good will. *Ethics and Information Technology, 8*(4), 253–262. doi:10.1007/s10676-006-9110-6

Forlizzi, J., & Battarbee, K. (2004). Understanding experience in interactive systems. In *DIS '04: Proceedings of the 5th conference on Designing Interactive Systems* (pp. 261-268). ACM.

Foster, I., Kesselman, C., & Tuecke, S. (2001). The anatomy of the grid-enabling scalable virtual organizations. *International Journal of High Performance Computing Applications, 15*(3), 200–222. doi:10.1177/109434200101500302

Foucault, M. (1977). *Discipline and Punish: The Birth of the Prison*. New York: Vintage.

Foucault, M. (1986). *Power/Knowledge: Selected interviews and other writings 1972-1977*. Sussex: The Harvester Press Limited.

Fowler, M. (2000). *The New Methodology* (Original). Retrieved April 14, from http://www.martinfowler.com/articles/newMethodologyOriginal.html#ShouldYouGoLight

Fox, E. M. (1986). *Monopolization and Dominance in the United States and the European Community: Efficiency, Opportunity and Fairness*, 61 NOTRE DAME L. REV. 981.

Francis, D. (2002). Privacy and anonymity: Perceptions and expectations of online students. In G. Richards (Ed.), *Proceedings of World Conference on E-learning in Corporate, Government, Healthcare, and Higher Education 2002* (pp. 1473-1476).

Fredberg, T., Elmquist, M., & Ollila, S. (2008). *Managing Open Innovation -Present Findings and Future Directions* (VINNOVA Report VR 2008:02). VINNOVA - Verket för Innovationssystem/Swedish Governmental Agency for Innovation Systems. Retrieved February 20, 2009 from http://www.openinnovation.eu/download/vr-08-02.pdf

Free Software. (2003). *Free Software* (Open Source). Retrieved April 14, 2009 from http://www.free-soft.org/

Friedman, D. (2000). *Contracts in cyberspace*. American Law and Economics Association meeting.

Fudenberg, D. A., & Tirole, J. (1983). Game Theory (Chapter 1, Section 2.4). MIT Press.

Furnas, G. W. (1997). Effective view navigation. In *Proceedings of the SIGCHI conference on Human Factors and Computing* (pp. 367-374). Atlanta: University of Georgia, United States.

Gan, Q., & Suel, T. (2007). Improving Web spam classifiers using link structure. In *AIRWeb '07: Proceedings of the 3rd Int. Workshop on Advers. Inf. Retrieval on the Web* (pp. 17-20). Banff, Alberta, Canada. Retrieved February 10, 2009, from http://airweb.cse.lehigh.edu/2007/papers/paper_124.pdf.

Ganame, A. K., Bourgeois, J., Bidou, R., & Spies, F. (2008). A global security architecture for intrusion detection on computer networks. *Computers & Security, 27*, 30–47. doi:10.1016/j.cose.2008.03.004

Gangemi, A. (2007). Design patterns for legal ontology construction. In *Proceedings of LOAIT '07 II Workshop on Legal Ontologies and Artificial Intelligence Techniques*. Retrieved from http://ftp.informatik.rwth-aachen.de/Publications/CEUR-WS/Vol-321/paper4.pdf.

García, F. J., et al. (2002) An Adaptive e-Commerce System Definition. In *Proceedings of the Second International Conference on Adaptive Hypermedia and Adaptive Web-Based Systems* (LNCS 2347, pp. 505-509).

García, R. (2007). *A Semantic Web Approach to Digital Rights Management*. PhD Thesis. Retrieved from http://rhizomik.net/~roberto/thesis

Gartner Inc. (2007). *Dataquest Insight: SaaS Demand Set to Outpace Enterprise Application Software Market Growth*. New York: Gartner.

Gentili, A. (2000). L'inefficacia del contratto telematico. In "Rivista di Diritto Civile", Anno XLVI –, Parte I, Padova-Cedam.

Geradin, D. (2004). Limiting the Scope of Article 82 EC: What Can The EU Learn From the US Supreme Court's Judgment in *Trinko*, in the Wake of Microsoft, IMS, and Deutsche Telekom? *Common Market Law Review, 41*(6), 1519–1533.

Gerhart, S. L. (2004). Do web search engines suppress controversy? *First Monday, 9*(1). Retrieved April 2, 2009, from http://firstmonday.org/htbin/cgiwrap/bin/ojs/index.php/fm/article/view/1111/1031.

Ghemawat, S., Gobioff, H., & Leung, S. (2003). The Google file system. In *SOSP '03: Proceedings of the nineteenth ACM symposium on Operating systems principles* (pp. 29-43). New York: ACM Press.

Ghosh, S. (2003). *Deprivatizing Copyright*. Retrieved April 29, 2009, from http://ssrn.com/abstract=443600.

Ghosh, S. (2006). *Decoding and Recoding Natural Monopoly, Deregulation, and Intellectual Property*. Retrieved April 29, 2009, from http://ssrn.com/abstract=935145.

Gibbs, W. W. (2005). Software's Chronic Crisis. In R. H. Thyler & M. Dorfman (Eds.) Software Engineering Volume 1: The Development Processes (3rd Ed.). IEEE Computer Society.

Gloor, A. P., Heckman, C., & Makedon, F. (2004). *Ethical Issues in Collaborative Innovation Networks*. Paper presented at MIT Center for Collective Intelligence. Retrieved April 03, 2009 from http://ccs.mit.edu/pgloor%20papers/COIN4Ethicomp.pdf

Gloor, P. Laubacher, R., Dynes, S., Zhao, Y. (2003). *Visualization of Communication Patterns inCollaborative Innovation Networks: Analysis of some W3C working groups*. Paper presented at Innovative Collaborative Knowledge Networks. Retrieved February 03, 2009 from http://www.ickn.org/documents/visualization_of_communication.pdf

Glorioso, A. (2008). Ethics on a chip? Some general remarks on DRM, Internet filtering and trusted computing. In T. W. Bynum, M. Calzarossa, I. Lotto & S. Rogerson (Eds.), ETHICOMP 2008: Living, Working and Learning Beyond Technology (pp. 287-297). Mantova: University of Pavia, Italy.

Goldstein, P. (2003). *Copyright's highway: from Gutenberg to the celestial jukebox*. Stanford University Press.

Gonçalves, C. (1929). *Tratado de Direito Civil – em comentário ao Código Civil Português* (*Vol. 1*). Coimbra Editora. (in Portuguese)

Goodman, J. W. (2003). *The pros and cons of online dispute resolution: an assessment of cyber-mediation websites*. Duke Law and Technology Review.

Google. (2006). *Our philosophy*. Resource document. Google. Retrieved February 20, 2009, from http://www.google.com/intl/en/corporate/tenthings.html.

Google. (2006). *Webmaster guidelines*. Resource document. Google. Retrieved April 4, 2009, from http://www.google.com/support/webmasters/bin/answer.py?answer=35769.

Google. (2008). *Security backgrounder: for Google security and compliance products*. Resource document. Google. Retrieved April 5, 2009, from https://www.postini.com/legal/Security_Backgrounder2.pdf.

Google. (2008). *Content policy management*. Resource document. Google. Retrieved March 17, 2009, from www.google.com/a/help/intl/nl/security/pdf/content_policy_management.pdf.

Google. (2009). *Google milestones*. Resource document. Google. Retrieved February 23, 2009, from http://www.google.com/intl/en/corporate/history.html.

Google. (2009). *Company overview*. Resource document. Google. Retrieved February 23, 2009, from http://www.google.com/corporate.

Google. (2009). *Technology overview*. Resource document. Google. Retrieved February 22, 2009, from http://www.google.com/corporate/tech.html.

Google. (2009). *Google blog*. Resource document. Google. Retrieved February 22, 2009, from http://googleblog.blogspot.com/.

Goolsby, K. (2008, November). Innovation and Economy: Trends Impacting Initial Stages of Outsourcing. *Outsourcing Journal*. Retrieved February 3, 2009 from http://www.outsourcing-journal.com/nov2008-trends.html

Gordon, L. A., & Martin, P. L. (2006). Budgeting process for information security expenditures. *Communications of the ACM, 49*(1), 121–125. doi:10.1145/1107458.1107465

Goulev, P., Stead, L., Mamdani, A., & Evans, C. (2004). Computer Aided Emotional Fashion. *Computers & Graphics, 28*(5), 657–666. doi:10.1016/j.cag.2004.06.005

Granstrand, O. (2003). *Innovation and Intellectual Property*. Preliminary 3rd Draft of the paper presented at the Concluding Roundtable Discussion on IPR at the DRUID Summer Conference on Creating, Sharing and transferring knowledge. The role of Geography, Institutions and Organizations, Copenhagen. Retrieved April 03, 2009 from http://www.druid.dk/conferences/summer2003/Papers/GRANDSTRAND.pdf

Greenough, C. (2009). *Software engineering*. Retrieved April 14, 2009 from http://www.cse.scitech.ac.uk/seg/

Grimmelmann, J. (2005). *Regulating search?* Resource document. Yale Law School. Retrieved March 14, 2009, from http://james.grimmelmann.net/presentations/2005-12-03-search-engines.pdf.

Grimmelmann, J. (2007). *The structure of search engine law*. Resource document. *University of Iowa College of Law*. Retrieved April 4, 2009, from http://works.bepress.com/cgi/viewcontent.cgi?article=1012&context=james_grimmelmann.

Griswold v. Connecticut, 381 U.S. 479 (1965).

Gross, R., & Acquisti, A. (2005). Information revelation and privacy in online social networks. *Workshop on Privacy in the Electronic Society (WPES)*. Retrieved April 17, 2009 from http://www.heinz.cmu.edu/~acquisti/papers/privacy-facebook-gross-acquisti.pdf.

Gruber, T. R. (1993). A Translation Approach to Portable Ontology Specifications. *Knowledge Acquisition*, 5(2), 199–220. doi:10.1006/knac.1993.1008

Guadamuz, A., & Usher, J. (2005). Electronic Money: the European regulatory approach. In Edwards, L. (Ed.), *The New Legal Framework for E-Commerce in Europe* (pp. 173–201). Oxford: Hart Publishing.

Gual, J., Hellwig, M., Perrot, A., Polo, M., Rey, P., Schmidt, K. & Stenbacka, R. (2005, July). *An Economic Approach to Article 82*. Report by the EAGCP.

Guarino, N. (1998). Formal Ontology and Information Systems. In N. Guarino (Ed.), *Formal Ontology in Information Systems. Proceedings of FOIS'98* (pp. 3-15). Trento, Italy, 6-8 June 1998. Amsterdam: IOS Press.

Guibault, L. (1998), *Limitations Found Outside of Copyright Law – General Report*. ALAI Studies Days, Cambridge. Retrieved April 29, 2009, from http://www.ivir.nl/publications/guibault/VUL5BOVT.doc

Gutierrez, C. (2008). Foundations of RDF Databases. *The Semantic Web: Research and Applications*. Koster, M. (1993). *Guidelines for Robot Writers*. Retrieved from http://www.robotstxt.org/guidelines.html

Gutmann, P. (2000). X.509 Style Guide. Retrieved April 20, 2009, from http://www.cs.auckland.ac.nz/~pgut001/pubs/x509guide.txt

Gutmann, P. (2004). How to build a PKI that works. 3rd Annual PKI R&D Workshop. NIST, Gaithersburg MD. April 12-14, 2004.

Guttman, R. H., Moukas, A. G., & Maes, P. (1998). Agent-mediated electronic commerce: A survey. *The Knowledge Engineering Review*, 13(2), 147–159. doi:10.1017/S0269888998002082

Gyselen (1990). Abuse of Monopoly Power within the Meaning of Article 86 of the EEC Treaty -- Recent Developments. In B. Hawk (Ed.), 1990 *Fordham Corporate Law Institute* (pp. 598-599).

Hagel, J., & Armstrong, A. G. (1999). *Negocios rentables a través de Internet*. Barcelona: Paidós.

Haggerty, K., & Ericson, R. (2000). The surveillant assemblage. *The British Journal of Sociology*, 51(4), 605–622. doi:10.1080/00071310020015280

Hall, B. H. (2002). On Copyright and Patent Protection for Software and Databases: A Tale of Two Worlds. In O. Granstrand (ed.), *Economics, Law, and Intellectual Property*. Kluwer. Retrieved on June 8, 2009, from http://www.iiasa.ac.at/docs/HOTP/Dec99/bhhiiasa4.pdf

Hall, T., & Bannon, L. (2005). Designing ubiquitous computing to enhance children's interaction in museums. In *Proceedings of the 2005 conference on Interaction design and children* (pp. 62-69). ACM.

Halpern, J., & van der Meyden, R. (1999). A Logic for SDSI's Linked Local Name Spaces. In *Proc. 12th IEEE Computer Security Foundations Workshop* (pp.111-122).

Hammond, A. M. (2003). How do you write "yes"? A study on the effectiveness of online dispute resolution. *Conflict Resolution Quarterly, 20*(3). doi:10.1002/crq.25

Hansen, M., & Nohria, N. (2004). How to Build Collaborative Advantage, SMR. *MIT Sloan Management Review.* Retrieved April 03, 2009 from http://sloanreview.mit.edu/the-magazine/files/pdfs/46105SxW.pdf

Harley, J. B. (1968). The evaluation of early maps: Towards a methodology. *Imago Mundi, 22*, 68–70.

Harley, J. B., & Woodward, D. (1987). Preface. In Harley, J. B., & Woodward, D. (Eds.), *The history of cartography: Cartography in prehistoric, ancient, and medieval Europe and the Mediterranean* (Vol. 1, pp. 15–21). Chicago, IL: The University of Chicago Press.

Harnad, S. (2004). Apercus of WOS Meeting: Making Ends Meet in the Creative Commons. *American-Scientist-Open-Access-Forum.* Retrieved April 14, 2009 from http://users.ecs.soton.ac.uk/harnad/Hypermail/Amsci/3758.html

Harnad, S. (2008). Open Access, Free/Open Software, Open Data, and Creative Commons Commonalities and Distinctions. *Free Software Free Society Conference on Freedom in Computing, Development and Culture.* Retrieved April 14, 2009 from http://fsfs.in/schedule/events/61.en.html

Harnad, S., Brody, T., Vallieres, F., Carr, L., Hitchcock, S., Gingras, Y., et al. (2004). The green and the gold roads to Open Access. *Nature Web Focus.* Retrieved April 16, 2009 from http://www.nature.com/nature/focus/accessdebate/21.html

Harvey, P. D. A. (1980). *Topographical maps. Symbols, pictures and surveys.* London: Thames and Hudson.

Hassanein, K., Head, M., & Centre, M. E. R. (2004). *Manipulating social presence through the Web interface and its impact on consumer attitude towards online shopping.* McMaster eBusiness Research Centre.

Hawker, N. (2008). *The proposed Google-Yahoo alliance: An anti-trust white paper.* Washington: The American Anti-Trust Institute.

Hayes-Roth, F., Waterman, D. A., & Lenat, D. B. (1983). *Building expert systems.* Boston, MA: Addison-Wesley Longman Publishing Co., Inc.

Health and Consumer Protection Directorate-General. European Commission. (2006). Summary report of the responses to the consultation regarding "Community action on health services". Retrieved April 20, 2009, from http://ec.europa.eu/health/ph_overview/co_operation/healthcare/cross-border_healthcare_en.htm

Health Information Privacy. (n.d.) Retrieved April 12, 2009, from http://www.hhs.gov/ocr/privacy/index.html

Health Insurance Portability and Accountability Act, 42 U.S.C. § 290dd-2 (1996).

Heere, E., 2006. The use of GIS with property maps. *e-Perimetron, 4*(1), 297-307.

Heise Security. (2009). *Heise Security.* Resource document. Heise. Retrieved February 2, 2009, from http://www.heise.de/security/

Himma, K. E. (2005). Information and intellectual property protection: Evaluating the claim that information should be free. Resource document. *Berkeley Center for Law and Technology.* Retrieved April 5, 2009, from http://repositories.cdlib.org/bclt/lts/12.

HM Revenues & Customs. (2007). A guide for people who sell items online, through classified advertisements and at car boot sales. Retrieved April 2, 2009, from http://www.hmrc.gov.uk/guidance/selling/index.htm

Hoffman, D. L., & Novak, T. P. (1998). Bridging the racial divide on the Internet. *Science, 280*(5362), 390–391. doi:10.1126/science.280.5362.390

Holsapple, C. W., & Joshi, K. D. (2004). A formal knowledge management ontology: Conduct, activities, resources, and influences. *Journal of the American Society for Information Science and Technology, 55*(7), 593–612. doi:10.1002/asi.20007

Holt, B. (2000). Creating Senior Friendly Websites. Issue Brief 1(4) Centre for Mediacare Education Retrieved May 25, 2009 from http://www.medicareed.org/PublicationFiles/V1N4.pdf

Hoofnagle, C. J. (2005). *Privacy Self Regulation: A Decade of Disappointment*. Retrieved on March 13, 2007 from http://www.epic.org/reports/decadedisappoint.html.

Hori, M., & Ohashi, M. (2005). Adaptive Collaborative Work and XML Web Services. In Guah, M. W., & Currie, W. L. (Eds.), *Internet Strategy: The Road to Web Services* (pp. 86–100). Hershey, PA: IRM Press.

Hori, M., & Ohashi, M. (2007). Knowledge Creation and Adaptive Collaboration Based on XML Web Services. In Putnik, G. D., & Cunha, M. M. (Eds.), *Knowledge and Technology Management Virtual Organizations: Issues, Trends, Opportunities, and Solutions* (pp. 292–305). Hershey, PA: IDEA Group Publishing.

Horton, S. (2002). Privacy in the online classroom. *Web Teaching Guide*. Retrieved April 17, 2009 from http://www.dartmouth.edu/~webteach/articles/restrict.

House of Lords. Minutes of proceedings, 29 November 2005. Retrieved on June 30 2009 from http://www.publications.parliament.uk/pa/ld200506/minutes/051129/ldminute.htm

Housley, R., Polk, W., Ford, W., & Solo, D. (2002, April). Internet X.509 Public Key Infrastructure Certificate and CRL Profile. IETF RFC 3280. Retrieved April 20, 2009, from http://www.ietf.org/rfc/rfc3280.txt

Howard, M., & Leblanc, D. (2003). *Writing Secure Code* (2nd ed.). Microsoft Press.

Huang, R., & Paturi, R. (2005). *Analysis of the benefits and drawbacks of the PageRank algorithm*. Resource document. University of California. Retrieved February 8, 2009, from http://www.cse.ucsd.edu/~paturi/cse91/Presents/rhuang.pdf.

Hugenholtz, P. B. (2001). Copyright and Freedom of Expression in Europe. In Dreyfuss, C. R., Zimmerman, D. L., & First, H. (Eds.), *Expanding the boundaries of intellectual property. Innovation policy for the knowledge society* (pp. 343–363). Oxford University Press.

Hugenholtz, P. B. (2004). *The balance of interests in copyright law*. Max Planck Institute for Intellectual Property, Competition and Tax Law. Retrieved April 29, 2009, from http://www.ip.mpg.de/ww/en/pub/research/publikationen/online_publikationen/3__externe_beschr_nkungen_exte.cfm?#hugenholtz

Hunt, K. (2007). This Land Is Not Your Land: Second Life, CopyBot, and the Looming Question of Virtual Property Rights. *Texas Review of Entertainment and Sports Law, 9*, 141–173.

Hurlbert, W. (2004). *SEO ethics: Which hat to wear*. Resource document. Search Optimization. Retrieved April 4, 2009, from http://www.seochat.com/c/a/Search-Engine-Optimization-Help/SEO-Ethics-Which-Hat-To-Wear/.

Huxley-Binns, R., & Martin, J. (2008). Unlocking the English Legal System (2nd ed.).

Iannella, R. (2002). Open Digital Rights Language (ODRL), Version: 1.1. Retrieved April 20, 2009, from http://odrl.net/1.1/ODRL-11.pdf

ICC Task Force on Privacy and Protection of Personal Data. (2004, October 28). ICC report on binding corporate rules for international transfers of personal data. Retrieved on June 30, 2009 from http://www.iccwbo.org/home/ebitt/FINAL_ICC_BCRs_report.pdf

ICC Task Force on Privacy and the Protection of Personal Data. (2006, July 5). Standard application for approval of binding corporate rules for the transfer of personal data outside the EU (to be used in all EU member states). Retrieved on June 30, 2009 from http://www.iccwbo.org/uploadedFiles/ICC/policy/e-business/pages/Standard_Application_for_Approval_of_BCRs.pdf

ICO. (2003). Technical Guidance. International transfers/Transborder Data Flows - Guidance on the Use of Model Contract Clauses – data controllers established in the EU to data processors in countries outside the EU. Retrieved on June 30 2009 from http://www.ico.gov.uk/upload/documents/library/data_protection/practical_application/model_contracts_for_data_processors_processing_personal_information_on_their_behalf001001.pdf

ICO. (2006, February 27). Technical Guidance. The "Durant" case and its impact on the interpretation of the Data Protection 1998. Retrieved on June 30 2009 from http://www.ico.gov.uk/upload/documents/library/data_protection/detailed_specialist_guides/the_durant_case_and_its_impact_on_the_interpretation_of_the_data_protection_act.pdf

ICO. (2006, June 30). Technical Guidance. The Eighth Data Protection Principle and international data transfers. Retrieved on June 30 2009 from http://www.ico.gov.uk/upload/documents/library/data_protection/detailed_specialist_guides/international_transfers_legal_guidance_v3.0_171208.pdf

ICO. (2007, August 21). Technical Guidance. Determining what is personal data. Retrieved on June 30 2009 from http://www.ico.gov.uk/upload/documents/library/data_protection/detailed_specialist_guides/personal_data_flowchart_v1_with_preface001.pdf

ICO. (2009, January 28). Technical Guidance. Determining what information is 'data' for the purposes of the DPA. Retrieved on June 30 2009 from http://www.ico.gov.uk/upload/documents/library/data_protection/detailed_specialist_guides/what_is_data_for_the_purposes_of_the_dpa.pdf

ICT for better Healthcare in Europe. (n.d.). Retrieved June 9, 2009, from http://ec.europa.eu/information_society/activities/health/index_en.htm

IEEE. Computer Society (2009). *IEEE CS Certification Programs*. Retrieved April 11, 2009 from http://www2.computer.org/portal/web/getcertified

Imperatore, C. (2009). Wikis and blogs: Your keys to student collaboration & engagement. *Techniques, 84*(3), 30.

Information Week. (2008). *The case of universal search: White paper*. Resource document. Information Week. Retrieved February 14, 2009, from http://www.informationweek.com/whitepaper/Internet/Search/the-case-for-universal-searc-wp1227642995192;jsessionid=0BRM2105ZCVD2QSNDLPCKHSCJUNN2JVN?articleID=50500003.

Innovaro. (2006). *Innovation briefing 2006*, Retrieved April 17, 2009 from http://www.innovaro.com/inno_updates/Innovation%20Briefing%2007-06.pdf

I-node. (2005). *Security of the Google search appliances*. Resource document. I-node. Retrieved April 7, 2009, from http://www.i-node.it/documenti/GSA-physical-security.pdf.

Institute of Medicine. (2003). Committee on data standards for patient safety: board of health care services. Key capabilities of an electronic health record system: letter report. The National Academy of Sciences. Retrieved April 7, 2009, from http://www.iom.edu/report.asp?id=14391

International Chamber of Commerce. (2008). *Current and emerging Intellectual Property issues for business: A roadmap for business and policy makers* (9th ed.). Retrieved April 03, 2009 from http://www.iccwbo.org/uploadedFiles/ICC/policy/intellectual_property/pages/IP_Roadmap-2005(1).pdf

International Organization for Standardization. (2005). *ISO 9000:2005 Quality management systems – fundamentals and vocabulary*. Available from http://www.iso.org/iso/catalogue_detail?csnumber=42180.

Internet Attorney. (2009). *Internet privacy law*. Retrieved April 17, 2009 from http://www.netatty.com/privacy/privacy.html.

Internet World Stats. (2008, December 31). *Internet World Statistics: World Internet Users and Population Statistics*. Retrieved March 25, 2009, from http://www.internetworldstats.com/stats.htm

Internet World Stats. (2009). *World Internet Users and Population Stats*. Retrieved April 2, 2009 from http://www.internetworldstats.com/stats.htm

Introna, L. D., & Nissenbaum, H. (2000). Shaping the Web: Why the politics of search engines matter. *The Information Society, 16*(3), 169–186. doi:10.1080/01972240050133634

Jackson, P. (1990). *Introduction to expert systems*. Boston, MA: Addison-Wesley Longman Publishing Co., Inc.

Jamieson, L. (2007, Spring). Engineering education in a changing world. *The Bridge*.

Janse, B. J., & Mullen, T. (2008). Sponsored search: An overview of the concept, history, and technology. *International Journal of Electronic Business, 6*(2), 114–131. doi:10.1504/IJEB.2008.018068

Jansen, B. J., Booth, D. E., & Spink, A. (2007). Determining the user intent of Web search engine queries. *WWW 2007*. May 8-12, Banff, Alberta, Canada. Retrieved March 3, 2009, from http://www2007.org/posters/poster989.pdf.

Jarvenpaa, S. L., & Staples, D. S. (2001). The use of collaborative media for information sharing: An exploratory study of determinants. *The Journal of Strategic Information Systems, 18*(1), 151–183.

Jehoram, H. C. (2004). Copyright and freedom of expression, abuse of rights and standard chicanery: American and Dutch approaches. *European Intellectual Property Review, 26*(7), 275–279.

Jennings, N. & Wooldridge, M. (1996, January). Software Agents. *IEEE Review*.

Jennings, N., Faratin, P., Lomuscio, A., Parsons, S., Wooldridge, M., & Sierra, C. (2001). Automated Negotiation: Prospects, Methods and Challenges. *Group Decision and Negotiation, 10*(2), 199–215. doi:10.1023/A:1008746126376

Jiang, X., & Landay, J. (2002). Modeling Privacy Control in Context-aware Systems Using Decentralized Information Spaces. *IEEE Pervasive Computing / IEEE Computer Society [and] IEEE Communications Society, 1*(3), 59–63. doi:10.1109/MPRV.2002.1037723

Johnson, M. K., Reeder, J. A., Raye, C. L., & Mitchell, K. J. (2002). Second thoughts versus second looks: An age-related deficit in selectively refreshing just-active information. *Psychological Science, 13*, 64–67. doi:10.1111/1467-9280.00411

Jonczy, J., & Haenni, R. (2005). Credential Networks: a General Model for Distributed Trust and Authenticity Management. In *Proceedings Third Annual Conference on Privacy, Security and Trust*.

Jordan, J. M., III. (2006). *EU Personal Data Protection Laws Require Deleting Data When No Longer Needed*. Retrieved from www.cyberscrub.com/.../Legal_Requirements_to_Delete_EU_Personal_Data_Jim.pdf

Jung, B. (2001). *Media, communication and electronic business*. Warsaw: Difin Publishing.

Kagal, L., Finin, T., & Joshi, A. (2003). A policy language for pervasive systems. *Fourth IEEE Int. Workshop on Policies for Distributed Systems and Networks*.

Kagan, R. L. (1998). *Imágenes urbanas del mundo hispánico, 1493-1780*. Madrid: Eds. El Viso.

Kalakota, R., & Robinson, M. (2000). *E-Business 2.0, roadmap to success*. Boston, MA: Addison-Wesley.

Kaldor, M. (2007). *Human security: Reflections on globalization and intervention*. Cambridge: Polity Press.

Kalpic, B., & Bernus, P. (2006). Business Process Modelling Through the Knowledge Management Perspective. *Journal of Knowledge Management, 10*(3), 40–56. doi:10.1108/13673270610670849

Kang, I.-H., & Kim, G. C. (2004). Integration of multiple evidences based on a query type for web search. *Information Processing and Management: An International Journal, 40*(3), 459–478. doi:10.1016/S0306-4573(03)00053-0

Karimi, J., Somers, T. M., & Bhattacherjee, A. (2009). The Role of ERP Implementation in Enabling Digital Options: A Theoretical and Empirical Analysis. *International Journal of Electronic Commerce, 13*(3), 7–42. doi:10.2753/JEC1086-4415130301

Karpowicz A. (2001). *Podręcznik Prawa Autorskiego dla Studentów Uczelni Artystycznych*. RTW 2001.

Kashyap, V. (1999). Design and creation of ontologies for environmental information retrieval. In *Proceedings of the 12th Workshop on Knowledge Acquisition, Modelling and Management*. Alberta, Ontario, Canada. Retrieved April 3, 2009 from http://eprints.kfupm.edu.sa/34189/1/34189.pdf.

Katsch, E., & Rifkin, J. (2001). *Online dispute resolution – resolving conflicts in cyberspace*. San Francisco, CA: Jossey-Bass Wiley Company.

Katsh, E., Rifkin, J., & Gaitenby, A. (1999). E-Commerce, E-Disputes, and E-Dispute Resolution: In the Shadow of eBay Law. *Ohio State Journal on Dispute Resolution, 15*, 705.

Katsh, M. E. (1995). *Law in a digital world*. Oxford University Press.

Kaufman, P. (1995). *New trading systems and methods*. London: Wiley.

Kauper, T. (1990). EC Competition law - the road to 1992: article 86, excessive prices, and refusals to deal. *59 Antitrust L.J., 441*.

Kawamoto, D. (2008). *Study: Fox Interactive tops digital display ad market*. Cnet News. Retrieved April 5, 2009, from http://news.cnet.com/8301-1023_3-10026578-93.html.

Kerbaj, R. (2005). *Telstra's secret dossiers on staff*. The Australian.

Kerr, O. S. (2007). Four models of fourth amendment protection. *Stanford Law Review, 60*(2), 503.

Kettunen, J., & Kulmala, R. (2007). Intellectual Property Protection in Software Business. In Pagani, M. (Ed.), *Encyclopedia of Multimedia Technology and Networking*. Hershey, PA: IGI Global.

Khare, R., & Rifkin, A. (1997). Weaving a web of trust. *World Wide Web Journal, 2*(3), 77–112.

Kitching, J., & Blackburn, R. (1998). Intellectual property management in the small and medium enterprise (SME). *Journal of Small Business and Enterprise Development, 5*(4), 327–335. doi:10.1108/EUM0000000006797

Kobrin, S. J. (2002, November). *The Trans-Atlantic Data Privacy Dispute, Territorial Jurisdiction and Global Governance*. Retrieved April 9, 2009 from http://ssrn.com/abstract=349561

Koch, S. (2006). Home telehealth—Current state and future trends. *International Journal of Medical Informatics, 75*(8), 565–576. doi:10.1016/j.ijmedinf.2005.09.002

Kohlbach, M. (2004). Making Sense of Electronic Money. *The Journal of Information, Law and Technology, 1*.

Kohler, G. K. (2003). La resolución de los litigios en línea – perspectivas y retos del contencioso internacional contemporáneo. Revista Latino-Americana de Mediación y Arbitraje, vol. III – Número 4

Kohnfelder, L. (1978). Toward a Practical Public Cryptosystem. *Bachelor's thesis* (pp. 39-44). Dept. Electrical Engineering, MIT, Cambridge, Mass. Lewis, J. (2003, March 1). Reinventing PKI: Federated Identity and the Path to Practical Public Key Security. Retrieved April 20, 2009, from http://www.burtongroup.com/

Kolodner, J. L. (1993). *Case-based Reasoning*. Morgan Kaufmann Publishers.

Kong, L. (2007). Online Privacy in China: A Survey on Information Practices of Chinese Websites. *Chinese Journal of International Law, 6*(1), 157–183. doi:10.1093/chinesejil/jml061

Korff, D. (2008). The Standard Approach under Articles 8 – 11 ECHR and Article 2 ECHR at http://ec.europa.eu/justice_home/news/events/conference_dp_2009/presentations_speeches/KORFF_Douwe_a.pdf

Kornai, A. (2008). On the proper definition of information. In T. W. Bynum, M. Calzarossa, I. Lotto & S. Rogerson (Eds.), ETHICOMP 2008: Living, Working and Learning Beyond Technology (pp. 488-495). Mantua: University of Pavia, Italy.

Kosta, E., & Peggy Valcke, P. (2006). Retaining the Data Retention Directive. *Computer Law & Security Report, 22*, 370–380. doi:10.1016/j.clsr.2006.07.002

Kowalski, R., & Sergot, M. (1985). Computer Representation of the Law. In. *Proceedings, IJCAI-85*, 1269–1270.

Kunreuther, H. C., & Heal, G. M. (2003). Interdependent security. *Journal of Risk and Uncertainty, 26*(2/3), 231–249. doi:10.1023/A:1024119208153

Kuusisto, J., Kulmala, R., & Päällysaho, S. (2006). Intellectual property protection and management in SMEs. In Pesonen, P. (Ed.), *Uutta tietoa ja osaamista innovaatiopolitiikan käyttöön. ProACT-tutkimusohjelma 2001-2005. Teknologiaohjelmaraportti 5/2006.*

Kwon, S. (2007). Common defects in information security management system of Korean companies. *Journal of Systems and Software, 80*(10), 1631–1638. doi:10.1016/j.jss.2007.01.015

Lakoff, G., & Johnson, M. (1980). *Metaphors we live by.* Chicago, IL: University of Chicago Press.

Lakshminarayana, S. (2009). Categorization of web pages- Performance enhancement to search engine. *Knowledge-Based Systems, 22*(1), 100–104. doi:10.1016/j.knosys.2008.07.006

Lallana, E. C. (2004). *An overview of ICT policies and e-strategies of select Asian economies.* New Delhi: APDIP.

Lämsä, T. (2008). *Knowledge creation and organizational learning communities of practice: An empirical analysis of a healthcare organization.* Faculty of Economics and Business Administration, Department of Management and Entrepreneurship, University of Oulu.

Lange, J., & Lappe, M. (2007). The role of spatial and temporal information in biological motion perception. *Advances in Cognitive Psychology, 3*(4), 419–428. doi:10.2478/v10053-008-0006-3

Langer, A. (2005). *The Importance of Mediators, Bridge Builders, Wall Vaulters and.* Frontier. Una Città.

Lastowka, F. G., & Hunter, H. (in press). The Laws of the Virtual Worlds. *California Law Review.* Retrieved March 1, 2009, from http://papers.ssrn.com/sol3/papers.cfm?abstract_id=402860

Lastowka, G. (2007). *Google's law.* Working Paper. Rutgers University. Retrieved February 20, 2009, from http://works.bepress.com/lastowka/4.

Lau, R. Y. K. (2007). Towards a web services and intelligent agents-based negotiation system for B2B eCommerce. *Electronic Commerce Research and Applications, 6*(3), 260–273. doi:10.1016/j.elerap.2006.06.007

Law 32/2008, July 17. Transposes to the national legal order Directive 2006/24/EC of the European Parliament and of the Council of 15 March 2006, on the retention of data generated or processed in connection with the provision of publicly available electronic communications services or of public communications networks at. Retrieved January 21, 2010 from http://www.anacom.pt/render.jsp?contentId=951486

Law no. 41/2004, August 18. Legal provisions transposing to the national legal order Directive 2002/58/EC, of the European Parliament and of the Council, of 12 July, concerning the processing of personal data and the protection of privacy in the electronic communications sector. Retrieved January 21 from http://www.anacom.pt/render.jsp?contentId=951486. View: 21.01.2010

Law no. 67/98, October 26. Transposing into the Portuguese legal system Directive 95/46/EC of the European Parliament and of the Council of 24 October 1995 on the protection of individuals with regard to the processing of personal data and on the free movement of such data. Retrieved January 21, 2010 from http://www.anacom.pt/render.jsp?contentId=951486

Lawrence, S., & Giles, C. L. (1998). Searching the World Wide Web. *Science, 280,* 98–100. doi:10.1126/science.280.5360.98

Lawson, P. (2008). Privacy & Public Health: Ensuring Public Trust. *Electronic Health and Information Privacy Conference* (pp. 45-55).

Lax, D., & Sebenius, J. (1986). *The Manager as Negotiator: Bargaining for Cooperation and Competitive Gain.* Free Press.

Lederer, S., Beckman, C., Dey, A., & Mankoff, J. (2003). *Managing personal information disclosure in ubiquitous computing environments* (Tech Rep IRB-TR-03-015). Intel Research, Berkeley.

Lederman, L. (2007). 'Stanger than fiction': Taxing Virtual Worlds. *New York University Law Review, 82,* 1620–1672.

Lederman, R. (2004). The Medical Privacy Rule: Can Hospitals Comply Using Current Health Information Systems? In *Proceedings of the 17th IEEE Symposium on Computer-Based Medical Systems.*

Legal Directives & European Commission papers COMMISSION STAFF WORKING: Paper on the review of the EC legal framework in the field of copyright and related rights. Directive 96/9/EC of the European Parliament and Council, on March 11th regarding the legal protection of databases. Directive 2001/29/EC of the European Parliament and Council, May 22nd 2001, dealing with the harmonisation of specific aspects of copyright and related rights in the information society.

Legal Information Institute. (2009). *Consumer privacy guide.* Cornell University Law School. Retrieved April 10, 2009 from http://topics.law.cornell.edu/wex/personal_Information

Legal Information Institute. (2009). *Privacy.* Cornell University Law School. Retrieved April 10, 2009 from http://topics.law.cornell.edu/wex/personal_Information

Lerouge, J. F. (2003). The use of electronic agents questioned under contractual law. Suggested solutions on a European and American level. *The John Marshall Journal of Computer & Information Law, 18*(2), 403–433.

Lessig, L. (2004). *Free culture: how big media uses technology and the law to lock down culture and control creativity.* Penguin Press. Retrieved from http://www.free-culture.cc/freecontent/

Lessig, L. (2006). *Code version 2.0.* New York: Basic Books.

Lévêque, F. (2004, September). The Application of Essential Facility and Leveraging Doctrines to Intellectual Property in the EU: The Microsoft's Refusal to License on Interoperability. *CERNA Working Paper.* Retrieved from http://www.cerna.ensmp.fr

Li, M., Du, X. Y., & Wang, S. (2005). Learning ontology from relational database. In D. S. Yeung, Z.-Q. Liu, X.-Z. Wang & H. Yan (Eds.), *Proceedings of the 4th International Conference on Machine Learning and Cybernetics* (pp. 3410-3415). Guangzhou: University of Guangzhou, China.

Li, N. (2000). Local names in SPKI/SDSI. In *Proc. 13th IEEE Computer Security Foundations Workshop* (pp. 2-15). IEEE Computer Society Press.

Li, N., & Grosof, B. (2000). A practically implementable and tractable delegation logic. Proc. *2000 IEEE Symposium on Security and Privacy* (pp. 29-44). IEEE Computer Society Press.

Liddy, E. D. (2003). Automating & evaluating metadata generation. *The Eighth Search Engine Meeting.* April 7-8. Boston, Massachusetts, USA.

Liebeskind, J. P. (1996). Knowledge, strategy, and the theory of the firm. *Strategic Management Journal, 17*, 93–107.

Lighthouse International. (2009). *The Aging Eye.* Retrieved March 9, 2009, from http://www.lighthouse.org/medical/the-aging-eye/

Lima, F., & Varela, J. (1987). *Código Civil Anotado* (*Vol. 1*). Coimbra Editora Limitada. (in Portuguese)

Lin, N. H., Korba, L., Yee, G., Shih, T. K., & Lin, H. W. (2004). Security and privacy technologies for distance education applications. In *Proceedings of the 18th International Conference on Advanced Information Networking and Application.*

Liotta, P. H. (2002). Boomerang effect: The converegence of national and human security. *Security Dialogue, 33*(4), 473–488. doi:10.1177/0967010602033004007

Lipsman, A. (2003). *ComScore Media Metrix launches breakthrough system to track actual consumer search queries.* Resource document. Retrieved February 2, 2009, from http://www.comscore.com/press/release.asp?id=325.

Litvinsky, M. (2009). *Internet boom in China has given citizens new avenues for self-expression.* NoticiasFinancieras.

Livieratos, E. (Ed.). (2006). *Digital Approaches to Cartographic Heritage.* Thessaloniki: National Centre for Maps and Cartographic Heritage. Microsoft Digital Asset Server (DAS). Retrieved January 12, 2009 from http://www.microsoft.com/reader/das/default.htm

Livingston, B. (2004). *Google grumbles*. Resource document. eWeek. Retrieved February 17, 2009, from www.eweek.com/article2/0,4149,1530367,00.asp.

Lodder, A. R. (2006). The Third Party and Beyond. An Analysis of the Different Parties, in particular The Fifth, Involved in Online Dispute Resolution. *Information & Communications Technology Law*, *15*(2), 143–155. doi:10.1080/13600830600676438

Lodder, A. R., & Thiessen, E. M. (2003). The role of Artificial Intelligence in Online Dispute Resolution. In D. Choi & E. Katsh (Eds.), *Proceedings UN forum on ODR*.

Lodder, A. R., & Zeleznikow, J. (2005). Developing an Online Dispute Resolution Environment: Dialogue Tools and Negotiation Systems in a Three Step Model. *The Harvard Negotiation Law Review*, *10*, 287–338.

Luttighuis, P. O., & Biemans, F. (1999). ERP in the e-commerce era. Foundation's 2nd USP Roundtable ERP and Beyond, Utrecht.

Machill, M., et al. (2003). Wegweiser im netz: Qualität und nutzung von Suchmaschinen. In M. Machill & C. Welp (Eds.), Wegweiser im Netz (pp. 13-490). Gütersloh: Bertelsmann Stiftung.

Machlup, F. (1962). *The production and distribution of knowledge in the United States*. Princeton: Princeton University Press.

Madhavan, & Grover, R. (1996). From embedded knowledge to embodied knowledge: New products development as knowledge management. *ISBM report, 3*.

Mamdani, A., Pitt, J., Vasalou, A., & Bhusate, A. (2008). Emotional Computing and the Open Agent Society. In L. Magdalena, M. Ojeda-Aciego, & J.-L. Verdegay (Eds.), *Proceedings of IPMU'08* (pp. 1575-1582). Torremolinos (Malaga), June 22–27, 2008.

Manpower (2005). *Confronting the coming talent crunch: What's next?* Retrieved from http://www.manpower.com/mpcom/files?name=Talent_Shortage_Whitepaper_Global_Final.pdf.

Mansour, Y. (2007, April). *The E-Money Directive and MNOs: Why it All Went Wrong*. Prepared for the Bileta 2007 Annual Conference. Retrieved March 1, 2009, from http://www.bileta.ac.uk/Document%20Library/1/The%20E-Money%20Directive%20and%20MNOs%20-%20Why%20it%20All%20Went%20Wrong.pdf

Manunta, G. (2000). Defining security. [Cranfield: Cranfield Security Centre.]. *Diogenes*, 1.

Martin, W. J. (1995). *The global information society. Brookfield, VT*. Aldershot: Aslib Gower.

Martins, C. S., & Martins, S. J. (2005). The Impact of the USA PATRIOT Act on Records Management. *Information Management Journal*, *39*(3), 52–58.

Marziali, E., Serafini, J. M., & McCleary, L. (2005). A systematic review of practice standards and research ethics in technology-based home health care intervention programs for older adults. *Journal of Aging and Health*, *17*, 679–696. doi:10.1177/0898264305281100

Mason, D. (2009). Chips Raise Privacy Concerns. *Ward's Auto World*, *45*(3), 15.

Mazziotti, G. (2008). *EU digital copyright law and the end-user*. Springer.

McConnel, S. (2004). *Code Complete* (2nd ed.). Redmon, WA: Microsoft Press.

McConnell, S., & Tripp, L. (2005). Professional Software Engineering: Fact or Fiction. In R.H. Thyler & M. Dorfman (Eds.), Software Engineering Volume 1: The Development Processes (3rd Ed.). IEEE Computer Society.

McEliece, R. J., & Sarwate, D. V. (1981). On Sharing Secrets and Reed-Solomon Codes. *Communications of the ACM*, 24.

McMillan, R. (2006). *Google's binary search helps identify malware*. Resource document. PC World. Retrieved March 17, 2009, from http://www.pcworld.com/article/126371/googles_binary_search_helps_identify_malware.html.

Meaños, F. (2006).Un shopping en el bolsillo. Publicación semanal de Editorial Perfil S.A. N° 148. Retrieved March 26, 2009 from http://www.fortuna.uol.com.ar/edicion_0148/management/nota_01.htm

Mehrabian, A. (1980). *Silent Messages: Implicit Communication of Emotions and Attitudes*. Wadsworth Pub Co.

Menezes, A., van Oorscht, P., & Vanstone, S. (1996). *Handbook of Applied Cryptography*. CRC Press.

Merrill, D. (2006). Mashups: The new breed of Web app, an introduction to mashups. *The ultimate mashup - Web services and the semantic Web*. 2006. Retrieved from http://www.ibm.com/developerworks/xml/library/x-mashups.html

Mervis, J. (2007). Congress passes massive measure to support research and education. *Science, 317*(5839), 736–737. doi:10.1126/science.317.5839.736

Mervis, J. (2008). A new bottom line for school science. *Science, 319*(5866), 1030–1033. doi:10.1126/science.319.5866.1030

Mesjasz, C. (2004). *Security as a property of social systems*. Resource document. ISA Convention. Retrieved February 25, 2009, from http://www.allacademic.com/meta/p72561_index.html.

Mestçi, A. (2005). Turkey Internet Report. Retrieved February 18, 2009, from www.internethaftasi.org.tr/hafta06/docs/turkiye-internet-raporu.pdf

Microsoft Security Home Page. (2009). Microsoft Security. Resource document. Microsoft. Retrieved February 20, 2009, from http://www.microsoft.com/security/default.mspx.

Mierzejewska, B. (2008). Barbarians at the gate. In Wunderlinch, W., & Schimd, B. (Eds.), *Die Zukunft der Gutenberg-Galaxis* (pp. 99–116). Bern, Stuttgart, Wien: Haupt Verlag.

Miglio, F., Onida, T., Romano, F., & Santoro, S. (2003). *Electronic agents and the law of agency*. Retrieved from http://www.cirfid.unibo.it/~lea-02/pp/DemiglioOnida-RomanoSantoro.pdf, visited 8/9/2003

Miles, I. (1998). *The management of intellectual property in Knowledge Intensive Business Service Firms. Final report to ESRC*. UK: University of Manchester.

Miles, I. (2003) *Knowledge Intensive Services' Suppliers and Clients*. Ministry of Trade and Industry, Finland.

Miles, I., Andersen, B., Boden, M., & Howells, J. (1999). Service production and intellectual property, *International Journal of services Technology and Management, 1*(1), 37-57.

Miles, M., & Huberman, M. (1984). Fit, Failure and the Hall of Fame. *California Management Review, 26*(3).

Miller, M., & Stiegler, M. (2003). *The digital path: smart contracts and the third world. Markets, Information and Communication. Austrian Perspectives on the Internet Economy*. Routledge.

Min, P. (2004). *A 3D model search engine*. PhD Thesis. Computer Science. *Princeton University*. Retrieved March 3, 2009, from http://www.cs.princeton.edu/~min/publications/min04.pdf.

Ministerial Declaration. (2003). In the framework of the eHealth. 2003 conference. Retrieved December 7, 2008, from http://ec.europa.eu/information_society/eeurope/ehealth/conference/2003/doc/min_dec_22_may_03.pdf.

Miniwatts Marketing Group. (2009). *Internet world stats*. Resource document. Miniwatts Marketing Group. Retrieved January 5, 2009, from http://www.internetworldstats.com/stats.htm.

Mogee, M. E. (2003). *Foreign patenting behaviour of small and large firms: An update*. Restron, Virginia: SBA.

Moore, G. W., & Berman, J. J. (2000). Anatomic pathology data mining. In Cios, K. J. (Ed.), *Medical data mining and knowledge discovery* (pp. 61–108). Heidelberg: Springer.

Moore, J. W. (2005). An Integrated Collection of Software Engineering Standards. In R.H. Thyler & M. Dorfman (Eds.), Software Engineering Volume 1: The Development Processes (3rd Ed.). IEEE Computer Society.

Morgenthau, H. J. (1960). *Politics among nations. The struggle for power and peace*. New York: Alfred A. Knopf.

Moses, M. L. (2008). *The principles and practice of international commercial arbitration.* Cambridge University Press.

Moses, T. (2005). eXtensible Access Control Markup Language (XACML) Version 2.0. Retrieved April 20, 2009, from http://docs.oasis-open.org/xacml/2.0/access_control-xacml-2.0-core-spec-os.pdf

Moskop, J. C., Marco, C. A., Geiderman, J. M., & Derse, A. R. (2005). From Hippocrates to HIPAA: Privacy and confidentiality in emergency medicine. I. Conceptual, moral and legal foundations. *Annals of Emergency Medicine, 45*(1), 53–59. doi:10.1016/j.annemergmed.2004.08.008

Mowery, D., & Rosenberg, N. (1998). *Paths of Innovation: Technological Change in 20th-Century America.* Cambridge, UK: Cambridge University Press.

Moye, S. (2006). Congress Assesses Data Security Proposals. *Information Management Journal, 40*(1), 20-23.

Nagy, M., Vargas-Vera, M., Stolarski, P., & Motta, E. (2008). DSSim results for OAEI 2008. In *Proceedings of the 3rd International Workshop on Ontology Matching (OM-2008), Karlsruhe, Germany, October 26, 2008, CEUR WS vol. 431.*

National Security Council. (2010). Cybersecurity. Retrieved May 10, 2010 from http//www.whitehouse.gov/cybersecurity.

Naumann, I., & Hogben, G. (2008). Privacy features of European eID card specifications. *Network Security,* (8): 9–13. doi:10.1016/S1353-4858(08)70097-7

Naylor, D., & Jaworski, A. (2007). Virtual worlds, real challenges. *Entertainment Law Review, 18*(8), 262–264.

Netanel, N. W. (2003). Impose a Noncommercial Use Levy to Allow Free Peer-to-Peer File Sharing. *Harvard Journal of Law & Technology, 17,* 1–83.

Networking Government in New Zeland. (2009). *New Zealand Government Web Standards.* Retrieved April 9, 2009 from http://www.e.govt.nz/standards/webguidelines

Neville, B., & Pitt, J. (2003). A computational framework for social agents in agent mediated E- commerce. In A. Omicini, P. Petta & J. Pitt (Eds.), Engineering Societies in the Agents World: 4th International Workshop, ESAW 2003 (LNAI 3071, pp. 376-391). Springer Verlag.

Neville, B., & Pitt, J. (2004). A simulation study of social agents in agent mediated e- commerce. In *Proceedings AAMAS Workshop on Deception, Fraud and Trust in Agent Societies* (pp. 83-91). New York.

New rules issued to require government transparency. (2007, April 24). Retrieved on March 18, 2009 from http://www.chinadaily.com.cn/china/2007-04/24/content_858745.htm.

New Zealand Privacy Commissioner. (1999). *Discussion paper 2: Information Privacy principles.* Retrieved April 12, 2009 from http://www.cdt.org/privacy/eudirective.

Newell, F. (2000). *Loyalty.com: Customer Relationship Management in the New Era of Internet Marketing.* McGraw-Hill.

Nickel, J. W. (2007). *Making sense of human rights.* Malden, Massachusetts: Blackwell Publishers.

Nielson, S., Fogarty, S. J., & Wallach, D. S. (2004). *Attacks on local searching tools.* Technical report. Department of Computer Science. Rice University. Retrieved March 17, 2009, from http://seclab.cs.rice.edu/pubs/gdesktop-tr-dec04.pdf.

NIH & NLM. (2002). *Making Your Web Site Senior Friendly: A Checklist.* National Institute on Aging and National Library of Medicine. Retrieved May 25, 2008 from http://www.nlm.nih.gov/pubs/checklist.pdf

Nilsson, L.-G. (2003). Memory function in normal aging. *Acta Neurologica Scandinavica, 107*(Suppl. 179), 7–13. doi:10.1034/j.1600-0404.107.s179.5.x

Nimmer, M. (1970). Does Copyright Abridge the First Amendment Guarantees of Free Speech and Press? *University of California Law Review, 17.*

Niven, D. (2009). *Peer Review Principles, EPSRC.* Retrieved April 14, 2009 from http://www.epsrc.ac.uk/ResearchFunding/ReviewingProposals/Principles.htm

Nonaka, I., & Takeuchi, H. (1995). *The knowledge creating company: How Japanese Companies Create the Dynamics of Innovation.* Oxford: Oxford University Press.

Nothdurft, W. E. (1992). *Going Global: How Europe Helps Small Firms Export.* Brookings Institution Press.

Novais, P., Brito, L., & Neves, J. (2005). Pre-Argumentative Reasoning. *The Knowledge-Based Systems Journal, 18*(2-3), 79–88. doi:10.1016/j.knosys.2004.07.007

Nuttall, G. (2007). Income earned in virtual worlds: taxation issues. *E-Commerce Law & Policy, 9*(5).

O'Donoghue, R. (2007, September). *Microsoft v. EU Commission*: Sounds Good In Theory But...." *eCCP Publication.* Retrieved from http://www.globalcompetitionpolicy.com/index.php

O'Neil, M. (2009). *The Social Impact of Online Tribal Bureaucracy.* Paper presented at the Fourth Oekonux Conference, University of Manchester, UK 27-29 MARCH 2009.

O'Reilly, T. (2004). *Open Source Paradigm Shift.* Retrieved on June 8, 2009, from http://tim.oreilly.com/articles/paradigmshift_0504.html

O'Riordan, C. (2006, January). Transcript of Opening session of first international GPLv3 conference. Retrieved April 20, 2009, from http://www.ifso.ie/documents/gplv3-launch-2006-01-16.html

O'Shea, D. C. (2003). The bloom is off the Google. *Optical Engineering (Redondo Beach, Calif.), 42*(4), 894. doi:10.1117/1.1569244

Office of the Privacy Commissioner. (2005). *2004-05 Annual Report of the Office of the Privacy Commissioner.*

Ohashi, M. (2003). *Time Business.* Tokyo, Japan: NTT Publication.

Ohashi, M. (2003). *Public iDC and c-Society.* Tokyo, Japan: Kogaku Tosho.

Ohashi, M. (2004). The Time Authentication of Digital Contents. *Journal of Policy and Culture, 11*, 69–85.

Ohashi, M. (Ed.). (2003). *Knowledge-Based Collaborative Work.* The Report of Supplementary Budget Project of the Ministry of Post and Telecommunications.

Ohashi, M. (Ed.). (2003). *The Report of Society for the Advance Study on e-Society.* The Society of the Basis for e-Community.

Ohashi, M. (Ed.). (2004). The Report of the Advanced Studies for the Social Capital of e-Society. The Society of theBasis for the e-Community, Japan.

Ohashi, M. (Ed.). (2005). *XML Web Services for Next Generation & A view of Citizen Centric.* Japan: Kinokuniya Co.Ltd.

Ohashi, M., & Hori, M. (2005). The Theory of Economics for Network Society (pp. 2-5; 106-118). Japan: Kinokuniya Co., Ltd.

Ohashi, M., & Nagai, M. (2001). *Internet Data Center Revolution.* Tokyo, Japan: Impress.

Ohashi, M., Sasaki, K., & Hori, M. (2004). On the Study of Knowledge Structualization and Adaptive process Based on Project Based Learning. *Journal of Policy Studies, 11*, 55–78.

Olsen, K. A., & Saetre, P. (2007). IT for niche companies: is an ERP system the solution? *Information Systems Journal, 17*(1), 37–58. doi:10.1111/j.1365-2575.2006.00229.x

Olson, G. M., Malone, T. W., & Smith, J. B. (Eds.). (2001). *Coordination Theory and Collaboration Technology.* Mahwah, NJ: Erlbaum.

Öngören, G. (2000). İnternet Yayıncılığında Hukuki Sorunlar. İnternet ve Hukuk Forumu'na Sunulan Yayınlanmamış Tebliğ, 14/04/2000, İstanbul.

Online Etymology Dictionary. (2001). *Content.* Resource document. Online Etymology Dictionary. Retrieved January 1, 2009, from http://www.etymonline.com/index.php?l=c&p=24.

Open Source Initiative. (2009). *Open Source Licenses.* Retrieved April 14, 2009 from http://www.opensource.org/licenses

Open, I. D. (2007, December 5). OpenID Authentication 2.0. Retrieved April 20, 2009, from http://openid.net/specs/openid-authentication-2_0.html

Orciani, M., Frazzica, V., Colosi, L., & Galletti, F. (2007). Gregoriano cadastre: transformation of old maps into Geographical Information System and their contribution in terms of acquisition, processing and communication of historical data. *e-Perimetron, 2*(2), 92-104.

Organization for Economic Co-operation and Development. (2002). *OECD guidelines for the security of information systems and networks: Towards a culture of security.* Resource document. Retrieved February 2, 2009, from http://www.oecd.org/document/42/0,2340, en_2649_34255_15582250_1_1_1_1,00.html.

Organization for Economic Co-operation and Development. (n.d.). Retrieved June 15, 2009, from http://www.oecd.org

Ortiz, T. (2008). *Curso de Comercio Electrónico.* Retrieved March 26, 2009 from http://www.scribd.com/doc/96477/fundamentos-del-comercio-electronico

Orwell, G. (1949). *Nineteen Eighty-Four.* New York: Penguin.

OUT-LAW. (2008). *Designing software for the disabled-ISO guidelines.* News from Out-laws IT and e-commerce legal help from international law firm Pinsent Masons. Retrieved March 20, 2009 from http://www.out-law.com/page-3625.

Oxford Dictionary. (2008). *Oxford English dictionary.* Oxford: Oxford University Press.

Pacheco, O., & Carmo, J. (2003). A Role Based Model for the Normative Specification of Organized Collective Agency and Agents Interaction. *Autonomous Agents and Multi-Agent Systems, 6*(2), 145–184. doi:10.1023/A:1021884118023

Padilla, J., & O'Donoghue, R. (2006). *The Law and Economics of Article 82 EC.* Oxford: Hart Publishing.

Palmer, M. (2008). EU targets online privacy fears. *Financial Times (North American Edition),* 20.

Paris (2008). *Paris Convention for the Protection of Industrial Property.*

Parnas, D. L. (2005). Software Engineering Programs Are Not Computer Science Programs. In R.H. Thyler & M. Dorfman (Eds.), Software Engineering Volume 2: The Supporting Processes (3rd Ed.). IEEE Computer Society.

Parsons, T. W. (2008). *Enhancing pharmaceutical innovation through the use of Knowledge Management.* Ph. D. Thesis, Loughborough University.

Patterson, C., Shepherd, M., & Watters, C. (2000). An ethical framework: mechanisms for user-enabled choice and normative claims. *INFOETHICS 2000.* Resource document. United Nations Educational Scientific and Cultural Organization, Paris. Retrieved March 8, 2009, from http://webworld.unesco.org/infoethics2000/report_151100.html#conley.

Paulen. A. (2009). Google Adsense Ontology. Resource document. *Enzine.* Retrieved April 5, 2009, from http://ezinearticles.com/?Google-Adsense-Ontology&id=290598.

Perkowitz, M., & Etzioni, O. (2000). Towards adaptive websites: Conceptual framework and case study. *Computer Networks, 31*(11), 1245–1258. doi:10.1016/S1389-1286(99)00017-1

Peruginelli, G., & Chiti, G. (2002). Artificial intelligence in alternative dispute resolution. In *Proceedings of LEA 2002. Workshop on the Law of Electronic Agents* (pp. 97–104). CIRSFID, Bologna.

Peterson, M. G. E. (2005, January). Privacy, Public Safety, and Medical Research. *Journal of Medical Systems, 29*(1), 81–90. doi:10.1007/s10916-005-1106-y

Pew internet (2009). *Generational Differences in Online Activities.* Retrieved April 4, 2009 from http://www.pewinternet.org

Pfleeger, S. L., Fenton, N., & Page, S. (2005). Evaluating Software Engineering Standards. In R. H. Thyler & M. Dorfman (Eds.), Software Engineering Volume 2: The Supporting Processes (3rd Ed.). IEEE Computer Society.

Physor. (2006). *Google buys a new search algorithm.* Resource document. Retrieved February 7, 2009, from http://www.physorg.com/news63882927.html.

Pinkerton, B. (1994). *Finding what people want: Experiences with the webcrawler.* The Second International WWW Conference Chicago, USA, October 17-20. Retrieved April 11, 2009, from http://www.webir.org/resources/phd/pinkerton_2000.pdf.

Pipino, L., Lee, Y. W., & Wang, R. Y. (2002). Data quality assessment. *Communications of the ACM, 45*(4), 211–218. doi:10.1145/505248.506010

Pírko, Š. (2004). Největší medvědí trh od roku 1929 před námi... (in Czech: The biggest bear market since 1929 ahead …). Retrieved April 10, 2009, from http://colosseum.cz/pdf_analyzy/200405_us-stocks.pdf.

Pirolli, P., & Crad, S. K. (1999). Information foraging. *Psychological Review, 106*, 643–675. doi:10.1037/0033-295X.106.4.643

Pitt, J. (2005). The open agent society as a platform for the user-friendly information society. *AI & Society, 19*(2), 123–158. doi:10.1007/s00146-004-0306-1

Plock v. Bd. of Educ. of Freeport Sch. Dist. No. 145, 545 F. Supp. 2d 755 (N.D. Ill. 2007).

Podlas, K. (2000). Global commerce or global liability? How e -commerce can lead to suit in foreign courts or under foreign law. *The Mid – Atlantic. The Journal of Business, 36*(2), 89–101.

Politics: Senate Gives Patriot Act Six More Months. (2005). Retrieved on March 13, 2007 from http://www.cnn.com/2005/POLITICS/12/21/patriot.act/index.html.

Poullet, I. (2009). Data protection legislation: What is at stake for our society and democracy? *Computer Law & Security Report, 25*(3), 211–226. doi:10.1016/j.clsr.2009.03.008

Prahalad, C. K., & Ramaswamy, V. (in press). *The Future of Competition: Co-Creating Unique Value with Customers.* Boston. *Harvard Business Press.*

Primedia. (2006). Media Announcement: Privacy Commissioner publishes case notes 5-9 for 2006. *Primedia Email list.*

Privacy Act, 5 U.S.C. § 552a (1974).

Privacy International. (2003). *Data Retention violates human rights convention.* Retrieved from http://www.privacyinternational.org/article.shtml?cmd%5B347%5D=x-347-57875

Privacy Protection Act, 42 U.S.C. § 2000aa et seq. (1980).

Prosser, W. L. (1971). Handbook of the law of torts: Chapter 20 §117 right of privacy (4th ed.). St. Paul, MN: West Publishing Co.

Pyman, A., O'Rourke, A., & Teicher, J. (2008). Information Privacy and Employee Records in Australia: Which Way Forward? *Australian Bulletin of Labour, 34*(1), 28–46.

Quaddus, M., & Xu, J. (2007). Adoption of e-Commerce: A decision theoretic framework and an illustrative application. In *Proceedings of 10th International Conference on Computer and Information Technology (ICCIT 2007)* (pp. 292-297).

Ragouzis, N., Hughes, J., Philpott, R., Maler, E., Madsen, P., & Scavo, T. (2008). Security Assertion Markup Language (SAML) V2.0 Technical Overview. Retrieved April 20, 2009, from http://www.oasis-open.org/committees/download.php/27819/sstc-saml-tech-overview-2.0-cd-02.pdf

Rahwan, I., Ramchurn, S., Jennings, N., McBurney, P., Parsons, S., & Sonenberg, L. (2004). *Argumentation-based negotiation.* The Knowledge Engineering Review.

Raiffa, H. (2002). *The Art and Science of Negotiation.* Harvard University Press.

Ramchurn, S. D., Huynh, D., & Jennings, N. (2004). Trust in multiagent systems. *The Knowledge Engineering Review, 19*(1), 1–25. doi:10.1017/S0269888904000116

Randeree, E. (2006). Knowledge management: securing the future. *Journal of Knowledge Management, 10*(4), 145–156. doi:10.1108/13673270610679435

Rankin, B. (2007, November). What is a Mashup? *Ask Bob Rankin*. Retrieved from http://askbobrankin.com/what_is_a_mashup.html von Ahn, L., Blum, M. & Langford, J. (2002). Telling Humans and Computers Apart (Automatically) or How Lazy Cryptograhpers do AI. *Communications of the ACM*. von Ahn, L., Maurer, B., McMillen, C. & Blum, M. (2008, September 12). reCAPTCHA: Human-Based Character Recognition via Web Security Measures. *Science, 321*.

Rawls, J. (1971). *A Theory of Justice*. The Belknap Press of Harvard University Press.

Reding, V. (2007). Scientific Information in the Digital Age: How Accessible Should Publicly Funded Research Be? *Conference on Scientific Publishing in the European Research Area Access, Dissemination and Preservation in the Digital Age*. Brussels, European Commission for Information Society and Media.

Reding, V. (2008). La bibliothèque numérique européenne: du rêve à la réalité. *Forum d'Avignon 2008 – Culture, facteur de croissance*. Retrieved January 12, 2009 from http://ec.europa.eu/commission_barroso/reding/index_fr.htm

Reed, D., & McAlpin, D. (2005). Extensible Resource Identifier (XRI) Syntax V2.0. Retrieved April 20, 2009, from http://www.oasis-open.org/committees/download.php/15377/xri-syntax-V2.0-cs.pdf

Regner, T., Barria, J., Pitt, J., & Neville, B. (forthcoming). An Artist Life-Cycle Model for Digital Media Content: Strategies for the Light Web and the Dark Web. *Electronic Commerce Research and Applications*.

Reidenberg, J. (2000). Resolving Conflicting International Data Privacy Rules in Cyberspace. *Stanford Law Review, 52*, 1315–1376. doi:10.2307/1229516

Rejas, R., & Cuadrado, J. (2007). Licencias Software. *Otrosí. Ilustre Colegio de Abogados de Madrid., 84*, 60–70.

Reporters Sans Frontières (RSF). (1999, August 9). *Press Release*. internetworldstats.com Web site (n.d.). Retrieved March 15, 2009, from http://www.internetworldstats.com/stats4.htm

Reynolds, C., & Picard, R. (2004). Affective Sensors, Privacy, and Ethical Contracts. *Conference on Human Factors in Computing Systems* (CHI 2004), Vienna, Austria.

Richardson, M. (2002). Whither breach of confidence: A right of privacy for Australia? *Melborne University Law Review*. Retrieved Nov. 25, 2008 from http://www.austlii.edu.au/au/journals/MULR/2002.

Rieder, B. (2005). Networked control: Search engines and the symmetry of confidence. *International Review of Information Ethics, 3*(1), 26–32.

Rifkin, J. (2001). Online dispute resolution: theory and practice of the fourth party. *Conflict Resolution Quarterly, 19*(1).

Right to Financial Privacy Act, 12 U.S.C. 3401 et seq. (1978).

Rivest, R. L., & Lampson, B. (1996). SDSI - A Simple Distributed Security Infrastructure. September 15, 1996. Retrieved April 20, 2009, from http://people.csail.mit.edu/rivest/sdsi10.html

Roe v. Wade, 410 U.S. 113 (1973).

Romer, P. (1993). Two Strategies for Economic Development: Using Ideas and Producing Ideas. In *Proceedings of the World Bank Annual Conference on Development Economics*. Vitrubio, M. (25, b.c.). *De Architectura*. Retrieved on June 26, 2009, from http://www.latin.it/autore/vitruvio/de_architectura

Roselló, R. (2001). *El Comercio Electrónico y la Protección de los Consumidores*. Barcelona: España. Editorial Cedecs.

Rotolo, A., Sartor, G., & Smith, C. (2005). Formalization of a 'Normative Version' of Good Faith. In A. Oskamp & C. Cevenini (Eds.), *Proc. LEA 2005*. Nijmegen: Wolf Legal Publishers.

Rouvini, J.-D. (2003). Adapting to the user's internet search strategy on small devices. In L. Johnson & E. Andre (Eds.). *International Conference on Intelligent User Interfaces 2003* (pp. 284-286). Miami, Florida, USA.

Rowley, J. (1998). What is information? *Information Services & Use, 18*(4), 243–254.

Rubin, D. L., Shah, N. H., & Noy, N. F. (2007). Biomedical ontologies: a functional perspective. *Briefings in Bioinformatics, 9*(1), 75–90. doi:10.1093/bib/bbm059

Russel, S., & Norvig, P. (2003). *Artificial Intelligence: A modern approach* (2nd ed.). Prentice-Hall.

Salk, J., & Salk, J. D. (1981). *World populations and human values*. New York: Harper & Row Publishers.

Saltzer, J. H., & Schroeder, M. D. (1975). The protection of information in computer systems. *Proceedings of the IEEE, 63*(9), 1278–1308. doi:10.1109/PROC.1975.9939

Samuelson, P. (2000). *Towards More Sensible Anti-circumvention Regulations.* Retrieved April 29, 2009, from http://people.ischool.berkeley.edu/~pam/papers/fincrypt2.pdf

Sandler, R. B. (1997). Privacy law in the USA. Retrieved April 10, 2009 from http://www.rbs2.com/privacy.htm

Sanger, D. E., & Markoff, J. (2009, May 30). Obama outlines coordinated cyber-security plan. *New York Times*. Retrieved June 6, 2009 from http://www.nytimes.com/2009/05/30/us/politics/30cyber.html

Santos, D., Doz, Y., & Williamson, P. (2004). Is Your Innovation Process Global. *MIT Sloan Management Review*. Retrieved April 03, 2009 from http://sloanreview.mit.edu

Sarbanes-Oxley Financial and Accounting Disclosure Information. (2007). Retrieved on March 13, 2007 from http://www.sarbanes-oxley.com/

Sartor, G. (2002). Agents in Cyberlaw. In *Proceedings of the Workshop on the Law of Electronic Agents* (LEA 2002) and "Gli agenti software: nuovi sogetti del ciberdiritto?" Retrieved from http://www.cirfid.unibo.it/~sartor/sartorpapers/gsartor2002_agenti_software.pdf

Schacht, W. (2000). *Industrial Competitiveness and Technological Advancement: Debate Over Government Policy.* Report from CRS Issue Brief for Congress, Resources, Science, and Industry Division. Retrieved April 03, 2009 from http://fas.org/sgp/crs/misc/RL33528.pdf.

Schlembach, I. (2008). *Reputation stat antivirus-software, URL-filter und blacklisting.* Resource document. SearchSecurity.de. Retrieved April 1, 2009, from http://www.searchsecurity.de/themenbereiche/plattformsicherheit/client-security/articles/120503/.

Schneier, B. (2002). Crypto-Gram Newsletter August 15, 2002. Retrieved April 20, 2009, from http://www.schneier.com/crypto-gram-0208.html

Schneier, B. (2003). *Practical Cryptography*. Wiley & Sons.

Schofield, J. (2006). *How does Google envisage the future?* Resource document. The Guardian. Retrieved March 17, 2009, from http://media.guardian.co.uk/newmedia/story/0,1726289,00.html.

Schultz, T. (2002). *Online Dispute Resolution: An Overview and Selected Issues.* Economic Commission for Europe. Retrieved from http://ssrn.com/abstract=898821

Schultz, T. (2006). *Information Technology and Arbitration: A Practitioner's Guide.* The Hague: Kluwer Law International.

Schultz, T., Kaufmann-Kohler, G., Langer, D., & Bonnet, V. (2001). *Online Dispute Resolution: The State of the Art and the Issues.* Geneva: Report of the E-Com / E-Law Research Project of the University of Geneva.

Scully, J. (2005). Software and the Law. In R. H. Thyler & M. Dorfman (Eds.), Software Engineering Volume 1: The Development Processes (3rd Ed.). IEEE Computer Society.

SearchIgnite. (2008). *Potential impact of Google-Yahoo! Partnership & cost to marketers.* Resource document. Retrieved February 22, 2009, from http://www.searchignite.com/si/cm/tracking/trackredirect.aspx?siclientid=76&redirecturl.

Section508.gov. (2008). Retrieved April 9, 2009 from http://www.section508.gov

Secure Web Portal. (2009). Retrieved April 12, 2009, from http://www.guvenliweb.org.tr

Seehusen, F., & Stolen, K. (2008). *A method for model driven information flow security.* Report. University of Oslo, Norway. Retrieved March 3, 2009, from http://folk.uio.no/fredrise/publications/4.report-seehusen.pdf.

Shafer, P. S. (2005). Planning an Effective Training Program. In R. H. Thyler & M. Dorfman (Eds.), Software Engineering Volume 2: The Supporting Processes (3rd Ed.). IEEE Computer Society.

Shannon, C. E. (1948). A mathematical theory of communication. *The Bell System Technical Journal, 27,* 379–423, 623–656.

Shapiro, A. (1999). *The Control Revolution.* New York: PublicAffairs.

Shen, X., Tan, B., & Zhai, C. (2006). Exploiting personal search history to improve search accuracy. In *Proceedings of 2006 ACM Conference on Research and Development on Information Retrieval- Personal Information Management Workshop (PIM'2006)* (pp. 94-97). Retrieved March 2, 2009, from http://pim.ischool.washington.edu/pim06/files/shen-paper.pdf.

Sheng, H., Nah, F. F., & Siau, K. (2008). An Experimental Study on Ubiquitous commerce Adoption: Impact of Personalization and Privacy Concerns. *Journal of the Association for Information Systems, 9*(6), 344–376.

Sherman, C., & Price, G. (2001). *The invisible Web.* Medford, NJ: Information Today, Inc.

Shiley, C. S. (2003). *Putting the rights into the Family Education Rights and Privacy Act: Enforcement and the private right of action.* Unpublished Thesis. Massachusetts Institute of Technology.

Sınar, H. (2000), İnternetin Ortaya Çıkardığı Hukuki Sorunlara Bir Ceza Hukuku Yaklaşımı. MHB – Yılmaz Altuğ'a Armağan, Yıl:17-18, İstanbul.

Sınar, H. (2001). *İnternet ve Ceza Hukuku.* İstanbul: Beta Yayınları.

Singh, R. (2005). The Software Life Cycle Processes Standard. In R.H. Thyler & M. Dorfman (Eds.), Software Engineering Volume 2: The Supporting Processes (3rd Ed.). IEEE Computer Society.

Sisson, D. (2004). *Google secrets: How to get a top 10 ranking on the most important search engine in the world.* Redmond, WA: Blue Moose Webworks, Inc.

Sitesi, D. P. T. W. (DPT) (n.d.). T.R. Prime Ministry State Planning Organization Web Site. Retrieved March 03, 2009, from http://ekutup.dpt.gov.tr/plan/plan8.pdf

Skelton, R. A. (1965). *Looking at an early map.* Lawrence, KS: University of Kansas Library.

Smith, B., & Komar, B. (2005). *Microsoft Windows Security.* Microsoft Press.

Smith, E. (2001). The role of tacit and explicit knowledge in the workplace. *Journal of Knowledge Management, 5*(4), 311–321. doi:10.1108/13673270110411733

Smith, I. M., & Griffiths, V. (2004). *Programming the Finite Element Method* (4th ed.). Wiley.

Smith, P. G., & Merritt, G. M. (2002). *Proactive Risk Management.* Productivity Press.

Sojyo, I. (2009). *IP and Management Strategies in the Era of Open Innovation.* Report on the International Patent Licensing Seminar 2009. Retrieved March 17, 2009 from http://www.ryutu.inpit.go.jp/seminar_a/2009/pdf/B1_e.pdf

SOPRANO project HIC. (2006). *Review of HIC Concepts* (pp. 83-85). Retrieved May 25, 2008 from http://www.soprano-ip.org/ecportal.asp?id=226&nt=18&lang=1

SOPRANO project SOC. (2006) *Review of social & cultural aspects* (pp. 12-42). Retrieved May 25, 2008 from http://www.soprano-ip.org/ecportal.asp?id=226&nt=18&lang=1

Sornlertlamvanich, V. Tongchim, S., & Isahara, H. (2007). Evaluation of Web search engines with Thai queries. In *Proceedings of Workshop on NTCIR-6 and EVIA-1, NII, National Center of Sciences* (pp. 17-21). Tokyo: Japan.

Sourdin, T. (2005). *Alternative Dispute Resolution* (2nd ed.). Lawbook Co.

Spellings, M. (2006). *Answering the challenge of a changing world.*

Sperduto, R. D., & Seigel, D. (1980). Senile lens and senile macular changes in a population-based sample. *Am J Ophthalmol, 90*(1), 86-91. Retrieved on March 11, 2009 from http://www.ncbi.nlm.nih.gov/pubmed/7395962

Sproule, S., & Archer, N. (2006). Defining Identity Theft–A Discussion Paper. *McMaster eBusiness Research Centre (MeRC), McMaster University.*

Spulber, D. (2007, September). Competition Policy in Europe: Harming Incentives to Innovate. *eCCP Case Note.* Retrieved from http://www.globalcompetition-policy.com/index.php

Stallman, R. M. (1997). The Right to Read. [from http://www.gnu.org/philosophy/right-to-read.html]. *Communications of the ACM, 40*(2), 85–87. Retrieved April 20, 2009. doi:10.1145/253671.253726

Stamp, M. (2003). Digital Rights Management: The Technology Behind The Hype. *Journal of Electronic Commerce Research, 4*(3), 102–112.

Starbuck, W. H. (1992). Learning by knowledge intensive firms. *Journal of Management Studies, 29*(6), 713–740. doi:10.1111/j.1467-6486.1992.tb00686.x

Stark, P. B. (2007). The effectiveness of Internet content filters. *A Journal of Law and Policy for the Information Society, 2*(3), 943-979.

Steeves, V. (2008). If the Supreme Court were on facebook: Evaluating the reasonable expectation of privacy test from a social perspective. *Canadian Journal of Criminology and Criminal Justice, 50*(3), 331–347. doi:10.3138/cjccj.50.3.331

Steg, H., Strese, H., Loroff, C., Hull, J., & Schmidt, S. (2006). Europe Is Facing a Demographic Challenge. Ambient Assisted Living Offers Solutions. In the framework of The Ambient Assisted Living (AAL) Joint Programme. Retrieved March 10, 2009, from http://www.aal-europe.eu/.

Stevens, G. M. (1999). *Online privacy protection: Issues and developments.* National Library for the Environment. CRS Report: RL30322. Retrieved April 11, 2009 from http://digital.library.unt.edu/govdocs/crs/permalink/meta-crs-895:1

Stewart, T. A. (1999). *Intellectual Capital: The New Wealth of Organizations.* New York: Doubleday.

Stewart, T. A. (2001). *The Wealth of Knowledge. Intellectual Capital and the Twenty-First Century Organization.* New York: Doubleday.

Stolarski, P., Tomaszewski, T., Zeleznikow, J., & Abramowicz, W. (2008). *A Description of Legal Interpretations in Risk Management with the Use of Ontology Alignment Formalisms. ODR Workshop 2008 (Vol. 430).* CEUR-WS.

Storey, V. A., & Tebes, M. L. (2008). Instructor's privacy in distance (online) teaching: Where do you draw the line? *Online Journal of Distance Learning Administration XI* (II). Retrieved April 8, 2009 from http://www.westga.edu/distance/ojdla/summer112/storey112.html

Stothers, C. (2001). Refusal to Supply as Abuse of a Dominant Position: Essential Facilities in the European Union. *European Competition Law Review, 22*(7).

Sullivan, B. (2006). *'La difference' is stark in EU, U.S. privacy laws.* MSNBC.

Sullivan, D. (2002). *Google tops in search hours ratings.* Resource document. Search Engine Watch. Retrieved February 21, 2009, from http://searchenginewatch.com/sereport/article.php/2164801.

Sullivan, D. (2005). *Search engine sizes.* Resource document. Search Engine Watch. Retrieved March 25, 2009, from http://searchenginewatch.com/2156481.

Surden, H., Genesereth, M., & Logu, B. (2007). *Research abstracts 2: Representational complexity in law* (pp. 193–194). ACM.

Sutin, A. N. (2007). Virtual Worlds: Issues and challenges presented by virtual worlds. *E-Commerce Law & Policy, 9*(3).

Swart, J., & Kinney, N. (2003). Knowledge Intensive Firms: the influent of the client on HR system. University of Bath. *Human Resource Management Journal, 13*(3), 37–55. doi:10.1111/j.1748-8583.2003.tb00097.x

Swartz, N. (2007, Sep/Oct). Google Reduces Data Retention Period. *Information Management Journal, 41*(5), 22.

Swisher, K. (2008). *Microsoft's trojan horse (also Google's): Display advertising.* Resource document. All Things Digital. Retrieved February 22, 2009, from http://kara.allthingsd.com/20080716/microsofts-trojan-horse-also-googles.

Szabo, N. (1996). *Smart contracts: building blocks for digital markets.* Retrieved from http://szabo.best.vwh.net/smart.contracts.2.html

Tan, K. S., Chong, S. C., Lin, B. S., & Eze, U. C. (2009). Internet-based ICT adoption: evidence from Malaysian SMEs. *Industrial Management & Data Systems, 109*(1-2), 224–244. doi:10.1108/02635570910930118

Tang, P., Adams, J., & Paré, D. (2001). *Patent protection of computer programmes.* Final Report, ECSC-EC-EAEC. Brussels, Luxembourg: OMPI-CEPAL. Retrieved on June 26, 2009, from http://eupat.ffii.org/papers/tangadpa00/tangadpa00.pdf

Tang, X. (2008, March). *Frontiers of Law in China: Vol 3. Personal health care and medical treatment information and protection of privacy right* (pp. 408-422).

Teece, D. J. (2000). *Managing Intellectual Capital: Organizational, Strategic, and Policy Dimensions.* Oxford: Oxford University Press.

Teece, D. J. (2002). Knowledge and Competencies as Strategic asset. In Holsapple, C. W. (Ed.), *Handbook of Knowledge Management* (*Vol. 1*, pp. 129–152). Berlin: Springer-Verlag.

Teevan, J., Dumais, S. T., & Horvitz, E. E. (2005). Personalizing search via automated analysis of interests and activites. In *Proceedings of 28th Annual International ACM SIGIR Conference on Research and Development in Information Retrieval* (pp. 449-456). New York: ACM Press.

Telecommunications Act, 47 U.S.C. §§ 153, 255. § 153 (1996).

Telekomünikasyon İletişim Başkanlığı (TİB). (2009). Telecommunication Council Web site. Retrieved March 22, 2009, from http://www.tib.gov.tr/baskanlik_gorevleri.html

Telephone Consumer Protection Act, 47 U.S.C. § 227 (1991).

Temple Lang, J. (1995). Defining Legitimate Competition: Companies' Duties to Supply Competitors, and Access to Essential Facilities. In B. Hawk (Ed.), 1994 Fordham Corporate Law Institute, 245.

Temple Lang, J., & O'Donoghue, R. (2005, June 10). The Concept of an Exclusionary Abuse under Article 82. *Research Paper on the Modernisation of Article 82 EC.* Colegio de Europa (Brujas).

Teubner, G. (2001). *Das Recht hybrider Netzwerke.* ZHR.

The BigInteger Library of Java. (n.d.). http://java.sun.com/j2se/1.4.2/docs/api/java/math/BigInteger.html

The Charter of Fundamental Rights of the European Union. (2000). Retrieved June 15, 2009, from http://www.europarl.europa.eu/charter/default_en.htm

The Economist. (2003). Asia: The right to know; China. *The Economist, 369,* 72.

The European Convention on Human Rights. (1950). Retrieved June 15, 2009, from http://conventions.coe.int/treaty/en/Treaties/Html/005.htm

The International Covenant on Civil and Political Rights. (1966). Retrieved June 15, 2009, from http://www2.ohchr.org/english/law/ccpr.htm

The International PGP Home Page. (n.d.). http://www.pgpi.org/

The Open Group. single sign-on. Retrieved June 8, 2009, from http://www.opengroup.org/security/sso/.

The Royal National Institute for Deaf People. (1996). *Statistics on deafness.* Retrieved April 6, 2009 from http://www.rnid.org/html/info-factsheets-general-statistics-on-deafness.html

The treaty on European Union. (1992). Retrieved June 8, 2009, from http://europa.eu/eur-lex/en/treaties/dat/EU_treaty.html

The Web Accessibility in Mind. (2009). *World laws.* Retrieved April 9, 2009 from http://www.webaim.org/articles/laws/world/

Thiessen, E., & Zeleznikow, J. (2004). Technical aspects of online dispute resolution challenges and opportunities. In M. Conley Tyler, E. Katsh, & D. Choi (Eds.), *Proceedings of the Third Annual Forum on Online Dispute Resolution.*

Thomas, J. L. (2009). Online, teaching, & academic research privacy policy. Retrieved from http://www.ccba.jsu.edu/Thomas/PrivacyPolicy.doc

Thornburgh, D., & Lin, H. S. (Eds.). (2002). *Youth, pornography and the Internet.* Washington, D.C.: National Academies Press.

Thoumyre, L. (1999). L'échange des consentements dans le commerce électronique. *Lex Electronica, 5*(1).

Thyler, R. H., & Dorfman, M. (Eds.). (a2005). Software Engineering Volume 1: The Development Processes (3rd Ed.). IEEE Computer Society.

Thyler, R. H., & Dorfman, M. (Eds.). (b2005). Software Engineering Volume 2: The Supporting Processes (3rd ed.). IEEE Computer Society.

Time Business Forum (Ed.). (2003). *Time Ausentication Infrastructure Guidelines.* Japan: Time Business Forum.

Tockey, S. (2005). Recommended Skills and Knowledge for Software Engineers. In R. H. Thyler & M. Dorfman (Eds.), Software Engineering Volume 1: The Development Processes (3rd Ed.). IEEE Computer Society.

Toffler, A. (1980). *The Third Wave.* Bantam Books.

Tomaszewski, T. (1998). *Wyszukiwanie Informacji Prawnej w Systemach Hipertekstu.* PhD Thesis. Poznan University of Economics.

Tomaszewski, T., & Stolarski, P. (2008). Legal Framework for eCommerce Tax Analysis. In L. M. Camarinha-Matos & W. Picard (Eds.), *Pervasive Collaborative Networks, IFIP TC 5 WG 5.5 Ninth Working Conference on Virtual Enterprises, Poznan, Poland.* Springer.

Torremans, P. (2004). Copyright as a human right. In *Copyright and human rights: freedom of expression, intellectual property, privacy* (pp. 1–20). Kluwer Law International.

Torrisi, S. (1998). *Industrial Organization and Innovation. An International Study of the Software Industry.* Cheltenham: Edward Elgar.

Treasury Board of Canada Secretariat. (2007). *Common Look and Feel for the Internet 2.0.* Retrieved April 9, 2009 from http://www.tbs-sct.gc.ca/clf2-nsi2/index-eng.asp

Trivino, G., & van der Heide, A. (2008). Linguistic summarization of the human activity using skin conductivity and accelerometers. In L. Magdalena, M. Ojeda-Aciego, & J.-L. Verdegay (Eds.), *Proceedings of IPMU'08* (pp. 1583-1589).

Tsilas., L., N. (2007). Enabling Open Innovation and Interoperability: Recommendations for Policy-Makers. In *Proceedings of the 1st international conference on Theory and practice of electronic governance.* ACM International Conference Proceeding Series, Vol. 232.

Türkiye Büyük Millet Meclisi (TBMM). (n.d.). The Grand National Assembly of Turkey Web Site. Retrieved March 22, 2009, http://www.tbmm.gov.tr/sirasayi/donem22/yil01/ss1397m.htm

Turban, E. (1993). *Decision support and expert systems: management support systems.* Upper Saddle River, NJ: Prentice Hall PTR.

Turban, E., McLean, E., & Wetherbe, J. (1996). *Information technology for management: Improving quality and productivity.* New York: John Wiley & Sons.

Tysver, D. (2008). The History of Software Patents: From Benson and Diehr to State Street and Bilski. *BitLaw Legal Resource.* Retrieved on May 2, 2009 from http://www.bitlaw.com/software-patent/history.html.

U.S. Census Bureau IDB. (2009). *International Data Base.* Retrieved March 1, 2009 from http://www.census.gov/ipc/www/idb/

UKCRC. (2006). *UK Universities Computing Research UKCRC Submission to the EPSRC International Review.* Retrieved April 5, 2009 from http://www.ukcrc.org.uk/resource/reports/ukcrc_part_a.pdf

UKCRC. (2007). *Response by UKCRC to RCUK Consultation on Efficiency and Effectiveness of Peer Review.* Retrieved April 14, 2009 from http://www.ukcrc.org.uk/resource/reports/2007-01.pdf

United Nations. (2008). Human development report 2007/2008. Report. *United Nations.* Retrieved January 5, 2009, from http://hdr.undp.org/en/media/HDR_20072008_EN_Complete.pdf.

United States District Court. (2006a). *Kinderstart.com LLC v. Google Inc. first amended complaint, C 06-2057 RS.* Resource document. United States District Court: Northern District of California. San Jose. Retrieved February 10, 2009, from http://docs.justia.com/cases/federal/district-courts/california/candce/5:2006cv02057/178063/3/0.pdf.

United States District Court. (2006b). *Kinderstart.com LLC v. Google Inc. judgement order, C 06-2057 JF (RS).* Resource document. United States District Court: Northern District of California. San Jose Division. Retrieved February 10, 2009, from http://docs.justia.com/cases/federal/district-courts/california/candce/5:2006cv02057/178063/43/0.pdf.

United States Government Accountability Office. *Personal Information.* (2006). Retrieved on March 25, 2007 from http://www.gao.gov/new.items/d06674.pdf.

United States v. Heckenamp, 482 F3d 1142, Ninth Circuit (2007).

United States v. Miami University, 294 F. 3d 797 (2002)

Universal City Studios v. Reimerdes 273 F.3d 429 (2d Cir. 2001).

University of Illinois Eye & Ear Infirmary. (2007). *Macular Degeneration Info, The Eye Digest.* Retrieved March 10, 2009, from http://www.agingeye.net/maculardegen/maculardegeninformation.php

US Department of Health and Human Services, Office for Civil Rights. Standards for privacy of individually identifiable health information. (2000). Retrieved June 15, 2009, from http://www.ihs.gov/AdminMngrResources/PrivacyAct/pdf/combinedregtext.pdf

US Department of Health and Human Services, Office for Civil Rights. Summary of the HIPAA privacy rule. (2004). Retrieved June 15, 2009, from http://www.hhs.gov/ocr/privacy/hipaa/understanding/summary/privacysummary.pdf

Uszok, A., Bradshaw, J., Johnson, M., Jeffers, R., Tate, A., Dalton, J., & Aitken, A. (2004). Kaos policy management for semantic web services. *IEEE Intelligent Systems, 19,* 32–41. doi:10.1109/MIS.2004.31

Vacca, R. (2008). Viewing Virtual Property Ownership through the Lens of Innovation. *Tennessee Law Review, 76.*

Vaccaro, A., & Madsen, P. (2006). Firm information transparency: ethical questions into the information age. In Berleur, J., Numinen, M. I., & Impagliazzo, J. (Eds.), *Social Informatics: An Information Society for All? In Remembrance of Rob Kling* (pp. 145–156). Boston: Springer. doi:10.1007/978-0-387-37876-3_12

van Eijk, N. (2007). Search engines, the new bottleneck for content access. In *Proceedings of International Telecommunications Society ITS 19th European Regional Conference,* 2-5 September 2007. Istanbul, Turkey. Retrieved March 14, 2009, from http://www.itseurope.org/ITS%20CONF/istanbul2007/index.php?page=abstracts.

van Eijk, N. (2009). A converged regulatory model for search engines? *International. Magazine of the Society for Computers and Law, 19*(6), 1–3.

Vanderburg, H. W. (2007). Technology and the Law: Who Rules? *Bulletin of Science Technology Society 2007, 27,* 322; DOI: 10.1177/0270467607302688: General Article: Published by SAGE at University from Toronto, Retrieved April 17, 2009 from http://www.sagepublications.com, http://bst.sagepub.com/cgi/content/abstract/27/4/322

Vascellaro, J. E., & Fowler, G. A. (2009). China Blocks Local Access To YouTube, Once Again. *Wall Street Journal. (Eastern edition)* B1.

Vázquez Maure, F., & Martín López, J. (1989). *Lectura de mapas*. Madrid: Instituto Geográfico Nacional.

Video Privacy Protection Act, 18 U.S.C. § 2710 (1988).

Visser, R. S. P., & Bench-Capon, J. M. J. (1999). *Ontologies in the Design of Legal Knowledge Systems*. Retrieved from https://eprints.kfupm.edu.sa/55792/1/55792.pdf

Visser, R.S.P., & Bench-capon, T. (1996). *On the Reusability of Ontologies in Knowledge-System Design.*

Vlosky, R. P., & Westbrook, T. (2002). E-business exchange between homecenter buyers and wood products suppliers. *Forest Products Journal, 52*(1), 38–43.

Volonino, L., & Robinson, S. R. (2004). *Principles and Practice of Information Security: Protecting Computers from Hackers and Lawyers*. Upper Saddle River, NJ: Pearson Prentice Hall.

W3C EOWG (2008), *Web Accessibility for Older Users: A Literature review (Working Draft)*. W3C Education and Outreach Working Group. World Wide Web Consortium, (Massachusetts Institute of Technology, European Research Consortium for Informatics and Mathematics, Keio University). Retrieved May 25, 2008 from http://www.w3.org/TR/wai-age-literature/

W3C Policies (2006). Policies Relating to Web Accessibility. World Wide Web Consortium, (Massachusetts Institute of Technology, European Research Consortium for Informatics and Mathematics, Keio University). Retrieved April 9, 2009 from http://www.w3.org/WAI/Policy/

W3C WAI-AGE Group (2009). WAI Guidelines and older users: findings from a litterature review. [Editor's DRAFT - 11 March 2009]. World Wide Web Consortium, (Massachusetts Institute of Technology, European Research Consortium for Informatics and Mathematics, Keio University). Retrieved April 6, 2009 from http://www.w3.org/WAI/WAI-AGE/comparative.html

W3C WCAG 1.0 Recommendation (1999). Web Content Accessibility Guidelines 1.0 - W3C Recommendation 5-May-1999. World Wide Web Consortium, (Massachusetts Institute of Technology, European Research Consortium for Informatics and Mathematics, Keio University). Retrieved April 6, 2009 from http://www.w3.org/TR/1999/WAI-WEBCONTENT-19990505

W3C WCAG 2.0 How to (2008). Web Content Accessibility Guidelines (WCAG) 2.0 - How to Meet WCAG 2.0 - A customizable quick reference to Web Content Accessibility Guidelines 2.0 requirements (success criteria) and techniques. World Wide Web Consortium, (Massachusetts Institute of Technology, European Research Consortium for Informatics and Mathematics, Keio University). Retrieved April 6, 2009 from http://www.w3.org/WAI/WCAG20/quickref/

W3C WCAG 2.0 Latest. Web Content Accessibility Guidelines (WCAG) 2.0 – W3C Latest Recommendation. Copyright © World Wide Web Consortium, (Massachusetts Institute of Technology, European Research Consortium for Informatics and Mathematics, Keio University). Retrieved April 6, 2009 from http://www.w3.org/TR/WCAG20/

W3C WCAG 2.0 Recommendation (2008). Web Content Accessibility Guidelines (WCAG) 2.0 - W3C Recommendation 11 December 2008. World Wide Web Consortium, (Massachusetts Institute of Technology, European Research Consortium for Informatics and Mathematics, Keio University). Retrieved April 6, 2009 from http://www.w3.org/TR/2008/REC-WCAG20-20081211/

Waelbroeck, D. (2008, January). The *Microsoft* Judgment: Article 82 Revisited? *GCP Online Magazine*. Retrieved from http://globalcompetitionpolicy.org

Walden, A. E. (2005). Intellectual Property Rights and Cannibalization in Information Technology Outsourcing Contracts. *Journal of MIS Quarterly, 29*(4), 699-720. Retrieved March 25, 2009 from http://www.misq.org/archivist/vol/no29/Issue4/Walden.html

Waldrop, M. M. (2008). Science 2.0. *Scientific American, 298*(5). doi:10.1038/scientificamerican0508-68

Walker, D. (1980). *Oxford Companion to Law* (p. 301). Oxford University Press.

Walker, J. (2003). The Digital imprimatur: How big brother and big media can put the Internet genie back in the bottle. Retrieved April 20, 2009, from http://www.fourmilab.ch/documents/digital-imprimatur/

Wall, B. (2002). An imperfect cybercrime treaty. *CIO, 15*(9), 102.

Wallace, L. (2007). Online teaching and university policy: Investigating the disconnect. *Journal of Distance Education, 22*(1) 87-100. Retrieved April 6, 2009 from http://www.jofde.ca/index.php/jde/article/viewFile/58/471.

Walton, P. R. E., & McKersie, R. B. (1991). *A behavioral theory of labor negotiations.* Cornell University Press.

Wang, W. J., Yuan, Y., Archer, N. P., & Centre, M. E. R. (2004). *A Theoretical Framework for Combating Identity Theft. McMaster eBusiness Research Centre (MeRC).* DeGroote School of Business.

Wang, W., Meng, W., & Yu, C. (2000). Concept hierarchy based text database categorization in a metasearch engine environment. In Q. Li, Z. M. Ozsoyoglu, R. Wagner, Y. Kambayashi & Y. Zhang (Eds.), *Proceedings of the First International Conference on Web Information Systems Engineering (WISE'00)* (Vol. 1, pp. 283-290). Hong Kong, China.

Wang, Y., & DeWitt, D. J. (2004). Computing PageRank in a distributed Internet search system. In *Proceedings of the 30th VLDB Conference* (pp. 420-431). August 29-September 3, Toronto, Ontario, Canada. Retrieved January 27, 2009, from http://www.vldb.org/conf/2004/RS11P1.PDF.

Warnier, M., Brazier, F., Apistola, M., & Oskamp, A. (2007). *Towards automatic identification of completeness and consistency in digital dossiers* (pp. 177–181). ACM.

Warren, S.D. & Brandeis, L.D. (1890). The right to privacy. *Harvard Law Review, 4*(5), 193-220. Posted February 8, 1999. Retrieved April 10, 2009.

WebSideStory. (2004). *Google's search referral market share reaches an all- time high.* Resource document. Retrieved February 2, 2009, from http://www.websidestory.com/pressroom/pressreleases.html.

Webster, F. (2006). *Theories of the information society* (3rd ed.). London: Routledge.

Weitzenboeck, E. (2001). Electronic Agents and the formation of contracts. *International Journal of Law and Information Technology, 9*(3), 204–234. doi:10.1093/ijlit/9.3.204

Welch, V., Foster, I., Kesselman, C., Mulmo, O., Pearlman, L., Tuecke, S., et al. (2004). X.509 Proxy Certificates for Dynamic Delegation. In *Proceedings of the 3rd Annual PKI R&D Workshop.* Gaithersburg MD: NIST Technical Publications.

Weld, D., & Etzioni, O. (1994). The first law of softbotics. In *Proc. 12th Nat. Conf. on A.I.*

Wellman, B. (2001). Changing connectivity: A future history of Y2.03K. *Sociological Research Online, 4*(4). Retrieved January 21, 2009, from http://www.socresonline.org.uk/4/4/wellman.html.

West, J., & Gallagher, S. (2004). Challenges of Open Innovation: The Paradox of Firm Investment in Open Source Software. *R&D Management, 36*(3). Retrieved April 03, 2009 from http://www.cob.sjsu.edu/opensource/research/

Wettig, S., & Zehendner, E. (2003). The Electronic Agent: A Legal Personality under German Law? In A. Oskamp & E. Weitzenböck (Eds.), *Proceedings of the Law and Electronic Agents workshop (LEA'03).*

Whitman, M. E. (2003). Enemy at the gate: Threats to information security. *Communications of the ACM, 46*(8), 91–95. doi:10.1145/859670.859675

Wielki, J. (2008). The impact of search engines on contemporary organizations- The social and ethical implications. In T. W. Bynum, M. Calzarossa, I. Lotto & S. Rogerson (Eds.), ETHICOMP 2008: Living, Working and Learning Beyond Technology (pp. 769-803). Mantova: University of Pavia, Italy.

Wiig, K. M. (1997). Integrating Intellectual Capital and Knowledge Management. *Long Range Planning, 30*, 399–406. doi:10.1016/S0024-6301(97)90256-9

Wikisource (n.d.). *Statute of Anne*. Retrieved on June 16, 2009, from http://en.wikisource.org/wiki/Statute_of_Anne

Wilson, G. (2005). *Software Carpentary*. Python Software Foundation. Retrieved April 13, 2009 from http://www.swc.scipy.org/

Wilson, G. (2006). Where's the Real Bottleneck in Scientific Computing? *American Scientist, 94*(1), 5. doi:. doi:10.1511/2006.1.5

Windley, P. (2005). *Digital Identity*. O'Reilly.

Witkowski, M., Pitt, J., Fehin, P., & Arafa, Y. (2001). Indicators to the Effects of Agent Technology on Consumer Loyalty. In Stanford-Smith, B., & Chiozza, E. (Eds.), *E-Work and E-Commerce: Novel Solutions and Practices for a Global Networked Economy* (pp. 1165–1171). IOS Press.

Wooldrige, M. (2002). *An Introduction to MultiAgent Systems*. John Wiley & Sons.

Wooldrige, M. (2002). *An Introduction to Multiagent Systems*. John Wiley & Sons.

Word Intellectual Property Organization (WIPO). (n.d.). Retrieved from http://www.wipo.org

World Digital Library. (n.d.). Retrieved April 16, 2009 from http://worlddigitallibrary.org/project/English/index.html

World Intellectual Property Organization. (n.d.). *Berne Convention for the Protection of Literary and Artistic Works*. Retrieved on June 10, 2009, from http://www.wipo.int/treaties/en/ip/berne/trtdocs_wo001.html

World Medical Association. World Medical Association statement on the use of computer in medicine [rescinded at the WMA General Assembly, Pilanesberg, South Africa, 2006]. Geneva (CH): WMA; 2006. Retrieved June 15, 2009, http://www.wma.net/e/policy/c9.htm

World Summit on the Information Society. (2003). *Declaration of principles: Document WSIS-03/GENEVA/DOC/4-E, 12 December*. Resource document. International Telecommunications Union. Retrieved April 5, 2009, from http://www.itu.int/wsis/docs/geneva/official/dop.html.

World Trade Organization. (n.d.). *Trade-Related Aspects of Intellectual Property Rights*. Retrieved on June 10, 2009, from http://www.wto.org/english/docs_e/legal_e/27-trips_01_e.htm

XrML. (2002, March 8). XrML 2.0 Technical Overview Version 1.0. Retrieved April 20, 2009, from http://www.xrml.org/Reference/XrMLTechnicalOverviewV1.pdf

Ye, J. (2008). Going Dark: China's Computer Screens. Retrieved March 25, 2009, from http://blogs.wsj.com/chinajournal/2008/10/21/going-dark-chinas-computer-screens/

Zack, M. H. (1999). *Knowledge and Strategy*. Boston, MA: Butterworth-Heinemann.

Zaphiris, P., Kurniawan, S., & Ghiawadwala, M. (2007) A Systematic Approach to the Development of Research-Based Web Design Guidelines for Older People. *Universal Access in the Information Society Journal, 6*(1), 59-76, Retrieved from http://www.springerlink.com/content/087050g2771rj416/fulltext.pdf

Zartman, I. W. (2007). *Peacemaking in international conflict*. US Institute of Peace Press.

Zeleznikow, J., & Bellucci, E. (2003). Family_Winner: integrating game theory and heuristics to provide negotiation support. In *Proceedings of Sixteenth International Conference on Legal Knowledge Based System* (pp. 21-30).

Zeleznikow, J., & Stranieri, A. (1996). Automating legal reasoning in discretionary domains. In Legal Knowledge Based Systems JURIX'96 Foundations of legal knowledge systems (pp. 101-110).

Zeller, T. J. (2006). A new campaign tactic: manipulating Google data. Resource document. *The New York Times (Late Edition (East Coast))*, 20. Retrieved February 28, 2009, from http://www.nytimes.com/2006/10/26/us/politics/26googlebomb.html.

Zentai, L. (2006). Preservation of modern cartographic products. *e-Perimetron, 4* (1), 308-313.

Zhang, M. (2007). University Student Sues Microsoft for Invasion of Privacy. *CHINA.ORG.CN.*

Zhang, Y., Vasconcelos, W., & Sleeman, D. (2004). Ontosearch: An ontology search engine. In M. Bramer, F. Coenen & T. Allen (Eds.9), *Proceedings of the 24th SGAI International Conference on Innovation Techniques and Applications of Artificial Intelligence* (pp. 58-69). Cambridge, United Kingdom.

Zien, J., et al. (2001). Web query characteristics and their implications on search engines. In *Proceedings of the 10th WWW International Conference.* May 1-5, Hong Kong, Hong Kong. Retrieved January 25, 2009, from http://www10.org/cdrom/posters/1077.pdf.

Zook, M. A. (2005). *The geography of the Internet industry venture capital, dot-coms, and local knowledge (Information Age Series).* Oxford: Blackwell Publishing.

About the Contributors

Irene Maria Portela is currently an Assistant Professor in the School of Management at the Polytechnic Institute of Cavado and Ave, Portugal. She is graduated in Law, holds has a Master in Public Administration and holds a PhD in Law, in the field of Anti-Terrorism Law from Universy of Santiago de Compostela (Spain). She teaches subjects related with Constitutional Law to undergraduated and post-graduated studies. She regularly publishes in international peer-reviewed journals and participates on international scientific conferences. Her work appears in several papers published in journals, book chapters and conference proceedings.

Maria Manuela Cruz-Cunha is currently an Associate Professor in the School of Technology at the Polytechnic Institute of Cavado and Ave, Portugal. She holds a Dipl. Eng. in the field of Systems and Informatics Engineering, an M.Sci. in the field of Information Society and a Dr.Sci in the field of Virtual Enterprises, all from the University of Minho (Portugal). She teaches subjects related with Information Systems, Information Technologies and Organizational Models to undergraduated and post-graduated studies. She supervises several PhD projects in the domain of Virtual Enterprises and Information Systems and Technologies. She regularly publishes in international peer-reviewed journals and participates on international scientific conferences. She serves as a member of Editorial Board and Associate Editor for several International Journals and for several Scientific Committees of International Conferences. She has authored and edited several books and her work appears in more than 70 papers published in journals, book chapters and conference proceedings.

***

Beatriz Sainz de Abajo is a young telecommunications researcher in the University of Valladolid (Spain). She is a PhD candidate in Telecommunications Engineering. She has devoted all her professional life to the investigation around telecommunication regulation matters and novel telecommunication systems. Her future research interests are e-commerce, e-government, telecommunications policy and also digital contents both from the user's standpoint and from the competitive market vision.

Isabel de la Torre was born in Zamora, Spain, in 1979. She received the Engineer degree in telecommunications engineering from the University of Valladolid, Valladolid, Spain, in 2003. Currently, she is an assistant professor in the Department of Signal Theory and Communications at the University of Valladolid, where she is working towards the Ph.D. degree. Her research has been mainly focused in development of telemedicine applications, EHRs (Electronic Health Records) standards in Ophthalmology, e-learning and e-commerce applications.

Miguel López is a telecommunications professor in the University of Valladolid (Spain). He was born in Barcelona, Spain; in 1950. He has a PhD in Telecommunications Engineering from the Polytechnic University of Madrid, in 1982. Since 1991 he has been devoted to the promotion of Information Society in Castille and Leon region from several positions: Director of the Technical School of Telecommunications, R&D General Manager of a Telecommunications Technological Centre and also CEO of a cable telecommunications operator. Now, his research interests are biomedical signal, Telemedicine, Information Society, and to contribute to the promotion of the entrepreneurial character of University.

Pilar Chias is professor at the Technical School of Architecture and Geodesy of the University of Alcalá (Spain). After a long tradition on implementing GIS about the Cultural Heritage in a wide sense, her particular interest has focused on the historical cartography as a main source for researches on the historical evolution of the Spanish territories and landscapes. Co-author (with T. Abad) of many books and academic journal articles as *Los caminos y la construcción del territorio en Zamora. Catálogo de puentes* (2004*), Eduardo Torroja. Obras y Proyectos* (2005), 'Las vías de comunicación en la cartografía histórica de la Cuenca del Duero: construcción del territorio y paisaje', *Ingeniería Civil*, no. 149 (2008). She conducts the Project of the Ancient Cartography e-Library of the Instituto de Estudios Latinoamericanos (IELAT) of the University of Alcalá, Spain.

Tomas Abad is searcher at the Technical School of Architecture and Geodesy of the University of Alcalá (Spain). Despite his technical background, his particular interest soon turned to the history of the civil works and the industrial heritage. He is an outstanding member of the team of searchers of the University of Alcalá and the co-director of the Ancient Cartography e-Library of the IELAT.

Elena Rivera is a young lawyer and a member of the searchers' team of the University of Alcalá. Her main interests are focused on the problematics of the intellectual property rights (IPR) and the online accessibility to the historical and cultural materials.

Jose Antonio Álvarez Bermejo is a Computer Architect that works as a Lecturer at the Dept of Computer Architecture and Electronic at University of Almería, Spain. He is developing his work as a researcher within the research team "Supercomputación: Algoritmos" that is supported by official institutions as the Spanish Government. His research interests are centered in several areas, ranging from supercomputing and parallel programming techniques and Multicore processor's applications to Object Oriented programming techniques and computers security issues. He is also the reference teacher for the Microsoft dotNet student's club in Universidad de Almería, a group in which MS technologies are studied and exploited.

Juan Antonio López-Ramos is an Associate Professor at the University of Almeria, Spain. He has got a Ph.D. in Mathematics in 1998. He is author of more than 20 papers on Pure and Applied Mathematics and his research interest lies on Cryptography and Coding Theory. He is a researcher of the group "Categorias, Computacion y Teoria de Anillos" that it is supported by serveral official institutions as the Spanish Government. He has collaborated in multiple researching projects, some of them supported by NATO and jointly, with several private enterprises, in the developing of secure communications systems.

Francisco Javier Gálvez Sánchez is a Computer Science Engineer by the University of Almería, whose job has been focused on the web development and the safety of applications and systems. Currently, he is studying a Master Degree in Biomedical Engineering at the "Universidad Politécnica de Valencia". His main interests area are centered in the treatment of the medical images, inter-hospitalary communication and the application of new technologies into the medical environment.

Sam De Silva is a Partner at Taylor Walton LLP. Taylor Walton is one of the largest law firms in the South East region outside London and has recently been voted UK Corporate Law Firm of the Year by the readers of leading corporate finance magazine *ACQ*. Dr De Silva specialises in technology projects including outsourcing (IT, BPO and off-shoring), system development and supply, system integration, software licensing and support and services agreements. He advises clients in both the public and private sector and has acted for both suppliers and users of technology. He has had experience and is admitted to practice law in New Zealand, Australia and the United Kingdom. Dr De Silva has published widely and speaks regularly on outsourcing and technology contracts and is an Associate Lecturer at the University of Surrey for the Surrey European Management School. He has also developed an on-line course on IT contracts for Central Law Training. Dr De Silva also regularly advises on IP, data protection and e-commerce issues.

Fernando Diez is Graduated in Law and Graduated in Economics and Business Studies by Universidad Pontificia Comillas. After being *Visiting Researcher* at Harvard Law School, he obtained his Ph. D. in Commercial Law in Universidad Autónoma of Madrid (Spain). He is currently Director of ICO-Nebrija Antitrust Law and Economics Chair, and author of a number of articles and publications on various topics of Antitrust Law and Economics. He is also Correspondent Member of Real Academia de Jurisprudencia y Legislación (Spain), Member of Editorial Board of the Journal "*Competencia, Distribución y Consumo*" (La Ley) and Commercial Law Professor at Universidad Antonio de Nebrija.

Áurea Anguera de Sojo has a Degree in Law (1995) and a Degree in Economics (1996) from ICADE Universidad Pontificia de Comillas. She worked at Facultad de Economics from Universidad Nacional de Educación a Distancia, teaching about Human Research and Organizational Theory, since 1998 until now. At present She is Associate Professor at Informatics and Law Department of Universidad Politécnica de Madrid, imparting classes in Electronic Commerce and Social, Professional, Legal and Ethics Aspects of Engineering. She is preparing her Thesis Dissertation about Serendipity in Search Engines in Artificial Intelligence Department from Facultad de Informática from Universidad Politécnica de Madrid.

Francisco Serradilla has a Degree in Computer Science from the Universidad Politécnica de Madrid (1992) and has a Doctorate in Computer Science from the same University (1997). At present, he's Professor at Intelligent Applied Systems Department of Universidad Politécnica de Madrid and Director of the Intelligent Agents and Ubiquitous Computing Research Group. He worked in Mobile Robotics, Machine Vision and Artificial Neural Networks until 1997. Since 1998 his main research fields are Intelligent Information Agents, including Software Robots, Search Engines and Collaborative Recommender Systems. He's very interested in the social and legal implications of developing Information Agents and in new kinds of intellectual rights.

Murat Erdal was born in Beşiktaş, Istanbul in 1970. He holds a B.Sc. in Electrical Engineering (1991) from the Faculty of Engineering, Yıldız University and a Ph.D. in Business Administration (2000) from the Faculty of Political Sciences, Istanbul University. Erdal lectures on E-Business, Management Information Systems, Logistics Information Systems, Production Management and Supply Chain Management. He is the author of "E-Health", "Electronic Government; E-Turkey and Institutional Transformation" and "Technology Management" books. He has participated in several projects and has published scientific papers in journals and conferences. He has been a member of the Information Association of Turkey. He is married and has two children.

Gülşah Ekiz was born in Aydin in 1986. She graduated from Robert College, an American high school in Istanbul in 2004. She is currently a third year law student, studying in Galatasaray University, Istanbul. She has participated in numerous debate competitions and has worked actively in student organizations throughout her university years. She hopes to continue her career as an academic.

Selim Aksin was born in Konya in 1969. He completed his elemantary education in Konya. He graduated from Police Academy on 1992. After graduation his first workplace was Kecioren – Ankara as a deputy inspector. He took seminars and educations about computer and software. He worked as a police manager in Agri. He took his master of public administration degree from TODAIE on 2002 on the subject "international definition problem of terrorism". He took part of the studies of legal regulations, Communication Law and auditing of communication in Turkish National Police. He started to work in Telecommunication Presidency as a communicaiton expert on 2006 and he still work in here. On 2009 He accepted to Ankara University Law School and he is still a student in this Faculty. He is married and has two children.

Necmi Murat Güngör was born in Ankara in 1978. He gratuated from Police Academy in 2000 and attended to Istanbul Police Department as Deputy Inspector. He took his master degree on the subject of "Within the concept of New Penal Code Cyber Crimes and Applications of Turkish National Police" from Istanbul University Department of Public Administration. He took part of the studies of open source intelligence, computer forensics and cyber crimes as chief of cyber crime section in Turkish National Police. After 8 years of working for Turkish National Police he is attended to Information and Communication Technologies Authority, Communication Presidency as Communication Expert in Internet Department and still works. He especially works on Internet Content Regulations and Access Filtering issues. Mr. Güngör is married and has a child.

Joanna Leng was at the University of Manchester from 1996-2008 working in the area between academic computer service provision and research and development. Although she is primarily a visualizer, she has an in-depth working experience of eScience, computational science and high performance computing (HPC). While at the University she worked on and contributed to many projects and was heavily involved with the CSAR service throughout its duration, a UK national HPC service running from 1999-2006. Her interest in cross-disciplinary research started during her first degree in Biophysics. Since her MSc in computer science her work has been cross-disciplinary and her publications are mainly in 'other' disciplines. These include 3 chapters for books, over 20 papers, 12 technical reports and 6 articles for newsletters. Her interest in the working practices of computational science and adoption of its technologies started during her part-time PhD. She is now a freelancer and an honorary researcher for the School of Sociology at the University of Manchester.

Wes Sharrock has been at the University of Manchester since 1965. He has been assistant lecturer, lecturer, senior lecturer, reader and professor in sociology there. His main interests are in the philosophy of social science, philosophy of mind, sociological theory, computer supported cooperative work and ethnomethodology. Recent publications include: *Studies of Work and the Workplace in HCI: Concepts and Techniques* (2009); *Mathematical Equations as Durheimian Facts* (2009); *Sociological Objects, (*Ashgate); *Closet Cartesianism in Discursive Psychology* (2009); *Brain, Mind and Human Behavior in Contemporary Cognitive Science* (2008); and *Where do the limits of experience lie? Abandoning the dualism of objectivity and subjectivity* (2008).

Daniel Torres Gonçalves earned a master's degree at the University of Edinburgh in 2008: LL.M. in Innovation, Technology and the Law. The present chapter was a part of the final LL.M. dissertation. He is editor of SCRIPTed – A Journal of Law, Technology and Society, based at the University of Edinburgh, since 2007. He was born in Porto, Portugal, where he graduated as the top student at Lusíada University of Porto. He published several articles in Portuguese journals and, currently, he is a lawyer at António Vilar & Associados, working mainly with ICT law, IP law and medical law.

Michele Tomaiuolo is a researcher at the University of Parma, Department of Information Engineering, since the 1st of November, 2008. He obtained a master degree in Information Engineering, on the 24th of April, 2001 at the University of Parma, defending a thesis on the "Definition and realization of tools to manage the security in multi-agent systems", about the introduction of multiuser capabilities, authentication and encryption in JADE, an agent framework developed in Java by the University of Parma in conjunction with Telecom Italia Lab. He obtained a PhD in "Information technologies", at the University of Parma, Department of Information Engineering, on the 31st of March, 2006, defending a thesis on "Models and Tools to Manage Security in Multiagent Systems". His current research activity is focused in particular on security and trust management, but it also deals with multi-agent systems, semantic web, rule-based systems, peer-to-peer networks.

Ricardo J. Rejas-Muslera received his Ph.D in Computer Science from the Alcalá University of Madrid, and his B.S. degree in Law from the Carlos III University of Madrid; also he is Master in Law (Complutense University of Madrid). He worked at American Telecom as legal advisor from 1999, in 2002. In the fall of 2005 he moved at the University of Francisco de Vitoria, Madrid, Spain where he was full Professor, and since 2007, assistant director at the Engineering Department until 2008. In addition since 2005 he has been professor in Master Program at the Alcalá University of Madrid. Dr. Rejas-Muslera research interests include different aspects of Information Technology especially software legal aspects. Since 2006 he is the head of the 6SPIN, an integrant part of the Software Process Improvement Network (Software Engineering Institute, University of Carnegie Mellon).

Elena Davara is Master of Information and Communications Technology Law and Graduate in Law from the University Comillas of Madrid. He has a relevant experience in IT Law as Partner in Davara & Davara Law Firm, in addition he is Associate Professor in Polytechnic University of Madrid, and in master program in University of Alcalá de Henares, University Center Escorial Maria Cristina and

University Comillas of Madrid (ICADE). Elena Davara is currently Coordinator of the 'Law & Technology' section in the 'Novática' magazine.

Alain Abran holds a Ph.D. in Electrical and Computer Engineering (1994) from École Polytechnique de Montréal (Canada) and master degrees in Management Sciences (1974) and Electrical Engineering (1975) from University of Ottawa. He is a Professor and the Director of the Software Engineering Research Laboratory at the École de Technologie Supérieure (ETS) – Université du Québec (Montréal, Canada). He has 15 years of experience in teaching in a university environment as well as more than 20 years of industry experience in information systems development and software engineering. His research interests include software productivity and estimation models, software engineering foundations, software quality, software functional size measurement, software risk management and software maintenance management. Dr. Abran is currently a co-editor of the Guide to the Software Engineering Body of Knowledge project and a Co-chair of the Common Software Measurement International Consortium (COSMIC).

Luigi Buglione is an Associate Professor at the École de Technologie Supérieure (ETS) – Université du Québec, Canada and is currently working as Process Improvement Specialist at Engineering.IT (formerly Atos Origin Italy) in Rome, Italy. Previously, he worked as a Software Process Engineer at the European Software Institute (ESI) in Bilbao, Spain, and Sema Group in Rome (Italy). Dr. Buglione is a regular speaker at international Conferences on Software Measurement, Process Improvement and Quality, and participates to several associations involved in those issues. He received a Ph.D in Management Information Systems from LUISS Guido Carli University (Rome, Italy) and a degree cum laude in Economics from the University of Rome "La Sapienza", Italy. He is a Certified Software Measurement Specialist (IFPUG CSMS) Level 3. Further info on SEMQ website: www.geocities.com/lbu_measure/.

Witold Abramowicz (http://www.kie.ae.poznan.pl/members/wabramowicz/) is the chair of Department of Information Systems at The Poznan University of Economics, Poland. His particular areas of interest are Information Retrieval and Filtering, Knowledge Management in MIS. He received his M.Sc. from The Technical University of Poznan, Poland, Ph.D. from The Wroclaw Technical University, Poland, and habilitation from The Humboldt University Berlin, Germany. He worked for three universities in the Switzerland and Germany for twelve years. He is an editor or co-author of twenty seven books (published mostly by Springer and Kluwer Academic Publishers) and over 170 book chapters, articles in various journals and conference proceedings. He chaired 17 scientific international conferences and was a member of the program committees of over 220 other conferences. He is member of the editorial boards in some international journals like Wirtschaftsinformatik (A list), Comparative Technology Transfer, International Journal of Web Services Practices, International Journal of Web-based Learning and Teaching Technology, Business & Information Systems Engineering. Currently Professor Abramowicz is involved in 4 research projects in the 7th Framework Program EU. Professor Abramowicz is vice president of the Polish Association of Management Information Systems and member of board of Semantic Technology Institutes International (responsible for strategic development and internationalization).

Tadeusz Tomaszewski has been working for the Department of Information Systems, University of Economics since 1989. His scientific interests concern around legal informatics in particular in methods of legal information acquisition and representation, methods of legal content analysis, with special consideration for automatic retrieval of their syntactics and semantics, forms of information stored within the system and their links, methods of information retrieval (access structures, methods of search and navigation), He has been a co-author of a model of the first Polish legal hypertext information system - HyperThemis - that contains legal acts published in Polish government gazettes.

Piotr Stolarski joined the Department of Information Systems, University of Economics in 2007 after experiences with working for the largest Polish e-commerce Allegro.pl. The co-author of a number of papers on legal ontologies and legal information systems with vast experience in ontology engineering. Holder of two M.Scs (Dept. of Law, Poznan University and Business Information Systems, Poznan University of Economics). Currently a doctoral student. His particular areas of interests include: legal information representation, semantic legal information, legal ontologies life-cycle, legal aspects of risk management.

Charlie Chen is an Associate Professor in the Department of Computer Information Systems and the Walker College of Business at Appalachian State University, Boone, NC. He has published articles in the Communications of the Association for Information Systems, the International Journal of Technology and Human Interaction, the Journal of Information Systems Education, the Journal of Knowledge Management Research and Practice, and the Encyclopedia of Information Systems. Dr. Chen has presented his papers at a number of conferences and is serving as a reviewer for MIS Quarterly, a leading journal in IS, and for AMCIS and DSI conferences.

Dawn Medlin is the Chair of the Department of Computer Information Systems and is an Associate Professor, John A. Walker College of Business, and Appalachian State University in Boone, NC. Her teaching and research activities have mainly been in the area of security, web design, health care informatics, and e-commerce. She has published in journals such as The Journal of Information Systems Security, Information Systems Security, International Journal of Electronic Marketing and Retailing, and the International Journal of Healthcare Information Systems and Informatics.

Riikka Kulmala is the lecturer of the Turku University of Applied Sciences in Finland. Between 2002-2005 she was working as a researcher in ProACT research programme in the area of science, technology and innovation research in Finland. The research programme was funded by Ministry of Trade and Industry and the National Technology Agency (TEKES). At the moment she is preparing her doctoral thesis at Lappeenranta University of Technology. Her doctoral thesis discusses of intellectual property protection and management in small knowledge intensive companies. Riikka Kulmala has been working as a lecturer since 2001. Her subject areas include knowledge management and project management.

Juha Kettunen is the Rector of the Turku University of Applied Sciences in Finland and Adjunct Professor of the University of Jyväskylä in Finland. He was previously the Director of the Vantaa Institute for Continuing Education of the University of Helsinki and Director of the Advanced Management Education Centre of the University of Jyväskylä. He holds a Ph.D. from the University of Bristol in the UK, and a DSc from the University of Jyväskylä in Finland. Earlier he was an economist, but his recent interest areas include how the approaches of strategic management, quality assurance and knowledge management have been applied in knowledge-intensive organizations.

Isabelle Motte is working as researcher and adviser in ICT in two neighbouring Belgian Universities in Namur and in Louvain-la-Neuve. She has scientific background and approaches ICT with positive and critical mind. She has a great experience as ICT professors trainer and as ICT adviser in e-learning projects. She addressed both Belgian professors and academics coming from developing countries. She therefore also works on increasing open source software awareness in education sphere. Ergonomy, standards and ICT legislation are a concerns that she interests in for a long time. Senior web accessibility is one of her recent research question. She investigated the accessibility legislation and standardization process regarding the seniors as a specific target group. Her work has been much motivated by her interactions in the W3C WAI-AGE working group specifically interesting in the seniors difficulties on the web.

Monique Noirhomme-Fraiture is Professor of Probability and Statistics as well as of Human Computer Interaction (HCI) at the Faculte d'Informatique of the University of Namur. She was Chairperson of WG 13.3, (Human Computer Interaction and Disability). She participates to projects where she has the task of co-ordination and of visual interface development. She co-operates also in projects in e-learning, evaluation of interface and in design for all. She has supervised many student works in design of software for disabled persons. She has realized two video to promote awareness of designers to accessibility of Web sites ("L'écran noir", also in Portuguese and English version and "Web Senior Surfer"). She has organized conferences on the HCI field like IHM 04 in Namur and has been member of many program committees (like IHM, INTERACT's, Ubimob). She has been several times expert for projects evaluation for CEE.

Masakazu Ohashi is a professor at Graduate School and Faculty of Policy Studies, Chuo University, Japan. He received BE, BS, ME, and Dr. Eng. degree from Chuo University, Japan. His research activity covers the system for the next generation networking social systems and Social Design. He is a vice-president of The Infosocionomics Society in Japan. He is a member of UN/CEFACT TBG6. He is top executive of Time Business Form and several chairs of ICT Initiatives in Japan. He published many books and presented many papers at the international journals and conferences regarding of the Information Systems and Social Design.

Mayumi Hori is a professor at Graduate School and Faculty of Business Management, Hakuoh University, Japan. She receives BE and ME degree in economics form Rikkyo University, Japan and Dr. Policy Studies degree from Chuo University, Japan. Her research activity covers telework(e-work) and labor economics, especially working women. She is a director of The Infosocionomics Society in Japan. She published many books and presented many papers at the international journals and conferences regarding a flexible working format and work-life balance.

Louis B. Swartz, J.D., Associate Professor of Legal Studies at Robert Morris University, Moon Township, PA. Mr. Swartz teaches Legal Environment of Business and The Constitution and Current Legal Issues at the undergraduate level and Legal Issues of Executive Management in the M.B.A. program. He received his Bachelors degree from the University of Wisconsin in Madison, Wisconsin (1966) and his Juris Doctorate from Duquesne University in Pittsburgh, PA (1969). He is the Coordinator of the Robert Morris University Pre-Law Advisory Program and a member of the Northeast Association of Pre-Law Advisers (NAPLA) and the Academy of Legal Studies in Business (ALSB). His research interests include online education, legal studies and business law.

Michele T. Cole, J.D., PhD, Director of the Masters program in Nonprofit Management and Associate Professor of Nonprofit Management at Robert Morris University, Moon Township, PA. She received her law degree in 1982 from Duquesne University and her doctorate in Public Administration with a concentration in Nonprofit Management in 1993 from the University of Pittsburgh. Her research interests include effective online instruction, nonprofit sector curriculum development, legal issues in personnel management and application of business best practices and research to the nonprofit sector as well as the application of technology to learning strategies.

David A. Lovejoy, Esquire is a Veteran of United States Marine Corps. He attended the University of Nebraska, receiving a B.A. in 1968. His law degree was received from Duquesne University in 1974. He is an adjunct Professor of Business Law, Robert Morris University (1982-2007) and was an instructor at Allegheny County Community College in 1981. He practices law at Swartz Lovejoy & Associates LLP, Pittsburgh, Pennsylvania. He is admitted to Bar (1974), all Pennsylvania Courts and the Western District of Pennsylvania Federal Courts; U.S. Supreme Court, 1980; Third Circuit Court of Appeals, 1982; U.S. Tax Court, 1989. He is a member of Allegheny County, Pennsylvania, Panel of Arbitrators since 1974; and is a member of United States District Court, Western District of Pennsylvania, panel of arbitrators. His areas of specialty include Commercial and Retail Litigation, Bankruptcy Litigation, Tax, Financial and Estate Planning and Administration.

Pawan Chhabra has over 9 years of professional experience in Enterprise Architecture, Application Design and Development. He works as a Sr. Technical Architect at the Java Enterprise Center of Excellence group in Research unit of Infosys Technologies Ltd., India. Currently, Pawan is involved in area of research and development, architecting and designing n-tier distributed applications. His recent work is also involved in defining architecture, designing and development of context aware enterprise framework based upon service orientation concepts that introduces SaaS based capabilities and adaptive services. He has over 9 years of professional experience in implementing large-scale, mission-critical, IT Solutions across enterprises. He helps enabling application of industry wide best practices to applications development, mentors application development teams in designing high performance Java applications and showcasing various proof of concepts.

Chetan Kothari works as a principal architect at the J2EE Center of Excellence at Infosys Technologies Limited, a global leader in IT and business consulting services. Chetan has more than 11 years of experience with expertise in J2EE application framework development and defining, architecting, and implementing large-scale, mission-critical IT solutions across a range of industries. Chetan is TOGAF Certified Enterprise Architect and has experience of doing research in cutting edge technologies like SaaS, Cloud Computing, SOA, Web 2.0 and providing solution for adoption of these technologies. Chetan has filed patents and published papers in leading industry journal.

Subhadip Sarkar is working as Senior Intellectual Property Officer with Infosys Technologies Ltd. Bangalore. He has almost a decade work experience in the field of technology and Intellectual Property management. He has held executive positions in reputed companies such as British Oxygen Company and General Electric. He specializes in Intellectual Property management, innovation management, valuation, pricing and licensing of IP. He has extensive experience in managing multi-scenario IP Management strategies, strategizing and implementing change in situations of uncertainty and rapid growth, developing and driving high-performance cross-functional teams, and influencing and leveraging key relationships. At Infosys, Subhadip has been instrumental in architecting IP vision, implementing a structured IP management system and establishing some key best practices in IP management. Subhadip's research interests are in the areas of Patent Strategy and Management, Valuation of IP and IP Analytics. He has several papers and articles to his credit. Subhadip has also delivered several invited talks in many conferences and institutes.

Georgios V. Lioudakis is a senior research associate of the Intelligent Communications and Broadband Networks Laboratory (ICBNet) of the National Technical University of Athens (NTUA), Greece. He received his Dr.-Ing. degree in Electrical and Computer Engineering from the NTUA in 2008. As a research fellow of the NTUA since 2000, he has participated in several European and national research projects. His research interests include privacy protection, mobile networks and services, software engineering, middleware and distributed technologies; he has several publications related to these fields. Since 2009, Dr. Lioudakis is also an adjunct lecturer at the Department of Telecommunications Science and Technology, University of Peloponnese, Greece.

Francesca Rubina Gaudino is an associate lawyer at Baker & McKenzie, practicing in the areas of Information Technology/Communications, IT outsourcing, Data Protection and Security. Francesca Rubina Gaudino holds a J.D. in 1998 from University of Parma. She holds a Master in Business Law and Economics from the LUISS University "Guido Carli" in Rome, and also a Master of Laws LL.M. from University College of London (2000). She was admitted to bar in 2003; she is specialized in the area of data protection and security, and she has been issuing a number of articles and holding several seminars and lecturers on the matter of E-commerce and IT technologies in the data protection field, security and data protection.

Elisa Boschi leads the Secure Systems group at Hitachi Europe and is an academic guest at ETH Zurich. She is involved in several industrial and publicly funded research projects in the areas of network data anonymization, privacy enhancing technologies, biometrics, network monitoring and network and system security. She is an active contributor to the IETF IP flow information export (IPFIX) working group where she co-authors several Internet-Drafts and RFCs and to the European Telecommunications Standards Institute (ETSI) where she is rapporteur for the guide on network performance metrics and measurement methods. Prior to Hitachi, Ms. Boschi was a scientist at Fraunhofer FOKUS, the national German research institute on open communication systems. Ms. Boschi holds a Master of Science in computer engineering from the University of Pisa.

Giuseppe Bianchi is Full Professor of Telecommunications at the School of Engineering of the University of Roma Tor Vergata, Italy, since January 2007. He has a Laurea degree in Electrical Engineering from Politecnico di Milano (1990) and a specialist degree in information technology from the CEFRIEL research center of Milan (1991). Before his current appointment, he was Research Consultant for CEFRIEL (1991–1993), Assistant Professor at the Politecnico di Milano (1994–1998), and Associate Professor at the University of Palermo (1999–2003) and at the University of Roma Tor Vergata (2004–2006). His research activity spans several areas, among which: design and performance evaluation of broadband networks; multiple access in wireless local area networks; network security and privacy.

Dimitra I. Kaklamani is a Professor at the School of Electrical and Computer Engineering (SECE) of the National Technical University of Athens (NTUA). She has received the Diploma and Ph.D. degrees from the SECE, NTUA. She has published over 150 journal and conference papers and led and participated in several EU and national research projects. Her research interests span across different fields and include the use of Object-Oriented methodologies and middleware technologies for the development of distributed systems and privacy-aware infrastructures, and the development of visualisation and real-time simulation techniques for solving complex, large scale modelling problems of microwave engineering and information transmission systems.

Iakovos S. Venieris is a professor at the School of Electrical and Computer Engineering of the National Technical University of Athens since 1994. He received the Dipl.-Ing. degree from the University of Patras, Greece in 1988, and the Ph.D. degree from the National Technical University of Athens in 1990, all in Electrical and Computer Engineering. His research interests are in the fields of distributed systems, service engineering, agent technology, multimedia, mobile communications and Intelligent Networks, internetworking, signalling, resource scheduling and allocation for network management, modelling, performance evaluation and queuing theory. He has over 150 publications in the above areas. Prof. Venieris has received several national and international awards for academic achievement. He is a member of the IEEE and the Technical Chamber of Greece.

Jaroslav Král graduated in 1959 at Faculty of Mathematics and Physics of the Charles University, Prague, Czech Republic. He has been working in computer science at Czech Academy of Sciences and several Czech universities. He is now a full professor at the Faculty of Mathematical Physics of Charles University Prague and a visiting professor at the Faculty of Informatics of Masaryk University Brno, Czech Republic. His current research interests include: theory of formal languages and compilers, service-oriented systems engineering, education of software experts. He published more than 160 scientific papers. Jaroslav Král took part as the project leader in several successful projects including compilers, flexible manufacturing and automated warehouse systems.

Michal Žemlička is a senior assistant professor at the Faculty of Mathematics and Physics of Charles University, Prague. He graduated in 1996. His current research interests are extensible compilers, theory of parsing, design of large software systems, data structures, and computational linguistics. He published more than 60 scientific papers.

Juan José Andrés-Gutiérrez is a technological specialist at the Digital Home department at Telefónica R&D. He has been working as a technical project leader in several research projects related with AI and eHealth such as the European and Spanish funded projects Share-It and AmIVital. Currently his work is focussed on home devices, intelligent systems for automating environments, sensors networks, user centric systems and eHealth. He is in charge of projects related to the next generation of managed homes. Currently he is studying a PhD degree at the University of Valladolid where he received the M.Sc. degree in Computer Science (2000).

Esteban Pérez-Castrejón is a technological expert at Telefónica R&D. Since 1990 he has been working in multimedia services field including videoconferencing over high speed networks. He has been actively involved in the definition and deployment telemedicine, telehealth and eInclusion services including several European and Spanish funded projects like ATTRACT, TEN-CARE, Emerald and Share-It projects. In this field, he is currently working in Ambient Assisted Living applications, Activities of Daily Living modelling and Home Services. Nowadays he is studying a PhD degree at the Polytechnic University of Madrid where he received a M.Sc. degree in Bioengineering and Telemedicine.

Ana Isabel Calvo-Alcalde is an analyst working as an external consultant for Telefónica R&D at the Digital Home department. She got her bachelor degree in Computer Science in 2005 when she prepared her bachelor thesis at the Catholic University College of Bruges-Ostend (KHBO), Belgium. Afterwards she got her M.Sc degree in Computer Science in 2008 at the University of Valladolid. Since 2007 she is working in projects related to eHealth and telemedicine, like AmIVital and Share-It projects, focused on Ambient Intelligence aspects. She also has been working in some other projects related to Digital Home area. Her research interests are eHealth, Artificial Intelligence and Semantic Web techniques, such as expert systems, software agents and ontologies. Currently she is studying a PhD degree in Computer Science at University of Valladolid.

Jesús M. Vegas-Hernández, is an Associate Professor of Informatics at the University of Valladolid, Spain. In this same university, he obtained its PhD degree in Computer Science in 1999. His research activities, centered in Information Retrieval, Digital Libraries, Users Interfaces and Mobile Web Search, have produced more than 30 papers and articles in international conferences and journals. He has been involved in more than 15 research projects and he has participated as member of Program Committee in several international conferences. In his academic activities, he has taught several subjects related with the Operating Systems and the Computer Networks in the Computing Engineering studies. He is the director of the Master in Digital Libraries since its foundation in 2005.

Miguel Ángel González-Rebollo received his degree in Physics from the University of Valladolid in 1977. From 1980 to 1982 he was a scholarship holder of investigation in the University of Montpellier. In 1983 he obtained the PhD from the University of Valladolid with a study of photoelectronic properties of GaAs (Extraordinary Ph.D. Award of University of Valladolid). He has been professor of the University of Marrakech from 1983 to 1985. From 2000 to 2002 he was Assistant-Director of Technical Scholl of Engineering at the University of Valladolid. In 2003 he was appointed as a full Professor of Physics in the School of Engineering at the University of Valladolid. He works in the research group of semiconductors developing new techniques for microscopic and nanoscopic characterization of semiconductors, like spatial resolved photoconductivity and photoluminescence, phase stepping microscopy (Award of 3M group in 2000).

Jeremy Pitt is Reader in Intelligent Systems in the Department of Electrical & Electronic Engineering (EEE) Imperial College London, Deputy Head of the Intelligent Systems & Networks Group, and Director of the Information Systems Engineering B.Eng./M.Eng. degree course. He received his Ph.D. from the Department of Computing in 1991, joined EEE in 1996, and was appointed to Reader in 2004. He has been an Investigator on over 20 research grants from national and international funding agencies, and the holder of Royal Society, EPSRC and UKIERI international travel grants to India and Japan. Dr. Pitt has published over 100 research articles, including works on agent communication, agent societies, trust, forgiveness, voting and opinion formation. His current research interests are in organized and organizational adaptation of multi-agent systems, intelligent transportation management, and computer law. Dr. Pitt is a Senior Member of the ACM, a member of the IET and of the UK Conflict Research Society.

Arvind Bhusate is a Research Assistant in Intelligent Systems & Networks Group of the Electrical & Electronic Engineering Department at Imperial College London, where he studied for a PhD in enhancing quality of experience using intelligent communication technologies. During this time, he worked on two European projects, DANAE (dynamic multimedia) and ALIS (intelligent legal systems). Prior to these appointments he had completed a Masters of Research in Telecommunications at University College London and his Bachelors of Science in Computer Systems and Digital Electronics at Queen Mary College, University of London.

Gonçalo Jorge Morais da Costa is doing PhD in Knowledge Management and Ethics in De Montfort University with supervision of Ms. Mary Prior and Professor Simon Rogerson. Plus, he holds a Degree in Economics, a Pos-Degree in E-Business and IT, and a Masters in Management. He is also a lecturer in several Portuguese universities and his current research areas are all the major appliances regarding IT and ethics as demonstrated throughout his published and presented work in several journals and conferences, or book chapters.

Nuno Sotero Alves da Silva is doing PhD in Computer Ethics and Education in De Montfort University with supervision of Professor Simon Rogerson and Dr. Bernd Stahl. Plus, he holds a Degree in Computer Science Engineering and a Pos-Degree in E-Business and IT. He is also a lecturer and IT Manager in Lusíada University of Lisbon, Portugal. His current research areas are e-learning, bionano-tecnhology, computer happiness bounded to ethics.

Piotr Pawlak holds a PhD title at the Adam Mickiewicz University of Poznan, Poland. His specializations are in Political Sciences, as well as Cultural Sciences, and during 2008 have achieved the PhD degree into the Social Science Faculty, at Adam Mickiewicz University of Poznan. His doctoral thesis concerns cultural, social and also political aspects of modern mass-media, namely the Internet. The basic scope of this research was to give a response concerning the influence of Information and Communication Technologies at the lives of individuals, and societies.

Francisco Andrade, Lecturer and Researcher at Universidade do Minho's Law School (Department of Private Law), is also a researcher at the CCTC – Centro de Ciências e Tecnologias da Computação (Center for Computing Science and Technologies). His research has been focused mainly in the field of private law and informatics. Current work is being undertaken in the field of Artificial Intelligence and Conflict Resolution. He has published books chapters, journal papers, articles in proceedings of scientific conferences. Member of APDI – Associação Portuguesa de Direito Intelectual (Intelectual Law Portuguese Association) and of APPIA – Associação Portuguesa para a Inteligência Artificial (Portuguese Association for Artificial Intelligence).

Paulo Novais is a Professor of Computer Science at the Department of Informatics at the University of Minho, Braga, Portugal. He received a PhD in Computer Science from the same university in 2003. His current research directions span the fields of Knowledge Representation and Reasoning, Multi-Agent Systems, Ambient Intelligence, Collaborative Networks and AI and The Law. He is involved in several research projects funded by the Foundation for Science and Technology (FCT). He has published more than seventy papers in international journals, conferences and workshops and two books, in the supervision of projects of doctoral and master's participation in various jury of PhD and Master's, and also the organization of several scientific meetings. He is Vice-president of APPIA, the Portuguese Association for Artificial Intelligence.

Davide Carneiro is a researcher at the CCTC – Computer Science and Technology Center, Department of Informatics, University of Minho, Braga, Portugal. His current research directions span the fields of Online Dispute Resolution, Multi-agent Systems and Ambient Intelligence.

José Neves is Full Professor of Computer Science at the Department of Informatics at the University of Minho, Braga, Portugal. He received a PhD in Computer Science from Herriot Watt University, Edinburgh, Scotland, in 1984. His current research directions span the fields of AI and The Law, Knowledge Representation and Reasoning and Multiagent Systems.

José Machado is Professor of Computer Science at the Department of Informatics at the University of Minho, Braga, Portugal. He received a PhD in Computer Science from the University of Minho in 2002. His current research directions span the fields of Artificial Intelligence and The Law, Medical Informatics, Databases and Multiagent Systems.

Pedro Pina is a lawyer and teaches law at the Oliveira do Hospital School of Technology and Management of the Polytechnic Institute of Coimbra. He holds a law degree from the University of Coimbra Law School and has done post-graduate work in Territorial Development, Urbanism and Environmental Law from the Territorial Development, Urbanism and Environmental Law Studies Center (CEDOUA) at the University of Coimbra Law School. He holds a master's degree in Procedural Law Studies from the University of Coimbra and is currently a PhD candidate in the Doctoral Programme "Law, Justice, and Citizenship in the Twenty First Century" from the University of Coimbra School of Law.

Index